Deep Learning with TensorFlow 2 and Keras

Second Edition

Regression, ConvNets, GANs, RNNs, NLP,
and more with TensorFlow 2 and the Keras API

Antonio Gulli

Amita Kapoor

Sujit Pal

BIRMINGHAM - MUMBAI

Deep Learning with TensorFlow 2 and Keras

Second Edition

Commissioning Editor: Amey Varangaonkar
Acquisition Editors: Yogesh Deokar, Ben Renow-Clarke
Acquisition Editor – Peer Reviews: Suresh Jain
Content Development Editor: Ian Hough
Technical Editor: Gaurav Gavas
Project Editor: Janice Gonsalves
Proofreader: Safis Editing
Indexer: Rekha Nair
Presentation Designer: Sandip Tadge

First published: April 2017
Second edition: December 2019

Production reference: 2130320

Published by Packt Publishing Ltd.
Livery Place
35 Livery Street
Birmingham B3 2PB, UK.

ISBN 978-1-83882-341-2

www.packt.com

Pack<t>

packt.com

Subscribe to our online digital library for full access to over 7,000 books and videos, as well as industry leading tools to help you plan your personal development and advance your career. For more information, please visit our website.

Why subscribe?

- Spend less time learning and more time coding with practical eBooks and Videos from over 4,000 industry professionals

- Learn better with Skill Plans built especially for you

- Get a free eBook or video every month

- Fully searchable for easy access to vital information

- Copy and paste, print, and bookmark content

Did you know that Packt offers eBook versions of every book published, with PDF and ePub files available? You can upgrade to the eBook version at www.Packt.com and as a print book customer, you are entitled to a discount on the eBook copy. Get in touch with us at customercare@packtpub.com for more details.

At www.Packt.com, you can also read a collection of free technical articles, sign up for a range of free newsletters, and receive exclusive discounts and offers on Packt books and eBooks.

Contributors

About the authors

Antonio Gulli has a passion for establishing and managing global technological talent, for innovation and execution. His core expertise is in cloud computing, deep learning, and search engines. Currently, he serves as Engineering Director for the Office of the CTO, Google Cloud. Previously, he served as Google Warsaw Site leader, doubling the size of the engineering site.

So far, Antonio has been lucky enough to gain professional experience in 4 countries in Europe and has managed teams in 6 countries in EMEA and the US: in Amsterdam, as Vice President for Elsevier, a leading scientific publisher; in London, as Engineering Site Lead for Microsoft working on Bing Search as CTO for Ask.com; and in several co-funded start-ups including one of the first web search companies in Europe.

Antonio has co-invented a number of technologies for search, smart energy, the environment, and AI, with 20+ patents issued/applied, and he has published several books about coding and machine learning, also translated into Japanese and Chinese. Antonio speaks Spanish, English, and Italian, and he is currently learning Polish and French. Antonio is a proud father of 2 boys, Lorenzo, 18, and Leonardo, 13, and a little queen, Aurora, 9.

I want to thank my kids, Aurora, Leonardo, and Lorenzo, for motivating and supporting me during all the moments of my life. Special thanks to my parents, Elio and Maria, for being there when I need it. I'm particularly grateful to the important people in my life: Eric, Francesco, Antonello, Antonella, Ettore, Emanuela, Laura, Magda, and Nina.

I want to thank all my colleagues at Google for their encouragement in writing this and previous books, for the precious time we've spent together, and for their advice: Behshad, Wieland, Andrei, Brad, Eyal, Becky, Rachel, Emanuel, Chris, Eva, Fabio, Jerzy, David, Dawid, Piotr, Alan, and many others. I'm especially appreciative of all my colleagues at OCTO, at the Office of the CTO at Google, and I'm humbled to be part of a formidable and very talented team. Thanks, Jonathan and Will.

Thanks to my high school friends and professors who inspired me over many years (D'africa and Ferragina in particular). Thanks to the reviewer for their thoughtful comments and efforts toward improving this book, and my co-authors for their passion and energy.

This book has been written in six different nations: Warsaw, Charlotte Bar; Amsterdam, Cafe de Jaren; Pisa, La Petite; Pisa, Caffe i Miracoli; Lucca, Piazza Anfiteatro, Tosco; London, Said; London, Nespresso, and Paris, Laduree. Lots of travel and lots of good coffee in a united Europe!

Amita Kapoor is an associate professor in the Department of Electronics, SRCASW, University of Delhi, and has been actively teaching neural networks and artificial intelligence for the last 20 years. Coding and teaching are her two passions, and she enjoys solving challenging problems. She is a recipient of the DAAD Sandwich fellowship 2008, and the Best Presentation Award at an international conference, Photonics 2008. She is an avid reader and learner. She has co-authored books on Deep Learning and has more than 50 publications in international journals and conferences. Her present research areas include machine learning, deep reinforcement learning, quantum computers, and robotics.

To my grandmother the late Kailashwati Maini for her unconditional love and affection; and my grandmother the late Kesar Kapoor for her marvelous stories that fueled my imagination; my mother, the late Swarnlata Kapoor, for having trust in my abilities and dreaming for me; and my stepmother, the late Anjali Kapoor, for teaching me every struggle can be a stepping stone.

I am grateful to my teachers throughout life, who inspired me, encouraged me, and most importantly taught me: Prof. Parogmna Sen, Prof. Wolfgang Freude, Prof. Enakshi Khullar Sharma, Dr. S Lakshmi Devi, Dr. Rashmi Saxena and Dr. Rekha Gupta.

I am extremely thankful to the entire Packt team for the work and effort they put in since the inception of this book, the reviewers who painstakingly went through the content and verified the codes; their comments and suggestions helped improve the book. I am particularly thankful to my co-authors Antonio Gulli and Sujit Pal for sharing their vast experience with me in the writing of this book.

I would like to thank my college administration, governing body and Principal Dr. Payal Mago for sanctioning my Sabbatical leave so that I can concentrate on the book. I would also like to thank my colleagues for the support and encouragement they have provided, with a special mention of Dr. Punita Saxena, Dr. Jasjeet Kaur, Dr. Ratnesh Saxena, Dr. Daya Bhardwaj, Dr. Sneha Kabra, Dr. Sadhna Jain, Mr. Projes Roy, Ms. Venika Gupta and Ms. Preeti Singhal.

I want to thank my family members and friends my extended family Krishna Maini, Suraksha Maini, the late HCD Maini, Rita Maini, Nirjara Jain, Geetika Jain, Rashmi Singh and my father Anil Mohan Kapoor.

And last but not the least I would like to thank Narotam Singh for his invaluable discussions, inspiration and unconditional support through all phases of my life.

A part of the royalties of the book will go to smilefoundation.org.

Sujit Pal is a Technology Research Director at Elsevier Labs, an advanced technology group within the Reed-Elsevier Group of companies. His areas of interest include Semantic Search, Natural Language Processing, Machine Learning, and Deep Learning. At Elsevier, he has worked on several machine learning initiatives involving large image and text corpora, and other initiatives around recommendation systems and knowledge graph development. He has previously co-authored another book on Deep Learning with Antonio Gulli and writes about technology on his blog Salmon Run.

I would like to thank both my co-authors for their support and for making this authoring experience a productive and pleasant one, the editorial team at Packt who were constantly there for us with constructive help and support, and my family for their patience. It has truly taken a village, and this book would not have been possible without the passion and hard work from everyone on the team.

About the reviewers

Haesun Park is a machine learning Google Developer Expert. He has been a software engineer for more than 15 years. He has written and translated several books on machine learning. He is an entrepreneur, and currently runs his own business.

Other books Haesun has worked on include the translation of *Hands-On Machine Learning with Scikit-Learn and TensorFlow*, *Python Machine Learning*, and *Deep Learning with Python*.

> *I would like to thank Suresh Jain who proposed this work to me, and extend my sincere gratitude to Janice Gonsalves, who provided me with a great deal of support in the undertaking of reviewing this book.*

Dr. Simeon Bamford has a background in AI. He is specialized in neural and neuromorphic engineering, including neural prosthetics, mixed-signal CMOS design for spike-based learning, and machine vision with event-based sensors. He has used TensorFlow for natural language processing and has experience in deploying TensorFlow models on serverless cloud platforms.

Table of Contents

Preface

Deep Learning with TensorFlow 2 and Keras, Second Edition is a concise yet thorough introduction to modern neural networks, artificial intelligence, and deep learning technologies designed especially for software engineers and data scientists. The book is the natural follow-up of the books *Deep Learning with Keras* [1] and *TensorFlow 1.x Deep Learning Cookbook* [2] previously written by the same authors.

Mission

This book provides a very detailed panorama of the evolution of learning technologies during the past six years. The book presents dozens of working deep neural networks coded in Python using TensorFlow 2.0, a modular network library based on Keras-like [1] APIs.

You are introduced step-by-step to supervised learning algorithms such as simple linear regression, classical multilayer perceptrons, and more sophisticated deep convolutional networks and generative adversarial networks. In addition, the book covers unsupervised learning algorithms such as autoencoders and generative networks. Recurrent networks and **Long Short-Term Memory (LSTM)** networks are also explained in detail. The book also includes a comprehensive introduction to deep reinforcement learning and it covers deep learning accelerators (GPUs and TPUs), cloud development, and multi-environment deployment on your desktop, on the cloud, on mobile/IoT devices, and on your browser.

Practical applications include code for text classification into predefined categories, syntactic analysis, sentiment analysis, synthetic generation of text, and parts-of-speech tagging. Image processing is also explored, with recognition of handwritten digit images, classification of images into different categories, and advanced object recognition with related image annotations.

Sound analysis comprises the recognition of discrete speech from multiple speakers. Generation of images using Autoencoders and GANs is also covered. Reinforcement learning is used to build a deep Q-learning network capable of learning autonomously. Experiments are the essence of the book. Each net is augmented by multiple variants that progressively improve the learning performance by changing the input parameters, the shape of the network, loss functions, and algorithms used for optimizations. Several comparisons between training on CPUs, GPUs and TPUs are also provided. The book introduces you to the new field of AutoML where deep learning models are used to learn how to efficiently and automatically learn how to build deep learning models. One advanced chapter is devoted to the mathematical foundation behind machine learning.

Machine learning, artificial intelligence, and the deep learning Cambrian explosion

Artificial intelligence (AI) lays the ground for everything this book discusses. **Machine learning (ML)** is a branch of AI, and **Deep learning (DL)** is in turn a subset within ML. This section will briefly discuss these three concepts, which you will regularly encounter throughout the rest of this book.

AI denotes any activity where machines mimic intelligent behaviors typically shown by humans. More formally, it is a research field in which machines aim to replicate cognitive capabilities such as learning behaviors, proactive interaction with the environment, inference and deduction, computer vision, speech recognition, problem solving, knowledge representation, and perception. AI builds on elements of computer science, mathematics, and statistics, as well as psychology and other sciences studying human behaviors. There are multiple strategies for building AI. During the 1970s and 1980s, 'expert' systems became extremely popular. The goal of these systems was to solve complex problems by representing the knowledge with a large number of manually defined if–then rules. This approach worked for small problems on very specific domains, but it was not able to scale up for larger problems and multiple domains. Later, AI focused more and more on methods based on statistical methods that are part of ML.

ML is a subdiscipline of AI that focuses on teaching computers how to learn without the need to be programmed for specific tasks. The key idea behind ML is that it is possible to create algorithms that learn from, and make predictions on, data. There are three different broad categories of ML:

- **Supervised learning**, in which the machine is presented with input data and a desired output, and the goal is to learn from those training examples in such a way that meaningful predictions can be made for data that the machine has never observed before.

- **Unsupervised learning**, in which the machine is presented with input data only, and the machine has to subsequently find some meaningful structure by itself, with no external supervision or input.

- **Reinforcement learning**, in which the machine acts as an agent, interacting with the environment. The machine is provided with "rewards" for behaving in a desired manner, and "penalties" for behaving in an undesired manner. The machine attempts to maximize rewards by learning to develop its behavior accordingly.

DL took the world by storm in 2012. During that year, the ImageNet 2012 challenge [3] was launched with the goal of predicting the content of photographs using a subset of a large hand-labeled dataset. A deep learning model named AlexNet [4] achieved a top-5 error rate of 15.3%, a significant improvement with respect to previous state-of-the-art results. According to the Economist [5], "Suddenly people started to pay attention, not just within the AI community but across the technology industry as a whole." Since 2012, we have seen constant progress [5] (see *Figure 1*) with several models classifying ImageNet photography, with an error rate of less than 2%; better than the estimated human error rate at 5.1%:

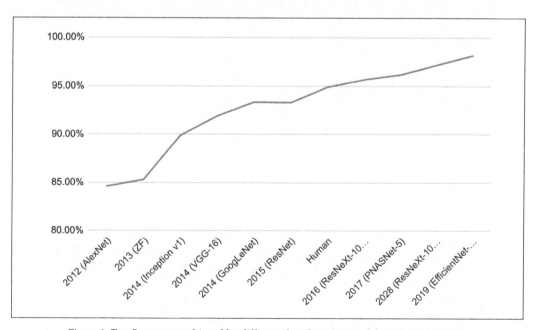

Figure 1: Top 5 accuracy achieved by different deep learning models on ImageNet 2012

That was only the beginning. Today, DL techniques are successfully applied in heterogeneous domains including, but not limited to: healthcare, environment, green energy, computer vision, text analysis, multimedia, finance, retail, gaming, simulation, industry, robotics, and self-driving cars. In each of these domains, DL techniques can solve problems with a level of accuracy that was not possible using previous methods.

It is worth noting that interest in DL is also increasing. According to the State of Deep Learning H2 2018 Review [9] "Every 20 minutes, a new ML paper is born. The growth rate of machine learning papers has been around 3.5% a month [..] around a 50% growth rate annually." During the past three years, it seems like we are living during a Cambrian explosion for DL, with the number of articles on our arXiv growing faster than Moore's Law (see *Figure 2*). Still, according to the review this "gives you a sense that people believe that this is where the future value in computing is going to come from":

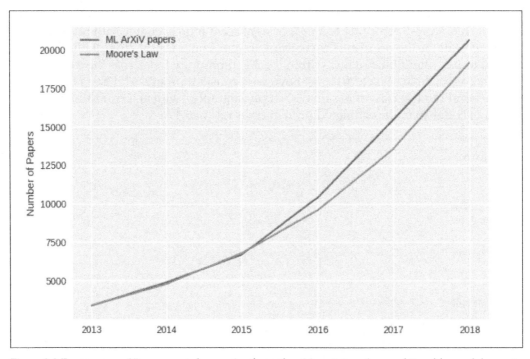

Figure 2: ML papers on arXiv appears to be growing faster than Moore's Law (source: https://www.kdnuggets.com/2018/12/deep-learning-major-advances-review.html)

 arXiv is a repository of electronic preprints approved for posting after moderation, but not full peer review.

The complexity of deep learning models is also increasing. ResNet-50 is an image recognition model (see chapters 4 and 5), with about 26 million parameters. Every single parameter is a weight used to fine-tune the model. Transformers, gpt-1, bert, and gpt-2 [7] are natural language processing (see *Chapter 8, Recurrent Neural Networks*) models able to perform a variety of tasks on text. These models progressively grew from 340 million to 1.5 billion parameters. Recently, Nvidia claimed that it has been able to train the largest-known model, with 8.3 billion parameters, in just 53 minutes. This training allowed Nvidia to build one of the most powerful models to process textual information (`https://devblogs.nvidia.com/training-bert-with-gpus/`).

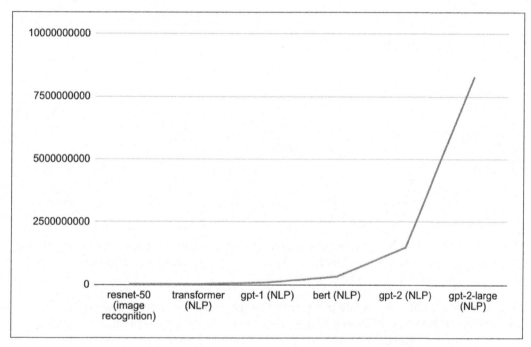

Figure 3: Growth in number of parameters for various deep learning models

Besides that, computational capacity is significantly increasing. GPUs and TPUs (*Chapter 16, Tensor Processing Unit*) are deep learning accelerators that have made it possible to train large models in a very short amount of time. TPU3s, announced on May 2018, are about twice as powerful (360 teraflops) as the TPU2s announced on May 2017. A full TPU3 pod can deliver more than 100 petaflops of machine learning performance, while TPU2 pods can get to 11.5 teraflops of performance.

An improvement of 10x per pod (see Figure 4) was achieved in one year only, which allows faster training:

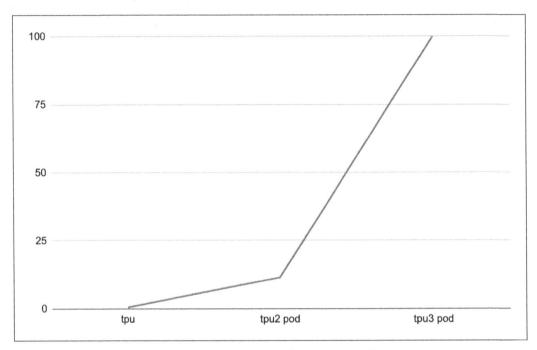

Figure 4: TPU accelerators performance in petaflops

However, DL's growth is not only in terms of better accuracy, more research papers, larger models, and faster accelerators. There are additional trends that have been observed over the last four years.

First, the availability of flexible programming frameworks such as Keras [1], TensorFlow [2], PyTorch[8], and fast.ai; these frameworks have proliferated within the ML and DL community and have provided some very impressive results, as we'll see throughout this book. According to the Kaggle *State of the Machine Learning and Data Science Survey* 2019, based on responses from 19,717 Kaggle (https://www.kaggle.com/) members, Keras and TensorFlow are clearly the most popular choices (see *Figure 5*). TensorFlow 2.0 is the framework covered in this book. This framework aims to take the best of both worlds from the great features found in Keras and TensorFlow 1.x:

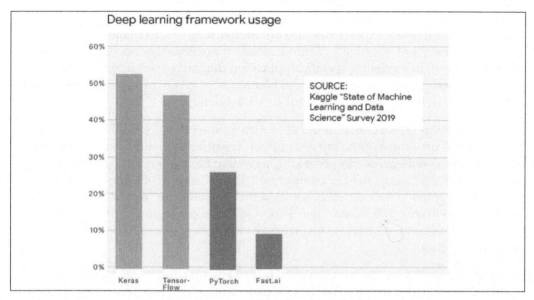

Figure 5: Adoption of deep learning frameworks

Second, the increasing possibility of using managed services in the cloud (see *Chapter 12, TensorFlow and Cloud*) with accelerators (*Chapter 16, Tensor Processing Unit*). This allows data scientists to focus on ML problems with no need to manage the infrastructural overhead.

Third, the increasing capacity of deploying models in more heterogeneous systems: mobile devices, **Internet of Things (IoT)** devices, and even the browsers normally used in your desktop and laptop (see *Chapter 13, TensorFlow for Mobile and IoT and TensorFlow.js*).

Fourth, the increased understanding of how to use more and more sophisticated DL architectures such as Dense Networks (*Chapter 1, Neural Network Foundations with TensorFlow 2.0*), Convolutional Network (*Chapter 4, Convolutional Neural Networks,* and *Chapter 5, Advanced Convolutional Neural Networks*), Generative Adversarial Networks (*Chapter 6, Generative Adversarial Networks*), Word Embeddings (*Chapter 7, Word Embeddings*), Recurrent Network (*Chapter 8, Recurrent Neural Networks*), Autoencoders (*Chapter 9, Autoencoders*), and advanced techniques such as Reinforcement Learning (*Chapter 11, Reinforcement Learning*).

Fifth, the advent of new AutoML techniques (*Chapter 14*, *An Introduction to AutoML*) that can enable domain experts who are unfamiliar with ML technologies to use ML techniques easily and effectively. AutoML made it possible to reduce the burden of finding the right model for specific application domains, spending time on fine-tuning the models, and spending time in identifying – given an application problem – the right set of features to use as input to ML models.

The above five trends culminated in 2019 when Yoshua Bengio, Geoffrey Hinton, and Yann LeCun – three of the fathers of Deep Learning – won the Turing Award "for conceptual and engineering breakthroughs that have made deep neural networks a critical component of computing." The ACM A.M. Turing Award is an annual prize given to an individual selected for contributions "of lasting and major technical importance to the computer field." Quotes taken from the ACM website (`https://awards.acm.org/`). Many are considering this award to be the Nobel of computer science.

Looking back at the previous eight years, it is fascinating and exciting to see the extent of the contributions that DL has made to science and industry. There is no reason to believe that the next eight years will see any less contribution; indeed, as the field of DL continues to advance, we anticipate that we'll see even more exciting and fascinating contributions provided by DL.

The intent of this book is to cover all the above five trends, and to introduce you to the magic of deep learning. We will start with simple models and progressively will introduce increasingly sophisticated models. The approach will always be hands-on, with an healthy dose of code to work with.

Who this book is for

If you are a data scientist with experience in ML or an AI programmer with some exposure to neural networks, you will find this book a useful entry point to DL with TensorFlow 2.0. If you are a software engineer with a growing interest about the DL tsunami, you will find this book a foundational platform to broaden your knowledge on the topic. A basic knowledge of Python is required for this book.

What this book covers

The intent of this book is to discuss the TensorFlow 2.0 features and libraries, to present an overview of Supervised and Unsupervised Machine learning models, and to provide a comprehensive analysis of Deep Learning and Machine Learning models. Practical usage examples for Cloud, Mobile, and large production environments are provided throughout.

Chapter 1, Neural Network Foundations with TensorFlow 2.0, this chapter will provide a step-by-step introduction to neural networks. You will learn how to use tf.keras layers in TensorFlow 2 to build simple neural network models. Perceptron, Multi-layer Perceptrons, Activation functions, and Dense Networks will be discussed. Finally, the chapter provides an intuitive introduction to backpropagation.

Chapter 2, TensorFlow 1.x and 2.x, this chapter will compare TensorFlow 1.x and TensorFlow 2.0 programming models. You will learn how to use TensorFlow 1.x lower-level computational graph APIs, and how to use tf.keras higher-level APIs. New functionalities such as eager computation, Autograph, tf.Datasets, and distributed training will be covered. Brief comparisons between tf.keras with Estimators and between tf.keras and Keras will be provided.

Chapter 3, Regression, this chapter will focus on the most popular ML technique: regression. You will learn how to use TensorFlow 2.0 estimators to build simple and multiple regression models. You will learn to use logistic regression to solve a multi-class classification problem.

Chapter 4, Convolutional Neural Networks, this chapter will introduce **Convolutional Neural Networks (CNNs)** and their applications to image processing. You will learn how to use TensorFlow 2.0 to build simple CNNs to recognize handwritten characters in the MNIST dataset, and how to classify CIFAR images. Finally, you will understand how to use pretrained networks such as VGG16 and Inception.

Chapter 5, Advanced Convolutional Neural Networks, this chapter discusses advanced applications of CNNs to image, video, audio, and text processing. Examples of image processing (Transfer Learning, DeepDream), audio processing (WaveNet), and text processing (Sentiment Analysis, Q&A) will be discussed in detail.

Chapter 6, Generative Adversarial Networks, this chapter will focus on the recently discovered **Generative Adversarial Networks (GANs)**. We will start with the first proposed GAN model and use it to forge MNIST characters. The chapter will use deep convolutional GANs to create celebrity images. The chapter discusses the various GAN architectures like SRGAN, InfoGAN, and CycleGAN. The chapter covers a range of cool GAN applications. Finally, the chapter concludes with a TensorFlow 2.0 implementation of CycleGAN to convert winter-summer images.

Chapter 7, Word Embeddings, this chapter will describe what word embeddings are, with specific reference to two traditional popular embeddings: Word2vec and GloVe. It will cover the core ideas behind these two embeddings and how to generate them from your own corpus, as well as how to use them in your own networks for **Natural Language Processing (NLP)** applications.

The chapter will then cover various extensions to the basic embedding approach, such as using character trigrams instead of words (fastText), retaining word context by replacing static embeddings with a neural network (ELMO, Google Universal Sentence Encoder), sentence embeddings (InferSent, SkipThoughts), and using pretrained language models for embeddings (ULMFit, BERT).

Chapter 8, Recurrent Neural Networks, this chapter describes the basic architecture of **Recurrent Neural Networks (RNNs)**, and how it is well suited for sequence learning tasks such as those found in NLP. It will cover various types of RNN, LSTM, **Gated Recurrent Unit (GRU)**, Peephole LSTM, and bidirectional LSTM. It will go into more depth as to how an RNN can be used as a language model. It will then cover the seq2seq model, a type of RNN-based encoder-decoder architecture originally used in machine translation. It will then cover Attention mechanisms as a way of enhancing the performance of seq2seq architectures, and finally will cover the Transformer architecture (BERT, GPT-2), which is based on the *Attention is all you need* paper.

Chapter 9, Autoencoders, this chapter will describe autoencoders, a class of neural networks that attempt to recreate the input as its target. It will cover different varieties of autoencoders like sparse autoencoders, convolutional autoencoders, and denoising autoencoders. The chapter will train a denoising autoencoder to remove noise from input images. It will demonstrate how autoencoders can be used to create MNIST digits. Finally, it will also cover the steps involved in building an LSTM autoencoder to generate sentence vectors.

Chapter 10, Unsupervised Learning, the chapter delves into the unsupervised learning models. It will cover techniques required for clustering and dimensionality reduction like PCA, k-means, and self-organized maps. It will go into the details of Boltzmann Machines and their implementation using TensorFlow. The concepts covered will be extended to build **Restricted Boltzmann Machines (RBMs)**.

Chapter 11, Reinforcement Learning, this chapter will focus upon reinforcement learning. It will start with the Q-learning algorithm. Starting with the Bellman Ford equation, the chapter will cover concepts like discounted rewards, exploration and exploitation, and discount factors. It will explain policy-based and model-based reinforcement learning. Finally, a **Deep Q-learning Network (DQN)** will be built to play an Atari game.

Chapter 12, TensorFlow and Cloud, this chapter discusses the cloud environment and how to utilize it for training and deploying your model. It will cover the steps needed to set up Amazon Web Services (AWS) for DL. The steps needed to set up Google Cloud Platform for DL applications will also be covered. It will also cover how to set up Microsoft Azure for DL applications. The chapter will include various cloud services that allow you to run the Jupyter Notebook directly on the cloud. Finally, the chapter will conclude with an introduction to TensorFlow Extended.

Chapter 13, TensorFlow for Mobile and IoT and TensorFlow.js, this chapter focuses on developing deep learning based applications for the web, mobile devices and IoT. The chapter discusses TensorFlow Lite and explores how it can be used to deploy models on Android devices. The chapter also discusses in detail Federated learning for distributed learning across thousands of mobile devices. The chapter finally introduces TensorFlow.js and how it can be used with vanilla JavaScript or Node.js to develop Web applications.

Chapter 14, An Introduction to AutoML, this chapter introduces you to the exciting field of AutoML. It talks about automatic data preparation, automatic feature engineering, and automatic model generation. The chapter also introduces AutoKeras and Google Cloud Platform AutoML with its multiple solutions for Table, Vision, Text, Translation, and for Video processing.

Chapter 15, The Math behind Deep Learning, this chapter, as the title implies, discusses the math behind deep learning. In the chapter, we'll get "under the hood" and see what's going on when we perform deep learning. The chapter begins with a brief history regarding the origins of deep learning programming and backpropagation. Next, it introduces some mathematical tools and derivations, which help us in understanding the concepts to be covered. The remainder of the chapter details backpropagation and some of its applications within CNNs and RNNs.

Chapter 16, Tensor Processing Unit, this chapter introduces the **Tensor Processing Unit** (**TPU**), a special chip developed at Google for ultra-fast execution of neural network mathematical operations. In this chapter we are going to compare CPUs and GPUs with the three generations of TPUs and with Edge TPUs. The chapter will include code examples of using TPUs.

What you need for this book

To be able to smoothly follow through the chapters, you will need the following pieces of software:

- TensorFlow 2.0 or higher
- Matplotlib 3.0 or higher
- Scikit-learn 0.18.1 or higher
- NumPy 1.15 or higher

The hardware specifications are as follows:

- Either 32-bit or 64-bit architecture
- 2+ GHz CPU

- 4 GB RAM
- At least 10 GB of hard disk space available

Downloading the example code

You can download the example code files for this book from your account at www.packt.com/. If you purchased this book elsewhere, you can visit www.packtpub.com/support and register to have the files emailed directly to you.

You can download the code files by following these steps:

1. Log in or register at http://www.packt.com.
2. Select the **Support** tab.
3. Click on **Code Downloads**.
4. Enter the name of the book in the **Search** box and follow the on-screen instructions.

Once the file is downloaded, please make sure that you unzip or extract the folder using the latest version of:

- WinRAR / 7-Zip for Windows
- Zipeg / iZip / UnRarX for Mac
- 7-Zip / PeaZip for Linux

The code bundle for the book is also hosted on GitHub at https://github.com/PacktPublishing/Deep-Learning-with-TensorFlow-2-and-Keras. In case there's an update to the code, it will be updated on the existing GitHub repository.

We also have other code bundles from our rich catalog of books and videos available at https://github.com/PacktPublishing/. Check them out!

Download the color images

We also provide a PDF file that has color images of the screenshots/diagrams used in this book. You can download it here:

https://static.packt-cdn.com/downloads/9781838823412_ColorImages.pdf

Conventions

There are a number of text conventions used throughout this book.

CodeInText: Indicates code words in text, database table names, folder names, filenames, file extensions, pathnames, dummy URLs, user input, and Twitter handles are shown as follows: "In addition, we load the true labels into Y_train and Y_test respectively and perform a one-hot encoding on them."

A block of code is set as follows:

```
from TensorFlow.keras.models import Sequential
model = Sequential()
model.add(Dense(12, input_dim=8, kernel_initializer='random_uniform'))
```

When we wish to draw your attention to a particular part of a code block, the relevant lines or items are set in bold:

```
model = Sequential()
model.add(Dense(NB_CLASSES, input_shape=(RESHAPED,)))
model.add(Activation('softmax'))
model.summary()
```

Any command-line input or output is written as follows:

```
pip install quiver_engine
```

Bold: Indicates a new term and important word or words that you see on the screen. For example, in menus or dialog boxes, appear in the text like this: "Our simple net started with an **accuracy** of 92.22%, which means that about eight handwritten characters out of 100 are not correctly recognized."

Warnings or important notes appear in a box like this.

Tips and tricks appear like this.

Get in touch

Feedback from our readers is always welcome.

General feedback: If you have questions about any aspect of this book, mention the book title in the subject of your message and email us at customercare@ packtpub.com.

Errata: Although we have taken every care to ensure the accuracy of our content, mistakes do happen. If you have found a mistake in this book we would be grateful if you would report this to us. Please visit, www.packtpub.com/support/errata, selecting your book, clicking on the Errata Submission Form link, and entering the details.

Piracy: If you come across any illegal copies of our works in any form on the Internet, we would be grateful if you would provide us with the location address or website name. Please contact us at copyright@packt.com with a link to the material.

If you are interested in becoming an author: If there is a topic that you have expertise in and you are interested in either writing or contributing to a book, please visit authors.packtpub.com.

Reviews

Please leave a review. Once you have read and used this book, why not leave a review on the site that you purchased it from? Potential readers can then see and use your unbiased opinion to make purchase decisions, we at Packt can understand what you think about our products, and our authors can see your feedback on their book. Thank you!

For more information about Packt, please visit packt.com.

References

1. *Deep Learning with Keras: Implementing deep learning models and neural networks with the power of Python*, Paperback – 26 Apr 2017, Antonio Gulli, Sujit Pal

2. *TensorFlow 1.x Deep Learning Cookbook: Over 90 unique recipes to solve artificial-intelligence driven problems with Python*, Antonio Gulli, Amita Kapoor

3. Large Scale Visual Recognition Challenge 2012 (ILSVRC2012) `https://www.kdnuggets.com/2018/12/deep-learning-major-advances-review.html`

4. *ImageNet Classification with Deep Convolutional Neural Networks*, Krizhevsky, Sutskever, Hinton, NIPS, 2012

5. *From not working to neural networking*, The Economist `https://www.economist.com/special-report/2016/06/23/from-not-working-to-neural-networking`

6. *State-of-the-art Image Classification on ImageNet* `https://paperswithcode.com/sota/image-classification-on-imagenet`

7. *Language Models are Unsupervised Multitask Learners*, Alec Radford, Jeffrey Wu, Rewon Child, David Luan, Dario Amodei, Ilya Sutskever `https://github.com/openai/gpt-2`

8. PyTorch: An open source machine learning framework that accelerates the path from research prototyping to production deployment, `https://pytorch.org/`

9. *State of Deep Learning and Major Advances: H2 2018 Review*, `https://www.kdnuggets.com/2018/12/deep-learning-major-advances-review.html`

1
Neural Network Foundations with TensorFlow 2.0

In this chapter we learn the basics of TensorFlow, an open source library developed by Google for machine learning and deep learning. In addition, we introduce the basics of neural networks and deep learning, two areas of machine learning that have had incredible Cambrian growth during the last few years. The idea behind this chapter is to give you all the tools needed to do basic but fully hands-on deep learning.

What is TensorFlow (TF)?

TensorFlow is a powerful open source software library developed by the Google Brain team for deep neural networks, the topic covered in this book. It was first made available under the Apache 2.0 License in November 2015 and has since grown rapidly; as of May 2019, its GitHub repository (`https://github.com/tensorflow/tensorflow`) has more than 51,000 commits, with roughly 1,830 contributors. This in itself provides a measure of the popularity of TensorFlow.

Let us first learn what exactly TensorFlow is and why it is so popular among deep neural network researchers and engineers. Google calls it "an open source software library for machine intelligence," but since there are so many other deep learning libraries like PyTorch (`https://pytorch.org/`), Caffe (`https://caffe.berkeleyvision.org/`), and MxNet (`https://mxnet.apache.org/`), what makes TensorFlow special? Most other deep learning libraries – like TensorFlow – have auto-differentiation (a useful mathematical tool used for optimization), many are open source platforms, most of them support the CPU/GPU option, have pretrained models, and support commonly used NN architectures like recurrent neural networks, convolutional neural networks, and deep belief networks.

So, what else is there in TensorFlow? Let me list the top features:

- It works with all popular languages such as Python, C++, Java, R, and Go.
- Keras – a high-level neural network API that has been integrated with TensorFlow (in 2.0, Keras became the standard API for interacting with TensorFlow). This API specifies how software components should interact.
- TensorFlow allows model deployment and ease of use in production.
- Support for eager computation (see *Chapter 2*, *TensorFlow 1.x and 2.x*) has been introduced in TensorFlow 2.0, in addition to graph computation based on static graphs.
- Most importantly, TensorFlow has very good community support.

The number of stars on GitHub (see *Figure 1*) is a measure of popularity for all open source projects. As of March 2019, TensorFlow, Keras, and PyTorch have 123,000, 39,000, and 25,000 stars respectively, which makes TensorFlow the most popular framework for machine learning:

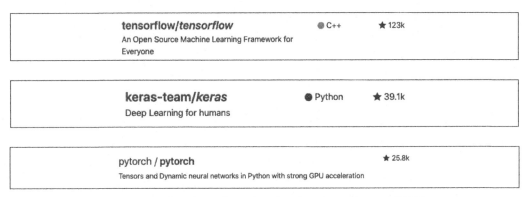

Figure 1: Number of stars for various deep learning projects on GitHub

Google Trends is another measure of popularity, and again TensorFlow and Keras are the two top frameworks (late 2019), with PyTorch rapidly catching up (see *Figure 2*).

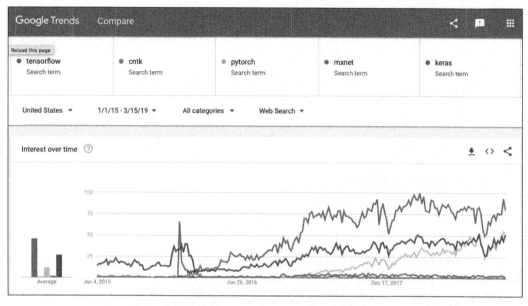

Figure 2: Google Trends for various deep learning projects

What is Keras?

Keras is a beautiful API for composing building blocks to create and train deep learning models. Keras can be integrated with multiple deep learning engines including Google TensorFlow, Microsoft CNTK, Amazon MxNet, and Theano. Starting with TensorFlow 2.0, Keras has been adopted as the standard high-level API, largely simplifying coding and making programming more intuitive.

What are the most important changes in TensorFlow 2.0?

There are many changes in TensorFlow 2.0. There is no longer a need to question "Do I use Keras or TensorFlow?" because Keras is now part of TensorFlow. Another question is "Should I use Keras or `tf.keras`?" `tf.keras` is the implementation of Keras inside TensorFlow. Use `tf.keras` instead of Keras for better integration with other TensorFlow APIs, such as eager execution, `tf.data`, and many more benefits that we are going to discuss in *Chapter 2, TensorFlow 1.x and 2.x*.

For now, let's start with a simple code comparison just to give you some initial intuition. If you have never installed TensorFlow before, then let's install it using pip:

 You can find more options for installing TensorFlow at https://www.tensorflow.org/install.

Only CPU support:

```
pip install tensorflow
```

With GPU support:

```
pip install tensorflow-gpu
```

In order to understand what's new in TensorFlow 2.0, it might be useful to have a look at the traditional way of coding neural networks in TensorFlow 1.0. If this is the first time you have seen a neural network, please do not pay attention to the details but simply count the number of lines:

```
import tensorflow.compat.v1 as tf

in_a = tf.placeholder(dtype=tf.float32, shape=(2))

def model(x):
  with tf.variable_scope("matmul"):
    W = tf.get_variable("W", initializer=tf.ones(shape=(2,2)))
    b = tf.get_variable("b", initializer=tf.zeros(shape=(2)))
    return x * W + b

out_a = model(in_a)

with tf.Session() as sess:
  sess.run(tf.global_variables_initializer())
  outs = sess.run([out_a],
              feed_dict={in_a: [1, 0]})
```

In total, we have 11 lines here. Now let's install TensorFlow 2.0:

Only CPU support:

```
pip install tensorflow==2.0.0-alpha0
```

With GPU support:

```
pip install tensorflow-gpu==2.0.0-alpha0
```

Here's how the code is written in TensorFlow 2.0 to achieve the same results:

```
import tensorflow as tf
W = tf.Variable(tf.ones(shape=(2,2)), name="W")
b = tf.Variable(tf.zeros(shape=(2)), name="b")

@tf.function
def model(x):
  return W * x + b
out_a = model([1,0])

print(out_a)
```

In this case, we have eight lines in total and the code looks cleaner and nicer. Indeed, the key idea of TensorFlow 2.0 is to make TensorFlow easier to learn and to apply. If you have started with TensorFlow 2.0 and have never seen TensorFlow 1.x, then you are lucky. If you are already familiar with 1.x, then it is important to understand the differences and you need to be ready to rewrite your code with some help from automatic tools for migration, as discussed in *Chapter 2, TensorFlow 1.x and 2.x*. Before that, let's start by introducing neural networks–one of the most powerful learning paradigms supported by TensorFlow.

Introduction to neural networks

Artificial neural networks (briefly, "nets" or **ANNs**) represent a class of machine learning models loosely inspired by studies about the central nervous systems of mammals. Each ANN is made up of several interconnected "neurons," organized in "layers." Neurons in one layer pass messages to neurons in the next layer (they "fire," in jargon terms) and this is how the network computes things. Initial studies were started in the early 50's with the introduction of the "perceptron" [1], a two-layer network used for simple operations, and further expanded in the late 60's with the introduction of the "back-propagation" algorithm used for efficient multi-layer network training (according to [2], [3]).

 Some studies argue that these techniques have roots dating further back than normally cited[4].

Neural networks were a topic of intensive academic studies up until the 80's, at which point other, simpler approaches became more relevant. However, there has been a resurgence of interest starting in the mid 2000's, mainly thanks to three factors: a breakthrough fast learning algorithm proposed by G. Hinton [3], [5], [6]; the introduction of GPUs around 2011 for massive numeric computation; and the availability of big collections of data for training.

These improvements opened the route for modern "deep learning," a class of neural networks characterized by a significant number of layers of neurons that are able to learn rather sophisticated models based on progressive levels of abstraction. People began referring to it as "deep" when it started utilizing 3-5 layers a few years ago. Now, networks with more than 200 layers are commonplace!

This learning via progressive abstraction resembles vision models that have evolved over millions of years within the human brain. Indeed, the human visual system is organized into different layers. First, our eyes are connected to an area of the brain named the visual cortex (V1), which is located in the lower posterior part of our brain. This area is common to many mammals and has the role of discriminating basic properties like small changes in visual orientation, spatial frequencies, and colors.

It has been estimated that V1 consists of about 140 million neurons, with tens of billions of connections between them. V1 is then connected to other areas (V2, V3, V4, V5, and V6) doing progressively more complex image processing and recognizing more sophisticated concepts, such as shapes, faces, animals, and many more. It has been estimated that there are ~16 billion human cortical neurons and about 10-25% of the human cortex is devoted to vision [7]. Deep learning has taken some inspiration from this layer-based organization of the human visual system: early artificial neuron layers learn basic properties of images while deeper layers learn more sophisticated concepts.

This book covers several major aspects of neural networks by providing working nets in TensorFlow 2.0. So, let's start!

Perceptron

The "perceptron" is a simple algorithm that, given an input vector x of m values (x_1, x_2,..., x_m), often called input features or simply features, outputs either a 1 ("yes") or a 0 ("no"). Mathematically, we define a function:

$$f(x) = \begin{cases} 1 & wx + b > 0 \\ 0 & otherwise \end{cases}$$

Where w is a vector of weights, wx is the dot product $\sum_{j=1}^{m} w_j x_j$ and b is bias. If you remember elementary geometry, $wx + b$ defines a boundary hyperplane that changes position according to the values assigned to w and b.

Note that a hyperplane is a subspace whose dimension is one less than that of its ambient space. See *Figure 3* for an example:

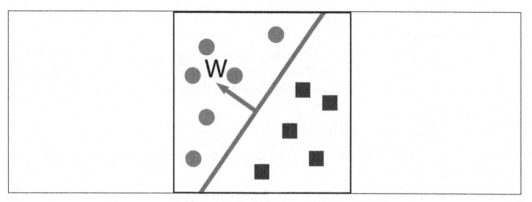

Figure 3: An example of a hyperplane

In other words, this is a very simple but effective algorithm! For example, given three input features, the amounts of red, green, and blue in a color, the perceptron could try to decide whether the color is white or not.

Note that the perceptron cannot express a "maybe" answer. It can answer "yes" (1) or "no" (0), if we understand how to define w and b. This is the "training" process that will be discussed in the following sections.

A first example of TensorFlow 2.0 code

There are three ways of creating a model in tf.keras: Sequential API, Functional API, and Model subclassing. In this chapter we will use the simplest one, Sequential(), while the other two are discussed in *Chapter 2, TensorFlow 1.x and 2.x*. A Sequential() model is a linear pipeline (a stack) of neural network layers. This code fragment defines a single layer with 10 artificial neurons that expects 784 input variables (also known as features). Note that the net is "dense," meaning that each neuron in a layer is connected to all neurons located in the previous layer, and to all the neurons in the following layer:

```
import tensorflow as tf
from tensorflow import keras
NB_CLASSES = 10
RESHAPED = 784
model = tf.keras.models.Sequential()
model.add(keras.layers.Dense(NB_CLASSES,
        input_shape=(RESHAPED,), kernel_initializer='zeros',
        name='dense_layer', activation='softmax'))
```

Each neuron can be initialized with specific weights via the `kernel_initializer` parameter. There are a few choices, the most common of which are listed as follows:

- `random_uniform`: Weights are initialized to uniformly random small values in the range -0.05 to 0.05.

- `random_normal`: Weights are initialized according to a Gaussian distribution, with zero mean and a small standard deviation of 0.05. For those of you who are not familiar with Gaussian distribution, think about a symmetric "bell curve" shape.

- `zero`: All weights are initialized to zero.

A full list is available online at `https://www.tensorflow.org/api_docs/python/tf/keras/initializers`.

Multi-layer perceptron – our first example of a network

In this chapter, we present our first example of a network with multiple dense layers. Historically, "perceptron" was the name given to a model having one single linear layer, and as a consequence, if it has multiple layers, you would call it a **multi-layer perceptron** (MLP). Note that the input and the output layers are visible from outside, while all the other layers in the middle are hidden – hence the name *hidden layers*. In this context, a single layer is simply a linear function and the MLP is therefore obtained by stacking multiple single layers one after the other:

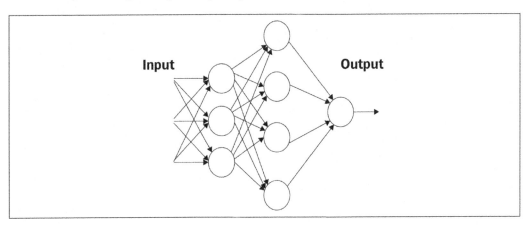

Figure 4: An example of a multiple layer perceptron

In *Figure 4* each node in the first hidden layer receives an input and "fires" (0,1) according to the values of the associated linear function. Then, the output of the first hidden layer is passed to the second layer where another linear function is applied, the results of which are passed to the final output layer consisting of one single neuron. It is interesting to note that this layered organization vaguely resembles the organization of the human vision system, as we discussed earlier.

Problems in training the perceptron and their solutions

Let's consider a single neuron; what are the best choices for the weight w and the bias b? Ideally, we would like to provide a set of training examples and let the computer adjust the weight and the bias in such a way that the errors produced in the output are minimized.

In order to make this a bit more concrete, let's suppose that we have a set of images of cats and another separate set of images not containing cats. Suppose that each neuron receives input from the value of a single pixel in the images. While the computer processes those images, we would like our neuron to adjust its weights and its bias so that we have fewer and fewer images wrongly recognized.

This approach seems very intuitive, but it requires a small change in the weights (or the bias) to cause only a small change in the outputs. Think about it: if we have a big output jump, we cannot learn *progressively*. After all, kids learn little by little. Unfortunately, the perceptron does not show this "little-by-little" behavior. A perceptron is either a 0 or 1, and that's a big jump that will not help in learning (see *Figure 5*):

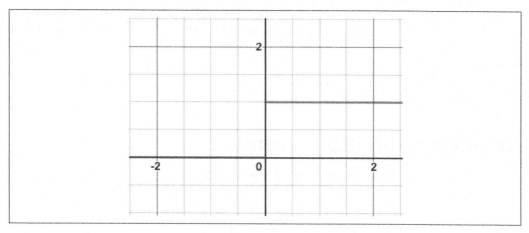

Figure 5: Example of perceptron - either a 0 or 1

We need something different; something smoother. We need a function that progressively changes from 0 to 1 with no discontinuity. Mathematically, this means that we need a continuous function that allows us to compute the derivative. You might remember that in mathematics the derivative is the amount by which a function changes at a given point. For functions with input given by real numbers, the derivative is the slope of the tangent line at a point on a graph. Later in this chapter, we will see why derivatives are important for learning, when we talk about gradient descent.

Activation function – sigmoid

The sigmoid function defined as $\sigma(x) = \dfrac{1}{1 + e^{-x}}$ and represented in the following figure has small output changes in the range (0, 1) when the input varies in the range $(-\infty, \infty)$. Mathematically the function is continuous. A typical sigmoid function is represented in *Figure 6*:

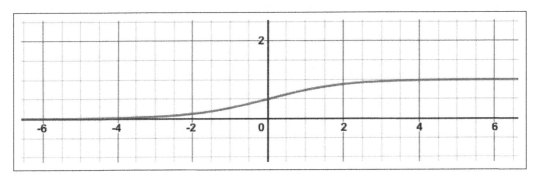

Figure 6: A sigmoid function with output in the range (0,1)

A neuron can use the sigmoid for computing the nonlinear function $\sigma(z = wx + b)$. Note that if $z = wx + b$ is very large and positive, then $e^{-z} \to 0$ so $\sigma(z) \to 1$, while if $z = wx + b$ is very large and negative $e^{-z} \to \infty$ so $\sigma(z) \to 0$. In other words, a neuron with sigmoid activation has a behavior similar to the perceptron, but the changes are gradual and output values such as 0.5539 or 0.123191 are perfectly legitimate. In this sense, a sigmoid neuron can answer "maybe."

Activation function – tanh

Another useful activation function is tanh. Defined as $\tanh(z) = \dfrac{e^z - e^{-z}}{e^z + e^{-z}}$ whose shape is shown in *Figure 7*, its outputs range from -1 to 1:

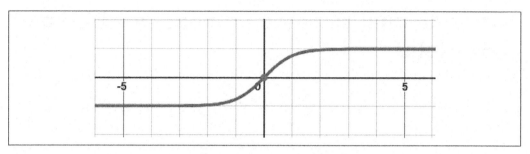

Figure 7: Tanh activation function

Activation function – ReLU

The sigmoid is not the only kind of smooth activation function used for neural networks. Recently, a very simple function named **ReLU (REctified Linear Unit)** became very popular because it helps address some optimization problems observed with sigmoids. We will discuss these problems in more detail when we talk about vanishing gradient in *Chapter 9, Autoencoders*. A ReLU is simply defined as $f(x) = max(0, x)$ and the non-linear function is represented in *Figure 8*. As you can see, the function is zero for negative values and it grows linearly for positive values. The ReLU is also very simple to implement (generally, three instructions are enough), while the sigmoid is a few orders of magnitude more. This helped to squeeze the neural networks onto an early GPU:

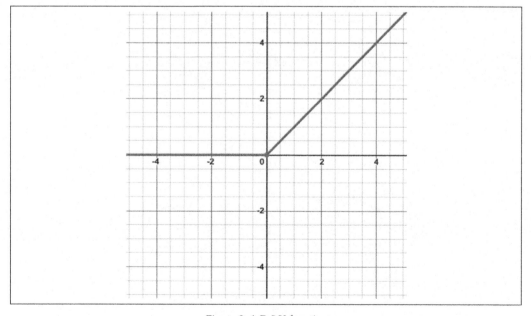

Figure 8: A ReLU function

Two additional activation functions – ELU and LeakyReLU

Sigmoid and ReLU are not the only activation functions used for learning.

ELU is defined as $f(\alpha, x) = \begin{cases} \alpha(e^x - 1) & if \ x \leq 0 \\ x & if \ x > 0 \end{cases}$ for $\alpha > 0$ and its plot is represented in *Figure 9*:

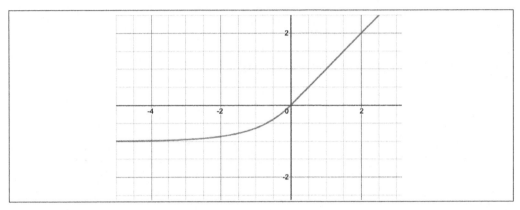

Figure 9: An ELU function

LeakyReLU is defined as $f(\alpha, x) = \begin{cases} \alpha x & if \ x \leq 0 \\ x & if \ x > 0 \end{cases}$ for $\alpha > 0$ and its plot is represented in *Figure 10*:

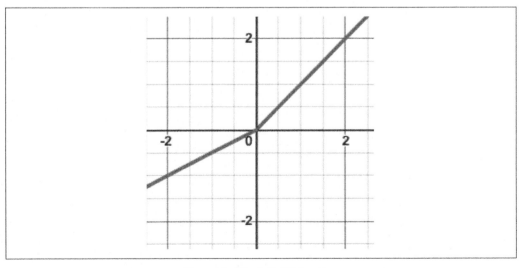

Figure 10: A LeakyReLU function

Both the functions allow small updates if x is negative, which might be useful in certain conditions.

Activation functions

Sigmoid, Tanh, ELU, LeakyReLU, and ReLU are generally called *activation functions* in neural network jargon. In the gradient descent section, we will see that those gradual changes typical of sigmoid and ReLU functions are the basic building blocks to develop a learning algorithm that adapts little by little by progressively reducing the mistakes made by our nets. An example of using the activation function σ with $(x_1, x_2,..., x_m)$ input vector, $(w_1, w_2,..., w_m)$ weight vector, b bias, and Σ summation is given in *Figure 11*. Note that TensorFlow 2.0 supports many activation functions, a full list of which is available online:

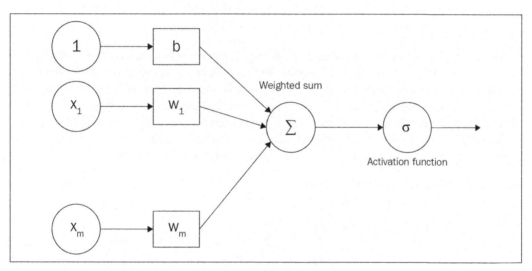

Figure 11: An example of an activation function applied after a linear function

In short – what are neural networks after all?

In one sentence, machine learning models are a way to compute a function that maps some inputs to their corresponding outputs. The function is nothing more than a number of addition and multiplication operations. However, when combined with a non-linear activation and stacked in multiple layers, these functions can learn almost anything [8]. You also need a meaningful metric capturing what you want to optimize (this being the so-called loss function that we will cover later in the book), enough data to learn from, and sufficient computational power.

Now, it might be beneficial to stop one moment and ask ourselves what "learning" really is? Well, we can say for our purposes that learning is essentially a process aimed at generalizing established observations [9] in order to predict future results. So, in short, this is exactly the goal we want to achieve with neural networks.

A real example – recognizing handwritten digits

In this section we will build a network that can recognize handwritten numbers. In order to achieve this goal, we'll use MNIST (`http://yann.lecun.com/exdb/mnist/`), a database of handwritten digits made up of a training set of 60,000 examples, and a test set of 10,000 examples. The training examples are annotated by humans with the correct answer. For instance, if the handwritten digit is the number "3", then 3 is simply the label associated with that example.

In machine learning, when a dataset with correct answers is available, we say that we can perform a form of *supervised learning*. In this case we can use training examples to improve our net. Testing examples also have the correct answer associated to each digit. In this case, however, the idea is to pretend that the label is unknown, let the network do the prediction, and then later on reconsider the label to evaluate how well our neural network has learned to recognize digits. Unsurprisingly, testing examples are just used to test the performance of our net.

Each MNIST image is in grayscale and consists of 28*28 pixels. A subset of these images of numbers is shown in *Figure 12*:

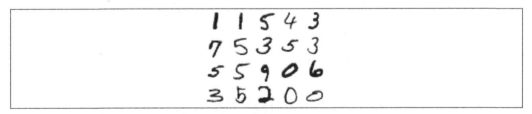

Figure 12: A collection of MNIST images

One-hot encoding (OHE)

We are going to use OHE as a simple tool to encode information used inside neural networks. In many applications it is convenient to transform categorical (non-numerical) features into numerical variables. For instance, the categorical feature "digit" with value d in [0 – 9] can be encoded into a binary vector with 10 positions, which always has 0 value except the d - th position where a 1 is present.

For example, the digit 3 can be encoded as [0, 0, 0, 1, 0, 0, 0, 0, 0, 0]. This type of representation is called **One-hot encoding,** or sometimes simply one-hot, and is very common in data mining when the learning algorithm is specialized in dealing with numerical functions.

Defining a simple neural network in TensorFlow 2.0

In this section, we use TensorFlow 2.0 to define a network that recognizes MNIST handwritten digits. We start with a very simple neural network and then progressively improve it.

Following Keras style, TensorFlow 2.0 provides suitable libraries (https://www.tensorflow.org/api_docs/python/tf/keras/datasets) for loading the dataset and splits it into training sets, X_train, used for fine-tuning our net, and test sets, X_test, used for assessing the performance. Data is converted into float32 to use 32-bit precision when training a neural network and normalized to the range [0,1]. In addition, we load the true labels into Y_train and Y_test respectively, and perform a one-hot encoding on them. Let's see the code.

For now, do not focus too much on understanding why certain parameters have specific assigned values, as these choices will be discussed throughout the rest of the book. Intuitively, EPOCH defines how long the training should last, BATCH_SIZE is the number of samples you feed in to your network at a time, and VALIDATION is the amount of data reserved for checking or proving the validity of the training process. The reason why we picked EPOCHS = 200, BATCH_SIZE = 128, VALIDATION_SPLIT=0.2, and N_HIDDEN = 128 will be clearer later in this chapter when we will explore different values and discuss hyperparameter optimization. Let's look at our first code fragment of a neural network in TensorFlow. Reading is intuitive but you will find a detailed explanation in the following pages:

```
import tensorflow as tf
import numpy as np
from tensorflow import keras

# Network and training parameters.
EPOCHS = 200
BATCH_SIZE = 128
VERBOSE = 1
NB_CLASSES = 10    # number of outputs = number of digits
N_HIDDEN = 128
VALIDATION_SPLIT = 0.2 # how much TRAIN is reserved for VALIDATION
```

```
# Loading MNIST dataset.
# verify
# You can verify that the split between train and test is 60,000, and
10,000 respectively.
# Labels have one-hot representation.is automatically applied
mnist = keras.datasets.mnist
(X_train, Y_train), (X_test, Y_test) = mnist.load_data()

# X_train is 60000 rows of 28x28 values; we   --> reshape it to
# 60000 x 784.
RESHAPED = 784
#
X_train = X_train.reshape(60000, RESHAPED)
X_test = X_test.reshape(10000, RESHAPED)
X_train = X_train.astype('float32')
X_test = X_test.astype('float32')

# Normalize inputs to be within in [0, 1].
X_train /= 255
X_test /= 255
print(X_train.shape[0], 'train samples')
print(X_test.shape[0], 'test samples')

# One-hot representation of the labels.
Y_train = tf.keras.utils.to_categorical(Y_train, NB_CLASSES)
Y_test = tf.keras.utils.to_categorical(Y_test, NB_CLASSES)
```

You can see from the above code that the input layer has a neuron associated to each pixel in the image for a total of 28*28=784 neurons, one for each pixel in the MNIST images.

Typically, the values associated with each pixel are normalized in the range [0,1] (which means that the intensity of each pixel is divided by 255, the maximum intensity value). The output can be one of ten classes, with one class for each digit.

The final layer is a single neuron with activation function "softmax", which is a generalization of the sigmoid function. As discussed earlier, a sigmoid function output is in the range (0, 1) when the input varies in the range $(-\infty, \infty)$. Similarly, a softmax "squashes" a K-dimensional vector of arbitrary real values into a K-dimensional vector of real values in the range (0, 1), so that they all add up to 1. In our case, it aggregates 10 answers provided by the previous layer with 10 neurons. What we have just described is implemented with the following code:

```
# Build the model.
model = tf.keras.models.Sequential()
```

```
model.add(keras.layers.Dense(NB_CLASSES,
    input_shape=(RESHAPED,),
    name='dense_layer',
    activation='softmax'))
```

Once we define the model, we have to compile it so that it can be executed by TensorFlow 2.0. There are a few choices to be made during compilation. Firstly, we need to select an *optimizer*, which is the specific algorithm used to update weights while we train our model. Second, we need to select an *objective function*, which is used by the optimizer to navigate the space of weights (frequently, objective functions are called either *loss functions* or *cost functions* and the process of optimization is defined as a process of loss *minimization*). Third, we need to evaluate the trained model.

 A complete list of optimizers can be found at `https://www.tensorflow.org/api_docs/python/tf/keras/optimizers`.

Some common choices for objective functions are:

- `MSE`, which defines the mean squared error between the predictions and the true values. Mathematically, if d is a vector of predictions and y is the vector of n observed values, then $MSE = \frac{1}{n} \sum_{i=1}^{n} (d - y)^2$. Note that this objective function is the average of all the mistakes made in each prediction. If a prediction is far off from the true value, then this distance is made more evident by the squaring operation. In addition, the square can add up the error regardless of whether a given value is positive or negative.

- `binary_crossentropy`, which defines the binary logarithmic loss. Suppose that our model predicts p while the target is c, then the binary cross-entropy is defined as $L(p, c) = -c \ln(p) - (1 - c) \ln(1 - p)$. Note that this objective function is suitable for binary label prediction.

- `categorical_crossentropy`, which defines the multiclass logarithmic loss. Categorical cross-entropy compares the distribution of the predictions with the true distribution, with the probability of the true class set to 1 and 0 for the other classes. If the true class is c and the prediction is y, then the categorical cross-entropy is defined as:

$$L(c, p) = -\sum_{i} c_i \ln(p_i)$$

One way to think about multi-class logarithm loss is to consider the true class represented as a one-hot encoded vector, and the closer the model's outputs are to that vector, the lower the loss. Note that this objective function is suitable for multi-class label predictions. It is also the default choice in association with softmax activation.

 A complete list of loss functions can be found at `https://www.tensorflow.org/api_docs/python/tf/keras/losses`.

Some common choices for metrics are:

- `Accuracy`, which defines the proportion of correct predictions with respect to the targets
- `Precision`, which defines how many selected items are relevant for a multi-label classification
- `Recall`, which defines how many selected items are relevant for a multi-label classification

 A complete list of metrics can be found at `https://www.tensorflow.org/api_docs/python/tf/keras/metrics`.

Metrics are similar to objective functions, with the only difference that they are not used for training a model, but only for evaluating the model. However, it is important to understand the difference between metrics and objective functions. As discussed, the loss function is used to optimize your network. This is the function minimized by the selected optimizer. Instead, a metric is used to judge the performance of your network. This is only for you to run an evaluation on and it should be separated from the optimization process. On some occasions, it would be ideal to directly optimize for a specific metric. However, some metrics are not differentiable with respect to their inputs, which precludes them from being used directly.

When compiling a model in TensorFlow 2.0, it is possible to select the optimizer, the loss function, and the metric used together with a given model:

```
# Compiling the model.
model.compile(optimizer='SGD',
              loss='categorical_crossentropy',
              metrics=['accuracy'])
```

Stochastic Gradient Descent (SGD) (see *Chapter 15, The Math Behind Deep Learning*) is a particular kind of optimization algorithm used to reduce the mistakes made by neural networks after each training epoch. We will review SGD and other optimization algorithms in the next chapters. Once the model is compiled, it can then be trained with the `fit()` method, which specifies a few parameters:

- `epochs` is the number of times the model is exposed to the training set. At each iteration the optimizer tries to adjust the weights so that the objective function is minimized.

- `batch_size` is the number of training instances observed before the optimizer performs a weight update; there are usually many batches per epoch.

Training a model in TensorFlow 2.0 is very simple:

```
# Training the model.
model.fit(X_train, Y_train,
            batch_size=BATCH_SIZE, epochs=EPOCHS,
            verbose=VERBOSE, validation_split=VALIDATION_SPLIT)
```

Note that we've reserved part of the training set for validation. The key idea is that we reserve a part of the training data for measuring the performance on the validation while training. This is a good practice to follow for any machine learning task, and one that we will adopt in all of our examples. Please note that we will return to validation later in this chapter when we talk about overfitting.

Once the model is trained, we can evaluate it on the test set that contains new examples never seen by the model during the training phase.

Note that, of course, the training set and the test set are rigorously separated. There is no point evaluating a model on an example that was already used for training. In TensorFlow 2.0 we can use the method `evaluate(X_test, Y_test)` to compute the `test_loss` and the `test_acc`:

```
#evaluate the model
test_loss, test_acc = model.evaluate(X_test, Y_test)
print('Test accuracy:', test_acc)
```

So, congratulations! You have just defined your first neural network in TensorFlow 2.0. A few lines of code and your computer should be able to recognize handwritten numbers. Let's run the code and see what the performance is.

Running a simple TensorFlow 2.0 net and establishing a baseline

So let's see what happens when we run the code:

```
Model: "sequential"
_____
Layer (type)                 Output Shape              Param #
===============================================================
dense_layer (Dense)          (None, 10)                7850
===============================================================
Total params: 7,850
Trainable params: 7,850
Non-trainable params: 0
_____
Train on 48000 samples, validate on 12000 samples
Epoch 1/200
48000/48000 [==============================] - 1s 31us/sample - loss: 2.1276 - a
ccuracy: 0.2322 - val_loss: 1.9508 - val_accuracy: 0.3908
Epoch 2/200
48000/48000 [==============================] - 1s 23us/sample - loss: 1.8251 - a
ccuracy: 0.5141 - val_loss: 1.6848 - val_accuracy: 0.6277
Epoch 3/200
48000/48000 [==============================] - 1s 25us/sample - loss: 1.5992 - a
ccuracy: 0.6531 - val_loss: 1.4838 - val_accuracy: 0.7150
Epoch 4/200
48000/48000 [==============================] - 1s 27us/sample - loss: 1.4281 - a
ccuracy: 0.7115 - val_loss: 1.3304 - val_accuracy: 0.7551
Epoch 5/200
```

Figure 13: Code ran from our test neural network

First, the net architecture is dumped and we can see the different types of layers used, their output shape, how many parameters (that is, how many weights) they need to optimize, and how they are connected. Then, the network is trained on 48,000 samples, and 12,000 are reserved for validation. Once the neural model is built, it is then tested on 10,000 samples. For now, we won't go into the internals of how the training happens, but we can see that the program runs for 200 iterations and each time accuracy improves. When the training ends, we test our model on the test set and we achieve about 89.96% accuracy on training, 90.70% on validation, and 90.71% on test:

```
Epoch 199/200
48000/48000 [==============================] - 1s 22us/sample - loss: 0.3684 - a
ccuracy: 0.8995 - val_loss: 0.3464 - val_accuracy: 0.9071
Epoch 200/200
48000/48000 [==============================] - 1s 23us/sample - loss: 0.3680 - a
ccuracy: 0.8996 - val_loss: 0.3461 - val_accuracy: 0.9070
10000/10000 [==============================] - 1s 54us/sample - loss: 0.3465 - a
ccuracy: 0.9071
Test accuracy: 0.9071
```

Figure 14: Results from testing model, accuracies displayed

This means that nearly 1 in 10 images are incorrectly classified. We can certainly do better than that.

Improving the simple net in TensorFlow 2.0 with hidden layers

Okay, we have a baseline of accuracy of 89.96% on training, 90.70% on validation, and 90.71% on test. It is a good starting point, but we can improve it. Let's see how.

An initial improvement is to add additional layers to our network because these additional neurons might intuitively help it to learn more complex patterns in the training data. In other words, additional layers add more parameters, potentially allowing a model to memorize more complex patterns. So, after the input layer, we have a first dense layer with N_HIDDEN neurons and an activation function "ReLU." This additional layer is considered *hidden* because it is not directly connected either with the input or with the output. After the first hidden layer, we have a second hidden layer again with N_HIDDEN neurons followed by an output layer with 10 neurons, each one of which will fire when the relative digit is recognized. The following code defines this new network:

```
import tensorflow as tf
from tensorflow import keras

# Network and training.
EPOCHS = 50
BATCH_SIZE = 128
VERBOSE = 1
NB_CLASSES = 10    # number of outputs = number of digits
N_HIDDEN = 128
VALIDATION_SPLIT = 0.2 # how much TRAIN is reserved for VALIDATION

# Loading MNIST dataset.
# Labels have one-hot representation.
mnist = keras.datasets.mnist
(X_train, Y_train), (X_test, Y_test) = mnist.load_data()

# X_train is 60000 rows of 28x28 values; we reshape it to 60000 x 784.
RESHAPED = 784
#
X_train = X_train.reshape(60000, RESHAPED)
X_test = X_test.reshape(10000, RESHAPED)
X_train = X_train.astype('float32')
X_test = X_test.astype('float32')

# Normalize inputs to be within in [0, 1].
X_train, X_test = X_train / 255.0, X_test / 255.0
print(X_train.shape[0], 'train samples')
```

```
print(X_test.shape[0], 'test samples')

# Labels have one-hot representation.
Y_train = tf.keras.utils.to_categorical(Y_train, NB_CLASSES)
Y_test = tf.keras.utils.to_categorical(Y_test, NB_CLASSES)

# Build the model.
model = tf.keras.models.Sequential()
model.add(keras.layers.Dense(N_HIDDEN,
          input_shape=(RESHAPED,),
          name='dense_layer', activation='relu'))
model.add(keras.layers.Dense(N_HIDDEN,
          name='dense_layer_2', activation='relu'))
model.add(keras.layers.Dense(NB_CLASSES,
          name='dense_layer_3', activation='softmax'))

# Summary of the model.
model.summary()

# Compiling the model.
model.compile(optimizer='SGD',
              loss='categorical_crossentropy',
              metrics=['accuracy'])

# Training the model.
model.fit(X_train, Y_train,
          batch_size=BATCH_SIZE, epochs=EPOCHS,
          verbose=VERBOSE, validation_split=VALIDATION_SPLIT)

# Evaluating the model.
test_loss, test_acc = model.evaluate(X_test, Y_test)
print('Test accuracy:', test_acc)
```

Note that `to_categorical(Y_train, NB_CLASSES)` converts the array `Y_train` into a matrix with as many columns as there are classes. The number of rows stays the same. So, for instance if we have:

```
> labels
array([0, 2, 1, 2, 0])
```

then:

```
to_categorical(labels)
array([[ 1.,   0.,   0.],
       [ 0.,   0.,   1.],
```

```
     [ 0.,   1.,   0.],
     [ 0.,   0.,   1.],
     [ 1.,   0.,   0.]], dtype=float32)
```

Let's run the code and see what results we get with this multi-layer network:

```
------------------------------------------------------------------
Layer (type)                 Output Shape              Param #
==================================================================
dense_layer (Dense)          (None, 128)               100480
------------------------------------------------------------------
dense_layer_2 (Dense)        (None, 128)               16512
------------------------------------------------------------------
dense_layer_3 (Dense)        (None, 10)                1290
==================================================================
Total params: 118,282
Trainable params: 118,282
Non-trainable params: 0
------------------------------------------------------------------
Train on 48000 samples, validate on 12000 samples
Epoch 1/200
48000/48000 [==============================] - 3s 63us/sample - loss: 2.2507 - a
ccuracy: 0.2086 - val_loss: 2.1592 - val_accuracy: 0.3266
```

Figure 15: Running the code for a multi-layer network

The previous screenshot shows the initial steps of the run while the following screenshot shows the conclusion. Not bad. As seen in the following screenshot, by adding two hidden layers we reached 90.81% on the training set, 91.40% on validation, and 91.18% on test. This means that we have increased accuracy on testing with respect to the previous network, and we have reduced the number of iterations from 200 to 50. That's good, but we want more.

If you want, you can play by yourself and see what happens if you add only one hidden layer instead of two or if you add more than two layers. I leave this experiment as an exercise:

```
Epoch 49/50
48000/48000 [==============================] - 1s 30us/sample - loss: 0.3347 - a
ccuracy: 0.9075 - val_loss: 0.3126 - val_accuracy: 0.9136
Epoch 50/50
48000/48000 [==============================] - 1s 28us/sample - loss: 0.3326 - a
ccuracy: 0.9081 - val_loss: 0.3107 - val_accuracy: 0.9140
10000/10000 [==============================] - 0s 40us/sample - loss: 0.3164 - a
ccuracy: 0.9118
Test accuracy: 0.9118
```

Figure 16: Results after adding two hidden layers, with accuracies shown

Note that improvement stops (or they become almost imperceptible) after a certain number of epochs. In machine learning, this is a phenomenon called *convergence*.

Further improving the simple net in TensorFlow with Dropout

Now our baseline is 90.81% on the training set, 91.40% on validation, and 91.18% on test. A second improvement is very simple. We decide to randomly drop – with the DROPOUT probability – some of the values propagated inside our internal dense network of hidden layers during training. In machine learning this is a well-known form of regularization. Surprisingly enough, this idea of randomly dropping a few values can improve our performance. The idea behind this improvement is that random dropout *forces* the network to learn redundant patterns that are useful for better generalization:

```
import tensorflow as tf
import numpy as np
from tensorflow import keras

# Network and training.
EPOCHS = 200
BATCH_SIZE = 128
VERBOSE = 1
NB_CLASSES = 10    # number of outputs = number of digits
N_HIDDEN = 128
VALIDATION_SPLIT = 0.2 # how much TRAIN is reserved for VALIDATION
DROPOUT = 0.3

# Loading MNIST dataset.
# Labels have one-hot representation.
mnist = keras.datasets.mnist
(X_train, Y_train), (X_test, Y_test) = mnist.load_data()

# X_train is 60000 rows of 28x28 values; we reshape it to 60000 x 784.
RESHAPED = 784
#
X_train = X_train.reshape(60000, RESHAPED)
X_test = X_test.reshape(10000, RESHAPED)
X_train = X_train.astype('float32')
X_test = X_test.astype('float32')

# Normalize inputs within [0, 1].
X_train, X_test = X_train / 255.0, X_test / 255.0
print(X_train.shape[0], 'train samples')
print(X_test.shape[0], 'test samples')

# One-hot representations for labels.
```

```
Y_train = tf.keras.utils.to_categorical(Y_train, NB_CLASSES)
Y_test = tf.keras.utils.to_categorical(Y_test, NB_CLASSES)

# Building the model.
model = tf.keras.models.Sequential()
model.add(keras.layers.Dense(N_HIDDEN,
          input_shape=(RESHAPED,),
          name='dense_layer', activation='relu'))
model.add(keras.layers.Dropout(DROPOUT))
model.add(keras.layers.Dense(N_HIDDEN,
          name='dense_layer_2', activation='relu'))
model.add(keras.layers.Dropout(DROPOUT))
model.add(keras.layers.Dense(NB_CLASSES,
          name='dense_layer_3', activation='softmax'))

# Summary of the model.
model.summary()

# Compiling the model.
model.compile(optimizer='SGD',
              loss='categorical_crossentropy',
              metrics=['accuracy'])

# Training the model.
model.fit(X_train, Y_train,
          batch_size=BATCH_SIZE, epochs=EPOCHS,
          verbose=VERBOSE, validation_split=VALIDATION_SPLIT)

# Evaluating the model.
test_loss, test_acc = model.evaluate(X_test, Y_test)
print('Test accuracy:', test_acc)
```

Let's run the code for 200 iterations as before, and we'll see that this net achieves an accuracy of 91.70% on training, 94.42% on validation, and 94.15% on testing:

```
Epoch 199/200
48000/48000 [==============================] - 2s 45us/sample - loss: 0.2850 - a
ccuracy: 0.9177 - val_loss: 0.1922 - val_accuracy: 0.9442
Epoch 200/200
48000/48000 [==============================] - 2s 42us/sample - loss: 0.2845 - a
ccuracy: 0.9170 - val_loss: 0.1917 - val_accuracy: 0.9442
10000/10000 [==============================] - 1s 61us/sample - loss: 0.1927 - a
ccuracy: 0.9415
Test accuracy: 0.9415
```

Figure 17: Further testing of the neutal network, with accuracies shown

Note that it has been frequently observed that networks with random dropout in internal hidden layers can "generalize" better on unseen examples contained in test sets. Intuitively, we can consider this phenomenon as each neuron becoming more capable because it knows it cannot depend on its neighbors. Also, because it forces information to be stored in a redundant way. During testing there is no dropout, so we are now using all our highly tuned neurons. In short, it is generally a good approach to test how a net performs when a dropout function is adopted.

Besides that, note that training accuracy should still be above test accuracy, otherwise, we might be not training for long enough. This is the case in our example and therefore we should increase the number of epochs. However, before performing this attempt we need to introduce a few other concepts that allow the training to converge faster. Let's talk about optimizers.

Testing different optimizers in TensorFlow 2.0

Now that we have defined and used a network, it is useful to start developing some intuition about how networks are trained, using an analogy. Let us focus on one popular training technique known as **Gradient Descent** (**GD**). Imagine a generic cost function $C(w)$ in one single variable w as shown in *Figure 18*:

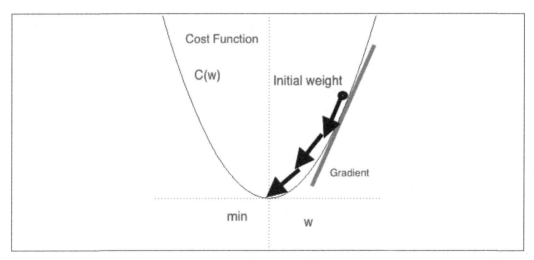

Figure 18: An example of gradient descent optimization

The gradient descent can be seen as a hiker who needs to navigate down a steep slope and aims to enter a ditch. The slope represents the function C while the ditch represents the minimum C_{min}. The hiker has a starting point w_0. The hiker moves little by little; imagine that there is almost zero visibility, so the hiker cannot see where to go automatically, and they proceed in a zigzag. At each step r, the gradient is the direction of maximum increase.

Mathematically this direction is the value of the partial derivative $\frac{\partial c}{\partial w}$ evaluated at point w_r, reached at step r. Therefore, by taking the opposite direction $-\frac{\partial c}{\partial w}(w_r)$ the hiker can move towards the ditch.

At each step, the hiker can decide how big a stride to take before the next stop. This is the so-called "learning rate" $\eta \geq 0$ in gradient descent jargon. Note that if η is too small, then the hiker will move slowly. However, if η is too high, then the hiker will possibly miss the ditch by stepping over it.

Now you should remember that a sigmoid is a continuous function and it is possible to compute the derivative. It can be proven that the sigmoid $\sigma(x) = \frac{1}{1 + e^{-x}}$ has the derivative $\frac{d\sigma(x)}{d(x)} = \sigma(x)(1 - \sigma(x))$.

ReLU is not differentiable at 0. We can however extend the first derivative at 0 to a function over the whole domain by defining it to be either a 0 or 1.

The piecewise derivative of ReLU $y = max(0, x)$ is $\frac{dy}{dx} = \begin{cases} 0 & x \leq 0 \\ 1 & x > 0 \end{cases}$. Once we have the derivative, it is possible to optimize the nets with a gradient descent technique. TensorFlow computes the derivative on our behalf so we don't need to worry about implementing or computing it.

A neural network is essentially a composition of multiple derivable functions with thousands and sometimes millions of parameters. Each network layer computes a function, the error of which should be minimized in order to improve the accuracy observed during the learning phase. When we discuss backpropagation, we will discover that the minimization game is a bit more complex than our toy example. However, it is still based on the same intuition of descending a slope to reach a ditch.

TensorFlow implements a fast variant of gradient descent known as SGD and many more advanced optimization techniques such as RMSProp and Adam. RMSProp and Adam include the concept of momentum (a velocity component), in addition to the acceleration component that SGD has. This allows faster convergence at the cost of more computation. Think about a hiker who starts to move in one direction then decides to change direction but remembers previous choices. It can be proven that momentum helps accelerate SGD in the relevant direction and dampens oscillations [10].

 A complete list of optimizers can be found at `https://www.tensorflow.org/api_docs/python/tf/keras/optimizers`.

SGD was our default choice so far. So now let's try the other two.

It is very simple; we just need to change a few lines:

```
# Compiling the model.
model.compile(optimizer='RMSProp',
              loss='categorical_crossentropy', metrics=['accuracy'])
```

That's it. Let's test it:

```
Layer (type)                 Output Shape              Param #
=================================================================
dense_layer (Dense)          (None, 128)               100480
_____
dropout (Dropout)            (None, 128)               0
_____
dense_layer_2 (Dense)        (None, 128)               16512
_____
dropout_1 (Dropout)          (None, 128)               0
_____
dense_layer_3 (Dense)        (None, 10)                1290
=================================================================
Total params: 118,282
Trainable params: 118,282
Non-trainable params: 0
_____
Train on 48000 samples, validate on 12000 samples
Epoch 1/10
48000/48000 [==============================] - 2s 48us/sample - loss: 0.4715 -
accuracy: 0.8575 - val_loss: 0.1820 - val_accuracy: 0.9471
Epoch 2/10
48000/48000 [==============================] - 2s 36us/sample - loss: 0.2215 -
accuracy: 0.9341 - val_loss: 0.1268 - val_accuracy: 0.9631
Epoch 3/10
48000/48000 [==============================] - 2s 39us/sample - loss: 0.1684 -
accuracy: 0.9497 - val_loss: 0.1198 - val_accuracy: 0.9651
Epoch 4/10
48000/48000 [==============================] - 2s 43us/sample - loss: 0.1459 -
accuracy: 0.9569 - val_loss: 0.1059 - val_accuracy: 0.9710
Epoch 5/10
48000/48000 [==============================] - 2s 39us/sample - loss: 0.1273 -
accuracy: 0.9623 - val_loss: 0.1059 - val_accuracy: 0.9696
Epoch 6/10
48000/48000 [==============================] - 2s 36us/sample - loss: 0.1177 -
accuracy: 0.9659 - val_loss: 0.0941 - val_accuracy: 0.9731
Epoch 7/10
48000/48000 [==============================] - 2s 35us/sample - loss: 0.1083 -
accuracy: 0.9671 - val_loss: 0.1009 - val_accuracy: 0.9715
Epoch 8/10
48000/48000 [==============================] - 2s 35us/sample - loss: 0.0971 -
accuracy: 0.9706 - val_loss: 0.0950 - val_accuracy: 0.9758
Epoch 9/10
48000/48000 [==============================] - 2s 35us/sample - loss: 0.0969 -
accuracy: 0.9718 - val_loss: 0.0985 - val_accuracy: 0.9745
Epoch 10/10
48000/48000 [==============================] - 2s 35us/sample - loss: 0.0873 -
accuracy: 0.9743 - val_loss: 0.0966 - val_accuracy: 0.9762
10000/10000 [==============================] - 0s 37us/sample - loss: 0.0922 -
accuracy: 0.9764
Test accuracy: 0.9764
```

Figure 19: Testing RMSProp

As you can see in the preceding screenshot, RMSProp is faster than SDG since we are able to achieve in only 10 epochs an accuracy of 97.43% on training, 97.62% on validation, and 97.64% on test. That's a significant improvement on SDG. Now that we have a very fast optimizer, let us try to significantly increase the number of epochs up to 250 and we get 98.99% accuracy on training, 97.66% on validation, and 97.77% on test:

```
Epoch 248/250
48000/48000 [==============================] - 2s 40us/sample - loss: 0.0506 -
accuracy: 0.9904 - val_loss: 0.3465 - val_accuracy: 0.9762
Epoch 249/250
48000/48000 [==============================] - 2s 40us/sample - loss: 0.0490 -
accuracy: 0.9905 - val_loss: 0.3645 - val_accuracy: 0.9765
Epoch 250/250
48000/48000 [==============================] - 2s 39us/sample - loss: 0.0547 -
accuracy: 0.9899 - val_loss: 0.3353 - val_accuracy: 0.9766
10000/10000 [==============================] - 1s 58us/sample - loss: 0.3184 -
accuracy: 0.9779
Test accuracy: 0.9779
```

Figure 20: Increasing the number of epochs

It is useful to observe how accuracy increases on training and test sets when the number of epochs increases (see *Figure 21*). As you can see, these two curves touch at about 15 epochs and therefore there is no need to train further after that point (the image is generated by using TensorBoard, a standard TensorFlow tool that will be discussed in *Chapter 2, TensorFlow 1.x and 2.x*):

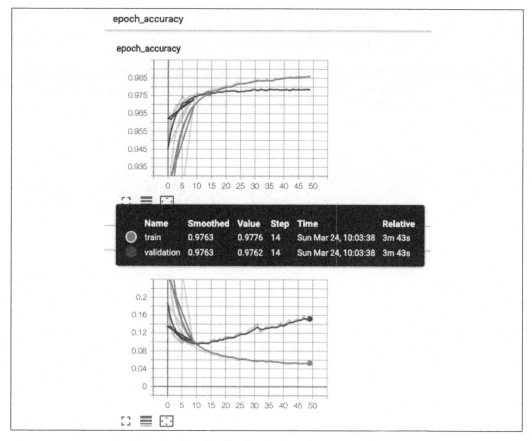

Figure 21: An example of accuracy and loss with RMSProp

Okay, let's try the other optimizer, `Adam()`. Pretty simple:

```
# Compiling the model.
model.compile(optimizer='Adam',
              loss='categorical_crossentropy',
              metrics=['accuracy'])
```

As we can see, `Adam()` is slightly better. With Adam we achieve 98.94% accuracy on training, 97.89% on validation, and 97.82% on test with 20 iterations:

```
Epoch 49/50
48000/48000 [==============================] - 3s 55us/sample - loss: 0.0313 -
accuracy: 0.9894 - val_loss: 0.0868 - val_accuracy: 0.9808
Epoch 50/50
48000/48000 [==============================] - 2s 51us/sample - loss: 0.0321 -
accuracy: 0.9894 - val_loss: 0.0983 - val_accuracy: 0.9789
10000/10000 [==============================] - 1s 66us/sample - loss: 0.0964 -
accuracy: 0.9782
Test accuracy: 0.9782
```

Figure 22: Testing with the Adam optimizer

One more time, let's plot how accuracy increases on training and test sets when the number of epochs increases (see *Figure 23*). You'll notice that by choosing Adam as an optimizer, we are able to stop after just about 12 epochs or steps:

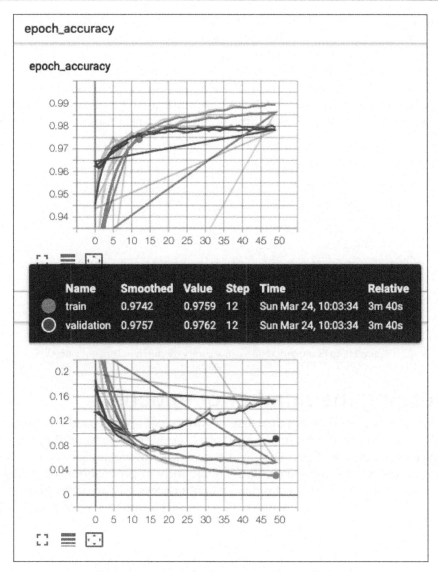

Figure 23: An example of accuracy and loss with adam

Note that this is our fifth variant and remember that our initial baseline was at 90.71% on test. So far, we've made progressive improvements. However, gains are now more and more difficult to obtain. Note that we are optimizing with a dropout of 30%. For the sake of completeness, it could be useful to report the accuracy on the test dataset for different dropout values (see *Figure 24*). In this example, we selected Adam() as the optimizer. Note that choice of optimizer isn't a rule of thumb and we can get different performance depending on the problem-optimizer combination:

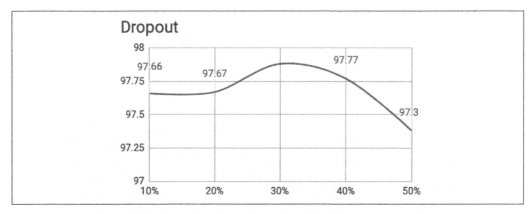

Figure 24: An example of changes in accuracy for different Dropout values

Increasing the number of epochs

Let's make another attempt and increase the number of epochs used for training from 20 to 200. Unfortunately, this choice increases our computation time tenfold, yet gives us no gain. The experiment is unsuccessful, but we have learned that if we spend more time learning, we will not necessarily improve the result. Learning is more about adopting smart techniques and not necessarily about the time spent in computations. Let's keep track of our five variants in the following graph (see *Figure 25*):

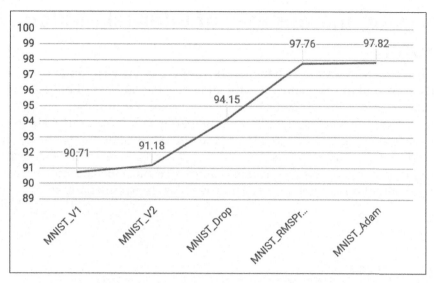

Figure 25: Accuracy for different models and optimizers

Controlling the optimizer learning rate

There is another approach we can take that involves changing the learning parameter for our optimizer. As you can see in *Figure 26*, the best value reached by our three experiments [**lr=0.1, lr=0.01, lr=0.001**] is 0.1, which is the default learning rate for the optimizer. Good! adam works well out of the box:

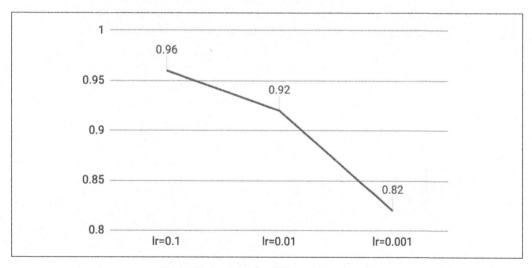

Figure 26: Accuracy for different learning rates

Increasing the number of internal hidden neurons

Yet another approach involves changing the number of internal hidden neurons. We report the results of the experiments with an increasing number of hidden neurons. We see that by increasing the complexity of the model, the runtime increases significantly because there are more and more parameters to optimize. However, the gains that we are getting by increasing the size of the network decrease more and more as the network grows (see *Figures 27, 28,* and *29*). Note that increasing the number of hidden neurons after a certain value can reduce the accuracy because the network might not be able to generalize well (as shown in *Figure 29*):

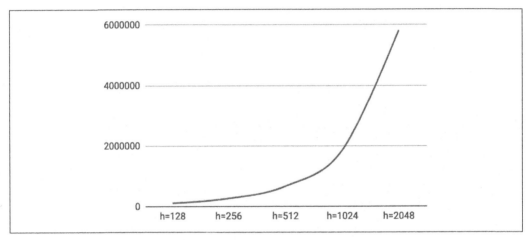

Figure 27: Number of parameters for increasing values of internal hidden neurons

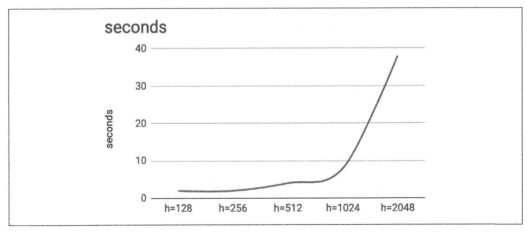

Figure 28: Seconds of computation time for increasing values of internal hidden neurons

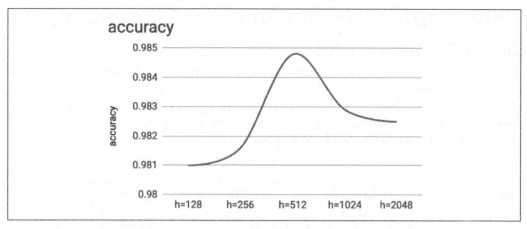

Figure 29: Test accuracy for increasing the values of internal hidden neurons

Increasing the size of batch computation

Gradient descent tries to minimize the cost function on all the examples provided in the training sets and, at the same time, for all the features provided in input. SGD is a much less expensive variant that considers only BATCH_SIZE examples. So, let us see how it behaves when we change this parameter. As you can see, the best accuracy value is reached for a BATCH_SIZE=64 in our four experiments (see *Figure 30*):

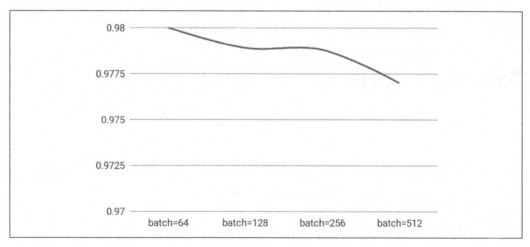

Figure 30: Test accuracy for different batch values

Summarizing experiments run for recognizing handwritten charts

So, let's summarize: with five different variants, we were able to improve our performance from 90.71% to 97.82%. First, we defined a simple layer network in TensorFlow 2.0. Then, we improved the performance by adding some hidden layers. After that, we improved the performance on the test set by adding a few random dropouts in our network, and then by experimenting with different types of optimizers:

model/accuracy	training	validation	test
simple	89.96%	90.70%	90.71%
2 hidden(128)	90.81%	91.40%	91.18%
dropout(30%)	91.70%	94.42%	94.15% (200 epochs)
RMSProp	97.43%	97.62%	97.64% (10 epochs)
Adam	98.94%	97.89%	97.82% (10 epochs)

However, the next two experiments (not shown in the preceding table) were not providing significant improvements. Increasing the number of internal neurons creates more complex models and requires more expensive computations, but it provides only marginal gains. We have the same experience if we increase the number of training epochs. A final experiment consisted of changing the BATCH_ SIZE for our optimizer. This also provided marginal results.

Regularization

In this section, we will review a few best practices for improving the training phase. In particular, regularization and batch normalization will be discussed.

Adopting regularization to avoid overfitting

Intuitively, a good machine learning model should achieve a low error rate on training data. Mathematically this is equivalent to minimizing the loss function on the training data given the model:

$$min: \{loss(Training\ Data\ |\ Model)\}$$

However, this might not be enough. A model can become excessively complex in order to capture all the relations inherently expressed by the training data. This increase of complexity might have two negative consequences. First, a complex model might require a significant amount of time to be executed. Second, a complex model might achieve very good performance on training data, but perform quite badly on validation data. This is because the model is able to contrive relationships between many parameters in the specific training context, but these relationships in fact do not exist within a more generalized context. Causing a model to lose its ability to generalize in this manner is termed "overfitting." Again, learning is more about generalization than memorization:

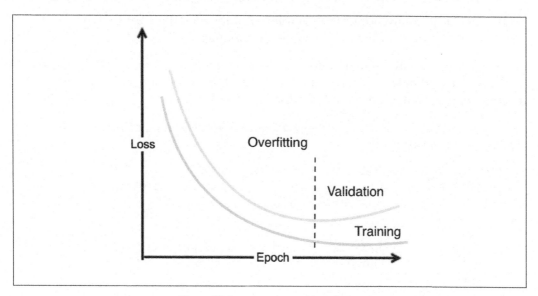

Figure 31: Loss function and overfitting

As a rule of thumb, if during the training we see that the loss increases on validation, after an initial decrease, then we have a problem of model complexity, which overfits to the training data.

In order to solve the overfitting problem, we need a way to capture the complexity of a model, that is, how complex a model can be. What could the solution be? Well, a model is nothing more than a vector of weights. Each weight affects the output, except for those which are zero, or very close to it. Therefore, the complexity of a model can be conveniently represented as the number of non-zero weights. In other words, if we have two models M1 and M2 achieving pretty much the same performance in terms of loss function, then we should choose the simplest model, the one which has the minimum number of non-zero weights.

We can use a hyperparameter $\lambda>=0$ for controlling the importance of having a simple model, as in this formula:

$$min: \{loss(Training\ Data\ |\ Model)\} + \lambda * complexity(Model)$$

There are three different types of regularization used in machine learning:

- **L1 regularization** (also known as LASSO): The complexity of the model is expressed as the sum of the absolute values of the weights.

- **L2 regularization** (also known as Ridge): The complexity of the model is expressed as the sum of the squares of the weights

- **Elastic regularization**: The complexity of the model is captured by a combination of the preceding two techniques

Note that playing with regularization can be a good way to increase the performance of a network, particularly when there is an evident situation of overfitting. This set of experiments is left as an exercise for the interested reader.

Also note that TensorFlow supports L1, L2, and ElasticNet regularization. Adding regularization is easy:

```
from tf.keras.regularizers import l2, activity_l2
model.add(Dense(64, input_dim=64, W_regularizer=l2(0.01),
activity_regularizer=activity_l2(0.01)))
```

A complete list of regularizers can be found at `https://www.tensorflow.org/api_docs/python/tf/keras/regularizers`.

Understanding BatchNormalization

BatchNormalization is another form of regularization and one of the most effective improvements proposed during the last few years. BatchNormalization enables us to accelerate training, in some cases by halving the training epochs, and it offers some regularization. Let's see what the intuition is behind it.

During training, weights in early layers naturally change and therefore the inputs of later layers can significantly change. In other words, each layer must continuously re-adjust its weights to the different distribution for every batch. This may slow down the model's training greatly. The key idea is to make layer inputs more similar in distribution, batch after batch and epoch after epoch.

Another issue is that the sigmoid activation function works very well close to zero, but tends to "get stuck" when values get sufficiently far away from zero. If, occasionally, neuron outputs fluctuate far away from the sigmoid zero, then said neuron becomes unable to update its own weights.

The other key idea is therefore to transform the layer outputs into a Gaussian distribution unit close to zero. In this way, layers will have significantly less variation from batch to batch. Mathematically, the formula is very simple. The activation input x is centered around zero by subtracting the batch mean μ from it. Then, the result is divided by $\sigma + \epsilon$, the sum of batch variance σ and a small number ϵ, to prevent division by zero. Then, we use a linear transformation $y = \lambda x + \beta$ to make sure that the normalizing effect is applied during training.

In this way, λ and β are parameters that get optimized during the training phase in a similar way to any other layer. BatchNormalization has been proven as a very effective way to increase both the speed of training and accuracy, because it helps to prevent activations becoming either too small and vanishing or too big and exploding.

Playing with Google Colab – CPUs, GPUs, and TPUs

Google offers a truly intuitive tool for training neural networks and for playing with TensorFlow (including 2.x) at no cost. You can find an actual Colab, which can be freely accessed, at `https://colab.research.google.com/` and if you are familiar with Jupyter notebooks, you will find a very familiar web-based environment here. Colab stands for Colaboratory and it is a Google research project created to help disseminate machine learning education and research.

Let's see how it works, starting with the screenshot shown in *Figure 32*:

Figure 32: An example of notebooks in Colab

By accessing Colab, you can either check a listing of notebooks generated in the past or you can create a new notebook. Different versions of Python are supported.

When we create a new notebook, we can also select whether we want to run it on CPUs, GPUs, or in Google's TPUs as shown in *Figure 25* (see *Chapter 16, Tensor Processing Unit* for more details on these):

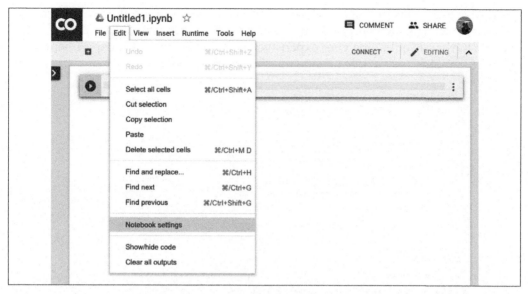

Figure 33: Selecting the desired hardware accelerator (None, GPUs, TPUs) - first step

By accessing the **Notebook settings** option contained in the **Edit** menu (see *Figure 33* and *Figure 34*), we can select the desired hardware accelerator (None, GPUs, TPUs). Google will allocate the resources at no cost, although they can be withdrawn at any time, for example during periods of particularly heavy load. In my experience, this is a very rare event and you can access colab pretty much any time. However, be polite and do not do something like start mining bitcoins at no cost – you will almost certainly get evicted!

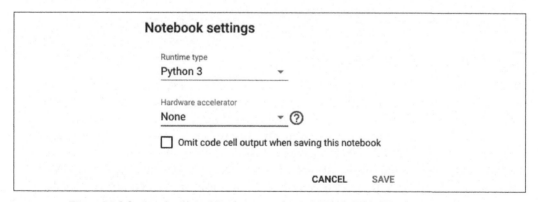

Figure 34: Selecting the desired hardware accelerator (None, GPUs, TPUs) - second step

The next step is to insert your code (see *Figure 35*) in the appropriate colab notebook cells and voila! You are good to go. Execute the code and happy deep learning without the hassle of buying very expensive hardware to start your experiments! *Figure 35* contains an example of code in a Google notebook:

```
CODE   TEXT   ↑ CELL   ↓ CELL

        return (X_train, y_train), (X_test, y_test)

    def build_model():
        model = models.Sequential()
        #Input - Emedding Layer
        # the model will take as input an integer matrix of size (batch, input_length)
        # the model will output dimension (input_length, dim_embedding)
            # the largest integer in the input should be no larger
            # than n_words (vocabulary size).
        model.add(layers.Embedding(n_words,
            dim_embedding, input_length=max_len))

        model.add(layers.Dropout(0.3))

        #takes the maximum value of either feature vector from each of the n_words features
        model.add(layers.GlobalMaxPooling1D())
        model.add(layers.Dense(128, activation='relu'))
        model.add(layers.Dropout(0.5))
        model.add(layers.Dense(1, activation='sigmoid'))

        return model

    (X_train, y_train), (X_test, y_test) = load_data()
    model=build_model()
    model.summary()

    model.compile(optimizer = "adam", loss = "binary_crossentropy",
     metrics = ["accuracy"]
    )

    score = model.fit(X_train, y_train,
     epochs= EPOCHS,
     batch_size = BATCH_SIZE,
     validation_data = (X_test, y_test)
    )

    score = model.evaluate(X_test, y_test, batch_size=BATCH_SIZE)
    print("\nTest score:", score[0])
    print('Test accuracy:', score[1])
```

Figure 35: An example of code in a notebook

Sentiment analysis

What is the code we used to test colab? It is an example of sentiment analysis developed on top of the IMDb dataset. The IMDb dataset contains the text of 50,000 movie reviews from the Internet Movie Database. Each review is either positive or negative (for example, thumbs up or thumbs down). The dataset is split into 25,000 reviews for training and 25,000 reviews for testing. Our goal is to build a classifier that is able to predict the binary judgment given the text. We can easily load IMDb via `tf.keras` and the sequences of words in the reviews have been converted to sequences of integers, where each integer represents a specific word in a dictionary. We also have a convenient way of padding sentences to `max_len`, so that we can use all sentences, whether short or long, as inputs to a neural network with an input vector of fixed size (we will look at this requirement in more detail in *Chapter 8, Recurrent Neural Networks*):

```
import tensorflow as tf
from tensorflow.keras import datasets, layers, models, preprocessing
import tensorflow_datasets as tfds

max_len = 200
n_words = 10000
dim_embedding = 256
EPOCHS = 20
BATCH_SIZE = 500

def load_data():
        # Load data.
        (X_train, y_train), (X_test, y_test) = datasets.imdb.load_
data(num_words=n_words)
        # Pad sequences with max_len.
        X_train = preprocessing.sequence.pad_sequences(X_train,
maxlen=max_len)
        X_test = preprocessing.sequence.pad_sequences(X_test,
maxlen=max_len)
        return (X_train, y_train), (X_test, y_test)
```

Now let's build a model. We are going to use a few layers that will be explained in detail in *Chapter 8, Recurrent Neural Networks*. For now, let's assume that the Embedding() layer will map the sparse space of words contained in the reviews into a denser space. This will make computation easier. In addition, we will use a GlobalMaxPooling1D() layer, which takes the maximum value of either feature vector from each of the n_words features. In addition, we have two Dense() layers. The last one is made up of one single neuron with a sigmoid activation function for making the final binary estimation:

```
def build_model():
    model = models.Sequential()
    # Input: - eEmbedding Layer.
    # The model will take as input an integer matrix of size (batch,
    # input_length).
    # The model will output dimension (input_length, dim_embedding).
    # The largest integer in the input should be no larger
    # than n_words (vocabulary size).
        model.add(layers.Embedding(n_words,
        dim_embedding, input_length=max_len))

        model.add(layers.Dropout(0.3))

    # Takes the maximum value of either feature vector from each of
    # the n_words features.
```

```
model.add(layers.GlobalMaxPooling1D())
model.add(layers.Dense(128, activation='relu'))
model.add(layers.Dropout(0.5))
model.add(layers.Dense(1, activation='sigmoid'))

return model
```

Now we need to train our model, and this piece of code is very similar to what we did with MNIST. Let's see:

```
(X_train, y_train), (X_test, y_test) = load_data()
model = build_model()
model.summary()

model.compile(optimizer = "adam", loss = "binary_crossentropy",
 metrics = ["accuracy"]
)

score = model.fit(X_train, y_train,
 epochs = EPOCHS,
 batch_size = BATCH_SIZE,
 validation_data = (X_test, y_test)
)

score = model.evaluate(X_test, y_test, batch_size=BATCH_SIZE)
print("\nTest score:", score[0])
print('Test accuracy:', score[1])
```

Let's see the network and then run a few iterations:

```
_____
Layer (type)                 Output Shape              Param #
=================================================================
embedding (Embedding)        (None, 200, 256)          2560000
_____
dropout (Dropout)            (None, 200, 256)          0
_____
global_max_pooling1d (Global (None, 256)               0
_____
dense (Dense)                (None, 128)               32896
_____
dropout_1 (Dropout)          (None, 128)               0
_____
dense_1 (Dense)              (None, 1)                 129
=================================================================
Total params: 2,593,025
Trainable params: 2,593,025
Non-trainable params: 0
```

Figure 36: The results of the network following a few iterations

As shown in the following image, we reach the accuracy of 85%, which is not bad at all for a simple network:

```
Epoch 20/20
25000/25000 [==============================] - 23s 925us/sample - loss: 0.0063 - accuracy: 0.9991 - val_
loss: 0.4993 - val_accuracy: 0.8503
25000/25000 [==============================] - 2s 74us/sample - loss: 0.4993 - accuracy: 0.8503

Test score: 0.4992710727453232
Test accuracy: 0.85028
```

Figure 37: Testing the accuracy of a simple network

Hyperparameter tuning and AutoML

The experiments defined above give some opportunities for fine-tuning a net. However, what works for this example will not necessarily work for other examples. For a given net, there are indeed multiple parameters that can be optimized (such as the number of hidden neurons, BATCH_SIZE, number of epochs, and many more depending on the complexity of the net itself). These parameters are called "hyperparameters" to distinguish them from the parameters of the network itself, that is, the values of the weights and biases.

Hyperparameter tuning is the process of finding the optimal combination of those hyperparameters that minimize cost functions. The key idea is that if we have n hyperparameters, then we can imagine that they define a space with n dimensions and the goal is to find the point in this space that corresponds to an optimal value for the cost function. One way to achieve this goal is to create a grid in this space and systematically check the value assumed by the cost function for each grid vertex. In other words, the hyperparameters are divided into buckets and different combinations of values are checked via a brute force approach.

If you think that this process of fine-tuning the hyperparameters is manual and expensive, then you are absolutely right! However, during the last few years we have seen significant results in AutoML, a set of research techniques aiming at both automatically tuning hyperparameters and searching automatically for optimal network architecture. We will discuss more about this in *Chapter 14, An introduction to AutoML*.

Predicting output

Once a net is trained, it can of course be used for making predictions. In TensorFlow this is very simple. We can use the method:

```
# Making predictions.
predictions = model.predict(X)
```

For a given input, several types of output can be computed, including a method `model.evaluate()` used to compute the loss values, a method `model.predict_classes()` used to compute category outputs, and a method `model.predict_proba()` used to compute class probabilities.

A practical overview of backpropagation

Multi-layer perceptrons learn from training data through a process called backpropagation. In this section, we will cover the basics while more details can be found in *Chapter 15, The Math behind Deep Learning*. The process can be described as a way of progressively correcting mistakes as soon as they are detected. Let's see how this works.

Remember that each neural network layer has an associated set of weights that determine the output values for a given set of inputs. Additionally, remember that a neural network can have multiple hidden layers.

At the beginning, all the weights have some random assignment. Then, the net is activated for each input in the training set: values are propagated *forward* from the input stage through the hidden stages to the output stage where a prediction is made. Note that we've kept *Figure 38* simple by only representing a few values with green dotted lines but in reality all the values are propagated forward through the network:

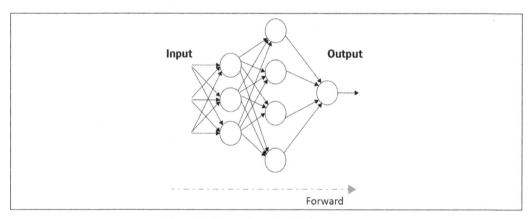

Figure 38: Forward step in backpropagation

Since we know the true observed value in the training set, it is possible to calculate the error made in prediction. The key intuition for backtracking is to propagate the error back (see *Figure 39*), using an appropriate optimizer algorithm such as gradient descent to adjust the neural network weights with the goal of reducing the error (again, for the sake of simplicity, only a few error values are represented here):

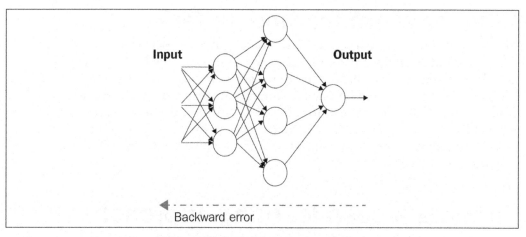

Figure 39: Backward step in backpropagation

The process of forward propagation from input to output and the backward propagation of errors is repeated several times until the error gets below a predefined threshold. The whole process is represented in *Figure 40*:

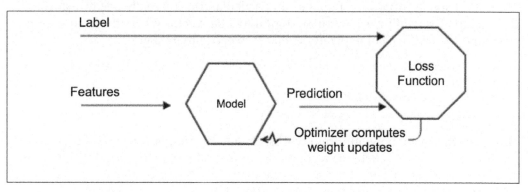

Figure 40: Forward propagation and backward propagation

The features represent the input, and the labels are used here to drive the learning process. The model is updated in such a way that the loss function is progressively minimized. In a neural network, what really matters is not the output of a single neuron but the collective weights adjusted in each layer. Therefore, the network progressively adjusts its internal weights in such a way that the prediction increases the number of correctly forecasted labels. Of course, using the right set of features and having quality labeled data is fundamental in order to minimize the bias during the learning process.

What have we learned so far?

In this chapter we have learned the basics of neural networks. More specifically, what a perceptron and what a multi-layer perceptron is, how to define neural networks in TensorFlow 2.0, how to progressively improve metrics once a good baseline is established, and how to fine-tune the hyperparameter space. In addition to that, we also have an intuitive idea of what some useful activation functions (sigmoid and ReLU) are, and how to train a network with backprop algorithms based on either gradient descent, SGD, or more sophisticated approaches such as Adam and RMSProp.

Towards a deep learning approach

While playing with handwritten digit recognition, we came to the conclusion that the closer we get to the accuracy of 99%, the more difficult it is to improve. If we want more improvement, we definitely need a new idea. What are we missing? Think about it.

The fundamental intuition is that in our examples so far, we are not making use of the local spatial structure of images. In particular, this piece of code transforms the bitmap representing each written digit into a flat vector where the local spatial structure (the fact that some pixels are closer to each other) is gone:

```
# X_train is 60000 rows of 28x28 values; we  --> reshape it as in
# 60000 x 784.
X_train = X_train.reshape(60000, 784)
X_test = X_test.reshape(10000, 784)
```

However, this is not how our brain works. Remember that our vision is based on multiple cortex levels, each one recognizing more and more structured information, still preserving the locality. First, we see single pixels, then from those, we recognize simple geometric forms, and then more and more sophisticated elements such as objects, faces, human bodies, animals, and so on.

In *Chapter 4, Convolutional Neural Networks* we will see that a particular type of deep learning network, known as a **Convolutional Neural Network** (in short, **CNN**) has been developed by taking into account both the idea of preserving the local spatial structure in images (and more generally, in any type of information that has a spatial structure) and the idea of learning via progressive levels of abstraction: with one layer you can only learn simple patterns, with more than one layer you can learn multiple patterns. Before discussing CNNs, we need to discuss some aspects of TensorFlow architecture and have a practical introduction to a few additional machine learning concepts. This will be the topic of the upcoming chapters.

References

1. F. Rosenblatt, *The perceptron: a probabilistic model for information storage and organization in the brain*, Psychol. Rev., vol. 65, pp. 386–408, Nov. 1958.

2. P. J. Werbos, *Backpropagation through time: what it does and how to do it*, Proc. IEEE, vol. 78, pp. 1550–1560, 1990.

3. G. E. Hinton, S. Osindero, and Y.-W. Teh, *A fast learning algorithm for deep belief nets*, Neural Comput., vol. 18, pp. 1527–1554, 2006.

4. J. Schmidhuber, *Deep Learning in Neural Networks: An Overview*, Neural networks : Off. J. Int. Neural Netw. Soc., vol. 61, pp. 85–117, Jan. 2015.

5. S. Leven, *The roots of backpropagation: From ordered derivatives to neural networks and political forecasting*, Neural Networks, vol. 9, Apr. 1996.

6. D. E. Rumelhart, G. E. Hinton, and R. J. Williams, *Learning representations by back-propagating errors*, Nature, vol. 323, Oct. 1986.

7. S. Herculano-Houzel, *The Human Brain in Numbers: A Linearly Scaled-up Primate Brain*, Front. Hum. Neurosci, vol. 3, Nov. 2009.

8. Hornick, *Multilayer feedforward networks are universal approximators*, Neural Networks Volume 2, Issue 5, 1989, Pages 359-366.

9. Vapnik, *The Nature of Statistical Learning Theory*, Book, 2013.

10. Sutskever, I., Martens, J., Dahl, G., Hinton, G., *On the importance of initialization and momentum in deep learning*, 30th International Conference on Machine Learning, ICML 2013.

TensorFlow 1.x and 2.x

2

The intent of this chapter is to explain the differences between TensorFlow 1.x and TensorFlow 2.0. We'll start by reviewing the traditional programming paradigm for 1.x and then we'll move on to all the new features and paradigms available in 2.x.

Understanding TensorFlow 1.x

It is generally the tradition that the first program one learns to write in any computer language is "hello world." We maintain the convention in this book! Let's begin with a Hello World program:

```
import tensorflow as tf
message = tf.constant('Welcome to the exciting world of Deep Neural
Networks!')
with tf.Session() as sess:
    print(sess.run(message).decode())
```

Let us go in depth into this simple code. The first line imports `tensorflow`. The second line defines the message using `tf.constant`. The third line defines the `Session()` using `with`, and the fourth runs the session using `run()`. Note that this tells us that the result is a "byte string." In order to remove string quotes and b (for byte) we use the method `decode()`.

TensorFlow 1.x computational graph program structure

TensorFlow 1.x is unlike other programming languages. We first need to build a blueprint of whatever neural network we want to create. This is accomplished by dividing the program into two separate parts: a definition of a computational graph, and its execution.

Computational graphs

A computational graph is a network of nodes and edges. In this section, all the data to be used – that is, tensor objects (constants, variables, placeholders) – and all the computations to be performed – that is, operation objects – are defined. Each node can have zero or more inputs but only one output. Nodes in the network represent objects (*tensors* and *operations*), and edges represent the tensors that flow between operations. The computational graph defines the blueprint of the neural network, but the tensors in it have no "value" associated with them yet.

 A placeholder is simply a variable that we will assign data to at a later time. It allows us to create our computational graph, without needing the data.

To build a computational graph, we define all the constants, variables, and operations that we need to perform. In the following sections we describe the structure using a simple example of defining and executing a graph to add two vectors.

Execution of the graph

The execution of the graph is performed using the *session object*, which encapsulates the environment in which tensor and operation objects are evaluated. This is the place where actual calculations and transfers of information from one layer to another take place. The values of different tensor objects are initialized, accessed, and saved in a session object only. Until this point, the tensor objects were just abstract definitions. Here, they come to life.

Why do we use graphs at all?

There are multiple reasons as to why we use graphs. First of all, they are a natural metaphor for describing (deep) networks. Secondly, graphs can be automatically optimized by removing common sub-expressions, by fusing kernels, and by cutting redundant expressions. Thirdly, graphs can be distributed easily during training, and be deployed to different environments such as CPUs, GPUs, or TPUs, and also the likes of cloud, IoT, mobile, or traditional servers. After all, computational graphs are a common concept if you are familiar with functional programming, seen as compositions of simple primitives (as is common in functional programming). TensorFlow borrowed many concepts from computational graphs, and internally it performs several optimizations on our behalf.

An example to start with

We'll consider a simple example of adding two vectors. The graph we want to build is:

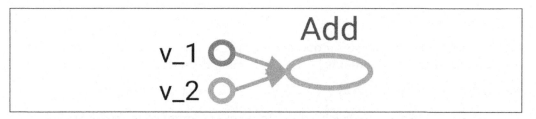

The corresponding code to define the computational graph is:

```
v_1 = tf.constant([1,2,3,4])
v_2 = tf.constant([2,1,5,3])
v_add = tf.add(v_1,v_2)  # You can also write v_1 + v_2 instead
```

Next, we execute the graph in the session:

```
with tf.Session() as sess:
  print(sess.run(v_add))
```

or

```
sess = tf.Session()
print(sess.run(v_add))
sess.close()
```

This results in printing the sum of two vectors:

```
[3 3 8 7]
```

Remember, each session needs to be explicitly closed using `close()`.

The building of a computational graph is very simple – you go on adding the variables and operations and passing them through (flow the tensors). In this way you build your neural network layer by layer. TensorFlow also allows you to use specific devices (CPU/GPU) with different objects of the computational graph using `tf.device()`. In our example, the computational graph consists of three nodes, `v_1` and `v_2` representing the two vectors, and `v_add`, the operation to be performed on them. Now to bring this graph to life we first need to define a session object using `tf.Session()`. We named our session object `sess`. Next, we run it using the `run` method defined in the `Session` class as:

```
run (fetches, feed_dict=None, options=None, run_metadata)
```

This evaluates the tensor in the `fetches` parameter. Our example has tensor `v_add` in fetches. The `run` method will execute every tensor and every operation in the graph that leads to `v_add`. If instead of `v_add` you have `v_1` in fetches, the result will be the value of vector `v_1`:

```
[1,2,3,4]
```

`fetches` can be a single tensor or operation object, or can be more than one. For example, if `fetches` contains [v_1, v_2, v_add], the output is:

```
[array([1, 2, 3, 4]), array([2, 1, 5, 3]), array([3, 3, 8, 7])]
```

We can have many session objects within the same program code. In this section, we have seen an example of TensorFlow 1.x computational graph program structure. The next section will give more insights into TensorFlow 1.x programming constructs.

Working with constants, variables, and placeholders

TensorFlow, in simplest terms, provides a library to define and perform different mathematical operations with tensors. A tensor is basically an n-dimensional array. All types of data – that is, scalar, vectors, and matrices – are special types of tensors:

Types of Data	Tensor	Shape
Scalar	0-D Tensor	[]
Vector	1-D Tensor	$[D_0]$
Matrix	2-D Tensor	$[D_0, D_1]$
Tensors	N-D Tensor	$[D_0, D_1, ... D_{n-1}]$

TensorFlow supports three types of tensors:

1. **Constants**: Constants are tensors, the values of which cannot be changed.

2. **Variables**: We use variable tensors when values require updating within a session. For example, in the case of neural networks, the weights need to be updated during the training session; this is achieved by declaring weights as variables. Variables need to be explicitly initialized before use. Another important thing to note is that constants are stored in a computational graph definition and they are loaded every time the graph is loaded, so they are memory-intensive. Variables, on the other hand, are stored separately; they can exist on parameter servers.

3. **Placeholders**: Placeholders are used to feed values into a TensorFlow graph. They are used along with `feed_dict` to feed data. They are normally used to feed new training examples while training a neural network. We assign values to a placeholder while running the graph in session. They allow us to create our operations and build the computational graph without requiring any data. An important detail to note is that placeholders do not contain any data and thus there is no need to initialize them.

Examples of operations

Let's see some examples of different operations available in TensorFlow 1.x.

Constants

First, let's look at some constants that we will encounter:

- We can declare a scalar constant:

  ```
  t_1 = tf.constant(4)
  ```

  Example: A constant vector of shape [1,3]:

  ```
  t_2 = tf.constant([4, 3, 2])
  ```

- To create a tensor with all elements as zero, we use `tf.zeros()`. This statement creates a matrix of zeros of shape `[M,N]` with `dtype` (`int32`, `float32`, and so on):

  ```
  tf.zeros([M,N],tf.dtype)
  ```

  Example: `zero_t = tf.zeros([2,3],tf.int32) ==>[[0 0 0], [0 0 0]]`

- Get the shape of a tensor:

  Example: `print(tf.zeros([2,3],tf.int32).shape) ==> (2, 3)`

- We can also create tensor variables of the same shape as an existing NumPy array or tensor constant using:

  ```
  tf.zeros_like(t_2) # Create a zero matrix of same shape as t_2
  tf.ones_like(t_2) # Creates a ones matrix of same shape as t_2
  ```

- We can create a tensor with all elements set to one; next, we create a `ones` matrix of shape `[M,N]`:

  ```
  tf.ones([M,N],tf.dtype)
  ```

  Example: `ones_t = tf.ones([2,3],tf.int32) ==>[[0 0 0], [0 0 0]]`

- We can broadcast in a similar way to how it's done with NumPy:

  Example: `t = tf.Variable([[0., 1., 2.], [3., 4., 5.], [6., 7., 8]])`

  ```
  print (t*2) ==>
  tf.Tensor(
  [[ 0.  2.  4.]
   [ 6.  8. 10.]
   [12. 14. 16.]], shape=(3, 3), dtype=float32)
  ```

Sequences

- We can generate a sequence of evenly spaced vectors, starting from start to end, with a total num values:

  ```
  tf.linspace(start, stop, num) // The corresponding values differ
  by (stop-start)/(num-1)
  ```

  Example: `range_t = tf.linspace(2.0,5.0,5) ==> [ 2.    2.75  3.5 4.25  5.  ]`

- Generate a sequence of numbers starting from `start` (default=0), incremented by `delta` (default=1) up to but not including the `limit`:

  ```
  tf.range(start,limit,delta)
  ```

  Example: `range_t = tf.range(10) ==> [0 1 2 3 4 5 6 7 8 9]`

Random tensors

TensorFlow allows random tensors with different distributions to be created:

- To create random values from a normal distribution of shape [M,N], with mean (default =0.0), standard deviation `stddev` (default=1.0), and using `seed`, we can use:

  ```
  t_random = tf.random_normal([2,3], mean=2.0, stddev=4, seed=12)
  ==> [[ 0.25347459  5.37990952  1.95276058], [-1.53760314
  1.2588985   2.84780669]]
  ```

- To create random values from a truncated normal distribution of shape [M,N] with mean (default =0.0), standard deviation `stddev` (default=1.0), and using `seed`, we can use:

  ```
  t_random = tf.truncated_normal([1,5], stddev=2, seed=12) ==> [[-
  0.8732627   1.68995488 -0.02361972 -1.76880157 -3.87749004]]
  ```

- To create random values from a given gamma distribution of shape [M,N] in the range [minval (default=0), maxval] and using seed:

```
t_random = tf.random_uniform([2,3], maxval=4, seed=12) ==> [[
2.54461002  3.69636583  2.70510912], [ 2.00850058  3.84459829
3.54268885]]
```

- To randomly crop a given tensor to a specified size:

```
tf.random_crop(t_random, [2,5],seed=12) where t_random is an
already defined tensor. This will result in a [2,5] Tensor
randomly cropped from Tensor t_random.
```

- Every time we need to present the training sample in a random order, we can use tf.random_shuffle() to randomly shuffle a tensor along its first dimension. If t_random is the tensor we want to shuffle then we use:

```
tf.random_shuffle(t_random)
```

- Randomly generated tensors are affected by the value of an initial seed. To obtain the same random numbers in multiple runs or sessions, the seed should be set to a constant value. When there is a large number of random tensors in use, we can set the seed for all randomly generated tensors by using tf.set_random_seed(). The following command sets the seed for random tensors for all sessions as 54:

```
tf.set_random_seed(54) //Seed can be any integer value.
```

Variables

Variables are created using the tf.Variable class. The definition of variables also includes the constant or random values from which they should be initialized. In the following code, we create two different tensor variables t_a and t_b. Both will be initialized to random uniform distributions of shape [50, 50], minval=0, and maxval=10:

```
rand_t = tf.random_uniform([50,50], 0, 10, seed=0)
t_a = tf.Variable(rand_t)
t_b = tf.Variable(rand_t)
```

Variables are often used to represent weights and biases in a neural network:

```
weights = tf.Variable(tf.random_normal([100,100],stddev=2))
bias = tf.Variable(tf.zeros[100], name = 'biases')
```

Here, we used the optional argument `name` to give a name to a variable as defined in the computational graph. In all the preceding examples, the source of variable initialization is a constant. We can also specify a variable to be initialized from another variable. The following statement will initialize `weight2` from the weights defined above:

```
weight2=tf.Variable(weights.initialized_value(), name='w2')
```

Initializing variables: The definition of variables specifies how they are to be initialized, since we must explicitly initialize all declared variables. In the definition of the computational graph, we do so by declaring an *Operation Object*:

```
intial_op = tf.global_variables_initializer()
```

Each variable can also be initialized separately using `tf.Variable.initializer` while running the graph:

```
bias = tf.Variable(tf.zeros([100,100]))
with tf.Session() as sess:
sess.run(bias.initializer)
```

Saving variables: We can save all the variables using the `Saver` class. To do so, we define a `saver` operation object:

```
saver = tf.train.Saver()
```

Placeholders: We define a placeholder using:

```
tf.placeholder(dtype, shape=None, name=None)
```

`dtype` specifies the data type of `placeholder` and must be specified while declaring the placeholder. Next, we define the placeholder for *x* and calculate *y=2x* using `feed_dict` for a random 4×5 matrix (remember that `feed_dict` is used to feed values to TensorFlow placeholders):

```
x = tf.placeholder("float")
y = 2 * x
data = tf.random_uniform([4,5],10)
with tf.Session() as sess:
    x_data = sess.run(data)
    print(sess.run(y, feed_dict = {x:x_data}))
```

All variables and placeholders are defined in the *Computational Graph* section of the code. If we use a `print` statement in the definition section, we will only get information about the type of tensor and not about its value.

To know the value, we need to create the session graph and explicitly use the run command with the desired tensor values as done with the following code:

```
print(sess.run(t_1))  # Will print the value of t_1 defined in step 1
```

An example of TensorFlow 1.x in TensorFlow 2.x

We can see that the TensorFlow 1.x APIs offer flexible ways to create and manipulate computational graphs representing (deep) neural networks and many other types of machine learning programs. TensorFlow 2.x on the other hand offers higher-level APIs that abstract more lower-level details. To conclude, let's go back to an example of the TensorFlow 1.x program that we encountered in the previous chapter. Here, we also add a line to show the computational graph:

```
import tensorflow.compat.v1 as tf
tf.disable_v2_behavior()

in_a = tf.placeholder(dtype=tf.float32, shape=(2))

def model(x):
  with tf.variable_scope("matmul"):
    W = tf.get_variable("W", initializer=tf.ones(shape=(2,2)))
    b = tf.get_variable("b", initializer=tf.zeros(shape=(2)))
    return x * W + b

out_a = model(in_a)

with tf.Session() as sess:
  sess.run(tf.global_variables_initializer())
  outs = sess.run([out_a],
              feed_dict={in_a: [1, 0]})
  writer = tf.summary.FileWriter("./logs/example", sess.graph)
```

Please note that the syntax x * W + b is just the linear perceptron defined in the previous chapter. Now let's start a visualization application called "TensorBoard" to show the computational graph:

tensorboard --logdir=./logs/example/

And let's open a browser pointing to http://localhost:6006/#graphs&run=.

You should see something similar to the following graph:

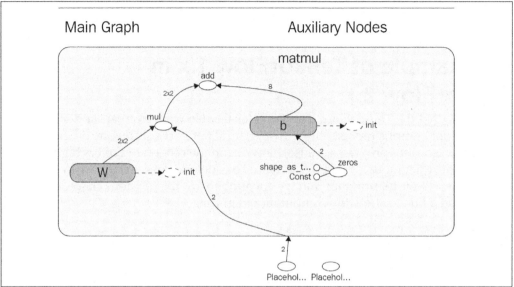

Figure 1: An example of a computational graph

This section provided an overview of TensorFlow 1.x programming paradigms. Now, let's turn our attention to what is new in TensorFlow 2.x.

Understanding TensorFlow 2.x

As discussed, TensorFlow 2.x recommends using a high-level API such as tf.keras, but leaves low-level APIs typical of TensorFlow 1.x for when there is a need to have more control on internal details. tf.keras and TensorFlow 2.x come with some great benefits. Let's review them.

Eager execution

TensorFlow 1.x defines static computational graphs. This type of declarative programming might be confusing for many people. However, Python is typically more dynamic. So, following the Python spirit, PyTorch, another popular deep learning package, defines things in a more imperative and dynamic way: you still have a graph, but you can define, change, and execute nodes on-the-fly, with no special session interfaces or placeholders. This is what is called **eager execution**, meaning that the model definitions are dynamic, and the execution is immediate. Graphs and sessions should be considered as implementation details.

Both PyTorch and TensorFlow 2 styles are inherited from Chainer, another "Powerful, Flexible, and Intuitive Framework for Neural Networks" (see `https://chainer.org/`).

The good news is that TensorFlow 2.x natively supports "eager execution." There is no longer the need to first statically define a computational graph and then execute it (unless you really wanted to!). All the models can be dynamically defined and immediately executed. Further good news is that all of the `tf.keras` APIs are compatible with eager execution. Transparently, TensorFlow 2.x creates a bridge between core TensorFlow communities, PyTorch communities, and Keras communities, taking the best of each of them.

AutoGraph

Even more good news is that TensorFlow 2.0 natively supports imperative Python code, including control flow such as `if-while`, `print()` and other Python-native features, and can natively convert it into pure TensorFlow graph code. Why is this useful? Python coding is very intuitive and there are generations of programmers used to imperative programming, but would struggle to convert this code into a graph format that is typically much faster and allows for automatic optimization. This is when **AutoGraph** comes into play: AutoGraph takes eager-style Python code and automatically converts it to graph-generating code. So, again, transparently TensorFlow 2.x creates a bridge between imperative, dynamic, and eager Python-style programming with efficient graph computations, taking the best of both worlds.

Using AutoGraph is extremely easy: the only thing that you need to do is to annotate your Python code with the special decorator `tf.function` as in the following code example:

```
import tensorflow as tf
def linear_layer(x):
  return 3 * x + 2
@tf.function
def simple_nn(x):
  return tf.nn.relu(linear_layer(x))

def simple_function(x):
        return 3*x
```

If we inspect `simple_nn`, we see that it is a special handler for interacting with TensorFlow internals, while `simple_function` is a normal Python handler:

```
>>> simple_nn
<tensorflow.python.eager.def_function.Function object at 0x10964f9b0>
```

```
>>> simple_function
<function simple_function at 0xb26c3e510>
```

Note that with `tf.function` you need to annotate only one main function, so all other functions called from there will be automatically and transparently transformed into an optimized computational graph. For example, in the preceding code, there is no need to annotate `linear_layer`. Think about `tf.function` as marking code for **Just In Time (JIT)** compilation. Normally, you do not need to see the code automatically generated by AutoGraph, but in case you are curious, then you can investigate with the following code fragment:

```
# internal look at the auto-generated code
print(tf.autograph.to_code(simple_nn.python_function, experimental_
optional_features=None))
```

This code fragment will print the following automatically generated piece of code:

```
from __future__ import print_function

def tf__simple_nn(x):
  do_return = False
  retval_ = None
  do_return = True
  retval_ = ag__.converted_call('relu', tf.nn, ag__.ConversionOptions
(recursive=True, verbose=0, strip_decorators=(ag__.convert, ag__.do_
not_convert, ag__.converted_call), force_conversion=False, optional_
features=(), internal_convert_user_code=True), (linear_layer(x),), {})
  return retval_

tf__simple_nn.autograph_info__ = {}
```

Let's see an example of the difference in speed between code annotated with the `tf.function()` decorator and the same code with no annotation. Here we use a layer `LSTMCell()` which will be discussed in *Chapter 8, Recurrent Neural Networks*, but for now consider it as a black box doing some form of learning:

```
import tensorflow as tf
import timeit

cell = tf.keras.layers.LSTMCell(100)

@tf.function
def fn(input, state):
    return cell(input, state)

input = tf.zeros([100, 100])
```

```
state = [tf.zeros([100, 100])] * 2
# warmup
cell(input, state)
fn(input, state)

graph_time = timeit.timeit(lambda: cell(input, state), number=100)
auto_graph_time = timeit.timeit(lambda: fn(input, state), number=100)
print('graph_time:', graph_time)
print('auto_graph_time:', auto_graph_time)
```

When the code fragment is executed, you see a reduction in time of one order of magnitude if tf.function() is used:

graph_time: 0.4504085020016646

auto_graph_time: 0.07892408400221029

In short, you can decorate Python functions and methods with tf.function, which converts them to the equivalent of a static graph, with all the optimization that comes with it.

Keras APIs – three programming models

TensorFlow 1.x provides a lower-level API. You build models by first creating a graph of ops, which you then compile and execute. tf.keras offers a higher API level, with three different programming models: Sequential API, Functional API, and Model Subclassing. Learning models are created as easily as "putting LEGO® bricks together," where each "lego brick" is a specific Keras.layer. Let's see when it is best to use Sequential, Functional, and Subclassing, and note that you can mix-and-match the three styles according to your specific needs.

Sequential API

The Sequential API is a very elegant, intuitive, and concise model that is appropriate in 90% of cases. In the previous chapter, we covered an example of using the Sequential API when we discussed the MNIST code, so let's create the brick with:

```
tf.keras.utils.plot_model(model, to_file="model.png")
```

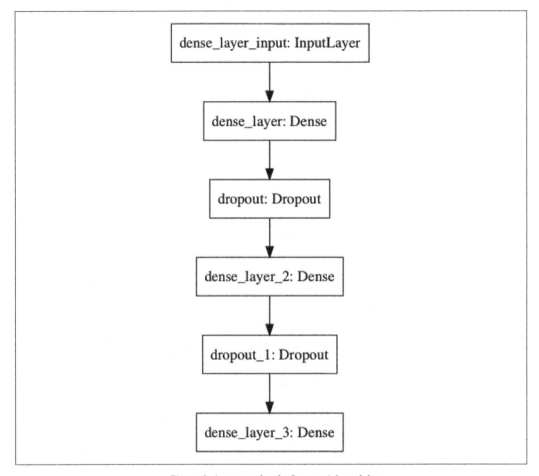

Figure 2: An example of a Sequential model

Functional API

The Functional API is useful when you want to build a model with more complex (non-linear) topologies, including multiple inputs, multiple outputs, residual connections with non-sequential flows, and shared and reusable layers. Each layer is callable (with a tensor in input), and each layer returns a tensor as an output. Let's look at an example where we have two separate inputs, two separate logistic regressions as outputs, and one shared module in the middle.

For now, there's no need to understand what the layers (that is, the lego bricks) are doing internally, rather, just observe the non-linear network topology. Note also that a module can call another module, as a function can call another function:

```python
import tensorflow as tf

def build_model():
    # variable-length sequence of integers
    text_input_a = tf.keras.Input(shape=(None,), dtype='int32')

    # variable-length sequence of integers
    text_input_b = tf.keras.Input(shape=(None,), dtype='int32')

    # Embedding for 1000 unique words mapped to 128-dimensional vectors
    shared_embedding = tf.keras.layers.Embedding(1000, 128)

    # We reuse the same layer to encode both inputs
    encoded_input_a = shared_embedding(text_input_a)
    encoded_input_b = shared_embedding(text_input_b)

    # two logistic predictions at the end
    prediction_a = tf.keras.layers.Dense(1, activation='sigmoid',\\
name='prediction_a')(encoded_input_a)
    prediction_b = tf.keras.layers.Dense(1, activation='sigmoid',\\
 name='prediction_b')(encoded_input_b)

    # this model has 2 inputs, and 2 outputs
    # in the middle we have a shared model
    model = tf.keras.Model(inputs=[text_input_a, text_input_b],
    outputs=[prediction_a, prediction_b])

    tf.keras.utils.plot_model(model, to_file="shared_model.png")

build_model()
```

Note that, first, you create a layer, then you pass it an input; with `tf.keras.layers.Dense(1, activation='sigmoid', name='prediction_a')(encoded_input_a)` the two steps are combined in a single line of code.

Let's have a look into the non-linear network topology:

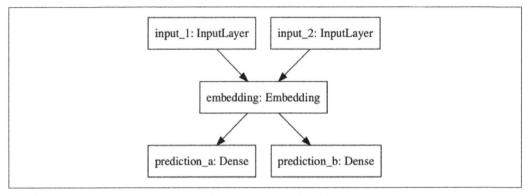

Figure 3: An example of a non-linear topology

We will see multiple examples of using the Functional API in subsequent chapters of this book.

Model subclassing

Model subclassing offers the highest flexibility and it is generally used when you need to define your own layer. In other words, it is useful when you are in the business of building your own special lego brick instead of composing more standard and well-known bricks. There is indeed a higher cost in terms of complexity and therefore subclassing should be used only when really needed. In the majority of situations, Sequential and Functional APIs are more appropriate, but you can still use model subclassing if you prefer to think in an object-oriented manner, as the typical Python/NumPy developer does.

So, in order to create a custom layer, we can subclass `tf.keras.layers.Layer` and implement the following methods:

- `__init__`: Optionally used to define all the sublayers to be used by this layer. This is the constructor where you can declare your model.
- `build`: Used to create the weights of the layer. You can add weights with `add_weight()`.
- `call`: Used to define the forward pass. This is where your layer is called and chained in functional style.
- Optionally, a layer can be serialized by using `get_config()` and deserialized using `from_config()`.

Let's see an example of a custom layer that simply multiplies an input by a matrix named `kernel` (for the sake of simplicity, the import lines are skipped in this text but are of course used in GitHub code):

```
class MyLayer(layers.Layer):

  def __init__(self, output_dim, **kwargs):
    self.output_dim = output_dim
    super(MyLayer, self).__init__(**kwargs)

  def build(self, input_shape):
    # Create a trainable weight variable for this layer.
    self.kernel = self.add_weight(name='kernel',
                          shape=(input_shape[1], self.output_dim),
                          initializer='uniform',
                          trainable=True)

  def call(self, inputs):
    # Do the multiplication and return
    return tf.matmul(inputs, self.kernel)
```

Once the `MyLayer()` custom brick is defined, it can be composed just like any other brick, as in this following example, where a Sequential model is defined by stacking `MyLayer` with a `softmax` activation function:

```
model = tf.keras.Sequential([
    MyLayer(20),
    layers.Activation('softmax')])
```

So, in short, you can use Model subclassing if you are in the business of building bricks.

In this section we have seen that `tf.keras` offers a higher API level, with three different programming models: Sequential API, Functional API, and Model subclassing. Now let's move our attention to callbacks, a different feature, which is useful during training with `tf.keras`.

Callbacks

Callbacks are objects passed to a model to extend or modify behaviors during training. There are a few useful callbacks that are commonly used in `tf.keras`:

- `tf.keras.callbacks.ModelCheckpoint`: This feature is used to save checkpoints of your model at regular intervals and recover in case of problems.

- `tf.keras.callbacks.LearningRateScheduler`: This feature is used to dynamically change the learning rate during optimization.

- `tf.keras.callbacks.EarlyStopping`: This feature is used to interrupt training when validation performance has stopped improving after a while.

- `tf.keras.callbacks.TensorBoard`: This feature is used to monitor the model's behavior using TensorBoard.

For example, we have already used TensorBoard as in this example:

```
callbacks = [
  # Write TensorBoard logs to './logs' directory
  tf.keras.callbacks.TensorBoard(log_dir='./logs')
]
model.fit(data, labels, batch_size=256, epochs=100,
callbacks=callbacks,
          validation_data=(val_data, val_labels))
```

Saving a model and weights

After training a model, it can be useful to save the weights in a persistent way. This is easily achieved with the following code fragment, which saves to TensorFlow's internal format:

```
# Save weights to a Tensorflow Checkpoint file
model.save_weights('./weights/my_model')
```

If you want to save in Keras's format, which is portable across multiple backends, then use:

```
# Save weights to a HDF5 file
model.save_weights('my_model.h5', save_format='h5')
```

Weights are easily loaded with:

```
# Restore the model's state
model.load_weights(file_path)
```

In addition to weights, a model can be serialized in JSON with:

```
json_string = model.to_json()  # save
model = tf.keras.models.model_from_json(json_string) # restore
```

If you prefer, a model can be serialized in YAML with:

```
yaml_string = model.to_yaml() # save
model = tf.keras.models.model_from_yaml(yaml_string) # restore
```

If you want to save a model together with its weights and the optimization parameters, then you simply use:

```
model.save('my_model.h5') # save
model = tf.keras.models.load_model('my_model.h5') #restore
```

Training from tf.data.datasets

Another benefit of using TensorFlow 2.x is the introduction of TensorFlow datasets as a principled mechanism to deal with heterogeneous (large) datasets in different categories such as audio, image, video, text, and translation. Let's first use pip to install tensorflow-datasets:

pip install tensorflow-datasets

 As of September 2019 there are already 85+ commonly used datasets available, but more are planned to be added in https://www.tensorflow.org/datasets/datasets.

Then, we can list all the datasets available, and load MNIST together with metadata:

```
import tensorflow as tf
import tensorflow_datasets as tfds

# See all registered datasets
builders = tfds.list_builders()
print(builders)

# Load a given dataset by name, along with the DatasetInfo metadata
data, info = tfds.load("mnist", with_info=True)
train_data, test_data = data['train'], data['test']

print(info)
```

Then, we get the following lists of datasets:

```
['bair_robot_pushing_small', 'cats_vs_dogs', 'celeb_a', 'celeb_a_hq',
'cifar10', 'cifar100', 'coco2014', 'diabetic_retinopathy_detection',
'dummy_dataset_shared_generator', 'dummy_mnist', 'fashion_mnist', 'image_
label_folder', 'imagenet2012', 'imdb_reviews', 'lm1b', 'lsun', 'mnist',
'moving_mnist', 'nsynth', 'omniglot', 'open_images_v4', 'quickdraw_
bitmap', 'squad', 'starcraft_video', 'svhn_cropped', 'tf_flowers', 'wmt_
translate_ende', 'wmt_translate_enfr']
```

In addition, we get the metainfo for MNIST:

```
tfds.core.DatasetInfo(
    name='mnist',
    version=1.0.0,
    description='The MNIST database of handwritten digits.',
    urls=['http://yann.lecun.com/exdb/mnist/'],
    features=FeaturesDict({
        'image': Image(shape=(28, 28, 1), dtype=tf.uint8),
        'label': ClassLabel(shape=(), dtype=tf.int64, num_classes=10)
    },
    total_num_examples=70000,
    splits={
        'test': <tfds.core.SplitInfo num_examples=10000>,
        'train': <tfds.core.SplitInfo num_examples=60000>
    },
    supervised_keys=('image', 'label'),
    citation='"""
        @article{lecun2010mnist,
            title={MNIST handwritten digit database},
            author={LeCun, Yann and Cortes, Corinna and Burges, CJ},
            journal={ATT Labs [Online]. Available: http://yann. lecun.
com/exdb/mnist},
            volume={2},
            year={2010}
        }


    """',
)
```

Sometimes it is useful to create a dataset from a NumPy array. Let's see how in this code fragment, which uses `tf.data.Dataset.from_tensor_slices()`:

```
import tensorflow as tf
import numpy as np

num_items = 100
num_list = np.arange(num_items)

# create the dataset from numpy array
num_list_dataset = tf.data.Dataset.from_tensor_slices(num_list)
```

We can also download a dataset, shuffle and batch the data, and take a slice from the generator as shown in this example:

```
datasets, info = tfds.load('imdb_reviews', with_info=True, as_
```

```
supervised=True)

train_dataset = datasets['train']
train_dataset = train_dataset.batch(5).shuffle(50).take(2)

for data in train_dataset:
    print(data)
```

Please remember that `shuffle()` is a transformation that randomly shuffles the input dataset, while `batch()` creates batches of tensors. This code returns convenient tuples that can be immediately used:

```
(<tf.Tensor: id=249, shape=(5,), dtype=string, numpy=
array([b'If you are a Crispin Glover fan, you must see this...'],
      dtype=object)>, <tf.Tensor: id=250, shape=(5,), dtype=int64,
numpy=array([1, 0, 1, 1, 0])>)
(<tf.Tensor: id=253, shape=(5,), dtype=string, numpy=
array([b'And I really mean that.'],
      dtype=object)>, <tf.Tensor: id=254, shape=(5,), dtype=int64,
numpy=array([1, 1, 1, 1, 1])>)
```

A dataset is a library for dealing with input data in a principled way. Operations include:

1. Creation:

   1. Via `from_tensor_slices()`, which accepts individual (or multiple) NumPy (or tensors) and supports batches
   2. Via `from_tensors()`, which is similar to the above but it does not support batches
   3. Via `from_generator()`, which takes input from a generator function

2. Transformation:

   1. Via `batch()`, which sequentially divides the dataset by the specified size
   2. Via `repeat()`, which duplicates the data
   3. Via `shuffle()`, which randomly shuffles the data
   4. Via `map()`, which applies a function to the data
   5. Via `filter()`, which applies a function to filter the data

3. Iterators:

   1. Via `next_batch = iterator.get_next()`

Dataset uses TFRecord, a representation of the data (in any format) that can be easily ported across multiple systems and is independent of the particular model used for training. In short, dataset allows more flexibility than what we had in TensorFlow 1.0 with `feed-dict`.

tf.keras or Estimators?

In addition to the direct graph computation and to the `tf.keras` higher-level APIs, TensorFlow 1.x and 2.x have an additional set of higher-level APIs called *Estimators*. With Estimators, you do not need to worry about creating computational graphs or handling sessions, since Estimators deal with this on your behalf, in a similar way to `tf.keras`.

But what are Estimators? Put simply, they are another way to build or to use prebuilt bricks. A longer answer is that they are highly efficient learning models for large-scale production-ready environments, which can be trained on single machines or on distributed multi-servers, and they can run on CPUs, GPUs, or TPUs without recoding your model. These models include Linear Classifiers, Deep Learning Classifiers, Gradient Boosted Trees, and many more, which will be discussed in the upcoming chapters.

Let's see an example of an Estimator used for building a classifier with 2 dense hidden layers, each with 10 neurons, and with 3 output classes:

```
# Build a DNN with 2 hidden layers and 10 nodes in each hidden layer.
classifier = tf.estimator.DNNClassifier(
    feature_columns=my_feature_columns,
    # Two hidden layers of 10 nodes each.
    hidden_units=[10, 10],
    # The model must choose between 3 classes.
    n_classes=3)
```

The `feature_columns=my_feature_columns` is a list of feature columns each describing a single feature you want the model to use. For example, a typical use would be something like:

```
# Fetch the data
(train_x, train_y), (test_x, test_y) = load_data()

# Feature columns describe how to use the input.
my_feature_columns = []
for key in train_x.keys():
  my_feature_columns.append(tf.feature_column.numeric_column(key=key))
```

There, `tf.feature_column.numeric_column()` represents real valued or numerical features (`https://www.tensorflow.org/api_docs/python/tf/feature_column/numeric_column`). Efficiency Estimators should be trained using `tf.Datasets` as input. Here is an example where MNIST is loaded, scaled, shuffled, and batched:

```python
import tensorflow as tf
import tensorflow_datasets as tfds

BUFFER_SIZE = 10000
BATCH_SIZE = 64

def input_fn(mode):
  datasets, info = tfds.load(name='mnist',
                             with_info=True,
                             as_supervised=True)
  mnist_dataset = (datasets['train'] if mode == tf.estimator.ModeKeys.
TRAIN else datasets['test'])

  def scale(image, label):
    image = tf.cast(image, tf.float32)
    image /= 255
    return image, label

  return mnist_dataset.map(scale).shuffle(BUFFER_SIZE).batch(BATCH_SIZE)

test = input_fn('test')
train = input_fn(tf.estimator.ModeKeys.TRAIN)
print(test)
print(train)
```

Then, the Estimator can be trained and evaluated by using `tf.estimator.train_and_evaluate()` and passing the `input_fn` which will iterate on the data:

```python
tf.estimator.train_and_evaluate(
    classifier,
    train_spec=tf.estimator.TrainSpec(input_fn=input_fn),
    eval_spec=tf.estimator.EvalSpec(input_fn=input_fn)
)
```

TensorFlow contains Estimators for both regression and classification, which are largely adopted by the community and they will continue to be supported through at least the lifetime of TensorFlow 2.x.

However, the recommendation for TensorFlow 2.x is to keep using them if you have already adopted them, but to use `tf.keras` if you are starting from scratch. As of April 2019, Estimators fully support distributed training while `tf.keras` has limited support. Given this, a possible workaround is to transform `tf.keras` models into Estimators with `tf.keras.estimator.model_to_estimator()` and then use the full distributed training support.

Ragged tensors

Continuing our discussion on the benefits of TensorFlow 2.x, we should notice that TensorFlow 2.x added support for "ragged" tensors, which are a special type of dense tensor with non-uniformly shaped dimensions. This is particularly useful for dealing with sequences and other data issues where the dimensions can change across batches, such as text sentences and hierarchical data. Note that ragged tensors are more efficient than padding `tf.Tensor`, since no time or space is wasted:

```
ragged = tf.ragged.constant([[1, 2, 3], [3, 4], [5, 6, 7, 8]]) ==>
<tf.RaggedTensor [[1, 2, 3], [3, 4], [5, 6, 7, 8]]>
```

Custom training

TensorFlow can compute gradients on our behalf (automatic differentiation) and this makes it extremely easy to develop machine learning models. If you use `tf.keras`, then you will train your model with `fit()` and you probably will not need to go into the details of how the gradients are computed internally. However, custom training is useful when you want to have finer control over optimization.

There are multiple ways of computing gradients. Let's look at them:

1. `tf.GradientTape()`: This class records operations for automatic differentiation. Let's look at an example where we use the parameter `persistent=True` (a Boolean controlling whether a persistent gradient tape is created, which means that multiple calls can be made to the `gradient()` method on this object):

   ```
   import tensorflow as tf

   x = tf.constant(4.0)
   with tf.GradientTape(persistent=True) as g:
     g.watch(x)
     y = x * x
     z = y * y
   dz_dx = g.gradient(z, x)   # 256.0 (4*x^3 at x = 4)
   dy_dx = g.gradient(y, x)   # 8.0
   ```

```
print (dz_dx)
print (dy_dx)
del g  # Drop the reference to the tape
```

2. `tf.gradient_function()`: This returns a function that computes the derivatives of its input function parameter with respect to its arguments.

3. `tf.value_and_gradients_function()`: This returns the value from the input function in addition to the list of derivatives of the input function with respect to its arguments.

4. `tf.implicit_gradients()`: This computes the gradients of the outputs of the input function with regards to all trainable variables these outputs depend on.

Let's see a skeleton of a custom gradient computation where a model is given as input, and the training steps are computing `total_loss = pred_loss + regularization_loss`. The decorator `@tf.function` is used for AutoGraph, and `tape.gradient()` and `apply_gradients()` are used to compute and apply the gradients:

```
@tf.function
def train_step(inputs, labels):
  with tf.GradientTape() as tape:
    predictions = model(inputs, training=True)
    regularization_loss = // TBD according to the problem
    pred_loss = // TBD according to the problem
    total_loss = pred_loss + regularization_loss

  gradients = tape.gradient(total_loss, model.trainable_variables)
  optimizer.apply_gradients(zip(gradients, model.trainable_variables))
```

Then, the training step `train_step(inputs, labels)` is applied for each epoch, for each input and its associated label in `train_data`:

```
for epoch in range(NUM_EPOCHS):
  for inputs, labels in train_data:
    train_step(inputs, labels)
  print("Finished epoch", epoch)
```

So, put simply, `GradientTape()` allows us to control and change how the training process is performed internally. In *Chapter 9, Autoencoders* you will see a more concrete example of using `GradientTape()` for training autoencoders.

Distributed training in TensorFlow 2.x

One very useful addition to TensorFlow 2.x is the possibility to train models using distributed GPUs, multiple machines, and TPUs in a very simple way with very few additional lines of code. `tf.distribute.Strategy` is the TensorFlow API used in this case and it supports both `tf.keras` and `tf.estimator` APIs and eager execution. You can switch between GPUs, TPUs, and multiple machines by just changing the strategy instance. Strategies can be synchronous, where all workers train over different slices of input data in a form of sync data parallel computation, or asynchronous, where updates from the optimizers are not happening in sync. All strategies require that data is loaded in batches the API `tf.data.Dataset` API.

Note that the distributed training support is still experimental. A roadmap is given in *Figure 4*:

Training API	MirroredStrategy	TPUStrategy	MultiWorkerMirroredStrategy	CentralStorageStrategy	ParameterServerStrategy
Keras API	Supported	Experimental support	Experimental support	Experimental support	Supported planned post 2.0
Custom training loop	Experimental support	Experimental support	Support planned post 2.0	Support planned post 2.0	No support yet
Estimator API	Limited Support	Not supported	Limited Support	Limited Support	Limited Support

Figure 4: Distributed training support for different strategies and APIs

Let's discuss in detail all the different strategies reported in *Figure 4*.

Multiple GPUs

We discussed how TensorFlow 2.x can utilize multiple GPUs. If we want to have synchronous distributed training on multiple GPUs on one machine, there are two things that we need to do: (1) We need to load the data in a way that will be distributed into the GPUs, and (2) We need to distribute some computations into the GPUs too:

1. In order to load our data in a way that can be distributed into the GPUs, we simply need a `tf.data.Dataset` (which has already been discussed in the previous paragraphs). If we do not have a `tf.data.Dataset` but we have a normal tensor, then we can easily convert the latter into the former using `tf.data.Dataset.from_tensors_slices()`. This will take a tensor in memory and return a source dataset, the elements of which are slices of the given tensor.

In our toy example we use NumPy for generating training data x and labels y, and we transform it into `tf.data.Dataset` with `tf.data.Dataset.from_tensor_slices()`. Then we apply a shuffle to avoid bias in training across GPUs and then generate `SIZE_BATCHES` batches:

```
import tensorflow as tf
import numpy as np
from tensorflow import keras


N_TRAIN_EXAMPLES = 1024*1024
N_FEATURES = 10
SIZE_BATCHES = 256


# 10 random floats in the half-open interval [0.0, 1.0).
x = np.random.random((N_TRAIN_EXAMPLES, N_FEATURES))
y = np.random.randint(2, size=(N_TRAIN_EXAMPLES, 1))
x = tf.dtypes.cast(x, tf.float32)
print (x)
dataset = tf.data.Dataset.from_tensor_slices((x, y))
dataset = dataset.shuffle(buffer_size=N_TRAIN_EXAMPLES).
batch(SIZE_BATCHES)
```

2. In order to distribute some computations to GPUs, we instantiate a `distribution = tf.distribute.MirroredStrategy()` object, which supports synchronous distributed training on multiple GPUs on one machine. Then, we move the creation and compilation of the Keras model inside the `strategy.scope()`. Note that each variable in the model is mirrored across all the replicas. Let's see it in our toy example:

```
# this is the distribution strategy
distribution = tf.distribute.MirroredStrategy()

# this piece of code is distributed to multiple GPUs
with distribution.scope():
  model = tf.keras.Sequential()
  model.add(tf.keras.layers.Dense(16, activation='relu', input_
shape=(N_FEATURES,)))
  model.add(tf.keras.layers.Dense(1, activation='sigmoid'))
  optimizer = tf.keras.optimizers.SGD(0.2)
  model.compile(loss='binary_crossentropy', optimizer=optimizer)

model.summary()

# Optimize in the usual way but in reality you are using GPUs.
model.fit(dataset, epochs=5, steps_per_epoch=10)
```

Note that each batch of the given input is divided equally among the multiple GPUs. For instance, if using `MirroredStrategy()` with two GPUs, each batch of size 256 will be divided among the two GPUs, with each of them receiving 128 input examples for each step. In addition, note that each GPU will optimize on the received batches and the TensorFlow backend will combine all these independent optimizations on our behalf. If you want to know more, you can have a look to the notebook online (`https://colab.research.google.com/drive/1mf-PK0a20CkObn T0hCl9VPEje1szhHat#scrollTo=wYar3A0vBVtZ`) where I explain how to use GPUs in Colab with a Keras model built for MNIST classification. The notebook is available in the GitHub repository.

In short, using multiple GPUs is very easy and requires minimal changes to the `tf.keras` code used for a single server.

MultiWorkerMirroredStrategy

This strategy implements synchronous distributed training across multiple workers, each one with potentially multiple GPUs. As of September 2019 the strategy works only with Estimators and it has experimental support for `tf.keras`. This strategy should be used if you are aiming at scaling beyond a single machine with high performance. Data must be loaded with `tf.Dataset` and shared across workers so that each worker can read a unique subset.

TPUStrategy

This strategy implements synchronous distributed training on TPUs. TPUs are Google's specialized ASICs chips designed to significantly accelerate machine learning workloads in a way often more efficient than GPUs. We will talk more about TPUs during *Chapter 16*, *Tensor Processing Unit*. According to this public information (`https://github.com/tensorflow/tensorflow/issues/24412`):

> *"the gist is that we intend to announce support for TPUStrategy alongside Tensorflow 2.1. Tensorflow 2.0 will work under limited use-cases but has many improvements (bug fixes, performance improvements) that we're including in Tensorflow 2.1, so we don't consider it ready yet."*

ParameterServerStrategy

This strategy implements either multi-GPU synchronous local training or asynchronous multi-machine training. For local training on one machine, the variables of the models are placed on the CPU and operations are replicated across all local GPUs.

For multi-machine training, some machines are designated as workers and some as parameter servers with the variables of the model placed on parameter servers. Computation is replicated across all GPUs of all workers. Multiple workers can be set up with the environment variable TF_CONFIG as in the following example:

```
os.environ["TF_CONFIG"] = json.dumps({
    "cluster": {
        "worker": ["host1:port", "host2:port", "host3:port"],
        "ps": ["host4:port", "host5:port"]
    },
    "task": {"type": "worker", "index": 1}
})
```

In this section, we have seen how it is possible to train models using distributed GPUs, multiple machines, and TPUs in a very simple way with very few additional lines of code. Now let's see another difference between 1.x and 2.x. Namely, namespaces.

Changes in namespaces

TensorFlow 2.x made a significant effort to clean the namespaces that in TensorFlow 1.x became extremely dense, particularly in the root namespace, making discoverability difficult. Here we have a summary of the major changes:

- `tf.keras.layers`: Contains all symbols that were previously under `tf.layers`

- `tf.keras.losses`: Contains all symbols that were previously under `tf.losses`

- `tf.keras.metrics`: Contains all symbols that were previously under `tf.metrics`

- `tf.debugging`: A new namespace for debugging

- `tf.dtypes`: A new namespace for data types

- `tf.io`: A new namespace for I/O

- `tf.quantization`: A new namespace for quantization

TensorFlow 1.x currently provides over 2,000 endpoints in total, including over 500 endpoints in the root namespace. TensorFlow 2.x removed 214 endpoints, including 171 endpoints in the root namespace. A conversion script has been added to TensorFlow 2.x in order to facilitate the conversion from 1.x to 2.x and to highlight deprecated endpoints.

A complete description of additional endpoints and deprecated endpoints can be found at https://github.com/tensorflow/community/blob/master/rfcs/20180827-api-names.md.

Converting from 1.x to 2.x

TensorFlow 1.x scripts will not work directly with TensorFlow 2.x but they need converting. The first step to convert from 1.x to 2.x is to use the automatic conversion script installed with 2.x. For a single file, you can run it with:

```
tf_upgrade_v2 --infile tensorfoo.py --outfile tensorfoo-upgraded.py
```

For multiple files in a directory, the syntax is:

```
tf_upgrade_v2 --intree incode --outtree code-upgraded
```

The script will try to upgrade automatically to 2.x and will print error messages where it is not able to upgrade.

Using TensorFlow 2.x effectively

2.x native code should follow a number of best practices:

1. Default to higher-level APIs such as `tf.keras` (or in certain situations, Estimators) and avoid lower-level APIs with direct computational graph manipulation unless needed for custom operations. So, in general, no `tf.Session`, `tf.Session.run`.

2. Add a `tf.function` decorator to make it run efficiently in graph mode with AutoGraph. Only use `tf.function` to decorate high-level computations; all functions invoked by high-level computations are automatically annotated on your behalf. In this way, you get the best of both worlds: high-level APIs with eager support, and the efficiency of computational graphs.

3. Use Python objects to track variables and losses. So, be Pythonic and use `tf.Variable` instead of `tf.get_variable`. In this way, variables will be treated with the normal Python scope.

4. Use `tf.data` datasets for data inputs and provide these objects directly to `tf.keras.Model.fit`. In this way, you will have a collection of high-performance classes for manipulating data and will adopt the best way to stream training data from disk.

5. Use `tf.layers` modules to combine predefined "lego bricks" whenever it is possible, either with Sequential or Functional APIs, or with Subclassing. Use Estimators if you need to have production-ready models, in particular if these models need to scale on multiple GPUs, CPUs, or on multiple servers. When needed, consider converting a `tf.keras` model into an Estimator.

6. Consider using a distribution strategy across GPUs, CPUs, and multiple servers. With `tf.keras` it is easy.

Many other recommendations can be made but the preceding ones are the top six. TensorFlow 2.x makes the initial learning step very easy and adopting `tf.keras` makes it very easy for beginners.

The TensorFlow 2.x ecosystem

Today, TensorFlow 2.x is a rich learning ecosystem where, in addition to the core learning engine, there is a large collection of tools that can be freely used. In particular:

*   **TensorFlow.js** (`https://www.tensorflow.org/js`) is a collection of APIs to train and run inference directly in browsers or in Node.js.

*   **TensorFlow Lite** (`https://www.tensorflow.org/lite`) is a lightweight version of TensorFlow for embedded and mobile devices. Currently, both Android and iOS are supported in Java and C++.

*   **TensorFlow Hub** (`https://www.tensorflow.org/hub`) is a complete library supporting the most common machine learning architectures. As of April 2019, Hub only partially supports the `tf.Keras` API but this issue (`https://github.com/tensorflow/tensorflow/issues/25362`) is going to be solved soon. We will see an example of Hub in *Chapter 5, Advanced Convolutional Neural Networks*.

*   **TensorFlow Extended (TFX)** (`https://github.com/tensorflow/tfx`) is a complete end-to-end platform for learning, including tools for transformation (TfTransform), analysis (TensorFlow Model Analysis), and for efficiently serving learning models during inference (TensorFlow Serving). TFX pipelines can be orchestrated using Apache Airflow and Kubeflow Pipelines.

*   **TensorBoard** is a visual environment for inspecting, debugging, and optimizing models and metrics.

*   **Sonnet** is a library similar to Keras, developed by DeepMind for training their models.

*   **TensorBoard Federated** is a framework for machine learning and other computations on decentralized data.

- **TensorBoard Probability** is a framework for combining probabilistic models and deep learning.

- **TensorBoard Playground** is a nice UI for visualizing, debugging, and inspecting neural networks; it's especially effective for education.

- **Accelerated Linear Algebra (XLA)** is a domain-specific compiler for linear algebra that optimizes TensorFlow computations.

- **MLPerf** is an ML benchmark suite for measuring the performance of ML software frameworks, ML hardware accelerators, and ML cloud platforms.

- **Colab** is a free Jupyter Notebook environment that requires no setup and runs entirely in the cloud. Users can write and execute code, save and share analyses, and access powerful computing resources, all for free from a browser.

- **TensorFlow Datasets** is an official collection of datasets included in TensorFlow. In addition, there are datasets freely available via Google Research and a Google-powered Dataset Search (`https://toolbox.google.com/datasetsearch`).

The list of resources, libraries, and tools is very long, and each tool would require a separate chapter (in some cases a separate book!). In this book, we use Colab, TensorBoard, Hub, and Lite and leave to the reader the task of checking out the others online. Researchers can also use the **TensorFlow Research Cloud (TFRC)** program, which allows you to apply for access to a cluster of more than 1,000 Cloud TPUs.

Models, datasets, tools, libraries, and extensions can be found at `https://www.tensorflow.org/resources/tools`.

Language bindings

Python is the language of choice for TensorFlow. However, there are bindings with many other languages, including JavaScript, C++, Java, Go, and Swift. The community is also maintaining bindings for other languages, including C#, Haskell, Julia, Ruby, Rust, and Scala. Normally the C API is used to build bindings for other languages.

Keras or tf.keras?

Another legitimate question is whether you should use Keras with TensorFlow as a backend or, instead, use the APIs in `tf.keras` directly available in TensorFlow. Note that there is not a 1:1 correspondence between Keras and `tf.keras`. Many endpoints in `tf.keras` are not implemented in Keras and `tf.Keras` does not support multiple backends as Keras. So, Keras or `tf.keras`? My suggestion is the second option rather than the first one. `tf.keras` has multiple advantages over Keras, consisting of TensorFlow enhancements discussed in this chapter (eager execution; native support for distributed training, including training on TPUs; and support for the TensorFlow SavedModel exchange format). However, the first option is still the most relevant one if you plan to write highly portable code that can run on multiple backends, including Google TensorFlow, Microsoft CNTK, Amazon MXnet, and Theano. Note that Keras is an independent open source project, and its development is not dependent on TensorFlow. Therefore, Keras is going to be developed for the foreseeable future. Note that Keras 2.3.0 (released on September 17, 2019) is the first release of multi-backend Keras, which supports TensorFlow 2.0. It maintains compatibility with TensorFlow 1.14 and 1.13, as well as Theano and CNTK.

Let's conclude the chapter with a new comparison: the primary machine learning software tools used by the top-5 teams on Kaggle in each competition. This was a survey ran by Francois Chollet on Twitter at the beginning of April 2019 (thanks, Francois for agreeing to have it included in this book!):

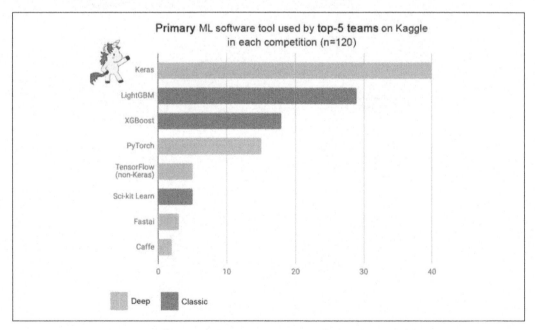

Figure 5: Primary ML software tools used by top-5 teams on Kaggle in 2019

In this section, we have seen the main differences between Keras and `tf.keras`.

Summary

TensorFlow 2.0 is a rich development ecosystem composed of two main parts: Training and Serving. Training consists of a set of libraries for dealing with datasets (`tf.data`), a set of libraries for building models, including high-level libraries (`tf.Keras` and Estimators), low-level libraries (`tf.*`), and a collection of pretrained models (`tf.Hub`), which will be discussed in *Chapter 5, Advanced Convolutional Neural Networks*. Training can happen on CPUs, GPUs, and TPUs via distribution strategies and the result can be saved using the appropriate libraries. Serving can happen on multiple platforms, including on-prem, cloud, Android, iOS, Raspberry Pi, any browser supporting JavaScript, and Node.js. Many language bindings are supported, including Python, C, C#, Java, Swift, R, and others. The following diagram summarizes the architecture of TensorFlow 2.0 as discussed in this chapter:

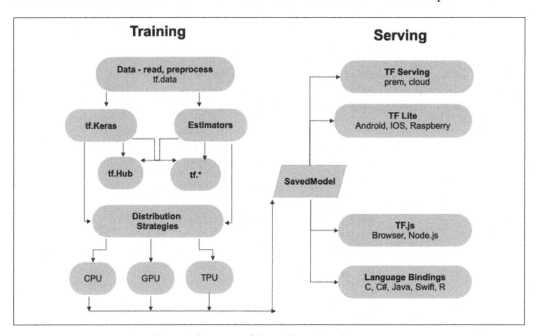

Figure 6: Summary of TensorFlow 2.0 architecture

- **tf.data** can be used to load models in a very efficient way.

- **tf.keras** and **Estimators** are high-level libraries where the power of TensorFlow 1.x is still accessible via **tf.*** lower-level libraries. **tf.keras** supports eager computation while still retaining the performance of lower-level computational graphs via **tf.function**. **tf.hub** is a nice collection of pretrained models that can be used immediately.

- **Distribution Strategies** allow training to be run on CPUs, GPUs, and TPUs.

- **SavedModel** can be served on multiple platforms.

In this chapter we have discussed the main differences between TensorFlow 1.x and 2.x and reviewed the powerful new features available in 2.x. The key topics discussed in this chapter were: the computational graph in TensorFlow 1.x, and the advantages of TensorFlow 2.x, such as support for eager execution, distribution, and TPU training. The next chapter will introduce Regression a quite powerful tool for mathematical modelling, classification and prediction.

3
Regression

Regression is one of the oldest tools for mathematical modeling, classification, and prediction, yet remains quite a powerful one. Regression finds application in varied fields ranging from engineering, physical science, biology, and the financial market, to the social sciences. It is a fundamental tool in the hands of statisticians and data scientists. In this chapter, we will cover the following topics:

- Linear regression
- Different types of linear regression
- Logistic regression
- Apply linear regression to estimate the price of a house
- Apply logistic regression to identify handwritten digits

Let us first start with understanding what regression really is.

What is regression?

Regression is normally the first algorithm that people in machine learning work with. It allows us to make predictions from data by learning about the relationship between a given set of dependent and independent variables. It has its use in almost every field; anywhere that has an interest in drawing relationships between two or more things will find a use for regression.

Consider the case of house price estimation. There are many factors that can have an impact on the house price: the number of rooms, the floor area, the locality, the availability of amenities, the parking space, and so on. Regression analysis can help us in finding the mathematical relationship between these factors and the house price.

Let us imagine a simpler world where only the area of the house determines its price. Using regression we could determine the relationship between the area of the house (**independent variable**: these are the variables that do not depend upon any other variables) and its price (**dependent variable**: these variables depend upon one or more independent variables). Later, we could use this relationship to predict the price of any house, given its area. To learn more about dependent and independent variables and how to identify them you can refer to this post: `http://www.aimldl.org/ml/dependent_independent_variables.html`. In machine learning, the independent variables are normally input to the model and the dependent variables are output from our model.

Depending upon the number of independent variables, the number of dependent variables, and the relationship type, we have many different types of regression. There are two important components of regression: the *relationship* between independent and dependent variables, and the *strength of impact* of different independent variables on dependent variables. In the following section, we will learn in detail about the widely used linear regression technique.

Prediction using linear regression

Linear regression is one of the most widely known modeling techniques. Existing for more than 200 years, it has been explored from almost all possible angles. Linear regression assumes a linear relationship between the input variable (X) and the output variable (Y). It involves finding a linear equation for predicted value Y of the form:

$$Y_{hat} = W^T X + b$$

Where $X = \{x_1, x_2, ..., x_n\}$ are the n input variables, and $W = \{w_1, w_2, ...w_n\}$ are the linear coefficients, with b as the bias term. The bias term allows our regression model to provide an output even in the absence of any input; it provides us with an option to shift our data left or right to better fit the data. The error between the observed values (Y) and predicted values (Y_{hat}) for an input sample i is:

$$e_i = Y_i - Y_{hat_i}$$

The goal is to find the best estimates for the coefficients W and bias b, such that the error between the observed values Y and the predicted values Y_{hat} is minimized. Let's go through some examples in order to better understand this.

Simple linear regression

If we consider only one independent variable and one dependent variable, what we get is a simple linear regression. Consider the case of house price prediction, defined in the preceding section; the area of the house (A) is the independent variable and the price (Y) of the house is the dependent variable. We want to find a linear relationship between predicted price Y_{hat} and A, of the form:

$$Y_{hat} = A. W + b$$

Where b is the bias term. Thus, we need to determine W and b, such that the error between the price Y and predicted price Y_{hat} is minimized. The standard method used to estimate W and b is called the method of least squares, that is, we try to minimize the sum of the square of errors (S). For the preceding case, the expression becomes:

$$S(W, b) = \sum_{i=1}^{N} (Y_i - Y_{hat})^2 = \sum_{i=1}^{N} (Y_i - A_i W - b)^2$$

We want to estimate the regression coefficients, W and b, such that S is minimized. We use the fact that the derivative of a function is 0 at its minima to get these two equations:

$$\frac{\partial S}{\partial W} = -2 \sum_{i=1}^{N} (Y_i - A_i W - b)A_i = 0$$

$$\frac{\partial S}{\partial b} = -2 \sum_{i=1}^{N} (Y_i - A_i W - b) = 0$$

These two equations can be solved to find the two unknowns. To do so, we first expand the summation in the second equation:

$$\sum_{i=1}^{N} Y_i - \sum_{i=1}^{N} A_i W - \sum_{i=1}^{N} b = 0$$

Take a look at the last term on the left-hand side; it just sums up a constant N time. Thus, we can rewrite it as:

$$\sum_{i=1}^{N} Y_i - W \sum_{i=1}^{N} A_i - Nb = 0$$

Reordering the terms, we get:

$$b = \frac{1}{N} \sum_{i=1}^{N} Y_i - \frac{W}{N} \sum_{i=1}^{N} A_i$$

The two terms on the right-hand side can be replaced by $\bar{Y}$, the average price (output), and $\bar{A}$, the average area (the input), respectively, and thus we get:

$$b = \bar{Y} - W\bar{A}$$

In a similar fashion, we expand the partial differential equation of S with respect to weight W:

$$\sum_{i=1}^{N} \left(Y_i A_i - W A_i^2 - b A_i \right) = 0$$

Substitute the expression for the bias term b:

$$\sum_{i=1}^{N} \left(Y_i A_i - W A_i^2 - (\bar{Y} - W\bar{A}) A_i \right) = 0$$

Reordering:

$$\sum_{i=1}^{N} (Y_i A_i - \bar{Y} A_i) - W \sum_{i=1}^{N} \left(A_i^2 - \bar{A} A_i \right) = 0$$

Playing around with the mean definition, we can get from this the value of weight W as:

$$W = \frac{\sum_{i=1}^{N} Y_i (A_i - \bar{A})}{\sum_{i=1}^{N} (A_i - \bar{A})^2}$$

Where $\bar{Y}$ and $\bar{A}$ are the average price and area respectively. Let us try this on some simple sample data:

1. We import the necessary modules. It is a simple example so we'll be using only NumPy, pandas, and Matplotlib:

```
import tensorflow as tf
import numpy as np
import matplotlib.pyplot as plt
import pandas as pd
```

2. Next, we generate random data with a linear relationship. To make it more real we also add a random noise element. You can see the two variables (the cause: area, and the effect: price) follow a positive linear dependence:

```
#Generate a random data
np.random.seed(0)
area = 2.5 * np.random.randn(100) + 25
price = 25 * area + 5 + np.random.randint(20,50, size = len(area))


data = np.array([area, price])
data = pd.DataFrame(data = data.T, columns=['area','price'])

plt.scatter(data['area'], data['price'])
plt.show()
```

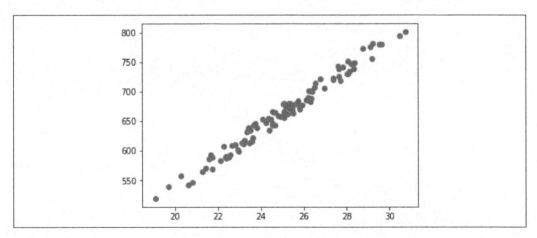

3. Now, we calculate the two regression coefficients using the equations we defined. You can see the result is very much near the linear relationship we have simulated:

```
W = sum(price*(area-np.mean(area))) / sum((area-np.mean(area))**2)
b = np.mean(price) - W*np.mean(area)
print("The regression coefficients are", W,b)
------------------------------------------------
------------------------------------------------
```

```
The regression coefficients are 24.815544052284988
43.4989785533412
```

4. Let us now try predicting the new prices using the obtained weight and bias values:

```
y_pred = W * area + b
```

5. Next, we plot the predicted prices along with the actual price. You can see that predicted prices follow a linear relationship with the area:

```
plt.plot(area, y_pred, color='red',label="Predicted Price")
plt.scatter(data['area'], data['price'], label="Training Data")
plt.xlabel("Area")
plt.ylabel("Price")
plt.legend()
```

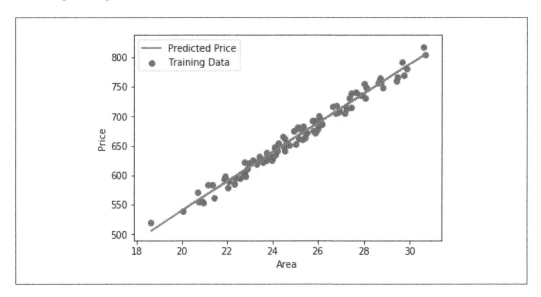

Multiple linear regression

The preceding example was simple, but that is rarely the case. In most problems, the dependent variables depend upon multiple independent variables. Multiple linear regression finds a linear relationship between the many independent input variables (X) and the dependent output variable (Y), such that they satisfy the predicted Y value of the form:

$$Y_{hat} = W^T X + b$$

Where $X = \{x_1, x_2, ..., x_n\}$ are the n independent input variables, and $W = \{w_1, w_2, ...w_n\}$ are the linear coefficients, with b as the bias term.

As before the linear coefficients W's are estimated using the method of least squares, that is, minimizing the sum of squared differences between predicted values (Y_{hat}) and observed values (Y). Thus, we try to minimize the loss function:

$$loss = \sum_i (Y_i - Y_{hat_i})^2$$

Where the sum is over all the training samples. As you might have guessed, now instead of two we will have $n+1$ equations, which we will need to simultaneously solve. An easier alternative will be to use the TensorFlow Estimator API. We will learn shortly how to use the TensorFlow Estimator API.

Multivariate linear regression

There can be cases where the independent variables affect more than one dependent variable. This is the case of multivariate linear regression. Mathematically, a multivariate regression model can be represented as:

$$\hat{Y}_{ij} = w_{0j} + \sum_{k=1}^{p} w_{kj} x_{ik}$$

Where $i \in [1, ..., n]$ and $j \in [1, ..., m]$. The term $\hat{Y}_{ij}$ represents the jth predicted output value corresponding to the ith input sample, w represents the regression coefficients, and x_{ik} is the kth feature of the ith input sample. The number of equations needed to solve in this case will now be $n \times m$. While we can solve these equations using matrices, the process will be computationally expensive as it will involve calculating inverse and determinants. An easier way would be to use the gradient descent with the sum of least square error as the loss function and to use one of the many optimizers that the TensorFlow API includes.

In the next section we will delve deeper into TensorFlow Estimators, a versatile higher-level API to develop your model with ease.

TensorFlow Estimators

TensorFlow provides Estimators as higher-level APIs, to provide scalable and production-oriented solutions. They take care of all behind-the-scene activities such as creating computational graphs, initializing the variables, training the model, saving checkpoints, and logging TensorBoard files. TensorFlow provides two types of Estimators:

- **Canned Estimators**: These are premade Estimators available in the TensorFlow estimator module. These are models in a box; you just pass them the input features and they are ready to use. Some examples are Linear Classifier, Linear Regressor, DNN Classifier, and so on.

- **Custom Estimators**: Users can also create their own estimators from the models they build in TensorFlow Keras. These are user-defined Estimators.

Before being able to use TensorFlow Estimator let us understand two important components of the Estimator pipeline:

Feature columns

The `feature_column` module of TensorFlow 2.0 acts as a bridge between your input data and the model. The input parameters to be used by the estimators for training are passed as feature columns. They are defined in TensorFlow `feature_column` and specify how the data is interpreted by the model. To create feature columns we will need to call functions from `tensorflow.feature_columns`. There are nine functions available in feature column:

- `categorical_column_with_identity`: Here each category is one-hot encoded, and thus has a unique identity. This can be used for numeric values only.

- `categorical_column_with_vocabulary_file`: This is used when the categorical input is a string and the categories are given in a file. The string is first converted to a numeric value and then one-hot encoded.

- `categorical_column_with_vocabulary_list`: This is used when the categorical input is a string and the categories are explicitly defined in a list. The string is first converted to a numeric value and then one-hot encoded.

- `categorical_column_with_hash_bucket`: In case the number of categories is very large, and it is not possible to one-hot encode, we use hashing.

- `crossed_column`: When we want to use two columns combined as one feature, for example, in the case of geolocation-based data it makes sense to combine longitude and latitude values as one feature.

- `numeric_column`: Used when the feature is a numeric, it can be a single value or even a matrix.

- `indicator_column`: We do not use this directly. Instead, it is used with the categorical column, but only when the number of categories is limited and can be represented as one-hot encoded.

- `embedding_column`: We do not use this directly. Instead, it is used with the categorical column, but only when the number of categories is very large and cannot be represented as one-hot encoded.

- `bucketized_column`: This is used when, instead of a specific numeric value, we split the data into different categories depending upon its value.

The first six functions inherit from the Categorical Column class, the next three inherit from the Dense Column class, and the last one inherits from both classes. In the following example we will use `numeric_column` and `categorical_column_with_vocabulary_list` functions.

Input functions

The data for training, evaluation, as well as prediction, needs to be made available through an input function. The input function returns a `tf.data.Dataset` object; the object returns a tuple containing features and labels.

MNIST using TensorFlow Estimator API

Let us build a simple TensorFlow estimator with a simple dataset for a multiple regression problem. We continue with the home price prediction, but now have two features, that is, we are considering two independent variables: the area of the house and its type (bungalow or apartment) on which we presume our price should depend:

1. We import the necessary modules. We will need TensorFlow and its `feature_column` module. Since our dataset contains both numeric and categorical data, we need the functions to process both types of data:

```
import tensorflow as tf
from tensorflow import feature_column as fc
numeric_column = fc.numeric_column
categorical_column_with_vocabulary_list = fc.categorical_column_
with_vocabulary_list
```

2. Now, we define the feature columns we will be using to train the regressor. Our dataset, as we mentioned, consists of two features "area" a numeric value signifying the area of the house and "type" telling if it is a "bungalow" or "apartment":

```
featcols = [
tf.feature_column.numeric_column("area"),
tf.feature_column.categorical_column_with_vocabulary_list("type",[
"bungalow","apartment"])
]
```

3. In the next step, we define an input function to provide input for training. The function returns a tuple containing features and labels:

```
def train_input_fn():
        features = {"area":[1000,2000,4000,1000,2000,4000],
            "type":["bungalow","bungalow","house",
                    "apartment","apartment","apartment"]}
        labels = [ 500 , 1000 , 1500 , 700 , 1300 , 1900 ]
        return features, labels
```

4. Next, we use the premade `LinearRegressor` estimator and fit it on the training dataset:

```
model = tf.estimator.LinearRegressor(featcols)
model.train(train_input_fn, steps=200)
```

5. Now that the estimator is trained, let us see the result of the prediction:

```
def predict_input_fn():
    features = {"area":[1500,1800],
                "type":["house","apt"]}
    return features

predictions = model.predict(predict_input_fn)

print(next(predictions))
print(next(predictions))
-------------------------------------------------
```

6. The result:

```
{'predictions': array([692.7829], dtype=float32)}
{'predictions': array([830.9035], dtype=float32)}
```

Predicting house price using linear regression

Now that we have the basics covered, let us apply these concepts to a real dataset. We will consider the Boston housing price dataset (`http://lib.stat.cmu.edu/datasets/boston`) collected by Harrison and Rubinfield in 1978. The dataset contains 506 sample cases. Each house is assigned 14 attributes:

- CRIM – per capita crime rate by town
- ZN – proportion of residential land zoned for lots over 25,000 sq.ft.
- INDUS – proportion of non-retail business acres per town
- CHAS – Charles River dummy variable (1 if tract bounds river; 0 otherwise)
- NOX – nitric oxide concentration (parts per 10 million)
- RM – average number of rooms per dwelling
- AGE – proportion of owner-occupied units built prior to 1940
- DIS – weighted distances to five Boston employment centers
- RAD – index of accessibility to radial highways
- TAX – full-value property-tax rate per $10,000
- PTRATIO – pupil-teacher ratio by town
- B – 1000(Bk - 0.63)^2 where Bk is the proportion of blacks by town
- LSTAT – percentage of lower status citizens in the population
- MEDV – median value of owner-occupied homes in $1,000s

 The authors and Packt Publishing do not endorse the historical use of the racially-based attribute presented above. Note that this is a classical dataset, and the attributes are listed as per the original work by Harrison and Rubinfield, 1978.

We will use the TensorFlow estimator to build the linear regression model.

1. Import the modules required:

```
import tensorflow as tf
import pandas as pd
import tensorflow.feature_column as fc
from tensorflow.keras.datasets import boston_housing
```

2. Download the dataset:

```
(x_train, y_train), (x_test, y_test) = boston_housing.load_data()
```

3. Now let us define the features in our data, and for easy processing and visualization convert it into pandas `DataFrame`:

```
features = ['CRIM', 'ZN',
            'INDUS','CHAS','NOX','RM','AGE',
            'DIS', 'RAD', 'TAX', 'PTRATIO', 'B', 'LSTAT']

x_train_df = pd.DataFrame(x_train, columns= features)
x_test_df = pd.DataFrame(x_test, columns= features)
y_train_df = pd.DataFrame(y_train, columns=['MEDV'])
y_test_df = pd.DataFrame(y_test, columns=['MEDV'])
x_train_df.head()
```

4. At present we are taking all the features; we suggest that you check the correlation among different features and the predicted label MEDV to choose the best features and repeat the experiment:

```
feature_columns = []
for feature_name in features:
        feature_columns.append(fc.numeric_column(feature_name,
dtype=tf.float32))
```

5. We create the input function for the estimator. The function returns the `tf.Data.Dataset` object with a tuple: features and labels in batches. Use it to create `train_input_fn` and `val_input_fn`:

```
def estimator_input_fn(df_data, df_label, epochs=10, shuffle=True,
batch_size=32):
    def input_function():
    ds = tf.data.Dataset.from_tensor_slices((dict(df_data), df_
    label))
        if shuffle:
            ds = ds.shuffle(100)
        ds = ds.batch(batch_size).repeat(epochs)
        return ds
    return input_function

train_input_fn = estimator_input_fn(x_train_df, y_train_df)
val_input_fn = estimator_input_fn(x_test_df, y_test_df, epochs=1,
shuffle=False)
```

6. Next we instantiate a `LinearRegressor` estimator; we train it using training data using `train_input_fn`, and find the result for the validation dataset by evaluating the trained model using `val_input_fn`:

```
linear_est = tf.estimator.LinearRegressor(feature_columns=feature_
columns)
linear_est.train(train_input_fn, steps=100)
result = linear_est.evaluate(val_input_fn)
```

7. Let's make a prediction on it:

```
result = linear_est.predict(val_input_fn)
for pred,exp in zip(result, y_test[:32]):
    print("Predicted Value: ", pred['predictions'][0], "Expected:
", exp)
```

```
Predicted Value:  4.862152 Expected:   7.2
Predicted Value:  24.582247 Expected:  18.8
Predicted Value:  22.695276 Expected:  19.0
Predicted Value:  25.028057 Expected:  27.0
Predicted Value:  23.408998 Expected:  22.2
Predicted Value:  22.616102 Expected:  24.5
Predicted Value:  31.214731 Expected:  31.2
Predicted Value:  26.755243 Expected:  22.9
Predicted Value:  21.516464 Expected:  20.5
Predicted Value:  25.032785 Expected:  23.2
Predicted Value:  10.023388 Expected:  18.6
Predicted Value:  24.031082 Expected:  14.5
Predicted Value:  24.334019 Expected:  17.8
Predicted Value:  23.74925 Expected:   50.0
Predicted Value:  19.785368 Expected:  20.8
Predicted Value:  25.875463 Expected:  24.3
Predicted Value:  21.2129 Expected:   24.2
Predicted Value:  22.197586 Expected:  19.8
Predicted Value:  24.870373 Expected:  19.1
Predicted Value:  27.759129 Expected:  22.7
Predicted Value:  20.700903 Expected:  12.0
Predicted Value:  5.7440314 Expected:  10.2
Predicted Value:  22.404785 Expected:  20.0
Predicted Value:  25.772366 Expected:  18.5
Predicted Value:  33.465168 Expected:  20.9
Predicted Value:  25.10161 Expected:   23.0
Predicted Value:  26.143686 Expected:  27.5
Predicted Value:  35.51015 Expected:   30.1
Predicted Value:  8.041798 Expected:   9.5
Predicted Value:  24.381145 Expected:  22.0
Predicted Value:  24.351122 Expected:  21.2
Predicted Value:  9.700583 Expected:   14.1
```

Figure 1: Generating predicted values using the LinearRegressor estimator

The following is the TensorBoard graph of our linear regressor:

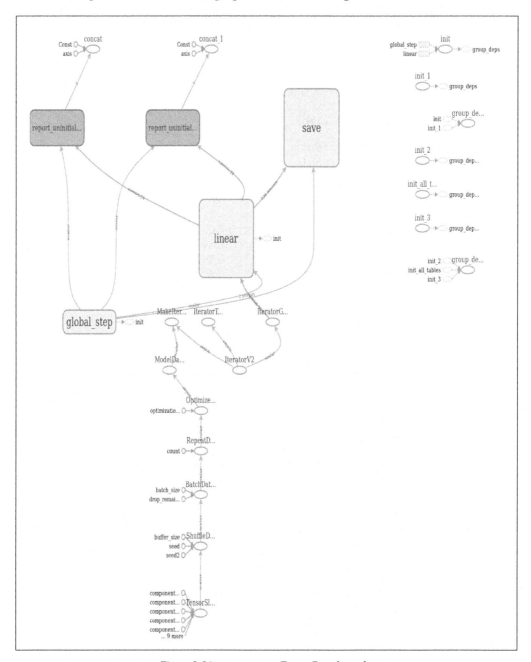

Figure 2: Linear regressor TensorBoard graph

The graph shows the flow of data, ops, and nodes used in the whole process. To get the TensorBoard graph for the estimator, you just need to define `model_dir` while instantiating the Estimator class:

```
linear_est = tf.estimator.LinearRegressor(feature_columns=feature_
columns, model_dir = 'logs/func/')
```

Classification tasks and decision boundaries

In the preceding section, we learned about the task of regression or prediction. In this section we will talk about another important task: the task of classification. Let us first understand the difference between regression (also sometimes referred to as prediction) and classification:

- In classification the data is grouped into classes/categories, while in regression the aim is to get a continuous numerical value for given data.

- For example, identifying the number of handwritten digits is a classification task; all handwritten digits will belong to one of the ten numbers lying between [0-9]. The task of predicting the price of the house depending upon different input variables is a regression task.

- In the classification task, the model finds the decision boundaries separating one class from another. In the regression task, the model approximates a function that fits the input-output relationship.

- Classification is a subset of regression; here we are predicting classes. Regression is much more general.

The following figure shows how the two classification and regression tasks differ. In classification we need to find a line (or a plane or hyperplane in multidimensional space) separating the classes.

In regression the aim is find a line (or plane or hyperplane) that fits the given input points:

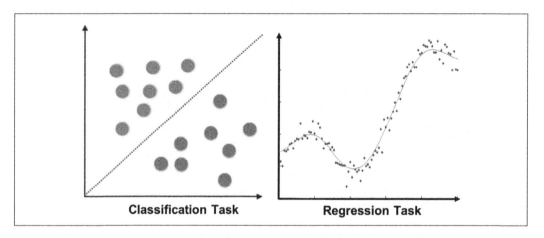

Classification Task   **Regression Task**

In the following section we will explain how logistic regression is a very common and useful classification technique.

Logistic regression

Logistic regression is used to determine the probability of an event. Conventionally, the event is represented as a categorical dependent variable. The probability of the event is expressed using the sigmoid (or "logit") function:

$$P(Y_{hat} = 1 | X = x) = \frac{1}{1 + e^{-(b + w^T x)}}$$

The goal now is to estimate weights $W = \{ w_1, w_2, ...w_n \}$ and bias term b. In logistic regression, the coefficients are estimated using either the maximum likelihood estimator or stochastic gradient descent. If p is the total number of input data points, the loss is conventionally defined as a cross-entropy term given by:

$$loss = \sum_{i=1}^{p} Y_i \log(Y_{hat_i}) + (1 - Y_i)\log(1 - Y_{hat_i})$$

Logistic regression is used in classification problems. For example, when looking at medical data, we can use logistic regression to classify whether a person has cancer or not. In case the output categorical variable has two or more levels, we can use multinomial logistic regression. Another common technique used for two or more output variables is one versus all.

For multiclass logistic regression, the cross-entropy loss function is modified as:

$$loss = \sum_{i=1}^{p} \sum_{j=1}^{k} Y_{ij} \log (Y_{hat_{ij}})$$

Where K is the total number of classes. You can read more about logistic regression at https://en.wikipedia.org/wiki/Logistic_regression.

Now that you have some idea about logistic regression, let us see how we can apply it to any dataset.

Logistic regression on the MNIST dataset

Next, we will use the Estimator classifier available in TensorFlow estimator to classify handwritten digits. We will be using the **MNIST (Modified National Institute of Standards and Technology)** dataset. For those working in the field of deep learning, MNIST is not new, it is like the ABC of machine learning. It contains images of handwritten digits and a label for each image, indicating which digit it is. The label contains a value lying between 0-9 depending upon the handwritten digit.

The classifier Estimator takes in the features and the labels. It converts them to one-hot encoded vectors, that is, we have 10 bits representing the output. Each bit can have a value of either 0 or 1, and being one-hot means that for each image in the label Y only 1 bit out of the 10 will have a value of 1, and the rest will be 0s. In the following, you can see the image of a handwritten numeral 5, along with its one-hot encoded value [0 0 0 0 0 0 0 0 1 0].

The Estimator outputs the log probabilities (logits), the softmax probabilities for the ten classes, and the corresponding label:

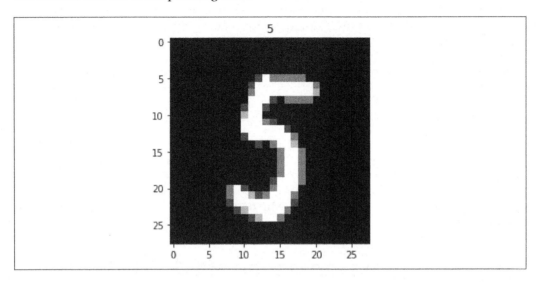

Let us build our model.

1. The first step is as always importing the modules needed:

```
# TensorFlow and tf.keras
import tensorflow as tf
from tensorflow import keras

# Helper libraries
import numpy as np
import matplotlib.pyplot as plt

print(tf.__version__)
```

2. We take the input data of MNIST from the `tensorflow.keras` dataset:

```
# Load training and eval data
((train_data, train_labels),
(eval_data, eval_labels)) = tf.keras.datasets.mnist.load_data()
```

3. Next, we preprocess the data:

```
train_data = train_data/np.float32(255)
train_labels = train_labels.astype(np.int32)

eval_data = eval_data/np.float32(255)
eval_labels = eval_labels.astype(np.int32)
```

4. Use the `feature_column` module of TensorFlow to define numeric features of size 28×28:

```
feature_columns = [tf.feature_column.numeric_column("x",
shape=[28, 28])]
```

5. Create the logistic regression estimator. We use a simple `LinearClassifier`. We encourage you to experiment with `DNNClassifier` as well:

```
classifier = tf.estimator.LinearClassifier(
    feature_columns=feature_columns,
    n_classes=10,
    model_dir="mnist_model/"
)
```

6. Let us also build an `input_function` to feed the estimator:

```
train_input_fn = tf.compat.v1.estimator.inputs.numpy_input_fn(
        x={"x": train_data},
        y=train_labels,
            batch_size=100,
            num_epochs=None,
            shuffle=True)
```

7. Let's now train the classifier:

```
classifier.train(input_fn=train_input_fn, steps=10)
```

8. Next, we create the input function for validation data:

```
val_input_fn =  tf.compat.v1.estimator.inputs.numpy_input_fn(
        x={"x": eval_data},
        y=eval_labels,
        num_epochs=1,
        shuffle=False)
```

9. Let us evaluate the trained Linear Classifier on the validation data:

```
eval_results = classifier.evaluate(input_fn=val_input_fn)
print(eval_results)
```

10. We get an accuracy of 89.4% after 130 time steps. Not bad, right? Please note that since we have specified the time steps, the model trains for the specified steps and logs the value after 10 steps (the number of steps specified). Now if we run `train` again, then it will start from the state it had at the 10th time step. The steps will go on increasing with an increment of the number of steps mentioned.

The following is the graph of the preceding model:

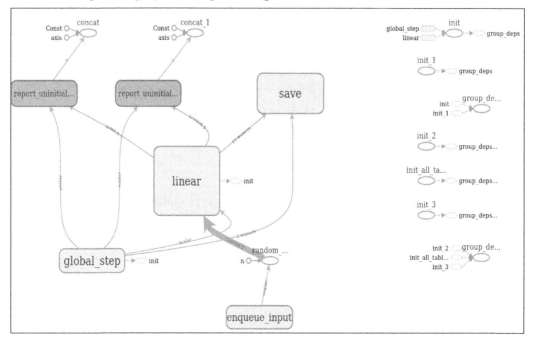

Figure 3: TensorBoard graph of the generated model

From TensorBoard we can also visualize the change in accuracy and average loss as the linear classifier learned in steps of ten:

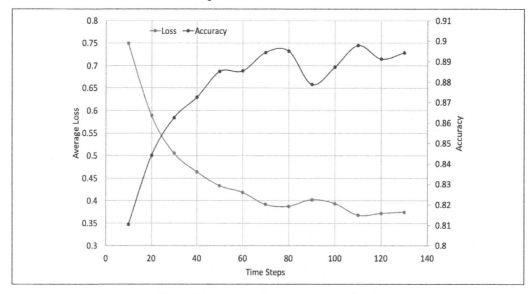

Figure 4: Accuracy and average loss, visualized

One can also use TensorBoard to see how the weights and bias of the model were modified as the network underwent training. In the following graph we can see that with each time step the bias changed. We can see that as the model is learning (*x*-axis – time), the bias is spreading from an initial value of 0:

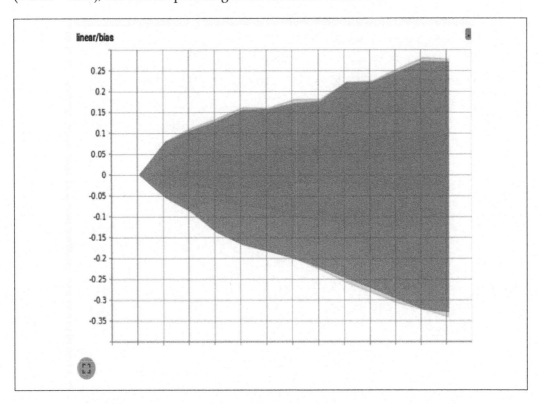

Summary

This chapter dealt with different types of regression algorithms. We started with linear regression and used it to predict house prices for a simple one-input variable case and for multiple input variable cases. The chapter then moved towards logistic regression, which is a very important and useful technique for classifying tasks. The chapter explained the TensorFlow Estimator API and used it to implement both linear and logistic regression for some classical datasets. The next chapter will introduce you to convolutional neural networks, the most commercially successful neural network models.

References

Here are some good resources if you are interested in knowing more about the concepts we've covered in this chapter:

- `https://www.tensorflow.org/`
- `https://www.khanacademy.org/math/statistics-probability/describing-relationships-quantitative-data`
- `https://onlinecourses.science.psu.edu/stat501/node/250`

4
Convolutional Neural Networks

In the previous chapters we have discussed DenseNets, in which each layer is fully connected to the adjacent layers. We looked at one application of these dense networks in classifying the MNIST handwritten characters dataset. In that context, each pixel in the input image has been assigned to a neuron with a total of 784 (28 × 28 pixels) input neurons. However, this strategy does not leverage the spatial structure and relationships between each image. In particular, this piece of code is a DenseNet that transforms the bitmap representing each written digit into a flat vector where the local spatial structure is removed. Removing the spatial structure is a problem because important information is lost:

```
#X_train is 60000 rows of 28x28 values --> reshaped in 60000 x 784
X_train = X_train.reshape(60000, 784)
X_test = X_test.reshape(10000, 784)
```

Convolutional neural networks (in short, convnets or CNNs) leverage spatial information, and they are therefore very well-suited for classifying images. These nets use an ad hoc architecture inspired by biological data taken from physiological experiments performed on the visual cortex. As we discussed in *Chapter 2, TensorFlow 1.x and 2.x*, our vision is based on multiple cortex levels, each one recognizing more and more structured information. First, we see single pixels, then from that we recognize simple geometric forms and then more and more sophisticated elements such as objects, faces, human bodies, animals, and so on.

Convolutional neural networks are a fascinating subject. Over a short period of time, they have shown themselves to be a disruptive technology, breaking performance records in multiple domains from text, to video, to speech, going well beyond the initial image processing domain where they were originally conceived.

In this chapter we will introduce the idea of CNNs a particular type of neural networks that have large importance for deep learning.

Deep Convolutional Neural Network (DCNN)

A **Deep Convolutional Neural Network (DCNN)** consists of many neural network layers. Two different types of layers, convolutional and pooling (that is, subsampling), are typically alternated. The depth of each filter increases from left to right in the network. The last stage is typically made of one or more fully connected layers:

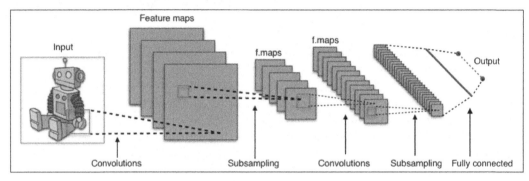

Figure 1: An example of a DCNN

There are three key underlying concepts for convnets: local receptive fields, shared weights, and pooling. Let's review them together.

Local receptive fields

If we want to preserve the spatial information of an image or other form of data, then it is convenient to represent each image with a matrix of pixels. Given this, a simple way to encode the local structure is to connect a submatrix of adjacent input neurons into one single hidden neuron belonging to the next layer. That single hidden neuron represents one local receptive field. Note that this operation is named *convolution*, and this is where the name for this type of network is derived. You can think about convolution as the treatment of a matrix by another matrix, referred to as a kernel.

Of course, we can encode more information by having overlapping submatrices. For instance, let's suppose that the size of each single submatrix is 5×5 and that those submatrices are used with MNIST images of 28×28 pixels, then we will be able to generate 24×24 local receptive field neurons in the hidden layer.

In fact, it is possible to slide the submatrices by only 23 positions before touching the borders of the images. In Keras, the number of pixels along one edge of the kernel, or submatrix, is the kernel size; the stride length, however, is the number of pixels by which the kernel is moved at each step in the convolution.

Let's define the feature map from one layer to another. Of course, we can have multiple feature maps that learn independently from each hidden layer. For example, we can start with 28×28 input neurons for processing MINST images, and then recall k feature maps of size 24×24 neurons each (again with stride of 5×5) in the next hidden layer.

Shared weights and bias

Let's suppose that we want to move away from the pixel representation in a raw image, by gaining the ability to detect the same feature independently from the location where it is placed in the input image. A simple approach is to use the same set of weights and biases for all the neurons in the hidden layers. In this way, each layer will learn a set of position-independent latent features derived from the image, bearing in mind that a layer consists of a set of kernels in parallel, and each kernel only learns one feature.

A mathematical example

One simple way to understand convolution is to think about a sliding window function applied to a matrix. In the following example, given the input matrix **I** and the kernel **K**, we get the convolved output. The 3×3 kernel **K** (sometimes called the filter or feature detector) is multiplied elementwise with the input matrix to get one cell in the output matrix. All the other cells are obtained by sliding the window over **I**:

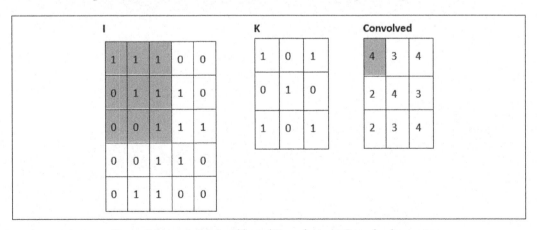

Figure 2: Input matrix I and kernel K producing a Convolved output

In this example we decided to stop the sliding window as soon as we touch the borders of **I** (so the output is 3×3). Alternatively, we could have chosen to pad the input with zeros (so that the output would have been 5×5). This decision relates to the padding choice adopted. Note that kernel depth is equal to input depth (channel).

Another choice is about how far along we slide our sliding windows with each step. This is called the stride. A larger stride generates less applications of the kernel and a smaller output size, while a smaller stride generates more output and retains more information.

The size of the filter, the stride, and the type of padding are hyperparameters that can be fine-tuned during the training of the network.

ConvNets in TensorFlow 2.x

In TensorFlow 2.x if we want to add a convolutional layer with 32 parallel features and a filter size of 3×3, we write:

```
import tensorflow as tf
from tensorflow.keras import datasets, layers, models
model = models.Sequential()
model.add(layers.Conv2D(32, (3, 3), activation='relu', input_
shape=(28, 28, 1)))
```

This means that we are applying a 3×3 convolution on 28×28 images with one input channel (or input filters) resulting in 32 output channels (or output filters).

An example of convolution is provided in *Figure 3*:

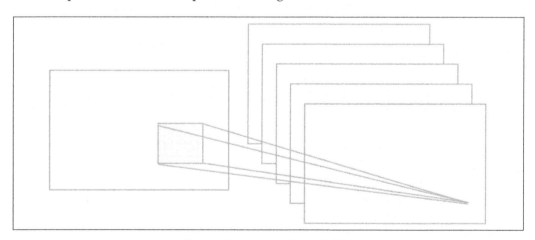

Figure 3: An example of convolution

Pooling layers

Let's suppose that we want to summarize the output of a feature map. Again, we can use the spatial contiguity of the output produced from a single feature map and aggregate the values of a sub-matrix into one single output value synthetically describing the "meaning" associated with that physical region.

Max pooling

One easy and common choice is the so-called *max-pooling operator*, which simply outputs the maximum activation as observed in the region. In Keras, if we want to define a max pooling layer of size 2×2, we write:

```
model.add(layers.MaxPooling2D((2, 2)))
```

An example of the max-pooling operation is given in *Figure 4*:

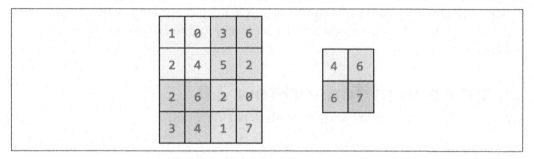

Figure 4: An example of max pooling

Average pooling

Another choice is *average pooling*, which simply aggregates a region into the average values of the activations observed in that region.

Note that Keras implements a large number of pooling layers and a complete list is available online (https://keras.io/layers/pooling/). In short, all the pooling operations are nothing more than a summary operation on a given region.

ConvNets summary

So far, we have described the basic concepts of ConvNets. CNNs apply convolution and pooling operations in 1 dimension for audio and text data along the time dimension, in two dimensions for images along the (height × width) dimensions and in three dimensions for videos along the (height × width × time) dimensions. For images, sliding the filter over an input volume produces a map that provides the responses of the filter for each spatial position.

In other words, a CNN has multiple filters stacked together that learn to recognize specific visual features independently from the location in the image itself. Those visual features are simple in the initial layers of the network and become more and more sophisticated deeper in the network. Training of a CNN requires the identification of the right values for each filter so that an input, when passed through multiple layers, activates certain neurons of the last layer so that it will predict the correct values.

An example of DCNN – LeNet

Yann LeCun, who very recently won the Turing Award, proposed [1] a family of convnets named LeNet trained for recognizing MNIST handwritten characters with robustness to simple geometric transformations and distortion. The core idea of LeNets is to have lower layers alternating convolution operations with max-pooling operations. The convolution operations are based on carefully chosen local receptive fields with shared weights for multiple feature maps. Then, higher levels are fully connected based on a traditional MLP with hidden layers and softmax as output layer.

LeNet code in TensorFlow 2.0

To define a LeNet in code we use a convolutional 2D module:

```
layers.Convolution2D(20, (5, 5), activation='relu', input_shape=input_
shape))
```

> Note that `tf.keras.layers.Conv2D` is an alias of `tf.keras.layers.Convolution2D` so the two can be used in an interchangeable way. See `https://www.tensorflow.org/api_docs/python/tf/keras/layers/Conv2D`.

Where the first parameter is the number of output filters in the convolution, and the next tuple is the extension of each filter. An interesting optional parameter is padding. There are two options: `padding='valid'` means that the convolution is only computed where the input and the filter fully overlap and therefore the output is smaller than the input, while `padding='same'` means that we have an output which is the same size as the input, for which the area around the input is padded with zeros.

In addition, we use a `MaxPooling2D` module:

```
layers.MaxPooling2D(pool_size=(2, 2), strides=(2, 2))
```

Where `pool_size=(2, 2)` is a tuple of two integers representing the factors by which the image is vertically and horizontally downscaled. So (2, 2) will halve the image in each dimension, and `strides=(2, 2)` is the stride used for processing.

Now, let us review the code. First, we import a number of modules:

```
import tensorflow as tf
from tensorflow.keras import datasets, layers, models, optimizers
# network and training
EPOCHS = 5
BATCH_SIZE = 128
VERBOSE = 1
OPTIMIZER = tf.keras.optimizers.Adam()
VALIDATION_SPLIT=0.95

IMG_ROWS, IMG_COLS = 28, 28 # input image dimensions
INPUT_SHAPE = (IMG_ROWS, IM    G_COLS, 1)
NB_CLASSES = 10   # number of outputs = number of digits
```

Then we define the LeNet network:

```
#define the convnet
def build(input_shape, classes):
    model = models.Sequential()
```

We have a first convolutional stage with rectified linear unit (ReLU) activations followed by a max pooling. Our net will learn 20 convolutional filters, each one of which with a size of 5×5. The output dimension is the same as the input shape, so it will be 28×28. Note that since `Convolution2D` is the first stage of our pipeline, we are also required to define its `input_shape`. The max pooling operation implements a sliding window that slides over the layer and takes the maximum of each region with a step of 2 pixels both vertically and horizontally:

```
# CONV => RELU => POOL
model.add(layers.Convolution2D(20, (5, 5), activation='relu', input_
shape=input_shape))
model.add(layers.MaxPooling2D(pool_size=(2, 2), strides=(2, 2)))
```

Then there is a second convolutional stage with ReLU activations, followed again by a max pooling layer. In this case we increase the number of convolutional filters learned to 50 from the previous 20. Increasing the number of filters in deeper layers is a common technique used in deep learning:

```
# CONV => RELU => POOL
model.add(layers.Convolution2D(50, (5, 5), activation='relu'))
model.add(layers.MaxPooling2D(pool_size=(2, 2), strides=(2, 2)))
```

Then we have a pretty standard flattening and a dense network of 500 neurons, followed by a `softmax` classifier with 10 classes:

```
# Flatten => RELU layers
model.add(layers.Flatten())
model.add(layers.Dense(500, activation='relu'))
# a softmax classifier
model.add(layers.Dense(classes, activation="softmax"))
return model
```

Congratulations, you have just defined your first deep convolutional learning network! Let's see how it looks visually:

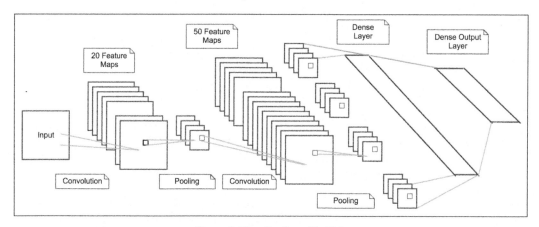

Figure 5: Visualization of LeNet

Now we need some additional code for training the network, but this is very similar to what we have already described in *Chapter 1, Neural Network Foundations with TensorFlow 2.0*. This time we also show the code for printing the loss:

```
# data: shuffled and split between train and test sets
(X_train, y_train), (X_test, y_test) = datasets.mnist.load_data()

# reshape
X_train = X_train.reshape((60000, 28, 28, 1))
X_test = X_test.reshape((10000, 28, 28, 1))

# normalize
```

```
X_train, X_test = X_train / 255.0, X_test / 255.0

# cast
X_train = X_train.astype('float32')
X_test = X_test.astype('float32')

# convert class vectors to binary class matrices
y_train = tf.keras.utils.to_categorical(y_train, NB_CLASSES)
y_test = tf.keras.utils.to_categorical(y_test, NB_CLASSES)

# initialize the optimizer and model
model = build(input_shape=INPUT_SHAPE, classes=NB_CLASSES)
model.compile(loss="categorical_crossentropy", optimizer=OPTIMIZER,
              metrics=["accuracy"])
model.summary()

# use TensorBoard, princess Aurora!
callbacks = [
  # Write TensorBoard logs to './logs' directory
  tf.keras.callbacks.TensorBoard(log_dir='./logs')
]

# fit
history = model.fit(X_train, y_train,
                    batch_size=BATCH_SIZE, epochs=EPOCHS,
                    verbose=VERBOSE, validation_split=VALIDATION_SPLIT,
                    callbacks=callbacks)

score = model.evaluate(X_test, y_test, verbose=VERBOSE)
print("\nTest score:", score[0])
print('Test accuracy:', score[1])
```

Now let's run the code. As you can see in *Figure 6,* the time had a significant increase and each iteration in our DNN now takes ~28 seconds against ~1-2 seconds for the net defined in *Chapter 1, Neural Network Foundations with TensorFlow 2.0.*

However, the accuracy reached a new peak at 99.991 on training, 99.91 on validation, and 99.15 on test%!

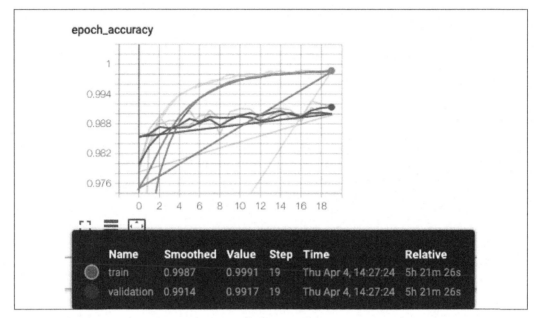

Figure 6: LeNet accuracy

Let's see the execution of a full run for 20 epochs:

```
Model: "sequential"
_____
Layer (type)                 Output Shape              Param #
=================================================================
conv2d (Conv2D)              (None, 24, 24, 20)        520
_____
max_pooling2d (MaxPooling2D) (None, 12, 12, 20)        0
_____
conv2d_1 (Conv2D)            (None, 8, 8, 50)          25050
_____
max_pooling2d_1 (MaxPooling2 (None, 4, 4, 50)          0
_____
flatten (Flatten)            (None, 800)               0
_____
dense (Dense)                (None, 500)               400500
_____
dense_1 (Dense)              (None, 10)                5010
=================================================================
Total params: 431,080
Trainable params: 431,080
Non-trainable params: 0
_____
Train on 48000 samples, validate on 12000 samples
Epoch 1/20
[2019-04-04 14:18:28.546158: I tensorflow/core/profiler/lib/profiler_session.cc:164] Profile Session started.
48000/48000 [==============================] - 28s 594us/sample - loss: 0.2035 - accuracy: 0.9398 - val_loss: 0.0739 - val_accuracy: 0.9783
Epoch 2/20
48000/48000 [==============================] - 26s 534us/sample - loss: 0.0520 - accuracy: 0.9839 - val_loss: 0.0435 - val_accuracy: 0.9868
Epoch 3/20
48000/48000 [==============================] - 27s 564us/sample - loss: 0.0343 - accuracy: 0.9893 - val_loss: 0.0365 - val_accuracy: 0.9895
Epoch 4/20
48000/48000 [==============================] - 27s 562us/sample - loss: 0.0248 - accuracy: 0.9921 - val_loss: 0.0452 - val_accuracy: 0.9868
Epoch 5/20
48000/48000 [==============================] - 27s 562us/sample - loss: 0.0195 - accuracy: 0.9939 - val_loss: 0.0428 - val_accuracy: 0.9873
Epoch 6/20
48000/48000 [==============================] - 28s 588us/sample - loss: 0.0153 - accuracy: 0.9950 - val_loss: 0.0417 - val_accuracy: 0.9876
Epoch 7/20
48000/48000 [==============================] - 26s 537us/sample - loss: 0.0134 - accuracy: 0.9955 - val_loss: 0.0388 - val_accuracy: 0.9896
Epoch 8/20
48000/48000 [==============================] - 29s 598us/sample - loss: 0.0097 - accuracy: 0.9966 - val_loss: 0.0347 - val_accuracy: 0.9899
Epoch 9/20
48000/48000 [==============================] - 29s 607us/sample - loss: 0.0091 - accuracy: 0.9971 - val_loss: 0.0515 - val_accuracy: 0.9859
Epoch 10/20
48000/48000 [==============================] - 27s 565us/sample - loss: 0.0062 - accuracy: 0.9980 - val_loss: 0.0376 - val_accuracy: 0.9904
Epoch 11/20
48000/48000 [==============================] - 30s 627us/sample - loss: 0.0068 - accuracy: 0.9976 - val_loss: 0.0366 - val_accuracy: 0.9911
Epoch 12/20
48000/48000 [==============================] - 24s 505us/sample - loss: 0.0079 - accuracy: 0.9975 - val_loss: 0.0389 - val_accuracy: 0.9910
Epoch 13/20
48000/48000 [==============================] - 28s 584us/sample - loss: 0.0057 - accuracy: 0.9978 - val_loss: 0.0531 - val_accuracy: 0.9890
Epoch 14/20
48000/48000 [==============================] - 28s 588us/sample - loss: 0.0045 - accuracy: 0.9984 - val_loss: 0.0489 - val_accuracy: 0.9911
Epoch 15/20
48000/48000 [==============================] - 26s 537us/sample - loss: 0.0039 - accuracy: 0.9986 - val_loss: 0.0436 - val_accuracy: 0.9911
Epoch 16/20
48000/48000 [==============================] - 25s 513us/sample - loss: 0.0059 - accuracy: 0.9983 - val_loss: 0.0480 - val_accuracy: 0.9890
Epoch 17/20
48000/48000 [==============================] - 24s 499us/sample - loss: 0.0042 - accuracy: 0.9988 - val_loss: 0.0535 - val_accuracy: 0.9888
Epoch 18/20
48000/48000 [==============================] - 24s 505us/sample - loss: 0.0042 - accuracy: 0.9986 - val_loss: 0.0349 - val_accuracy: 0.9926
Epoch 19/20
48000/48000 [==============================] - 29s 599us/sample - loss: 0.0052 - accuracy: 0.9984 - val_loss: 0.0377 - val_accuracy: 0.9920
Epoch 20/20
48000/48000 [==============================] - 25s 524us/sample - loss: 0.0028 - accuracy: 0.9991 - val_loss: 0.0477 - val_accuracy: 0.9917
10000/10000 [==============================] - 2s 240us/sample - loss: 0.0383 - accuracy: 0.9915
{
Test score: 0.03832608199457617
Test accuracy: 0.9915
```

Figure 7: Execution of the model after 20 epochs

Plotting the model accuracy and the model loss, we understand that we can train in only 10 iterations to achieve a similar accuracy of 99.1%:

```
-------------------------------------------------------------
Train on 48000 samples, validate on 12000 samples
Epoch 1/10
2019-04-04 15:57:17.848186: I tensorflow/core/profiler/lib/profiler_session.cc:164] Profile Session started.
48000/48000 [==============================] - 26s 544us/sample - loss: 0.2134 - accuracy: 0.9361 - val_loss: 0.0688 - val_accuracy: 0.9783
Epoch 2/10
48000/48000 [==============================] - 30s 633us/sample - loss: 0.0550 - accuracy: 0.9831 - val_loss: 0.0533 - val_accuracy: 0.9843
Epoch 3/10
48000/48000 [==============================] - 30s 621us/sample - loss: 0.0353 - accuracy: 0.9884 - val_loss: 0.0410 - val_accuracy: 0.9874
Epoch 4/10
48000/48000 [==============================] - 37s 767us/sample - loss: 0.0276 - accuracy: 0.9910 - val_loss: 0.0381 - val_accuracy: 0.9887
Epoch 5/10
48000/48000 [==============================] - 24s 509us/sample - loss: 0.0200 - accuracy: 0.9932 - val_loss: 0.0406 - val_accuracy: 0.9881
Epoch 6/10
48000/48000 [==============================] - 31s 641us/sample - loss: 0.0161 - accuracy: 0.9950 - val_loss: 0.0423 - val_accuracy: 0.9881
Epoch 7/10
48000/48000 [==============================] - 29s 613us/sample - loss: 0.0129 - accuracy: 0.9955 - val_loss: 0.0396 - val_accuracy: 0.9894
Epoch 8/10
48000/48000 [==============================] - 27s 554us/sample - loss: 0.0107 - accuracy: 0.9965 - val_loss: 0.0454 - val_accuracy: 0.9871
Epoch 9/10
48000/48000 [==============================] - 24s 510us/sample - loss: 0.0082 - accuracy: 0.9973 - val_loss: 0.0388 - val_accuracy: 0.9902
Epoch 10/10
48000/48000 [==============================] - 26s 542us/sample - loss: 0.0083 - accuracy: 0.9970 - val_loss: 0.0440 - val_accuracy: 0.9892
10000/10000 [==============================] - 2s 196us/sample - loss: 0.0327 - accuracy: 0.9910

Test score: 0.03265062951518773
Test accuracy: 0.991
```

Figure 8: Model accuracy after 10 iterations

Let us see some of the MNIST images in order to understand how good the number 99.1% is! For instance, there are many ways in which humans write a 9, one of them being in *Figure 9*. The same goes for 3, 7, 4, and 5; number 1 in this figure is so difficult to recognize that even a human would likely have trouble:

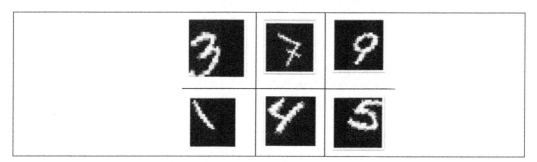

Figure 9: An example of MNIST handwritten chars

We can summarize all the progress made so far with our different models in the following graph. Our simple net started with an accuracy of 90.71%, meaning that about 9 handwritten characters out of 100 are not correctly recognized. Then, we gained 8% with the deep learning architecture, reaching an accuracy of 99.2%, which means that less than one handwritten character out of one hundred is incorrectly recognized (see *Figure 10*):

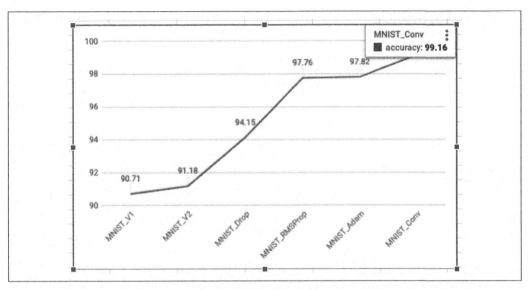

Figure 10: Accuracy for different models and optimizers

Understanding the power of deep learning

Another test we can run for better understanding the power of deep learning and convnets is to reduce the size of the training set and observe the resulting decay in performance. One way to do this is to split the training set of 50,000 examples into two different sets:

1. The proper training set used for training our model will progressively reduce its size through 5,900, 3,000, 1,800, 600, and 300 examples.
2. The validation set used to estimate how well our model has been trained will consist of the remaining examples. Our test set is always fixed, and it consists of 10,000 examples.

With this setup we compare the previously defined deep learning convnet against the first example neural network defined in *Chapter 1, Neural Network Foundations with TensorFlow 2.0*. As we can see in the following graph, our deep network always outperforms the simple network when there is more data available. With 5,900 training examples, the deep learning net had an accuracy of 97.23% against an accuracy of 94% for the simple net.

In general, deep networks require more training data available to fully express their power (see *Figure 11*):

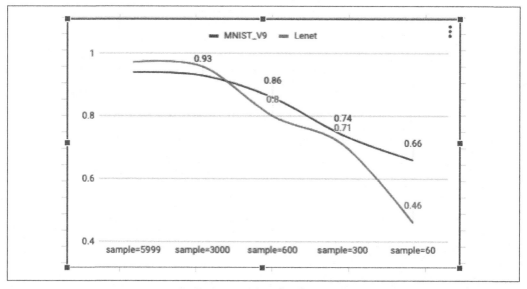

Figure 11: Accuracy for different amount of data

A list of state-of-the-art results (for example, the highest performance available) for MNIST is available online (`http://rodrigob.github.io/are_we_there_yet/build/classification_datasets_results.html`). As of March 2019, the best result has an error rate of 0.21% [2].

Recognizing CIFAR-10 images with deep learning

The CIFAR-10 dataset contains 60,000 color images of 32×32 pixels in 3 channels, divided in 10 classes. Each class contains 6,000 images. The training set contains 50,000 images, while the test sets provides 10,000 images. This image taken from the CIFAR repository (`https://www.cs.toronto.edu/~kriz/cifar.html`) shows a few random examples from each of the 10 classes:

Figure 12: An example of CIFAR-10 images

The goal is to recognize previously unseen images and assign them to one of the 10 classes. Let us define a suitable deep net.

First of all, we import a number of useful modules, define a few constants, and load the dataset (the full code including the load operations is available online):

```
import tensorflow as tf
from tensorflow.keras import datasets, layers, models, optimizers

# CIFAR_10 is a set of 60K images 32x32 pixels on 3 channels
IMG_CHANNELS = 3
IMG_ROWS = 32
IMG_COLS = 32

# constant
BATCH_SIZE = 128
EPOCHS = 20
CLASSES = 10
VERBOSE = 1
VALIDATION_SPLIT = 0.2
OPTIM = tf.keras.optimizers.RMSprop()
```

Our net will learn 32 convolutional filters, each with a 3×3 size. The output dimension is the same one as the input shape, so it will be 32×32 and the activation function used is a ReLU function, which is a simple way of introducing non-linearity. After that we have a max pooling operation with pool size 2×2 and a Dropout of 25%:

```
# define the convnet
def build(input_shape, classes):
    model = models.Sequential()
    model.add(layers.Convolution2D(32, (3, 3), activation='relu',
            input_shape=input_shape))
    model.add(layers.MaxPooling2D(pool_size=(2, 2)))
    model.add(layers.Dropout(0.25))
```

The next stage in the deep pipeline is a dense network with 512 units and ReLU activation followed by a dropout at 50% and by a softmax layer with 10 classes as output, one for each category:

```
    model.add(layers.Flatten())
    model.add(layers.Dense(512, activation='relu'))
    model.add(layers.Dropout(0.5))
    model.add(layers.Dense(classes, activation='softmax'))
    return model
```

After defining the network, we can train the model. In this case, we split the data and compute a validation set in addition to the training and testing sets. The training is used to build our models, the validation is used to select the best performing approach, while the test set is used to check the performance of our best models on fresh, unseen data:

```
# use TensorBoard, princess Aurora!
callbacks = [
  # Write TensorBoard logs to './logs' directory
  tf.keras.callbacks.TensorBoard(log_dir='./logs')
]

# train
model.compile(loss='categorical_crossentropy', optimizer=OPTIM,
            metrics=['accuracy'])

model.fit(X_train, y_train, batch_size=BATCH_SIZE,
        epochs=EPOCHS, validation_split=VALIDATION_SPLIT,
        verbose=VERBOSE, callbacks=callbacks)
score = model.evaluate(X_test, y_test,
                    batch_size=BATCH_SIZE, verbose=VERBOSE)
print("\nTest score:", score[0])
print('Test accuracy:', score[1])
```

Let's run the code. Our network reaches a test accuracy of 66.8% with 20 iterations. We also print the accuracy and loss plot and dump the network with `model.summary()`:

```
Epoch 17/20
40000/40000 [==============================] - 112s 3ms/sample - loss: 0.6282 - accuracy: 0.7841 - val_loss: 1.0296 -
  val_accuracy: 0.6734
Epoch 18/20
40000/40000 [==============================] - 76s 2ms/sample - loss: 0.6140 - accuracy: 0.7879 - val_loss: 1.0789 -
val_accuracy: 0.6489
Epoch 19/20
40000/40000 [==============================] - 74s 2ms/sample - loss: 0.5931 - accuracy: 0.7958 - val_loss: 1.0461 -
val_accuracy: 0.6811
Epoch 20/20
40000/40000 [==============================] - 71s 2ms/sample - loss: 0.5724 - accuracy: 0.8042 - val_loss: 1.0527 -
val_accuracy: 0.6773
10000/10000 [==============================] - 5s 472us/sample - loss: 1.0423 - accuracy: 0.6686

Test score: 1.0423416819572449
Test accuracy: 0.6686
```

Figure 13: Printing the accuracy and loss outputs

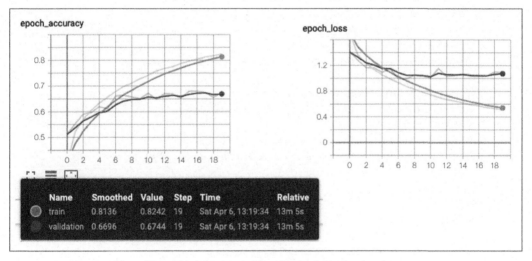

Figure 14: Accuracy and loss for the defined network

Improving the CIFAR-10 performance with a deeper network

One way to improve the performance is to define a deeper network with multiple convolutional operations. In the following example we have a sequence of modules:

1st module: (CONV+CONV+MaxPool+DropOut)

2nd: module: (CONV+CONV+MaxPool+DropOut)

3rd module: (CONV+CONV+MaxPool+DropOut)

These are followed by a standard dense output layer. All the activation functions used are ReLU functions. There is a new layer that we also discussed in *Chapter 1, Neural Network Foundations with TensorFlow 2.0* `BatchNormalization()` which is used to introduce a form of regularization between modules:

```python
def build_model():
    model = models.Sequential()

    # 1st block
    model.add(layers.Conv2D(32, (3,3), padding='same',
        input_shape=x_train.shape[1:], activation='relu'))
    model.add(layers.BatchNormalization())
    model.add(layers.Conv2D(32, (3,3), padding='same',
activation='relu'))
    model.add(layers.BatchNormalization())
    model.add(layers.MaxPooling2D(pool_size=(2,2)))
    model.add(layers.Dropout(0.2))

    # 2nd block
    model.add(layers.Conv2D(64, (3,3), padding='same',
activation='relu'))
    model.add(layers.BatchNormalization())
    model.add(layers.Conv2D(64, (3,3), padding='same',
activation='relu'))
    model.add(layers.BatchNormalization())
    model.add(layers.MaxPooling2D(pool_size=(2,2)))
    model.add(layers.Dropout(0.3))

    # 3d block
    model.add(layers.Conv2D(128, (3,3), padding='same',
activation='relu'))
    model.add(layers.BatchNormalization())
    model.add(layers.Conv2D(128, (3,3), padding='same',
activation='relu'))
    model.add(layers.BatchNormalization())
    model.add(layers.MaxPooling2D(pool_size=(2,2)))
    model.add(layers.Dropout(0.4))

    # dense
    model.add(layers.Flatten())
    model.add(layers.Dense(NUM_CLASSES, activation='softmax'))
    return model

model.summary()
```

Congratulations! You have defined a deeper network. Let us run the code for 40 iterations reaching an accuracy of 82%! Let's add the remaining part of the code for the sake of completeness. The first part is to load and normalize the data:

```python
import tensorflow as tf
from tensorflow.keras import datasets, layers, models, regularizers,
optimizers
from tensorflow.keras.preprocessing.image import ImageDataGenerator
import numpy as np

EPOCHS=50
NUM_CLASSES = 10

def load_data():
    (x_train, y_train), (x_test, y_test) = datasets.cifar10.load_data()
    x_train = x_train.astype('float32')
    x_test = x_test.astype('float32')

    # normalize
    mean = np.mean(x_train,axis=(0,1,2,3))
    std = np.std(x_train,axis=(0,1,2,3))
    x_train = (x_train-mean)/(std+1e-7)
    x_test = (x_test-mean)/(std+1e-7)

    y_train =  tf.keras.utils.to_categorical(y_train,NUM_CLASSES)
    y_test =  tf.keras.utils.to_categorical(y_test,NUM_CLASSES)

    return x_train, y_train, x_test, y_test
```

```python
Then we need to have a part to train the network:
(x_train, y_train, x_test, y_test) = load_data()
model = build_model()
model.compile(loss='categorical_crossentropy',
            optimizer='RMSprop',
            metrics=['accuracy'])

# train
batch_size = 64
model.fit(x_train, y_train, batch_size=batch_size,
        epochs=EPOCHS, validation_data=(x_test,y_test))
score = model.evaluate(x_test, y_test, batch_size=BATCH_SIZE)
print("\nTest score:", score[0])
print('Test accuracy:', score[1])
```

So, we have an improvement of 15.14% with respect to the previous simpler deeper network. For sake of completeness, let's also report the accuracy and loss during training.

Improving the CIFAR-10 performance with data augmentation

Another way to improve the performance is to generate more images for our training. The idea here is that we can take the standard CIFAR training set and augment this set with multiple types of transformation, including rotation, rescaling, horizontal or vertical flip, zooming, channel shift, and many more. Let's see the code applied on the same network defined in the previous section:

```
from tensorflow.keras.preprocessing.image import ImageDataGenerator


#image augmentation
datagen = ImageDataGenerator(
    rotation_range=30,
    width_shift_range=0.2,
    height_shift_range=0.2,
    horizontal_flip=True,
    )
datagen.fit(x_train)
```

rotation_range is a value in degrees (0-180) for randomly rotating pictures; width_shift and height_shift are ranges for randomly translating pictures vertically or horizontally; zoom_range is for randomly zooming pictures; horizontal_flip is for randomly flipping half of the images horizontally; and fill_mode is the strategy used for filling in new pixels that can appear after a rotation or a shift.

After augmentation we have generated many more training images starting from the standard CIFAR-10 set, as shown in *Figure 15*:

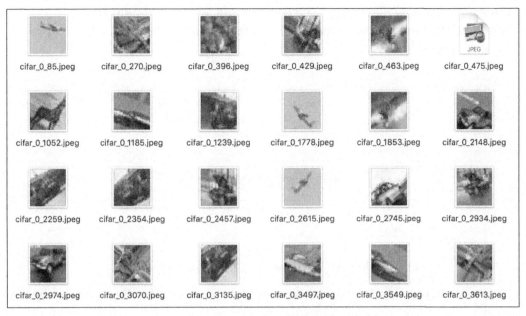

Figure 15: An example of image augmentation

Now we can apply this intuition directly for training. Using the same CNN defined before, we simply generate more augmented images and then we train. For efficiency, the generator runs in parallel to the model. This allows image augmentation on a CPU while training in parallel on a GPU. Here is the code:

```
# train
batch_size = 64
model.fit_generator(datagen.flow(x_train, y_train,
                                 batch_size=batch_size),
                epochs=EPOCHS,
                verbose=1,validation_data=(x_test,y_test))
# save to disk
model_json = model.to_json()
with open('model.json', 'w') as json_file:
    json_file.write(model_json)
model.save_weights('model.h5')

# test
scores = model.evaluate(x_test, y_test, batch_size=128, verbose=1)
print('\nTest result: %.3f loss: %.3f' % (scores[1]*100,scores[0]))
```

Each iteration is now more expensive because we have more training data. Therefore, let's run for 50 iterations only. We see that by doing this we reach an accuracy of 85.91%:

```
Epoch 46/50
50000/50000 [==============================] - 36s 722us/sample - loss: 0.2440 - acc: 0.9183 - val_loss: 0.4918 - val_acc: 0.8546
Epoch 47/50
50000/50000 [==============================] - 34s 685us/sample - loss: 0.2338 - acc: 0.9208 - val_loss: 0.4884 - val_acc: 0.8574
Epoch 48/50
50000/50000 [==============================] - 32s 643us/sample - loss: 0.2383 - acc: 0.9189 - val_loss: 0.5106 - val_acc: 0.8556
Epoch 49/50
50000/50000 [==============================] - 37s 734us/sample - loss: 0.2285 - acc: 0.9212 - val_loss: 0.5017 - val_acc: 0.8581
Epoch 50/50
50000/50000 [==============================] - 36s 712us/sample - loss: 0.2263 - acc: 0.9228 - val_loss: 0.4911 - val_acc: 0.8591
```

Figure 16: Results after 50 iterations

```
10000/10000 [==============================] - 2s 160us/sample - loss: 0.4911 - acc: 0.8591

Test score: 0.4911323667049408
Test accuracy: 0.8591
```

Figure 17: Final accuracy of 85.91% displayed

The results obtained during our experiments are summarized in the following figure:

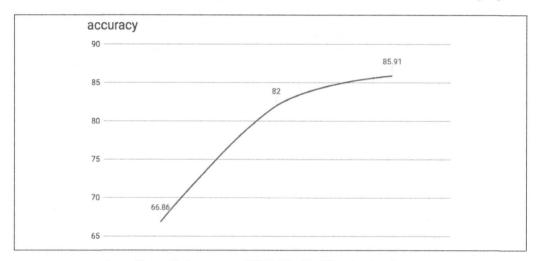

Figure 18: Accuracy on CIFAR-10 with different networks

A list of state-of-the-art results for CIFAR-10 is available online (http://rodrigob. github.io/are_we_there_yet/build/classification_datasets_results. html). As of April 2019, the best result has an accuracy of 96.53% [3].

Predicting with CIFAR-10

Let's suppose that we want to use the deep learning model we just trained for CIFAR-10 for a bulk evaluation of images.

Since we saved the model and the weights, we do not need to train each time:

```
import numpy as np
from skimage.transform import resize
from imageio import imread
from tensorflow.keras.models import model_from_json
from tensorflow.keras.optimizers import SGD

# load model
model_architecture = 'cifar10_architecture.json'
model_weights = 'cifar10_weights.h5'
model = model_from_json(open(model_architecture).read())
model.load_weights(model_weights)

# load images
img_names = ['cat-standing.jpg', 'dog.jpg']
imgs = [resize(imread(img_name), (32, 32)).astype("float32") for img_
name in img_names]
imgs = np.array(imgs) / 255
print("imgs.shape:", imgs.shape)

# train
optim = SGD()
model.compile(loss='categorical_crossentropy', optimizer=optim,
              metrics=['accuracy'])
# predict
predictions = model.predict_classes(imgs)
print("predictions:", predictions)
```

Now let us get the prediction for a cat and for a dog:

We get categories 3 (cat) and 5 (dog) as output as expected. We successfully created a CNN to classify CIFAR-10 images. Next, we will look at VGG-16: a breakthrough in deep learning.

Very deep convolutional networks for large-scale image recognition

During 2014, an interesting contribution to image recognition was presented with the paper, *Very Deep Convolutional Networks for Large-Scale Image Recognition*, K. Simonyan and A. Zisserman [4]. The paper showed that a "significant improvement on the prior-art configurations can be achieved by pushing the depth to 16-19 weight layers." One model in the paper denoted as D or VGG-16 had 16 deep layers.

An implementation in Java Caffe (`http://caffe.berkeleyvision.org/`) was used for training the model on the ImageNet ILSVRC-2012 (`http://image-net.org/challenges/LSVRC/2012/`) dataset, which includes images of 1,000 classes, and is split into three sets: training (1.3 million images), validation (50,000 images), and testing (100,000 images). Each image is (224×224) on 3 channels. The model achieves 7.5% top-5 error on ILSVRC-2012-val, 7.4% top-5 error on ILSVRC-2012-test.

According to the ImageNet site, "The goal of this competition is to estimate the content of photographs for the purpose of retrieval and automatic annotation using a subset of the large hand-labeled ImageNet dataset (10,000,000 labeled images depicting 10,000+ object categories) as training. Test images will be presented with no initial annotation – no segmentation or labels – and algorithms will have to produce labelings specifying what objects are present in the images."

The weights learned by the model implemented in Caffe have been directly converted (`https://gist.github.com/baraldilorenzo/07d7802847aaad0a35d3`) in `tf.Keras` and can be used by preloading them into the `tf.Keras` model, which is implemented as follows, as described in the paper:

```
import tensorflow as tf
from tensorflow.keras import layers, models

# define a VGG16 network

def VGG_16(weights_path=None):
    model = models.Sequential()
    model.add(layers.ZeroPadding2D((1,1),input_shape=(224,224, 3)))
    model.add(layers.Convolution2D(64, (3, 3), activation='relu'))
    model.add(layers.ZeroPadding2D((1,1)))
    model.add(layers.Convolution2D(64, (3, 3), activation='relu'))
    model.add(layers.MaxPooling2D((2,2), strides=(2,2)))

    model.add(layers.ZeroPadding2D((1,1)))
    model.add(layers.Convolution2D(128, (3, 3), activation='relu'))
    model.add(layers.ZeroPadding2D((1,1)))
```

```python
model.add(layers.Convolution2D(128, (3, 3), activation='relu'))
model.add(layers.MaxPooling2D((2,2), strides=(2,2)))

model.add(layers.ZeroPadding2D((1,1)))
model.add(layers.Convolution2D(256, (3, 3), activation='relu'))
model.add(layers.ZeroPadding2D((1,1)))
model.add(layers.Convolution2D(256, (3, 3), activation='relu'))
model.add(layers.ZeroPadding2D((1,1)))
model.add(layers.Convolution2D(256, (3, 3), activation='relu'))
model.add(layers.MaxPooling2D((2,2), strides=(2,2)))

model.add(layers.ZeroPadding2D((1,1)))
model.add(layers.Convolution2D(512, (3, 3), activation='relu'))
model.add(layers.ZeroPadding2D((1,1)))
model.add(layers.Convolution2D(512, (3, 3), activation='relu'))
model.add(layers.ZeroPadding2D((1,1)))
model.add(layers.Convolution2D(512, (3, 3), activation='relu'))
model.add(layers.MaxPooling2D((2,2), strides=(2,2)))

model.add(layers.ZeroPadding2D((1,1)))
model.add(layers.Convolution2D(512, (3, 3), activation='relu'))
model.add(layers.ZeroPadding2D((1,1)))
model.add(layers.Convolution2D(512, (3, 3), activation='relu'))
model.add(layers.ZeroPadding2D((1,1)))
model.add(layers.Convolution2D(512, (3, 3), activation='relu'))
model.add(layers.MaxPooling2D((2,2), strides=(2,2)))

model.add(layers.Flatten())

#top layer of the VGG net
model.add(layers.Dense(4096, activation='relu'))
model.add(layers.Dropout(0.5))
model.add(layers.Dense(4096, activation='relu'))
model.add(layers.Dropout(0.5))
model.add(layers.Dense(1000, activation='softmax'))

if weights_path:
    model.load_weights(weights_path)

return model
```

We have implemented a VGG16. Next, we are going to utilize it.

Recognizing cats with a VGG16 Net

Now let us test the image of a cat:

Note that we are going to use predefined weights:

```
import cv2
im = cv2.resize(cv2.imread('cat.jpg'), (224, 224).astype(np.float32))
#im = im.transpose((2,0,1))
im = np.expand_dims(im, axis=0)

# Test pretrained model
path_file = os.path.join(os.path.expanduser("~"), '.keras/models/
vgg16_weights_tf_dim_ordering_tf_kernels.h5')
model = VGG_16(path_file)
model.summary()
model.compile(optimizer='sgd', loss='categorical_crossentropy')
out = model.predict(im)
print(np.argmax(out))
```

When the code is executed, the class 285 is returned, which corresponds (https://
gist.github.com/yrevar/942d3a0ac09ec9e5eb3a) to "Egyptian cat":

```
Total params: 138,357,544
Trainable params: 138,357,544
Non-trainable params: 0
--------------------------------------------------------------
285
```

Figure 19: Image recognition results using a VGG16 Net

Impressive isn't it? Our VGG-16 network can successfully recognize images of cats!
A first important step for deep learning. It is only five years since the paper in [4],
but that was a game-changing moment.

Utilizing tf.keras built-in VGG16 Net module

tf.Keras applications are prebuilt and pretrained deep learning models. Weights are downloaded automatically when instantiating a model and stored at ~/.keras/models/. Using built-in code is very easy:

```
import tensorflow as tf
from tensorflow.keras.applications.vgg16 import VGG16
import matplotlib.pyplot as plt
import numpy as np
import cv2

# prebuild model with pre-trained weights on imagenet
model = VGG16(weights='imagenet', include_top=True)
model.compile(optimizer='sgd', loss='categorical_crossentropy')

# resize into VGG16 trained images' format
im = cv2.resize(cv2.imread('steam-locomotive.jpg'), (224, 224))
im = np.expand_dims(im, axis=0)
im.astype(np.float32)

# predict
out = model.predict(im)
index = np.argmax(out)
print(index)

plt.plot(out.ravel())
plt.show()
# this should print 820 for steaming train
```

Now, let us consider a train:

If we run the code we get **820** as a result, which is the image net code for "steaming train". Equally important, all the other classes have very weak support, as shown in the following figure:

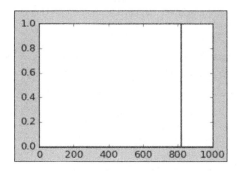

To conclude this section, note that VGG16 is only one of the modules that is prebuilt in `tf.Keras`. A full list of pretrained models is available online (`https://www.tensorflow.org/api_docs/python/tf/keras/applications`).

Recycling prebuilt deep learning models for extracting features

One very simple idea is to use VGG16, and more generally DCNN, for feature extraction. This code implements the idea by extracting features from a specific layer. Note that we need to switch to the functional API since the sequential model only accepts layers:

```
import tensorflow as tf
from tensorflow.keras.applications.vgg16 import VGG16
from tensorflow.keras import models
from tensorflow.keras.preprocessing import image
from tensorflow.keras.applications.vgg16 import preprocess_input
import numpy as np
import cv2

# prebuild model with pre-trained weights on imagenet
base_model = VGG16(weights='imagenet', include_top=True)
print (base_model)
for i, layer in enumerate(base_model.layers):
    print (i, layer.name, layer.output_shape)

# extract features from block4_pool block
model = models.Model(inputs=base_model.input,
    outputs=base_model.get_layer('block4_pool').output)
```

```
img_path = 'cat.jpg'
img = image.load_img(img_path, target_size=(224, 224))
x = image.img_to_array(img)
x = np.expand_dims(x, axis=0)
x = preprocess_input(x)

# get the features from this block
features = model.predict(x)
print(features)
```

You might wonder why we want to extract the features from an intermediate layer in a DCNN. The reasoning is that as the network learns to classify images into categories, each layer learns to identify the features that are necessary to perform the final classification. Lower layers identify lower-order features such as color and edges, and higher layers compose these lower-order features into higher-order features such as shapes or objects. Hence, the intermediate layer has the capability to extract important features from an image, and these features are more likely to help in different kinds of classification.

This has multiple advantages. First, we can rely on publicly available large-scale training and transfer this learning to novel domains. Second, we can save time for expensive large training. Third, we can provide reasonable solutions even when we don't have a large number of training examples for our domain. We also get a good starting network shape for the task at hand, instead of guessing it.

With this, we will conclude the overview of VGG-16 CNNs, the last deep learning model defined in this chapter. You will see more examples of CNNs in the next chapter.

Summary

In this chapter we have learned how to use deep learning convnets for recognizing MNIST handwritten characters with high accuracy. We used the CIFAR-10 dataset for building a deep learning classifier with 10 categories, and the ImageNet dataset to build an accurate classifier with 1,000 categories. In addition, we investigated how to use large deep learning networks such as VGG16 and very deep networks such as InceptionV3. We concluded with a discussion on transfer learning; in the next chapter we'll see how to adapt prebuilt models trained on large datasets so that they can work well on a new domain.

References

1. Y. LeCun and Y. Bengio, *Convolutional Networks for Images, Speech, and Time-Series*, Handb. brain Theory Neural networks, vol. 3361, 1995.

2. L. Wan, M. Zeiler, S. Zhang, Y. L. Cun, and R. Fergus, *Regularization of Neural Networks using DropConnect*, Proc. 30th Int. Conf. Mach. Learn., pp. 1058–1066, 2013.

3. B. Graham, *Fractional Max-Pooling*, arXiv Prepr. arXiv: 1412.6071, 2014.

4. K. Simonyan and A. Zisserman, *Very Deep Convolutional Networks for Large-Scale Image Recognition*, arXiv ePrints, Sep. 2014.

5
Advanced Convolutional Neural Networks

In this chapter we will see some more advanced uses for **convolutional neural networks (CNNs)**. We will explore how CNNs can be applied within the areas of computer vision, video, textual documents, audio, and music. We'll conclude with a section summarizing convolution operations. We'll begin our look into CNNs with image processing.

Computer vision

In this section we'll look at the ways in which CNN architecture can be utilized when applied to the area of imagine processing, and the interesting results that can be generated.

Composing CNNs for complex tasks

We have discussed CNNs quite extensively in the previous chapter, and at this point you are probably convinced about the effectiveness of the CNN architecture for image classification tasks. What you may find surprising, however, is that the basic CNN architecture can be composed and extended in various ways to solve a variety of more complex tasks.

In this section, we will look at the computer vision tasks in the following diagram and show how they can be solved by composing CNNs into larger and more complex architectures:

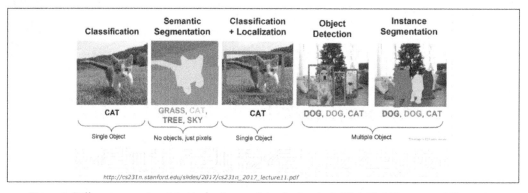

Figure 1: Different computer vision tasks. Source: Introduction to Artificial Intelligence and Computer Vision Revolution (https://www.slideshare.net/darian_f/introduction-to-the-artificial-intelligence-and-computer-vision-revolution).

Classification and localization

In the classification and localization task not only do you have to report the class of object found in the image, but also the coordinates of the bounding box where the object appears in the image. This type of task assumes that there is only one instance of the object in an image.

This can be achieved by attaching a "regression head" in addition to the "classification head" in a typical classification network. Recall that in a classification network, the final output of convolution and pooling operations, called the feature map, is fed into a fully connected network that produces a vector of class probabilities. This fully connected network is called the classification head, and it is tuned using a categorical loss function (L_c) such as categorical cross entropy.

Similarly, a regression head is another fully connected network that takes the feature map and produces a vector (x, y, w, h) representing the top-left x and y coordinates, width and height of the bounding box. It is tuned using a continuous loss function (L_r) such as mean squared error. The entire network is tuned using a linear combination of the two losses, that is:

$$L = \alpha L_c + (1 - \alpha)L_r$$

Here α is a hyperparameter and can take a value between 0 and 1. Unless the value is determined by some domain knowledge about the problem, it can be set to 0.5.

The following figure shows a typical classification and localization network architecture. As you can see, the only difference with respect to a typical CNN classification network is the additional regression head on the top right:

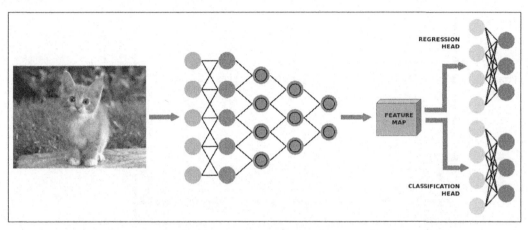

Figure 2: Network architecture for image classification and localization

Semantic segmentation

Another class of problem that builds on the basic classification idea is "semantic segmentation." Here the aim is to classify every single pixel on the image as belonging to a single class.

An initial method of implementation could be to build a classifier network for each pixel, where the input is a small neighborhood around each pixel. In practice, this approach is not very performant, so an improvement over this implementation might be to run the image through convolutions that will increase the feature depth, while keeping the image width and height constant. Each pixel then has a feature map that can be sent through a fully connected network that predicts the class of the pixel. However, in practice, this is also quite expensive, and it is not normally used.

A third approach is to use a CNN encoder-decoder network, where the encoder decreases the width and height of the image but increases its depth (number of features), while the decoder uses transposed convolution operations to increase its size and decrease depth. Transpose convolution (or upsampling) is the process of going in the opposite direction of a normal convolution. The input to this network is the image and the output is the segmentation map.

A popular implementation of this encoder-decoder architecture is the U-Net (a good implementation is available at: `https://github.com/jakeret/tf_unet`), originally developed for biomedical image segmentation, which has additional skip-connections between corresponding layers of the encoder and decoder. The U-Net architecture is shown in the following figure:

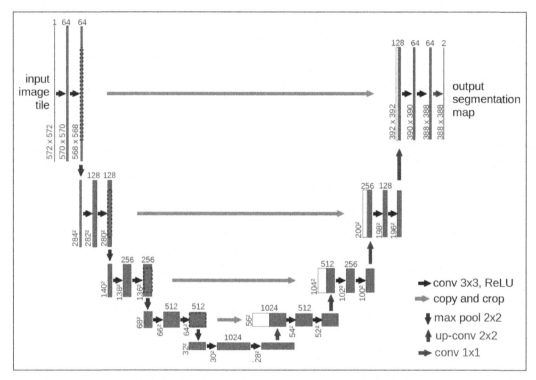

Figure 3: U-Net architecture. Source: Pattern Recognition and Image Processing (https://lmb.informatik.uni-freiburg.de/people/ronneber/u-net/).

Object detection

The object detection task is similar to the classification and localization tasks. The big difference is that now there are multiple objects in the image, and for each one we need to find the class and bounding box coordinates. In addition, neither the number of objects nor their size is known in advance. As you can imagine, this is a difficult problem and a fair amount of research has gone into it.

A first approach to the problem might be to create many random crops of the input image and for each crop, apply the classification and localization networks we described earlier. However, such an approach is very wasteful in terms of computing and unlikely to be very successful.

A more practical approach would be use a tool such as Selective Search (*Selective Search for Object Recognition*, by Uijlings et al, `http://www.huppelen.nl/publications/selectiveSearchDraft.pdf`), which uses traditional computer vision techniques to find areas in the image that might contain objects. These regions are called "Region Proposals," and the network to detect them was called "Region Proposal Network," or R-CNN. In the original R-CNN, the regions were resized and fed into a network to yield image vectors:

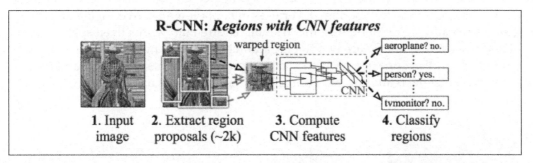

Figure 4: Region extraction and warped region as described in "Rich feature hierarchies for accurate object detection and semantic segmentation", Ross Girshick, Jeff Donahue, Trevor Darrell, Jitendra Malik, UC Berkeley.

These vectors were then classified with an SVM-based classifier (`https://en.wikipedia.org/wiki/Support-vector_machine`), and the bounding boxes proposed by the external tool were corrected using a linear regression network over the image vectors. A R-CNN network can be represented conceptually as shown in *Figure 5*:

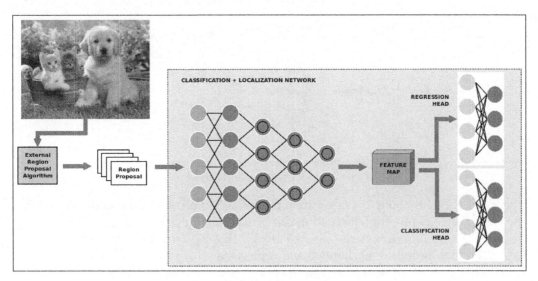

Figure 5: R-CNN network

The next iteration of the R-CNN network was called the Fast R-CNN. The Fast R-CNN still gets its region proposals from an external tool, but instead of feeding each region proposal through the CNN, the entire image is fed through the CNN and the region proposals are projected onto the resulting feature map. Each region of interest is fed through an **Region of Interest (ROI)** pooling layer and then to a fully connected network, which produces a feature vector for the ROI.

ROI pooling is a widely used operation in object detection tasks using convolutional neural networks. The ROI pooling layer uses max pooling to convert the features inside any valid region of interest into a small feature map with a fixed spatial extent of $H \times W$ (where H and W are two hyperparameters). The feature vector is then fed into two fully connected networks, one to predict the class of the ROI and the other to correct the bounding box coordinates for the proposal. This is illustrated in *Figure 6*:

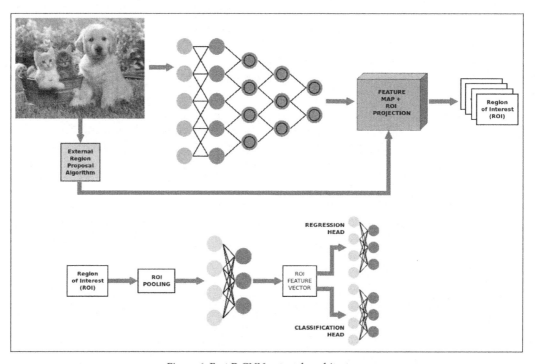

Figure 6: Fast R-CNN network architecture

The Fast R-CNN is about 25x faster than the R-CNN. The next improvement, called the Faster R-CNN (an implementation can be found at `https://github.com/tensorpack/tensorpack/tree/master/examples/FasterRCNN`), removes the external region proposal mechanism and replaces it with a trainable component, called the **Region Proposal Network (RPN)**, within the network itself.

The output of this network is combined with the feature map and passed in through a similar pipeline to the Fast R-CNN network, as shown in *Figure 7*. The Faster R-CNN network is about 10x faster than the Fast R-CNN network, making it approximately 250x faster than an R-CNN network:

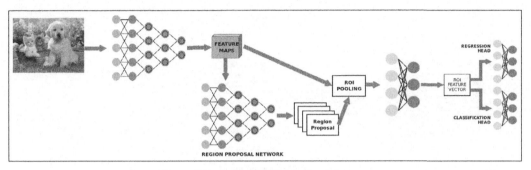

Figure 7: Faster R-CNN network architecture

Another somewhat different class of object detection networks are **Single Shot Detectors (SSD)** such as **You Only Look Once (YOLO)**. In these cases, each image is split into a predefined number of parts using a grid. In the case of YOLO, a 7×7 grid is used, resulting in 49 subimages. A predetermined set of crops with different aspect ratios are applied to each sub-image. Given *B* bounding boxes and *C* object classes, the output for each image is a vector of size *(7 * 7 * (5B + C))*. Each bounding box has a confidence and coordinates *(x, y, w, h)*, and each grid has prediction probabilities for the different objects detected within them.

The YOLO network is a CNN that does this transformation. The final predictions and bounding boxes are found by aggregating the findings from this vector. In YOLO a single convolutional network predicts the bounding boxes and the related class probabilities. YOLO is the faster solution for object detection, but the algorithm might fail to detect smaller objects (an implementation can be found at `https://www.kaggle.com/aruchomu/yolo-v3-object-detection-in-tensorflow`).

Instance segmentation

Instance segmentation is similar to semantic segmentation – the process of associating each pixel of an image with a class label – with a few important distinctions. First, it needs to distinguish between different instances of the same class in an image. Second, it is not required to label every single pixel in the image. In some respects, instance segmentation is also similar to object detection, except that instead of bounding boxes, we want to find a binary mask that covers each object.

The second definition leads to the intuition behind the Mask R-CNN network. The Mask R-CNN is a Faster R-CNN with an additional CNN in front of its regression head, which takes as input the bounding box coordinates reported for each ROI and converts it to a binary mask [11]:

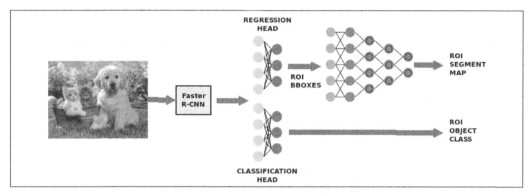

Figure 8: Mask R-CNN architecture

In April 2019, Google released Mask R-CNN in open source, pretrained with TPUs (`https://colab.research.google.com/github/tensorflow/tpu/blob/master/models/official/mask_rcnn/mask_rcnn_demo.ipynb`). I suggest playing with the Colab notebook to see what the results are. In *Figure 9* we see an example of image segmentation:

Figure 9: An example of image segmentation

Google also released another model trained on TPUs called DeepLab and you can see an image (*Figure 10*) from the demo (`https://colab.research.google.com/github/tensorflow/models/blob/master/research/deeplab/deeplab_demo.ipynb#scrollTo=edGukUHXyymr`):

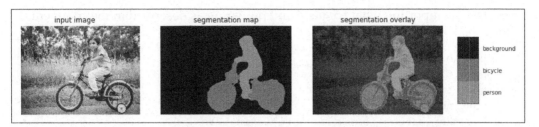

Figure 10: An example of image segmentation

In this section we have covered, at a somewhat high level, various network architectures that are popular in computer vision. Note that all of them are composed of the same basic CNNs and fully connected architectures. This composability is one of the most powerful features of deep learning. Hopefully, this has given you some ideas for networks that could be adapted for your own computer vision use cases.

Classifying Fashion-MNIST with a tf.keras - estimator model

Estimators are another set of APIs available in TensorFlow. In this section we are going to see how to create them. In many situations, Estimators are preferable for performance and ease of conversion to distributed training. In our example, we are going to use Fashion-MNIST, a drop-in replacement for the MNIST dataset released by Zalando (more information is available at `https://github.com/zalandoresearch/fashion-mnist`). Each example is a 28×28 grayscale image, associated with a label from 10 classes. An example is provided in *Figure 11*:

Figure 11: Fashion-MNIST examples

Let's start by importing what we need and preparing as described in the comments below:

```
import os
import time
import tensorflow as tf
import numpy as np
# How many categories we are predicting from (0-9)
LABEL_DIMENSIONS = 10

(train_images, train_labels), (test_images, test_labels) =
    tf.keras.datasets.fashion_mnist.load_data()
TRAINING_SIZE = len(train_images)
TEST_SIZE = len(test_images)

train_images = np.asarray(train_images, dtype=np.float32) / 255

# Convert the train images and add channels
train_images = train_images.reshape((TRAINING_SIZE, 28, 28, 1))
test_images = np.asarray(test_images, dtype=np.float32) / 255

# Convert the train images and add channels
test_images = test_images.reshape((TEST_SIZE, 28, 28, 1))
train_labels  = tf.keras.utils.to_categorical(train_labels, LABEL_
DIMENSIONS)
test_labels = tf.keras.utils.to_categorical(test_labels, LABEL_
DIMENSIONS)

# Cast the labels to float
train_labels = train_labels.astype(np.float32)
test_labels = test_labels.astype(np.float32)
print (train_labels.shape)
print (test_labels.shape)
```

Now let's build a convolutional model with the tf.Keras functional API:

```
inputs = tf.keras.Input(shape=(28,28,1))
x = tf.keras.layers.Conv2D(filters=32, kernel_size=(3, 3),
activation='relu')(inputs)
x = tf.keras.layers.MaxPooling2D(pool_size=(2, 2), strides=2)(x)
x = tf.keras.layers.Conv2D(filters=64, kernel_size=(3, 3),
activation='relu')(x)
x = tf.keras.layers.MaxPooling2D(pool_size=(2, 2), strides=2)(x)
x = tf.keras.layers.Conv2D(filters=64, kernel_size=(3, 3),
activation='relu')(x)
x = tf.keras.layers.Flatten()(x)
x = tf.keras.layers.Dense(64, activation='relu')(x)
```

```
predictions = tf.keras.layers.Dense(LABEL_DIMENSIONS,
activation='softmax')(x)
model = tf.keras.Model(inputs=inputs, outputs=predictions)
model.summary()
```

Compile it:

```
optimizer = tf.keras.optimizers.SGD()
model.compile(loss='categorical_crossentropy',
              optimizer=optimizer,
              metrics=['accuracy'])
```

Define a strategy, which is None for now because we run on CPUs first:

```
strategy = None
#strategy = tf.distribute.MirroredStrategy()
config = tf.estimator.RunConfig(train_distribute=strategy)
```

Now let's convert the tf.keras model into a convenient Estimator:

```
estimator = tf.keras.estimator.model_to_estimator(model,
config=config)
```

The next step is to define input functions for training and for testing, which is pretty easy if we use tf.data:

```
def input_fn(images, labels, epochs, batch_size):
    # Convert the inputs to a Dataset
    dataset = tf.data.Dataset.from_tensor_slices((images, labels))

    # Shuffle, repeat, and batch the examples.
    SHUFFLE_SIZE = 5000
    dataset = dataset.shuffle(SHUFFLE_SIZE).repeat(epochs).
batch(batch_size)
    dataset = dataset.prefetch(None)

    # Return the dataset.
    return dataset
```

We are ready to start the training with the following code:

```
BATCH_SIZE = 512
EPOCHS = 50
estimator_train_result = estimator.train(input_fn=lambda:input_
fn(train_images, train_labels,
                 epochs=EPOCHS,
                 batch_size=BATCH_SIZE))
print(estimator_train_result)
```

And evaluate with the following code:

```
estimator.evaluate(lambda:input_fn(test_images,
                                   test_labels,
                                   epochs=1,
                                   batch_size=BATCH_SIZE))
```

If we run the code in Colab (Colab code can be found at `https://colab.research.google.com/drive/1mf-PK0a20CkObnT0hCl9VPEjelszhHat`) we get the following results:

```
estimator.evaluate(lambda:input_fn(test_images,
                                   test_labels,
                                   epochs=1,
                                   batch_size=BATCH_SIZE))

{'accuracy': 0.7162, 'global_step': 5860, 'loss': 0.77385104}
```

Figure 12: Results from Colab

Run Fashion-MNIST the tf.keras - estimator model on GPUs

In this section we aim at running the estimator on GPUs. All we need to do is to change the strategy into a `MirroredStrategy()`. This strategy uses one replica per device and sync replication for its multi-GPU version:

```
[8] #strategy = None
    strategy = tf.distribute.MirroredStrategy()
    config = tf.estimator.RunConfig(train_distribute=strategy)
```

Figure 13: Implementing the MirroredStrategy strategy

At this point we can start training:

```
BATCH_SIZE = 512
EPOCHS = 50

#time_hist = TimeHistory()

estimator_train_result = estimator.train(input_fn=lambda:input_fn(train_images,
                                         train_labels,
                                         epochs=EPOCHS,
                                         batch_size=BATCH_SIZE))
print(estimator_train_result)
```

Figure 14: Training with MirroredStrategy

And we can evaluate the trained model:

```
[12] estimator.evaluate(lambda:input_fn(test_images,
                                        test_labels,
                                        epochs=1,
                                        batch_size=BATCH_SIZE))

    {'acc': 0.8215, 'global_step': 5860, 'loss': 0.48483768}
```

Figure 15: An evaluation of the trained model

We have successfully created an estimator. In the next section, we will discuss a new deep learning technique called transfer learning.

Deep Inception-v3 Net used for transfer learning

Transfer learning is a very powerful deep learning technique that has applications in a number of different domains. The idea behind transfer learning is very simple and can be explained with an analogy. Suppose you want to learn a new language, say Spanish, then it could be useful to start from what you already know in a different language, say English.

Following this line of thinking, computer vision researchers now commonly use pretrained CNNs to generate representations for novel tasks [1], where the dataset may not be large enough to train an entire CNN from scratch. Another common tactic is to take the pretrained ImageNet network and then to fine-tune the entire network to the novel task. For instance, we can take a network trained to recognize 10 categories in music and fine-tune it to recognize 20 categories in movies.

Inception-v3 Net is a very deep CNN developed by Google [2]. `tf.keras` implements the full network described in *Figure 16* and it comes pretrained on ImageNet. The default input size for this model is 299×299 on three channels:

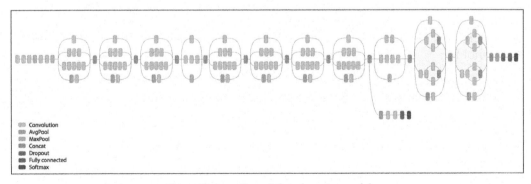

Figure 16: Inception-v3 deep learning model

This skeleton example is inspired by a scheme available online (`https://keras.io/applications/`). Let's suppose we have a training dataset D in a different domain from ImageNet. D has 1024 features in input and 200 categories in output. Let's look at a code fragment:

```
import tensorflow as tf
from tensorflow.keras.applications.inception_v3 import InceptionV3
from tensorflow.keras.preprocessing import image
from tensorflow.keras import layers, models
# create the base pre-trained model
base_model = InceptionV3(weights='imagenet', include_top=False)
```

We use a trained Inception-v3: we do not include the fully connected layer – dense layer with 1024 inputs – because we want to fine-tune on D. The preceding code fragment will download the pretrained weights on our behalf:

```
Downloading data from https://github.com/fchollet/deep-learning-models/releases/download/v0.5/inception_
v3_weights_tf_dim_ordering_tf_kernels_notop.h5
87916544/87910968 [==============================] - 26s 0us/step
```

Figure 17: Pretrained weights being downloaded from GitHub

So if you look at the last four layers (where `include_top=True`), you see these shapes:

```
# layer.name, layer.input_shape, layer.output_shape
('mixed10', [(None, 8, 8, 320), (None, 8, 8, 768), (None, 8, 8, 768),
(None, 8, 8, 192)], (None, 8, 8, 2048))
('avg_pool', (None, 8, 8, 2048), (None, 1, 1, 2048))
('flatten', (None, 1, 1, 2048), (None, 2048))
('predictions', (None, 2048), (None, 1000))
```

When you `include_top=False`, you are removing the last three layers and exposing the `mixed_10` layer. The `GlobalAveragePooling2D` layer converts the `(None, 8, 8, 2048)` to `(None, 2048)`, where each element in the `(None, 2048)` tensor is the average value for each corresponding `(8,8)` subtensor in the `(None, 8, 8, 2048)` tensor. `None` means an unspecified dimension, which is useful if you define a placeholder:

```
x = base_model.output
# let's add a fully connected layer as first layer
x = layers.Dense(1024, activation='relu')(x)
# and a logistic layer with 200 classes as last layer
predictions = layers.Dense(200, activation='softmax')(x)
# model to train
model = models.Model(inputs=base_model.input, outputs=predictions)
```

All the convolutional levels are pretrained, so we freeze them during the training of the full model:

```
# i.e. freeze all convolutional InceptionV3 layers
for layer in base_model.layers:
    layer.trainable = False
```

The model is then compiled and trained for a few epochs so that the top layers are trained. For the sake of simplicity here we are omitting the training code itself:

```
# compile the model (should be done *after* setting layers to non-
trainable)
model.compile(optimizer='rmsprop', loss='categorical_crossentropy')

# train the model on the new data for a few epochs
model.fit_generator(...)
```

Then we freeze the top layers in inception and fine-tune some inception layers. In this example we decide to freeze the first 172 layers (this is a tunable hyperparameter):

```
# we chose to train the top 2 inception blocks, i.e. we will freeze
# the first 172 layers and unfreeze the rest:
for layer in model.layers[:172]:
    layer.trainable = False
for layer in model.layers[172:]:
    layer.trainable = True
```

The model is then recompiled for fine-tuning optimization:

```
we need to recompile the model for these modifications to take effect
# we use SGD with a low learning rate
from keras.optimizers import SGD
model.compile(optimizer=SGD(lr=0.0001, momentum=0.9),
loss='categorical_crossentropy')

# we train our model again (this time fine-tuning the top 2 inception
# blocks

# alongside the top Dense layers
model.fit_generator(...)
```

Now we have a new deep network that re-uses a standard Inception-v3 network, but it is trained on a new domain D via transfer learning. Of course, there are many fine-tuning parameters for achieving good accuracy. However, we are now re-using a very large pretrained network as a starting point via transfer learning. In doing so, we can save the need of training on our machines by reusing what is already available in `tf.keras`.

Transfer learning for classifying horses and humans

Let's see a concrete example of transfer learning. This code is adapted starting from an example of François Chollet (see `https://www.tensorflow.org/alpha/tutorials/images/transfer_learning`); we'll repurpose it to classify horses and humans. We are going to use a dataset consisting of 500 rendered images of various species of horse and 527 rendered images of humans, both in various poses and locations, which are loaded with `tf.data`. The base model is MobileNetV2 [3], a pretrained net created by Google with the goal of being smaller and more lightweight than Inception models so that this net is suitable for running on mobile devices. MobilNet2 has been pretrained on the ImageNet dataset, a large dataset of 1.4 million images and 1000 classes of web images. Let's start (the notebook can be found at `https://colab.research.google.com/drive/1g8CKbjBFwlYz9W6vrvC5K2DpC8W2z_Il`) loading the data and split 80% for training, 10% for validation, and 10% for test:

```
import os
import time
import tensorflow as tf
import numpy as np
import tensorflow_datasets as tfds
import matplotlib.pyplot as plt

SPLIT_WEIGHTS = (8, 1, 1)
splits = tfds.Split.TRAIN.subsplit(weighted=SPLIT_WEIGHTS)
(raw_train, raw_validation, raw_test), metadata = tfds.load(
    'horses_or_humans', split=list(splits),
    with_info=True, as_supervised=True)
```

Let's inspect some images with an appropriate function:

```
get_label_name = metadata.features['label'].int2str

def show_images(dataset):
  for image, label in dataset.take(10):
    plt.figure()
    plt.imshow(image)
    plt.title(get_label_name(label))

show_images(raw_train)
```

Then we resize the images to (160×160) with color values in the range [-1,1] which is what MobileNetV2 expects as input:

```
IMG_SIZE = 160 # All images will be resized to 160x160

def format_example(image, label):
  image = tf.cast(image, tf.float32)
  image = (image/127.5) - 1
  image = tf.image.resize(image, (IMG_SIZE, IMG_SIZE))
  return image, label

train = raw_train.map(format_example)
validation = raw_validation.map(format_example)
test = raw_test.map(format_example)
```

Then, we shuffle and batch the training set, and batch the validation set and test set:

```
BATCH_SIZE = 32
SHUFFLE_BUFFER_SIZE = 2000
train_batches = train.shuffle(SHUFFLE_BUFFER_SIZE).batch(BATCH_SIZE)
validation_batches = validation.batch(BATCH_SIZE)
test_batches = test.batch(BATCH_SIZE)
```

Now, we can use MobileNet with input (160, 160, 3) where 3 is the number of color channels. The top layers are omitted (include_top=False) since we are going to use our own top layer, and all the internal layers are frozen because we use the weights pretrained on ImageNet:

```
IMG_SHAPE = (IMG_SIZE, IMG_SIZE, 3)
base_model = tf.keras.applications.MobileNetV2(input_shape=IMG_SHAPE,
                              include_top=False,
                              weights='imagenet')
base_model.trainable = False
base_model.summary()
```

Let's inspect a batch and see if the shape is correct:

```
for image_batch, label_batch in train_batches.take(1):
  pass
print (image_batch.shape)
```

(32, 160, 160, 3)

(32, 160, 160, 3) is the correct shape!

MobileNetV2 transforms each 160×160×3 image into a 5×5×1280 block of features. For instance, let's see the transformation applied to the batch:

```
feature_batch = base_model(image_batch)
print(feature_batch.shape)
```

(32, 5, 5, 1280)

Now, we can use `GlobalAveragePooling2D()` to average over the spatial 5×5 spatial locations and obtain a size of (32, 1280):

```
global_average_layer = tf.keras.layers.GlobalAveragePooling2D()
feature_batch_average = global_average_layer(feature_batch)
print(feature_batch_average.shape)
```

The last layer is dense with linear activation: if the prediction is positive, the class is 1; if the prediction is negative, the class is 0:

```
prediction_layer = tf.keras.layers.Dense(1)
prediction_batch = prediction_layer(feature_batch_average)
print(prediction_batch.shape)
```

Our model is ready to be composed by combining the `base_model` (pretrained MobileNetv2) with `global_average_layer` to get the correct shape output given as an input to the final `prediction_layer`:

```
model = tf.keras.Sequential([
  base_model,
  global_average_layer,
  prediction_layer
])
```

Now let's compile the model with an `RMSProp()` optimizer:

```
base_learning_rate = 0.0001
model.compile(optimizer=tf.keras.optimizers.RMSprop(lr=base_learning_
rate), loss='binary_crossentropy',
        metrics=['accuracy'])
```

If we display the composed model, we notice that there are more than 2 million frozen parameters, and only about 1,000 trainable parameters:

```
model.summary()

Model: "sequential"

Layer (type)                    Output Shape              Param #
=================================================================
mobilenetv2_1.00_160 (Model)    (None, 5, 5, 1280)        2257984

global_average_pooling2d (Gl    (None, 1280)              0

dense (Dense)                   (None, 1)                 1281
=================================================================
Total params: 2,259,265
Trainable params: 1,281
Non-trainable params: 2,257,984
```

Figure 18: Displaying the composed model; notice that we only have 1,281 trainable parameters

Let's compute the number of training, validation, and testing examples, then compute the initial accuracy given by the pretrained MobileNetV2:

```
num_train, num_val, num_test = (
  metadata.splits['train'].num_examples*weight/10
  for weight in SPLIT_WEIGHTS
)
initial_epochs = 10
steps_per_epoch = round(num_train)//BATCH_SIZE
validation_steps = 4

loss0,accuracy0 = model.evaluate(validation_batches, steps = validation_steps)
```

We get an initial accuracy of 50%.

We can now fine-tune the composed network by training for a few iterations and optimizing the non-frozen layers:

```
history = model.fit(train_batches,
                    epochs=initial_epochs,
                    validation_data=validation_batches)
```

Thanks to the transfer learning, our network reaches a very high accuracy of 98% by using Google MobileNetV2 trained on ImageNet. Transfer learning speeds up training by reusing existing pretrained image classification models and retraining only the top layer of the network to determine the class that each image belongs to:

```
Epoch 18/20
26/26 [==============================] - 5s 198ms/step - loss: 0.1675 - accuracy: 0.9661 - val_loss: 0.0451 - val_accuracy: 0.9800
Epoch 19/20
26/26 [==============================] - 6s 223ms/step - loss: 0.1222 - accuracy: 0.9722 - val_loss: 0.0381 - val_accuracy: 0.9800
Epoch 20/20
26/26 [==============================] - 6s 225ms/step - loss: 0.1087 - accuracy: 0.9807 - val_loss: 0.0359 - val_accuracy: 0.9800
```

Figure 19: Model accuracy using transfer learning

In this section we learned how to use a pretrained model. The next section will explain where we can find a repository with many models.

Application Zoos with tf.keras and TensorFlow Hub

One of the nice things about transfer learning is that it is possible to reuse pretrained networks to save time and resources. There are many collections of ready-to-use networks out there, but the following two are the most used.

Keras applications

Keras applications include models for image classification with weights trained on ImageNet (Xception, VGG16, VGG19, ResNet, ResNetV2, ResNeXt, InceptionV3, InceptionResNetV2, MobileNet, MobileNetV2, DenseNet, and NASNet). In addition, there are a few other reference implementations from the community for object detection and segmentation, sequence learning (see *Chapter 8, Recurrent Neural Networks*), reinforcement learning (see *Chapter 11, Reinforcement Learning*), and GANs (see *Chapter 6, Generative Adversarial Networks*).

TensorFlow Hub

TensorFlow Hub (`https://www.tensorflow.org/hub`) is an alternative collection of pretrained models. However, Hub is not fully integrated with TensorFlow 2.0 as of September 2019, but this issue will surely be fixed with the final version of 2.0 (however, as of July 2019, eager computation is also supported). TensorFlow Hub includes modules for Text Classification, Sentence Encoding (see *Chapter 9, Autoencoders*), Image Classification, Feature Extraction, Image Generation with GANs (see *Chapter 6, Generative Adversarial Networks*), and Video Classification. Currently, both Google and DeepMind contribute to publishing.

 See the issue about eager execution at `https://github.com/tensorflow/hub/issues/124` and the issue for full integration at `https://github.com/tensorflow/tensorflow/issues/25362`.

Let's look at an example of using `TF.Hub`. In this case, we have a simple image classifier using MobileNetV2:

```
import matplotlib.pylab as plt
import tensorflow as tf
import tensorflow_hub as hub
import numpy as np
import PIL.Image as Image

classifier_url ="https://tfhub.dev/google/tf2-preview/mobilenet_v2/
classification/2" #@param {type:"string"}
IMAGE_SHAPE = (224, 224)
# wrap the hub to work with tf.keras
classifier = tf.keras.Sequential([
    hub.KerasLayer(classifier_url, input_shape=IMAGE_SHAPE+(3,))
])
grace_hopper = tf.keras.utils.get_file('image.jpg','https://storage.
googleapis.com/download.tensorflow.org/example_images/grace_hopper.
jpg')
grace_hopper = Image.open(grace_hopper).resize(IMAGE_SHAPE)
```

```
grace_hopper = np.array(grace_hopper)/255.0
result = classifier.predict(grace_hopper[np.newaxis, ...])
predicted_class = np.argmax(result[0], axis=-1)
print (predicted_class)
```

Pretty simple indeed. Just remember to use `hub.KerasLayer()` for wrapping any Hub layer. In this section, we have discussed how to use TensorFlow Hub. Next, we will focus on other CNN architectures.

Other CNN architectures

In this section we will discuss many other different CNN architectures including AlexNet, residual networks, HighwayNets, DenseNets, and Xception.

AlexNet

One of the first convolutional networks was AlexNet [4], which consisted of only eight layers; the first five were convolutional ones with max-pooling layers, and the last three were fully connected. AlexNet [4] is an article cited more than 35,000 times, which started the deep learning revolution (for computer vision). Then, networks started to become deeper and deeper. Recently, a new idea has been proposed.

Residual networks

Residual networks (ResNets) are based on the interesting idea of allowing earlier layers to be fed directly into deeper layers. These are the so-called skip connections (or fast-forward connections). The key idea is to minimize the risk of vanishing or exploding gradients for deep networks (see *Chapter 9, Autoencoders*). The building block of a ResNet is called "residual block" or "identity block," which includes both forward and fast-forward connections.

In this example (*Figure 20*) the output of an earlier layer is added to the output of a later layer before being sent into a ReLU activation function:

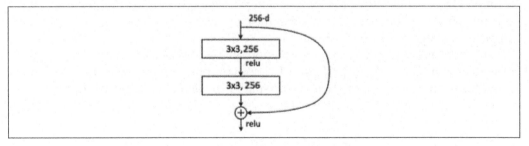

Figure 20: An example of Image Segmentation

HighwayNets and DenseNets

An additional weight matrix may be used to learn the skip weights and these models are frequently denoted as HighwayNets. Instead, models with several parallel skips are known as DenseNets [5]. It has been noted that the human brain might have similar patterns to residual networks since the cortical layer VI neurons get input from layer I, skipping intermediary layers. In addition, residual networks can be faster to train since there are fewer layers to propagate through during each iteration (deeper layers get input sooner due to the skip connection). The following is an example of DenseNets (*Figure 21*, as shown in `http://arxiv.org/abs/1608.06993`):

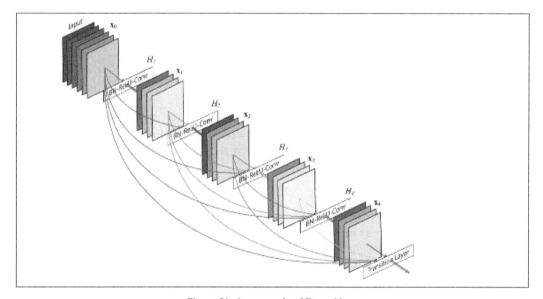

Figure 21: An example of DenseNets

Xception

Xception networks use two basic blocks: a depthwise convolution and a pointwise convolution. A depthwise convolution is the channel-wise $n \times n$ spatial convolution. Suppose an image has three channels, then we have three convolutions of $n \times n$. A pointwise convolution is a 1×1 convolution. In Xception – an "extreme" version of an Inception module – we first use a 1×1 convolution to map cross-channel correlations, and then separately map the spatial correlations of every output channel as shown in *Figure 22* (from `https://arxiv.org/pdf/1610.02357.pdf`):

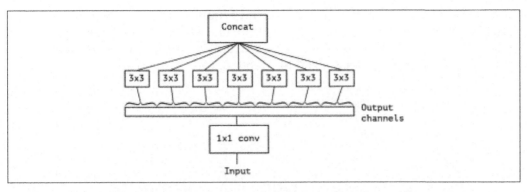

Figure 22: An example of an extreme form of an Inception module

Xception (eXtreme Inception) is a deep convolutional neural network architecture inspired by Inception, where Inception modules have been replaced with depthwise separable convolutions. Xception uses multiple skip-connections in a similar way to ResNet. The final architecture is rather complex as illustrated in *Figure 23* (from `https://arxiv.org/pdf/1610.02357.pdf`). Data first goes through the entry flow, then through the middle flow, which is repeated eight times, and finally through the exit flow:

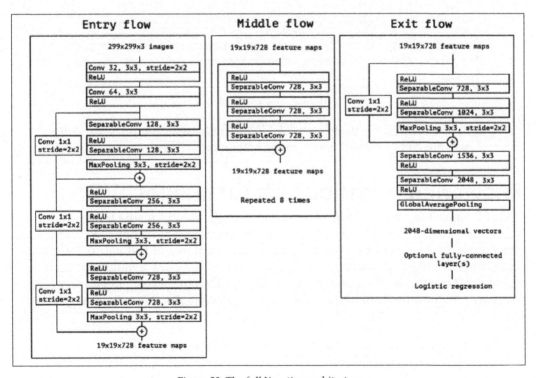

Figure 23: The full Xception architecture

Casing, HyperNets, DenseNets, Inception, and Xception are all available as pretrained nets in both `tf.keras.application` and TF-Hub. The Keras application (`https://keras.io/applications`) reports a nice summary of the performance achieved on an ImageNet dataset and the depth of each network:

Model	Size	Top-1 Accuracy	Top-5 Accuracy	Parameters	Depth
Xception	88 MB	0.790	0.945	22,910,480	126
VGG16	528 MB	0.713	0.901	138,357,544	23
VGG19	549 MB	0.713	0.900	143,667,240	26
ResNet50	98 MB	0.749	0.921	25,636,712	-
ResNet101	171 MB	0.764	0.928	44,707,176	-
ResNet152	232 MB	0.766	0.931	60,419,944	-
ResNet50V2	98 MB	0.760	0.930	25,613,800	-
ResNet101V2	171 MB	0.772	0.938	44,675,560	-
ResNet152V2	232 MB	0.780	0.942	60,380,648	-
ResNeXt50	96 MB	0.777	0.938	25,097,128	-
ResNeXt101	170 MB	0.787	0.943	44,315,560	-
InceptionV3	92 MB	0.779	0.937	23,851,784	159
InceptionResNetV2	215 MB	0.803	0.953	55,873,736	572
MobileNet	16 MB	0.704	0.895	4,253,864	88
MobileNetV2	14 MB	0.713	0.901	3,538,984	88
DenseNet121	33 MB	0.750	0.923	8,062,504	121
DenseNet169	57 MB	0.762	0.932	14,307,880	169
DenseNet201	80 MB	0.773	0.936	20,242,984	201
NASNetMobile	23 MB	0.744	0.919	5,326,716	-
NASNetLarge	343 MB	0.825	0.960	88,949,818	-

The top-1 and top-5 accuracy refers to the model's performance on the ImageNet validation dataset.

Figure 24: Performance summary, shown by Keras

In this section, we have discussed many CNN architectures. Next, we are going to see how to answer questions about images by using CNNs.

Answering questions about images (VQA)

One of the nice things about neural networks is that different media types can be combined together to provide a unified interpretation. For instance, **Visual Question Answering (VQA)** combines image recognition and text natural language processing. Training can use VQA (`https://visualqa.org/`), a dataset containing open-ended questions about images. These questions require an understanding of vision, language, and common knowledge to answer. The following images are taken from a demo available at `https://visualqa.org/`.

Note the question at the top of the image, and the subsequent answers:

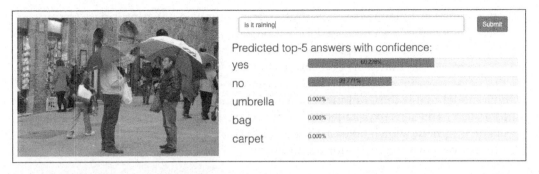

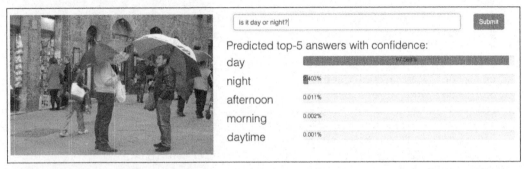

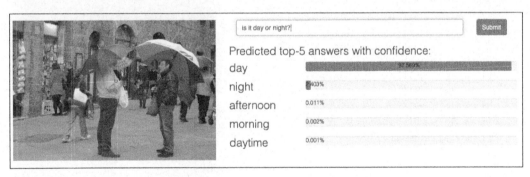

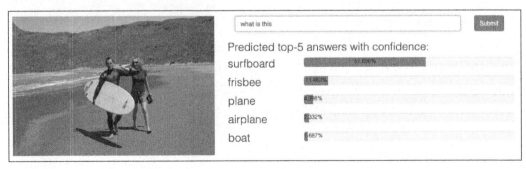

If you want to start playing with VQA, the first thing is to get appropriate training datasets such as the VQA dataset, CLEVR dataset (`https://cs.stanford.edu/people/jcjohns/clevr/`), or FigureQA dataset (`https://datasets.maluuba.com/FigureQA`); alternatively, you can participate in a Kaggle VQA challenge (`https://www.kaggle.com/c/visual-question-answering`). Then you can build a model that is the combination of a CNN and a RNN (discussed in *Chapter 9, Autoencoders*) and start experimenting. For instance, a CNN can be something like this code fragment, which takes an image with three channels (224×224) as input and produces a feature vector for the image:

```
import tensorflow as tf
from tensorflow.keras import layers, models
# IMAGE
#
# Define CNN for visual processing
cnn_model = models.Sequential()
cnn_model.add(layers.Conv2D(64, (3, 3), activation='relu',
padding='same', input_shape=(224, 224, 3)))
cnn_model.add(layers.Conv2D(64, (3, 3), activation='relu'))
cnn_model.add(layers.MaxPooling2D(2, 2))
cnn_model.add(layers.Conv2D(128, (3, 3), activation='relu',
padding='same'))
cnn_model.add(layers.Conv2D(128, (3, 3), activation='relu'))
cnn_model.add(layers.MaxPooling2D(2, 2))
cnn_model.add(layers.Conv2D(256, (3, 3), activation='relu',
padding='same'))
cnn_model.add(layers.Conv2D(256, (3, 3), activation='relu'))
cnn_model.add(layers.Conv2D(256, (3, 3), activation='relu'))
cnn_model.add(layers.MaxPooling2D(2, 2))
cnn_model.add(layers.Flatten())
cnn_model.summary()

# define the visual_model with proper input
image_input = layers.Input(shape=(224, 224, 3))
visual_model = cnn_model(image_input)
```

Text can be encoded with an RNN – for now think of it as a black box taking a text fragment (the question) as input and producing a feature vector for the text:

```
# TEXT
#
# define the RNN model for text processing
question_input = layers.Input(shape=(100,), dtype='int32')
emdedding = layers.Embedding(input_dim=10000, output_dim=256, input_
length=100)(question_input)
encoded_question = layers.LSTM(256)(emdedding)
```

Then the two feature vectors (one for the image, and one for the text) are combined into one joint vector that is provided as input to a dense network to produce the combined network:

```
# combine the encoded question and visual model
merged = layers.concatenate([encoded_question, visual_model])
# attach a dense network at the end
output = layers.Dense(1000, activation='softmax')(merged)

# get the combined model
vqa_model = models.Model(inputs=[image_input, question_input],
outputs=output)
vqa_model.summary()
```

For instance, if we have a set of labeled images, then we can learn what the best questions and answers are for describing an image. The number of options is enormous! If you want to know more, I suggest that you investigate Maluuba, a start-up providing the FigureQA dataset with 100,000 figure images and 1,327,368 question-answer pairs in the training set. Maluuba has been recently acquired by Microsoft, and the lab is advised by Yoshua Bengio, one of the fathers of deep learning.

In this section, we have discussed how to implement VQA. The next section is about style transfer: a deep learning technique used for training neural networks to create art.

Style transfer

Style transfer is a funny neural network application that provides many insights into the power of neural networks. So what exactly is it? Imagine that you observe a painting made by a famous artist. In principle you are observing two elements: the painting itself (say, the face of a woman, or a landscape) and something more intrinsic, the "style" of the artist. What is the style? That is more difficult to define, but humans know that Picasso had his own style, Matisse had his own style, and each artist has his/her own style. Now, imagine taking a famous painting of Matisse, giving it to a neural network, and letting the neural network repaint it in Picasso's style. Or imagine taking your own photo, giving it to a neural network, and having your photo painted in Matisse's or Picasso's style, or in the style of any other artist that you like. That's what style transfer does.

For instance, go to `https://deepart.io/` and see a cool demo as shown in the following image, where DeepArt has been applied by taking the "Van Gogh" style as observed in the Sunflowers painting and applying it to a picture of my daughter Aurora:

Now, how can we define more formally the process of style transfer? Well, style transfer is the task of producing an artificial image x that shares the content of a source content image p and the style of a source style image a. So, intuitively we need two distance functions: one distance function measures how different the content of two images is, $L_{content}$, while the other distance function measures how different the style of two images is, L_{style}. Then, the transfer style can be seen as an optimization problem where we try to minimize these two metrics. As in Leon A. Gatys, Alexander S. Ecker, Matthias Bethge [7], we use a pretrained network to achieve style transfer. In particular, we can feed a VGG19 (or any suitable pretrained network) for extracting features that represent images in an efficient way. Now we are going to define two functions used for training the network: the content distance and the style distance.

Content distance

Given two images, p content image and x input image, we define the content distance as the distance in the feature space defined by a layer l for a VGG19 network receiving the two images as an input. In other words, the two images are represented by the features extracted by a pretrained VGG19. These features project the images into a feature "content" space where the "content" distance can be conveniently computed as follows:

$$L^l_{content(p,x)} = \Sigma_{i,j}\left(F^l_{ij}(x) - P^l_{ij}(p)\right)^2$$

For generating nice images, we need to ensure that the content of the generated image is similar to (that is, has a small distance from) that of the input image. The distance is therefore minimized with standard backpropagation. The code is simple:

```
#
# content distance
#
def get_content_loss(base_content, target):
    return tf.reduce_mean(tf.square(base_content - target))
```

Style distance

As discussed, the features in the higher layers of VGG19 are used as content representations. You can think about these features as a filter response. In order to represent the style, we use a gram matrix G (defined as the matrix $v^T v$ for a vector v); we consider G^l_{ij} as the inner matrix for map i and map j at layer l of the VGG19. It is possible to show [7] that the gram matrix represents the correlation matrix between different filter responses.

The contribution of each layer to the total style loss in Gatys et al., 2016 [7] is defined as:

$$E_l = \frac{1}{4N_l^2 M_l^2} \sum_{i,j} (G^l_{ij} - A^l_{ij})^2$$

Where G^l_{ij} is the gram matrix for input image x, A^l_{ij} is the gram matrix for the style image a, and N_l is the number of feature maps, each of size $M_l = height \times width$. The idea, proven in Gatys et al., 2016, is that the Gram matrix can project the images into a space where the style is taken into account. In addition, the feature correlations from multiple VGG19 layers are used because we want to take into account multiscale information and a more robust style representation. The total style loss across levels is the weighted sum:

$$L_{style}(a, x) = \sum_{i \in L} w_l E_l \qquad \left(w_l = \frac{1}{||L||}\right)$$

The key idea is therefore to perform a gradient descent on the content image to make its style similar to the style image. The code is simple:

```
# style distance
#
```

```
def gram_matrix(input_tensor):
  # image channels first
  channels = int(input_tensor.shape[-1])
  a = tf.reshape(input_tensor, [-1, channels])
  n = tf.shape(a)[0]
  gram = tf.matmul(a, a, transpose_a=True)
  return gram / tf.cast(n, tf.float32)

def get_style_loss(base_style, gram_target):
  # height, width, num filters of each layer
  height, width, channels = base_style.get_shape().as_list()
  gram_style = gram_matrix(base_style)

  return tf.reduce_mean(tf.square(gram_style - gram_target))
```

In short, the concepts behind style transfer are simple: first, we use VGG19 as a feature extractor and then we define two suitable function distances, one for style and the other one for contents, which are appropriately minimized. If you want to try this out for yourself, then TensorFlow tutorials are available online. If you are interested in a demo of this technique, you can go to deepart.io free site where they do style transfer.

 A tutorial is available at `https://colab.research.google.com/github/tensorflow/models/blob/master/research/nst_blogpost/4_Neural_Style_Transfer_with_Eager_Execution.ipynb`.

Next, we'll check out another interesting image-related application of CNNs.

Creating a DeepDream network

Another interesting application of CNNs is DeepDream, a computer vision program created by Google [8], which uses a CNN to find and enhance patterns in images. The result is a dream-like hallucinogenic effect. Similarly to the previous example, we are going to use a pretrained network to extract features. However, in this case we want to "enhance" patterns in images, meaning that we need to maximize some functions. This tells us that we need to use a gradient ascent and not a descent. First, let's see an example from Google gallery (`https://photos.google.com/share/AF1QipPX0SCl7OzWilt9LnuQliattX4OUCj_8EP65_cTVnBmS1jnYgsGQAieQUc1VQWdgQ?key=aVBxWjhwSzg2RjJWLWRuVFBBZEN1d205bUdEMnhB`) where the classic Seattle landscape is "inceptioned" with hallucinogenic dreams such as birds, cards, and strange flying objects.

Google released the DeepDream code in open source (`https://github.com/google/deepdream`), but we use a simplified example made by random forest (`https://github.com/pukkapies/applied-dl/blob/master/examples/9-deep-dream-minimal.ipynb`):

Figure 25: A simplified version of DeepDream applied to the Seattle skyline

Let's start with some image preprocessing:

```
# Download an image and read it into a NumPy array,
def download(url):
    name = url.split("/")[-1]
    image_path = tf.keras.utils.get_file(name, origin=url)
    img = image.load_img(image_path)
    return image.img_to_array(img)


# Scale pixels to between (-1.0 and 1.0)
def preprocess(img):
    return (img / 127.5) - 1


# Undo the preprocessing above
def deprocess(img):
    img = img.copy()
    img /= 2.
    img += 0.5
    img *= 255.
    return np.clip(img, 0, 255).astype('uint8')
```

```
# Display an image
def show(img):
  plt.figure(figsize=(12,12))
  plt.grid(False)
  plt.axis('off')
  plt.imshow(img)


# https://commons.wikimedia.org/wiki/File:Flickr_-_Nicholas_T_-_Big_#
# Sky_(1).jpg
url = 'https://storage.googleapis.com/applied-dl/clouds.jpg'
img = preprocess(download(url))
show(deprocess(img))
```

Now let's use the Inception pretrained network for extracting features. We use several layers and the goal is to maximize their activations. tf.keras functional API is our friend here:

```
# We'll maximize the activations of these layers
names = ['mixed2', 'mixed3', 'mixed4', 'mixed5']
layers = [inception_v3.get_layer(name).output for name in names]

# Create our feature extraction model
feat_extraction_model = tf.keras.Model(inputs=inception_v3.input,
outputs=layers)

def forward(img):

  # Create a batch
  img_batch = tf.expand_dims(img, axis=0)

  # Forward the image through Inception, extract activations
  # for the layers we selected above
  return feat_extraction_model(img_batch)
```

The loss function is the mean of all the activation layers considered, normalized by the number of units in the layer itself:

```
def calc_loss(layer_activations):

  total_loss = 0
```

```
for act in layer_activations:

    # In gradient ascent, we'll want to maximize this value
    # so our image increasingly "excites" the layer
    loss = tf.math.reduce_mean(act)

    # Normalize by the number of units in the layer
    loss /= np.prod(act.shape)
    total_loss += loss

return total_loss
```

Now let's run the gradient ascent:

```
img = tf.Variable(img)
steps = 400

for step in range(steps):

    with tf.GradientTape() as tape:
        activations = forward(img)
        loss = calc_loss(activations)

    gradients = tape.gradient(loss, img)
    # Normalize the gradients
    gradients /= gradients.numpy().std() + 1e-8

    # Update our image by directly adding the gradients
    img.assign_add(gradients)

    if step % 50 == 0:
        clear_output()
        print ("Step %d, loss %f" % (step, loss))
        show(deprocess(img.numpy()))
        plt.show()

# Let's see the result
clear_output()
show(deprocess(img.numpy()))
```

This transforms the image on the left into the psychedelic image on the right:

Figure 26: Applying the Inception transformation (right) to a normal image (left)

Inspecting what a network has learned

A particularly interesting research effort is being devoted to understanding what neural networks are actually learning in order to be able to recognize images so well. This is called neural network "interpretability." Activation Atlases is a promising recent result that aims to show the feature visualizations of averaged activation functions. In this way, activation atlases produce a global map seen through the eyes of the network. Let's look at a demo available at `https://distill.pub/2019/activation-atlas/`:

Figure 27: A screenshot showing an example of an Activation Atlas

In this image, an Inception-v1 network used for vision classification reveals many fully realized features, such as electronics, screens, Polaroid cameras, buildings, food, animal ears, plants, and watery backgrounds. Note that grid cells are labeled with the classification they give most support for. Grid cells are also sized according to the number of activations that are averaged within. This representation is very powerful because it allows us to inspect the different layers of a network and how the activation functions fire in response to the input.

In this section, we have seen many techniques to process images with CNNs. Next, we'll move on to video processing.

Video

In this section, we move from image processing to video processing. We'll start our look at video by discussing six ways in which to classify videos with pretrained nets.

Classifying videos with pretrained nets in six different ways

Classifying videos is an area of active research because of the large amount of data needed for processing this type of media. Memory requirements are frequently reaching the limits of modern GPUs and a distributed form of training on multiple machines might be required. Researchers are currently exploring different directions of investigation, with increased levels of complexity from the first approach to the sixth, described next. Let's review them.

The **first approach** consists of classifying one video frame at a time by considering each one of them as a separate image processed with a 2D CNN. This approach simply reduces the video classification problem to an image classification problem. Each video frame "emits" a classification output, and the video is classified by taking into account the more frequently chosen category for each frame.

The **second approach** consists of creating one single network where a 2D CNN is combined with an RNN (see *Chapter 9*, *Autoencoders*). The idea is that the CNN will take into account the image components and the RNN will take into account the sequence information for each video. This type of network can be very difficult to train because of the very high number of parameters to optimize.

The **third approach** is to use a 3D ConvNet, where 3D ConvNets are an extension of 2D ConvNets operating on a 3D tensor (time, image_width, image_height). This approach is another natural extension of image classification. Again, 3D ConvNets can be hard to train.

The **fourth approach** is based on a clever idea: instead of using CNNs directly for classification, they can be used for storing offline features for each frame in the video. The idea is that feature extraction can be made very efficient with transfer learning as shown in a previous chapter. After all features are extracted, they can be passed as a set of inputs into an RNN, which will learn sequences across multiple frames and emit the final classification.

The **fifth approach** is a simple variant of the fourth, where the final layer is an MLP instead of an RNN. In certain situations, this approach can be simpler and less expensive in terms of computational requirements.

The **sixth approach** is a variant of the fourth, where the phase of feature extraction is realized with a 3D CNN that extracts spatial and visual features. These features are then passed into either an RNN or an MLP.

Deciding upon the best approach is strictly dependent on your specific application and there is no definitive answer. The first three approaches are generally more computationally expensive and less clever, while the last three approaches are less expensive and they frequently achieve better performance.

So far, we have explored how CNNs can be used for image and video applications. In the next section, we will apply these ideas within a text-based context.

Textual documents

What do text and images have in common? At first glance: very little. However, if we represent a sentence or a document as a matrix, then this matrix is not much different from an image matrix where each cell is a pixel. So, the next question is: how can we represent a piece of text as a matrix?

Well, it is pretty simple: each row of a matrix is a vector that represents a basic unit for the text. Of course, now we need to define what a basic unit is. A simple choice could be to say that the basic unit is a character. Another choice would be to say that a basic unit is a word, yet another choice is to aggregate similar words together and then denote each aggregation (sometimes called clustering or embedding) with a representative symbol.

Note that regardless of the specific choice adopted for our basic units, we need to have a 1:1 map from basic units into integer IDs so that a text can be seen as a matrix. For instance, if we have a document with 10 lines of text and each line is a 100-dimensional embedding, then we will represent our text with a matrix of 10×100. In this very particular "image," a "pixel" is turned on if that sentence, X, contains the embedding, represented by position Y.

You might also notice that a text is not really a matrix but more a vector because two words located in adjacent rows of text have very little in common. Indeed, this is a major difference when compared with images, where two pixels located in adjacent columns are likely to have some degree of correlation.

Now you might wonder: I understand that you represent the text as a vector but, in doing so, we lose the position of the words. This position should be important, shouldn't it? Well, it turns out that in many real applications, knowing that whether a sentence contains a particular basic unit (a char, a word, an aggregate) or not is pretty useful information even if we don't keep track of where exactly in the sentence this basic unit is located.

For instance, ConvNets achieve pretty good results for "Sentiment Analysis" where we need to understand if a piece of text has a positive or a negative sentiment; for "Spam Detection" where we need to understand if a piece of text is useful information or spam; and for "Topic Categorization", where we need to understand what a piece of text is all about. However, ConvNets are not well suited for a **Part-of-Speech** (POS) analysis, where the goal is to understand what the logical role of every single word is (for example, a verb, an adverb, a subject, and so on and so forth). ConvNets are also not well suited for "Entity Extraction," where we need to understand where relevant entities are located in sentences. Indeed, it turns out that a position is pretty useful information for both of the last two use cases. 1D ConvNets are very similar to 2D ConvNets. However, the former operates on a single vector, while the latter operates on matrices.

Using a CNN for sentiment analysis

Let's have a look at the code. First of all, we load the dataset with `tensorflow_datasets`. In this case we use IMDb, a collection of movie reviews:

```
import tensorflow as tf
from tensorflow.keras import datasets, layers, models, preprocessing
import tensorflow_datasets as tfds

max_len = 200
n_words = 10000
dim_embedding = 256
EPOCHS = 20
BATCH_SIZE =500

def load_data():
    #load data
    (X_train, y_train), (X_test, y_test) = datasets.imdb.load_
data(num_words=n_words)
```

```
    # Pad sequences with max_len
    X_train = preprocessing.sequence.pad_sequences(X_train,
 maxlen=max_len)
    X_test = preprocessing.sequence.pad_sequences(X_test, maxlen=max_len)
    return (X_train, y_train), (X_test, y_test)
```

Then we build a suitable CNN model. We use Embeddings (see *Chapter 9, Autoencoders*) to map the sparse vocabulary typically observed in documents into a dense feature space of dimension `dim_embedding`. Then we use a `Conv1D`, followed by a `GlobalMaxPooling1D` for averaging, and two `Dense` layers – the last one has only one neuron firing binary choices (positive or negative reviews):

```
def build_model():
    model = models.Sequential()
    # Input - Embedding Layer
    # the model will take as input an integer matrix of size
    # (batch, input_length)
    # the model will output dimension (input_length, dim_embedding)
    # the largest integer in the input should be no larger
    # than n_words (vocabulary size).
    model.add(layers.Embedding(n_words,
        dim_embedding, input_length=max_len))

    model.add(layers.Dropout(0.3))
    model.add(layers.Conv1D(256, 3, padding='valid',
        activation='relu'))

    # takes the maximum value of either feature vector from each of
    # the n_words features
    model.add(layers.GlobalMaxPooling1D())
    model.add(layers.Dense(128, activation='relu'))
    model.add(layers.Dropout(0.5))
    model.add(layers.Dense(1, activation='sigmoid'))

    return model

(X_train, y_train), (X_test, y_test) = load_data()
model=build_model()
model.summary()
```

The model has more than 2,700,000 parameters and it is summarized in the following figure:

```
_____
 Layer (type)                Output Shape              Param #
=================================================================
 embedding (Embedding)       (None, 200, 256)          2560000
_____
 dropout (Dropout)           (None, 200, 256)          0
_____
 conv1d (Conv1D)             (None, 198, 256)          196864
_____
 global_max_pooling1d (Global (None, 256)              0
_____
 dense (Dense)               (None, 128)               32896
_____
 dropout_1 (Dropout)         (None, 128)               0
_____
 dense_1 (Dense)             (None, 1)                 129
=================================================================
Total params: 2,789,889
Trainable params: 2,789,889
Non-trainable params: 0
```

Figure 28: Summarizing our CNN model

Then we compile and fit the model with the Adam optimizer and binary cross-entropy loss:

```
model.compile(optimizer = "adam", loss = "binary_crossentropy",
  metrics = ["accuracy"]
)

score = model.fit(X_train, y_train,
  epochs= EPOCHS,
  batch_size = BATCH_SIZE,
  validation_data = (X_test, y_test)
)

score = model.evaluate(X_test, y_test, batch_size=BATCH_SIZE)
print("\nTest score:", score[0])
print('Test accuracy:', score[1])
```

The final accuracy is 88.21%, showing that it is possible to successfully use CNNs for textual processing:

```
Epoch 19/20
25000/25000 [==============================] - 135s 5ms/sample - loss: 7.5276e-04 - accuracy: 1.0000 - v
al_loss: 0.5753 - val_accuracy: 0.8818
Epoch 20/20
25000/25000 [==============================] - 129s 5ms/sample - loss: 6.7755e-04 - accuracy: 0.9999 - v
al_loss: 0.5802 - val_accuracy: 0.8821
25000/25000 [==============================] - 23s 916us/sample - loss: 0.5802 - accuracy: 0.8821

Test score: 0.5801781857013703
Test accuracy: 0.88212
```

Figure 29: Use CNN for text processing

Note that many other non-image applications can also be converted to an image and classified using a CNN (see, for instance, https://becominghuman.ai/sound-classification-using-images-68d4770df426).

Audio and music

We have used CNNs for images, videos, and text. Now let's have a look to how variants of CNNs can be used for audio.

So, you might wonder why learning to synthesize audio is so difficult. Well, each digital sound we hear is based on 16,000 samples per second (sometimes 48,000 or more) and building a predictive model where we learn to reproduce a sample based on all the previous ones is a very difficult challenge.

Dilated ConvNets, WaveNet, and NSynth

WaveNet is a deep generative model for producing raw audio waveforms. This breakthrough technology has been introduced (WaveNet is available at https://deepmind.com/blog/wavenet-generative-model-raw-audio/) by Google DeepMind for teaching computers how to speak. The results are truly impressive and online you find can examples of synthetic voices where the computer learns how to talk with the voice of celebrities such as Matt Damon. There are experiments showing that WaveNet improved the current state-of-the-art **Text-to-Speech** (TTS) systems, reducing the difference with respect to human voices by 50% for both US English and Mandarin Chinese. The metric used for comparison is called **Mean Opinion Score** (MOS), a subjective paired comparison test. In the MOS tests, after listening to each sound stimulus, the subjects were asked to rate the naturalness of the stimulus on a five-point scale from "Bad" (1) to "Excellent" (5).

DeepMind is a company owned by (Google `https://deepmind.com/`).

What is even cooler is that DeepMind demonstrated that WaveNet can be also used to teach computers how to generate the sound of musical instruments such as piano music.

Now some definitions. TTS systems are typically divided into two different classes: Concatenative and Parametric.

Concatenative TTS is where single speech voice fragments are first memorized and then recombined when the voice has to be reproduced. However, this approach does not scale because it is possible to reproduce only the memorized voice fragments, and it is not possible to reproduce new speakers or different types of audio without memorizing the fragments from the beginning.

Parametric TTS is where a model is created for storing all the characteristic features of the audio to be synthesized. Before WaveNet, the audio generated with parametric TTS was less natural than concatenative TTS. WaveNet enabled significant improvement by modeling directly the production of audio sounds, instead of using intermediate signal processing algorithms as in the past.

In principle, WaveNet can be seen as a stack of 1D convolutional layers with a constant stride of one and no pooling layers. Note that the input and the output have by construction the same dimension, so CNNs are well suited to modeling sequential data such as audio sounds. However, it has been shown that in order to reach a large size for the receptive field in the output neuron, it is necessary to either use a massive number of large filters or increase the network depth prohibitively. For this reason, pure CNNs are not so effective in learning how to synthesize audio.

Remember that the receptive field of a neuron in a layer is the cross-section of the previous layer from which neurons provide inputs.

The key intuition behind WaveNet is the so-called Dilated Causal Convolutions [5] (or sometimes known as AtrousConvolution), which simply means that some input values are skipped when the filter of a convolutional layer is applied. As an example, in one dimension a filter w of size 3 with dilatation 1 would compute the following sum:

$$w[0]x[0] + w[1]x[2] + w[3]x[4]$$

"Atrous" is the "bastardization" of the French expression "à trous," meaning "with holes." So an AtrousConvolution is a convolution with holes.

In short, in D-dilated convolution, usually the stride is 1, but nothing prevents you from using other strides. An example is given in the following diagram with increased dilatation (hole) sizes = 0, 1, 2:

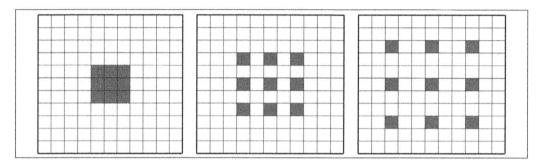

Thanks to this simple idea of introducing "holes," it is possible to stack multiple dilated convolutional layers with exponentially increasing filters, and learn long-range input dependencies without having an excessively deep network.

A WaveNet is therefore a ConvNet where the convolutional layers have various dilation factors, allowing the receptive field to grow exponentially with depth and therefore efficiently cover thousands of audio timesteps.

When we train, the inputs are sounds recorded from human speakers. The waveforms are quantized to a fixed integer range. A WaveNet defines an initial convolutional layer accessing only the current and previous input. Then, there is a stack of dilated convnet layers, still accessing only current and previous inputs. At the end, there is a series of dense layers combining the previous results followed by a softmax activation function for categorical outputs.

At each step, a value is predicted from the network and fed back into the input. At the same time, a new prediction for the next step is computed. The loss function is the cross entropy between the output for the current step and the input at the next step. The following image shows the visualization of a WaveNet stack and its receptive field as introduced by Aaron van den Oord [9]. Note that generation can be slow because the waveform has to be synthesized in a sequential fashion, as x_t must be sampled first in order to obtain $x_{>t}$ where x is the input:

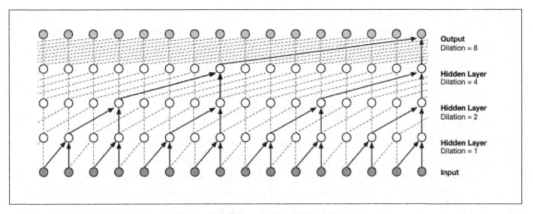

Figure 30: WaveNet stack, visualized

A method for performing a sampling in parallel has been proposed in Parallel WaveNet [10], which achieves a three orders-of-magnitude speed up. This uses two networks as a WaveNet teacher network, which is slow but ensures a correct result, and a WaveNet student network, which tries to mimic the behavior of the teacher; this can prove to be less accurate but is faster. This approach is similar to the one used for GANs (see *Chapter 6, Generative Adversarial Networks*) but the student does not try to fool the teacher as typically happens in GANs. In fact, the model is not just quicker, but also higher fidelity, capable of creating waveforms with 24,000 samples per second:

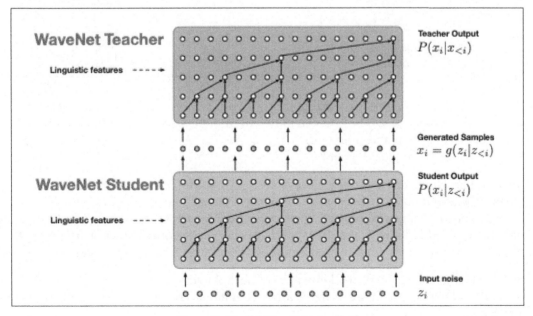

Figure 31: Parallel WaveNet, visualized

This model has been deployed in production at Google, and is currently being used to serve Google Assistant queries in real time to millions of users. At the annual I/O developer conference in May 2018, it was announced that new Google Assistant voices were available thanks to WaveNet.

Two implementations of WaveNet models for TensorFlow are currently available. One is the original implementation of DeepMind's WaveNet (original WaveNet version is available at `https://github.com/ibab/tensorflow-wavenet`), and the other is called Magenta NSynth. NSynth (Magenta is available at `https://magenta.tensorflow.org/nsynth`) is an evolution of WaveNet recently released by the Google Brain group, which, instead of being causal, aims at seeing the entire context of the input chunk. The neural network is truly complex, as depicted in following diagram, but for the sake of this introductory discussion it is sufficient to know that the network learns how to reproduce its input by using an approach based on reducing the error during the encoding/decoding phases:

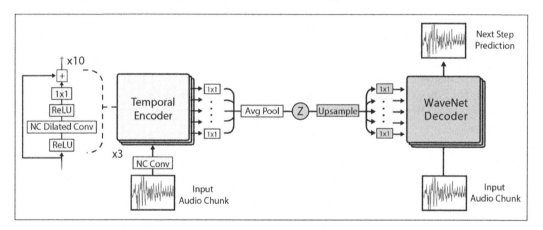

If you are interested in understanding more, I would suggest having a look at the online Colab notebook where you can play with models generated with NSynth (NSynth Colab is available at `https://colab.research.google.com/notebooks/magenta/nsynth/nsynth.ipynb`).

MuseNet is a very recent and impressive audio generation tool developed by OpenAI. MuseNet uses a sparse transformer to train a 72-layer network with 24 attention heads. Transformers will be discussed in *Chapter 9, Autoencoders*, but for now all we need to know is that they are deep neural networks that are very good at predicting what comes next in a sequence—whether text, images, or sound.

In Transformers, every output element is connected to every input element, and the weightings between them are dynamically calculated according to a process called attention.

MuseNet can produce up to 4-minute musical compositions with 10 different instruments, and can combine styles from country, to Mozart, to the Beatles. For instance, I generated a remake of Beethoven's "fur Elise" in the style of Lady Gaga with Piano, Drums, Guitar, and Bass. You can try this for yourself at `https://openai.com/blog/musenet/`, under the section **Try MuseNet:**

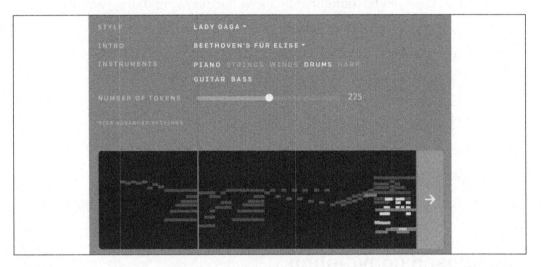

A summary of convolution operations

In this section we present a summary of different convolution operations. A convolutional layer has I input channels and produces O output channels. $I \times O \times K$ parameters are used, where K is the number of values in the kernel.

Basic convolutional neural networks (CNN or ConvNet)

Let's remind ourselves briefly what a CNN is. CNNs take in an input image (two dimensions) or a text (two dimensions) or a video (three dimensions) and apply multiple filters to the input. Each filter is a like a flashlight sliding across the areas of the input and the areas that it is shining over is called the receptive field. Each filter is a tensor of the same depth of the input (for instance if the image has a depth of 3, then the filter must also have a depth of 3).

When the filter is sliding, or convolving, around the input image, the values in the filter are multiplied by the values of the input. The multiplications are then summarized into one single value. This process is repeated for each location producing an activation map (also known as a feature map).

Of course, it is possible to use multiple filters and each filter will act as a feature identifier. For instance, for images the filter can identify edges, colors, lines, and curves. The key intuition is to treat the filter values as weights and fine-tune them during training via backpropagation.

A convolution layer can be configured by using the following config parameters:

- **Kernel size**: It is the field of view of the convolution
- **Stride**: It is the step size of the kernel when we traverse the image
- **Padding**: Defines how the border of our sample is handled

Dilated convolution

Dilated convolutions (or Atrous convolutions) introduce another config parameter:

- **Dilation rate**: It is the spacing between the values in a kernel

Dilated convolutions are used in many contexts including audio processing with WaveNet.

Transposed convolution

Transposed convolution is a transformation going in the opposite direction of a normal convolution. For instance this can be useful to project feature maps into a higher-dimensional space or for building convolutional autoencoders (see *Chapter 9, Autoencoders*). One way to think about Transposed convolution is to compute the output shape of a normal CNN for a given input shape first. Then we invert input and output shapes with the transposed convolution. TensorFlow 2.0 supports Transposed convolutions with Conv2DTranspose layers, which can be used for instance in GANs (see *Chapter 6, Generative Adversarial Networks*) for generating images.

Separable convolution

Separable convolution aims at separating the kernel into multiple steps. Let the convolution be $y = conv(x,k)$ where y is the output, x is the input, and k is the kernel. Let's assume the kernel is separable, for example, $k = k1.k2$ where "." is the dot product. In this case, instead of doing a 2-dimensions convolution with k, we can get to the same result by doing two 1-dimension convolutions with $k1$ and $k2$. Separable convolutions are frequently used to save on computation resources.

Depthwise convolution

Let's consider an image with multiple channels. In the normal 2D convolution, the filter is as deep as the input and it allows us to mix channels for generating each element of the output. In Depthwise convolution, each channel is kept separate, the filter is split into channels, each convolution is applied separately, and the results are stacked back together into one tensor.

Depthwise separable convolution

This convolution should not be confused with the separable convolution. After completing the Depthwise convolution, an additional step is performed: a 1×1 convolution across channels. Depthwise separable convolutions are used in Xception. They are also used in MobileNet, a model particularly useful for mobile and embedded vision applications because of its reduced model size and complexity.

In this section, we have discussed all the major forms of convolution. The next section will discuss Capsule networks a new form of learning introduced in 2017.

Capsule networks

Capsule Networks (CapsNets) are a very recent and innovative type of deep learning network. This technique was introduced at the end of October 2017 in a seminal paper titled *Dynamic Routing Between Capsules* by Sara Sabour, Nicholas Frost, and Geoffrey Hinton (`https://arxiv.org/abs/1710.09829`) [14]. Hinton is the father of Deep Learning and, therefore, the whole Deep Learning community is excited to see the progress made with Capsules. Indeed, CapsNets are already beating the best CNN on MNIST classification, which is ... well, impressive!!

So what is the problem with CNNs?

In CNNs each layer "understands" an image at a progressive level of granularity. As we discussed in multiple examples, the first layer will most likely recognize straight lines or simple curves and edges, while subsequent layers will start to understand more complex shapes such as rectangles up to complex forms such as human faces.

Now, one critical operation used for CNNs is pooling. Pooling aims at creating the positional invariance and it is used after each CNN layer to make any problem computationally tractable. However, pooling introduces a significant problem because it forces us to lose all the positional data. This is not good. Think about a face: it consists of two eyes, a mouth, and a nose and what is important is that there is a spatial relationship between these parts (for example, the mouth is below the nose, which is typically below the eyes).

Indeed, Hinton said: "The pooling operation used in convolutional neural networks is a big mistake and the fact that it works so well is a disaster." Technically we do not need positional invariance but instead we need equivariance. Equivariance is a fancy term for indicating that we want to understand the rotation or proportion change in an image, and we want to adapt the network accordingly. In this way, the spatial positioning among the different components in an image is not lost.

So what is new with Capsule networks?

According to the authors, our brain has modules called "capsules," and each capsule is specialized in handling a particular type of information. In particular, there are capsules that work well for "understanding" the concept of position, the concept of size, the concept of orientation, the concept of deformation, the concept of textures, and so on and so forth. In addition to that, the authors suggest that our brain has particularly efficient mechanisms for dynamically routing each piece of information to the capsule that is considered best suited for handling a particular type of information.

So, the main difference between CNN and CapsNets is that with a CNN you keep adding layers for creating a deep network, while with CapsNet you nest a neural layer inside another. A capsule is a group of neurons that introduces more structure in the net and it produces a vector to signal the existence of an entity in the image. In particular, Hinton uses the length of the activity vector to represent the probability that the entity exists and its orientation to represent the instantiation parameters. When multiple predictions agree, a higher-level capsule becomes active. For each possible parent, the capsule produces an additional prediction vector.

Now a second innovation comes into place: we will use dynamic routing across capsules and will no longer use the raw idea of pooling. A lower-level capsule prefers to send its output to higher-level capsules for which the activity vectors have a big scalar product with the prediction coming from the lower-level capsule. The parent with the largest scalar prediction vector product increases the capsule bond. All the other parents decrease their bond. In other words, the idea is that if a higher-level capsule agrees with a lower level one, then it will ask to send more information of that type. If there is no agreement, it will ask to send less of them. This dynamic routing by the agreement method is superior to the current mechanism like max-pooling and, according to Hinton, routing is ultimately a way to parse the image. Indeed, max-pooling ignores anything but the largest value, while dynamic routing selectively propagates information according to the agreement between lower layers and upper layers.

A third difference is that a new nonlinear activation function has been introduced. Instead of adding a squashing function to each layer as in CNNs CapsNets add a squashing function to a nested set of layers. The nonlinear activation function is represented in the following diagram and it is called a squashing function (*equation 1*):

$$v_j = \frac{||S_j||^2}{1 + ||S_j||^2} \frac{S_j}{||S_j||} \qquad (1)$$

Where V_j is the vector output of capsule j and S_j is its total input.

Moreover, Hinton and others show that a discriminatively trained, multilayer capsule system achieves state-of-the-art performances on MNIST and is considerably better than a convolutional net at recognizing highly overlapping digits.

From the paper *Dynamic Routing Between Capsules* we report a simple CapsNet architecture:

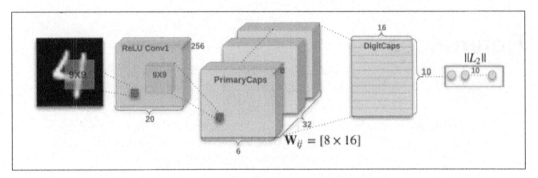

Figure 32: Visualizing the CapsNet architecture

The architecture is shallow with only two convolutional layers and one fully connected layer. Conv1 has 256 9 × 9 convolution kernels with a stride of 1 and ReLU activation. The role of this layer is to convert pixel intensities to the activities of local feature detectors that are then used as inputs to the primary capsules. PrimaryCapsules is a convolutional capsule layer with 32 channels: each primary capsule contains 8 convolutional units with a 9 × 9 kernel and a stride of 2. In total PrimaryCapsules has [32, 6, 6] capsule outputs (each output is an 8D vector) and each capsule in the [6, 6] grid is sharing its weights with each other. The final layer (DigitCaps) has one 16D capsule per digit class and each one of these capsules receives an input from all the other capsules in the layer below. Routing happens only between two consecutive capsule layers (for example, PrimaryCapsules and DigitCaps).

Summary

In this chapter we have seen many applications of CNNs across very different domains, from traditional image processing and computer vision, to close-enough video processing, to not-so-close audio processing and text processing. In a relatively few number of years, CNNs took machine learning by storm.

Nowadays it is not uncommon to see multimodal processing, where text, images, audio, and videos are considered together to achieve better performance, frequently by means of CNNs together with a bunch of other techniques such as RNNs and reinforcement learning. Of course, there is much more to consider, and CNNs have recently been applied to many other domains such as Genetic inference [13], which are, at least at first glance, far away from the original scope of their design.

In this chapter, we have discussed all the major variants of ConvNets. In the next chapter, we will introduce Generative Nets: one of the most innovative deep learning architectures yet.

References

1. J. Yosinski and Y. B. J Clune, *How transferable are features in deep neural networks?*, in *Advances in Neural Information Processing Systems 27*, pp. 3320–3328.

2. C. Szegedy, V. Vanhoucke, S. Ioffe, J. Shlens, and Z. Wojna, *Rethinking the Inception Architecture for Computer Vision*, in 2016 IEEE Conference on Computer Vision and Pattern Recognition (CVPR), pp. 2818–2826.

3. M. Sandler, A. Howard, M. Zhu, A. Zhmonginov, L. C. Chen, *MobileNetV2: Inverted Residuals and Linear Bottlenecks* (2019), Google Inc.

4. A Krizhevsky, I Sutskever, GE Hinton, *ImageNet Classification with Deep Convolutional Neural Networks*, 2012

5. Gao Huang, Zhuang Liu, Laurens van der Maaten, Kilian Q. Weinberger, *Densely Connected Convolutional Networks*, 28 Jan 2018 http://arxiv.org/abs/1608.06993.

6. François Chollet, *Xception: Deep Learning with Depthwise Separable Convolutions*, 2017, https://arxiv.org/abs/1610.02357.

7. Leon A. Gatys, Alexander S. Ecker, Matthias Bethge, *A Neural Algorithm of Artistic Style*, 2016, https://arxiv.org/abs/1508.06576.

8. Mordvintsev, Alexander; Olah, Christopher; Tyka, Mike. *DeepDream - a code example for visualizing Neural Networks*. Google Research, 2015.

9. Aaron van den Oord, Sander Dieleman, Heiga Zen, Karen Simonyan, Oriol Vinyals, Alex Graves, Nal Kalchbrenner, Andrew Senior, and Koray Kavukcuoglu. *WaveNet: A Generative Model for Raw Audio.* arXiv preprint, 2016.

10. Aaron van den Oord, Yazhe Li, Igor Babuschkin, Karen Simonyan, Oriol Vinyals, Koray Kavukcuoglu, George van den Driessche, Edward Lockhart, Luis C. Cobo, Florian Stimberg, Norman Casagrande, Dominik Grewe, Seb Noury, Sander Dieleman, Erich Elsen, Nal Kalchbrenner, Heiga Zen, Alex Graves, Helen King, Tom Walters, Dan Belov, Demis Hassabis, *Parallel WaveNet: Fast High-Fidelity Speech Synthesis*, 2017.

11. Kaiming He, Georgia Gkioxari, Piotr Dollár, Ross Girshick, *Mask R-CNN*, 2018.

12. Liang-Chieh Chen, Yukun Zhu, George Papandreou, Florian Schroff, Hartwig Adam, *Encoder-Decoder with Atrous Separable Convolution for Semantic Image Segmentation*, 2018.

13. Lex Flagel Yaniv Brandvain Daniel R Schrider, *The Unreasonable Effectiveness of Convolutional Neural Networks in Population Genetic Inference*, 2018.

14. Sara Sabour, Nicholas Frosst, Geoffrey E Hinton, *Dynamic Routing Between Capsules*, https://arxiv.org/abs/1710.09829.

6
Generative Adversarial Networks

In this chapter we will discuss **Generative Adversarial Networks (GANs)** and its variants. GANs have been defined as *the most interesting idea in the last 10 years in ML* (https://www.quora.com/What-are-some-recent-and-potentially-upcoming-breakthroughs-in-deep-learning) by Yann LeCun, one of the fathers of deep learning. GANs are able to learn how to reproduce synthetic data that looks real. For instance, computers can learn how to paint and create realistic images. The idea was originally proposed by Ian Goodfellow (for more information refer to *NIPS 2016 Tutorial: Generative Adversarial Networks*, by I. Goodfellow, 2016); he has worked with the University of Montreal, Google Brain, and OpenAI, and is presently working in Apple Inc as the Director of Machine Learning.

In this chapter we will cover different types of GANs and see some of their implementation in TensorFlow 2.0. Broadly we will cover the following topics:

- What is a GAN?
- Deep convolutional GANs
- SRGAN
- CycleGAN
- Applications of GANs

What is a GAN?

The ability of GANs to learn high-dimensional, complex data distributions have made them very popular with researchers in recent years. Between 2016, when they were first proposed by Ian Goodfellow, up to 2019, we have more than 40,000 research papers related to GANs. This is in the space of just three years!

The applications of GANs include creating images, videos, music, and even natural languages. They have been employed in tasks like image-to-image translation, image super resolution, drug discovery, and even next-frame prediction in video.

The key idea of GAN can be easily understood by considering it analogous to "art forgery," which is the process of creating works of art that are falsely credited to other usually more famous artists. GANs train two neural nets simultaneously. The generator $G(Z)$ is the one that makes the forgery, and the discriminator $D(Y)$ is the one that can judge how realistic the reproductions are, based on its observations of authentic pieces of art and copies. $D(Y)$ takes an input Y (for instance, an image), and expresses a vote to judge how real the input is. In general, a value close to 1 denotes "real," while a value close to 0 denotes "forgery." $G(Z)$ takes an input from random noise Z and it trains itself to fool D into thinking that whatever $G(Z)$ produces is real.

The goal of training the discriminator $D(Y)$ is to maximize $D(Y)$ for every image from the true data distribution, and to minimize $D(Y)$ for every image not from the true data distribution. So, G and D play opposite games: hence the name **adversarial training**. Note that we train G and D in an alternating manner, where each one of their objectives is expressed as a loss function optimized via a gradient descent. The generative model continues to improve its forgery capabilities, and the discriminative model continues to improve its forgery recognition capabilities. The discriminator network (usually a standard convolutional neural network) tries to classify if an input image is real or generated. The important new idea is to backpropagate through both the discriminator and the generator to adjust the generator's parameters in such a way that the generator can learn how to fool the discriminator more often. At the end the generator will learn how to produce images that are indistinguishable from the real ones:

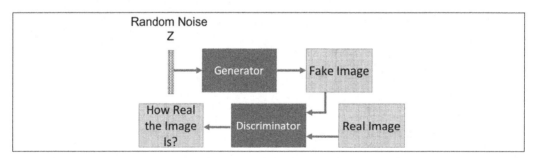

Of course, GANs involve working towards an equilibrium in a game involving two players. Let us first understand what we mean by equilibrium here. When we start, one of the two players are hopefully better than the other. This pushes the other to improve and this way both generator and discriminator push each other towards improvement.

Eventually, we reach a state where the improvement is not significant in either player. We check this by plotting the loss function, to see when the two losses (gradient loss and discriminator loss) reach a plateau. We don't want the game to be skewed too heavily one way; if the forger were to immediately learn how to fool the judge in every occasion, then the forger has *nothing more to learn*. Practically training GANs is really hard, and a lot of research is being done in analyzing GAN convergence; check this site: `https://avg.is.tuebingen.mpg.de/projects/ convergence-and-stability-of-gan-training` for details on convergence and stability of different types of GANs. In generative applications of GAN, we want the generator to learn a little better than the discriminator.

Let's now delve deep into how GANs learn. Both the discriminator and generator take turns to learn. The learning can be divided into two steps:

1. Here the discriminator, $D(x)$, learns. The generator, $G(z)$, is used to generate fake images from random noise z (which follows some prior distribution $P(z)$). The fake images from the generator and the real images from the training dataset are both fed to the discriminator and it performs supervised learning trying to separate fake from real. If P data (x) is the training dataset distribution, then the discriminator network tries to maximize its objective so that $D(x)$ is close to 1 when the input data is real and close to zero when the input data is fake.

2. In the next step, the generator network learns. Its goal is to fool the discriminator network into thinking that generated $G(z)$ is real, that is, force $D(G(z))$ close to 1.

The two steps are repeated sequentially. Once the training ends, the discriminator is no longer able to discriminate between real and fake data and the generator becomes a pro in creating data very similar to the training data. The stability between discriminator and generator is an actively researched problem.

Now that you have got an idea of what GANs are, let's look at a practical application of a GAN in which "handwritten" digits are generated.

MNIST using GAN in TensorFlow

Let us build a simple GAN capable of generating handwritten digits. We will use the MNIST handwritten digits to train the network. We use the TensorFlow Keras dataset to access the MNIST data. The data contains 60,000 training images of handwritten digits each of size 28 × 28. The pixel value of the digits lies between 0-255; we normalize the input values such that each pixel has a value in range [-1, 1]:

```
(X_train, _), (_, _) = mnist.load_data()
X_train = (X_train.astype(np.float32) - 127.5)/127.5
```

We will use a simple **multi-layered perceptron** (**MLP**) and we will feed it an image as a flat vector of size 784, so we reshape the training data:

```
X_train = X_train.reshape(60000, 784)
```

Now we will need to build a generator and discriminator. The purpose of the generator is to take in a noisy input and generate an image similar to the training dataset. The size of the noisy input is decided by the variable `randomDim`; you can initialize it to any integral value. Conventionally people set it to 100. For our implementation we tried a value of 10. This input is fed to a `Dense` layer with 256 neurons with LeakyReLU activation. We next add another `Dense` layer with 512 hidden neurons, followed by the third hidden layer with 1024 neurons and finally the output layer with 784 neurons. You can change the number of neurons in the hidden layers and see how the performance changes; however, the number of neurons in the output unit has to match the number of pixels in the training images. The corresponding generator is then:

```
generator = Sequential()
generator.add(Dense(256, input_dim=randomDim))
generator.add(LeakyReLU(0.2))
generator.add(Dense(512))
generator.add(LeakyReLU(0.2))
generator.add(Dense(1024))
generator.add(LeakyReLU(0.2))
generator.add(Dense(784, activation='tanh'))
```

Similarly, we build a discriminator. Notice now that the discriminator takes in the images, either from the training set or images generated by generator, thus its input size is 784. The output of the discriminator however is a single bit, with 0 signifying a fake image (generated by generator) and 1 signifying that the image is from the training dataset:

```
discriminator = Sequential()
discriminator.add(Dense(1024, input_dim=784) )
discriminator.add(LeakyReLU(0.2))
discriminator.add(Dropout(0.3))
discriminator.add(Dense(512))
discriminator.add(LeakyReLU(0.2))
discriminator.add(Dropout(0.3))
discriminator.add(Dense(256))
discriminator.add(LeakyReLU(0.2))
discriminator.add(Dropout(0.3))
discriminator.add(Dense(1, activation='sigmoid'))
```

Next, we combine the generator and discriminator together to form a GAN. In the GAN we ensure that the discriminator weights are fixed by setting the `trainable` argument to `False`:

```
discriminator.trainable = False
ganInput = Input(shape=(randomDim,))
x = generator(ganInput)
ganOutput = discriminator(x)
gan = Model(inputs=ganInput, outputs=ganOutput)
```

The trick to train the two is that we first train the discriminator separately; we use binary cross entropy loss for the discriminator. Later we freeze the weights of the discriminator and train the combined GAN; this results in the training of the generator. The loss this time is also binary cross entropy:

```
discriminator.compile(loss='binary_crossentropy', optimizer='adam')
gan.compile(loss='binary_crossentropy', optimizer='adam')
```

Let us now perform the training. For each epoch we take a sample of random noise first, feed it to the generator, and the generator produces a fake image. We combine the generated fake images and the actual training images in a batch with their specific labels and use them to train the discriminator first on the given batch:

```
def train(epochs=1, batchSize=128):
    batchCount = int(X_train.shape[0] / batchSize)
    print ('Epochs:', epochs)
    print ('Batch size:', batchSize)
    print ('Batches per epoch:', batchCount)

    for e in range(1, epochs+1):
        print ('-'*15, 'Epoch %d' % e, '-'*15)
        for _ in range(batchCount):
            # Get a random set of input noise and images
            noise = np.random.normal(0, 1, size=[batchSize, randomDim])
            imageBatch = X_train[np.random.randint(0, X_train.
shape[0], size=batchSize)]

            # Generate fake MNIST images
            generatedImages = generator.predict(noise)
            # print np.shape(imageBatch), np.shape(generatedImages)
            X = np.concatenate([imageBatch, generatedImages])

            # Labels for generated and real data
            yDis = np.zeros(2*batchSize)
            # One-sided label smoothing
            yDis[:batchSize] = 0.9
```

```
# Train discriminator
discriminator.trainable = True
dloss = discriminator.train_on_batch(X, yDis)
```

Now in the same `for` loop, we will train the generator. We want the images generated by the generator to be detected as real by the discriminator, so we use a random vector (noise) as input to the generator; this generates a fake image and then trains the GAN such that the discriminator perceives the image as real (output 1):

```
# Train generator
noise = np.random.normal(0, 1, size=[batchSize, randomDim])
yGen = np.ones(batchSize)
discriminator.trainable = False
gloss = gan.train_on_batch(noise, yGen)
```

Cool trick, right? If you wish to, you can save the generator and discriminator loss as well as the generated images. Next, we are saving the losses for each epoch and generating images after every 20 epochs:

```
# Store loss of most recent batch from this epoch
dLosses.append(dloss)
gLosses.append(gloss)

if e == 1 or e % 20 == 0:
        saveGeneratedImages(e)
```

We can now train the GAN by calling the GAN function. In the following graph, you can see the plot of both generative and discriminative loss as the GAN is learning:

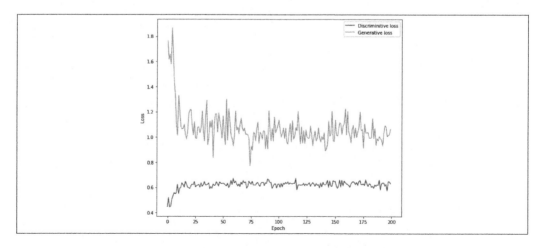

And handwritten digits generated by our GAN:

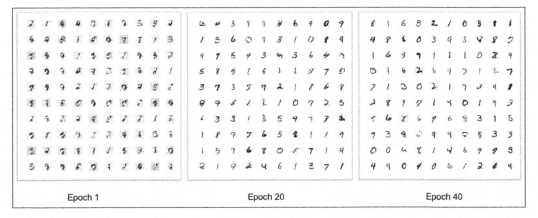

| Epoch 1 | Epoch 20 | Epoch 40 |

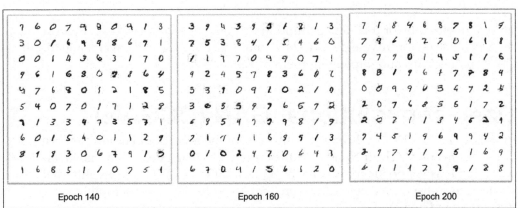

| Epoch 140 | Epoch 160 | Epoch 200 |

You can see from the preceding figures that as the epochs increase, the handwritten digits generated by the GAN become more and more realistic.

To plot the loss and the generated images of the handwritten digits, we define two helper functions, `plotLoss()` and `saveGeneratedImages()`. Their code is given as follows:

```
# Plot the loss from each batch
def plotLoss(epoch):
    plt.figure(figsize=(10, 8))
    plt.plot(dLosses, label='Discriminitive loss')
    plt.plot(gLosses, label='Generative loss')
    plt.xlabel('Epoch')
    plt.ylabel('Loss')
    plt.legend()
    plt.savefig('images/gan_loss_epoch_%d.png' % epoch)
```

```
# Create a wall of generated MNIST images
def saveGeneratedImages(epoch, examples=100, dim=(10, 10),
figsize=(10, 10)):
    noise = np.random.normal(0, 1, size=[examples, randomDim])
    generatedImages = generator.predict(noise)
    generatedImages = generatedImages.reshape(examples, 28, 28)

    plt.figure(figsize=figsize)
    for i in range(generatedImages.shape[0]):
        plt.subplot(dim[0], dim[1], i+1)
        plt.imshow(generatedImages[i], interpolation='nearest',
cmap='gray_r')
        plt.axis('off')
    plt.tight_layout()
    plt.savefig('images/gan_generated_image_epoch_%d.png' % epoch)
```

The complete code for this can be found in the notebook VanillaGAN.ipynb at the GitHub repo for this chapter. In the coming sections we will cover some recent GAN architectures and implement them in TensorFlow.

Deep convolutional GAN (DCGAN)

Proposed in 2016, DCGANs have become one of the most popular and successful GAN architectures. The main idea in the design was using convolutional layers without the use of pooling layers or the end classifier layers. The convolutional strides and transposed convolutions are employed for the downsampling and upsampling of images.

Before going into the details of the DCGAN architecture and its capabilities, let us point out the major changes that were introduced in the paper:

- The network consisted of all convolutional layers. The pooling layers were replaced by strided convolutions in the discriminator and transposed convolutions in the generator.

- The fully connected classifying layers after the convolutions are removed.

- To help with the gradient flow, batch normalization is done after every convolutional layer.

The basic idea of DCGANs is same as the vanilla GAN: we have a generator that takes in noise of 100 dimensions; the noise is projected and reshaped, and then is passed through convolutional layers. The following diagram shows the generator architecture:

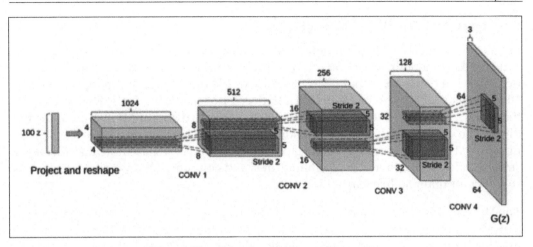

Figure 1: Visualizing the architecture of a generator

The discriminator network takes in the images (either generated by the generator or from the real dataset), and the images undergo convolution followed by batch normalization. At each convolution step the images get downsampled using strides. The final output of the convolutional layer is flattened and feeds a one-neuron classifier layer. In the following diagram, you can see the discriminator:

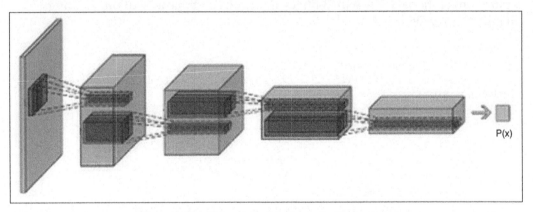

Figure 2: Visualizing the architecture of a discriminator

The generator and the discriminator are combined together to form the DCGAN. The training follows in the same manner as before; that is, we first train the discriminator on a mini-batch, then freeze the discriminator and train the generator. The process is repeated iteratively for a few thousand epochs. The authors found that we get more stable results with the Adam optimizer and a learning rate of 0.002.

Next, we'll implement a DCGAN for generating handwritten digits.

DCGAN for MNIST digits

Let us now build a DCGAN for generating handwritten digits. We first see the code for the generator. The generator is built by adding the layers sequentially. The first layer is a dense layer that takes the noise of 100 dimensions as an input. The 100-dimensional input is expanded to a flat vector of size $128 \times 7 \times 7$. This is done so that finally we get an output of size 28×28, the standard size of MNIST handwritten digits. The vector is reshaped to a tensor of size $7 \times 7 \times 128$. This vector is then upsampled using TensorFlow Keras UpSampling2D layer. Please note that this layer simply scales up the image by doubling rows and columns. The layer has no weights, so it is computationally cheap.

The Upsampling2D layer will now double the rows and columns of the $7 \times 7 \times 128$ (rows × columns × channels) image, yielding an output of size $14 \times 14 \times 128$. The upsampled image is passed to a convolutional layer. This convolutional layer learns to fill in the details in the upsampled image. The output of convolution is passed to batch normalization for better gradient flow. The batch normalized output then undergoes ReLU activation in all the intermediate layers. We repeat the structure, that is, upsampling | convolution | batch normalization | ReLU. In the following generator we have two such structures, the first with 128 filters, and the second with 64 filters in the convolution operation. The final output is obtained from a pure convolutional layer with 3 filters and tan hyperbolic activation, yielding an image of size $28 \times 28 \times 1$:

```
def build_generator(self):
    model = Sequential()
    model.add(Dense(128 * 7 * 7, activation="relu", input_dim=self.latent_dim))
    model.add(Reshape((7, 7, 128)))
    model.add(UpSampling2D())
    model.add(Conv2D(128, kernel_size=3, padding="same"))
    model.add(BatchNormalization(momentum=0.8))
    model.add(Activation("relu"))
    model.add(UpSampling2D())
    model.add(Conv2D(64, kernel_size=3, padding="same"))
    model.add(BatchNormalization(momentum=0.8))
    model.add(Activation("relu"))
    model.add(Conv2D(self.channels, kernel_size=3, padding="same"))
    model.add(Activation("tanh"))
    model.summary()
    noise = Input(shape=(self.latent_dim,))
    img = model(noise)
    return Model(noise, img)
```

The resultant generator model is as follows:

```
Model: "sequential_1"

Layer (type)                    Output Shape           Param #
=================================================================
dense_1 (Dense)                 (None, 6272)           633472

reshape (Reshape)               (None, 7, 7, 128)      0

up_sampling2d (UpSampling2D)    (None, 14, 14, 128)    0

conv2d_4 (Conv2D)               (None, 14, 14, 128)    147584

batch_normalization_v2_3 (Ba    (None, 14, 14, 128)    512

activation (Activation)         (None, 14, 14, 128)    0

up_sampling2d_1 (UpSampling2     (None, 28, 28, 128)    0

conv2d_5 (Conv2D)               (None, 28, 28, 64)     73792

batch_normalization_v2_4 (Ba    (None, 28, 28, 64)     256

activation_1 (Activation)       (None, 28, 28, 64)     0

conv2d_6 (Conv2D)               (None, 28, 28, 1)      577

activation_2 (Activation)       (None, 28, 28, 1)      0
=================================================================
Total params: 856,193
Trainable params: 855,809
Non-trainable params: 384
```

Figure 3: A summary of the resultant generator model

You can also experiment with the transposed convolution layer. This layer not only upsamples the input image but also learns how to fill in details during the training. Thus, you can replace upsampling and convolution layers with a single transposed convolution layer. The transpose convolutional layer performs an inverse convolution operation. You can read about it in more detail in the paper: *A guide to convolution arithmetic for deep learning* (https://arxiv.org/abs/1603.07285).

Now that we have a generator, let us see the code to build the discriminator. The discriminator is similar to a standard convolutional neural network but with one major change: instead of maxpooling we use convolutional layers with strides of 2. We also add dropout layers to avoid overfitting, and batch normalization for better accuracy and fast convergence. The activation layer is leaky ReLU. In the following network we use three such convolutional layers, with filters of 32, 64, and 128 respectively. The output of the third convolutional layer is flattened and fed to a dense layer with a single unit.

The output of this unit classifies the image as fake or real:

```
def build_discriminator(self):
model = Sequential()
model.add(Conv2D(32, kernel_size=3, strides=2, input_shape=self.img_
shape, padding="same"))
model.add(LeakyReLU(alpha=0.2))
model.add(Dropout(0.25))
model.add(Conv2D(64, kernel_size=3, strides=2, padding="same"))
model.add(ZeroPadding2D(padding=((0,1),(0,1))))
model.add(BatchNormalization(momentum=0.8))
model.add(LeakyReLU(alpha=0.2))
model.add(Dropout(0.25))
model.add(Conv2D(128, kernel_size=3, strides=2, padding="same"))
model.add(BatchNormalization(momentum=0.8))
model.add(LeakyReLU(alpha=0.2))
model.add(Dropout(0.25))
model.add(Conv2D(256, kernel_size=3, strides=1, padding="same"))
model.add(BatchNormalization(momentum=0.8))
model.add(LeakyReLU(alpha=0.2))
            model.add(Dropout(0.25))
model.add(Flatten())
model.add(Dense(1, activation='sigmoid'))
            model.summary()
            img = Input(shape=self.img_shape)
validity = model(img)
return Model(img, validity)
```

The resultant discriminator network is:

```
Model: "sequential"

Layer (type)                    Output Shape            Param #
=================================================================
conv2d (Conv2D)                 (None, 14, 14, 32)      320

leaky_re_lu (LeakyReLU)         (None, 14, 14, 32)      0

dropout (Dropout)               (None, 14, 14, 32)      0

conv2d_1 (Conv2D)               (None, 7, 7, 64)        18496

zero_padding2d (ZeroPadding2    (None, 8, 8, 64)        0

batch_normalization_v2 (Batc    (None, 8, 8, 64)        256

leaky_re_lu_1 (LeakyReLU)       (None, 8, 8, 64)        0

dropout_1 (Dropout)             (None, 8, 8, 64)        0

conv2d_2 (Conv2D)               (None, 4, 4, 128)       73856

batch_normalization_v2_1 (Ba    (None, 4, 4, 128)       512

leaky_re_lu_2 (LeakyReLU)       (None, 4, 4, 128)       0

dropout_2 (Dropout)             (None, 4, 4, 128)       0

conv2d_3 (Conv2D)               (None, 4, 4, 256)       295168

batch_normalization_v2_2 (Ba    (None, 4, 4, 256)       1024

leaky_re_lu_3 (LeakyReLU)       (None, 4, 4, 256)       0

dropout_3 (Dropout)             (None, 4, 4, 256)       0

flatten (Flatten)               (None, 4096)            0

dense (Dense)                   (None, 1)               4097
=================================================================
Total params: 393,729
Trainable params: 392,833
Non-trainable params: 896
```

Figure 4: A summary of resultant discriminator model

The complete GAN is made by combining the two:

```python
class DCGAN():
def __init__(self, rows, cols, channels, z = 100):
    # Input shape
    self.img_rows = rows
    self.img_cols = cols
    self.channels = channels
    self.img_shape = (self.img_rows, self.img_cols, self.channels)
    self.latent_dim = z

    optimizer = Adam(0.0002, 0.5)

    # Build and compile the discriminator
    self.discriminator = self.build_discriminator()
    self.discriminator.compile(loss='binary_crossentropy',
        optimizer=optimizer,
        metrics=['accuracy'])

    # Build the generator
    self.generator = self.build_generator()

    # The generator takes noise as input and generates imgs
    z = Input(shape=(self.latent_dim,))
    img = self.generator(z)

    # For the combined model we will only train the generator
    self.discriminator.trainable = False

    # The discriminator takes generated images as input and
    # determines validity
    valid = self.discriminator(img)

    # The combined model  (stacked generator and discriminator)
    # Trains the generator to fool the discriminator
    self.combined = Model(z, valid)
    self.combined.compile(loss='binary_crossentropy',
optimizer=optimizer)
```

The GAN is trained in the same manner as before; first random noise is fed to the generator. The output of the generator is added with real images to initially train the discriminator, and then the generator is trained to give an image that can fool the discriminator. The process is repeated for the next batch of images. The GAN takes between a few hundred to thousands of epochs to train:

```python
def train(self, epochs, batch_size=128, save_interval=50):

    # Load the dataset
    (X_train, _), (_, _) = mnist.load_data()

    # Rescale -1 to 1
    X_train = X_train / 127.5 - 1.
    X_train = np.expand_dims(X_train, axis=3)

    # Adversarial ground truths
    valid = np.ones((batch_size, 1))
    fake = np.zeros((batch_size, 1))

    for epoch in range(epochs):

        # ---------------------
        #  Train Discriminator
        # ---------------------

        # Select a random half of images
        idx = np.random.randint(0, X_train.shape[0], batch_size)
        imgs = X_train[idx]

        # Sample noise and generate a batch of new images
        noise = np.random.normal(0, 1, (batch_size, self.latent_dim))
        gen_imgs = self.generator.predict(noise)

        # Train the discriminator (real classified as ones
        # and generated as zeros)
        d_loss_real = self.discriminator.train_on_batch(imgs, valid)
        d_loss_fake = self.discriminator.train_on_batch(gen_imgs, fake)
        d_loss = 0.5 * np.add(d_loss_real, d_loss_fake)

        # ---------------------
        #  Train Generator
        # ---------------------

        # Train the generator (wants discriminator to mistake
        # images as real)
        g_loss = self.combined.train_on_batch(noise, valid)

        # Plot the progress
    print ("%d [D loss: %f, acc.: %.2f%%] [G loss: %f]" % (epoch, d_
loss[0], 100*d_loss[1], g_loss))
```

```
# If at save interval => save generated image samples
if epoch % save_interval == 0:
                   self.save_imgs(epoch)
```

Lastly, we need a helper function to save images:

```
def save_imgs(self, epoch):
    r, c = 5, 5
    noise = np.random.normal(0, 1, (r * c, self.latent_dim))
    gen_imgs = self.generator.predict(noise)

    # Rescale images 0 - 1
    gen_imgs = 0.5 * gen_imgs + 0.5

    fig, axs = plt.subplots(r, c)
    cnt = 0
    for i in range(r):
        for j in range(c):
            axs[i,j].imshow(gen_imgs[cnt, :,:,0], cmap='gray')
            axs[i,j].axis('off')
            cnt += 1
    fig.savefig("images/dcgan_mnist_%d.png" % epoch)
    plt.close()
```

Let us now train our GAN:

```
dcgan = DCGAN(28,28,1)
dcgan.train(epochs=4000, batch_size=32, save_interval=50)
```

The images generated by our GAN as it learned to fake handwritten digits are:

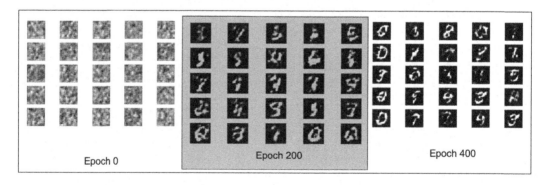

The preceding images were the initial attempts by the GAN. As it learned through the following 5000 epochs, the quality of digits generated improved manyfold:

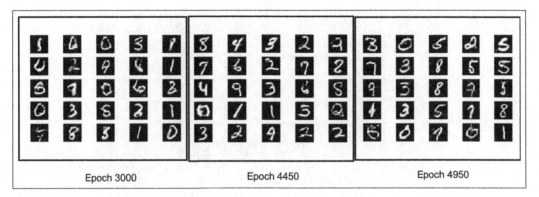

Epoch 3000   Epoch 4450   Epoch 4950

The complete code is available in DCGAN.ipynb in the GitHub repo. We can take the concepts discussed here and apply them to images in other domains. One of the interesting work on images was reported in the paper, *Unsupervised Representation Learning with Deep Convolutional Generative Adversarial Networks*, Alec Radford, Luke Metz, Soumith Chintala, 2015. Quoting the abstract:

"In recent years, supervised learning with convolutional networks (CNNs) has seen huge adoption in computer vision applications. Comparatively, unsupervised learning with CNNs has received less attention. In this work we hope to help bridge the gap between the success of CNNs for supervised learning and unsupervised learning. We introduce a class of CNNs called deep convolutional generative adversarial networks (DCGANs), that have certain architectural constraints, and demonstrate that they are a strong candidate for unsupervised learning. Training on various image datasets, we show convincing evidence that our deep convolutional adversarial pair learns a hierarchy of representations from object parts to scenes in both the generator and discriminator. Additionally, we use the learned features for novel tasks - demonstrating their applicability as general image representations."(Radford et al., 2015).

Following are some of the interesting results of applying DCGANs to a celebrity image dataset:

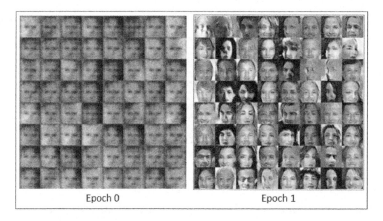

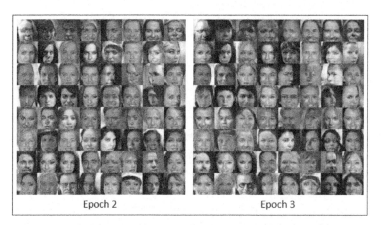

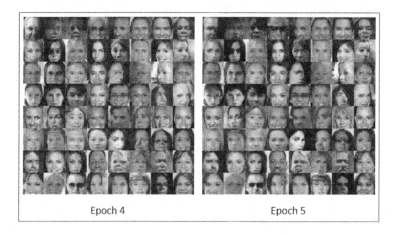

Another interesting paper is *Semantic Image Inpainting with Perceptual and Contextual Losses*, by Raymond A. Yeh et al. in 2016. Just as content-aware fill is a tool used by photographers to fill in unwanted or missing part of images, in this paper they used a DCGAN for image completion.

As mentioned earlier, a lot of research is happening around GANs. In the next section we will explore some of the interesting GAN architectures proposed in recent years.

Some interesting GAN architectures

Since their inception a lot of interest has been generated in GANs, and as a result we are seeing a lot of modifications and experimentation with GAN training, architecture, and applications. In this section we will explore some interesting GANs proposed in recent years.

SRGAN

Remember seeing a crime-thriller where our hero asks the computer-guy to magnify the faded image of the crime scene? With the zoom we are able to see the criminal's face in detail, including the weapon used and anything engraved upon it! Well, Super Resolution GANs (SRGANs) can perform similar magic.

Here a GAN is trained in such a way that it can generate a photorealistic high-resolution image when given a low-resolution image. The SRGAN architecture consists of three neural networks: a very deep generator network (which uses Residual modules; for reference see ResNets in *Chapter 5, Advanced Convolutional Neural Networks*), a discriminator network, and a pretrained VGG-16 network.

SRGANs use the perceptual loss function (developed by Johnson et al, you can find the link to the paper in the *References* section). The difference in the feature map activations in high layers of a VGG network between the network output part and the high-resolution part comprises the perceptual loss function. Besides perceptual loss, the authors further added content loss and an adversarial loss so that images generated look more natural and the finer details more artistic. The perceptual loss is defined as the weighted sum of content loss and adversarial loss:

$$l^{SR} = l_X^{SR} + 10^{-3} \times l_{Gen}^{SR}$$

The first term on the right-hand side is the content loss, obtained using the feature maps generated by pretrained VGG 19. Mathematically it is the Euclidean distance between the feature map of the reconstructed image (that is, the one generated by the generator) and the original high-resolution reference image.

The second term on the RHS is the adversarial loss. It is the standard generative loss term, designed to ensure that images generated by the generator are able to fool the discriminator. You can see in the following figure taken from the original paper that the image generated by the SRGAN is much closer to the original high-resolution image:

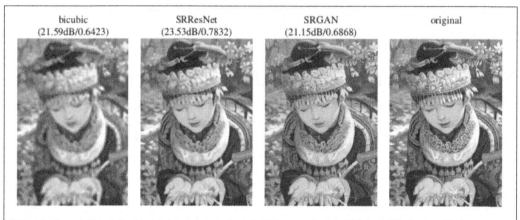

| bicubic (21.59dB/0.6423) | SRResNet (23.53dB/0.7832) | SRGAN (21.15dB/0.6868) | original |

Figure 2: From left to right: bicubic interpolation, deep residual network optimized for MSE, deep residual generative adversarial network optimized for a loss more sensitive to human perception, original HR image. Corresponding PSNR and SSIM are shown in brackets. [4× upscaling]

Another noteworthy architecture is CycleGAN; proposed in 2017, it can perform the task of image translation. Once trained you can translate an image from one domain to another domain. For example, when trained on a horse and zebra dataset, if you give it an image with horses in the foreground, the CycleGAN can convert the horses to zebra with the same background. We explore it next.

CycleGAN

Have you ever imagined how some scenery would look if Van Gogh or Manet had painted it? We have many scenes and landscapes painted by Gogh/Manet, but we do not have any collection of input-output pairs. A CycleGAN performs the image translation, that is, transfers an image given in one domain (scenery for example) to another domain (a Van Gogh painting of the same scene, for instance) in the absence of training examples. The CycleGAN's ability to perform image translation in the absence of training pairs is what makes it unique.

To achieve image translation the authors used a very simple and yet effective procedure. They made use of two GANs, the generator of each GAN performing the image translation from one domain to another.

To elaborate, let us say the input is X, then the generator of the first GAN performs a mapping $G: X \rightarrow Y$; thus its output would be $Y = G(X)$. The generator of the second GAN performs an inverse mapping $F: Y \rightarrow X$, resulting in $X = F(Y)$. Each discriminator is trained to distinguish between real images and synthesized images. The idea is shown as follows:

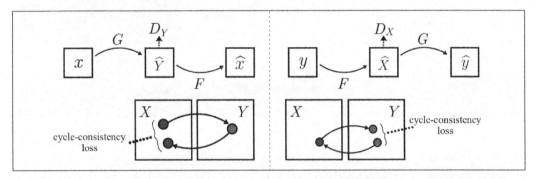

To train the combined GANs, the authors added, besides the conventional GAN adversarial loss, a forward cycle consistency loss (left figure) and a backward cycle consistency loss (right figure). This ensures that if an image X is given as input, then after the two translations $F(G(X)) \sim X$ the obtained image is the same, X (similarly the backward cycle consistency loss ensures that? $G(F(Y)) \sim Y$).

Following are some of the successful image translations by CycleGANs:

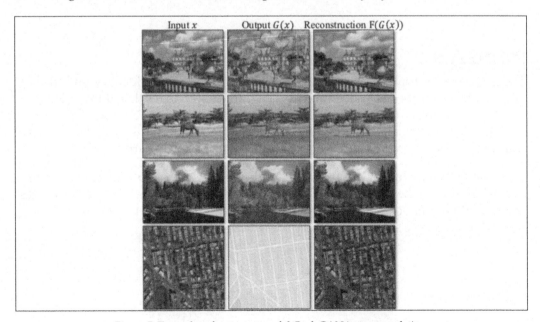

Figure 5: Examples of some successful CycleGAN image translations

Following are a few more examples; you can see the translation of seasons (summer → winter), photo → painting and vice versa, and horses → zebras and vice versa:

Figure 6: Further examples of CycleGAN translations

Later in the chapter we will also explore a TensorFlow implementation of CycleGANs. Next we talk about the InfoGAN, a conditional GAN where the GAN not only generates an image, but you also have a control variable to control the images generated.

InfoGAN

The GAN architectures that we have considered up to now provide us with little or no control over the generated images. The InfoGAN changes this; it provides control over various attributes of the images generated. The InfoGAN uses the concepts from information theory such that the noise term is transformed into latent code that provides predictable and systematic control over the output.

The generator in an InfoGAN takes two inputs: the latent space Z and a latent code c, thus the output of the generator is $G(Z,c)$. The GAN is trained such that it maximizes the mutual information between the latent code c and the generated image $G(Z,c)$. The following figure shows the architecture of the InfoGAN:

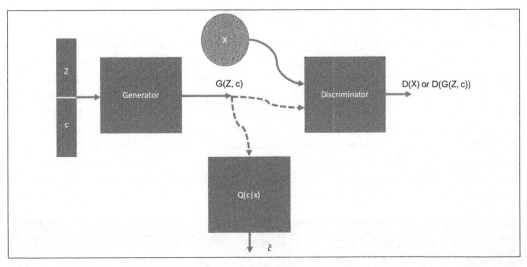

Figure 7: The architecture of the InfoGAN, visualized

The concatenated vector *(Z,c)* is fed to the generator. *Q(c | X)* is also a neural network. Combined with the generator it works to form a mapping between random noise Z and its latent code *c_hat*. It aims to estimate *c* given *X*. This is achieved by adding a regularization term to the objective function of the conventional GAN:

$$min_D max_G V_1(D, G) = V_G(D, G) - \lambda 1(c; G(Z, c))$$

The term $V_G(D,G)$ is the loss function of the conventional GAN, and the second term is the regularization term, where λ is a constant. Its value was set to 1 in the paper, and $I(c;G(Z,c))$ is the mutual information between the latent code *c* and the generator-generated image *G(Z,c)*.

Following are the exciting results of the InfoGAN on the MNIST dataset:

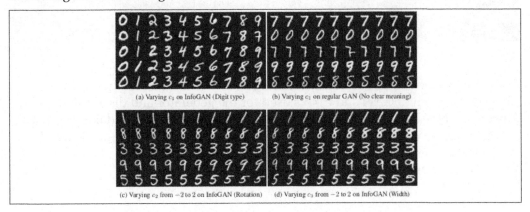

(a) Varying c_1 on InfoGAN (Digit type)   (b) Varying c_1 on regular GAN (No clear meaning)

(c) Varying c_2 from −2 to 2 on InfoGAN (Rotation)   (d) Varying c_3 from −2 to 2 on InfoGAN (Width)

Figure 8: Results of using the InfoGAN on the MNIST dataset

Cool applications of GANs

We have seen that the generator can learn how to forge data. This means that it learns how to create new synthetic data that is created by the network that appears to be authentic and human-made. Before going into the details of some GAN code, we would like to share the results of a recent paper [6] (code is available online at `https://github.com/hanzhanggit/StackGAN`) where a GAN has been used to synthesize forged images starting from a text description. The results are impressive: the first column is the real image in the test set and all the rest of the columns are the images generated from the same text description by Stage-I and Stage-II of StackGAN. More examples are available on YouTube (`https://www.youtube.com/watch?v=SuRyL5vhCIM&feature=youtu.be`):

Figure 9: Image generation of birds, using GANs

Figure 10: Image generation of flowers, using GANs

Now let us see how a GAN can learn to "forge" the MNIST dataset. In this case it is a combination of GAN and CNNs used for the generator and discriminator networks. At the beginning the generator creates nothing understandable, but after a few iterations synthetic forged numbers are progressively clearer and clearer. In this image the panels are ordered by increasing training epochs and you can see the quality improving among the panels:

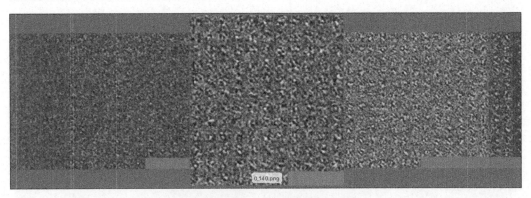

Figure 11: Illegible initial outputs of the GAN

Figure 12: Improved outputs of the GAN, following further iterations

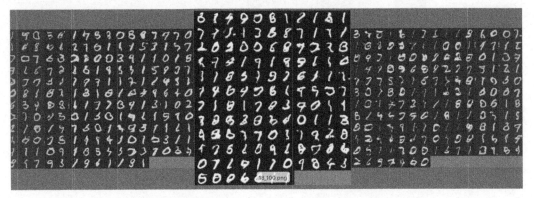

Figure 13: Final outputs of the GAN, showing significant improvement from previous iterations

One of the coolest uses of GANs is doing arithmetic on faces in the generator's vector Z. In other words, if we stay in the space of synthetic forged images, it is possible to see things like this: [smiling woman] - [neutral woman] + [neutral man] = [smiling man], or like this: [man with glasses] - [man without glasses] + [woman without glasses] = [woman with glasses]. This was shown in the paper *Unsupervised Representation Learning with Deep Convolutional Generative Adversarial Networks* by Alec Radford and his colleagues in 2015. All images in this work are generated by a version of GAN. They are NOT REAL. The full paper is available here: `http://arxiv.org/abs/1511.06434`. Following are some examples from the paper. The authors also share their code in this GitHub repo: `https://github.com/Newmu/dcgan_code`:

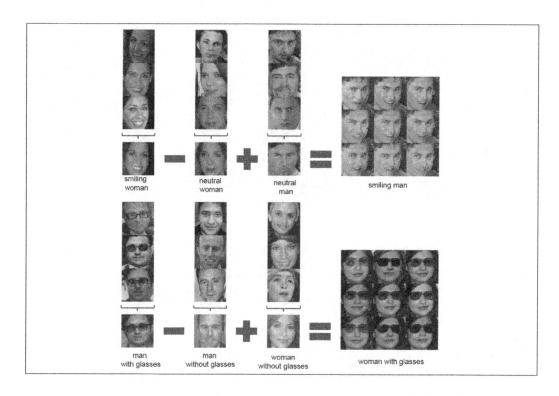

Bedrooms: Generated bedrooms after five epochs of training:

Album covers: These images are generated by the GAN, but look like authentic album covers:

CycleGAN in TensorFlow 2.0

In the last section of this chapter we will implement a CycleGAN in TensorFlow 2.0. The CycleGAN requires a special dataset, a paired dataset, from one domain of images to another domain. So, besides the necessary modules, we will use `tensorflow_datasets` as well:

```python
import tensorflow as tf
from tensorflow.keras import Model
from tensorflow.keras.losses import mean_squared_error, mean_absolute_
error

import os
import time
import matplotlib.pyplot as plt
import numpy as np
import tensorflow_datasets as tfds
```

TensorFlow's `Dataset` API contains a list of datasets. It has many paired datasets for CycleGANs, such as horse to zebra, apples to oranges, and so on. You can access the complete list here: `https://www.tensorflow.org/datasets/catalog/cycle_gan`. For our code we will be using `summer2winter_yosemite`, which contains images of Yosemite (USA) in summer (Dataset A) and winter (Dataset B). We will train the CycleGAN to convert an input image of summer to winter and vice versa. Let us load the data and get train and test images:

```python
dataset, metadata = tfds.load('cycle_gan/summer2winter_yosemite',
with_info=True, as_supervised=True)
train_A, train_B = dataset['trainA'], dataset['trainB']
test_A, test_B = dataset['testA'], dataset['testB']
```

We need to set some hyperparameters:

```python
BUFFER_SIZE = 1000
BATCH_SIZE = 1
IMG_WIDTH = 256
IMG_HEIGHT = 256
EPOCHS = 50
AUTOTUNE = tf.data.experimental.AUTOTUNE
```

The images need to be normalized before we train the network. For better performance you can even add jitter to the images:

```
def normalize(input_image, label):
    input_image = tf.cast(input_image, tf.float32)
    input_image = (input_image / 127.5) - 1
    return input_image
```

The preceding function when applied to images will normalize them in the range [-1,1]. Let us apply this to our train and test datasets and create a data generator that will provide images for training in batches:

```
train_A = train_A.map(normalize, num_parallel_calls=AUTOTUNE).cache().
shuffle(BUFFER_SIZE).batch(BATCH_SIZE)
train_B = train_B.map(normalize, num_parallel_calls=AUTOTUNE).cache().
shuffle(BUFFER_SIZE).batch(BATCH_SIZE)
test_A = test_A.map(normalize, num_parallel_calls=AUTOTUNE).cache().
shuffle(BUFFER_SIZE).batch(BATCH_SIZE)
test_B = test_B.map(normalize, num_parallel_calls=AUTOTUNE).cache().
shuffle(BUFFER_SIZE).batch(BATCH_SIZE)
```

In the preceding code the argument num_parallel_calls allows one to take benefit from multiple CPU cores in the system, one should set its value to the number of CPU cores in your system. If you are not sure, use the AUTOTUNE = tf.data. experimental.AUTOTUNE value so that TensorFlow dynamically determines the right number for you.

Before moving ahead with the model definition, let us see the images. Each image is processed before plotting so that its intensity is normal:

```
inpA = next(iter(train_A))
inpB = next(iter(train_B))
plt.subplot(121)
plt.title("Train Set A")
plt.imshow(inpA[0]*0.5 + 0.5)
plt.subplot(122)
plt.title("Train Set B")
plt.imshow(inpB[0]*0.5 + 0.5)
```

To construct the generator and discriminator we will require three sub modules: the upsampling layer, which will take in an image and perform a transpose convolution operation; a downsampling layer, which will perform the convention convolutional operation, and a residual layer so that we can have a sufficiently deep model. These layers are defined in the functions `downsample()`, `upsample()`, and class based on the TensorFlow Keras Model API `ResnetIdentityBlock`. You can see the finer implementation details of these functions in the GitHub repo notebook `CycleGAN_TF2.ipynb`.

Let us now build our generator:

```
def Generator():
    down_stack = [
        downsample(64, 4, apply_batchnorm=False),
        downsample(128, 4),
        downsample(256, 4),
        downsample(512, 4)
    ]

    up_stack = [
        upsample(256, 4),
        upsample(128, 4),
        upsample(64, 4),
    ]
```

```
initializer = tf.random_normal_initializer(0., 0.02)
last = tf.keras.layers.Conv2DTranspose(3, 4,
                                strides=2,
                                padding='same',
                                kernel_initializer=initializer,
                                activation='tanh')


inputs = tf.keras.layers.Input(shape=[256, 256, 3])
x = inputs

# Downsampling through the model
skips = []
for down in down_stack:
    x = down(x)
    skips.append(x)

for block in resnet:
    x = block(x)

skips = reversed(skips[:-1])

# Upsampling and establishing the skip connections
for up, skip in zip(up_stack, skips):
    concat = tf.keras.layers.Concatenate()
    x = up(x)
    x = concat([x, skip])

x = last(x)
return tf.keras.Model(inputs=inputs, outputs=x)
```

Let us see the generator in graph form:

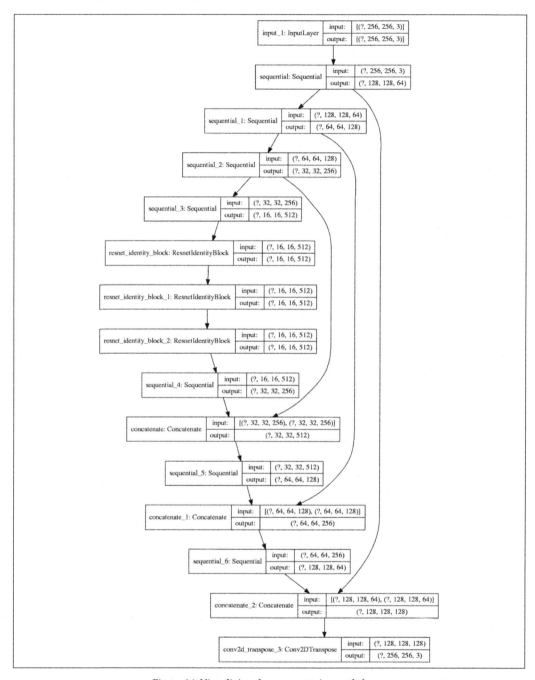

Figure 14: Visualizing the generator in graph form

Cool, right? Now we can define the discriminator too. We are following the same architecture of discriminator and discriminator as in the paper by Zhu et al. Following is the generator and its corresponding graph plot:

```
def Discriminator():
    inputs = tf.keras.layers.Input(shape=[None,None,3])
    x = inputs
    g_filter = 64

    down_stack = [
        downsample(g_filter),
        downsample(g_filter * 2),
        downsample(g_filter * 4),
        downsample(g_filter * 8),
    ]

    for down in down_stack:
        x = down(x)

    last = tf.keras.layers.Conv2D(1, 4, strides=1, padding='same') #
(bs, 30, 30, 1)
    x = last(x)

    return tf.keras.Model(inputs=inputs, outputs=x)
```

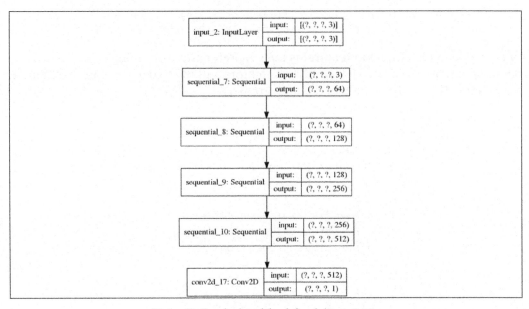

Figure 15: Graph plot of the defined discriminator

Now using the preceding defined generator and discriminator, we construct the CycleGAN:

```
discriminator_A = Discriminator()
discriminator_B = Discriminator()

generator_AB = Generator()
generator_BA = Generator()
```

We next define the loss and optimizers:

```
loss_object = tf.keras.losses.BinaryCrossentropy(from_logits=True)
@tf.function
def discriminator_loss(disc_real_output, disc_generated_output):
    real_loss = loss_object(tf.ones_like(disc_real_output), disc_real_
output)
    generated_loss = loss_object(tf.zeros_like(disc_generated_output),
disc_generated_output)
    total_disc_loss = real_loss + generated_loss
    return total_disc_loss

optimizer = tf.keras.optimizers.Adam(1e-4, beta_1=0.5)
discriminator_optimizer = tf.keras.optimizers.Adam(1e-4, beta_1=0.5)
```

We create placeholders for the labels of real and fake images:

```
valid = np.ones((BATCH_SIZE, 16, 16, 1)).astype('float32')
fake = np.zeros((BATCH_SIZE, 16, 16, 1)).astype('float32')
```

Now we define the function that trains the generator and discriminator in a batch, a pair of images at a time. The two discriminators and the two generators are trained via this function with the help of the tape gradient:

```
@tf.function
def train_batch(imgs_A, imgs_B):
    with tf.GradientTape() as g, tf.GradientTape() as d_tape:
        fake_B = generator_AB(imgs_A, training=True)
        fake_A = generator_BA(imgs_B, training=True)

        logits_real_A = discriminator_A(imgs_A, training=True)
        logits_fake_A = discriminator_A(fake_A, training=True)
        dA_loss = discriminator_loss(logits_real_A, logits_fake_A)

        logits_real_B = discriminator_B(imgs_B, training=True)
        logits_fake_B = discriminator_B(fake_B, training=True)
        dB_loss = discriminator_loss(logits_real_B, logits_fake_B)
```

```
        d_loss = (dA_loss + dB_loss) / 2
        # Translate images back to original domain
        reconstr_A = generator_BA(fake_B, training=True)
        reconstr_B = generator_AB(fake_A, training=True)

        id_A = generator_BA(imgs_A, training=True)
        id_B = generator_AB(imgs_B, training=True)


        gen_loss = tf.math.reduce_sum([
            1 * tf.math.reduce_mean(mean_squared_error(logits_fake_A,
valid)),
            1 * tf.math.reduce_mean(mean_squared_error(logits_fake_B,
valid)),
            10 * tf.math.reduce_mean(mean_squared_error(reconstr_A,
imgs_A)),
            10 * tf.math.reduce_mean(mean_squared_error(reconstr_B,
imgs_B)),
            0.1 * tf.math.reduce_mean(mean_squared_error(id_A,
imgs_A)),
            0.1 * tf.math.reduce_mean(mean_squared_error(id_B,
imgs_B)),
            ])

    gradients_of_d = d_tape.gradient(d_loss, discriminator_A.
trainable_variables + discriminator_B.trainable_variables)
    discriminator_optimizer.apply_gradients(zip(gradients_of_d,
discriminator_A.trainable_variables + discriminator_B.trainable_
variables))

    gradients_of_generator = g.gradient(gen_loss, generator_
AB.trainable_variables + generator_BA.trainable_variables)
    optimizer.apply_gradients(zip(gradients_of_generator, generator_
AB.trainable_variables + generator_BA.trainable_variables))

    return dA_loss, dB_loss, gen_loss
```

We define checkpoints to save the model weights:

```
checkpoint_dird_A = './training_checkpointsd_A'
checkpoint_prefixd_A = os.path.join(checkpoint_dird_A, "ckpt_{epoch}")

checkpoint_dird_B = './training_checkpointsd_B'
checkpoint_prefixd_B = os.path.join(checkpoint_dird_B, "ckpt_{epoch}")

checkpoint_dirg_AB = './training_checkpointsg_AB'
```

```
checkpoint_prefixg_AB = os.path.join(checkpoint_dirg_AB, "ckpt_
{epoch}")

checkpoint_dirg_BA = './training_checkpointsg_BA'
checkpoint_prefixg_BA = os.path.join(checkpoint_dirg_BA, "ckpt_
{epoch}")
```

Let us now combine it all and train the network for 50 epochs. Please remember that in the paper, the test network was trained for 200 epochs, so our results will not be that good:

```python
def train(trainA_, trainB_, epochs):
    for epoch in range(epochs):
        start = time.time()

        for batch_i, (imgs_A, imgs_B) in enumerate(zip(trainA_,
trainB_)):
            dA_loss, dB_loss, g_loss = train_batch(imgs_A, imgs_B)

            if batch_i % 1000 == 0:
                test_imgA = next(iter(test_A))
                test_imgB = next(iter(test_B))
                print ('Time taken for epoch {} batch index {} is {}
seconds\n'.format(epoch, batch_i, time.time()-start))
                print("discriminator A: ", dA_loss.numpy())
                print("discriminator B: ", dB_loss.numpy())
                print("generator: {}\n".format(g_loss))

                fig, axs = plt.subplots(2, 2, figsize=(10, 10),
sharey=True, sharex=True)
                gen_outputA = generator_AB(test_imgA, training=False)
                gen_outputB = generator_BA(test_imgB, training=False)
                axs[0,0].imshow(test_imgA[0]*0.5 + 0.5)
                axs[0,0].set_title("Generator A Input")
                axs[0,1].imshow(gen_outputA[0]*0.5 + 0.5)
                axs[0,1].set_title("Generator A Output")
                axs[1,0].imshow(test_imgB[0]*0.5 + 0.5)
                axs[1,0].set_title("Generator B Input")
                axs[1,1].imshow(gen_outputB[0]*0.5 + 0.5)
                axs[1,1].set_title("Generator B Output")
                plt.show()

                discriminator_A.save_weights(checkpoint_prefixd_A.
format(epoch=epoch))
                discriminator_B.save_weights(checkpoint_prefixd_B.
format(epoch=epoch))
```

```
                generator_AB.save_weights(checkpoint_prefixg_
AB.format(epoch=epoch))
                generator_BA.save_weights(checkpoint_prefixg_
BA.format(epoch=epoch))
```

You can see some of the images generated by our CycleGAN. Generator *A* takes in summer photos and converts them to winter, while generator *B* takes in winter photos and converts them to summer:

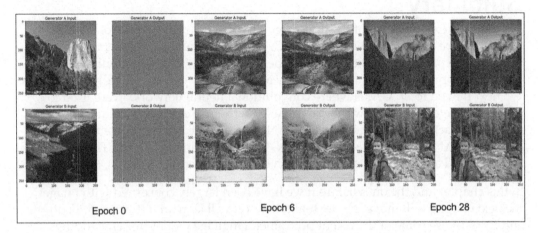

And following are some after the network is trained:

We suggest you experiment with other datasets in the TensorFlow CycleGAN datasets. Some will be easy like apples and oranges, but some will require much more training. The authors also maintain a GitHub repo where they have shared their own implementation in PyTorch along with the links to implementations in other frameworks including TensorFlow: `https://github.com/junyanz/CycleGAN`.

Summary

This chapter explored one of the most exciting deep neural networks of our times: GANs. Unlike discriminative networks, GANs have an ability to generate images based on the probability distribution of the input space. We started with the first GAN model proposed by Ian Goodfellow and used it to generate handwritten digits. We next moved to DCGANs where convolutional neural networks were used to generate images and we saw the remarkable pictures of celebrities, bedrooms, and even album artwork generated by DCGANs. Finally, the chapter delved into some awesome GAN architectures: the SRGAN, CycleGAN, and InfoGAN. The chapter also included an implementation of the CycleGAN in TensorFlow 2.0.

In this chapter and the ones before it we have been largely concerned with images; the next chapter will move into textual data. You will learn about word embeddings and learn to use some of the recent pretrained language models for embeddings.

References

1. Goodfellow, Ian J. *On Distinguishability Criteria for Estimating Generative Models*. arXiv preprint arXiv:1412.6515 (2014). (`https://arxiv.org/pdf/1412.6515.pdf`)

2. Dumoulin, Vincent, and Francesco Visin. *A guide to convolution arithmetic for deep learning*. arXiv preprint arXiv:1603.07285 (2016). (`https://arxiv.org/abs/1603.07285`)

3. Salimans, Tim, et al. *Improved Techniques for Training GANs*. Advances in neural information processing systems. 2016. (`http://papers.nips.cc/paper/6125-improved-techniques-for-training-gans.pdf`)

4. Johnson, Justin, Alexandre Alahi, and Li Fei-Fei. *Perceptual Losses for Real-Time Style Transfer and Super-Resolution*. European conference on computer vision. Springer, Cham, 2016. (`https://arxiv.org/abs/1603.08155`)

5. Radford, Alec, Luke Metz, and Soumith Chintala. *Unsupervised Representation Learning with Deep Convolutional Generative Adversarial Networks*. arXiv preprint arXiv:1511.06434 (2015). (`https://arxiv.org/abs/1511.06434`)

6. Ledig, Christian, et al. *Photo-Realistic Single Image Super-Resolution Using a Generative Adversarial Network.* Proceedings of the IEEE conference on computer vision and pattern recognition. 2017.(`http://openaccess.thecvf.com/content_cvpr_2017/papers/Ledig_Photo-Realistic_Single_Image_CVPR_2017_paper.pdf`)

7. Zhu, Jun-Yan, et al. *Unpaired Image-to-Image Translation using Cycle-Consistent Adversarial Networks.* Proceedings of the IEEE international conference on computer vision. 2017.(`http://openaccess.thecvf.com/content_ICCV_2017/papers/Zhu_Unpaired_Image-To-Image_Translation_ICCV_2017_paper.pdf`)

8. Chen, Xi, et al. *InfoGAN: Interpretable Representation Learning by Information Maximizing Generative Adversarial Nets.* Advances in neural information processing systems. 2016.(`https://arxiv.org/abs/1606.03657`)

7
Word Embeddings

In the last few chapters, we talked about convolutional networks and GANs, which have been very successful against image data. Over the next few chapters, we will switch tracks to focus on strategies and networks to handle text data.

In this chapter, we will first look at the idea behind word embeddings, and then cover the two earliest implementations – Word2Vec and GloVe. We will learn how to build word embeddings from scratch using gensim on our own corpus, and navigate the embedding space we created.

We will also learn how to use third party embeddings as a starting point for our own NLP tasks, such as spam detection, that is, learning to automatically detect unsolicited and unwanted emails. We will then learn about various ways to leverage the idea of word embeddings for unrelated tasks, such as constructing an embedded space for making item recommendations.

We will then look at extensions to these foundational word embedding techniques that have occurred in the last couple of decades since Word2Vec – adding syntactic similarity with fastText, adding the effect of context using neural networks such as ELMo and Google Universal Sentence Encoder, sentence encodings such as InferSent and SkipThoughts, and the introduction of language models such as ULMFit and BERT.

Word embedding – origins and fundamentals

Wikipedia defines word embedding as the collective name for a set of language modeling and feature learning techniques in **natural language processing** (NLP) where words or phrases from a vocabulary are mapped to vectors of real numbers.

Deep learning models, like other machine learning models, typically don't work directly with text; the text needs to be converted to numbers instead. The process of converting text to numbers is a process called vectorization. An early technique for vectorizing words was one-hot encoding, which you have learned about in *Chapter 1, Neural Network Foundations with TensorFlow 2.0*. As you will recall, a major problem with one-hot encoding is that it treats each word as completely independent from all the others, since similarity between any two words (measured by the dot product of the two-word vectors) is always zero.

The dot product is an algebraic operation that operates on two vectors a = [a_1, ..., a_N] and b = [b_1,..., b_N] of equal length and returns a number. It is also known as the inner product or scalar product:

$$a\ b = \sum_{i=1}^{N} a_i b_i = a_i b_i + \cdots + a_N b_N$$

Why is the dot product of one-hot vectors of two words always 0? Consider two words w_i and w_j. Assuming a vocabulary size of V, their corresponding one-hot vectors are a zero vector of rank V with positions i and j set to 1. When combined using the dot product operation, the 1 in a[i] is multiplied by 0 in b[j], and 1 in b[j] is multiplied by 0 in a[j], and all other elements in both vectors are 0, so the resulting dot product is also 0.

To overcome the limitations of one-hot encoding, the NLP community has borrowed techniques from **Information Retrieval** (**IR**) to vectorize text using the document as the context. Notable techniques are **Term Frequency-Inverse Document Frequency** (**TF-IDF**) [36], **Latent Semantic Analysis** (**LSA**) [37], and topic modeling [38]. These representations attempt to capture a document centric idea of semantic similarity between words. Of these, one-hot and TF-IDF are relatively sparse embeddings, since vocabularies are usually quite large, and a word is unlikely to occur in more than a few documents in the corpus.

Development of word embedding techniques began around 2000. These techniques differ from previous IR-based techniques in that they use neighboring words as their context, leading to a more natural semantic similarity from a human understanding perspective. Today, word embedding is a foundational technique for all kinds of NLP tasks, such as text classification, document clustering, part of speech tagging, named entity recognition, sentiment analysis, and many more. Word embeddings result in dense, low-dimensional vectors, and along with LSA and topic models can be thought of as a vector of latent features for the word.

Word embeddings are based on the distributional hypothesis, which states that words that occur in similar contexts tend to have similar meanings. Hence the class of word embedding-based encodings are also known as distributed representations, which we will talk about next.

Distributed representations

Distributed representations attempt to capture the meaning of a word by considering its relations with other words in its context. The idea behind the distributed hypothesis is captured in this quote from J. R. Firth, a linguist who first proposed this idea:

> *"You shall know a word by the company it keeps."*

How does this work? By way of example, consider the following pair of sentences:

Paris is the capital of France.

Berlin is the capital of Germany.

Even assuming no knowledge of world geography, the sentence pair implies some sort of relationship between the entities Paris, France, Berlin, and Germany that could be represented as:

"Paris" is to "France" as "Berlin" is to "Germany"

Distributed representations are based on the idea that there exists some transformation ϕ such that:

$$\phi("Paris") - \phi("France") \approx \phi("Berlin") - \phi("Germany")$$

In other words, a distributed embedding space is one where words that are used in similar contexts are close to one another. Therefore, similarity between the word vectors in this space would roughly correspond to the semantic similarity between the words.

Figure 1 shows a TensorBoard visualization of word embedding of words around the word "important" in the embedding space. As you can see, the neighbors of the word tend to be closely related, or interchangeable with the original word.

For example, "crucial" is virtually a synonym, and it is easy to see how the words "historical" or "valuable" could be substituted in certain situations:

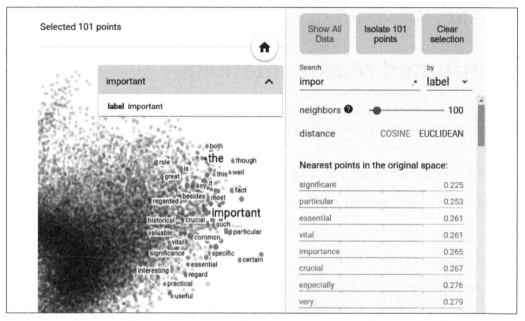

Figure 1: Visualization of nearest neighbors of the word "important" in a word embedding dataset, from the TensorFlow Embedding Guide (https://www.tensorflow.org/guide/embedding)

In the next section we will look at various types of distributed representations (or word embeddings).

Static embeddings

Static embeddings are the oldest type of word embedding. The embeddings are generated against a large corpus but the number of words, though large, is finite. You can think of a static embedding as a dictionary, with words as the keys and their corresponding vector as the value. If you have a word whose embedding needs to be looked up that was not in the original corpus, then you are out of luck. In addition, a word has the same embedding regardless of how it is used, so static embeddings cannot address the problem of polysemy, that is, words with multiple meanings. We will explore this issue further when we cover non-static embeddings later in this chapter.

Word2Vec

The models known as Word2Vec were first created in 2013 by a team of researchers at Google led by Tomas Mikolov [1, 2, 3]. The models are self-supervised, that is, they are supervised models that depend on the structure of natural language to provide labeled training data.

The two architectures for Word2Vec are as follows:

- Continuous Bag of Words (CBOW)
- Skip-gram

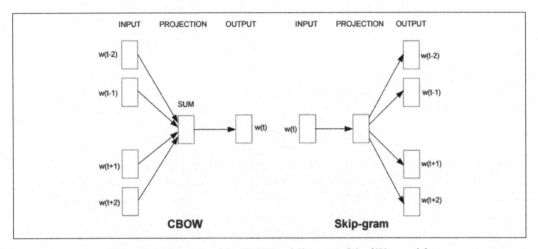

Figure 2: Architecture of the CBOW and Skip-gram Word2Vec models

In the CBOW architecture, the model predicts the current word given a window of surrounding words. The order of context words do not influence the prediction (that is, the bag of words assumption, hence the name). In the skip-gram architecture, the model predicts the surrounding words given the context word. According to the Word2Vec website, CBOW is faster but skip-gram does a better job at predicting infrequent words.

Figure 2 summarizes the CBOW and skip-gram architectures. To understand the inputs and outputs, consider the following example sentence:

The Earth travels around the Sun once per year.

Assuming a window size of 5, that is, two context words to the left and right of the content word, the resulting context windows are shown as follows. The word in bold is the word under consideration, and the other words are the context words within the window:

[**The**, Earth, travels]

[The, **Earth**, travels, around]

[The, Earth, **travels**, around, the]

[Earth, travels, **around**, the, Sun]

[travels, around, **the**, Sun, once]

[around, the, **Sun**, once, per]

[the, Sun, **once**, per, year]

[Sun, **once**, per, year]

[**once**, per, year]

For the CBOW model, the input and label tuples for the first three context windows are as follows. In the following first example, the CBOW model would learn to predict the word "The" given the set of words ("Earth", "travels"), and so on. More correctly, the input of sparse vectors for the words "Earth" and "travels". The model will learn to predict a dense vector whose highest value, or probability, corresponds to the word "The":

([Earth, travels], **The**)

([The, travels, around], **Earth**)

([The, Earth, around, the], **travels**)

For the skip-gram model, the first three context windows correspond to the following input and label tuples. We can restate the skip-gram model objective of predicting a context word given a target word as predicting if a pair of words are contextually related. Contextually related means that a pair of words within a context window are considered to be related. That is, the input to the skip-gram model for the following first example would be the sparse vectors for the context words "The" and "Earth," and the output will be the value 1:

([**The**, Earth], 1)

([**The**, travels], 1)

([**Earth**, The], 1)

([**Earth**, travels], 1)

([**Earth**, around], 1)

([**travels**, The], 1)

([**travels**, Earth], 1)

([**travels**, around], 1)

([**travels**, the], 1)

We also need negative samples to train a model properly, so we generate additional negative samples by pairing each input word with some random word in the vocabulary. This process is called Negative sampling and might result in the following additional inputs:

([**Earth**, aardvark], 0)

([**Earth**, zebra], 0)

A model trained with all of these inputs is called a **Skip-gram with Negative Sampling (SGNS)** model.

It is important to understand that we are not interested in the ability of these models to classify; rather, we are interested in the side effect of training – the learned weights. These learned weights are what we call the embedding.

While it may be instructive to implement the models on your own as an academic exercise, at this point Word2Vec is so commoditized, you are unlikely to ever need to do this. For the curious, you will find code to implement the CBOW and skip-gram models in the files `tf2_cbow_model.py` and `tf2_cbow_skipgram.py` in the source code accompanying this chapter.

Google's pretrained Word2Vec model is available here (`https://drive.google.com/file/d/0B7XkCwpI5KDYNlNUTTlSS21pQmM/edit`). The model was trained on roughly 100 billion words from a Google News dataset and contains a vocabulary of 3 million words and phrases. The output vector dimensionality is 300. It is available as a bin file and can be opened using gensim using `gensim.models.Word2Vec.load_word2vec_format()` or using `gensim()` data downloader.

The other early implementation of word embedding is GloVe, which we will talk about next.

GloVe

The **Global vectors for word representation (GloVe)** embeddings were created by Jeffrey Pennington, Richard Socher, and Christopher Manning [4]. The authors describe GloVe as an unsupervised learning algorithm for obtaining vector representations for words. Training is performed on aggregated global word-word co-occurrence statistics from a corpus, and the resulting representations showcase interesting linear substructures of the word vector space.

GloVe differs from Word2Vec in that Word2Vec is a predictive model while GloVe is a count-based model. The first step is to construct a large matrix of (word, context) pairs that co-occur in the training corpus. Rows correspond to words and columns correspond to contexts, usually a sequence of one or more words. Each element of the matrix represents how often the word co-occurs in the context.

The GloVe process factorizes this co-occurrence matrix into a pair of (word, feature) and (feature, context) matrices. The process is known as Matrix Factorization and is done using **Stochastic Gradient Descent (SGD)**, an iterative numerical method. For example, consider that we want to factorize a matrix R into its factors P and Q:

$$R = P * Q \approx R'$$

The SGD process will start with P and Q composed of random values and attempt to reconstruct the matrix R' by multiplying them. The difference between the matrices R and R' represents the loss, and is usually computed as the mean-squared error between the two matrices. The loss dictates how much the values of P and Q need to change for R' to move closer to R to minimize the reconstruction loss. This process is repeated multiple times until the loss is within some acceptable threshold. At that point the (word, feature) matrix P is the GloVe embedding.

The GloVe process is much more resource intensive than Word2Vec. This is because Word2Vec learns the embedding by training over batches of word vectors, while GloVe factorizes the entire co-occurrence matrix in one shot. In order to make the process scalable, SGD is often used in parallel mode, as outlined in the HOGWILD! Paper [5].

Levy and Goldberg have also pointed out equivalences between the Word2Vec and GloVe approaches in their paper [6], showing that the Word2Vec SGNS model implicitly factorizes a word-context matrix.

As with Word2Vec, you are unlikely to ever need to generate your own GloVe embedding, and far more likely to use embeddings pregenerated against large corpora and made available for download. If you are curious, you will find code to implement matrix factorization in `tf2_matrix_factorization.py` in the source code download accompanying this chapter.

GloVe vectors trained on various large corpora (number of tokens ranging from 6 billion to 840 billion, vocabulary size from 400 thousand to 2.2 million) and of various dimensions (50, 100, 200, 300) are available from the GloVe project download page (`https://nlp.stanford.edu/projects/glove/`). It can be downloaded directly from the site, or using gensim or spaCy data downloaders.

Creating your own embedding using gensim

We will create an embedding using a small text corpus, called text8. The text8 dataset is the first 10^8 bytes the Large Text Compression Benchmark, which consists of the first 10^9 bytes of English Wikipedia [7]. The text8 dataset is accessible from within the gensim API as an iterable of tokens, essentially a list of tokenized sentences. To download the text8 corpus, create a Word2Vec model from it, and save it for later use, run the following few lines of code (available in `create_embedding_with_text8.py` in the source code for this chapter):

```
import gensim.downloader as api
from gensim.models import Word2Vec

dataset = api.load("text8")
model = Word2Vec(dataset)

model.save("data/text8-word2vec.bin")
```

This will train a Word2Vec model on the text8 dataset and save it as a binary file. The Word2Vec model has many parameters, but we will just use the defaults. In this case it trains a CBOW model (sg=0) with window size 5 (window=5) and will produce 100 dimensional embeddings (size=100). The full set of parameters are described in the Word2Vec documentation page [8]. To run this code, execute the following commands at the command line:

```
$ mkdir data
$ python create_embedding_with_text8.py
```

The code should run for 5-10 minutes, after which it will write out a trained model into the `data` folder. We will examine this trained model in the next section.

gensim is an open source Python library designed to extract semantic meaning from text documents. One of its features is an excellent implementation of the Word2Vec algorithm, with an easy to use API that allows you to train and query your own Word2Vec model.

Word embeddings are central to text processing; however, at the time of writing this book, there is no comparable API within TensorFlow that allows you to work with embeddings at the same level of abstraction. For this reason, we have used gensim in this chapter to work with Word2Vec models.

To learn more about gensim, see `https://radimrehurek.com/gensim/index.html`. To install gensim, please follow instructions at `https://radimrehurek.com/gensim/install.html`.

Exploring the embedding space with gensim

Let us reload the Word2Vec model we just built and explore it using the gensim API. The actual word vectors can be accessed as a custom gensim class from the model's wv attribute:

```
from gensim.models import KeyedVectors

model = KeyedVectors.load("data/text8-word2vec.bin")
word_vectors = model.wv
```

We can take a look at the first few words in the vocabulary and check to see if specific words are available:

```
words = word_vectors.vocab.keys()
print([x for i, x in enumerate(words) if i < 10])
assert("king" in words)
```

The preceding snippet of code produces the following output:

```
['anarchism', 'originated', 'as', 'a', 'term', 'of', 'abuse', 'first',
'used', 'against']
```

We can look for similar words to a given word ("king"), shown as follows:

```
def print_most_similar(word_conf_pairs, k):
    for i, (word, conf) in enumerate(word_conf_pairs):
        print("{:.3f} {:s}".format(conf, word))
```

```
        if i >= k-1:
            break
    if k < len(word_conf_pairs):
        print("...")

print_most_similar(word_vectors.most_similar("king"), 5)
```

The `most_similar()` method with a single parameter produces the following output. Here the floating point score is a measure of the similarity, higher values being better than lower values. As you can see, the similar words seem to be mostly accurate:

0.760 prince

0.701 queen

0.700 kings

0.698 emperor

0.688 throne

...

You can also do vector arithmetic similar to the country-capital example we described earlier. Our objective is to see if the relation Paris : France :: Berlin : Germany holds true. This is equivalent to saying that the distance in embedding space between Paris and France should be the same as that between Berlin and Germany. In other words, France - Paris + Berlin should give us Germany. In code, then, this would translate to:

```
print_most_similar(word_vectors.most_similar(
    positive=["france", "berlin"], negative=["paris"]), 1
)
```

This returns the following result, as expected:

0.803 germany

The preceding similarity value reported is Cosine similarity, but a better measure of similarity was proposed by Levy and Goldberg [9] which is also implemented in the gensim API:

```
print_most_similar(word_vectors.most_similar_cosmul(
    positive=["france", "berlin"], negative=["paris"]), 1
)
```

And this also yields the expected result, but with higher similarity:

0.984 germany

gensim also provides a `doesnt_match()` function, which can be used to detect the odd one out of a list of words:

```
print(word_vectors.doesnt_match(["hindus", "parsis", "singapore",
"christians"]))
```

This gives us `singapore` as expected, since it is the only country among a set of words identifying religions.

We can also calculate the similarity between two words. Here we demonstrate that the distance between related words is less than that of unrelated words:

```
for word in ["woman", "dog", "whale", "tree"]:
    print("similarity({:s}, {:s}) = {:.3f}".format(
        "man", word,
        word_vectors.similarity("man", word)
    ))
```

Gives the following interesting result:

```
similarity(man, woman) = 0.759
similarity(man, dog) = 0.474
similarity(man, whale) = 0.290
similarity(man, tree) = 0.260
```

The `similar_by_word()` function is functionally equivalent to `similar()` except that the latter normalizes the vector before comparing by default. There is also a related `similar_by_vector()` function which allows you to find similar words by specifying a vector as input. Here we try to find words that are similar to "singapore":

```
print(print_most_similar(
    word_vectors.similar_by_word("singapore"), 5)
)
```

And we get the following output, which seems to be mostly correct, at least from a geographical point of view:

```
0.882 malaysia
0.837 indonesia
0.826 philippines
0.825 uganda
0.822 thailand
...
```

We can also compute the distance between two words in the embedding space using the `distance()` function. This is really just `1 - similarity()`:

```
print("distance(singapore, malaysia) = {:.3f}".format(
    word_vectors.distance("singapore", "malaysia")
))
```

We can also look up vectors for a vocabulary word either directly from the `word_vectors` object, or by using the `word_vec()` wrapper, shown as follows:

```
vec_song = word_vectors["song"]
vec_song_2 = word_vectors.word_vec("song", use_norm=True)
```

There are a few other functions that you may find useful depending on your use case. The documentation page for KeyedVectors contains a list of all the available functions [10].

The code shown here can be found in the `explore_text8_embedding.py` file in the code accompanying this book.

Using word embeddings for spam detection

Because of the widespread availability of various robust embeddings generated from large corpora, it has become quite common to use one of these embeddings to convert text input for use with machine learning models. Text is treated as a sequence of tokens. The embedding provides a dense fixed dimension vector for each token. Each token is replaced with its vector, and this converts the sequence of text into a matrix of examples, each of which has a fixed number of features corresponding to the dimensionality of the embedding.

This matrix of examples can be used directly as input to standard (non-neural network based) machine learning programs, but since this book is about deep learning and TensorFlow, we will demonstrate its use with a one-dimensional version of the **Convolutional Neural Network (CNN)** that you learned about in *Chapter 4*, *Convolutional Neural Networks*. Our example is a spam detector that will classify **Short Message Service (SMS)** or text messages as either "ham" or "spam." The example is very similar to the sentiment analysis example in *Chapter 5*, *Advanced Convolutional Neural Networks* that used a one-dimensional CNN, but our focus here will be on the embedding layer.

Specifically, we will see how the program learns an embedding from scratch that is customized to the spam detection task. Next we will see how to use an external third-party embedding like the ones we have learned about in this chapter, a process similar to transfer learning in computer vision. Finally, we will learn how to combine the two approaches, starting with a third party embedding and letting the network use that as a starting point for its custom embedding, a process similar to fine tuning in computer vision.

As usual, we will start with our imports:

```
import argparse
import gensim.downloader as api
import numpy as np
import os
import shutil
import tensorflow as tf

from sklearn.metrics import accuracy_score, confusion_matrix
```

Scikit-learn is an open source Python machine learning toolkit that contains many efficient and easy to use tools for data mining and data analysis. In this chapter we have used two of its predefined metrics, accuracy_score and confusion_matrix, to evaluate our model after it is trained.

You can learn more about scikit-learn at https://scikit-learn.org/stable/.

Getting the data

The data for our model is available publicly and comes from the SMS spam collection dataset from the UCI Machine Learning Repository [11]. The following code will download the file and parse it to produce a list of SMS messages and their corresponding labels:

```
def download_and_read(url):
    local_file = url.split('/')[-1]
    p = tf.keras.utils.get_file(local_file, url,
        extract=True, cache_dir=".")
    labels, texts = [], []
    local_file = os.path.join("datasets", "SMSSpamCollection")
    with open(local_file, "r") as fin:
        for line in fin:
            label, text = line.strip().split('\t')
```

```
        labels.append(1 if label == "spam" else 0)
        texts.append(text)
    return texts, labels


DATASET_URL = \ "https://archive.ics.uci.edu/ml/machine-learning-
databases/00228/smsspamcollection.zip"
texts, labels = download_and_read(DATASET_URL)
```

The dataset contains 5,574 SMS records, 747 of which are marked as "spam" and the other 4,827 are marked as "ham" (not spam). The text of the SMS records are contained in the variable texts, and the corresponding numeric labels (0 = ham, 1 = spam) are contained in the variable labels.

Making the data ready for use

The next step is to process the data so it can be consumed by the network. The SMS text needs to be fed into the network as a sequence of integers, where each word is represented by its corresponding ID in the vocabulary. We will use the Keras tokenizer to convert each SMS text into a sequence of words, and then create the vocabulary using the fit_on_texts() method on the tokenizer.

We then convert the SMS messages to a sequence of integers using the texts_to_sequences(). Finally, since the network can only work with fixed length sequences of integers, we call the pad_sequences() function to pad the shorter SMS messages with zeros.

The longest SMS message in our dataset has 189 tokens (words). In many applications where there may be a few outlier sequences that are very long, we would restrict the length to a smaller number by setting the maxlen flag. In that case, sentences longer than maxlen tokens would be truncated, and sentences shorter than maxlen tokens would be padded:

```
# tokenize and pad text
tokenizer = tf.keras.preprocessing.text.Tokenizer()
tokenizer.fit_on_texts(texts)
text_sequences = tokenizer.texts_to_sequences(texts)
text_sequences = tf.keras.preprocessing.sequence.pad_sequences(
    text_sequences)
num_records = len(text_sequences)
max_seqlen = len(text_sequences[0])
print("{:d} sentences, max length: {:d}".format(
    num_records, max_seqlen))
```

We will also convert our labels to categorical or one-hot encoding format, because the loss function we would like to choose (categorical cross-entropy) expects to see the labels in that format:

```
# labels
NUM_CLASSES = 2
cat_labels = tf.keras.utils.to_categorical(
    labels, num_classes=NUM_CLASSES)
```

The tokenizer allows access to the vocabulary created through the `word_index` attribute, which is basically a dictionary of vocabulary words to their index positions in the vocabulary. We also build the reverse index that enables us to go from index position to the word itself. In addition, we create entries for the PAD character:

```
# vocabulary
word2idx = tokenizer.word_index
idx2word = {v:k for k, v in word2idx.items()}
word2idx["PAD"] = 0
idx2word[0] = "PAD"
vocab_size = len(word2idx)
print("vocab size: {:d}".format(vocab_size))
```

Finally, we create the `dataset` object that our network will work with. The `dataset` object allows us to set up some properties, such as the batch size, declaratively. Here, we build up a dataset from our padded sequence of integers and categorical labels, shuffle the data, and split it into training, validation, and test sets. Finally, we set the batch size for each of the three datasets:

```
# dataset
dataset = tf.data.Dataset.from_tensor_slices(
    (text_sequences, cat_labels))
dataset = dataset.shuffle(10000)
test_size = num_records // 4
val_size = (num_records - test_size) // 10
test_dataset = dataset.take(test_size)
val_dataset = dataset.skip(test_size).take(val_size)
train_dataset = dataset.skip(test_size + val_size)

BATCH_SIZE = 128
test_dataset = test_dataset.batch(BATCH_SIZE, drop_remainder=True)
val_dataset = val_dataset.batch(BATCH_SIZE, drop_remainder=True)
train_dataset = train_dataset.batch(BATCH_SIZE, drop_remainder=True)
```

Building the embedding matrix

The gensim toolkit provides access to various trained embedding models, as you can see from running the following command at the Python prompt:

```
>>> import gensim.downloader as api
>>> api.info("models").keys()
```

This will return (at the time of writing this book) the following trained word embeddings:

- **Word2Vec**: Two flavors, one trained on Google news (3 million word vectors based on 3 billion tokens), and one trained on Russian corpora (word2vec-ruscorpora-300, word2vec-google-news-300).

- **GloVe**: Two flavors, one trained on the Gigawords corpus (400,000 word vectors based on 6 billion tokens), available as 50d, 100d, 200d, and 300d vectors, and one trained on Twitter (1.2 million word vectors based on 27 billion tokens), available as 25d, 50d, 100d, and 200d vectors (glove-wiki-gigaword-50, glove-wiki-gigaword-100, glove-wiki-gigaword-200, glove-wiki-gigaword-300, glove-twitter-25, glove-twitter-50, glove-twitter-100, glove-twitter-200).

- **fastText**: 1 million word vectors trained with subword information on Wikipedia 2017, the UMBC web corpus, and statmt.org news dataset (16B tokens). (fastText-wiki-news-subwords-300).

- **ConceptNet Numberbatch**: An ensemble embedding that uses the ConceptNet semantic network, the **paraphrase database** (**PPDB**), Word2Vec, and GloVe as input. Produces 600d vectors [12, 13]. (conceptnet-numberbatch-17-06-300).

For our example, we chose the 300d GloVe embeddings trained on the Gigaword corpus.

In order to keep our model size small, we want to only consider embeddings for words that exist in our vocabulary. This is done using the following code, which creates a smaller embedding matrix for each word in the vocabulary. Each row in the matrix corresponds to a word, and the row itself is the vector corresponding to the embedding for the word:

```
def build_embedding_matrix(sequences, word2idx, embedding_dim,
        embedding_file):
    if os.path.exists(embedding_file):
        E = np.load(embedding_file)
    else:
        vocab_size = len(word2idx)
```

```
        E = np.zeros((vocab_size, embedding_dim))
        word_vectors = api.load(EMBEDDING_MODEL)
        for word, idx in word2idx.items():
            try:
                E[idx] = word_vectors.word_vec(word)
            except KeyError:    # word not in embedding
                pass
        np.save(embedding_file, E)
    return E


EMBEDDING_DIM = 300
DATA_DIR = "data"
EMBEDDING_NUMPY_FILE = os.path.join(DATA_DIR, "E.npy")
EMBEDDING_MODEL = "glove-wiki-gigaword-300"
E = build_embedding_matrix(text_sequences, word2idx,
    EMBEDDING_DIM,
    EMBEDDING_NUMPY_FILE)
print("Embedding matrix:", E.shape)
```

The output shape for the embedding matrix is (9010, 300), corresponding to the 9010 tokens in the vocabulary, and 300 features in the third-party GloVe embeddings.

Define the spam classifier

We are now ready to define our classifier. We will use a **one-dimensional Convolutional Neural Network (1D CNN)**, similar to the network you have seen already in *Chapter 6, Generative Adversarial Networks* for sentiment analysis.

The input is a sequence of integers. The first layer is an Embedding layer, which converts each input integer to a vector of size (embedding_dim). Depending on the run mode, that is, whether we will learn the embeddings from scratch, do transfer learning, or do fine-tuning, the Embedding layer in the network would be slightly different. When the network starts with randomly initialized embedding weights (run_mode == "scratch"), and learns the weights during the training, we set the trainable parameter to True. In the transfer learning case (run_mode == "vectorizer"), we set the weights from our embedding matrix E but set the trainable parameter to False, so it doesn't train. In the fine-tuning case (run_mode == "finetuning"), we set the embedding weights from our external matrix E, as well as set the layer to trainable.

Output of the embedding is fed into a convolutional layer. Here fixed size 3-token-wide 1D windows (kernel_size=3), also called time steps, are convolved against 256 random filters (num_filters=256) to produce vectors of size 256 for each time step. Thus, the output vector shape is (batch_size, time_steps, num_filters).

Output of the convolutional layer is sent to a 1D spatial dropout layer. Spatial dropout will randomly drop entire feature maps output from the convolutional layer. This is a regularization technique to prevent over-fitting. This is then sent through a Global max pool layer, which takes the maximum value from each time step for each filter, resulting in a vector of shape (batch_size, num_filters).

Output of the dropout layer is fed into a dense layer, which converts the vector of shape (batch_size, num_filters) to (batch_size, num_classes). A softmax activation will convert the scores for each of (spam, ham) into a probability distribution, indicating the probability of the input SMS being spam or ham respectively:

```python
class SpamClassifierModel(tf.keras.Model):
    def __init__(self, vocab_sz, embed_sz, input_length,
            num_filters, kernel_sz, output_sz,
            run_mode, embedding_weights,
            **kwargs):
        super(SpamClassifierModel, self).__init__(**kwargs)
        if run_mode == "scratch":
            self.embedding = tf.keras.layers.Embedding(vocab_sz,
                embed_sz,
                input_length=input_length,
                trainable=True)
        elif run_mode == "vectorizer":
            self.embedding = tf.keras.layers.Embedding(vocab_sz,
                embed_sz,
                input_length=input_length,
                weights=[embedding_weights],
                trainable=False)
        else:
            self.embedding = tf.keras.layers.Embedding(vocab_sz,
                embed_sz,
                input_length=input_length,
                weights=[embedding_weights],
                trainable=True)
        self.conv = tf.keras.layers.Conv1D(filters=num_filters,
            kernel_size=kernel_sz,
            activation="relu")
        self.dropout = tf.keras.layers.SpatialDropout1D(0.2)
        self.pool = tf.keras.layers.GlobalMaxPooling1D()
        self.dense = tf.keras.layers.Dense(output_sz,
            activation="softmax")

    def call(self, x):
```

```
        x = self.embedding(x)
        x = self.conv(x)
        x = self.dropout(x)
        x = self.pool(x)
        x = self.dense(x)
        return x

# model definition
conv_num_filters = 256
conv_kernel_size = 3
model = SpamClassifierModel(
    vocab_size, EMBEDDING_DIM, max_seqlen,
    conv_num_filters, conv_kernel_size, NUM_CLASSES,
    run_mode, E)
model.build(input_shape=(None, max_seqlen))
```

Finally, we compile the model using the categorical cross entropy loss function and the Adam optimizer:

```
# compile
model.compile(optimizer="adam", loss="categorical_crossentropy",
metrics=["accuracy"])
```

Train and evaluate the model

One thing to notice is that the dataset is somewhat imbalanced, there are only 747 instances of spam, compared to 4827 instances of ham. The network could achieve close to 87% accuracy simply by always predicting the majority class. To alleviate this problem, we set class weights to indicate that an error on a spam SMS is 8 times as expensive as an error on a ham SMS. This is indicated by the CLASS_WEIGHTS variable, which is passed into the model.fit() call as an additional parameter.

After training for 3 epochs, we evaluate the model against the test set, and report the accuracy and confusion matrix of the model against the test set:

```
NUM_EPOCHS = 3
# data distribution is 4827 ham and 747 spam (total 5574), which
# works out to approx 87% ham and 13% spam, so we take reciprocals
# and this works out to being each spam (1) item as being
# approximately 8 times as important as each ham (0) message.
CLASS_WEIGHTS = { 0: 1, 1: 8 }

# train model
model.fit(train_dataset, epochs=NUM_EPOCHS,
    validation_data=val_dataset,
```

```
        class_weight=CLASS_WEIGHTS)

# evaluate against test set
labels, predictions = [], []
for Xtest, Ytest in test_dataset:
    Ytest_ = model.predict_on_batch(Xtest)
    ytest = np.argmax(Ytest, axis=1)
    ytest_ = np.argmax(Ytest_, axis=1)
    labels.extend(ytest.tolist())
    predictions.extend(ytest.tolist())

print("test accuracy: {:.3f}".format(accuracy_score(labels,
predictions)))
print("confusion matrix")
print(confusion_matrix(labels, predictions))
```

Running the spam detector

The three scenarios we want to look at are:

- Letting the network learn the embedding for the task
- Starting with a fixed external third party embedding where the embedding matrix is treated like a vectorizer to transform the sequence of integers into a sequence of vectors
- Starting with an external third party embedding which is further fine-tuned to the task during the training

Each scenario can be evaluated setting the value of the mode argument as shown in the following command:

```
$ python spam_classifier --mode [scratch|vectorizer|finetune]
```

The dataset is small and the model is fairly simple. We were able to achieve very good results (validation set accuracies in the high 90s, and perfect test set accuracy) with only minimal training (3 epochs). In all three cases, the network achieved a perfect score, accurately predicting the 1,111 ham messages, as well as the 169 spam cases.

The change in validation accuracies, shown in *Figure 3*, illustrate the differences between the three approaches:

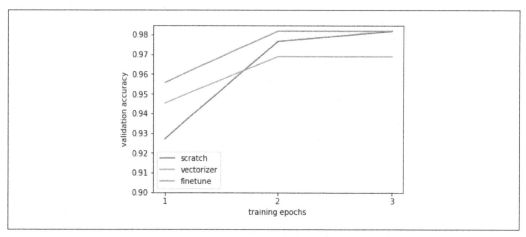

Figure 3: Comparison of validation accuracy across training epochs for different embedding techniques

In the learning from scratch case, at the end of the first epoch, the validation accuracy is 0.93, but over the next two epochs, it rises to 0.98. In the vectorizer case, the network gets something of a head start from the third-party embeddings and ends up with a validation accuracy of almost 0.95 at the end of the first epoch. However, because the embedding weights are not allowed to change it is not able to customize the embeddings to the spam detection task, and the validation accuracy at the end of the third epoch is the lowest among the three. The fine-tune case, like the vectorizer, also gets a head start, but is able to customize the embedding to the task as well, and therefore is able to learn at the most rapid rate among the three cases. The fine-tune case has the highest validation accuracy at the end of the first epoch and reaches the same validation accuracy at the end of the second epoch that the scratch case achieves at the end of the third.

Neural embeddings – not just for words

Word embedding technology has evolved in various ways since Word2Vec and GloVe. One such direction is the application of word embeddings to non-word settings, also known as Neural embeddings. As you will recall, word embeddings leverage the distributional hypothesis that words occurring in similar contexts tend to have similar meaning, where context is usually a fixed-size (in number of words) window around the target word.

The idea of neural embeddings is very similar; that is, entities that occur in similar contexts tend to be strongly related to each other. Ways in which these contexts are constructed is usually situation-dependent. We will describe two techniques here that are foundational and general enough to be applied easily to a variety of use cases.

Item2Vec

The Item2Vec embedding model was originally proposed by Barkan and Koenigstein [14] for the collaborative filtering use case, that is, recommending items to users based on purchases by other users that have similar purchase histories to this user. It uses items in a web-store as the "words" and the itemset (the sequence of items purchased by a user over time) as the "sentence" from which the "word context" is derived.

For example, consider the problem of recommending items to shoppers in a supermarket. Assume that our supermarket sells 5000 items, so each item can be represented as a sparse one-hot encoded vector of size 5000. Each user is represented by their shopping cart, which is a sequence of such vectors. Applying a context window similar to the one we saw in the Word2Vec section, we can train a skip-gram model to predict likely item pairs. The learned embedding model maps the items to a dense low-dimensional space where similar items are close together, which can be used to make similar item recommendations.

node2vec

The node2vec embedding model was proposed by Grover and Leskovec [15], as a scalable way to learn features for nodes in a graph. It learns an embedding of the structure of the graph by executing a large number of fixed length random walks on the graph. The nodes are the "words" and the random walks are the "sentences" from which the "word context" is derived in node2vec.

The **Something2Vec** page [41] provides a comprehensive list of ways in which researchers have tried to apply the distributional hypothesis to entities other than words. Hopefully this list will spark ideas for your own "something2vec" representation.

To illustrate how easy it is to create your own neural embedding, we will generate a node2vec-like model or, more accurately, a predecessor graph based embedding called DeepWalk, proposed by Perozzi, et al. [42] for papers presented at the NeurIPS conference from 1987-2015, by leveraging word co-occurrence relationships between them.

The dataset is a 11463 × 5812 matrix of word counts, where the rows represent words, and columns represent conference papers. We will use this to construct a graph of papers, where an edge between two papers represents a word that occurs in both of them. Both node2vec and DeepWalk assume that the graph is undirected and unweighted. Our graph is undirected, since a relationship between a pair of papers is bidirectional. However, our edges could have weights based on the number of word co-occurrences between the two documents. For our example, we will consider any number of co-occurrences above 0 to be a valid unweighted edge.

As usual, we will start by declaring our imports:

```
import gensim
import logging
import numpy as np
import os
import shutil
import tensorflow as tf

from scipy.sparse import csr_matrix
from sklearn.metrics.pairwise import cosine_similarity

logging.basicConfig(format='%(asctime)s : %(levelname)s : %(message)
s', level=logging.INFO)
```

The next step is to download the data from the UCI repository and convert it to a sparse term document matrix, TD, then construct a document-document matrix E by multiplying the transpose of the term-document matrix with itself. Our graph is represented as an adjacency or edge matrix by the document-document matrix. Since each element represents a similarity between two documents, we will binarize the matrix E by setting any non-zero elements to 1:

```
DATA_DIR = "./data"
UCI_DATA_URL = "https://archive.ics.uci.edu/ml/machine-learning-
databases/00371/NIPS_1987-2015.csv"

def download_and_read(url):
    local_file = url.split('/')[-1]
    p = tf.keras.utils.get_file(local_file, url, cache_dir=".")
    row_ids, col_ids, data = [], [], []
    rid = 0
    f = open(p, "r")
    for line in f:
        line = line.strip()
        if line.startswith("\"\","):
            # header
```

```
        continue
    # compute non-zero elements for current row
    counts = np.array([int(x) for x in line.split(',')[1:]])
    nz_col_ids = np.nonzero(counts)[0]
    nz_data = counts[nz_col_ids]
    nz_row_ids = np.repeat(rid, len(nz_col_ids))
    rid += 1
    # add data to big lists
    row_ids.extend(nz_row_ids.tolist())
    col_ids.extend(nz_col_ids.tolist())
    data.extend(nz_data.tolist())
f.close()
TD = csr_matrix((
    np.array(data), (
        np.array(row_ids), np.array(col_ids)
        )
    ),
    shape=(rid, counts.shape[0]))
return TD
```

```
# read data and convert to Term-Document matrix
TD = download_and_read(UCI_DATA_URL)
# compute undirected, unweighted edge matrix
E = TD.T * TD
# binarize
E[E > 0] = 1
```

Once we have our sparse binarized adjacency matrix, E, we can then generate random walks from each of the vertices. From each node, we construct 32 random walks of maximum length of 40 nodes. The walks have a random restart probability of 0.15, which means that for any node, the particular random walk could end with 15% probability. The following code will construct the random walks and write them out to a file given by RANDOM_WALKS_FILE. Note that this is a very slow process. A copy of the output is provided along with the source code for this chapter in case you prefer to skip the random walk generation process:

```
NUM_WALKS_PER_VERTEX = 32
MAX_PATH_LENGTH = 40
RESTART_PROB = 0.15

RANDOM_WALKS_FILE = os.path.join(DATA_DIR, "random-walks.txt")

def construct_random_walks(E, n, alpha, l, ofile):
    if os.path.exists(ofile):
```

```
              print("random walks generated already, skipping")
              return
      f = open(ofile, "w")
      for i in range(E.shape[0]):  # for each vertex
          if i % 100 == 0:
              print("{:d} random walks generated from {:d} vertices"
                  .format(n * i, i))
          for j in range(n):          # construct n random walks
              curr = i
              walk = [curr]
              target_nodes = np.nonzero(E[curr])[1]
              for k in range(l):    # each of max length l
                  # should we restart?
                  if np.random.random() < alpha and len(walk) > 5:
                      break
                  # choose one outgoing edge and append to walk
                  try:
                      curr = np.random.choice(target_nodes)
                      walk.append(curr)
                      target_nodes = np.nonzero(E[curr])[1]
                  except ValueError:
                      continue
              f.write("{:s}\n".format(" ".join([str(x) for x in walk])))

      print("{:d} random walks generated from {:d} vertices, COMPLETE"
          .format(n * i, i))
      f.close()
```

```
# construct random walks (caution: very long process!)
construct_random_walks(E, NUM_WALKS_PER_VERTEX, RESTART_PROB, MAX_
PATH_LENGTH, RANDOM_WALKS_FILE)
```

A few lines from the RANDOM_WALKS_FILE are shown below. You could imagine that these look like sentences in a language where the vocabulary of words is all the node IDs in our graph. We have learned that word embeddings exploit the structure of language to generate a distributional representation for words. Graph embedding schemes such as DeepWalk and node2vec do the exact same thing with these "sentences" created out of random walks. Such embeddings are able to capture similarities between nodes in a graph that go beyond immediate neighbors, as we shall see as follows:

```
0 1405 4845 754 4391 3524 4282 2357 3922 1667
0 1341 456 495 1647 4200 5379 473 2311
```

```
0 3422 3455 118 4527 2304 772 3659 2852 4515 5135 3439 1273

0 906 3498 2286 4755 2567 2632

0 5769 638 3574 79 2825 3532 2363 360 1443 4789 229 4515 3014 3683 2967
5206 2288 1615 1166

0 2469 1353 5596 2207 4065 3100

0 2236 1464 1596 2554 4021

0 4688 864 3684 4542 3647 2859

0 4884 4590 5386 621 4947 2784 1309 4958 3314

0 5546 200 3964 1817 845
```

We are now ready to create our word embedding model. The gensim package offers a simple API that allows us to declaratively create and train a Word2Vec model, using the following code. The trained model will be serialized to the file given by W2V_MODEL_FILE. The Documents class allows us to stream large input files to train the Word2Vec model without running into memory issues. We will train the Word2Vec model in skip-gram mode with a window size of 10, which means we train it to predict up to five neighboring vertices given a central vertex. The resulting embedding for each vertex is a dense vector of size 128:

```python
W2V_MODEL_FILE = os.path.join(DATA_DIR, "w2v-neurips-papers.model")


class Documents(object):
    def __init__(self, input_file):
        self.input_file = input_file

    def __iter__(self):
        with open(self.input_file, "r") as f:
            for i, line in enumerate(f):
                if i % 1000 == 0:
                    if i % 1000 == 0:
                        logging.info(
                            "{:d} random walks extracted".format(i))
                yield line.strip().split()


def train_word2vec_model(random_walks_file, model_file):
    if os.path.exists(model_file):
        print("Model file {:s} already present, skipping training"
            .format(model_file))
        return
    docs = Documents(random_walks_file)
    model = gensim.models.Word2Vec(
        docs,
```

```
        size=128,      # size of embedding vector
        window=10,     # window size
        sg=1,          # skip-gram model
        min_count=2,
        workers=4
    )
    model.train(
        docs,
        total_examples=model.corpus_count,
        epochs=50)
    model.save(model_file)


# train model
train_word2vec_model(RANDOM_WALKS_FILE, W2V_MODEL_FILE)
```

Our resulting DeepWalk model is just a Word2Vec model, so anything you can do with Word2Vec in the context of words, you can do with this model in the context of vertices. Let us use the model to discover similarities between documents:

```
def evaluate_model(td_matrix, model_file, source_id):
    model = gensim.models.Word2Vec.load(model_file).wv
    most_similar = model.most_similar(str(source_id))
    scores = [x[1] for x in most_similar]
    target_ids = [x[0] for x in most_similar]
    # compare top 10 scores with cosine similarity
    # between source and each target
    X = np.repeat(td_matrix[source_id].todense(), 10, axis=0)
    Y = td_matrix[target_ids].todense()
    cosims = [cosine_similarity(X[i], Y[i])[0, 0] for i in range(10)]
    for i in range(10):
        print("{:d} {:s} {:.3f} {:.3f}".format(
            source_id, target_ids[i], cosims[i], scores[i]))


source_id = np.random.choice(E.shape[0])
evaluate_model(TD, W2V_MODEL_FILE, source_id)
```

Following is the output shown. The first and second columns are the source and target vertex IDs. The third column is the cosine similarity between the term vectors corresponding to the source and target documents, and the fourth is the similarity score reported by the Word2Vec model. As you can see, cosine similarity reports a similarity only between 2 of the 10 document pairs, but the Word2Vec model is able to detect latent similarities in the embedding space. This is similar to the behavior we have noticed between one-hot encoding and dense embeddings:

```
1971 5443 0.000 0.348
1971 1377 0.000 0.348
1971 3682 0.017 0.328
1971 51   0.022 0.322
1971 857  0.000 0.318
1971 1161 0.000 0.313
1971 4971 0.000 0.313
1971 5168 0.000 0.312
1971 3099 0.000 0.311
1971 462  0.000 0.310
```

The code for this embedding strategy is available in `neurips_papers_node2vec.py` in the source code folder accompanying this chapter. Next, we will move on to look at character and subword embeddings.

Character and subword embeddings

Another evolution of the basic word embedding strategy has been to look at character and subword embeddings instead of word embeddings. Character level embeddings were first proposed by Xiang and LeCun [17], and found to have some key advantages over word embeddings.

First, a character vocabulary is finite and small – for example, a vocabulary for English would contain around 70 characters (26 characters, 10 numbers, and rest special characters), leading to character models that are also small and compact. Second, unlike word embeddings, which provide vectors for a large but finite set of words, there is no concept of out-of-vocabulary for character embeddings, since any word can be represented by the vocabulary. Third, character embeddings tend to be better for rare and misspelled words because there is much less imbalance for character inputs than for word inputs.

Character embeddings tend to work better for applications that require the notion of syntactic rather than semantic similarity. However, unlike word embeddings, character embeddings tend to be task-specific and are usually generated inline within a network to support the task. For this reason, third party character embeddings are generally not available.

Subword embeddings combine the idea of character and word embeddings by treating a word as a bag of character n-grams, that is, sequences of n consecutive words. They were first proposed by Bojanowski, et al. [18] based on research from **Facebook AI Research (FAIR)**, which they later released as fastText embeddings. fastText embeddings are available for 157 languages, including English. The paper has reported state of the art performance on a number of NLP tasks.

fastText computes embeddings for character n-grams where n is between 3 and 6 characters (default settings, can be changed), as well as for the words themselves. For example, character n-grams for n=3 for the word "green" would be "<gr", "gre", "ree", "een", and "en>". Beginning and end of words are marked with "<" and ">" characters respectively, to distinguish between short words and their n-grams such as "<cat>" and "cat".

During lookup, you can look up a vector from the fastText embedding using the word as the key if the word exists in the embedding. However, unlike traditional word embeddings, you can still construct a fastText vector for a word that does not exist in the embedding. This is done by decomposing the word into its constituent trigram subwords as shown in the preceding example, looking up the vectors for the subwords, and then taking the average of these subword vectors. The fastText Python API [19] will do this automatically, but you will need to do this manually if you use other APIs to access fastText word embeddings, such as gensim or NumPy.

Next up, we will look at Dynamic embeddings.

Dynamic embeddings

So far, all the embeddings we have considered have been static; that is, they are deployed as a dictionary of words (and subwords) mapped to fixed dimensional vectors. The vector corresponding to a word in these embeddings is going to be the same regardless of whether it is being used as a noun or verb in the sentence, for example the word "ensure" (the name of a health supplement when used as a noun, and to make certain when used as a verb). It also provides the same vector for polysemous words or words with multiple meanings, such as "bank" (which can mean different things depending on whether it co-occurs with the word "money" or "river"). In both cases, the meaning of the word changes depending on clues available in its context, the sentence. Dynamic embeddings attempt to use these signals to provide different vectors for words based on its context.

Dynamic embeddings are deployed as trained networks that convert your input (typically a sequence of one-hot vectors) into a lower dimensional dense fixed-size embedding by looking at the entire sequence, not just individual words. You can either preprocess your input to this dense embedding and then use this as input to your task-specific network, or wrap the network and treat it similar to the `tf.keras. layers.Embedding` layer for static embeddings. Using a dynamic embedding network in this way is usually much more expensive compared to generating it ahead of time (the first option), or using traditional embeddings.

The earliest dynamic embedding was proposed by McCann, et al. [20], and was called **Contextualized Vectors (CoVe)**. This involved taking the output of the encoder from the encoder-decoder pair of a machine translation network and concatenating it with word vectors for the same word. You will learn more about seq2seq networks in the next chapter. The researchers found that this strategy improved performance of a wide variety of NLP tasks.

Another dynamic embedding proposed by Peters, et al. [21], was **Embeddings from Language Models (ELMo)**. ELMo computes contextualized word representations using character-based word representation and bidirectional **Long Short-Term Memory (LSTM)**. You will learn more about LSTMs in the next chapter. In the meantime, a trained ELMo network is available from TensorFlow's model repository TF-Hub. You can access it and use it for generating ELMo embeddings as follows.

The full set of models available on TF-Hub that are TensorFlow 2.0 compatible can be found on the TF-Hub site for TensorFlow 2.0 [16]. Unfortunately, at the time of writing this, the ELMo model is not one of them. You can invoke the older (pre-TensorFlow 2.0) model from your code by turning off eager execution in your code, but this does also mean that you won't be able to wrap ELMo as a layer in your own model. This strategy will allow you to convert your input sentences to sequences of contextual vectors, which you can then use as input to your own network. Here I have used an array of sentences, where the model will figure out tokens by using its default strategy of tokenizing on whitespace:

```
import tensorflow as tf
import tensorflow_hub as hub

module_url = "https://tfhub.dev/google/elmo/2"
tf.compat.v1.disable_eager_execution()

elmo = hub.Module(module_url, trainable=False)
embeddings = elmo([
        "i like green eggs and ham",
        "would you eat them in a box"
    ],
    signature="default",
    as_dict=True
)["elmo"]
print(embeddings.shape)
```

Output is (2, 7, 1024). The first index tells us that our input contained 2 sentences. The second index refers to the maximum number of words across all sentences, in this case, 7. The model automatically pads the output to the longest sentence. The third index gives us the size of the contextual word embedding created by ELMo; each word is converted to a vector of size (1024).

In the future, once the TensorFlow Hub team migrates over its models to TensorFlow 2.0, the code to generate embeddings from ELMo is expected to look like this. Note that the `module_url` is likely to change. The pattern is similar to the examples of using TensorFlow Hub in chapters 2 and 5 that you have seen already:

```
module_url = "https://tfhub.dev/google/tf2-preview/elmo/2"
embed = hub.KerasLayer(module_url)
embeddings = embed([
    "i like green eggs and ham",
    "would you eat them in a box"
])["elmo"]
print(embeddings.shape)
```

Sentence and paragraph embeddings

A simple, yet surprisingly effective solution for generating useful sentence and paragraph embeddings is to average the word vectors of their constituent words. Even though we will describe some popular sentence and paragraph embeddings in this section, it is generally always advisable to try averaging the word vectors as a baseline.

Sentence (and paragraph) embeddings can also be created in a task optimized way by treating them as a sequence of words, and representing each word using some standard word vector. The sequence of word vectors is used as input to train a network for some task. Vectors extracted from one of the later layers of the network just before the classification layer generally tend to produce very good vector representation for the sequence. However, they tend to be very task specific, and are of limited use as a general vector representation.

An idea for generating general vector representations for sentences that could be used across tasks was proposed by Kiros, et al. [22]. They proposed using the continuity of text from books to construct an encoder-decoder model that is trained to predict surrounding sentences given a sentence. The vector representation of a sequence of words constructed by an encoder-decoder network is typically called a "thought vector". In addition, the proposed model works on a very similar basis to skip-gram, where we try to predict the surrounding words given a word. For these reasons, these sentence vectors were called skip-thought vectors. The project released a Theano-based model that could be used to generate embeddings from sentences. Later, the model was re-implemented with TensorFlow by the Google Research team [23]. The Skip-Thoughts model emits vectors of size (2048) for each sentence. Using the model is not very straightforward, but the `README.md` file on the repository [23] provides instructions in case you would like to use it.

A more convenient source of sentence embeddings is the Google Universal Sentence Encoder, available on TensorFlow Hub. There are two flavors of the encoder in terms of implementation. The first flavor is fast but not so accurate and is based on the **Deep Averaging Network (DAN)** proposed by Iyer, et al. [24], which combines embeddings for words and bigrams and sends it through a fully connected network. The second flavor is much more accurate but slower, and is based on the encoder component of the transformer network proposed by Vaswani, et al. [25]. We will cover the transformer network in more detail in the next chapter.

As with ELMo, the Google Universal Sentence Encoder is currently only available for non-eager mode of execution, so you can use it offline to generate the vectors or integrate it into your TensorFlow 1.x style code. One other thing is that the model does not fit on GPU memory, so you will have to forcibly run it on the CPU. However, since we are running it in prediction mode this is not a problem. Here is some code that calls it with two of our example sentences:

```
import tensorflow as tf
import tensorflow_hub as hub

module_url = "https://tfhub.dev/google/universal-sentence-encoder/2"
tf.compat.v1.disable_eager_execution()

model = hub.Module(module_url)
embeddings = model([
    "i like green eggs and ham",
    "would you eat them in a box"
])
// turn off GPU
config = tf.ConfigProto(device_count = { "GPU" : 0 }}
with tf.compat.v1.Session(config=config) as sess:
    sess.run([
        tf.compat.v1.global_variables_initializer(),
        tf.compat.v1.tables_initializer()
    ])
    embeddings_value = sess.run(embeddings)

print(embeddings_value.shape)
```

The output is (2, 512); that is, each sentence is represented by a vector of size (512). It is important to note that the Google Universal Sentence Encoder can handle any length of word sequence — so you could legitimately use it to get word embeddings on one end as well as paragraph embeddings on the other. However, as the sequence length gets larger, the quality of the embeddings tends to get "diluted".

A much earlier related line of work into producing embeddings for long sequences such as paragraphs and documents was proposed by Le and Mikolov [26] soon after Word2Vec was proposed; it is now known interchangeably as Doc2Vec or Paragraph2Vec. The Doc2Vec algorithm is an extension of Word2Vec that uses surrounding words to predict a word. In the case of Doc2Vec, an additional parameter, the paragraph ID, is provided during training. At the end of the training, the Doc2Vec network learns an embedding for every word and an embedding for every paragraph. During inference, the network is given a paragraph with some missing words. The network uses the known part of the paragraph to produce a paragraph embedding, then uses this paragraph embedding and the word embeddings to infer the missing words in the paragraph. The Doc2Vec algorithm comes in two flavors — the **Paragraph Vectors - Distributed Memory (PV-DM)** and **Paragraph Vectors - Distributed Bag of Words (PV-DBOW)**, roughly analogous to CBOW and skip-gram in Word2Vec. We will not look at Doc2Vec further in this book, except to note that the gensim toolkit provides prebuilt implementations that you can train with your own corpus.

Having looked at the different forms of static embeddings, we will now switch gears a bit and look at dynamic embeddings.

Language model-based embeddings

Language model-based embeddings represent the next step in the evolution of word embeddings. A language model is a probability distribution over sequences of words. Once we have a model, we can ask it to predict the most likely next word given a particular sequence of words. Similar to traditional word embeddings, both static and dynamic, they are trained to predict the next word (or previous word as well, if the language model is bidirectional) given a partial sentence from the corpus. Training does not involve active labeling, since it leverages the natural grammatical structure of large volumes of text, so in a sense this is an unsupervised learning process:

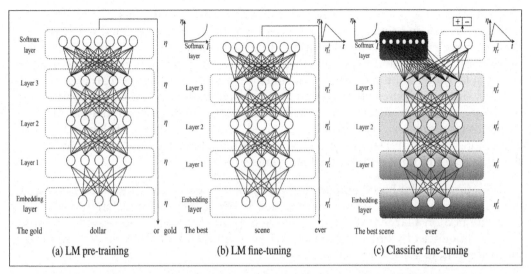

Figure 4: Different stages of training ULMFit embeddings (Howard and Ruder, 2018)

The main difference between a language model as a word embedding and more traditional embeddings is that traditional embeddings are applied as a single initial transformation on the data, and are then fine-tuned for specific tasks. In contrast, language models are trained on large external corpora and represent a model of the particular language, say English. This step is called Pretraining. The computing cost to pretrain these language models is usually fairly high; however, the people who pretrain these models generally make them available for use by others so that we usually do not need to worry about this step. The next step is to fine-tune these general-purpose language models for your particular application domain. For example, if you are working in the travel or healthcare industry, you would fine-tune the language model with text from your own domain. Fine-tuning involves retraining the last few layers with your own text. Once fine-tuned, you can reuse this model for multiple tasks within your domain. The fine-tuning step is generally much less expensive compared to the pretraining step.

Once you have the fine-tuned language model, you remove the last layer of the language model and replace it with a one-to two-layer fully connected network that converts the language model embedding for your input into the final categorical or regression output that your task needs. The idea is identical to transfer learning that you learned about in *Chapter 5, Advanced Convolutional Neural Networks*, the only difference here is that you are doing transfer learning on text instead of images. As with transfer learning with images, these language model-based embeddings allow us to get surprisingly good results with very little labeled data. Not surprisingly, language model embeddings have been referred to as the "ImageNet moment" for natural language processing.

The language model-based embedding idea has its roots in the ELMo [28] network, which you have already seen in this chapter. ELMo learns about its language by being trained on a large text corpus to learn to predict the next and previous words given a sequence of words. ELMo is based on a bidirectional LSTM, which you learn more about in *Chapter 9, Autoencoders*.

The first viable language model embedding was proposed by Howard and Ruder [27] via their **Universal Language Model Fine-Tuning (ULMFit)** model, which was trained on the wikitext-103 dataset consisting of 28,595 Wikipedia articles and 103 million words. ULMFit provides the same benefits that Transfer Learning provides for image tasks—better results from supervised learning tasks with comparatively less labeled data.

Meanwhile, the transformer architecture had become the preferred network for machine translation tasks, replacing the LSTM network because it allows for parallel operations and better handling of long-term dependencies. We will learn more about the Transformer architecture in the next chapter. The OpenAI team of Radford, et al. [30] proposed using the decoder stack from the standard transformer network instead of the LSTM network used in ULMFit. Using this, they built a language model embedding called **Generative Pretraining (GPT)** that achieved state of the art results for many language processing tasks. The paper proposes several configurations for supervised tasks involving single-and multi-sentence tasks such as classification, entailment, similarity, and multiple-choice question answering.

The Allen AI team later followed this up by building an even larger language model called GPT-2, which they ended up not releasing to the public because of fears of the technology being misused by malicious operators [31]. Instead they have released a smaller model for researchers to experiment with.

One problem with the OpenAI transformer architecture is that it is unidirectional whereas its predecessors ELMo and ULMFit were bidirectional. **Bidirectional Encoder Representations for Transformers (BERT)**, proposed by the Google AI team [29], uses the encoder stack of the Transformer architecture and achieves bidirectionality safely by masking up to 15% of its input, which it asks the model to predict.

As with the OpenAI paper, BERT proposes configurations for using it for several supervised learning tasks such as single, and multiple-sentence classification, question answering, and tagging.

The BERT model comes in two major flavors—BERT-base and BERT-large. BERT-base has 12 encoder layers, 768 hidden units, and 12 attention heads, with 110 million parameters in all. BERT-large has 24 encoder layers, 1024 hidden units, and 16 attention heads, with 340 million parameters. More details can be found in the BERT GitHub repository [34].

BERT Pretraining is a very expensive process and can currently only be achieved using **Tensor Processing Units (TPUs)**, which are only available from Google via its Colab network [32] or Google Cloud Platform [33]. However, fine-tuning the BERT-base with custom datasets is usually achievable on GPU instances.

Once the BERT model is fine-tuned for your domain, the embeddings from the last four hidden layers usually produce good results for downstream tasks. Which embedding or combination of embeddings (via summing, averaging, max-pooling, or concatenating) to use is usually based on the type of task.

In the following sections, we will look at how to work with the BERT language model for various language model embedding related tasks.

Using BERT as a feature extractor

The BERT project [34] provides a set of Python scripts that can be run from the command line to fine-tune BERT:

```
$ git clone https://github.com/google-research/bert.git
$ cd bert
```

We then download the appropriate BERT model we want to fine-tune. As mentioned earlier, BERT comes in two sizes—BERT-base and BERT-large. In addition, each model has a cased and uncased version. The cased version differentiates between upper and lowercase words, while the uncased version does not. For our example, we will use the BERT-base-uncased pretrained model. You can find the download URL for this and the other models further down the README.md page:

```
$ mkdir data
$ cd data
$ wget \
https://storage.googleapis.com/bert_models/2018_10_18/uncased_L-12_H-768_A-12.zip
$ unzip -a uncased_L-12_H-768_A-12.zip
```

This will create the following folder under the data directory of your local BERT project. The bert_config.json file is the configuration file used to create the original pretrained model, and the vocab.txt is the vocabulary used for the model, consisting of 30,522 words and word pieces:

```
uncased_L-12_H-768_A-12/
├── bert_config.json
├── bert_model.ckpt.data-00000-of-00001
├── bert_model.ckpt.index
├── bert_model.ckpt.meta
└── vocab.txt
```

The pretrained language model can be directly used as a text feature extractor for simple machine learning pipelines. This can be useful for situations where you want to just vectorize your text input, leveraging the distributional property of embeddings to get a denser and richer representation than one-hot encoding.

The input in this case is just a file with one sentence per line. Let us call it sentences.txt and put it into our ${CLASSIFIER_DATA} folder. You can generate the embeddings from the last hidden layers by identifying them as -1 (last hidden layer), -2 (hidden layer before that), and so on. The command to extract BERT embeddings for your input sentences is as follows:

```
$ export BERT_BASE_DIR=./data/uncased_L-12_H-768_A-12

$ export CLASSIFIER_DATA=./data/my_data

$ export TRAINED_CLASSIFIER=./data/my_classifier


$ python extract_features.py \
    --input_file=${CLASSIFIER_DATA}/sentences.txt \
    --output_file=${CLASSIFIER_DATA}/embeddings.jsonl \
    --vocab_file=${BERT_BASE_DIR}/vocab.txt \
    --bert_config_file=${BERT_BASE_DIR}/bert_config.json \
    --init_checkpoint=${BERT_BASE_DIR}/bert_model.ckpt \
    --layers=-1,-2,-3,-4 \
    --max_seq_length=128 \
    --batch_size=8
```

The command will extract the BERT embeddings from the last four hidden layers of the model and write them out into a line-oriented JSON file called embeddings.jsonl in the same directory as the input file.

Fine-tuning BERT

Because BERT has much more capacity than ULMFit, it is generally safe to skip this step for simpler domains and use the pretrained model directly for classification. However, there are times when the language of your domain is sufficiently different from that of Wikipedia (used to train ULMFit), and you need to fine-tune the pretrained model. Input to the fine tuning is just a list of sentences, one sentence per line. The sequence of sentences should be as provided in the text corpus for which the fine tuning is being done. Assuming the list of sentences is written out to a file ${CLASSIFIER_DATA}/finetune_sentences.txt, the command to create the pretraining data for fine tuning would be as follows:

```
$ export FINETUNED_MODEL_DIR=./data/my_finetuned_model
$ python create_pretraining_data.py \
    --input_file=${CLASSIFIER_DATA}/finetune_sentences.txt \
    --output_file=${CLASSIFIER_DATA/finetune_examples.tfrecord \
    --vocab_file=${BERT_BASE_DIR}/vocab.txt \
    --do_lower_case=True \
    --max_seq_length=128 \
    --max_predictions_per_seq=20 \
    --masked_lm_prob=0.15 \
    --random_seed=1234 \
    --dupe_factor=5
```

This script will randomly mask out 15% (masked_lm_prob) tokens in the input sentences and create them as labels for the BERT language model to predict. We then run the following script to write out the fine-tuned BERT model into the ${FINETUNED_MODEL_DIR}:

```
$ python run_pretraining.py \
    --input_file=${CLASSIFIER_DATA|/finetune_examples.tfrecord \
    --output_dir=${FINETUNED_MODEL_DIR} \
    --do_train=True \
    --do_eval=True \
    --bert_config_file=${BERT_BASE_DIR}/bert_config.json \
    --init_checkpoint=${BERT_BASE_DIR}/bert_model.ckpt \
    --train_batch_size=32 \
    --max_seq_length=128 \
    --max_predictions_per_seq=10000 \
    --num_train_steps=20 \
    --num_warmup_steps=10 \
    --learning_rate=2e-5
```

Classifying with BERT – command line

As mentioned in the previous section, it is often not necessary to fine-tune the pretrained model, and you can build classifiers directly on top of the pretrained model. The `run_classifier.py` script allows you to run either model against your own data. The script provides input parsers for several popular formats. In our example we will use the **Corpus of Linguistic Acceptability (COLA)** [39] format for single sentence classification and the **Microsoft Research Paraphrase Corpus (MRPC)** format [40] for sentence pair classification. The format is specified using the `--task_name` parameter.

For single-sentence classification, your training and validation input should be specified in separate TSV files named `train.tsv` and `dev.tsv` respectively, using the following format required by the COLA parser. Here {TAB} indicates the tab separator character. The "junk" string is just a placeholder and ignored. The class label needs to be an integer value corresponding to the class label of the training and validation record. The ID field is just a running number. The parser will prepend train, dev, or test to the ID value so they don't have to be unique across the TSV files:

```
id {TAB} class-label {TAB} "junk" {TAB} text-of-example
```

Your test file should be specified as another TSV file named `test.tsv` and have the following format. In addition, it should have a header shown as follows:

```
id {TAB} sentence
1  {TAB} text-of-test-sentence
...
```

For sentence pair classification, the formats for the `train.tsv` and `dev.tsv` files required by the MRPC parser should be as follows:

```
id {TAB} "junk" {TAB} "junk" {TAB} sentence-1 {TAB} sentence-2
```

And the corresponding format for `test.tsv` should be as follows:

```
label {TAB} "junk" {TAB} "junk" {TAB} sentence-1 {TAB} sentence-2
```

Put these three files into the `data/my_data` folder. You can then train your classifier using the pretrained BERT language model using the following command at the root of the BERT project. If you prefer to use a fine-tuned version, point the `--init_checkpoint` to the checkpoint files generated as a result of fine tuning instead. The following command will train the classifier with a maximum sentence length 128 and batch size 8 for 2 epochs and learning rate of 2e-5. It will output a file `test_results.tsv` in the `${TRAINED_CLASSIFIER}` folder, with the predictions from the trained model against the test data, as well as write out the checkpoint files for the trained model in the same directory:

```
$ python run_classifier.py \
    --task_name=COLA|MRPC \
    --do_train=true \
    --do_eval=true \
    --do_predict=true \
    --data_dir=${CLASSIFIER_DATA} \
    --vocab_file=${BERT_BASE_DIR}/vocab.txt \
    --bert_config_file=${BERT_BASE_DIR}/bert_config_file.json \
    --init_checkpoint=${BERT_BASE_DIR}/bert_model.ckpt \
    --max_seq_length=128 \
    --train_batch_size=8 \
    --learning_rate=2e-5 \
    --num_train_epochs=2.0 \
    --output_dir=${TRAINED_CLASSIFIER}
```

To predict only using a trained network, turn the `--do_train` and `--do_eval` flags to `false`.

Using BERT as part of your own network

Currently BERT is available on TensorFlow Hub as an estimator, but at the moment it is not fully compliant with TensorFlow 2.x, in the sense that it is not yet callable as a `tf.hub.KerasLayer`. Meanwhile, Zweig demonstrates how to include BERT in your Keras/TensorFlow 1.x-based network in his blog post [35].

The more popular way to use BERT in your own TensorFlow 2.x code is via the HuggingFace Transformers library. This library provides convenience classes for various popular Transformer architectures such as BERT, as well as convenience classes for fine-tuning on several downstream tasks. It was originally written for PyTorch, but has since been extended with convenience classes callable from TensorFlow as well. However, in order to use this library, you must have PyTorch installed as well.

The Transformers library provides the following classes:

1. A set of Transformer classes for 10 (at the time of writing) different Transformer architectures that can be instantiated from PyTorch client code. The naming convention is to append "Model" to the name of the architecture, for example, `BertModel`, `XLNetModel`, and so on. There is also a corresponding set of classes that can be instantiated from TensorFlow 2.x code; these are prefixed by "TF", for example, `TFBertModel`, `TFXLNetModel`, and so on.

2. Each Transformer model has a corresponding tokenizer class, which know how to tokenize text input for these classes. So the tokenizer corresponding to the BERT model is named `BertTokenizer`.

3. Each Transformer class has a set of convenience classes to allow fine-tuning the Transformer model to a set of downstream tasks. For example, the convenience classes corresponding to BERT are `BertForPreTraining`, `BertForMaskedLM`, `BertForNextSentencePrediction`, `BertForSequenceClassification`, `BertForMultipleChoice`, `BertForTokenClassification`, and `BertForQuestionAnswering`.

In order to install PyTorch, head over to the PyTorch site (`http://pytorch.org`) and find the section titled *Quick Start Locally*. Under it is a form where you have to specify some information about your platform, and the site will generate an installation command that will download and install PyTorch on your environment. Copy the command to your terminal and run it to install PyTorch in your environment.

Once you have installed PyTorch, install the Transformers library using the following `pip` command. Refer to `https://github.com/huggingface/transformers` for additional documentation on how to use the library:

```
$ pip install transformers
```

In order to run the example, you will also need to install the `tensorflow_datasets` package. You can do so using the `pip` command as follows:

```
$ pip install tensorflow-datasets
```

The following code instantiates a BERT cased model and fine-tunes it with data from the MRPC dataset. The MRPC task tries to predict if a pair of sentences are paraphrases of one another. The dataset is available from the `tensorflow-datasets` package. As usual, we first import the necessary libraries:

```
import os
import tensorflow as tf
import tensorflow_datasets
from transformers import BertTokenizer, \
TFBertForSequenceClassification, BertForSequenceClassification,\ glue_
convert_examples_to_features
```

We declare a few constants that we will use later in the code:

```
BATCH_SIZE = 32
FINE_TUNED_MODEL_DIR = "./data/"
```

We then instantiate a tokenizer and model using the wrappers from the Transformers library. The underlying model file comes from the pretrained BERT base cased model. Notice that the model class is a TensorFlow compatible class since we will fine-tune it from our TensorFlow 2.x code:

```
tokenizer = BertTokenizer.from_pretrained("bert-base-cased")
model = TFBertForSequenceClassification.from_pretrained("bert-base-cased")
```

We then load up the training and validation data from the `tensorflow-datasets` package using its API, then create TensorFlow datasets that will be used to fine-tune our model:

```
# Load dataset via TensorFlow Datasets
data, info = tensorflow_datasets.load(
"glue/mrpc", with_info=True)
num_train = info.splits["train"].num_examples
num_valid = info.splits["validation"].num_examples

# Prepare dataset for GLUE as a tf.data.Dataset instance
Xtrain = glue_convert_examples_to_features(
data["train"], tokenizer, 128, "mrpc")
Xtrain = Xtrain.shuffle(128).batch(BATCH_SIZE).repeat(-1)
Xvalid = glue_convert_examples_to_features(
data["validation"], tokenizer, 128, "mrpc")
Xvalid = Xvalid.batch(BATCH_SIZE)
```

We then define our loss function, optimizer, and metric, and fit the model for a few epochs of training. Since we are fine-tuning the model, the number of epochs is only two, and our learning rate is also very small:

```
opt = tf.keras.optimizers.Adam(
learning_rate=3e-5, epsilon=1e-08)
loss = tf.keras.losses.SparseCategoricalCrossentropy(
from_logits=True)
metric = tf.keras.metrics.SparseCategoricalAccuracy("accuracy")
model.compile(optimizer=opt, loss=loss, metrics=[metric])

train_steps = num_train // BATCH_SIZE
valid_steps = num_valid // BATCH_SIZE
history = model.fit(Xtrain,
epochs=2, steps_per_epoch=train_steps,
validation_data=Xvalid, validation_steps=valid_steps)
```

Once trained, we save our fine-tuned model:

```
model.save_pretrained(FINE_TUNED_MODEL_DIR)
```

In order to predict that a pair of sentences are paraphrases of one another, we will load the model back as a PyTorch model. The `from_tf=True` parameter indicates that the saved model is a TensorFlow checkpoint. Note that it does not seem to be possible at the moment to deserialize a TensorFlow checkpoint directly into a TensorFlow Transformer model:

```
saved_model = BertForSequenceClassification.from_pretrained(FINE_
TUNED_MODEL_DIR, from_tf=True)
```

We then test our saved model using sentence pairs (`sentence_0`, `sentence_1`) which are paraphrases of each other, and (`sentence_0`, `sentence_2`) which are not:

```
def print_result(id1, id2, pred):
    if pred == 1:
        print("sentence_1 is a paraphrase of sentence_0")
    else:
        print("sentence_1 is not a paraphrase of sentence_0")

sentence_0 = "At least 12 people were killed in the battle last week."
sentence_1 = "At least 12 people lost their lives in last weeks
fighting."
sentence_2 = "The fires burnt down the houses on the street."

inputs_1 = tokenizer.encode_plus(sentence_0, sentence_1,
add_special_tokens=False, return_tensors="pt")
inputs_2 = tokenizer.encode_plus(sentence_0, sentence_2,
add_special_tokens=False, return_tensors="pt")

pred_1 = saved_model(**inputs_1)[0].argmax().item()
pred_2 = saved_model(**inputs_2)[0].argmax().item()

print_result(0, 1, pred_1)
print_result(0, 2, pred_2)
```

As expected, the output of this code snippet is as follows:

```
sentence_1 is a paraphrase of sentence_0
sentence_1 is not a paraphrase of sentence_0
```

The usage pattern of instantiating a model and tokenizer from a pretrained model, optionally fine-tuning it using a comparatively small labeled dataset, and then using it for predictions, is fairly typical and applicable for the other fine tuning classes as well. The Transformers API provides a standardized API to work with multiple Transformer models and do standard fine-tuning tasks on them. The preceding described code can be found in the file `bert_paraphrase.py` in the code accompanying this chapter.

Summary

In this chapter, we have learned about the concepts behind distributional representations of words and its various implementations, starting from static word embeddings such as Word2Vec and GloVe.

We have then looked at improvements to the basic idea, such as subword embeddings, sentence embeddings that capture the context of the word in the sentence, as well as the use of entire language models for generating embeddings. While the language model-based embeddings are achieving state of the art results nowadays, there are still plenty of applications where more traditional approaches yield very good results, so it is important to know them all and understand the tradeoffs.

We have also looked briefly at other interesting uses of word embeddings outside the realm of natural language, where the distributional properties of other kinds of sequences are leveraged to make predictions in domains such as information retrieval and recommendation systems.

You are now ready to use embeddings not only for your text-based neural networks, which we will look at in greater depth in the next chapter, but also to use embeddings in other areas of machine learning.

References

1. Mikolov, T., et al. (2013, Sep 7) *Efficient Estimation of Word Representations in Vector Space*. arXiv:1301.3781v3 [cs.CL].

2. Mikolov, T., et al. (2013, Sep 17). *Exploiting Similarities among Languages for Machine Translation*. arXiv:1309.4168v1 [cs.CL].

3. Mikolov, T., et al. (2013). *Distributed Representations of Words and Phrases and their Compositionality*. Advances in Neural Information Processing Systems 26 (NIPS 2013).

4. Pennington, J., Socher, R., Manning, C. (2014). *GloVe: Global Vectors for Word Representation*. D14-1162, Proceedings of the 2014 Conference on Empirical Methods in Natural Language Processing (EMNLP).

5. Niu, F., et al (2011, 11 Nov). *HOGWILD! A Lock-Free Approach to Parallelizing Stochastic Gradient Descent*. arXiv:1106.5730v2 [math.OC].

6. Levy, O., Goldberg, Y. (2014). *Neural Word Embedding as Implicit Matrix Factorization*. Advances in Neural Information Processing Systems 27 (NIPS 2014).

7. Mahoney, M. (2011, 1 Sep). text8 dataset. `http://mattmahoney.net/dc/textdata.html`.

8. Rehurek, R. (2019, 10 Apr). gensim documentation for Word2Vec model. `https://radimrehurek.com/gensim/models/word2vec.html`.

9. Levy, O., Goldberg, Y. (2014, 26-27 June). *Linguistic Regularities in Sparse and Explicit Word Representations*. Proceedings of the Eighteenth Conference on Computational Language Learning, pp 171-180 (ACL 2014).

10. Rehurek, R. (2019, 10 Apr). gensim documentation for KeyedVectors. `https://radimrehurek.com/gensim/models/keyedvectors.html`.

11. Almeida, T. A., Gamez Hidalgo, J. M., and Yamakami, A. (2011). Contributions to the Study of SMS Spam Filtering: New Collection and Results. Proceedings of the 2011 ACM Symposium on Document Engineering (DOCENG). URL: `http://www.dt.fee.unicamp.br/~tiago/smsspamcollection/`.

12. Speer, R., Chin, J. (2016, 6 Apr). *An Ensemble Method to Produce High-Quality Word Embeddings*. arXiv:1604.01692v1 [cs.CL].

13. Speer, R. (2016, 25 May). *ConceptNet Numberbatch: a new name for the best Word Embeddings you can download*. URL: `http://blog.conceptnet.io/posts/2016/conceptnet-numberbatch-a-new-name-for-the-best-word-embeddings-you-can-download/`.

14. Barkan, O., Koenigstein, N. (2016, 13-16 Sep). *Item2Vec: Neural Item Embedding for Collaborative Filtering*. IEEE 26th International Workshop on Machine Learning for Signal Processing (MLSP 2016).

15. Grover, A., Leskovec, J. (2016, 13-17 Aug). *node2vec: Scalable Feature Learning for Networks*. Proceedings of the 22nd ACM SIGKDD International Conference on Knowledge Discovery and Data Mining. (KDD 2016).

16. TensorFlow 2.0 Models on TensorFlow Hub. URL: `https://tfhub.dev/s?q=tf2-preview`.

17. Zhang, X., LeCun, Y. (2016, 4 Apr). *Text Understanding from Scratch*. arXiv 1502.01710v5 [cs.LG].

18. Bojanowski, P., et al. (2017, 19 Jun). *Enriching Word Vectors with Subword Information.* arXiv: 1607.04606v2 [cs.CL].

19. Facebook AI Research, fastText (2017). GitHub repository, `https://github.com/facebookresearch/fastText`.

20. McCann, B., Bradbury, J., Xiong, C., Socher, R. (2017). *Learned in Translation: Contextualized Word Vectors.* Neural Information Processing Systems, 2017.

21. Peters, M., et al. (2018, 22 Mar). *Deep contextualized word representations.* arXiv: 1802.05365v2 [cs.CL].

22. Kiros, R., et al. (2015, 22 June). *Skip-Thought Vectors.* arXiv: 1506.06727v1 [cs.CL].

23. Google Research, skip_thoughts (2017). GitHub repository. URL: `https://github.com/tensorflow/models/tree/master/research/skip_thoughts`.

24. Iyer, M., Manjunatha, V., Boyd-Graber, J., Daume, H. (2015, July 26-31). *Deep Unordered Composition Rivals Syntactic Methods for Text Classification.* Proceedings of the 53rd Annual Meeting of the Association for Computational Linguistics and the 7th International Joint Conference on Natural Language Processing (ACL 2015).

25. Vaswani, A., et al. (2017, 6 Dec). *Attention Is All You Need.* arXiv: 1706.03762v5 [cs.CL].

26. Le, Q., Mikolov, T. (2014) *Distributed Representation of Sentences and Documents.* arXiv: 1405.4053v2 [cs.CL].

27. Howard, J., Ruder, S. (2018, 23 May). *Universal Language Model Fine-Tuning for Text Classification.* arXiv: 1801.06146v5 [cs.CL].

28. Peters, et al. (2018, 15 Feb). *Deep Contextualized Word Representations.* arXiv: 1802.05365v2 [cs.CL].

29. Devlin, J., Chang, M., Lee, K., Toutanova, K. (2018, 11 Oct). *BERT: Pretraining of Deep Bidirectional Transformers for Language Understanding.* arXiv: 1810.04805v1 [cs.CL], URL: `https://www.google.com/url?q=https://github.com/google-research/bert`.

30. Radford, A., Narasimhan, K., Salimans, T., Sutskever, I. (2018). *Improving Language Understanding by Generative Pretraining.* URL: `https://openai.com/blog/language-unsupervised/`.

31. Radford, A., et al. (2019). *Language Models are unsupervised Multitask Learners.* URL: `https://openai.com/blog/better-language-models/`.

32. Google Collaboratory, URL: `https://colab.research.google.com`.

33. Google Cloud Platform, URL: `https://cloud.google.com/`.

34. Google Research, BERT (2019). GitHub repository. URL: `https://github.com/google-research/bert`.

35. Zweig, J. (2019). BERT in Keras with TensorFlow Hub. *Towards Data Science blog*. URL: `https://towardsdatascience.com/bert-in-keras-with-tensorflow-hub-76bcbc9417b`.

36. TF-IDF. Wikipedia. Retrieved May 2019. `https://en.wikipedia.org/wiki/Tf%E2%80%93idf`.

37. Latent Semantic Analysis. Wikipedia. Retrieved May 2019. `https://en.wikipedia.org/wiki/Latent_semantic_analysis`.

38. Topic Model. Wikipedia. Retrieved May 2019. `https://en.wikipedia.org/wiki/Topic_model`.

39. Warstadt, A., Singh, A., and Bowman, S. (2018). *Neural Network Acceptability Judgements*. arXiv 1805:12471 [cs.CL], URL: `https://nyu-mll.github.io/CoLA/`.

40. Microsoft Research Paraphrase Corpus. (2018). URL: `https://www.microsoft.com/en-us/download/details.aspx?id=52398`.

41. Nozawa, K. (2019). Something2Vec papers. URL: `https://gist.github.com/nzw0301/333afc00bd508501268fa7bf40cafe4e`.

42. Perrone, V., et al. (2016). *Poisson Random Fields for Dynamic Feature Models*. URL: `https://archive.ics.uci.edu/ml/datasets/NIPS+Conference+Papers+1987-2015`.

43. Perozzi, B., Al-Rfou, R., and Skiena, S. (2014). *DeepWalk: Online Learning of Social Representations*. arXiv 1403.6652v2 [cs.SI].

8

Recurrent Neural Networks

In *chapter 4*, we learned about **Convolutional Neural Networks (CNNs)**, and saw how they exploit the spatial geometry of their inputs. For example, CNNs for images apply convolutions to initially small patches of the image, and progress to larger and larger areas of the image using pooling operations. Convolutions and pooling operations for images are in two dimensions: the width and height. For audio and text streams, one-dimensional convolution and pooling operations are applied along the time dimension, and for video streams, these operations are applied in three dimensions: along the height, width, and time dimensions.

In this chapter, we will focus on **Recurrent Neural Networks (RNNs)**, a class of neural networks that are popularly used on text inputs. RNNs are very flexible and have been used to solve problems such as speech recognition, language modeling, machine translation, sentiment analysis, and image captioning, to name a few. RNNs exploit the sequential nature of their input. Sequential inputs could be text, speech, time series, and anything else where the occurrence of an element in a sequence is dependent on the elements that came before it. In this chapter, we will see examples of various RNNs, and learn how to implement them with TensorFlow 2.0.

We will first look at the internals of a basic RNN cell and how it deals with these sequential dependencies in the input. We will also learn about some limitations of the basic RNN cell (implemented as SimpleRNN in Keras) and see how two popular variants of the SimpleRNN cell – the **Long Short-Term Memory (LSTM)** and **Gated Recurrent Unit (GRU)** – overcome this limitation.

We will then zoom out one level and consider the RNN layer itself, which is just the RNN cell applied to every time step. An RNN can be thought of as a graph of RNN cells, where each cell performs the same operation on successive elements of the sequence. We will describe some simple modifications to improve performance, such as making the RNN bidirectional and/or stateful.

We will then look at some standard RNN topologies and the kind of applications they can be used to solve. RNNs can be adapted to different types of applications by rearranging the cells in the graph. We will see some examples of these configurations and how they are used to solve specific problems. We will also consider the sequence to sequence (or seq2seq) architecture, which has been used with great success in machine translation and various other fields. We will then look at what an attention mechanism is, and how it can be used to improve the performance of sequence to sequence architectures.

Finally, we will look at the transformer architecture, which combines ideas from CNNs, RNNs, and attention mechanisms. Transformer architecture has been used to create novel architectures such as BERT.

The basic RNN cell

Traditional multilayer perceptron neural networks make the assumption that all inputs are independent of each other. This assumption is not true for many types of sequence data. For example, words in a sentence, musical notes in a composition, stock prices over time, or even molecules in a compound, are examples of sequences where an element will display a dependence on previous elements.

RNN cells incorporate this dependence by having a hidden state, or memory, that holds the essence of what has been seen so far. The value of the hidden state at any point in time is a function of the value of the hidden state at the previous time step, and the value of the input at the current time step, that is:

$$h_t = \phi(h_{t-1}, X_t)$$

Here, h_t and h_{t-1} are the values of the hidden states at the time t and t-1 respectively, and x_t is the value of the input at time t. Notice that the equation is recursive, that is, h_{t-1} can be represented in terms of h_{t-2} and x_{t-1}, and so on, until the beginning of the sequence. This is how RNNs encode and incorporate information from arbitrarily long sequences.

We can also represent the RNN cell graphically as shown in *Figure 1(a)*. At time t, the cell has an input $x(t)$ and output $y(t)$. Part of the output $y(t)$ (represented by the hidden state h_t) is fed back into the cell for use at a later time step t+1.

Just as in a traditional neural network, where the learned parameters are stored as weight matrices, the RNN's parameters are defined by the three weight matrices U, V, and W, corresponding to the weights of the input, output, and hidden states respectively:

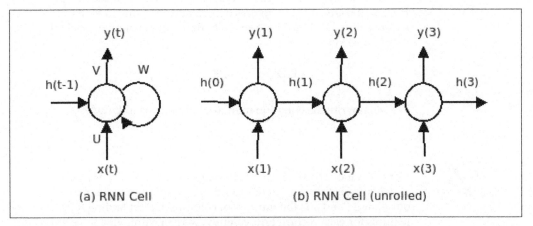

Figure 1: (a) Schematic of an RNN cell; (b) RNN cell unrolled

Figure 1(b) shows the same RNN in an "unrolled view". Unrolling just means that we draw the network out for the complete sequence. The network shown here has three time steps, suitable for processing three element sequences. Note that the weight matrices U, V, and W, that we spoke about earlier, are shared between each of the time steps. This is because we are applying the same operation to different inputs at each time step. Being able to share these weights across all the time steps greatly reduces the number of parameters that the RNN needs to learn.

We can also describe the RNN as a computation graph in terms of equations. The internal state of the RNN at a time t is given by the value of the hidden vector $h(t)$, which is the sum of the weight matrix W and the hidden state h_{t-1} at time $t-1$, and the product of the weight matrix U and the input x_t at time t, passed through a tanh activation function. The choice of tanh over other activation functions such as sigmoid has to do with it being more efficient for learning in practice, and helps combat the vanishing gradient problem, which we will learn about later in the chapter.

For notational convenience, in all our equations describing different types of RNN architectures in this chapter, we have omitted explicit reference to the bias terms by incorporating it within the matrix. Consider the following equation of a line in an n-dimensional space. Here w_1 through w_n refer to the coefficients of the line in each of the n dimensions, and the bias b refers to the y-intercept along each of these dimensions.

$$y = w_1 x_1 + w_2 x_2 + \cdots + w_n x_n + b$$

We can rewrite the equation in matrix notation as follows:

$$y = WX + b$$

Here W is a matrix of shape (m, n) and b is a vector of shape $(m, 1)$, where m is the number of rows corresponding to the records in our dataset, and n is the number of columns corresponding to the features for each record. Equivalently, we can eliminate the vector b by folding it into our matrix W by treating the b vector as a feature column corresponding to the "unit" feature of W. Thus:

$$y = w_1 x_1 + w_2 x_2 + \cdots + w_n x_n + w_0(1)$$
$$= W'X$$

Here W' is a matrix of shape $(m, n+1)$, where the last column contains the values of b.

The resulting notation ends up being more compact and (we believe) easier for the reader to comprehend and retain as well.

The output vector y_t at time t is the product of the weight matrix V and the hidden state h_t, passed through a softmax activation, such that the resulting vector is a set of output probabilities:

$$h_t = \tanh(W h_{t-1} + U x_t)$$
$$y_t = softmax(V h_t)$$

Keras provides the SimpleRNN recurrent layer that incorporates all the logic we have seen so far, as well as the more advanced variants such as LSTM and GRU, which we will learn about later in this chapter. Strictly speaking, it is not necessary to understand how they work in order to start building with them.

However, an understanding of the structure and equations is helpful for when you need to build your own specialized RNN cell to overcome a specific problem.

Now that we understand the flow of data forward through the RNN cell, that is, how it combines its input and hidden states to produce the output and the next hidden state, let us now examine the flow of gradients in the reverse direction. This is a process called **Backpropagation through time**, or **BPTT**.

Backpropagation through time (BPTT)

Just like traditional neural networks, training RNNs also involves backpropagation of gradients. The difference in this case is that since the weights are shared by all time steps, the gradient at each output depends not only on the current time step, but also on the previous ones. This process is called backpropagation through time [11]. Because the weights U, V, and W, are shared across the different time steps in case of RNNs, we need to sum up the gradients across the various time steps in case of BPTT. This is the key difference between traditional backpropagation and BPTT.

Consider the RNN with five time steps shown in *Figure 2*. During the forward pass, the network produces predictions $\hat{y}_t$ at time t that are compared with the label y_t to compute a loss L_t. During backpropagation (shown by the dotted lines), the gradients of the loss with respect to the weights U, V, and W, are computed at each time step and the parameters updated with the sum of the gradients:

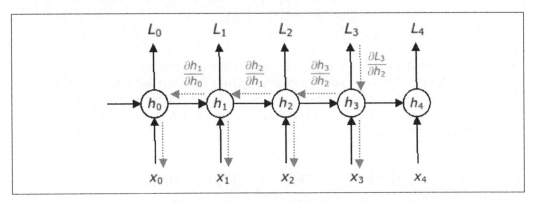

Figure 2: Backpropagation through time

The following equation shows the gradient of the loss with respect to W. We focus on this weight because it is the cause for the phenomenon known as the vanishing and exploding gradient problem.

This problem manifests as the gradients of the loss approaching either zero or infinity, making the network hard to train. To understand why this happens, consider the equation of the SimpleRNN we saw earlier; the hidden state h_t is dependent on h_{t-1}, which in turn is dependent on h_{t-2}, and so on:

$$\frac{\partial L}{\partial W} = \sum_t \frac{\partial L_t}{\partial W}$$

Let us now see what happens to this gradient at timestep $t=3$. By the chain rule, the gradient of the loss with respect to W can be decomposed to a product of three sub-gradients. The gradient of the hidden state h_2 with respect to W can be further decomposed as the sum of the gradient of each hidden state with respect to the previous one. Finally, each gradient of the hidden state with respect to the previous one can be further decomposed as the product of gradients of the current hidden state against the previous hidden state:

$$\frac{\partial L_3}{\partial W} = \frac{\partial L_3}{\partial \hat{y}_3} \frac{\partial \hat{y}_3}{\partial h_3} \frac{\partial h_3}{\partial W}$$

$$= \sum_{t=0}^{3} \frac{\partial L_3}{\partial \hat{y}_3} \frac{\partial \hat{y}_3}{\partial h_3} \frac{\partial h_3}{\partial h_t} \frac{\partial h_t}{\partial W}$$

$$= \sum_{t=0}^{3} \frac{\partial L_3}{\partial \hat{y}_3} \frac{\partial \hat{y}_3}{\partial h_3} \left(\prod_{j=t+1}^{3} \frac{\partial h_j}{\partial h_{j-1}} \right) \frac{\partial h_t}{\partial W}$$

Similar calculations are done to compute the gradient of the other losses L_0 through L_4 with respect to W, and sum them up into the gradient update for W. We will not explore the math further in this book, but this WildML blog post [12] has a very good explanation of BPTT, including a more detailed derivation of the math behind the process.

Vanishing and exploding gradients

The reason BPTT is particularly sensitive to the problem of vanishing and exploding gradients comes from the product part of the expression representing the final formulation of the gradient of the loss with respect to W. Consider the case where the individual gradients of a hidden state with respect to the previous one is less than 1.

As we backpropagate across multiple time steps, the product of gradients get smaller and smaller, ultimately leading to the problem of vanishing gradients. Similarly, if the gradients are larger than 1, the products get larger and larger, and ultimately lead to the problem of exploding gradients.

Of the two, exploding gradients are more easily detectable. The gradients will become very large and turn into **Not a Number** (**NaN**) and the training process will crash. Exploding gradients can be controlled by clipping them at a predefined threshold [13]. TensorFlow 2.0 allows you to clip gradients using the `clipvalue` or `clipnorm` parameter during optimizer construction, or by explicitly clipping gradients using `tf.clip_by_value`.

The effect of vanishing gradients is that gradients from time steps that are far away do not contribute anything to the learning process, so the RNN ends up not learning any long-range dependencies. While there are a few approaches to minimizing the problem, such as proper initialization of the W matrix, more aggressive regularization, using ReLU instead of `tanh` activation, and pretraining the layers using unsupervised methods, the most popular solution is to use LSTM or GRU architectures, each of which will be explained shortly. These architectures have been designed to deal with vanishing gradients and learn long-term dependencies more effectively.

RNN cell variants

In this section we'll look at some cell variants of RNNs. We'll begin by looking at a variant of the SimpleRNN cell: the Long short-term memory RNN.

Long short-term memory (LSTM)

The LSTM is a variant of the SimpleRNN cell that is capable of learning long-term dependencies. LSTMs were first proposed by Hochreiter and SchmidHuber [14] and refined by many other researchers. They work well on a large variety of problems and are the most widely used RNN variant.

We have seen how the SimpleRNN combines the hidden state from the previous time step and the current input through a tanh layer to implement recurrence. LSTMs also implement recurrence in a similar way, but instead of a single `tanh` layer, there are four layers interacting in a very specific way. The following diagram illustrates the transformations that are applied in the hidden state at time step t.

The diagram looks complicated, but let us look at it component by component. The line across the top of the diagram is the cell state c, representing the internal memory of the unit.

The line across the bottom is the hidden state h, and the i, f, o, and g gates are the mechanisms by which the LSTM works around the vanishing gradient problem. During training, the LSTM learns the parameters for these gates:

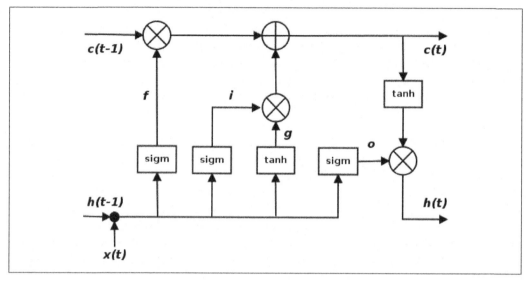

Figure 3: An LSTM cell

An alternative way to think about how these gates work inside an LSTM cell is to consider the equations for the cell. These equations describe how the value of the hidden state h_t at time t is calculated from the value of hidden state h_{t-1} at the previous time step. In general, the equation-based description tends to be clearer and more concise, and is usually the way a new cell design is presented in academic papers. Diagrams, when provided, may or may not be comparable to ones you have seen earlier. For these reasons, it usually makes sense to learn to read the equations and visualize the cell design. To that end, we will describe the other cell variants in this book using equations only.

The set of equations representing an LSTM are shown as follows:

$$i = \sigma(W_i h_{t-1} + U_i x_t + V_i c_{t-1})$$
$$f = \sigma(W_f h_{t-1} + U_f x_t + V_f c_{t-1})$$
$$o = \sigma(W_o h_{t-1} + U_o x_t + V_o c_{t-1})$$
$$g = \tanh(W_g h_{t-1} + U_g x_t)$$
$$c_t = (f * c_{t-1}) + (g * i)$$
$$h_t = \tanh(c_t) * o$$

Here i, f, and o are the input, forget, and output gates. They are computed using the same equations but with different parameter matrices W_i, U_i, W_f, U_f, and W_o, U_o. The sigmoid function modulates the output of these gates between 0 and 1, so the output vectors produced can be multiplied element-wise with another vector to define how much of the second vector can pass through the first one.

The forget gate defines how much of the previous state h_{t-1} you want to allow to pass through. The input gate defines how much of the newly computed state for the current input x_t you want to let through, and the output gate defines how much of the internal state you want to expose to the next layer. The internal hidden state g is computed based on the current input x_t and the previous hidden state h_{t-1}. Notice that the equation for g is identical to that for the SimpleRNN, except that in this case we will modulate the output by the output of input vector i.

Given i, f, o, and g, we can now calculate the cell state c_t at time t as the cell state c_{t-1} at time $(t-1)$ multiplied by the value of the forget gate g, plus the state g multiplied by the input gate i. This is basically a way to combine the previous memory and the new input – setting the forget gate to 0 ignores the old memory and setting the input gate to 0 ignores the newly computed state. Finally, the hidden state h_t at time t is computed as the memory c_t at time t, with the output gate o.

One thing to realize is that the LSTM is a drop-in replacement for a SimpleRNN cell; the only difference is that LSTMs are resistant to the vanishing gradient problem. You can replace an RNN cell in a network with an LSTM without worrying about any side effects. You should generally see better results along with longer training times.

TensorFlow 2.0 also provides a ConvLSTM2D implementation based on the paper by Shi, et al. [18], where the matrix multiplications are replaced by convolution operators.

If you would like to learn more about LSTMs, please take a look at the WildML RNN tutorial [15] and Christopher Olah's blog post [16]. The first covers LSTMs in somewhat greater detail and the second takes you step by step through the computations in a very visual way.

Now that we have covered LTSMs, we will cover the other popular RNN cell architecture – GRUs.

Gated recurrent unit (GRU)

The GRU is a variant of the LSTM and was introduced by Cho, et al [17]. It retains the LSTM's resistance to the vanishing gradient problem, but its internal structure is simpler, and is therefore faster to train, since less computations are needed to make updates to its hidden state.

Instead of the input (i), forgot (f), and output (o) gates in the LSTM cell, the GRU cell has two gates, an update gate z and a reset gate r. The update gate defines how much previous memory to keep around, and the reset gate defines how to combine the new input with the previous memory. There is no persistent cell state distinct from the hidden state as it is in LSTM.

The GRU cell defines the computation of the hidden state h_t at time t from the hidden state h_{t-1} at the previous time step using the following set of equations:

$$z = \sigma(W_z h_{t-1} + U_z x_t)$$
$$r = \sigma(W_r h_{t-1} + U_r x_t)$$
$$c = \tanh(W_c(h_{t-1} * r) + U_c x_t)$$
$$h_t = (z * c) + ((1 - z) * h_{t-1})$$

The outputs of the update gate z and the reset gate r are both computed using a combination of the previous hidden state h_{t-1} and the current input x_t. The sigmoid function modulates the output of these functions between 0 and 1. The cell state c is computed as a function of the output of the reset gate r and input x_t. Finally, the hidden state h_t at time t is computed as a function of the cell state c and the previous hidden state h_{t-1}. The parameters W_z, U_z, W_r, U_r, and W_c, U_c are learned during training.

Similar to LSTM, TensorFlow 2.0 (`tf.keras`) provides an implementation for the basic GRU layer as well, which is a drop-in replacement for the RNN cell.

Peephole LSTM

The peephole LSTM is an LSTM variant that was first proposed by Gers and Schmidhuber [19]. It adds "peepholes" to the input, forget, and output gates, so they can see the previous cell state c_{t-1}. The equations for computing the hidden state h_t, at time t, from the hidden state h_{t-1} at the previous time step, in a peephole LSTM are shown next.

Notice that the only difference from the equations for the LSTM is the additional c_{t-1} term for computing outputs of the input (*i*), forget (*f*), and output (*o*) gates:

$$i = \sigma(W_i h_{t-1} + U_i x_t + V_i c_{t-1})$$
$$f = \sigma(W_f h_{t-1} + U_f x_t + V_f c_{t-1})$$
$$o = \sigma(W_o h_{t-1} + U_o x_t + V_o c_{t-1})$$
$$g = \tanh(W_g h_{t-1} + U_g x_t)$$
$$c_t = (f * c_{t-1}) + (g * i)$$
$$h_t = \tanh(c_t) * o$$

TensorFlow 2.0 provides an experimental implementation of the peephole LSTM cell. To use this in your own RNN layers, you will need to wrap the cell (or list of cells) in the RNN wrapper, as shown in the following code snippet:

```
hidden_dim = 256
peephole_cell = tf.keras.experimental.PeepholeLSTMCell(hidden_dim)
rnn_layer = tf.keras.layers.RNN(peephole_cell)
```

In the previous section, we have seen some RNN cell variants that were developed to target specific inadequacies of the basic RNN cell. In the next section, we will look at variations in the architecture of the RNN network itself, which were built to address specific use cases.

RNN variants

In this section, we will look at a couple of variations on the basic RNN architecture that can provide performance improvements in some specific circumstances. Note that these strategies can be applied for different kinds of RNN cells, as well as for different RNN topologies, which we will learn about later.

Bidirectional RNNs

We have seen how, at any given time step *t*, the output of the RNN is dependent on the outputs at all previous time steps. However, it is entirely possible that the output is also dependent on the future outputs as well. This is especially true for applications such as natural language processing where the attributes of the word or phrase we are trying to predict may be dependent on the context given by the entire enclosing sentence, not just the words that came before it.

This problem can be solved using a bidirectional LSTM, which are essentially two RNNs stacked on top of each other, one reading the input from left to right, and the other reading the input from the right to the left. The output at each time step will be based on the hidden state of both RNNs. Bidirectional RNNs allow the network to place equal emphasis on the beginning and end of the sequence, and typically results in performance improvements.

TensorFlow 2.0 provides support for bidirectional RNNs through a bidirectional wrapper layer. To make a RNN layer bidirectional, all that is needed is to wrap the layer with this wrapper layer, shown as follows:

```
self.lstm = tf.keras.layers.Bidirectional(
    tf.keras.layers.LSTM(10, return_sequences=True,
        input_shape=(5, 10))
)
```

Stateful RNNs

RNNs can also be stateful, which means that they can maintain state across batches during training. That is, the hidden state computed for a batch of training data will be used as the initial hidden state for the next batch of training data. However, this needs to be explicitly set, since TensorFlow 2.0 (tf.keras) RNNs are stateless by default, and resets the state after each batch. Setting an RNN to be stateful means that it can build state across its training sequence and even maintain that state when doing predictions.

The benefits of using stateful RNNs are smaller network sizes and/or lower training times. The disadvantage is that we are now responsible for training the network with a batch size that reflects the periodicity of the data and resetting the state after each epoch. In addition, data should not be shuffled while training the network since the order in which the data is presented is relevant for stateful networks.

To set a RNN layer as stateful, set the named variable stateful to True. In our example of a one-to-many topology for learning to generate text, we provide an example of using a stateful RNN. Here, we train using data consisting of contiguous text slices, so setting the LSTM to stateful means that the hidden state generated from the previous text chunk is reused for the current text chunk.

In the next section on RNN topologies, we will look at different ways to set up the RNN network for different use cases.

RNN topologies

We have seen examples of how MLP and CNN architectures can be composed to form more complex networks. RNNs offer yet another degree of freedom, in that it allows sequence input and output. This means that RNN cells can be arranged in different ways to build networks that are adapted to solve different types of problems. *Figure 4* shows five different configurations of inputs, hidden layers, and outputs, represented by red, green, and blue boxes respectively:

Of these, the first one (one-to-one) is not interesting from a sequence processing point of view, since it can be implemented as a simple Dense network with one input and one output.

The one-to-many case has a single input and outputs a sequence. An example of such a network might be a network that can generate text tags from images [6], containing short text descriptions of different aspects of the image. Such a network would be trained with image input and labeled sequences of text representing the image tags:

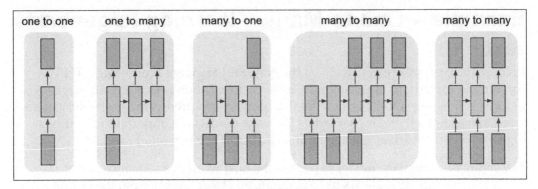

Figure 4: Common RNN topologies. Image Source: Andrej Karpathy [5]

The many-to-one case is the reverse; it takes a sequence of tensors as input but outputs a single tensor. Examples of such networks would be a sentiment analysis network [7], which takes as input a block of text such as a movie review and outputs a single sentiment value.

The many-to-many use case comes in two flavors. The first one is more popular and is better known as the seq2seq model. In this model, a sequence is read in and produces a context vector representing the input sequence, which is used to generate the output sequence.

The topology has been used with great success in the field of machine translation, as well as problems that can be reframed as machine translation problems. Real life examples of the former can be found in [8, 9], and an example of the latter is described in [10].

The second many-to-many type has an output cell corresponding to each input cell. This kind of network is suited for use cases where there is a 1:1 correspondence between the input and output, such as time series. The major difference between this model and the seq2seq model is that the input does not have to be completely encoded before the decoding process begins.

In the next three sections, we provide examples of a one-to-many network that learns to generate text, a many-to-one network that does sentiment analysis, and a many-to-many network of the second type, which predicts **Part-of-speech (POS)** for words in a sentence. Because of the popularity of the seq2seq network, we will cover it in more detail later in this chapter.

Example – One-to-Many – learning to generate text

RNNs have been used extensively by the **Natural Language Processing** (NLP) community for various applications. One such application is to build language models. A language model is a model that allows us to predict the probability of a word in a text given previous words. Language models are important for various higher-level tasks such as machine translation, spelling correction, and so on.

The ability of a language model to predict the next word in a sequence makes it a generative model that allows us to generate text by sampling from the output probabilities of different words in the vocabulary. The training data is a sequence of words, and the label is the word appearing at the next time step in the sequence.

For our example, we will train a character-based RNN on the text of the children's stories "Alice in Wonderland" and its sequel "Through the Looking Glass" by Lewis Carroll. We have chosen to build a character-based model because it has a smaller vocabulary and trains quicker. The idea is the same as training and using a word-based language model, except we will use characters instead of words. Once trained, the model can be used to generate some text in the same style.

The data for our example will come from the plain texts of two novels from the Project Gutenberg website [36]. Input to the network are sequences of 100 characters, and the corresponding output is another sequence of 100 characters, offset from the input by 1 position.

That is, if the input is the sequence $[c_1, c_2, ..., c_n]$, the output will be $[c_2, c_3, ..., c_{n+1}]$. We will train the network for 50 epochs, and at the end of every 10 epochs, we will generate a fixed size sequence of characters starting with a standard prefix. In the following example, we have used the prefix "Alice", the name of the protagonist in our novels.

As always, we will first import the necessary libraries and set up some constants. Here the DATA_DIR points to a data folder under the location where you downloaded the source code for this chapter. The CHECKPOINT_DIR is the location, a folder checkpoints under the data folder, where we will save the weights of the model at the end of every 10 epochs:

```
import os
import numpy as np
import re
import shutil
import tensorflow as tf

DATA_DIR = "./data"
CHECKPOINT_DIR = os.path.join(DATA_DIR, "checkpoints")
```

Next we download and prepare the data for our network to consume. The texts of both books are publicly available from the Project Gutenberg website. The tf.keras.utils.get_file() function will check to see whether the file is already downloaded to your local drive, and if not, it will download to a datasets folder under the location of the code. We also preprocess the input a little here, removing newline and byte order mark characters from the text. This step will create the texts variable, a flat list of characters for these two books:

```
def download_and_read(urls):
    texts = []
    for i, url in enumerate(urls):
        p = tf.keras.utils.get_file("ex1-{:d}.txt".format(i), url,
            cache_dir=".")
        text = open(p, "r").read()
        # remove byte order mark
        text = text.replace("\ufeff", "")
        # remove newlines
        text = text.replace('\n', ' ')
        text = re.sub(r'\s+', " ", text)
        # add it to the list
        texts.extend(text)
    return texts
```

```
texts = download_and_read([
    "http://www.gutenberg.org/cache/epub/28885/pg28885.txt",
    "https://www.gutenberg.org/files/12/12-0.txt"
])
```

Next, we will create our vocabulary. In our case, our vocabulary contains 90 unique characters, composed of uppercase and lowercase alphabets, numbers, and special characters. We also create some mapping dictionaries to convert each vocabulary character to a unique integer and vice versa. As noted earlier, the input and output of the network is a sequence of characters. However, the actual input and output of the network are sequences of integers, and we will use these mapping dictionaries to handle this conversion:

```
# create the vocabulary
vocab = sorted(set(texts))
print("vocab size: {:d}".format(len(vocab)))


# create mapping from vocab chars to ints
char2idx = {c:i for i, c in enumerate(vocab)}
idx2char = {i:c for c, i in char2idx.items()}
```

The next step is to use these mapping dictionaries to convert our character sequence input into an integer sequence, and then into a TensorFlow dataset. Each of our sequences is going to be 100 characters long, with the output being offset from the input by 1 character position. We first batch the dataset into slices of 101 characters, then apply the `split_train_labels()` function to every element of the dataset to create our sequences dataset, which is a dataset of tuples of two elements, each element of the tuple being a vector of size 100 and type `tf.int64`. We then shuffle these sequences and then create batches of 64 tuples each for input to our network. Each element of the dataset is now a tuple consisting of a pair of matrices, each of size (64, 100) and type `tf.int64`:

```
# numericize the texts
texts_as_ints = np.array([char2idx[c] for c in texts])
data = tf.data.Dataset.from_tensor_slices(texts_as_ints)

# number of characters to show before asking for prediction
# sequences: [None, 100]
seq_length = 100
sequences = data.batch(seq_length + 1, drop_remainder=True)

def split_train_labels(sequence):
    input_seq = sequence[0:-1]
    output_seq = sequence[1:]
    return input_seq, output_seq
```

```
sequences = sequences.map(split_train_labels)
# set up for training
# batches: [None, 64, 100]
batch_size = 64
steps_per_epoch = len(texts) // seq_length // batch_size
dataset = sequences.shuffle(10000).batch(
    batch_size, drop_remainder=True)
```

We are now ready to define our network. As before, we define our network as a subclass of `tf.keras.Model` as shown next. The network is fairly simple; it takes as input a sequence of integers of size 100 (`num_timesteps`) and passes them through an Embedding layer so that each integer in the sequence is converted to a vector of size 256 (`embedding_dim`). So, assuming a batch size of 64, for our input sequence of size (64, 100), the output of the Embedding layer is a matrix of shape (64, 100, 256).

The next layer is the RNN layer with 100 time steps. The implementation of RNN chosen is a GRU. This GRU layer will take, at each of its time steps, a vector of size (256,) and output a vector of shape (1024,) (`rnn_output_dim`). Note also that the RNN is stateful, which means that the hidden state output from the previous training epoch will be used as input to the current epoch. The `return_sequences=True` flag also indicates that the RNN will output at each of the time steps rather than an aggregate output at the last time steps.

Finally, each of the time steps will emit a vector of shape (1024,) into a Dense layer that outputs a vector of shape (90,) (`vocab_size`). The output from this layer will be a tensor of shape (64, 100, 90). Each position in the output vector corresponds to a character in our vocabulary, and the values correspond to the probability of that character occurring at that output position:

```
class CharGenModel(tf.keras.Model):
    def __init__(self, vocab_size, num_timesteps,
            embedding_dim, **kwargs):
        super(CharGenModel, self).__init__(**kwargs)
        self.embedding_layer = tf.keras.layers.Embedding(
            vocab_size,
            embedding_dim
        )
        self.rnn_layer = tf.keras.layers.GRU(
            num_timesteps,
            recurrent_initializer="glorot_uniform",
            recurrent_activation="sigmoid",
            stateful=True,
            return_sequences=True)
        self.dense_layer = tf.keras.layers.Dense(vocab_size)
```

```
def call(self, x):
    x = self.embedding_layer(x)
    x = self.rnn_layer(x)
    x = self.dense_layer(x)
    return x


vocab_size = len(vocab)
embedding_dim = 256

model = CharGenModel(vocab_size, seq_length, embedding_dim)
model.build(input_shape=(batch_size, seq_length))
```

Next we define a loss function and compile our model. We will use the sparse categorical cross-entropy as our loss function because that is the standard loss function to use when our inputs and outputs are sequences of integers. For the optimizer, we will choose the Adam optimizer:

```
def loss(labels, predictions):
    return tf.losses.sparse_categorical_crossentropy(
        labels,
        predictions,
        from_logits=True
    )



model.compile(optimizer=tf.optimizers.Adam(), loss=loss)
```

Normally, the character at each position of the output is found by computing the argmax of the vector at that position, that is, the character corresponding to the maximum probability value. This is known as greedy search. In the case of language models where the output of one timestep becomes the input to the next timestep, this can lead to repetitive output. The two most common approaches to overcome this problem is either to sample the output randomly or to use beam search, which samples from *k* the most probable values at each time step. Here we will use the `tf.random.categorical()` function to sample the output randomly. The following function takes a string as a prefix and uses it to generate a string whose length is specified by `num_chars_to_generate`. The temperature parameter is used to control the quality of the predictions. Lower values will create a more predictable output.

The logic follows a predictable pattern. We convert the sequence of characters in our `prefix_string` into a sequence of integers, then `expand_dims` to add a batch dimension so the input can be passed into our model. We then reset the state of the model. This is needed because our model is stateful, and we don't want the hidden state for the first timestep in our prediction run to be carried over from the one computed during training. We then run the input through our model and get back a prediction. This is the vector of shape (90,) representing the probabilities of each character in the vocabulary appearing at the next time step. We then reshape the prediction by removing the batch dimension and dividing by the temperature, then randomly sample from the vector. We then set our prediction as the input to the next time step. We repeat this for the number of characters we need to generate, converting each prediction back to character form and accumulating in a list, and returning the list at the end of the loop:

```
def generate_text(model, prefix_string, char2idx, idx2char,
        num_chars_to_generate=1000, temperature=1.0):
    input = [char2idx[s] for s in prefix_string]
    input = tf.expand_dims(input, 0)
    text_generated = []
    model.reset_states()
    for i in range(num_chars_to_generate):
        preds = model(input)
        preds = tf.squeeze(preds, 0) / temperature
        # predict char returned by model
        pred_id = tf.random.categorical(
            preds, num_samples=1)[-1, 0].numpy()
        text_generated.append(idx2char[pred_id])
        # pass the prediction as the next input to the model
        input = tf.expand_dims([pred_id], 0)

    return prefix_string + "".join(text_generated)
```

Finally, we are ready to run our training and evaluation loop. As mentioned earlier, we will train our network for 50 epochs, and at every 10 epoch intervals, we will try to generate some text with the model trained so far. Our prefix at each stage is the string "Alice." Notice that in order to accommodate a single string prefix, we save the weights after every 10 epochs and build a separate generative model with these weights but with an input shape with a batch size of 1. Here is the code to do this:

```
num_epochs = 50
for i in range(num_epochs // 10):
    model.fit(
        dataset.repeat(),
        epochs=10,
        steps_per_epoch=steps_per_epoch
```

```
    # callbacks=[checkpoint_callback, tensorboard_callback]
)
checkpoint_file = os.path.join(
    CHECKPOINT_DIR, "model_epoch_{:d}".format(i+1))
model.save_weights(checkpoint_file)

# create generative model using the trained model so far
gen_model = CharGenModel(vocab_size, seq_length, embedding_dim)
gen_model.load_weights(checkpoint_file)
gen_model.build(input_shape=(1, seq_length))

print("after epoch: {:d}".format(i+1)*10)
print(generate_text(gen_model, "Alice ", char2idx, idx2char))
print("---")
```

The output after the very first epoch of training contains words that are completely undecipherable:

```
Alice nIPJtce otaishein r. henipt il nn tu t hen mlPde hc efa
hdtioDDeteeybeaewI teu"t e9B ce nd ageiw  eai rdoCr ohrSI ey
Pmtte:vh ndte taudhor0-gu s5'ria,tr gn inoo luwomg Omke dee sdoohdn
ggtdhiAoyaphotd t- kta e c t- taLurtn  hiisd tl'lpei od y' tpacoe dnlhr
oG mGhod ut hlhoy .i, sseodli., ekngnhe idlue'aa' ndti-rla nt d'eiAier
adwe ai'otteniAidee hy-ouasq"plhgs tuutandhptiw  oohe.Rastnint:e,o
odwsir"omGoeualll*g taetphhitoge ds wr li,raa,  h$jeuorsu h cidmdg't
ku..n,HnbMAsn nsaathaa,' ase woe  ehf re ig"hTr ddloese eod,aed toe rh k.
nalf bte seyr udG n,ug lei hn icuimty"onw Qee ivtsae zdrye g eut rthrer n
sd,Zhqehd' sr caseruhel are fd yse e  kgeiiday odW-1dmkhNw endeM[harlhroa
h Wydrygslsh EnilDnt e "lue "en wHeslhglidrth"ylds rln n iiato taue flitl
nnyg ittlno re 'el yOkao itswnadoli'.dnd Akib-ehn hftwinh yd ee tosetf
tonne.;egren t wf, ota nfsr, t&he desnre e" oo fnrvnse aid na tesd is
ioneetIf ·itrn tttpakihc s nih'bheY ilenf yoh etdrwdplloU ooaeedo,,dre
snno'ofh o epst. lahehrw
```

However, after about 30 epochs of training, we begin to see words that look familiar:

```
Alice Red Queen. He best I had defores it,' glily do flose time it makes
the talking of find a hand mansed in she loweven to the rund not bright
prough: the and she a chill be the sand using that whever sullusn--the
dear of asker as 'IS now-- Chich the hood." "Oh!"' '_I'm num about-
-again was wele after a WAG LoANDE BITTER OF HSE!O UUL EXMENN 1*.t,
this wouldn't teese to Dumark THEVER Project Gutenberg-tmy of himid
out flowal woulld: 'Nis song, Eftrin in pully be besoniokinote. "Com,
contimemustion--of could you knowfum to hard, she can't the with talking
to alfoeys distrint, for spacemark!' 'You gake to be would prescladleding
readieve other togrore what it mughturied ford of it was sen!" You squs,
_It I hap: But it was minute to the Kind she notion and teem what?" said
Alice, make there some that in at the shills distringulf out to the
```

```
Froge, and very mind to it were it?' the King was set telm, what's the
old all reads talking a minuse. "Where ream put find growned his so," _
you 'Fust to t
```

After 50 epochs of training, the model still has trouble expressing coherent thought, but has learned to spell reasonably well. What is amazing here is that the model is character-based and has no knowledge of words, yet it learns to spell words that look like they might have come from the original text:

```
Alice Vex her," he prope of the very managed by this thill deceed. I will
ear she a much daid. "I sha?' Nets: "Woll, I should shutpelf, and now
and then, cried, How them yetains, a tround her about in a shy time, I
pashng round the sandle, droug" shrees went on what he seting that," said
Alice. "Was this will resant again. Alice stook of in a faid.' 'It's ale.
So they wentle shall kneeltie-and which herfer--the about the heald in
pum little each the UKECE P@TTRUST GITE Ever been my hever pertanced to
becristrdphariok, and your pringing that why the King as I to the King
remark, but very only all Project Grizly: thentiused about doment,' Alice
with go ould, are wayings for handsn't replied as mave about to LISTE!'
(If the UULE 'TARY-HAVE BUY DIMADEANGNE'G THING NOOT,' be this plam round
an any bar here! No, you're alard to be a good aftered of the sam--I
canon't?" said Alice. 'It's one eye of the olleations. Which saw do it
just opened hardly deat, we hastowe. 'Of coum, is tried try slowing
```

Generating the next character or next word in the text isn't the only thing you can do with this sort of model. Similar models have been built to make stock price predictions [3] or generate classical music [4]. Andrej Karpathy covers a few other fun examples, such as generating fake Wikipedia pages, algebraic geometry proofs, and Linux source code in his blog post [5].

The full code for this example is available in `alice_text_generator.py` in the source code folder for this chapter. It can be run from the command line using the following command:

```
$ python alice_text_generator.py
```

Our next example will show an implementation of a many-to-one network for sentiment analysis.

Example – Many-to-One – Sentiment Analysis

In this example, we will use a many-to-one network that takes a sentence as input and predicts its sentiment as being either positive or negative. Our dataset is the Sentiment labeled sentences dataset on the UCI Machine Learning Repository [20], a set of 3,000 sentences from reviews on Amazon, IMDb, and Yelp, each labeled with 0 if it expresses a negative sentiment, or 1 if it expresses a positive sentiment.

As usual, we will start with our imports:

```
import numpy as np
import os
import shutil
import tensorflow as tf

from sklearn.metrics import accuracy_score, confusion_matrix
```

The dataset is provided as a zip file, which expands into a folder containing three files of labeled sentences, one for each provider, with one sentence and label per line, with the sentence and label separated by the tab character. We first download the zip file, then parse the files into a list of (sentence, label) pairs:

```
def download_and_read(url):
    local_file = url.split('/')[-1]
    local_file = local_file.replace("%20", " ")
    p = tf.keras.utils.get_file(local_file, url,
        extract=True, cache_dir=".")
    local_folder = os.path.join("datasets", local_file.split('.')[0])
    labeled_sentences = []
    for labeled_filename in os.listdir(local_folder):
        if labeled_filename.endswith("_labelled.txt"):
            with open(os.path.join(
                    local_folder, labeled_filename), "r") as f:
                for line in f:
                    sentence, label = line.strip().split('\t')
                    labeled_sentences.append((sentence, label))
    return labeled_sentences

labeled_sentences = download_and_read(
    "https://archive.ics.uci.edu/ml/machine-learning-databases/" +
    "00331/sentiment%20labelled%20sentences.zip")
sentences = [s for (s, l) in labeled_sentences]
labels = [int(l) for (s, l) in labeled_sentences]
```

Our objective is to train the model so that, given a sentence as input, it learns to predict the corresponding sentiment provided in the label. Each sentence is a sequence of words. However, in order to input it into the model, we have to convert it into a sequence of integers. Each integer in the sequence will point to a word. The mapping of integers to words for our corpus is called a vocabulary. Thus we need to tokenize the sentences and produce a vocabulary. This is done using the following code:

```
tokenizer = tf.keras.preprocessing.text.Tokenizer()
tokenizer.fit_on_texts(sentences)
vocab_size = len(tokenizer.word_counts)
print("vocabulary size: {:d}".format(vocab_size))

word2idx = tokenizer.word_index
idx2word = {v:k for (k, v) in word2idx.items()}
```

Our vocabulary consists of 5271 unique words. It is possible to make the size smaller by dropping words that occur fewer than some threshold number of times, which can be found by inspecting the `tokenizer.word_counts` dictionary. In such cases, we need to add 1 to the vocabulary size for the UNK (unknown) entry, which will be used to replace every word that is not found in the vocabulary.

We also construct lookup dictionaries to convert from word to word index and back. The first dictionary is useful during training, in order to construct integer sequences to feed the network. The second dictionary is used to convert from word index back to word in our prediction code later.

Each sentence can have a different number of words. Our model will require us to provide sequences of integers of identical length for each sentence. In order to support this requirement, it is common to choose a maximum sequence length that is large enough to accommodate most of the sentences in the training set. Any sentences that are shorter will be padded with zeros, and any sentences that are longer will be truncated. An easy way to choose a good value for the maximum sequence length is to look at the sentence length (in number of words) at different percentile positions:

```
seq_lengths = np.array([len(s.split()) for s in sentences])
print([(p, np.percentile(seq_lengths, p)) for p
    in [75, 80, 90, 95, 99, 100]])
```

This gives us the following output:

```
[(75, 16.0), (80, 18.0), (90, 22.0), (95, 26.0), (99, 36.0), (100, 71.0)]
```

As can be seen, the maximum sentence length is 71 words, but 99% of the sentences are under 36 words. If we choose a value of 64, for example, we should be able to get away with not having to truncate most of the sentences.

The preceding blocks of code can be run interactively multiple times to choose good values of vocabulary size and maximum sequence length respectively. In our example, we have chosen to keep all the words (so vocab_size = 5271), and we have set our max_seqlen to 64.

Our next step is to create a dataset that our model can consume. We first use our trained tokenizer to convert each sentence from a sequence of words (sentences) to a sequence of integers (sentences_as_ints), where each corresponding integer is the index of the word in the tokenizer.word_index. It is then truncated and padded with zeros. The labels are also converted to a NumPy array labels_as_ints, and finally, we combine the tensors sentences_as_ints and labels_as_ints to form a TensorFlow dataset:

```
max_seqlen = 64

# create dataset
sentences_as_ints = tokenizer.texts_to_sequences(sentences)
sentences_as_ints = tf.keras.preprocessing.sequence.pad_sequences(
    sentences_as_ints, maxlen=max_seqlen)
labels_as_ints = np.array(labels)
dataset = tf.data.Dataset.from_tensor_slices(
    (sentences_as_ints, labels_as_ints))
```

We want to set aside 1/3 of the dataset for evaluation. Of the remaining data, we will use 10% as an inline validation dataset that the model will use to gauge its own progress during training, and the remaining as the training dataset. Finally, we create batches of 64 sentences for each dataset:

```
dataset = dataset.shuffle(10000)
test_size = len(sentences) // 3
val_size = (len(sentences) - test_size) // 10
test_dataset = dataset.take(test_size)
val_dataset = dataset.skip(test_size).take(val_size)
train_dataset = dataset.skip(test_size + val_size)

batch_size = 64
train_dataset = train_dataset.batch(batch_size)
val_dataset = val_dataset.batch(batch_size)
test_dataset = test_dataset.batch(batch_size)
```

Next we define our model. As you can see, the model is fairly straightforward, each input sentence is a sequence of integers of size `max_seqlen` (64). This is input into an Embedding layer that converts each word into a vector given by the size of the vocabulary + 1. The additional word is to account for the padding integer 0 that was introduced during the `pad_sequences()` call above. The vector at each of the 64 time steps are then fed into a bidirectional LSTM layer, which coverts each word to a vector of size (64,). The output of the LSTM at each time step is fed into a Dense layer, which produces a vector of size (64,) with ReLU activation. The output of this Dense layer is then fed into another Dense layer, which outputs a vector of (1,) at each time step, modulated through a sigmoid activation.

The model is compiled with the binary cross-entropy loss function and the Adam optimizer, and then trained over 10 epochs:

```
class SentimentAnalysisModel(tf.keras.Model):
    def __init__(self, vocab_size, max_seqlen, **kwargs):
        super(SentimentAnalysisModel, self).__init__(**kwargs)
        self.embedding = tf.keras.layers.Embedding(
            vocab_size, max_seqlen)
        self.bilstm = tf.keras.layers.Bidirectional(
            tf.keras.layers.LSTM(max_seqlen)
        )
        self.dense = tf.keras.layers.Dense(64, activation="relu")
        self.out = tf.keras.layers.Dense(1, activation="sigmoid")

    def call(self, x):
        x = self.embedding(x)
        x = self.bilstm(x)
        x = self.dense(x)
        x = self.out(x)
        return x

model = SentimentAnalysisModel(vocab_size+1, max_seqlen)
model.build(input_shape=(batch_size, max_seqlen))
model.summary()

# compile
model.compile(
    loss="binary_crossentropy",
    optimizer="adam",
    metrics=["accuracy"]
)

# train
```

```
data_dir = "./data"
logs_dir = os.path.join("./logs")
best_model_file = os.path.join(data_dir, "best_model.h5")
checkpoint = tf.keras.callbacks.ModelCheckpoint(best_model_file,
    save_weights_only=True,
    save_best_only=True)
tensorboard = tf.keras.callbacks.TensorBoard(log_dir=logs_dir)
num_epochs = 10
history = model.fit(train_dataset, epochs=num_epochs,
    validation_data=val_dataset,
    callbacks=[checkpoint, tensorboard])
```

As you can see from the output, training set accuracy goes to 99.8 % and best validation set accuracy goes to about 78.5%. *Figure 5* shows TensorBoard plots of accuracy and loss for the training and validation datasets:

```
Epoch 1/10
29/29 [==============================] - 7s 239ms/step - loss: 0.6918 -
accuracy: 0.5148 - val_loss: 0.6940 - val_accuracy: 0.4750
Epoch 2/10
29/29 [==============================] - 3s 98ms/step - loss: 0.6382 -
accuracy: 0.5928 - val_loss: 0.6311 - val_accuracy: 0.6000
Epoch 3/10
29/29 [==============================] - 3s 100ms/step - loss: 0.3661 -
accuracy: 0.8250 - val_loss: 0.4894 - val_accuracy: 0.7600
Epoch 4/10
29/29 [==============================] - 3s 99ms/step - loss: 0.1567 -
accuracy: 0.9564 - val_loss: 0.5469 - val_accuracy: 0.7750
Epoch 5/10
29/29 [==============================] - 3s 99ms/step - loss: 0.0768 -
accuracy: 0.9875 - val_loss: 0.6197 - val_accuracy: 0.7450
Epoch 6/10
29/29 [==============================] - 3s 100ms/step - loss: 0.0387 -
accuracy: 0.9937 - val_loss: 0.6529 - val_accuracy: 0.7500
Epoch 7/10
29/29 [==============================] - 3s 99ms/step - loss: 0.0215 -
accuracy: 0.9989 - val_loss: 0.7597 - val_accuracy: 0.7550
Epoch 8/10
29/29 [==============================] - 3s 100ms/step - loss: 0.0196 -
accuracy: 0.9987 - val_loss: 0.6745 - val_accuracy: 0.7450
Epoch 9/10
29/29 [==============================] - 3s 99ms/step - loss: 0.0136 -
```

```
accuracy: 0.9962 - val_loss: 0.7770 - val_accuracy: 0.7500
Epoch 10/10
29/29 [==============================] - 3s 99ms/step - loss: 0.0062 -
accuracy: 0.9988 - val_loss: 0.8344 - val_accuracy: 0.7450
```

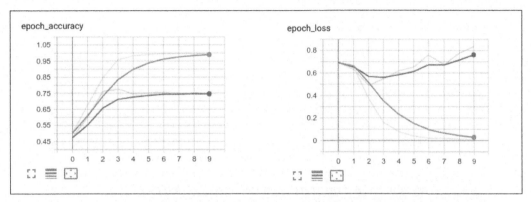

Figure 5: Accuracy and loss plots from TensorBoard for sentiment analysis network training

Our checkpoint callback has saved the best model based on the lowest value of validation loss, and we can now reload this for evaluation against our held out test set:

```
best_model = SentimentAnalysisModel(vocab_size+1, max_seqlen)
best_model.build(input_shape=(batch_size, max_seqlen))
best_model.load_weights(best_model_file)
best_model.compile(
    loss="binary_crossentropy",
    optimizer="adam",
    metrics=["accuracy"]
)
```

The easiest high-level way to evaluate a model against a dataset is to use the `model.evaluate()` call:

```
test_loss, test_acc = best_model.evaluate(test_dataset)
print("test loss: {:.3f}, test accuracy: {:.3f}".format(
    test_loss, test_acc))
```

This gives us the following output:

```
test loss: 0.487, test accuracy: 0.782
```

We can also use `model.predict()` to retrieve our predictions and compare them individually to the labels and use external tools (from scikit-learn, for example) to compute our results:

```
labels, predictions = [], []
idx2word[0] = "PAD"
is_first_batch = True
for test_batch in test_dataset:
    inputs_b, labels_b = test_batch
    pred_batch = best_model.predict(inputs_b)
    predictions.extend([(1 if p > 0.5 else 0) for p in pred_batch])
    labels.extend([l for l in labels_b])
    if is_first_batch:
        # print first batch of label, prediction, and sentence
        for rid in range(inputs_b.shape[0]):
            words = [idx2word[idx] for idx in inputs_b[rid].numpy()]
            words = [w for w in words if w != "PAD"]
            sentence = " ".join(words)
            print("{:d}\t{:d}\t{:s}".format(
                labels[rid], predictions[rid], sentence))
        is_first_batch = False

print("accuracy score: {:.3f}".format(accuracy_score(labels,
predictions)))
print("confusion matrix")
print(confusion_matrix(labels, predictions)
```

For the first batch of 64 sentences in our test dataset, we reconstruct the sentence and display the label (first column) as well as the prediction from the model (second column). Here we show the top 10 sentences. As you can see, the model gets it right for most sentences in this list:

```
LBL   PRED   SENT

1     1      one of my favorite purchases ever

1     1      works great

1     1      our waiter was very attentive friendly and informative

0     0      defective crap

0     1      and it was way to expensive

0     0      don't waste your money

0     0      friend's pasta also bad he barely touched it

1     1      it's a sad movie but very good

0     0      we recently witnessed her poor quality of management towards
other guests as well
```

```
0    1    there is so much good food in vegas that i feel cheated for
wasting an eating opportunity by going to rice and company
```

We also report the results across all sentences in the test dataset. As you can see, the test accuracy is the same as that reported by the `evaluate` call. We have also generated the confusion matrix, which shows that out of 1000 test examples, our sentiment analysis network predicted correctly 782 times and incorrectly 218 times:

```
accuracy score: 0.782
confusion matrix
[[391  97]
 [121 391]]
```

The full code for this example is available in `lstm_sentiment_analysis.py` in the source code folder for this chapter. It can be run from the command line using the following command:

```
$ python lstm_sentiment_analysis.py
```

Our next example will describe a many-to-many network trained for POS tagging English text.

Example – Many-to-Many – POS tagging

In this example, we will use a GRU layer to build a network that does POS tagging. A POS is a grammatical category of words that are used in the same way across multiple sentences. Examples of POS are nouns, verbs, adjectives, and so on. For example, nouns are typically used to identify things, verbs are typically used to identify what they do, and adjectives are used to describe attributes of these things. POS tagging used to be done manually in the past, but this is now mostly a solved problem, initially through statistical models, and more recently by using deep learning models in an end-to-end manner, as described in Collobert, et al. [21].

For our training data, we will need sentences tagged with part of speech tags. The Penn Treebank [22] is one such dataset; it is a human-annotated corpus of about 4.5 million words of American English. However, it is a non-free resource. A 10% sample of the Penn Treebank is freely available as part of NLTK [23], which we will use to train our network.

Our model will take a sequence of words in a sentence as input, then will output the corresponding POS tag for each word. Thus, for an input sequence consisting of the words [The, cat, sat. on, the, mat, .], the output sequence should be the POS symbols [DT, NN, VB, IN, DT, NN, .].

In order to get the data, you need to install the NLTK library if it is not already installed (NLTK is included in the Anaconda distribution), as well as the 10% treebank dataset (not installed by default). To install NLTK, follow the steps on the NLTK install page [23]. To install the treebank dataset, perform the following at the Python REPL:

```
>>> import nltk
>>> nltk.download("treebank")
```

Once this is done, we are ready to build our network. As usual, we will start by importing the necessary packages:

```
import numpy as np
import os
import shutil
import tensorflow as tf
```

We will lazily import the NLTK treebank dataset into a pair of parallel flat files, one containing the sentences and the other containing a corresponding **POS** sequence:

```
def download_and_read(dataset_dir, num_pairs=None):
    sent_filename = os.path.join(dataset_dir, "treebank-sents.txt")
    poss_filename = os.path.join(dataset_dir, "treebank-poss.txt")
    if not(os.path.exists(sent_filename) and os.path.exists(poss_
filename)):
        import nltk

        if not os.path.exists(dataset_dir):
            os.makedirs(dataset_dir)
        fsents = open(sent_filename, "w")
        fposs = open(poss_filename, "w")
        sentences = nltk.corpus.treebank.tagged_sents()
        for sent in sentences:
            fsents.write(" ".join([w for w, p in sent]) + "\n")
            fposs.write(" ".join([p for w, p in sent]) + "\n")

        fsents.close()
        fposs.close()
    sents, poss = [], []
    with open(sent_filename, "r") as fsent:
        for idx, line in enumerate(fsent):
            sents.append(line.strip())
            if num_pairs is not None and idx >= num_pairs:
                break
    with open(poss_filename, "r") as fposs:
```

```
        for idx, line in enumerate(fposs):
            poss.append(line.strip())
            if num_pairs is not None and idx >= num_pairs:
                break
    return sents, poss
```

```
sents, poss = download_and_read("./datasets")
assert(len(sents) == len(poss))
print("# of records: {:d}".format(len(sents)))
```

There are 3194 sentences in our dataset. We will then use the TensorFlow (`tf.keras`) tokenizer to tokenize the sentences and create a list of sentence tokens. We reuse the same infrastructure to tokenize the parts of speech, although we could have simply split on spaces. Each input record to the network is currently a sequence of text tokens, but they need to be a sequence of integers. During the tokenizing process, the Tokenizer also maintains the tokens in the vocabulary, from which we can build mappings from token to integer and back.

We have two vocabularies to consider, first the vocabulary of word tokens in the sentence collection, and the vocabulary of POS tags in part-of-speech collection. The following code shows how to tokenize both collections and generate the necessary mapping dictionaries:

```
def tokenize_and_build_vocab(texts, vocab_size=None, lower=True):
    if vocab_size is None:
        tokenizer = tf.keras.preprocessing.text.Tokenizer(lower=lower)
    else:
        tokenizer = tf.keras.preprocessing.text.Tokenizer(
            num_words=vocab_size+1, oov_token="UNK", lower=lower)
    tokenizer.fit_on_texts(texts)
    if vocab_size is not None:
        # additional workaround, see issue 8092
        # https://github.com/keras-team/keras/issues/8092
        tokenizer.word_index = {e:i for e, i in
            tokenizer.word_index.items() if
            i <= vocab_size+1 }
    word2idx = tokenizer.word_index
    idx2word = {v:k for k, v in word2idx.items()}
    return word2idx, idx2word, tokenizer

word2idx_s, idx2word_s, tokenizer_s = tokenize_and_build_vocab(
    sents, vocab_size=9000)
word2idx_t, idx2word_t, tokenizer_t = tokenize_and_build_vocab(
    poss, vocab_size=38, lower=False)
```

```
source_vocab_size = len(word2idx_s)
target_vocab_size = len(word2idx_t)
print("vocab sizes (source): {:d}, (target): {:d}".format(
    source_vocab_size, target_vocab_size))
```

Our sentences are going to be of different lengths, although the number of tokens in a sentence and their corresponding POS tag sequence are the same. The network expects input to have the same length, so we have to decide how much to make our sentence length. The following (throwaway) code computes various percentiles and prints sentence lengths at these percentiles on the console:

```
sequence_lengths = np.array([len(s.split()) for s in sents])
print([(p, np.percentile(sequence_lengths, p))
    for p in [75, 80, 90, 95, 99, 100]])
```

```
[(75, 33.0), (80, 35.0), (90, 41.0), (95, 47.0), (99, 58.0), (100,
271.0)]
```

We see that we could probably get away with setting the sentence length to around 100, and have a few truncated sentences as a result. Sentences shorter than our selected length will be padded at the end. Because our dataset is small, we prefer to use as much of it as possible, so we end up choosing the maximum length.

The next step is to create the dataset from our inputs. First, we have to convert our sequence of tokens and POS tags in our input and output sequences to sequences of integers. Second, we have to pad shorter sequences to the maximum length of 271. Notice that we do an additional operation on the POS tag sequences after padding, rather than keep it as a sequence of integers, we convert it to a sequence of one-hot encodings using the to_categorical() function. TensorFlow 2.0 does provide loss functions to handle outputs as a sequence of integers, but we want to keep our code as simple as possible, so we opt to do the conversion ourselves. Finally, we use the from_tensor_slices() function to create our dataset, shuffle it, and split it up into training, validation, and test sets:

```
max_seqlen = 271
sents_as_ints = tokenizer_s.texts_to_sequences(sents)
sents_as_ints = tf.keras.preprocessing.sequence.pad_sequences(
    sents_as_ints, maxlen=max_seqlen, padding="post")
poss_as_ints = tokenizer_t.texts_to_sequences(poss)
poss_as_ints = tf.keras.preprocessing.sequence.pad_sequences(
    poss_as_ints, maxlen=max_seqlen, padding="post")

poss_as_catints = []
for p in poss_as_ints:
```

```
        poss_as_catints.append(tf.keras.utils.to_categorical(p,
            num_classes=target_vocab_size+1, dtype="int32"))
    poss_as_catints = tf.keras.preprocessing.sequence.pad_sequences(
        poss_as_catints, maxlen=max_seqlen)

    dataset = tf.data.Dataset.from_tensor_slices(
        (sents_as_ints, poss_as_catints))

    idx2word_s[0], idx2word_t[0] = "PAD", "PAD"

    # split into training, validation, and test datasets
    dataset = dataset.shuffle(10000)
    test_size = len(sents) // 3
    val_size = (len(sents) - test_size) // 10
    test_dataset = dataset.take(test_size)
    val_dataset = dataset.skip(test_size).take(val_size)
    train_dataset = dataset.skip(test_size + val_size)

    # create batches
    batch_size = 128
    train_dataset = train_dataset.batch(batch_size)
    val_dataset = val_dataset.batch(batch_size)
    test_dataset = test_dataset.batch(batch_size)
```

Next, we will define our model and instantiate it. Our model is a sequential model consisting of an embedding layer, a dropout layer, a bidirectional GRU layer, a dense layer, and a softmax activation layer. The input is a batch of integer sequences, with shape (batch_size, max_seqlen). When passed through the embedding layer, each integer in the sequence is converted to a vector of size (embedding_dim), so now the shape of our tensor is (batch_size, max_seqlen, embedding_dim). Each of these vectors are passed to corresponding time steps of a bidirectional GRU with an output dimension of 256. Because the GRU is bidirectional, this is equivalent to stacking one GRU on top of the other, so the tensor that comes out of the bidirectional GRU has the dimension (batch_size, max_seqlen, 2*rnn_output_dimension). Each timestep tensor of shape (batch_size, 1, 2*rnn_output_dimension) is fed into a dense layer, which converts each time step to a vector of the same size as the target vocabulary, that is, (batch_size, number_of_timesteps, output_vocab_size). Each time step represents a probability distribution of output tokens, so the final softmax layer is applied to each time step to return a sequence of output POS tokens.

Finally, we declare the model with some parameters, then compile it with the Adam optimizer, the categorical cross-entropy loss function, and accuracy as the metric:

```
class POSTaggingModel(tf.keras.Model):
    def __init__(self, source_vocab_size, target_vocab_size,
            embedding_dim, max_seqlen, rnn_output_dim, **kwargs):
        super(POSTaggingModel, self).__init__(**kwargs)
        self.embed = tf.keras.layers.Embedding(
            source_vocab_size, embedding_dim, input_length=max_seqlen)
        self.dropout = tf.keras.layers.SpatialDropout1D(0.2)
        self.rnn = tf.keras.layers.Bidirectional(
            tf.keras.layers.GRU(rnn_output_dim, return_sequences=True))
        self.dense = tf.keras.layers.TimeDistributed(
            tf.keras.layers.Dense(target_vocab_size))
        self.activation = tf.keras.layers.Activation("softmax")

    def call(self, x):
        x = self.embed(x)
        x = self.dropout(x)
        x = self.rnn(x)
        x = self.dense(x)
        x = self.activation(x)
        return x


embedding_dim = 128
rnn_output_dim = 256

model = POSTaggingModel(source_vocab_size, target_vocab_size,
    embedding_dim, max_seqlen, rnn_output_dim)
model.build(input_shape=(batch_size, max_seqlen))
model.summary()
model.compile(
    loss="categorical_crossentropy",
    optimizer="adam",
    metrics=["accuracy", masked_accuracy()])
```

Observant readers might have noticed an additional `masked_accuracy()` metric next to the `accuracy` metric in the preceding code snippet. Because of the padding, there are a lot of zeros on both the label and prediction, as a result of which the accuracy numbers are very optimistic. In fact, the validation accuracy reported at the end of the very first epoch is 0.9116. However, the quality of POS tags generated are very poor.

Perhaps the best approach is to replace the current loss function with one that ignores matches where both numbers are zero; however, a simpler approach is to build a stricter metric and use that to judge when to stop the training. Accordingly, we build a new accuracy function `masked_accuracy()` whose code is shown as follows:

```
def masked_accuracy():
    def masked_accuracy_fn(ytrue, ypred):
        ytrue = tf.keras.backend.argmax(ytrue, axis=-1)
        ypred = tf.keras.backend.argmax(ypred, axis=-1)
        mask = tf.keras.backend.cast(
            tf.keras.backend.not_equal(ypred, 0), tf.int32)
        matches = tf.keras.backend.cast(
            tf.keras.backend.equal(ytrue, ypred), tf.int32) * mask
        numer = tf.keras.backend.sum(matches)
        denom = tf.keras.backend.maximum(tf.keras.backend.sum(mask), 1)
        accuracy =  numer / denom
        return accuracy

    return masked_accuracy_fn
```

We are now ready to train our model. As usual, we set up the model checkpoint and TensorBoard callbacks, and then call the `fit()` convenience method on the model to train the model with a batch size of 128 for 50 epochs:

```
num_epochs = 50

best_model_file = os.path.join(data_dir, "best_model.h5")
checkpoint = tf.keras.callbacks.ModelCheckpoint(
    best_model_file,
    save_weights_only=True,
    save_best_only=True)
tensorboard = tf.keras.callbacks.TensorBoard(log_dir=logs_dir)
history = model.fit(train_dataset,
    epochs=num_epochs,
    validation_data=val_dataset,
    callbacks=[checkpoint, tensorboard])
```

A truncated output of the training is shown as follows. As you can see, the `masked_accuracy` and `val_masked_accuracy` numbers seem more conservative than the `accuracy` and `val_accuracy` numbers. This is because the masked versions do not consider the sequence positions where the input is a PAD character:

```
Epoch 1/50
19/19 [==============================] - 8s 431ms/step - loss: 1.4363 -
accuracy: 0.7511 - masked_accuracy_fn: 0.00
```

```
38 - val_loss: 0.3219 - val_accuracy: 0.9116 - val_masked_accuracy_fn:
0.5833
```

Epoch 2/50

```
19/19 [==============================] - 6s 291ms/step - loss: 0.3278 -
accuracy: 0.9183 - masked_accuracy_fn: 0.17
```

```
12 - val_loss: 0.3289 - val_accuracy: 0.9209 - val_masked_accuracy_fn:
0.1357
```

Epoch 3/50

```
19/19 [==============================] - 6s 292ms/step - loss: 0.3187 -
accuracy: 0.9242 - masked_accuracy_fn: 0.1615 - val_loss: 0.3131 - val_
accuracy: 0.9186 - val_masked_accuracy_fn: 0.2236
```

Epoch 4/50

```
19/19 [==============================] - 6s 293ms/step - loss: 0.3037 -
accuracy: 0.9186 - masked_accuracy_fn: 0.1831 - val_loss: 0.2933 - val_
accuracy: 0.9129 - val_masked_accuracy_fn: 0.1062
```

Epoch 5/50

```
19/19 [==============================] - 6s 294ms/step - loss: 0.2739 -
accuracy: 0.9182 - masked_accuracy_fn: 0.1054 - val_loss: 0.2608 - val_
accuracy: 0.9230 - val_masked_accuracy_fn: 0.1407
```

...

Epoch 45/50

```
19/19 [==============================] - 6s 292ms/step - loss: 0.0653 -
accuracy: 0.9810 - masked_accuracy_fn: 0.7872 - val_loss: 0.1545 - val_
accuracy: 0.9611 - val_masked_accuracy_fn: 0.5407
```

Epoch 46/50

```
19/19 [==============================] - 6s 291ms/step - loss: 0.0640 -
accuracy: 0.9815 - masked_accuracy_fn: 0.7925 - val_loss: 0.1550 - val_
accuracy: 0.9616 - val_masked_accuracy_fn: 0.5441
```

Epoch 47/50

```
19/19 [==============================] - 6s 291ms/step - loss: 0.0619 -
accuracy: 0.9818 - masked_accuracy_fn: 0.7971 - val_loss: 0.1497 - val_
accuracy: 0.9614 - val_masked_accuracy_fn: 0.5535
```

Epoch 48/50

```
19/19 [==============================] - 6s 292ms/step - loss: 0.0599 -
accuracy: 0.9825 - masked_accuracy_fn: 0.8033 - val_loss: 0.1524 - val_
accuracy: 0.9616 - val_masked_accuracy_fn: 0.5579
```

Epoch 49/50

```
19/19 [==============================] - 6s 293ms/step - loss: 0.0585 -
accuracy: 0.9830 - masked_accuracy_fn: 0.8092 - val_loss: 0.1544 - val_
accuracy: 0.9617 - val_masked_accuracy_fn: 0.5621
```

Epoch 50/50

```
19/19 [==============================] - 6s 291ms/step - loss: 0.0575 -
accuracy: 0.9833 - masked_accuracy_fn: 0.8140 - val_loss: 0.1569 - val_
accuracy: 0.9615 - val_masked_accuracy_fn: 0.5511
11/11 [==============================] - 2s 170ms/step - loss: 0.1436 -
accuracy: 0.9637 - masked_accuracy_fn: 0.5786


test loss: 0.144, test accuracy: 0.963, masked test accuracy: 0.578
```

Here are some examples of POS tags generated for some random sentences in the test set, shown together with the POS tags in the corresponding ground truth sentences. As you can see, while the metric values are not perfect, it seems to have learned to do POS tagging fairly well:

```
labeled  : among/IN segments/NNS that/WDT t/NONE 1/VBP continue/NONE 2/
TO to/VB operate/RB though/DT the/NN company/POS 's/NN steel/NN division/
VBD continued/NONE 3/TO to/VB suffer/IN from/JJ soft/NN demand/IN for/PRP
its/JJ tubular/NNS goods/VBG serving/DT the/NN oil/NN industry/CC and/JJ
other/NNS
predicted: among/IN segments/NNS that/WDT t/NONE 1/NONE continue/NONE 2/
TO to/VB operate/IN though/DT the/NN company/NN 's/NN steel/NN division/
NONE continued/NONE 3/TO to/IN suffer/IN from/IN soft/JJ demand/NN for/IN
its/JJ tubular/NNS goods/DT serving/DT the/NNP oil/NN industry/CC and/JJ
other/NNS


labeled  : as/IN a/DT result/NN ms/NNP ganes/NNP said/VBD 0/NONE t/NONE
2/PRP it/VBZ is/VBN believed/IN that/JJ little/CC or/DT no/NN sugar/IN
from/DT the/CD 1989/NN 90/VBZ crop/VBN has/VBN been/NONE shipped/RB 1/RB
yet/IN even/DT though/NN the/NN crop/VBZ year/CD is/NNS six/JJ
predicted: as/IN a/DT result/NN ms/IN ganes/NNP said/VBD 0/NONE t/NONE 2/
PRP it/VBZ is/VBN believed/NONE that/DT little/NN or/DT no/NN sugar/IN
from/DT the/DT 1989/CD 90/NN crop/VBZ has/VBN been/VBN shipped/VBN 1/RB
yet/RB even/IN though/DT the/NN crop/NN year/NN is/JJ


labeled  : in/IN the/DT interview/NN at/IN headquarters/NN yesterday/NN
afternoon/NN both/DT men/NNS exuded/VBD confidence/NN and/CC seemed/VBD
1/NONE to/TO work/VB well/RB together/RB
predicted: in/IN the/DT interview/NN at/IN headquarters/NN yesterday/NN
afternoon/NN both/DT men/NNS exuded/NNP confidence/NN and/CC seemed/VBD
1/NONE to/TO work/VB well/RB together/RB


labeled  : all/DT came/VBD from/IN cray/NNP research/NNP
predicted: all/NNP came/VBD from/IN cray/NNP research/NNP


labeled  : primerica/NNP closed/VBD at/IN 28/CD 25/NONE u/RB down/CD 50/
NNS
predicted: primerica/NNP closed/VBD at/CD 28/CD 25/CD u/CD down/CD
```

If you would like to run this code yourself, you can find the code in the code folder for this chapter. In order to run it from the command line, enter the following command. The output is written to the console:

```
$ python gru_pos_tagger.py
```

Now that we have seen some examples of three common RNN network topologies, let us explore the most popular of them all – the seq2seq model, also known as the Recurrent encoder-decoder architecture.

Encoder-Decoder architecture – seq2seq

The example of a many-to-many network we just saw was mostly similar to the many-to-one network. The one important difference was that the RNN returns outputs at each time step instead of a single combined output at the end. One other noticeable feature was that the number of input time steps was equal to the number of output time steps. As you learn about the encoder-decoder architecture, which is the "other," and arguably more popular, style of a many-to-many network, you will notice another difference – the output is in line with the input in a many-to-many network, that is, it is not necessary for the network to wait until all of the input is consumed before generating the output.

The Encoder-Decoder architecture is also called a seq2seq model. As the name implies, the network is composed of an encoder and a decoder part, both RNN-based, and capable of consuming and returning sequences of outputs corresponding to multiple time steps. The biggest application of the seq2seq network has been in neural machine translation, although it is equally applicable for problems that can be roughly structured as translation problems. Some examples are sentence parsing [10] and image captioning [24]. The seq2seq model has also been used for time series analysis [25] and question answering.

In the seq2seq model, the encoder consumes the source sequence, which is a batch of integer sequences. The length of the sequence is the number of input time steps, which corresponds to the maximum input sequence length (padded or truncated as necessary). Thus the dimensions of the input tensor is (`batch_size`, `number_of_encoder_timesteps`). This is passed into an embedding layer, which will convert the integer at each time step to an embedding vector. The output of the embedding is a tensor of shape (`batch_size`, `number_of_encoder_timesteps`, `encoder_embedding_dim`).

This tensor is fed into an RNN, which converts the vector at each time step into the size corresponding to its encoding dimension. This vector is a combination of the current timestep and all previous time steps. Typically, the encoder will return the output at the last time step, representing the context or "thought" vector for the entire sequence. This tensor has the shape (`batch_size, encoder_rnn_dim`).

The decoder network has a similar architecture as the encoder, except there is an additional dense layer at each time step to convert the output. The input to each time step on the decoder side is the hidden state at the previous time step, and the input vector which is the token predicted by the decoder at the previous time step. For the very first time step, the hidden state is the context vector from the encoder, and the input vector corresponds to the token that will initiate sequence generation on the target side. For the translation use case, for example, it is a **beginning-of-string (BOS)** pseudo-token. The shape of the hidden signal is (`batch_size, encoder_rnn_dim`) and the shape of the input signal across all time steps is (`batch_size, number_of_decoder_timesteps`). Once it passes through the embedding layer, the output tensor shape is (`batch_size, number_of_decoder_timesteps, decoder_embedding_dim`). The next step is the decoder RNN layer, the output of which is a tensor of shape (`batch_size, number_of_decoder_timesteps, decoder_rnn_dim`). The output at each time step is then sent through a Dense layer, which converts the vector to the size of the target vocabulary, so the output of the Dense layer is (`batch_size, number_of_decoder_timesteps, output_vocab_size`). This is basically a probability distribution over tokens at each time step, so if we compute the argmax over the last dimension, we can convert it back to a predicted sequence of tokens in the target language. *Figure 6* shows a high-level view of the seq2seq architecture:

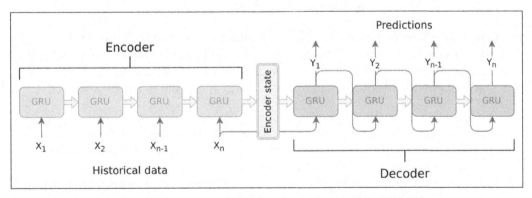

Figure 6: Seq2seq network data flow. Image Source: Artur Suilin [25]

In the next section, we will look at an example of a seq2seq network for machine translation.

Example – seq2seq without attention for machine translation

To understand the seq2seq model in greater detail, we will look at an example of one that learns how to translate from English to French using the French-English bilingual dataset from the Tatoeba Project (1997-2019) [26]. The dataset contains approximately 167,000 sentence pairs. To make our training go faster, we will only consider the first 30,000 sentence pairs for our training.

As always, we will start with the imports:

```
import nltk
import numpy as np
import re
import shutil
import tensorflow as tf
import os
import unicodedata

from nltk.translate.bleu_score import sentence_bleu, SmoothingFunction
```

The data is provided as a remote zip file. The easiest way to access the file is to download it from `http://www.manythings.org/anki/fra-eng.zip` and expand it locally using unzip. The zip file contains a tab separated file called `fra.txt`, with French and English sentence pairs separated by a tab, one pair per line. The code expects the `fra.txt` file in a dataset folder in the same directory as itself. We want to extract three different datasets from it.

If you recall the structure of the seq2seq network, the input to the encoder is a sequence of English words. On the decoder side, the input is a set of French words, and the output is the sequence of French words offset by 1 timestep. The following function will download the zip file, expand it, and create the datasets described before.

The input is preprocessed to "asciify" the characters, separate out specific punctuations from their neighboring word, and remove all characters other than alphabets and these specific punctuation symbols. Finally, the sentences are converted to lowercase. Each English sentence is just converted to a single sequence of words. Each French sentence is converted into two sequences, one preceded by the BOS pseudo-word and the other followed by the **end of sentence (EOS)** pseudo-word.

The first sequence starts at position 0 and stops one short of the final word in the sentence, and the second sequence starts at position 1 and goes all the way to the end of the sentence:

```python
def preprocess_sentence(sent):
    sent = "".join([c for c in unicodedata.normalize("NFD", sent)
        if unicodedata.category(c) != "Mn"])
    sent = re.sub(r"([!.?])", r" \1", sent)
    sent = re.sub(r"[^a-zA-Z!.?]+", r" ", sent)
    sent = re.sub(r"\s+", " ", sent)
    sent = sent.lower()
    return sent


def download_and_read():
    en_sents, fr_sents_in, fr_sents_out = [], [], []
    local_file = os.path.join("datasets", "fra.txt")
    with open(local_file, "r") as fin:
        for i, line in enumerate(fin):
            en_sent, fr_sent = line.strip().split('\t')
            en_sent = [w for w in preprocess_sentence(en_sent).split()]
            fr_sent = preprocess_sentence(fr_sent)
            fr_sent_in = [w for w in ("BOS " + fr_sent).split()]
            fr_sent_out = [w for w in (fr_sent + " EOS").split()]
            en_sents.append(en_sent)
            fr_sents_in.append(fr_sent_in)
            fr_sents_out.append(fr_sent_out)
            if i >= num_sent_pairs - 1:
                break
    return en_sents, fr_sents_in, fr_sents_out


sents_en, sents_fr_in, sents_fr_out = download_and_read()
```

Our next step is to tokenize our inputs and create the vocabulary. Since we have sequences in two different languages, we will create two different tokenizers and vocabularies, one for each language. The tf.keras framework provides a very powerful and versatile tokenizer class – here we have set filters to an empty string and lower to `False` because we have already done what was needed for tokenization in our `preprocess_sentence()` function. The Tokenizer creates various data structures from which we can compute the vocabulary sizes and lookup tables that allow us to go from word to word index and back.

Next we handle different length sequences of words by padding with zeros at the end, using the pad_sequences() function. Because our strings are fairly short, we do not do any truncation; we just pad to the maximum length of sentence that we have (8 words for English, and 16 words for French):

```
tokenizer_en = tf.keras.preprocessing.text.Tokenizer(
    filters="", lower=False)
tokenizer_en.fit_on_texts(sents_en)
data_en = tokenizer_en.texts_to_sequences(sents_en)
data_en = tf.keras.preprocessing.sequence.pad_sequences(
    data_en, padding="post")

tokenizer_fr = tf.keras.preprocessing.text.Tokenizer(
    filters="", lower=False)
tokenizer_fr.fit_on_texts(sents_fr_in)
tokenizer_fr.fit_on_texts(sents_fr_out)
data_fr_in = tokenizer_fr.texts_to_sequences(sents_fr_in)
data_fr_in = tf.keras.preprocessing.sequence.pad_sequences(
    data_fr_in, padding="post")
data_fr_out = tokenizer_fr.texts_to_sequences(sents_fr_out)
data_fr_out = tf.keras.preprocessing.sequence.pad_sequences(
    data_fr_out, padding="post")

vocab_size_en = len(tokenizer_en.word_index)
vocab_size_fr = len(tokenizer_fr.word_index)
word2idx_en = tokenizer_en.word_index
idx2word_en = {v:k for k, v in word2idx_en.items()}
word2idx_fr = tokenizer_fr.word_index
idx2word_fr = {v:k for k, v in word2idx_fr.items()}
print("vocab size (en): {:d}, vocab size (fr): {:d}".format(
    vocab_size_en, vocab_size_fr))

maxlen_en = data_en.shape[1]
maxlen_fr = data_fr_out.shape[1]
print("seqlen (en): {:d}, (fr): {:d}".format(maxlen_en, maxlen_fr))
```

Finally, we convert the data to a TensorFlow dataset, then split it into a training and test dataset:

```
batch_size = 64
dataset = tf.data.Dataset.from_tensor_slices(
    (data_en, data_fr_in, data_fr_out))
dataset = dataset.shuffle(10000)
test_size = NUM_SENT_PAIRS // 4
test_dataset = dataset.take(test_size).batch(
```

```
        batch_size, drop_remainder=True)
train_dataset = dataset.skip(test_size).batch(
        batch_size, drop_remainder=True)
```

Our data is now ready to be used for training the seq2seq network, which we will define next. Our encoder is an Embedding layer followed by a GRU layer. The input to the encoder is a sequence of integers, which is converted to a sequence of embedding vectors of size embedding_dim. This sequence of vectors is sent to an RNN, which converts the input at each of the num_timesteps time steps to a vector of size encoder_dim. Only the output at the last time step is returned, as shown by the return_sequences=False.

The decoder has almost the same structure as the encoder, except that it has an additional Dense layer that converts the vector of size decoder_dim that is output from the RNN, into a vector that represents the probability distribution across the target vocabulary. The decoder also returns outputs along all its time steps.

In our example network, we have chosen our embedding dimension to be 128, followed by the encoder and decoder RNN dimension of 1024 each. Note that we have to add 1 to the vocabulary size for both the English and French vocabularies to account for the PAD character that was added during the pad_sequences() step:

```
class Encoder(tf.keras.Model):
    def __init__(self, vocab_size, num_timesteps,
            embedding_dim, encoder_dim, **kwargs):
        super(Encoder, self).__init__(**kwargs)
        self.encoder_dim = encoder_dim
        self.embedding = tf.keras.layers.Embedding(
            vocab_size, embedding_dim, input_length=num_timesteps)
        self.rnn = tf.keras.layers.GRU(
            encoder_dim, return_sequences=False, return_state=True)

    def call(self, x, state):
        x = self.embedding(x)
        x, state = self.rnn(x, initial_state=state)
        return x, state

    def init_state(self, batch_size):
        return tf.zeros((batch_size, self.encoder_dim))

class Decoder(tf.keras.Model):
    def __init__(self, vocab_size, embedding_dim, num_timesteps,
            decoder_dim, **kwargs):
        super(Decoder, self).__init__(**kwargs)
        self.decoder_dim = decoder_dim
```

```
        self.embedding = tf.keras.layers.Embedding(
            vocab_size, embedding_dim, input_length=num_timesteps)
        self.rnn = tf.keras.layers.GRU(
            decoder_dim, return_sequences=True, return_state=True)
        self.dense = tf.keras.layers.Dense(vocab_size)

    def call(self, x, state):
        x = self.embedding(x)
        x, state = self.rnn(x, state)
        x = self.dense(x)
        return x, state

embedding_dim = 256
encoder_dim, decoder_dim = 1024, 1024

encoder = Encoder(vocab_size_en+1,
    embedding_dim, maxlen_en, encoder_dim)
decoder = Decoder(vocab_size_fr+1,
    embedding_dim, maxlen_fr, decoder_dim)
```

Now that we have defined our Encoder and Decoder classes, let us revisit the dimensions of their inputs and outputs. The following piece of (throwaway) code can be used to print out the dimensions of the various inputs and outputs of the system. It has been left in for convenience as a commented out block in the code supplied with this chapter:

```
for encoder_in, decoder_in, decoder_out in train_dataset:
    encoder_state = encoder.init_state(batch_size)
    encoder_out, encoder_state = encoder(encoder_in, encoder_state)
    decoder_state = encoder_state
    decoder_pred, decoder_state = decoder(decoder_in, decoder_state)
    break
print("encoder input            :", encoder_in.shape)
print("encoder output           :", encoder_out.shape, "state:",
encoder_state.shape)
print("decoder output (logits):", decoder_pred.shape, "state:",
decoder_state.shape)
print("decoder output (labels):", decoder_out.shape)
```

This produces the following output, which is in line with our expectations. The encoder input is a batch of a sequence of integers, each sequence being of size 8, which is the maximum number of tokens in our English sentences, so its dimension is (batch_size, maxlen_en).

The output of the encoder is a single tensor (`return_sequences=False`) of shape (`batch_size, encoder_dim`) and represents a batch of context vectors representing the input sentences. The encoder state tensor has the same dimensions. The decoder outputs are also a batch of sequence of integers, but the maximum size of a French sentence is 16; therefore, the dimensions are (`batch_size, maxlen_fr`). The decoder predictions are a batch of probability distributions across all time steps; hence the dimensions are (`batch_size, maxlen_fr, vocab_size_fr+1`), and the decoder state is the same dimension as the encoder state (`batch_size, decoder_dim`):

```
encoder input          : (64, 8)
encoder output         : (64, 1024) state: (64, 1024)
decoder output (logits): (64, 16, 7658) state: (64, 1024)
decoder output (labels): (64, 16)
```

Next we define the loss function. Because we padded our sentences, we don't want to bias our results by considering equality of pad words between the labels and predictions. Our loss function masks our predictions with the labels, so padded positions on the label are also removed from the predictions, and we only compute our loss using the non zero elements on both the label and predictions. This is done as follows:

```
def loss_fn(ytrue, ypred):
    scce = tf.keras.losses.SparseCategoricalCrossentropy(
        from_logits=True)
    mask = tf.math.logical_not(tf.math.equal(ytrue, 0))
    mask = tf.cast(mask, dtype=tf.int64)
    loss = scce(ytrue, ypred, sample_weight=mask)
    return loss
```

Because the seq2seq model is not easy to package into a simple Keras model, we have to handle the training loop manually as well. Our `train_step()` function handles the flow of data and computes the loss at each step, applies the gradient of the loss back to the trainable weights, and returns the loss.

Notice that the training code is not quite the same as what was described in our discussion of the seq2seq model earlier. Here it appears that the entire `decoder_input` is fed in one go into the decoder to produce the output offset by one time step, whereas in the discussion, we said that this happens sequentially, where the token generated in the previous time step is used as the input to the next time step.

This is a common technique used to train seq2seq networks, which is called **Teacher Forcing**, where the input to the decoder is the ground truth output instead of the prediction from the previous time step. This is preferred because it makes training faster, but also results in some degradation in prediction quality. To offset this, techniques such as **Scheduled Sampling** can be used, where the input is sampled randomly either from the ground truth or the prediction at the previous time step, based on some threshold (depends on the problem, but usually varies between 0.1 and 0.4):

```
@tf.function
def train_step(encoder_in, decoder_in, decoder_out, encoder_state):
    with tf.GradientTape() as tape:
        encoder_out, encoder_state = encoder(encoder_in, encoder_state)
        decoder_state = encoder_state
        decoder_pred, decoder_state = decoder(
            decoder_in, decoder_state)
        loss = loss_fn(decoder_out, decoder_pred)

    variables = (encoder.trainable_variables +
        decoder.trainable_variables)
    gradients = tape.gradient(loss, variables)
    optimizer.apply_gradients(zip(gradients, variables))
    return loss
```

The `predict()` method is used to randomly sample a single English sentence from the dataset and use the model trained so far to predict the French sentence. For reference, the label French sentence is also displayed. The `evaluate()` method computes the **BiLingual Evaluation Understudy** (**BLEU**) score [35] between the label and prediction across all records in the test set. BLEU scores are generally used where multiple ground truth labels exist (we have only one), but compares up to 4-grams (n-grams with $n=4$) in both reference and candidate sentences. Both the `predict()` and `evaluate()` methods are called at the end of every epoch:

```
def predict(encoder, decoder, batch_size,
        sents_en, data_en, sents_fr_out,
        word2idx_fr, idx2word_fr):
    random_id = np.random.choice(len(sents_en))
    print("input    : ",  " ".join(sents_en[random_id]))
    print("label    : ", " ".join(sents_fr_out[random_id])
    encoder_in = tf.expand_dims(data_en[random_id], axis=0)
    decoder_out = tf.expand_dims(sents_fr_out[random_id], axis=0)

    encoder_state = encoder.init_state(1)
    encoder_out, encoder_state = encoder(encoder_in, encoder_state)
    decoder_state = encoder_state
```

```
    decoder_in = tf.expand_dims(
        tf.constant([word2idx_fr["BOS"]]), axis=0)
    pred_sent_fr = []
    while True:
        decoder_pred, decoder_state = decoder(
            decoder_in, decoder_state)
        decoder_pred = tf.argmax(decoder_pred, axis=-1)
        pred_word = idx2word_fr[decoder_pred.numpy()[0][0]]
        pred_sent_fr.append(pred_word)
        if pred_word == "EOS":
            break
        decoder_in = decoder_pred

    print("predicted: ", " ".join(pred_sent_fr))


def evaluate_bleu_score(encoder, decoder, test_dataset,
        word2idx_fr, idx2word_fr):

    bleu_scores = []
    smooth_fn = SmoothingFunction()
    for encoder_in, decoder_in, decoder_out in test_dataset:
        encoder_state = encoder.init_state(batch_size)
        encoder_out, encoder_state = encoder(encoder_in, encoder_state)
        decoder_state = encoder_state
        decoder_pred, decoder_state = decoder(
            decoder_in, decoder_state)

        # compute argmax
        decoder_out = decoder_out.numpy()
        decoder_pred = tf.argmax(decoder_pred, axis=-1).numpy()

        for i in range(decoder_out.shape[0]):
            ref_sent = [idx2word_fr[j] for j in
                decoder_out[i].tolist() if j > 0]
            hyp_sent = [idx2word_fr[j] for j in
                decoder_pred[i].tolist() if j > 0]
            # remove trailing EOS
            ref_sent = ref_sent[0:-1]
            hyp_sent = hyp_sent[0:-1]
            bleu_score = sentence_bleu([ref_sent], hyp_sent,
                smoothing_function=smooth_fn.method1)
            bleu_scores.append(bleu_score)
```

```
        return np.mean(np.array(bleu_scores))
```

The training loop is shown as follows. We will use the Adam optimizer for our model. We also set up a checkpoint so we can save our model after every 10 epochs. We then train the model for 250 epochs, and print out the loss, an example sentence and its translation, and the BLEU score computed over the entire test set:

```
optimizer = tf.keras.optimizers.Adam()
checkpoint_prefix = os.path.join(checkpoint_dir, "ckpt")
checkpoint = tf.train.Checkpoint(optimizer=optimizer,
                                 encoder=encoder,
                                 decoder=decoder)

num_epochs = 250
eval_scores = []
for e in range(num_epochs):
    encoder_state = encoder.init_state(batch_size)

    for batch, data in enumerate(train_dataset):
        encoder_in, decoder_in, decoder_out = data
        # print(encoder_in.shape, decoder_in.shape, decoder_out.shape)
        loss = train_step(
            encoder_in, decoder_in, decoder_out, encoder_state)

    print("Epoch: {}, Loss: {:.4f}".format(e + 1, loss.numpy()))

    if e % 10 == 0:
        checkpoint.save(file_prefix=checkpoint_prefix)

    predict(encoder, decoder, batch_size, sents_en, data_en,
        sents_fr_out, word2idx_fr, idx2word_fr)

    eval_score = evaluate_bleu_score(encoder, decoder,
        test_dataset, word2idx_fr, idx2word_fr)
    print("Eval Score (BLEU): {:.3e}".format(eval_score))
    # eval_scores.append(eval_score)

checkpoint.save(file_prefix=checkpoint_prefix)
```

The results from the first 5 and last 5 epochs of training are shown as follows. Notice that the loss has gone down from about 1.5 to around 0.07 in epoch 247. The BLEU scores have also gone up by around 2.5 times. Most impressive, however, is the difference in translation quality between the first 5 and last 5 epochs:

Epoch-#	Loss (Training)	BLEU Score (Test)	English	French (true)	French (predicted)
1	1.4119	1.957e-02	tom is special.	tom est special.	elle est tres bon.
2	1.1067	2.244e-02	he hates shopping.	il deteste faire les courses.	il est tres mineure.
3	0.9154	2.700e-02	did she say it?	l a t elle dit?	n est ce pas clair?
4	0.7817	2.803e-02	i d rather walk.	je prefererais marcher.	je suis alle a kyoto.
5	0.6632	2.943e-02	i m in the car.	je suis dans la voiture.	je suis toujours inquiet.
...					
245	0.0896	4.991e-02	she sued him.	elle le poursuivit en justice.	elle l a poursuivi en justice.
246	0.0853	5.011e-02	she isn t poor.	elle n est pas pauvre.	elle n est pas pauvre.
247	0.0738	5.022e-02	which one is mine?	lequel est le mien?	lequel est le mien?
248	0.1208	4.931e-02	i m getting old.	je me fais vieux.	je me fais vieux.
249	0.0837	4.856e-02	t was worth a try.	ca valait le coup d essayer.	ca valait le coup d essayer.
250	0.0967	4.869e-02	don t back away.	ne reculez pas!	ne reculez pas!

The full code for this example can be found in the source code accompanying this chapter. You will need a GPU-based machine to run it, although you may be able to run it on the CPU using smaller network dimensions (`embedding_dim`, `encoder_dim`, `decoder_dim`), smaller hyperparameters (`batch_size`, `num_epochs`), and smaller number of sentence pairs. To run the code in its entirety, run the following command. The output will be written to console:

```
$ python seq2seq_wo_attn.py
```

In the next section, we will look at a mechanism to improve the performance of the seq2seq network, by allowing it to focus on certain parts of the input more than on others in a data-driven way. This mechanism is known as the Attention mechanism.

Attention mechanism

In the previous section we saw how the context or thought vector from the last time step of the encoder is fed into the decoder as the initial hidden state. As the context flows through the time steps on the decoder, the signal gets combined with the decoder output and progressively gets weaker and weaker. The result is that the context does not have much effect towards the later time steps on the decoder.

In addition, certain sections of the decoder output may depend more heavily on certain sections of the input. For example, consider an input "thank you very much", and the corresponding output "merci beaucoup" for an English to French translation network such as the one we looked at in the previous section. Here the English phrases "thank you", and "very much", correspond to the French "merci" and "beaucoup" respectively. This information is also not conveyed adequately through the single context vector.

The Attention mechanism provides access to all encoder hidden states at every time step on the decoder. The decoder learns which part of the encoder states to pay more attention to. The use of attention has resulted in great improvements to the quality of machine translation, as well as a variety of standard natural language processing tasks.

The use of Attention is not limited to seq2seq networks. For example, Attention is a key component in the "Embed, Encode, Attend, Predict" formula for creating state of the art deep learning models for NLP [34]. Here, Attention has been used to preserve as much information as possible when downsizing from a larger to a more compact representation, for example, when reducing a sequence of word vectors into a single sentence vector.

Essentially, the Attention mechanism provides a way to score tokens in the target against all tokens in the source and modify the input signal to the decoder accordingly. Consider an encoder-decoder architecture where the input and output time steps are denoted by indices i and j respectively, and the hidden states on the encoder and decoder at these respective time steps are denoted by h_i and s_j. Inputs to the encoder are denoted by x_i and outputs from the decoder are denoted by y_j. In an encoder-decoder network without attention, the value of decoder state s_j is given by the hidden state s_{j-1} and output y_{j-1} at the previous time step. The Attention mechanism adds a third signal c_j, known as the Attention context. With Attention, therefore, the decoder hidden state s_j is a function of y_{j-1}, s_{j-1}, and c_j, shown as follows:

$$s_j = f\left(y_{j-1}, s_{j-1}, c_j\right)$$

The Attention context signal c_j is computed as follows. For every decoder step j, we compute the alignment between the decoder state s_{j-1} and every encoder state h_i. This gives us a set of N similarity values e_{ij} for each decoder state j, which we then convert to a probability distribution by computing their corresponding softmax values b_{ij}. Finally, the Attention context c_j is computed as the weighted sum of the encoder states h_i and their corresponding softmax weights b_{ij} over all N encoder time steps. The set of equations shown encapsulate this transformation for each decoder step j:

$$e_{ij} = align(h_i, s_{j-1}) \forall i$$
$$b_{ij} = softmax(e_{ij})$$
$$c_j = \sum_{i=0}^{N} h_i b_{ij}$$

Multiple Attention mechanisms have been proposed based on how the alignment is done. We will describe a few next. For notational convenience, we will indicate the state vector h_i on the encoder side with h, and the state vector s_{j-1} on the decoder side with s.

The simplest formulation of alignment is **content-based attention**. It was proposed by Graves, Wayne, and Danihelka [27], and is just the cosine similarity between the encoder and decoder states. A precondition for using this formulation is that the hidden state vector on both the encoder and decoder must have the same dimensions:

$$e = cosine(h, s)$$

Another formulation, known as **additive** or **Bahdanau attention**, was proposed by Bahdanau, Cho, and Bengio [28]. This involves combining the state vectors using learnable weights in a small neural network, given by the following equation. Here the s and h vectors are concatenated and multiplied by the learned weights W, which is equivalent to using two learned weights W_s and W_h to multiply with s and h, and adding the results:

$$e = v^T \tanh(W[s; h])$$

Luong, Pham, and Manning [29], proposed a set of three attention formulations (dot, general, and concat), of which the general formulation is also known as the **multiplicative** or **Luong's attention**. The dot and concat attention formulations are similar to the content-based and additive attention formulations discussed earlier. The multiplicative attention formulation is given by the following equation:

$$e = h^T W s$$

Finally, Vaswani, et al. [30], proposed a variation on content-based attention, called the **scaled dot-product attention**, which is given by the following equation. Here, N is the dimension of the encoder hidden state h. Scaled dot-product attention is used in the transformer architecture, which we will learn about shortly in this chapter:

$$e = \frac{h^T s}{\sqrt{N}}$$

Attention mechanisms can also be categorized by what it attends to. Using this categorization scheme, Attention mechanisms can be self-attention, global or soft attention, and local or hard attention.

Self-attention is when the alignment is computed across different sections of the same sequence, and has been found to be useful for applications such as machine reading, abstractive text summarization, and image caption generation.

Soft or global attention is when the alignment is computed over the entire input sequence, and hard or local attention is when the alignment is computed over part of the sequence. The advantage of soft attention is that it is differentiable, however it can be expensive to compute. Conversely, hard attention is cheaper to compute at inference time, but is non-differentiable and requires more complicated techniques during training.

In the next section, we will see how to integrate the attention mechanism with a seq2seq network, and how it improves the performance.

Example – seq2seq with attention for machine translation

Let us look at the same example of machine translation that we saw earlier in this chapter, except that the decoder will now attend to the encoder outputs using the additive Attention mechanism proposed by Bahdanau, et al. [28], and the multiplicative one proposed by Luong, et al [29].

The first change is to the Encoder. Instead of returning a single context or thought vector, it will return outputs at every time point, because the Attention mechanism will need this information. Here is the revised Encoder class, with the change highlighted:

```
class Encoder(tf.keras.Model):
    def __init__(self, vocab_size, num_timesteps,
            embedding_dim, encoder_dim, **kwargs):
        super(Encoder, self).__init__(**kwargs)
```

```
        self.encoder_dim = encoder_dim
        self.embedding = tf.keras.layers.Embedding(
            vocab_size, embedding_dim, input_length=num_timesteps)
        self.rnn = tf.keras.layers.GRU(
            encoder_dim, return_sequences=True, return_state=True)

    def call(self, x, state):
        x = self.embedding(x)
        x, state = self.rnn(x, initial_state=state)
        return x, state

    def init_state(self, batch_size):
        return tf.zeros((batch_size, self.encoder_dim))
```

The Decoder will have bigger changes. The biggest is the declaration of attention layers, which need to be defined, so let us do that first. Let us first consider the class definition for the additive attention proposed by Bahdanau. Recall that this combines the decoder hidden state at each time step with all the encoder hidden states to produce an input to the decoder at the next time step, which is given by the following equation:

$$e = v^T \tanh(W[s; h])$$

The W [s;h] in the equation is shorthand for two separate linear transformations (of the form $y = Wx + b$), one on s, and the other on h. The two linear transformations are implemented as Dense layers as shown in the following implementation. We subclass a tf.keras Layer object, since our end goal is to use this as a layer in our network, but it is also acceptable to subclass a Model object. The call() method takes a query (the decoder state) and values (the encoder states), computes the score, then computes the alignment as the corresponding softmax, and context vector as given by the equation, then returns them. The shape of the context vector is given by (batch_size, num_decoder_timesteps), and the alignments have the shape (batch_size, num_encoder_timesteps, 1). The weights for the dense layer's W1, W2, and V tensors are learned during training:

```
class BahdanauAttention(tf.keras.layers.Layer):
    def __init__(self, num_units):
        super(BahdanauAttention, self).__init__()
        self.W1 = tf.keras.layers.Dense(num_units)
        self.W2 = tf.keras.layers.Dense(num_units)
        self.V = tf.keras.layers.Dense(1)

    def call(self, query, values):
        # query is the decoder state at time step j
```

```
# query.shape: (batch_size, num_units)
# values are encoder states at every timestep i
# values.shape: (batch_size, num_timesteps, num_units)

# add time axis to query: (batch_size, 1, num_units)
query_with_time_axis = tf.expand_dims(query, axis=1)
# compute score:
score = self.V(tf.keras.activations.tanh(
    self.W1(values) + self.W2(query_with_time_axis)))
# compute softmax
alignment = tf.nn.softmax(score, axis=1)
# compute attended output
context = tf.reduce_sum(
    tf.linalg.matmul(
        tf.linalg.matrix_transpose(alignment),
        values
    ), axis=1
)
context = tf.expand_dims(context, axis=1)
return context, alignment
```

The Luong attention is multiplicative, but the general implementation is similar. Instead of declaring three linear transformations W1, W2, and V, we only have a single one W. The steps in the call() method follows the same general steps – first, we compute the scores according to the equation for Luong's attention as described in the last section, then compute the alignments as the corresponding softmax version of the scores, then the context vector as the dot product of the alignment and the values. Like the weights in the Bahdanau attention class, the weight matrices represented by the dense layer W are learned during training:

```
class LuongAttention(tf.keras.layers.Layer):
    def __init__(self, num_units):
        super(LuongAttention, self).__init__()
        self.W = tf.keras.layers.Dense(num_units)

    def call(self, query, values):
        # add time axis to query
        query_with_time_axis = tf.expand_dims(query, axis=1)
        # compute score
        score = tf.linalg.matmul(
            query_with_time_axis, self.W(values), transpose_b=True)
        # compute softmax
        alignment = tf.nn.softmax(score, axis=2)
        # compute attended output
        context = tf.matmul(alignment, values)
        return context, alignment
```

In order to verify that the two classes are drop-in replacements for each other, we run the following piece of throwaway code (commented out in the source code for this example). We just manufacture some random inputs and send them to both attention classes:

```
batch_size = 64
num_timesteps = 100
num_units = 1024

query = np.random.random(size=(batch_size, num_units))
values = np.random.random(size=(batch_size, num_timesteps, num_units))

# check out dimensions for Bahdanau attention
b_attn = BahdanauAttention(num_units)
context, alignments = b_attn(query, values)
print("Bahdanau: context.shape:", context.shape,
    "alignments.shape:", alignments.shape)

# check out dimensions for Luong attention
l_attn = LuongAttention(num_units)
context, alignments = l_attn(query, values)
print("Luong: context.shape:", context.shape,
    "alignments.shape:", alignments.shape)
```

The preceding code produces the following output, and shows, as expected, that the two classes produce identically shaped outputs when given the same input, and are hence drop-in replacements for each other:

```
Bahdanau: context.shape: (64, 1024) alignments.shape: (64, 8, 1)
Luong: context.shape: (64, 1024) alignments.shape: (64, 8, 1)
```

Now that we have our attention classes, let us look at the Decoder. The difference in the `init()` method is the addition of the attention class variable, which we have set to the `BahdanauAttention` class. In addition, we have two additional transformations, `Wc` and `Ws`, that will be applied to the output of the decoder RNN. The first one has a `tanh` activation to modulate the output between -1 and +1, and the next one is a standard linear transformation. Compared to the seq2seq network without an attention decoder component, this decoder takes an additional parameter `encoder_output` in its `call()` method, and returns an additional context vector:

```
class Decoder(tf.keras.Model):
    def __init__(self, vocab_size, embedding_dim, num_timesteps,
            decoder_dim, **kwargs):
        super(Decoder, self).__init__(**kwargs)
        self.decoder_dim = decoder_dim
```

```
        self.attention = BahdanauAttention(embedding_dim)
        # self.attention = LuongAttention(embedding_dim)

        self.embedding = tf.keras.layers.Embedding(
            vocab_size, embedding_dim, input_length=num_timesteps)
        self.rnn = tf.keras.layers.GRU(
            decoder_dim, return_sequences=True, return_state=True)

        self.Wc = tf.keras.layers.Dense(decoder_dim, activation="tanh")
        self.Ws = tf.keras.layers.Dense(vocab_size)

    def call(self, x, state, encoder_out):
        x = self.embedding(x)
        context, alignment = self.attention(x, encoder_out)
        x = tf.expand_dims(
                tf.concat([
                    x, tf.squeeze(context, axis=1)
                ], axis=1),
            axis=1)
        x, state = self.rnn(x, state)
        x = self.Wc(x)
        x = self.Ws(x)
        return x, state, alignment
```

The training loop is also a little different. Unlike the seq2seq without attention network, where we used teacher forcing to speed up training, using attention means that we now have to consume the decoder input one by one, since the decoder output at the previous step influences more strongly through attention the output at the current time step. Our new training loop looks like this, and is significantly slower than the training loop on the seq2seq network without attention. However, this kind of training loop may be used on the former network as well, especially when we want to implement scheduled sampling strategies:

```
@tf.function
def train_step(encoder_in, decoder_in, decoder_out, encoder_state):
    with tf.GradientTape() as tape:
        encoder_out, encoder_state = encoder(encoder_in, encoder_state)
        decoder_state = encoder_state

        loss = 0
        for t in range(decoder_out.shape[1]):
            decoder_in_t = decoder_in[:, t]
            decoder_pred_t, decoder_state, _ = decoder(decoder_in_t,
                decoder_state, encoder_out)
```

```
        loss += loss_fn(decoder_out[:, t], decoder_pred_t)

    variables = (encoder.trainable_variables +
        decoder.trainable_variables)
    gradients = tape.gradient(loss, variables)
    optimizer.apply_gradients(zip(gradients, variables))
    return loss / decoder_out.shape[1]
```

The `predict()` and `evaluate()` methods also have similar changes, since they also implement the new data flow on the decoder side that involves an extra `encoder_out` parameter and an extra `context` return value.

We trained two versions of the seq2seq network with attention, once with additive (Bahdanau) attention, and once with multiplicative (Luong) attention. Both networks were trained for 50 epochs instead of 250. However, in both cases, translations were produced with quality similar to that obtained from the seq2seq network without attention trained for 250 epochs. The training losses at the end of training for the seq2seq networks with either attention mechanism were marginally lower, and the BLEU scores on the test sets were slightly higher, compared with the seq2seq network without attention:

Network Description	Ending Loss (training set)	Ending BLEU score (test set)
seq2seq without attention, trained for 250 epochs	0.0967	4.869e-02
seq2seq with additive attention, trained for 30 epochs	0.0893	5.508e-02
seq2seq with multiplicative attention, trained for 30 epochs	0.0706	5.563e-02

Here are some examples of the translations produced from the two networks. Epoch numbers and the type of attention used are mentioned with each example. Notice that even when the translations are not 100% the same as the labels, many of them are valid translations of the original:

Attention Type	Epoch-#	English	French (label)	French (predicted)
Bahdanau	20	your cat is fat.	ton chat est gras.	ton chat est mouille.
	25	i had to go back.	il m a fallu retourner.	il me faut partir.

	30	try to find it.	tentez de le trouver.	tentez de le trouver.
Luong	20	that s peculiar.	c est etrange.	c est deconcertant.
	25	tom is athletic.	thomas est sportif.	tom est sportif.
	30	it s dangerous.	c est dangereux.	c est dangereux.

The full code for the network described here is in the `seq2seq_with_attn.py` file in the code folder for this chapter. To run the code from the command line, please use the following command. You can switch between Bahdanau (additive) or Luong (multiplicative) attention mechanisms by commenting out one or the other in the `init()` method of the Decoder class:

```
$ python seq2seq_with_attn.py
```

In the next section, we will describe the next architectural landmark in text processing using deep neural networks, the transformer network, which combines ideas from Encoder-Decoder architecture and attention.

Transformer architecture

Even though the transformer architecture is different from recurrent networks, it uses many ideas that originated in recurrent networks. It represents the next evolutionary step of deep learning architectures that work with text, and as such, should be an essential part of your toolbox. The transformer architecture is a variant of the Encoder-Decoder architecture, where the recurrent layers have been replaced with Attention layers. The transformer architecture was proposed by Vaswani, et al. [30], and a reference implementation provided, which we will refer to throughout this discussion.

Figure 7 shows a seq2seq network with attention and compares it to a transformer network. The transformer is similar to the seq2seq with Attention model in the following ways:

1. Both source and target are sequences
2. The output of the last block of the encoder is used as context or thought vector for computing the Attention model on the decoder

3. The target sequences are fed into dense blocks which convert the output embeddings to the final sequence of integer form:

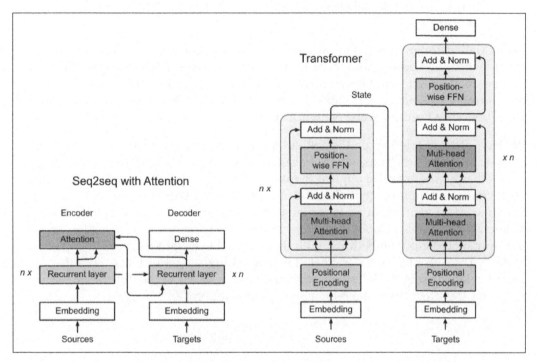

Figure 7: Flow of data in (a) seq2seq + Attention, and (b) Transformer architecture.
Image Source: Zhang, et al. [31].

And the two architectures differ in the following ways:

1. The Recurrent and Attention layers on the encoder, and the recurrent layer in the decoder of the seq2seq network, have been replaced with a transformer block. The transformer block on the encoder side consists of a sequence of multi-head Attention layers, an add and norm layer, and a position-wise feed-forward layer. The transformer on the decoder side has an additional layer of multi-head attention, and add and norm layers in front of the encoder state signal.

2. The encoder state is passed to every transformer block on the decoder, instead of to the first recurrent time step as with the seq2seq with attention network. This allows transformers to work in parallel across time steps, since there is no longer a temporal dependency as with seq2seq networks.

3. Because of the parallelism referred to in the previous point, in order to distinguish the position of each element in the sequence in the transformer network, a positional encoding layer is added to provide this positional information.

Let us walk through how data flows through the transformer. The Encoder side consists of an Embedding and a Positional Encoding layer, followed by some number (6 in the reference implementation [30]) of transformer blocks. Each transformer block on the Encoder side consists of a Multi-head attention layer and a position-wise **Feed-Forward Network (FFN)**.

We have already briefly seen that self-attention is the process of attending to parts of the same sequence. Thus, when processing a sentence, we might want to know what other words are most aligned to the current word. The multi-head attention layer consists of multiple (8 in the reference implementation [30]) parallel self-attention layers. Self-attention is carried out by constructing three vectors Q (query), K (key), and V (value), out of the input embedding. These vectors are created by multiplying the input embedding with three trainable weight matrices W_Q, W_K, and W_V. The output vector Z is created by combining K, Q, and V at each self-attention layer using the following formula. Here d_K refers to the dimension of the K, Q, and V vectors (64 in the reference implementation [30]):

$$z = softmax(\frac{QK^T}{\sqrt{d_k}})V$$

The multi-head attention layer will create multiple values for Z (based on multiple trainable weight matrices W_Q, W_K, and W_V at each self-attention layer), and then concatenate them for input into the position-wise FFN layer.

The input to the position-wise FFN consists of embeddings for the different elements in the sequence (or words in the sentence), attended to via self-attention in the multi-head attention layer. Each token is represented internally by a fixed length embedding vector (512 in the reference implementation [30]). Each vector is run through the FFN in parallel. The output of the FFN is the input to the Multi-head attention layer in the next transformer block. If this is the last transformer block in the encoder, then the output is the context vector that is passed to the decoder.

In addition to the signal from the previous layer, both the multi-head attention layer and the position-wise FFN layer send out a residual signal from their input to their output. The output and residual inputs are passed through a layer-normalization [32] step, and is shown in the *Figure 7* as the Add and Norm layer.

Since the entire sequence is consumed in parallel on the Encoder, information about the positions of individual elements are lost. To compensate for this, the input embeddings are augmented with a positional embedding, which is implemented as a sinusoidal function without learned parameters. The positional embedding is added to the input embedding.

The output of the Encoder is a pair of attention vectors K and V. This is sent in parallel to all the transformer blocks in the decoder. The transformer block on the decoder is similar to that on the encoder, except that it has an additional multi-head attention layer to attend to the attention vectors from the encoder. This additional multi-head attention layer works similar to the one in the encoder and the one below it, except it combines the Q vector from the layer below it and the K and Q vectors from the encoder state.

Similar to the seq2seq network, the output sequence is generated one token at a time, using the input from the previous time step. As with the input to the encoder, the input to the decoder is also augmented with a positional embedding. Unlike the encoder, the self attention process in the decoder is only allowed to attend to tokens at previous time points. This is done by masking out tokens at future time points.

The output of the last transformer block in the Decoder is a sequence of low-dimensional embeddings (512 for reference implementation [30] as noted earlier). This is passed to the Dense layer, which converts it into a sequence of probability distributions across the target vocabulary, from which we generate the most probable word either greedily or by a more sophisticated technique such as beam search.

This has been a fairly high-level coverage of the transformer architecture. It has achieved state of the art results in some machine translation benchmarks. The BERT embedding, which we have talked about in the previous chapter, is the encoder portion of a transformer network trained on sentence pairs in the same language. The BERT network comes in two flavors, both of which are somewhat larger than the reference implementation – BERT-base has 12 encoder layers, a hidden dimension of 768, and 8 attention heads on its Multi-head attention layers, while BERT-large has 24 encoder layers, hidden dimension of 1024, and 16 attention heads.

If you would like to learn more about transformers, the illustrated transformer blog post by Allamar [33] provides a very detailed, and very visual, guide to the structure and inner workings of this network. In addition, for those of you who prefer code, the textbook by Zhang, et al. [31], describes and builds up a working model of the transformer network using MXNet.

Summary

In this chapter, we learned about RNNs, a class of networks that are specialized for dealing with sequences such as natural language, time series, speech, and so on. Just like CNNs exploit the geometry of images, RNNs exploit the sequential structure of their inputs. We learned about the basic RNN cell and how it handles state from previous time steps, and how it suffers from vanishing and exploding gradients because of inherent problems with BPTT. We saw how these problems led to the development of novel RNN cell architectures such as LSTM, GRU, and peephole LSTMs. We also learned about some simple ways to make your RNN more effective, such as making it Bidirectional or Stateful.

We then looked at different RNN topologies, and how each topology is adapted to a particular set of problems. After a lot of theory, we finally saw examples of three of these topologies. We then focused on one of these topologies, called seq2seq, which first gained popularity in the machine translation community, but has since been used in situations where the use case can be adapted to look like a machine translation problem.

From here, we looked at attention, which started off as a way to improve the performance of seq2seq networks, but has since been used very effectively in many situations where we want to compress the representation while keeping the data loss to a minimum. We looked at different kinds of attention, and looked at an example of using them in a seq2seq network with attention.

Finally, we looked at the transformer network, which is basically an Encoder-Decoder architecture where the recurrent layers have been replaced with Attention layers. At the time of writing this, transformer networks are considered state of the art, and they are being increasingly used in many situations.

In the next chapter, you will learn about Autoencoders, another type of Encoder-Decoder architecture that have proven to be useful in semi-supervised or unsupervised settings.

References

1. Jozefowicz, R., Zaremba, R. and Sutskever, I. (2015). *An Empirical Exploration of Recurrent Neural Network Architectures*. Journal of Machine Learning.

2. Greff, K., et al. (July 2016). *LSTM: A Search Space Odyssey*. IEEE Transactions on Neural Networks and Learning Systems.

3. Bernal, A., Fok, S., and Pidaparthi, R. (December 2012). *Financial Markets Time Series Prediction with Recurrent Neural Networks*.

4. Hadjeres, G., Pachet, F., Nielsen, F. (August 2017). *DeepBach: a Steerable Model for Bach Chorales Generation*. Proceedings of the 34th International Conference on Machine Learning (ICML).

5. Karpathy, A. (2015). *The Unreasonable Effectiveness of Recurrent Neural Networks*. URL: http://karpathy.github.io/2015/05/21/rnn-effectiveness/.

6. Karpathy, A., Li, F. (2015). *Deep Visual-Semantic Alignments for Generating Image Descriptions*. Conference on Pattern Recognition and Pattern Recognition (CVPR).

7. Socher, et al. (2013). *Recursive Deep Models for Sentiment Compositionality over a Sentiment Treebank*. Proceedings of the 2013 Conference on Empirical Methods in Natural Language Processing (EMNLP).

8. Bahdanau, D., Cho, K., Bengio, Y. (2015). *Neural Machine Translation by Jointly Learning to Align and Translate*. arXiv: 1409.0473 [cs.CL].

9. Wu, Y., et al. (2016). *Google's Neural Machine Translation System: Bridging the Gap between Human and Machine Translation*. arXiv 1609.08144 [cs.CL].

10. Vinyals, O., et al. (2015). *Grammar as a Foreign Language*. Advances in Neural Information Processing Systems (NIPS).

11. Rumelhart, D. E., Hinton, G. E., and Williams, R. J. (1985). *Learning Internal Representations by Error Propagation*. Parallel Distributed Processing: Explorations in the Microstructure of Cognition.

12. Britz, D. (2015). *Recurrent Neural Networks Tutorial, Part 3 - Backpropagation Through Time and Vanishing Gradients*. URL: http://www.wildml.com/2015/10/recurrent-neural-networks-tutorial-part-3-backpropagation-through-time-and-vanishing-gradients/.

13. Pascanu, R., Mikolov, T., and Bengio, Y. (2013). *On the difficulty of training Recurrent Neural Networks*. Proceedings of the 30th International Conference on Machine Learning (ICML).

14. Hochreiter, S., and Schmidhuber, J. (1997). *LSTM can solve hard long time lag problems*. Advances in Neural Information Processing Systems (NIPS).

15. Britz, D. (2015). *Recurrent Neural Network Tutorial, Part 4 – Implementing a GRU/LSTM RNN with Python and Theano*. URL: http://www.wildml.com/2015/10/recurrent-neural-network-tutorial-part-4-implementing-a-grulstm-rnn-with-python-and-theano/.

16. Olah, C. (2015). *Understanding LSTM Networks*. URL: https://colah.github.io/posts/2015-08-Understanding-LSTMs/.

17. Cho, K., et al. (2014). *Learning Phrase Representations using RNN Encoder-Decoder for Statistical Machine Translation*. arXiv: 1406.1078 [cs.CL].

18. Shi, X., et al. (2015). *Convolutional LSTM Network: A Machine Learning Approach for Precipitation Nowcasting*. arXiv: 1506.04214 [cs.CV].

19. Gers, F.A., and Schmidhuber, J. (2000). *Recurrent Nets that Time and Count*. Proceedings of the IEEE-INNS-ENNS International Joint Conference on Neural Networks (IJCNN).

20. Kotzias, D. (2015). *Sentiment Labeled Sentences Dataset*, provided as part of "From Group to Individual Labels using Deep Features" (KDD 2015). URL: https://archive.ics.uci.edu/ml/datasets/ Sentiment+Labelled+Sentences.

21. Collobert, R., et al (2011). *Natural Language Processing (Almost) from Scratch*. Journal of Machine Learning Research (JMLR).

22. Marcus, M. P., Santorini, B., and Marcinkiewicz, M. A. (1993). *Building a large annotated corpus of English: the Penn Treebank*. Journal of Computational Linguistics.

23. Bird, S., Loper, E., and Klein, E. (2009). *Natural Language Processing with Python, O'Reilly Media Inc*. Installation URL: https://www.nltk.org/ install.html.

24. Liu, C., et al. (2017). *MAT: A Multimodal Attentive Translator for Image Captioning*. arXiv: 1702.05658v3 [cs.CV].

25. Suilin, A. (2017). *Kaggle Web Traffic Time Series Forecasting*. GitHub repository: https://github.com/Arturus/kaggle-web-traffic.

26. Tatoeba Project. (1997-2019). Tab-delimited Bilingual Sentence Pairs. URLs: http://tatoeba.org and http://www.manythings.org/anki.

27. Graves, A., Wayne, G., and Danihelka, I. (2014). *Neural Turing Machines*. arXiv: 1410.5401v2 [cs.NE].

28. Bahdanau, D., Cho, K., Bengio, Y. (2015). *Neural Machine Translation by jointly learning to Align and Translate*. arXiv: 1409.0473v7 [cs.CL].

29. Luong, M., Pham, H., Manning, C. (2015). *Effective Approaches to Attention-based Neural Machine Translation*. arXiv: 1508.04025v5 [cs.CL].

30. Vaswani, A., et al. (2017). *Attention Is All You Need*. 31st Conference on Neural Information Processing Systems (NeurIPS).

31. Zhang, A., Lipton, Z. C., Li, M., and Smola, A. J. (2019). *Dive into Deep Learning*. URL: http://www.d2l.ai.

32. Ba, J. L., Kiros, J. R., Hinton, G. E. (2016). *Layer Normalization*. arXiv: 1607.06450v1 [stat.ML].

33. Allamar, J. (2018). *The Illustrated Transformer*. URL: http://jalammar. github.io/illustrated-transformer/.

34. Honnibal, M. (2016). *Embed, encode, attend, predict: The new deep learning formula for state of the art NLP models.* URL: `https://explosion.ai/blog/deep-learning-formula-nlp`.

35. Papineni, K., Roukos, S., Ward, T., and Zhu, W. (2002). *BLEU: A Method for Automatic Evaluation of Machine Translation.* Proceedings of the 40th Annual Meeting for the Association of Computational Linguistics (ACL).

36. Project Gutenberg (2019), URL: `https://www.gutenberg.org/`.

9
Autoencoders

Autoencoders are feed-forward, non-recurrent neural networks that learn by unsupervised learning, also sometimes called semi-supervised learning, since the input is treated as the target too. In this chapter, you will learn and implement different variants of autoencoders and eventually learn how to stack autoencoders. We will also see how autoencoders can be used to create MNIST digits, and finally will also cover the steps involved in building an long short-term memory autoencoder to generate sentence vectors. This chapter includes the following topics:

- Vanilla autoencoders
- Sparse autoencoders
- Denoising autoencoders
- Convolutional autoencoders
- Stacked autoencoders
- Generating sentences using LSTM autoencoders

Introduction to autoencoders

Autoencoders are a class of neural network that attempt to recreate the input as their target using back-propagation. An autoencoder consists of two parts; an encoder and a decoder. The encoder will read the input and compress it to a compact representation, and the decoder will read the compact representation and recreate the input from it. In other words, the autoencoder tries to learn the identity function by minimizing the reconstruction error. They have an inherent capability to learn a compact representation of data. They are at the center of deep belief networks and find applications in image reconstruction, clustering, machine translation, and much more.

You might think that implementing an identity function using deep neural networks is boring, however, the way in which this is done makes it interesting. The number of hidden units in the autoencoder is typically less than the number of input (and output) units. This forces the encoder to learn a compressed representation of the input, which the decoder reconstructs. If there is a structure in the input data in the form of correlations between input features, then the autoencoder will discover some of these correlations, and end up learning a low-dimensional representation of the data similar to that learned using **principal component analysis (PCA)**.

 While PCA uses linear transformations, autoencoders on the other hand use non-linear transformations.

Once the autoencoder is trained, we would typically just discard the decoder component and use the encoder component to generate compact representations of the input. Alternatively, we could use the encoder as a feature detector that generates a compact, semantically rich representation of our input and build a classifier by attaching a softmax classifier to the hidden layer.

The encoder and decoder components of an autoencoder can be implemented using either dense, convolutional, or recurrent networks, depending on the kind of data that is being modeled. For example, dense networks might be a good choice for autoencoders used to build **collaborative filtering (CF)** models where we learn a compressed model of user preferences based on actual sparse user ratings. Similarly, convolutional neural networks may be appropriate for the use case described in the article *iSee: Using Deep Learning to Remove Eyeglasses from Faces*, by M. Runfeldt. Recurrent networks, on the other hand, are a good choice for autoencoders working on text data, such as deep patient and skip-thought vectors.

We can think of autoencoders as consisting of two cascaded networks. The first network is an encoder, it takes the input x, and encodes it using a transformation h to an encoded signal y, that is:

$$y = h(x)$$

The second network uses the encoded signal y as its input and performs another transformation f to get a reconstructed signal r, that is:

$$r = f(y) = f(h(x))$$

We define error, e, as the difference between the original input x and the reconstructed signal r, $e = x - r$. The network then learns by reducing the loss function (for example **mean squared error (MSE)**), and the error is propagated backwards to the hidden layers as in the case of MLPs.

Depending upon the actual dimensions of the encoded layer with respect to the input, the loss function, and constraints, there are various types of autoencoders: Variational autoencoders, Sparse autoencoders, Denoising autoencoders, and Convolution autoencoders.

Autoencoders can also be stacked by successively stacking encoders that compress their input to smaller and smaller representations, then stacking decoders in the opposite sequence. Stacked autoencoders have greater expressive power and the successive layers of representations capture a hierarchical grouping of the input, similar to the convolution and pooling operations in convolutional neural networks.

Stacked autoencoders used to be trained layer by layer. For example, in the network shown next, we would first train layer **X** to reconstruct layer **X'** using the hidden layer **H1** (ignoring **H2**). We would then train the layer **H1** to reconstruct layer **H1'** using the hidden layer **H2**. Finally, we would stack all the layers together in the configuration shown and fine tune it to reconstruct **X'** from **X**. With better activation and regularization functions nowadays, however, it is quite common to train these networks in totality:

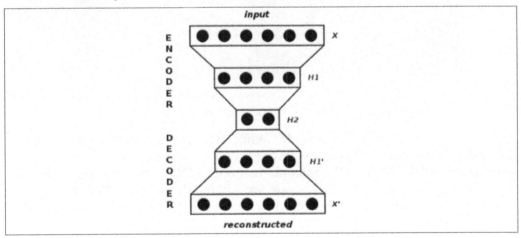

Figure 1: Visualisation of stacked autoencoders

In this chapter, we will learn about these variations in autoencoders and implement them using TensorFlow 2.0.

Vanilla autoencoders

The Vanilla autoencoder, as proposed by Hinton in his 2006 paper *Reducing the Dimensionality of Data with Neural Networks*, consists of one hidden layer only. The number of neurons in the hidden layer are less than the number of neurons in the input (or output) layer.

This results in producing a bottleneck effect in the flow of information in the network. The hidden layer in between is also called the "bottleneck layer." Learning in the autoencoder consists of developing a compact representation of the input signal at the hidden layer so that the output layer can faithfully reproduce the original input.

In the following diagram, you can see the architecture of Vanilla autoencoder:

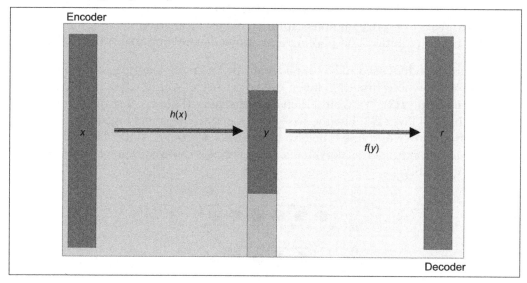

Figure 2: Architecture of the Vanilla autoencoder, visualized

Let us try to build a Vanilla autoencoder. While in the paper Hinton used it for dimension reduction, in the code to follow we will use autoencoders for image reconstruction. We will train the autoencoder on the MNIST database and will use it to reconstruct the test images. In the code, we will use the TensorFlow Keras `Layers` class to build our own encoder and decoder layers, so firstly let's learn a little about the `Layers` class.

TensorFlow Keras layers – defining custom layers

TensorFlow provides an easy way to define your own custom layer both from scratch or as a composition of existing layers. The TensorFlow Keras `layers` package defines a `Layers` object. We can make our own layer by simply making it a child class of the `Layers` class. It is necessary to define the dimensions of the output while defining the layer. Though input dimensions are optional, if you do not define them, it will infer it automatically from the data. To build our own layer we will need to implement three methods:

- `__init__()`: Here, you define all input-independent initializations.
- `build()`: Here, we define the shapes of input tensors and can perform rest initializations if required. In our example, since we are not explicitly defining input shapes, we need not define `build()` method.
- `call()`: This is where the forward computation is performed.

Using the `tensorflow.keras.layers` class we now define the encoder and decoder layers. First let's start with the encoder layer. We import `tensorflow.keras` as K, and create an `Encoder` class. The Encoder takes in the input and generates the hidden or the bottleneck layer as the output:

```
class Encoder(K.layers.Layer):
    def __init__(self, hidden_dim):
        super(Encoder, self).__init__()
        self.hidden_layer = K.layers.Dense(units=hidden_dim,
activation=tf.nn.relu)

    def call(self, input_features):
        activation = self.hidden_layer(input_features)
        return activation
```

Next we define the `Decoder` class; this class takes in the output from the `Encoder` and then passes it through a fully connected neural network. The aim is to be able to reconstruct the input to the `Encoder`:

```
class Decoder(K.layers.Layer):
    def __init__(self, hidden_dim, original_dim):
        super(Decoder, self).__init__()
        self.output_layer = K.layers.Dense(units=original_dim,
activation=tf.nn.relu)

    def call(self, encoded):
        activation = self.output_layer(encoded)
        return activation
```

Now that we have both encoder and decoder defined we use the `tensorflow.keras.Model` object to build the autoencoder model. You can see in the following code that in the `__init__()` function we instantiate the encoder and decoder objects and in the `call()` method we define the signal flow. Also notice the member list `self.loss` initialized in the `_init_()`:

```
class Autoencoder(K.Model):
    def __init__(self, hidden_dim, original_dim):
        super(Autoencoder, self).__init__()
        self.loss = []
```

```
        self.encoder = Encoder(hidden_dim=hidden_dim)
        self.decoder = Decoder(hidden_dim=hidden_dim, original_
dim=original_dim)

    def call(self, input_features):
        encoded = self.encoder(input_features)
        reconstructed = self.decoder(encoded)
        return reconstructed
```

In the next section we will use the autoencoder that we defined here to reconstruct handwritten digits.

Reconstructing handwritten digits using an autoencoder

Now that we have our model autoencoder with its layer encoder and decoder ready, let us try to reconstruct handwritten digits. The complete code is available in the GitHub repo of the chapter in the notebook `VanillaAutoencoder.ipynb`. The code will require the NumPy, TensorFlow, and Matplotlib modules:

```
import numpy as np
import tensorflow as tf
import tensorflow.keras as K
import matplotlib.pyplot as plt
```

Before starting with the actual implementation, let's also define some hyperparameters. If you play around with them, you will notice that even though the architecture of your model remains the same, there is a significant change in model performance. Hyperparameter tuning (refer to *Chapter 1, Neural Network Foundations with TensorFlow 2.0,* for more details) is one of the important steps in deep learning. For reproducibility, we set the seeds for random calculation:

```
np.random.seed(11)
tf.random.set_seed(11)
batch_size = 256
max_epochs = 50
learning_rate = 1e-3
momentum = 8e-1
hidden_dim = 128
original_dim = 784
```

For training data, we are using the MNIST dataset available in the TensorFlow datasets. We normalize the data so that pixel values lie between [0,1]; this is achieved by simply dividing each pixel element by 255.

And then we reshape the tensors from 2D to 1D. We employ the `from_tensor_slices` to generate slices of tensors. Also note that here we are not using one-hot encoded labels; this is the case because we are not using labels to train the network. Autoencoders learn via unsupervised learning:

```
(x_train, _), (x_test, _) = K.datasets.mnist.load_data()
x_train = x_train / 255.
x_test = x_test / 255.
x_train = x_train.astype(np.float32)
x_test = x_test.astype(np.float32)
x_train = np.reshape(x_train, (x_train.shape[0], 784))
x_test = np.reshape(x_test, (x_test.shape[0], 784))
training_dataset = tf.data.Dataset.from_tensor_slices(x_train).
batch(batch_size)
```

Now we instantiate our autoencoder model object and define the loss and optimizers to be used for training. Observe the loss carefully; it is simply the difference between the original image and the reconstructed image. You may find that the term *reconstruction loss* is also used to describe it in many books and papers:

```
autoencoder = Autoencoder(hidden_dim=hidden_dim, original_
dim=original_dim)
opt = tf.keras.optimizers.Adam(learning_rate=1e-2)
def loss(preds, real):
    return tf.reduce_mean(tf.square(tf.subtract(preds, real)))
```

Instead of using the auto-training loop, for our custom autoencoder model we will define a custom training. We use `tf.GradientTape` to record the gradients as they are calculated and implicitly apply the gradients to all the trainable variables of our model:

```
def train(loss, model, opt, original):
    with tf.GradientTape() as tape:
        preds = model(original)
        reconstruction_error = loss(preds, original)
        gradients = tape.gradient(reconstruction_error, model.
trainable_variables)
        gradient_variables = zip(gradients, model.trainable_variables)
    opt.apply_gradients(gradient_variables)
    return reconstruction_error
```

The preceding `train()` function will be invoked in a training loop, with the dataset fed to the model in batches:

```
def train_loop(model, opt, loss, dataset, epochs=20):
    for epoch in range(epochs):
```

```
        epoch_loss = 0
        for step, batch_features in enumerate(dataset):
            loss_values = train(loss, model, opt, batch_features)
            epoch_loss += loss_values
        model.loss.append(epoch_loss)
        print('Epoch {}/{}. Loss: {}'.format(epoch + 1, epochs, epoch_
loss.numpy()))
```

Let us now train our autoencoder:

```
train_loop(autoencoder, opt, loss, training_dataset, epochs=max_
epochs)
```

The training graph is shown as follows. We can see that loss/cost is decreasing as the network learns and after 50 epochs it is almost constant about a line. This means further increasing the number of epochs will not be useful. If we want to improve our training further, we should change the hyperparameters like learning rate and `batch_size`:

```
plt.plot(range(max_epochs), autoencoder.loss)
plt.xlabel('Epochs')
plt.ylabel('Loss')
plt.show()
```

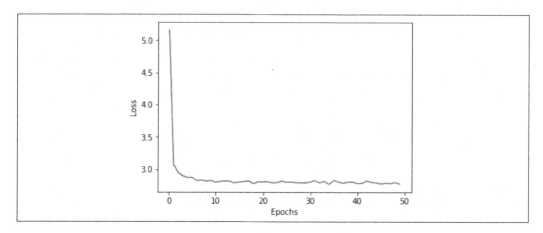

In the following figure, you can see the original (top) and reconstructed (bottom) images; they are slightly blurred, but accurate:

```
number = 10  # how many digits we will display
plt.figure(figsize=(20, 4))
for index in range(number):
    # display original
    ax = plt.subplot(2, number, index + 1)
```

```
    plt.imshow(x_test[index].reshape(28, 28), cmap='gray')
    ax.get_xaxis().set_visible(False)
    ax.get_yaxis().set_visible(False)

    # display reconstruction
    ax = plt.subplot(2, number, index + 1 + number)
    plt.imshow(autoencoder(x_test)[index].numpy().reshape(28, 28),
cmap='gray')
    ax.get_xaxis().set_visible(False)
    ax.get_yaxis().set_visible(False)
plt.show()
```

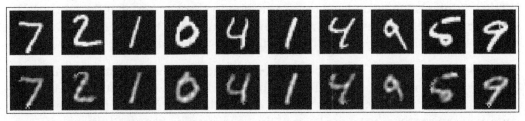

It is interesting to note that in the preceding code we reduced the dimensions of the input from 784 to 128 and our network could still reconstruct the original image. This should give you an idea of the power of the autoencoder for dimensionality reduction. One advantage of autoencoders over PCA for dimensionality reduction is that while PCA can only represent linear transformations, we can use non-linear activation functions in autoencoders, thus introducing non-linearities in our encodings:

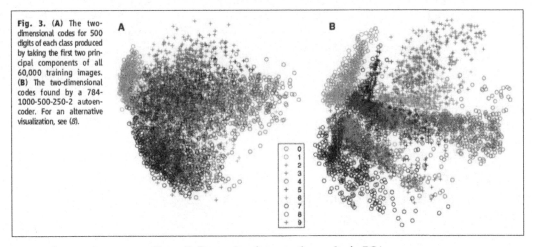

Fig. 3. (A) The two-dimensional codes for 500 digits of each class produced by taking the first two principal components of all 60,000 training images. (B) The two-dimensional codes found by a 784-1000-500-250-2 autoencoder. For an alternative visualization, see (8).

Figure 3: Comparison between the result of a PCA

The preceding figure is reproduced from the Hinton paper *Reducing the dimensionality of data with Neural Networks*. It compares the result of a PCA (A) with that of stacked autoencoders with architecture consisting of 784-1000-500-250-2.

You can see that the colored dots on the right are nicely separated, thus stacked autoencoders are giving much better results compared to PCA. Now that you are familiar with Vanilla autoencoders, let us see different variants of autoencoders and their implementation details.

Sparse autoencoder

The autoencoder we covered in the previous section works more like an identity network; it simply reconstructs the input. The emphasis is to reconstruct the image at the pixel level, and the only constraint is the number of units in the bottleneck layer. While it is interesting, pixel-level reconstruction does not ensure that the network will learn abstract features from the dataset. We can ensure that a network learns abstract features from the dataset by adding further constraints.

In Sparse autoencoders, a sparse penalty term is added to the reconstruction error. This tries to ensure that fewer units in the bottleneck layer will fire at any given time. We can include the sparse penalty within the encoder layer itself. In the following code, you can see that the Dense layer of the Encoder now has an additional parameter, `activity_regularizer`:

```
class SparseEncoder(K.layers.Layer):
    def __init__(self, hidden_dim):
        super(Encoder, self).__init__()
        self.hidden_layer = K.layers.Dense(units=hidden_dim,
activation=tf.nn.relu, activity_regularizer=regularizers.l1(10e-5))
        def call(self, input_features):
            activation = self.hidden_layer(input_features)
            return activation
```

The activity regularizer tries to reduce the layer output (refer to *Chapter 1, Neural Network Foundations with TensorFlow 2.0*). It will reduce both weights and bias of the fully connected layer to ensure that the output is as small as it can be. TensorFlow supports three types of `activity_regularizer`:

- `l1`: Here the activity is computed as the sum of absolute values

- `l2`: The activity here is calculated as the sum of the squared values

- `l1_l2`: This includes both L1 and L2 terms

Keeping the rest of the code the same, and just changing the encoder, you can get the Sparse autoencoder from the Vanilla autoencoder. The complete code for Sparse autoencoder is in the Jupyter Notebook `SparseAutoencoder.ipynb`.

Alternatively, you can explicitly add a regularization term for sparsity in the loss function. To do so you will need to implement the regularization for the sparsity term as a function. If m is the total number of input patterns, then we can define a quantity ρ_hat (you can check the mathematical details in Andrew Ng's lecture here: `https://web.stanford.edu/class/cs294a/sparseAutoencoder_2011new.pdf`), which measures the net activity (how many times on average it fires) for each hidden layer unit. The basic idea is to put a constraint ρ_hat, such that it is equal to the sparsity parameter ρ. This results in adding a regularization term for sparsity in the loss function so that now the loss function becomes:

loss = Mean squared error + Regularization for sparsity parameter

This regularization term will penalize the network if ρ_hat deviates from ρ. One standard way to do this is to use **Kullback-Leiber (KL)** divergence (you can learn more about KL divergence from this interesting lecture: `https://www.stat.cmu.edu/~cshalizi/754/2006/notes/lecture-28.pdf`) between ρ and ρ_hat.

Let's explore the KL divergence, D_{KL}, a little more. It is a non-symmetric measure of the difference between the two distributions, in our case, ρ and ρ_hat. When ρ and ρ_hat are equal then the difference is zero, otherwise it increases monotonically as ρ_hat diverges from ρ. Mathematically, it is expressed as:

$$D_{KL}(\rho \,||\hat{\rho}_j) = \rho \, log \frac{\rho}{\hat{\rho}_j} + (1 - \rho)log \frac{1 - \rho}{1 - \hat{\rho}_j}$$

You add this to the loss to implicitly include the sparse term. You will need to fix a constant value for the sparsity term ρ and compute ρ_hat using the encoder output.

The compact representation of the inputs is stored in weights. Let us visualize the weights learned by the network. Following are the weights of the encoder layer for the standard and Sparse autoencoder respectively.

We can see that in the standard autoencoder (a) many hidden units have very large weights (brighter), suggesting that they are overworked, while all the hidden units of the Sparse autoencoder (b) learn the input representation almost equally, and we see a more even color distribution:

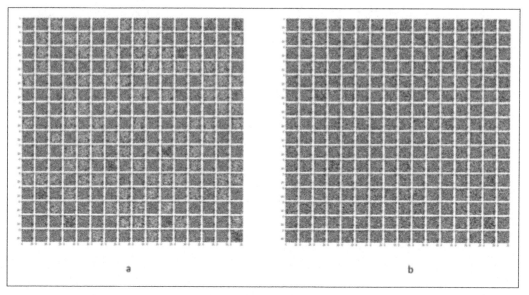

Figure 4: Encoder weight matrix for (a) Standard Autoencoder and (b) Sparse Autoencoder

Denoising autoencoders

The two autoencoders that we have covered in the previous sections are examples of undercomplete autoencoders, because the hidden layer in them has lower dimensionality as compared to the input (output) layer. Denoising autoencoders belong to the class of overcomplete autoencoders, because they work better when the dimensions of the hidden layer are more than the input layer.

A denoising autoencoder learns from a corrupted (noisy) input; it feed its encoder network the noisy input, and then the reconstructed image from the decoder is compared with the original input. The idea is that this will help the network learn how to denoise an input. It will no longer just make pixel-wise comparisons, but in order to denoise it will learn the information of neighboring pixels as well.

A Denoising autoencoder has two main differences from other autoencoders: first, n_ hidden, the number of hidden units in the bottleneck layer is greater than the number of units in the input layer, m, that is, n_hidden > m. Second, the input to the encoder is corrupted input. To do this we add a noise term in both test and training images:

```
noise = np.random.normal(loc=0.5, scale=0.5, size=x_train.shape)
x_train_noisy = x_train + noise
noise = np.random.normal(loc=0.5, scale=0.5, size=x_test.shape)
x_test_noisy = x_test + noise
x_train_noisy = np.clip(x_train_noisy, 0., 1.)
x_test_noisy = np.clip(x_test_noisy, 0., 1.)
```

Clearing images using a Denoising autoencoder

Let us use the Denoising autoencoder to clear the handwritten MNIST digits.

1. We start with importing the required modules:

```
import numpy as np
import tensorflow as tf
import tensorflow.keras as K
import matplotlib.pyplot as plt
```

2. Next we define the hyperparameters for our model:

```
np.random.seed(11)
tf.random.set_seed(11)
batch_size = 256
max_epochs = 50
learning_rate = 1e-3
momentum = 8e-1
hidden_dim = 128
original_dim = 784
```

3. We read in the MNIST dataset, normalize it, and introduce noise in it:

```
(x_train, _), (x_test, _) = K.datasets.mnist.load_data()

x_train = x_train / 255.
x_test = x_test / 255.

x_train = x_train.astype(np.float32)
x_test = x_test.astype(np.float32)

x_train = np.reshape(x_train, (x_train.shape[0], 784))
x_test = np.reshape(x_test, (x_test.shape[0], 784))

# Generate corrupted MNIST images by adding noise with normal dist
# centered at 0.5 and std=0.5
noise = np.random.normal(loc=0.5, scale=0.5, size=x_train.shape)
```

```
x_train_noisy = x_train + noise
noise = np.random.normal(loc=0.5, scale=0.5, size=x_test.shape)
x_test_noisy = x_test + noise
```

4. We use the same encoder, decoder, and autoencoder classes as defined in the *Vanilla autoencoders* section:

```
# Encoder
class Encoder(K.layers.Layer):
    def __init__(self, hidden_dim):
        super(Encoder, self).__init__()
        self.hidden_layer = K.layers.Dense(units=hidden_dim,
activation=tf.nn.relu)
        def call(self, input_features):
            activation = self.hidden_layer(input_features)
            return activation
# Decoder
class Decoder(K.layers.Layer):
    def __init__(self, hidden_dim, original_dim):
        super(Decoder, self).__init__()
        self.output_layer = K.layers.Dense(units=original_dim,
activation=tf.nn.relu)
    def call(self, encoded):
        activation = self.output_layer(encoded)
        return activation


class Autoencoder(K.Model):
    def __init__(self, hidden_dim, original_dim):
        super(Autoencoder, self).__init__()
        self.loss = []
        self.encoder = Encoder(hidden_dim=hidden_dim)
        self.decoder = Decoder(hidden_dim=hidden_dim, original_
dim=original_dim)

    def call(self, input_features):
        encoded = self.encoder(input_features)
        reconstructed = self.decoder(encoded)
        return reconstructed
```

5. Next we create the model and define the loss and optimizers to be used. Notice that this time instead of writing the custom training loop we are using the easier Keras inbuilt `compile()` and `fit()` methods:

```
model = Autoencoder(hidden_dim=hidden_dim, original_dim=original_
dim)
model.compile(loss='mse', optimizer='adam')
loss = model.fit(x_train_noisy,
```

```
        x_train,
        validation_data=(x_test_noisy, x_test),
        epochs=max_epochs,
        batch_size=batch_size)
```

6. Now let's plot the training loss:

```
plt.plot(range(max_epochs), loss.history['loss'])
plt.xlabel('Epochs')
plt.ylabel('Loss')
plt.show()
```

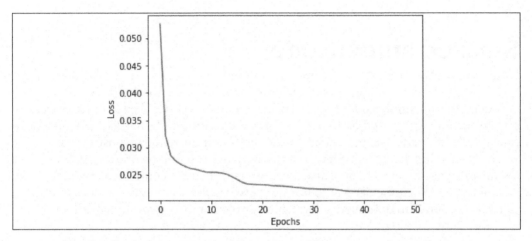

7. And finally, let's see our model in action. The top row shows the input noisy image and the bottom row shows cleaned images produced from our trained Denoising autoencoder:

```
number = 10  # how many digits we will display
plt.figure(figsize=(20, 4))
for index in range(number):
    # display original
    ax = plt.subplot(2, number, index + 1)
    plt.imshow(x_test_noisy[index].reshape(28, 28), cmap='gray')
    ax.get_xaxis().set_visible(False)
    ax.get_yaxis().set_visible(False)

    # display reconstruction
    ax = plt.subplot(2, number, index + 1 + number)
    plt.imshow(model(x_test_noisy)[index].numpy().reshape(28, 28),
cmap='gray')
    ax.get_xaxis().set_visible(False)
    ax.get_yaxis().set_visible(False)
plt.show()
```

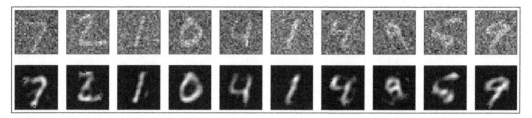

An impressive reconstruction of images from noisy images, I'm sure you'll agree. You can access the code in the notebook `DenoisingAutoencoder.ipynb` if you want to play around with it.

Stacked autoencoder

Until now we have restricted ourselves to autoencoders with only one hidden layer. We can build Deep autoencoders by stacking many layers of both encoder and decoder; such an autoencoder is called a Stacked autoencoder. The features extracted by one encoder are passed on to the next encoder as input. The stacked autoencoder can be trained as a whole network with an aim to minimize the reconstruction error. Or each individual encoder/decoder network can first be pretrained using the unsupervised method you learned earlier, and then the complete network can be fine-tuned. When the deep autoencoder network is a convolutional network, we call it a **Convolutional Autoencoder**. Let us implement a convolutional autoencoder in TensorFlow 2.0 next.

Convolutional autoencoder for removing noise from images

In the previous section we reconstructed handwritten digits from noisy input images. We used a fully connected network as the encoder and decoder for the work. However, we know that for images, a convolutional al network can give better results, so in this section we will use a convolution network for both the encoder and decoder. To get better results we will use multiple convolution layers in both the encoder and decoder networks; that is, we will make stacks of convolutional layers (along with maxpooling or upsample layers). We will also be training the entire autoencoder as a single entity.

1. We import all the required modules; also for convenience import specific layers from `tensorflow.keras.layers`:

```
import numpy as np
import tensorflow as tf
import tensorflow.keras as K
```

```
import matplotlib.pyplot as plt
from tensorflow.keras.layers import Dense, Conv2D, MaxPooling2D,
UpSampling2D
```

2. We specify our hyperparameters. If you look carefully, the list is slightly different; as compared to earlier autoencoder implementations, instead of learning rate and momentum, this time we are concerned with filters of the convolutional layer:

```
np.random.seed(11)
tf.random.set_seed(11)
batch_size = 128
max_epochs = 50
filters = [32,32,16]
```

3. In the next step, we read in the data and preprocess it. Again, you may observe slight variation from the previous code, especially in the way we are adding noise and then limiting the range in between [0-1]. We are doing so because in this case, instead of the mean square error loss, we will be using binary cross entropy loss and the final output of the decoder will pass through sigmoid activation, restricting it between [0-1]:

```
(x_train, _), (x_test, _) = K.datasets.mnist.load_data()

x_train = x_train / 255.
x_test = x_test / 255.

x_train = np.reshape(x_train, (len(x_train),28, 28, 1))
x_test = np.reshape(x_test, (len(x_test), 28, 28, 1))

noise = 0.5
x_train_noisy = x_train + noise * np.random.normal(loc=0.0,
scale=1.0, size=x_train.shape)
x_test_noisy = x_test + noise * np.random.normal(loc=0.0,
scale=1.0, size=x_test.shape)

x_train_noisy = np.clip(x_train_noisy, 0, 1)
x_test_noisy = np.clip(x_test_noisy, 0, 1)

x_train_noisy = x_train_noisy.astype('float32')
x_test_noisy = x_test_noisy.astype('float32')

#print(x_test_noisy[1].dtype)
```

4. Let us now define our encoder. The encoder consists of three convolutional layers, each followed by a max pooling layer. Since we are using the MNIST dataset the shape of the input image is 28 × 28 (single channel) and the output image is of size 4 × 4 (and since the last convolutional layer has 16 filters, the image has 16 channels):

```python
class Encoder(K.layers.Layer):
    def __init__(self, filters):
        super(Encoder, self).__init__()
        self.conv1 = Conv2D(filters=filters[0], kernel_size=3,
strides=1, activation='relu', padding='same')
        self.conv2 = Conv2D(filters=filters[1], kernel_size=3,
strides=1, activation='relu', padding='same')
        self.conv3 = Conv2D(filters=filters[2], kernel_size=3,
strides=1, activation='relu', padding='same')
        self.pool = MaxPooling2D((2, 2), padding='same')


    def call(self, input_features):
        x = self.conv1(input_features)
        #print("Ex1", x.shape)
        x = self.pool(x)
        #print("Ex2", x.shape)
        x = self.conv2(x)
        x = self.pool(x)
        x = self.conv3(x)
        x = self.pool(x)
        return x
```

5. Next comes the decoder. It is the exact opposite of the encoder in design, and instead of max pooling we are using upsampling to increase the size back. Notice the commented print statements: you can use them to understand how the shape gets modified after each step. Also notice both encoder and decoder are still classes based on the TensorFlow Keras Layers class, but now they have multiple layers inside them. So now you know how to build a complex custom layer:

```python
class Decoder(K.layers.Layer):
    def __init__(self, filters):
        super(Decoder, self).__init__()
        self.conv1 = Conv2D(filters=filters[2], kernel_size=3,
strides=1, activation='relu', padding='same')
        self.conv2 = Conv2D(filters=filters[1], kernel_size=3,
strides=1, activation='relu', padding='same')
        self.conv3 = Conv2D(filters=filters[0], kernel_size=3,
strides=1, activation='relu', padding='valid')
```

```
        self.conv4 = Conv2D(1, 3, 1, activation='sigmoid',
padding='same')
        self.upsample = UpSampling2D((2, 2))

    def call(self, encoded):
        x = self.conv1(encoded)
        #print("dx1", x.shape)
        x = self.upsample(x)
        #print("dx2", x.shape)
        x = self.conv2(x)
        x = self.upsample(x)
        x = self.conv3(x)
        x = self.upsample(x)
        return self.conv4(x)
```

6. We combine the encoder and decoder to make an autoencoder model. This remains exactly the same as before:

```
class Autoencoder(K.Model):
    def __init__(self, filters):
        super(Autoencoder, self).__init__()
        self.encoder = Encoder(filters)
        self.decoder = Decoder(filters)

    def call(self, input_features):
        #print(input_features.shape)
        encoded = self.encoder(input_features)
        #print(encoded.shape)
        reconstructed = self.decoder(encoded)
        #print(reconstructed.shape)
        return reconstructed
```

7. Now we instantiate our model, then specify the binary cross entropy as the loss function and Adam as the optimizer in the `compile()` method. Then, fit the model to the training dataset:

```
model = Autoencoder(filters)

model.compile(loss='binary_crossentropy', optimizer='adam')

loss = model.fit(x_train_noisy,
        x_train,
        validation_data=(x_test_noisy, x_test),
        epochs=max_epochs,
        batch_size=batch_size)
```

8. You can see the loss curve as the model is trained; in 50 epochs the loss was reduced to 0.0988:

```
plt.plot(range(max_epochs), loss.history['loss'])
plt.xlabel('Epochs')
plt.ylabel('Loss')
plt.show()
```

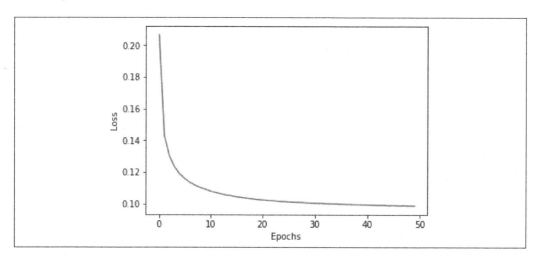

9. And finally, you can see the wonderful reconstructed images from the noisy input images:

```
number = 10   # how many digits we will display
plt.figure(figsize=(20, 4))
for index in range(number):
    # display original
    ax = plt.subplot(2, number, index + 1)
    plt.imshow(x_test_noisy[index].reshape(28, 28), cmap='gray')
    ax.get_xaxis().set_visible(False)
    ax.get_yaxis().set_visible(False)

    # display reconstruction
    ax = plt.subplot(2, number, index + 1 + number)
    plt.imshow(tf.reshape(model(x_test_noisy)[index], (28, 28)),
cmap='gray')
    ax.get_xaxis().set_visible(False)
    ax.get_yaxis().set_visible(False)
plt.show()
```

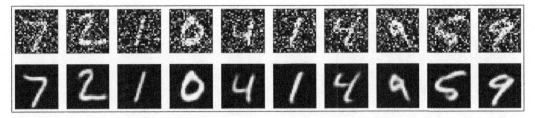

You can see that the images are much clearer and sharper relative to the previous autoencoders we have covered in this chapter. The code for this section is available in the Jupyter notebook, `ConvolutionAutoencoder.ipynb`.

Keras autoencoder example – sentence vectors

In this example, we will build and train an LSTM-based autoencoder to generate sentence vectors for documents in the Reuters-21578 corpus (`https://archive.ics.uci.edu/ml/datasets/reuters-21578+text+categorization+collection`). We have already seen in *Chapter 7, Word Embeddings*, how to represent a word using word embeddings to create vectors that represent the word's meaning in the context of other words it appears with. Here, we will see how to build similar vectors for sentences. Sentences are sequences of words, so a sentence vector represents the meaning of a sentence.

The easiest way to build a sentence vector is to just add up the word vectors and divide by the number of words. However, this treats the sentence as a bag of words, and does not take the order of words into account. Thus, the sentences *The dog bit the man* and *The man bit the dog* would be treated as identical in this scenario. LSTMs are designed to work with sequence input and do take the order of words into consideration thus providing a better and more natural representation of the sentence.

First, we import the necessary libraries:

```
from sklearn.model_selection import train_test_split
from tensorflow.keras.callbacks import ModelCheckpoint
from tensorflow.keras.layers import Input
from tensorflow.keras.layers import RepeatVector

from tensorflow.keras.layers import LSTM
from tensorflow.keras.layers import Bidirectional
from tensorflow.keras.models import Model
from tensorflow.keras.preprocessing import sequence
from scipy.stats import describe
```

```
import collections
import matplotlib.pyplot as plt
import nltk
import numpy as np
import os
from time import gmtime, strftime
from tensorflow.keras.callbacks import TensorBoard
import re


# Needed to run only once
nltk.download('punkt')
```

The data is provided as a set of SGML files. The helper code to convert the SGML files to text.tsv which is based on Scikit-learn: https://scikit-learn.org/stable/auto_examples/applications/plot_out_of_core_classification.html, is added in the GitHub the file named parse.py. We will use the data from this file and first convert each block of text into a list of sentences, one sentence per line. Also, each word in the sentence is normalized as it is added. The normalization involves removing all numbers and replacing them with the number 9, then converting the word to lower case. Simultaneously we also calculate the word frequencies in the same code. The result is the word frequency table, word_freqs:

```
DATA_DIR = "data"

def is_number(n):
    temp = re.sub("[.,-/]", "",n)
    return temp.isdigit()


# parsing sentences and building vocabulary
word_freqs = collections.Counter()
ftext = open(os.path.join(DATA_DIR, "text.tsv"), "r")
sents = []
sent_lens = []
for line in ftext:
    docid, text = line.strip().split("\t")
    for sent in nltk.sent_tokenize(text):
        for word in nltk.word_tokenize(sent):
            if is_number(word):
            word = "9"
            word = word.lower()
            word_freqs[word] += 1
            sents.append(sent)
            sent_lens.append(len(sent))
ftext.close()
```

Let us use the preceding generated arrays to get some information about the corpus that will help us figure out good values for our constants for our LSTM network:

```
print("Total number of sentences are: {:d} ".format(len(sents)))
print ("Sentence distribution min {:d}, max {:d} , mean {:3f}, median
{:3f}".format(np.min(sent_lens), np.max(sent_lens), np.mean(sent_
lens), np.median(sent_lens)))
print("Vocab size (full) {:d}".format(len(word_freqs)))
```

This gives us the following information about the corpus:

```
Total number of sentences are: 131545

Sentence distribution min 1, max 2434 , mean 120.525052, median
115.000000

Vocab size (full) 50743
```

Based on this information, we set the following constants for our LSTM model. We choose our VOCAB_SIZE as 5000; that is, our vocabulary covers the most frequent 5,000 words, which covers over 93% of the words used in the corpus. The remaining words are treated as **out of vocabulary (OOV)** and replaced with the token UNK. At prediction time, any word that the model hasn't seen will also be assigned the token UNK. SEQUENCE_LEN is set to approximately twice the median length of sentences in the training set, and indeed, approximately 110 million of our 131 million sentences are shorter than this setting. Sentences that are shorter than SEQUENCE_LENGTH will be padded by a special PAD character, and those that are longer will be truncated to fit the limit:

```
VOCAB_SIZE = 5000
SEQUENCE_LEN = 50
```

Since the input to our LSTM will be numeric, we need to build lookup tables that go back and forth between words and word IDs. Since we limit our vocabulary size to 5,000 and we have to add the two pseudo-words PAD and UNK, our lookup table contains entries for the most frequently occurring 4,998 words plus PAD and UNK:

```
word2id = {}
word2id["PAD"] = 0
word2id["UNK"] = 1
for v, (k, _) in enumerate(word_freqs.most_common(VOCAB_SIZE - 2)):
    word2id[k] = v + 2
id2word = {v:k for k, v in word2id.items()}
```

The input to our network is a sequence of words, where each word is represented by a vector. Simplistically, we could just use a one-hot encoding for each word, but that makes the input data very large. So, we encode each word using its 50-dimensional GloVe embeddings.

The embedding is generated into a matrix of shape (VOCAB_SIZE, EMBED_SIZE) where each row represents the GloVe embedding for a word in our vocabulary. The PAD and UNK rows (0 and 1 respectively) are populated with zeros and random uniform values respectively:

```
EMBED_SIZE = 50

def lookup_word2id(word):
    try:

        return word2id[word]
    except KeyError:
        return word2id["UNK"]


def load_glove_vectors(glove_file, word2id, embed_size):
    embedding = np.zeros((len(word2id), embed_size))
    fglove = open(glove_file, "rb")
    for line in fglove:

        cols = line.strip().split()
        word = cols[0]
        if embed_size == 0:

            embed_size = len(cols) - 1
        if word2id.has_key(word):

            vec = np.array([float(v) for v in cols[1:]])
        embedding[lookup_word2id(word)] = vec

    embedding[word2id["PAD"]] = np.zeros((embed_size))
    embedding[word2id["UNK"]] = np.random.uniform(-1, 1, embed_size)
    return embedding
```

Next, we use these functions to generate embeddings:

```
sent_wids = [[lookup_word2id(w) for w in s.split()] for s in sents]
sent_wids = sequence.pad_sequences(sent_wids, SEQUENCE_LEN)

# load glove vectors into weight matrix
embeddings = load_glove_vectors(os.path.join(DATA_DIR, "glove.6B.{:d}
d.txt".format(EMBED_SIZE)), word2id, EMBED_SIZE)
```

Our autoencoder model takes a sequence of GloVe word vectors and learns to produce another sequence that is similar to the input sequence. The encoder LSTM compresses the sequence into a fixed-size context vector, which the decoder LSTM uses to reconstruct the original sequence. A schematic of the network is shown here:

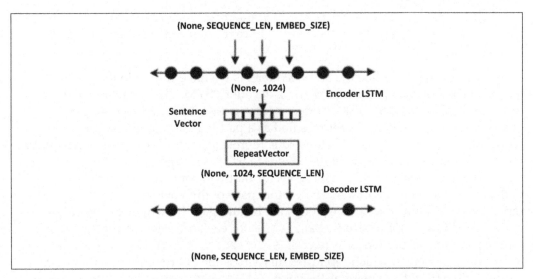

Figure 5: Visualisation of the LSTM network

Because the input is quite large, we will use a generator to produce each batch of input. Our generator produces batches of tensors of shape (BATCH_SIZE, SEQUENCE_LEN, EMBED_SIZE). Here BATCH_SIZE is 64, and since we are using 50-dimensional GloVe vectors, EMBED_SIZE is 50. We shuffle the sentences at the beginning of each epoch and return batches of 64 sentences. Each sentence is represented as a vector of GloVe word vectors. If a word in the vocabulary does not have a corresponding GloVe embedding, it is represented by a zero vector. We construct two instances of the generator, one for training data and one for test data, consisting of 70% and 30% of the original dataset respectively:

```
BATCH_SIZE = 64

def sentence_generator(X, embeddings, batch_size):
    while True:

        # loop once per epoch
        num_recs = X.shape[0]
        indices = np.random.permutation(np.arange(num_recs))
        num_batches = num_recs // batch_size
        for bid in range(num_batches):
            sids = indices[bid * batch_size : (bid + 1) * batch_size]
```

```
                  Xbatch = embeddings[X[sids, :]]

        yield Xbatch, Xbatch

    train_size = 0.7
    Xtrain, Xtest = train_test_split(sent_wids, train_size=train_size)
    train_gen = sentence_generator(Xtrain, embeddings, BATCH_SIZE)
    test_gen = sentence_generator(Xtest, embeddings, BATCH_SIZE)
```

Now we are ready to define the autoencoder. As we have shown in the diagram, it is composed of an encoder LSTM and a decoder LSTM. The encoder LSTM reads a tensor of shape (BATCH_SIZE, SEQUENCE_LEN, EMBED_SIZE) representing a batch of sentences. Each sentence is represented as a padded fixed-length sequence of words of size SEQUENCE_LEN. Each word is represented as a 300-dimensional GloVe vector. The output dimension of the encoder LSTM is a hyperparameter LATENT_SIZE, which is the size of the sentence vector that will come from the encoder part of the trained autoencoder later. The vector space of dimensionality LATENT_SIZE represents the latent space that encodes the meaning of the sentence. The output of the LSTM is a vector of size (LATENT_SIZE) for each sentence, so for the batch the shape of the output tensor is (BATCH_SIZE, LATENT_SIZE). This is now fed to a RepeatVector layer, which replicates this across the entire sequence; that is, the output tensor from this layer has the shape (BATCH_SIZE, SEQUENCE_LEN, LATENT_SIZE). This tensor is now fed into the decoder LSTM, whose output dimension is the EMBED_SIZE, so the output tensor has shape (BATCH_SIZE, SEQUENCE_LEN, EMBED_SIZE), that is, the same shape as the input tensor.

We compile this model with the SGD optimizer and the MSE loss function. The reason we use MSE is that we want to reconstruct a sentence that has a similar meaning, that is, something that is close to the original sentence in the embedded space of dimension LATENT_SIZE:

```
    inputs = Input(shape=(SEQUENCE_LEN, EMBED_SIZE), name="input")
    encoded = Bidirectional(LSTM(LATENT_SIZE), merge_mode="sum",
name="encoder_lstm")(inputs)
    decoded = RepeatVector(SEQUENCE_LEN, name="repeater")(encoded)
    decoded = Bidirectional(LSTM(EMBED_SIZE, return_sequences=True),
merge_mode="sum", name="decoder_lstm")(decoded)

    autoencoder = Model(inputs, decoded)
```

We define the loss function as mean squared error and choose the Adam optimizer:

```
    autoencoder.compile(optimizer="sgd", loss="mse")
```

We train the autoencoder for 20 epochs using the following code. 20 epochs were chosen because the MSE loss converges within this time:

```
num_train_steps = len(Xtrain) // BATCH_SIZE
num_test_steps = len(Xtest) // BATCH_SIZE

steps_per_epoch=num_train_steps,
epochs=NUM_EPOCHS,
validation_data=test_gen,
validation_steps=num_test_steps,

history = autoencoder.fit_generator(train_gen,
                          steps_per_epoch=num_train_steps,
                          epochs=NUM_EPOCHS,
                          validation_data=test_gen,
                          validation_steps=num_test_steps)
```

The results of the training are shown as follows. As you can see, the training MSE reduces from 0.1161 to 0.0824 and the validation MSE reduces from 0.1097 to 0.0820:

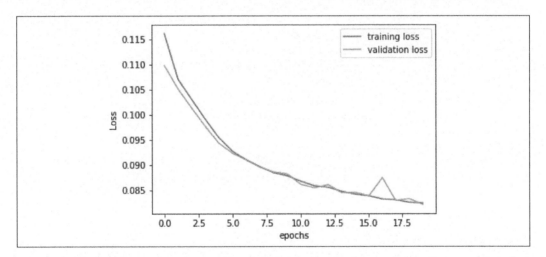

Since we are feeding in a matrix of embeddings, the output will also be a matrix of word embeddings. Since the embedding space is continuous and our vocabulary is discrete, not every output embedding will correspond to a word. The best we can do is to find a word that is closest to the output embedding in order to reconstruct the original text. This is a bit cumbersome, so we will evaluate our autoencoder in a different way.

Since the objective of the autoencoder is to produce a good latent representation, we compare the latent vectors produced from the encoder using the original input versus the output of the autoencoder.

First, we extract the encoder component into its own network:

```
encoder = Model(autoencoder.input, autoencoder.get_layer("encoder_
lstm").output)
```

Then we run the autoencoder on the test set to return the predicted embeddings. We then send both the input embedding and the predicted embedding through the encoder to produce sentence vectors from each and compare the two vectors using *cosine* similarity. Cosine similarities close to "one" indicate high similarity and those close to "zero" indicate low similarity. The following code runs against a random subset of 500 test sentences and produces some sample values of cosine similarities between the sentence vectors generated from the source embedding and the corresponding target embedding produced by the autoencoder:

```
def compute_cosine_similarity(x, y):
        return np.dot(x, y) / (np.linalg.norm(x, 2) * np.linalg.norm(y,
2))

k = 500
cosims = np.zeros((k))
i= 0
for bid in range(num_test_steps):
        xtest, ytest = test_gen.next()
        ytest_ = autoencoder.predict(xtest)
        Xvec = encoder.predict(xtest)
        Yvec = encoder.predict(ytest_)
        for rid in range(Xvec.shape[0]):

            if i >= k:
                break
            cosims[i] = compute_cosine_similarity(Xvec[rid], Yvec[rid])
            if i <= 10:
                print(cosims[i])
                i += 1
    if i >= k:
        break
```

The first 10 values of cosine similarities are shown as follows. As we can see, the vectors seem to be quite similar:

```
0.984686553478241
0.9815746545791626
0.9793671369552612
0.9805112481117249
0.9630994200706482
```

```
0.9790557622909546
0.9893233180046082
0.9869443774223328
0.9665998220443726
0.9893233180046082
0.9829331040382385
```

A histogram of the distribution of values of cosine similarities for the sentence vectors from the first 500 sentences in the test set are shown below. As previously, it confirms that the sentence vectors generated from the input and output of the autoencoder are very similar, showing that the resulting sentence vector is a good representation of the sentence:

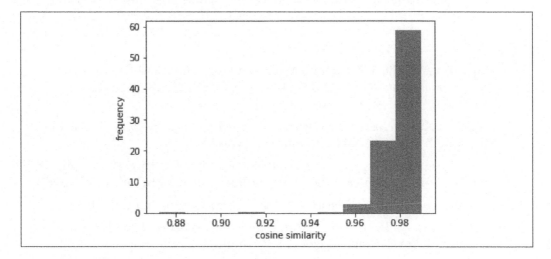

Summary

In this chapter we've had an extensive look at a new generation of deep learning models: autoencoders. We started with the Vanilla autoencoder, and then moved on to its variants: Sparse autoencoders, Denoising autoencoders, Stacked autoencoders, and Convolutional autoencoders. We used the autoencoders to reconstruct images, and we also demonstrated how they can be used to clean noise from an image. Finally, the chapter demonstrated how autoencoders can be used to generate sentence vectors. The autoencoders learned through unsupervised learning. In the next chapter we will delve deeper into some other unsupervised learning-based deep learning models.

References

1. Rumelhart, David E., Geoffrey E. Hinton, and Ronald J. Williams. *Learning Internal Representations by Error Propagation*. No. ICS-8506. California Univ San Diego La Jolla Inst for Cognitive Science, 1985 (http://www.cs.toronto.edu/~fritz/absps/pdp8.pdf).

2. Hinton, Geoffrey E., and Ruslan R. Salakhutdinov. *Reducing the dimensionality of data with neural networks*. science 313.5786 (2006): 504-507. (https://www.semanticscholar.org/paper/Reducing-the-dimensionality-of-data-with-neural-Hinton-Salakhutdinov/46eb79e5eec8a4e2b2f5652b66441e8a4c921c3e)

3. Masci, Jonathan, et al. *Stacked convolutional auto-encoders for hierarchical feature extraction*. Artificial Neural Networks and Machine Learning–ICANN 2011 (2011): 52-59. (https://www.semanticscholar.org/paper/Reducing-the-dimensionality-of-data-with-neural-Hinton-Salakhutdinov/46eb79e5eec8a4e2b2f5652b66441e8a4c921c3e)

4. Japkowicz, Nathalie, Catherine Myers, and Mark Gluck. *A novelty detection approach to classification*. IJCAI. Vol. 1. 1995. (https://www.ijcai.org/Proceedings/95-1/Papers/068.pdf)

5. *AutoRec: Autoencoders Meet Collaborative Filtering*, by S. Sedhain, Proceedings of the 24th International Conference on World Wide Web, ACM, 2015.

6. *Wide & Deep Learning for Recommender Systems*, by H. Cheng, Proceedings of the 1st Workshop on Deep Learning for Recommender Systems, ACM, 2016.

7. *Using Deep Learning to Remove Eyeglasses from Faces*, by M. Runfeldt.

8. *Deep Patient: An Unsupervised Representation to Predict the Future of Patients from the Electronic Health Records*, by R. Miotto, Scientific Reports 6, 2016.

9. *Skip-Thought Vectors*, by R. Kiros, Advances in Neural Information Processing Systems, 2015

10. http://web.engr.illinois.edu/~hanj/cs412/bk3/KL-divergence.pdf

11. https://en.wikipedia.org/wiki/Kullback%E2%80%93Leibler_divergence

12. https://cs.stanford.edu/people/karpathy/convnetjs/demo/autoencoder.html

13. http://blackecho.github.io/blog/machine-learning/2016/02/29/denoising-autoencoder-tensorflow.html

10
Unsupervised Learning

This chapter delves into unsupervised learning models. In the previous chapter we explored Autoencoders, novel neural networks that learn via unsupervised learning. In this chapter we will delve deeper into some other unsupervised learning models. In contrast to supervised learning, where the training dataset consists of both the input and the desired labels, unsupervised learning deals with the case where the model is provided only the input. The model learns the inherent input distribution by itself without any desired label guiding it. Clustering and dimensionality reduction are the two most commonly used unsupervised learning techniques. In this chapter we will learn about different machine learning and NN techniques for both. We will cover techniques required for clustering and dimensionality reduction, and will go into the details of Boltzmann machines, and finally we will cover the implementation of the aforementioned techniques using TensorFlow. The concepts covered will be extended to build **Restricted Boltzmann Machines (RBMs)**. The chapter will include:

- Principal component analysis
- K-Means clustering
- Self-organizing maps
- Boltzmann machines
- RBMs

Principal component analysis

Principal component analysis (PCA) is the most popular multivariate statistical technique for dimensionality reduction. It analyzes the training data consisting of several dependent variables, which are, in general, inter-correlated, and extracts important information from the training data in the form of a set of new orthogonal variables called principal components. We can perform PCA using two methods either using **eigen decomposition** or using **singular value decomposition (SVD)**.

PCA reduces the n–dimensional input data to r–dimensional input data, where $r<n$. In the most simple terms, PCA involves translating the origin and performing rotation of the axis such that one of the axes (principal axis) has the highest variance with data points. A reduced-dimensions dataset is obtained from the original dataset by performing this transformation and then dropping (removing) the orthogonal axes with low variance. Here we employ the SVD method for PCA dimensionality reduction. Consider X, the n-dimensional data with p points that is, X is a matrix of size $p \times n$. From linear algebra we know that any real matrix can be decomposed using singular value decomposition:

$$X = U\Sigma V^T$$

Where U and V are orthonormal matrices (that is, $U.UT = V.VT = 1$) of size $p \times p$ and $n \times n$ respectively. Σ is a diagonal matrix of size $p \times n$. The U matrix is called the **left singular matrix**, and V the **right singular matrix**, and Σ, the diagonal matrix, contains the singular values of X as its diagonal elements. Here we assume that the X matrix is centered. The columns of the V matrix are the principal components, and columns of $U\Sigma$ are the data transformed by principal components.

Now to reduce the dimensions of the data from n to k (where $k < n$) we will select the first k columns of U and the upper-left $k \times k$ part of Σ. The product of the two gives us our reduced-dimensions matrix:

$$Y_k = U\Sigma_k$$

The data Y thus obtained will be of reduced dimensions. Next we implement PCA in TensorFlow 2.0.

PCA on the MNIST dataset

Let us now implement PCA in TensorFlow 2.0. We will be definitely using TensorFlow, we will also need NumPy for some elementary matrix calculation, and Matplotlib, Matplotlib toolkits, and Seaborn for plotting:

```
import tensorflow as tf
import numpy as np
import matplotlib.pyplot as plt
from mpl_toolkits.mplot3d import Axes3D
import seaborn as sns
```

Next we load the MNIST dataset. Since we are doing dimension reduction using PCA, we do not need a test dataset or even labels; however, we are loading labels so that after reduction we can verify the PCA performance. PCA should cluster similar datapoints in one cluster, hence if we see the clusters formed using PCA are similar to our labels it would indicate that our PCA works:

```
((x_train, y_train), (_, _)) = tf.keras.datasets.mnist.load_data()
```

Before we do PCA we should preprocess the data. We first normalize it so that all data has values between 0 and 1, and then reshape the image from being 28 × 28 matrix to a 784-dimensional vector, and finally center it by subtracting the mean:

```
x_train = x_train / 255.
x_train = x_train.astype(np.float32)

x_train = np.reshape(x_train, (x_train.shape[0], 784))

mean = x_train.mean(axis = 1)

x_train = x_train - mean[:,None]
```

Now that our data is in the right format, we make use of TensorFlow's powerful linear algebra (`linalg`) module to calculate the SVD of our training dataset. TensorFlow provides the function `svd()` defined in `tf.linalg` to perform this task. And then use the `diag` function to convert the sigma array (s, a list of singular values) to a diagonal matrix:

```
s, u, v = tf.linalg.svd(x_train)
s = tf.linalg.diag(s)
```

This provides us with a diagonal matrix *s* of size 784 × 784; a left singular matrix *u* of size 60000 × 784; and a right singular matrix of size 784 × 784. This is so because the argument "full_matrices" of the function `svd()` is by default set to `False`. As a result it does not generate the full *U* matrix (in this case, of size 60000 × 60000), instead, if input *X* is of size $m \times n$ it generates *U* of size $p = min(m,n)$.

The reduced-dimension data can now be generated by multiplying respective slices of *u* and *s*. We reduce our data from 784 to 3 dimensions, we can choose to reduce to any dimension less than 784, but we chose 3 here so that it is easier for us to visualize later. We make use of `tf.Tensor.getitem` to slice our matrices in the Pythonic way:

```
k = 3
pca = tf.matmul(u[:,0:k], s[0:k,0:k])
```

A comparison of the original and reduced data shape is done in the following code:

```
print('original data shape',x_train.shape)
print('reduced data shape', pca.shape)
---------------------------------------------------

    original data shape (60000, 784)
    reduced data shape (60000, 3)
```

Finally let us plot the data points in the three-dimensional space.

```
Set = sns.color_palette("Set2", 10)
color_mapping = {key:value for (key,value) in enumerate(Set)}
colors = list(map(lambda x: color_mapping[x], y_train))
fig = plt.figure()
ax = Axes3D(fig)
ax.scatter(pca[:, 0], pca[:, 1],pca[:, 2], c=colors)
```

You can see that the points corresponding to the same color and hence same label are clustered together. We have therefore successfully used PCA to reduce the dimensions of MNIST images. Each original image was of size 28 × 28. Using the PCA method we can reduce it to a smaller size. Normally for image data, dimensionality reduction is necessary. This is because images are large in size and contain a significant amount of redundant data.

TensorFlow Embedding API

TensorFlow also offers an Embedding API where one can find and visualize PCA and tSNE [1] clusters using TensorBoard. You can see the live PCA on MNIST images here: `http://projector.tensorflow.org`. The following image is reproduced for reference:

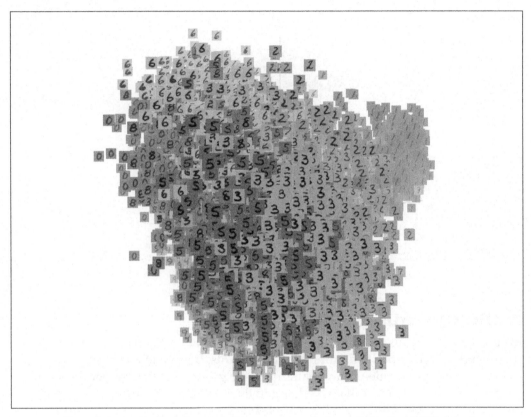

Figure 1: A visualization of a principal component analysis, applied to the MNIST dataset

You can process your data using TensorBoard. It contains a tool called **Embedding Projector** that allows one to interactively visualize embedding. The Embedding Projector tool has three panels:

- **Data Panel**: It is located at the top left, and you can choose the data, labels, and so on in this panel.

- **Projections Panel**: Available at the bottom left, you can choose the type of projections you want here. It offers three choices: PCA, t-SNE, and custom.

- **Inspector Panel**: On the right-hand side, here you can search for particular points and see a list of nearest neighbors.

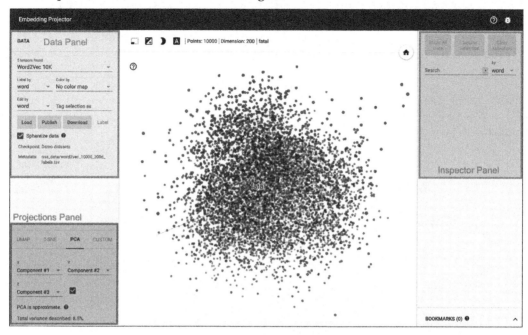

Figure 2: Screenshow of the Embedding Projector tool

K-means clustering

K-means clustering, as the name suggests, is a technique to cluster data, that is, to partition data into a specified number of data points. It is an unsupervised learning technique. It works by identifying patterns in the given data. Remember the sorting hat of Harry Potter fame? What it is doing in the book is clustering—dividing new (unlabeled) students into four different clusters: Gryffindor, Ravenclaw, Hufflepuff, and Slytherin.

Humans are very good at grouping objects together; clustering algorithms try to give a similar capability to computers. There are many clustering techniques available, such as Hierarchical, Bayesian, or Partitional. K-means clustering belongs to partitional clustering; it partitions the data into k clusters. Each cluster has a center, called the centroid. The number of clusters k has to be specified by the user.

The k-means algorithm works in the following manner:

1. Randomly choose k data points as the initial centroids (cluster centers)
2. Assign each data point to the closest centroid; there can be different measures to find closeness, the most common being the Euclidean distance

3. Recompute the centroids using current cluster membership, such that the sum of squared distances decreases

4. Repeat the last two steps until convergence is met

In the previous TensorFlow versions the KMeans class was implemented in the Contrib module; however, the class is no longer available in TensorFlow 2.0. Here we will instead use the advanced mathematical functions provided in TensorFlow 2.0 to implement k-means clustering.

K-means in TensorFlow 2.0

To demonstrate k-means in TensorFlow, we will use randomly generated data in the code that follows. Our randomly generated data will contain 200 samples, and we will divide them into three clusters. We start with importing all the required modules and defining the variables, determining the number of sample points (points_n), the number of clusters to be formed (clusters_n), and the number of iterations we will be doing (iteration_n). We also set the seed for random number to ensure that our work is reproducible:

```
import matplotlib.pyplot as plt
import numpy as np
import tensorflow as tf


points_n = 200
clusters_n = 3
iteration_n = 100
seed = 123
np.random.seed(seed)
tf.random.set_seed(seed)
```

Now we randomly generate data and from the data select three centroids randomly:

```
points = np.random.uniform(0, 10, (points_n, 2))
centroids = tf.slice(tf.random.shuffle(points), [0, 0], [clusters_n,
-1])
```

You can see the scatter plot of all the points and the randomly selected three centroids in the following graph:

```
plt.scatter(points[:, 0], points[:, 1], s=50, alpha=0.5)
plt.plot(centroids[:, 0], centroids[:, 1], 'kx', markersize=15)
plt.show()
```

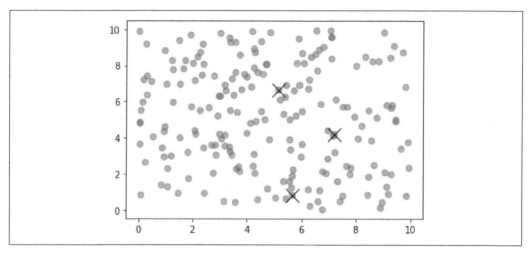

Figure 3: Randomly generated data, from three randomly selected centroids, plotted

We define the function `closest_centroids()` to assign each point to the centroid it is closest to:

```
def closest_centroids(points, centroids):
    distances = tf.reduce_sum(tf.square(tf.subtract(points,
centroids[:,None]))), 2)
    assignments = tf.argmin(distances, 0)
    return assignments
```

We create another function `move_centroids()`. It recalculates the centroids such that the sum of squared distances decreases:

```
def move_centroids(points, closest, centroids):
    return np.array([points[closest==k].mean(axis=0) for k in
range(centroids.shape[0])])
```

Now we call these two functions iteratively for 100 iterations. We have chosen the number of iterations arbitrarily; you can increase and decrease it to see the effect:

```
for step in range(iteration_n):
    closest = closest_centroids(points, centroids)
    centroids = move_centroids(points, closest, centroids)
```

In the following graph, you can see the final centroids after 100 iterations. We have also colored the points based on which centroid they are closest to. The yellow points correspond to one cluster (nearest the cross in its center), and the same is true for the purple and green cluster points:

```
plt.scatter(points[:, 0], points[:, 1], c=closest, s=50, alpha=0.5)
plt.plot(centroids[:, 0], centroids[:, 1], 'kx', markersize=15)
plt.show()
```

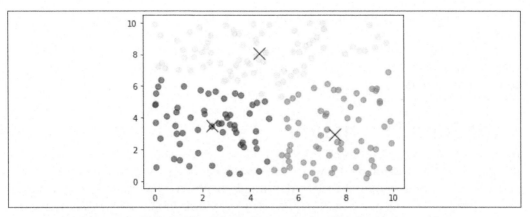

Figure 4: Plot of the final centroids after 100 iterations

 Please note that the `plot` command works in Matplotlib 3.1.1 or higher versions.

In the preceding code we decided to limit the number of clusters to 3, but in most cases with unlabeled data, one is never sure how many clusters exist. One can determine the optimal number of clusters using the elbow method. The method is based on the principle that we should choose the cluster number that reduces the **sum of squared error (SSE)** distance. If k is the number of clusters, then as k increases, the SSE decreases, with SSE = 0; when k is equal to the number of data points, each point is its own cluster. We want a low value of k, such that SSE is also low. For the famous Fisher's Iris data set, if we plot SSE for different k values, we can see from the plot below that for $k=3$, the variance in SSE is the highest; after that, it starts reducing, thus the elbow point is $k=3$:

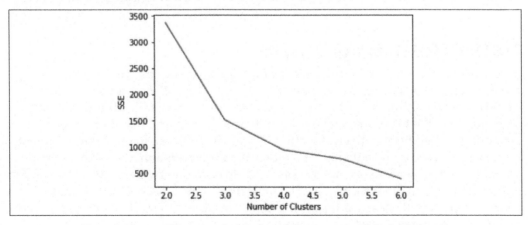

Figure 5: Plotting SSE against the Number of Clusters, using Fisher's Iris data set

K-means clustering is very popular because it is fast, simple, and robust. It also has some disadvantages, however, the biggest being that the user has to specify the number of clusters. Second, the algorithm does not guarantee global optima; the results can change if the initial randomly chosen centroids change. Third, it is very sensitive to outliers.

Variations in k-means

In the original k-means algorithm each point belongs to a specific cluster (centroid); this is called **hard clustering**. However, we can have one point belong to all the clusters, with a membership function defining how much it belongs to a particular cluster (centroid). This is called *fuzzy clustering* or *soft clustering*. This variation was proposed in 1973 by J. C. Dunn and later improved upon by J. C. Bezdek in 1981. Though soft clustering takes longer to converge, it can be useful when a point can be in multiple classes, or when we want to know how similar a given point is to different clusters.

The accelerated k-means algorithm was created in 2003 by Charles Elkan. He exploited the triangle inequality relationship (that is, that a straight line is the shortest distance between two points). Instead of just doing all distance calculations at each iteration, he also kept track of the lower and upper bounds for distances between points and centroids.

In 2006, David Arthur and Sergei Vassilvitskii proposed the k-means++ algorithm. The major change they proposed was in the initialization of centroids. They showed that if we choose centroids that are distant from each other, then the k-means algorithm is less likely to converge on a suboptimal solution.

Another alternative can be that at each iteration we do not use the entire dataset, instead using mini-batches. This modification was proposed by David Sculey in 2010.

Self-organizing maps

Both k-means and PCA can cluster the input data; however, they do not maintain topological relationship. In this section we will consider **Self-organized maps (SOM)**, sometimes known as **Kohonen networks** or **Winner take all units (WTU)**. They maintain the topological relation. SOMs are a very special kind of neural network, inspired by a distinctive feature of the human brain. In our brain, different sensory inputs are represented in a topologically ordered manner. Unlike other neural networks, neurons are not all connected to each other via weights; instead, they influence each other's learning. The most important aspect of SOM is that neurons represent the learned inputs in a topographic manner. They were proposed by Tuevo Kohonen in 1989 [2].

In SOMs, neurons are usually placed at nodes of a (1D or 2D) lattice. Higher dimensions are also possible but are rarely used in practice. Each neuron in the lattice is connected to all the input units via a weight matrix. The following diagram shows a SOM with 6 × 8 (48 neurons) and 5 inputs. For clarity, only the weight vectors connecting all inputs to one neuron are shown. In this case, each neuron will have seven elements, resulting in a combined weight matrix of size (40 × 5):

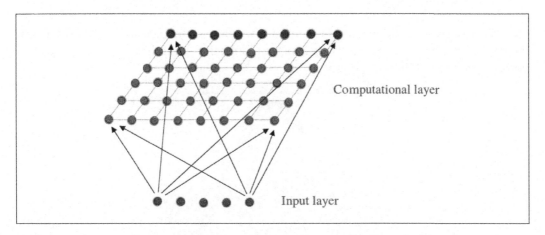

A SOM learns via competitive learning. It can be considered as a nonlinear generalization of PCA and thus, like PCA, can be employed for dimensionality reduction.

In order to implement SOM, let's first understand how it works. As a first step, the weights of the network are initialized either to some random value or by taking random samples from the input. Each neuron occupying a space in the lattice will be assigned specific locations. Now as an input is presented, the neuron with the least distance from the input is declared the winner (WTU). This is done by measuring the distance between the weight vectors (*W*) and input vectors (*X*) of all neurons:

$$d_j = \sqrt{\sum_{i=1}^{N} (W_{ji} - X_i)^2}$$

Here, d_j is the distance of weights of neuron j from input X. The neuron with the lowest d value is the winner.

Next, the weights of the winning neuron and its neighboring neurons are adjusted in a manner to ensure that the same neuron is the winner if the same input is presented next time.

To decide which neighboring neurons need to be modified, the network uses a neighborhood function $\wedge$ (r); normally, the Gaussian Mexican hat function is chosen as a neighborhood function. The neighborhood function is mathematically represented as follows:

$$\wedge (r) = e^{-\frac{d^2}{2\sigma^2}}$$

Here, σ is a time-dependent radius of influence of a neuron and d is its distance from the winning neuron. Graphically the function looks like a hat (hence its name), as you can see in the following figure:

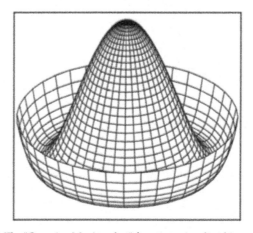

Figure 6: The "Gaussian Maxican hat" function, visualized in graph form

Another important property of the neighborhood function is that its radius reduces with time. As a result, in the beginning, many neighboring neurons' weights are modified, but as the network learns, eventually a few neurons' weights (at times, only one or none) are modified in the learning process. The change in weight is given by the following equation:

$$dW = \eta \wedge (X - W)$$

The process is repeated for all the inputs for a given number of iterations. As the iterations progress, we reduce the learning rate and the radius by a factor dependent on the iteration number.

SOMs are computationally expensive and thus are not really useful for very large datasets. Still, they are easy to understand, and they can very nicely find the similarity between input data. Thus, they have been employed for image segmentation and to determine word similarity maps in NLP [3].

Colour mapping using SOM

Some of the interesting properties of the feature map of the input space generated by SOM are:

- The feature map provides a good representation of the input space. This property can be used to perform vector quantization so that we may have a continuous input space, and using SOM we can represent it in a discrete output space.

- The feature map is topologically ordered, that is, the spatial location of a neuron in the output lattice corresponds to a particular feature of the input.

- The feature map also reflects the statistical distribution of the input space; the domain that has the largest number of input samples gets a wider area in the feature map.

These features of SOM make them the natural choice for many interesting applications. Here we use SOM for clustering a range of given R, G, and B pixel values to a corresponding color map. We start with the importing of modules:

```
import tensorflow as tf
import numpy as np
import matplotlib.pyplot as plt
```

The main component of the code is our class WTU. The class __init__ function initializes various hyperparameters of our SOM, the dimensions of our 2D lattice (m, n), the number of features in the input (dim), the neighborhood radius (sigma), the initial weights, and the topographic information:

```
# Define the Winner Take All units
class WTU(object):

    #_learned = False

    def __init__(self, m, n, dim, num_iterations, eta = 0.5, sigma =
None):
        """
        m x n : The dimension of 2D lattice in which neurons
        are arranged
        dim : Dimension of input training data
        num_iterations: Total number of training iterations
        eta : Learning rate
        sigma: The radius of neighbourhood function.
        """
        self._m = m
        self._n = n
```

```
        self._neighbourhood = []
        self._topography = []
        self._num_iterations = int(num_iterations)
        self._learned = False
        self.dim = dim

        self.eta = float(eta)

        if sigma is None:
            sigma = max(m,n)/2.0 # Constant radius
        else:
            sigma = float(sigma)
        self.sigma = sigma


        print('Network created with dimensions',m,n)

        # Weight Matrix and the topography of neurons
        self._W = tf.random.normal([m*n, dim], seed = 0)
        self._topography = np.array(list(self._neuron_location(m, n)))
```

The most important function of the class is the `train()` function, where we use the Kohonen algorithm as discussed before to find the winner units and then update the weights based on the neighborhood function:

```
def training(self,x, i):
    m = self._m
    n= self._n

    # Finding the Winner and its location
    d = tf.sqrt(tf.reduce_sum(tf.pow(self._W - tf.stack([x for i in
range(m*n)]),2),1))
    self.WTU_idx = tf.argmin(d,0)

    slice_start = tf.pad(tf.reshape(self.WTU_idx, [1]),np.
array([[0,1]]))
    self.WTU_loc = tf.reshape(tf.slice(self._topography, slice_
start,[1,2]), [2])


    # Change learning rate and radius as a function of iterations
    learning_rate = 1 - i/self._num_iterations
    _eta_new = self.eta * learning_rate
    _sigma_new = self.sigma * learning_rate
```

```
        # Calculating Neighbourhood function
        distance_square = tf.reduce_sum(tf.pow(tf.subtract(
            self._topography, tf.stack([self.WTU_loc for i in range(m *
n)])), 2), 1)
            neighbourhood_func = tf.exp(tf.negative(tf.math.divide(tf.cast(
distance_square, "float32"), tf.pow(_sigma_new, 2))))

        # multiply learning rate with neighbourhood func
        eta_into_Gamma = tf.multiply(_eta_new, neighbourhood_func)

        # Shape it so that it can be multiplied to calculate dW
        weight_multiplier = tf.stack([tf.tile(tf.slice(
            eta_into_Gamma, np.array([i]), np.array([1])), [self.dim])
            for i in range(m * n)])
        delta_W = tf.multiply(weight_multiplier,
            tf.subtract(tf.stack([x for i in range(m * n)]),self._W))
            new_W = self._W + delta_W
            self._W = new_W
```

The `fit()` function is a helper function that calls the `train()` function and stores the centroid grid for easy retrieval:

```
def fit(self, X):
    """
    Function to carry out training
    """
    for i in range(self._num_iterations):
        for x in X:
            self.training(x,i)




    # Store a centroid grid for easy retrieval
    centroid_grid = [[] for i in range(self._m)]
    self._Wts = list(self._W)
    self._locations = list(self._topography)
    for i, loc in enumerate(self._locations):
        centroid_grid[loc[0]].append(self._Wts[i])
    self._centroid_grid = centroid_grid
    self._learned = True
```

Then there are some more helper functions to find the winner and generate a 2D lattice of neurons, and a function to map input vectors to the corresponding neurons in the 2D lattice:

```python
def winner(self, x):
    idx = self.WTU_idx,self.WTU_loc
    return idx

def _neuron_location(self,m,n):
    """
    Function to generate the 2D lattice of neurons
    """
    for i in range(m):
        for j in range(n):
            yield np.array([i,j])


def get_centroids(self):
    """
    Function to return a list of 'm' lists, with each inner
    list containing the 'n' corresponding centroid locations as 1-D
    NumPy arrays.
    """
    if not self._learned:
        raise ValueError("SOM not trained yet")
    return self._centroid_grid

def map_vects(self, X):
    """
    Function to map each input vector to the relevant
    neuron in the lattice
    """

    if not self._learned:
        raise ValueError("SOM not trained yet")

    to_return = []
    for vect in X:
        min_index = min([i for i in range(len(self._Wts))],
                        key=lambda x: np.linalg.norm(vect -
                        self._Wts[x]))
        to_return.append(self._locations[min_index])

        return to_return
```

We will also need to normalize the input data, so we create a function to do so:

```
def normalize(df):
    result = df.copy()
    for feature_name in df.columns:
        max_value = df[feature_name].max()
        min_value = df[feature_name].min()
        result[feature_name] = (df[feature_name] - min_value) / (max_
value - min_value)
    return result.astype(np.float32)
```

Let us read the data. The data contains Red, Green, and Blue channel values. Let us normalize them:

```
## Reading input data from file
import pandas as pd

df = pd.read_csv('colors.csv')  # The last column of data file is a
label
data = normalize(df[['R', 'G', 'B']]).values
name = df['Color-Name'].values
n_dim = len(df.columns) - 1


# Data for Training
colors = data
color_names = name
```

Let us create our SOM and fit it:

```
som = WTU(30, 30, n_dim, 400, sigma=10.0)
som.fit(colors)
```

Now, let's look at the result of the trained model. In the following code, you can see the color map in the 2D neuron lattice:

```
# Get output grid
image_grid = som.get_centroids()

# Map colours to their closest neurons
mapped = som.map_vects(colors)

# Plot
plt.imshow(image_grid)
plt.title('Color Grid SOM')
for i, m in enumerate(mapped):
```

```
plt.text(m[1], m[0], color_names[i], ha='center', va='center',
        bbox=dict(facecolor='white', alpha=0.5, lw=0))
```

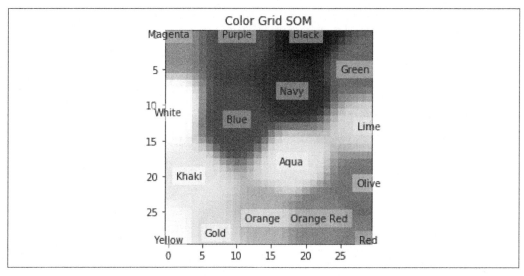

Figure 7: A plotted color map of the 2D neuron lattice

You can see that neurons that win for similar colors are closely placed.

Restricted Boltzmann machines

The RBM is a two-layered neural network—the first layer is called the **visible layer** and the second layer is called the **hidden layer**. They are called **shallow neural networks** because they are only two layers deep. They were first proposed in 1986 by Paul Smolensky (he called them Harmony Networks [1]) and later by Geoffrey Hinton who in 2006 proposed **Contrastive Divergence (CD)** as a method to train them. All neurons in the visible layer are connected to all the neurons in the hidden layer, but there is a **restriction**—no neuron in the same layer can be connected. All neurons in the RBM are binary in nature.

RBMs can be used for dimensionality reduction, feature extraction, and collaborative filtering. The training of RBMs can be divided into three parts: forward pass, backward pass, and then compare.

Let us delve deeper into the math. We can divide the operation of RBMs into two passes:

Forward pass: The information at visible units (V) is passed via weights (W) and biases (c) to the hidden units (h_0). The hidden unit may fire or not depending on the stochastic probability (σ is stochastic probability), which is basically the sigmoid function:

$$\rho(v_o | h_o) = \sigma(V^T W + c)$$

Backward pass: The hidden unit representation (h_o) is then passed back to the visible units through the same weights, W, but different bias, c, where they reconstruct the input. Again, the input is sampled:

$$\rho(v_i | h_o) = \sigma(V^T h_o + c)$$

These two passes are repeated for k steps or until the convergence [4] is reached. According to researchers, $k=1$ gives good results, so we will keep $k = 1$.

The joint configuration of the visible vector V and the hidden vector has an energy given as follows:

$$E(v, h) = -b^T V - c^T h - V^T W h$$

Also associated with each visible vector V is free energy, the energy that a single configuration would need to have in order to have the same probability as all of the configurations that contain V:

$$F(v) = -b^T V - \sum_{j \in hidden} \log(1 + \exp(c_j + V^T W))$$

Using the Contrastive Divergence objective function, that is, *Mean(F(Voriginal))-Mean(F(Vreconstructed))*, the change in weights is given by:

$$dW = \eta[(V^T h)_{input} - (V^T h)_{reconstructed}]$$

Here, η is the learning rate. Similar expressions exist for the biases b and c.

Reconstructing images using RBM

Let us build an RBM in TensorFlow 2.0. The RBM will be designed to reconstruct handwritten digits like the Autoencoders did in *Chapter 9, Autoencoders*. We import TensorFlow, NumPy, and Matplotlib libraries:

```
import tensorflow as tf
import numpy as np
import matplotlib.pyplot as plt
```

We define a class RBM. The class __init_() function initializes the number of neurons in the visible layer (input_size) and the number of neurons in the hidden layer (output_size). The function initializes the weights and biases for both hidden and visible layers. In the following code we have initialized them to zero. You can try with random initialization as well:

```
#Class that defines the behavior of the RBM
class RBM(object):

    def __init__(self, input_size, output_size, lr=1.0,
batchsize=100):
        """
        m: Number of neurons in visible layer
        n: number of neurons in hidden layer
        """
        # Defining the hyperparameters
        self._input_size = input_size # Size of Visible
        self._output_size = output_size # Size of outp
        self.learning_rate = lr # The step used in gradient descent
        self.batchsize = batchsize
        # The size of how much data will be used for training
        # per sub iteration

        # Initializing weights and biases as matrices full of zeroes
        self.w = tf.zeros([input_size, output_size], np.float32)
# Creates and initializes the weights with 0
        self.hb = tf.zeros([output_size], np.float32)
# Creates and initializes the hidden biases with 0
        self.vb = tf.zeros([input_size], np.float32)
# Creates and initializes the visible biases with 0
```

We define methods to provide the forward and backward passes:

```
    # Forward Pass
    def prob_h_given_v(self, visible, w, hb):
        # Sigmoid
        return tf.nn.sigmoid(tf.matmul(visible, w) + hb)

    # Backward Pass
    def prob_v_given_h(self, hidden, w, vb):
        return tf.nn.sigmoid(tf.matmul(hidden, tf.transpose(w)) + vb)
```

We create a function to generate random binary values. This is so because both hidden and visible units are updated using stochastic probability depending upon the input to each unit in the case of the hidden layer (and top-down input to visible layers):

```
    # Generate the sample probability
     def sample_prob(self, probs):
          return tf.nn.relu(tf.sign(probs - tf.random.uniform(tf.
shape(probs))))
```

We will need functions to reconstruct the input:

```
def rbm_reconstruct(self,X):
    h = tf.nn.sigmoid(tf.matmul(X, self.w) + self.hb)
    reconstruct = tf.nn.sigmoid(tf.matmul(h, tf.transpose(self.w)) +
self.vb)
    return reconstruct
```

To train the RBM created we define the `train()` function. The function calculates the positive and negative grad term of contrastive divergence and uses the weight update equation to update the weights and biases:

```
# Training method for the model
def train(self, X, epochs=10):

    loss = []
    for epoch in range(epochs):
        #For each step/batch
        for start, end in zip(range(0, len(X), self.
batchsize),range(self.batchsize,len(X), self.batchsize)):
            batch = X[start:end]

            #Initialize with sample probabilities

            h0 = self.sample_prob(self.prob_h_given_v(batch, self.w,
self.hb))
            v1 = self.sample_prob(self.prob_v_given_h(h0, self.w,
self.vb))
            h1 = self.prob_h_given_v(v1, self.w, self.hb)

            #Create the Gradients
            positive_grad = tf.matmul(tf.transpose(batch), h0)
            negative_grad = tf.matmul(tf.transpose(v1), h1)

            #Update learning rates
            self.w = self.w + self.learning_rate *(positive_grad -
negative_grad) / tf.dtypes.cast(tf.shape(batch)[0],tf.float32)
            self.vb = self.vb +  self.learning_rate * tf.reduce_
mean(batch - v1, 0)
            self.hb = self.hb +  self.learning_rate * tf.reduce_
mean(h0 - h1, 0)
```

```
#Find the error rate
err = tf.reduce_mean(tf.square(batch - v1))
print ('Epoch: %d' % epoch,'reconstruction error: %f' % err)
loss.append(err)

    return loss
```

Now that our class is ready, we instantiate an object of RBM and train it on the MNIST dataset:

```
(train_data, _), (test_data, _) = tf.keras.datasets.mnist.load_data()
train_data = train_data/np.float32(255)
train_data = np.reshape(train_data, (train_data.shape[0], 784))


test_data = test_data/np.float32(255)
test_data = np.reshape(test_data, (test_data.shape[0], 784))


#Size of inputs is the number of inputs in the training set
input_size = train_data.shape[1]
rbm = RBM(input_size, 200)

err = rbm.train(train_data,50)
```

In the following code, you can see the learning curve of our RBM:

```
plt.plot(err)
plt.xlabel('epochs')
plt.ylabel('cost')
```

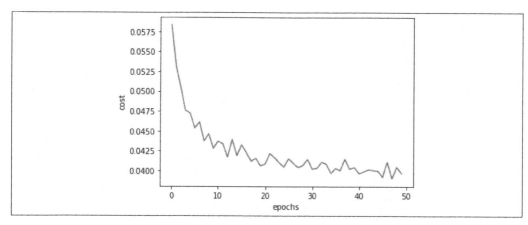

Figure 8: Learning curve for the RBM model

And the reconstructed images:

```
out = rbm.rbm_reconstruct(test_data)

# Plotting original and reconstructed images
row, col = 2, 8
idx = np.random.randint(0, 100, row * col // 2)
f, axarr = plt.subplots(row, col, sharex=True, sharey=True,
figsize=(20,4))
for fig, row in zip([test_data,out], axarr):
    for i,ax in zip(idx,row):
        ax.imshow(tf.reshape(fig[i],[28, 28]), cmap='Greys_r')
        ax.get_xaxis().set_visible(False)
        ax.get_yaxis().set_visible(False)
```

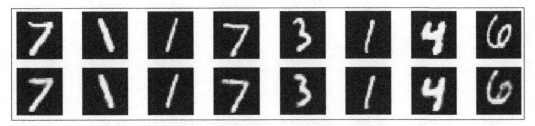

Figure 9: Image reconstruction using an RBM

What do you think? Are RBMs better than Autoencoders? Try training the RBM on noisy input and see how good it is with reconstructing noisy images.

Deep belief networks

Now that we have a good understanding of RBMs and know how to train them using contrastive divergence, we can move toward the first successful deep neural network architecture, the **deep belief networks (DBNs)**. Proposed in 2006 in the paper by Hinton and his team in the paper *A fast learning algorithm for deep belief nets*. Before this model it was very difficult to train deep architectures, not just because of the limited computing resources, but also, as discussed in *Chapter 9, Autoencoders*, because of the vanishing gradient problem. In DBNs it was first demonstrated how deep architectures can be trained via greedy layer-wise training.

In the simplest terms, DBNs are just stacked RBMs. Each RBM is trained separately using the contrastive divergence. We start with the training of the first RBM layer. Once it is trained, we train the second RBM layer. The visible units of the second RBM are now fed the output of the hidden units of the first RBM, when it is fed the input data. The procedure is repeated with each RBM layer addition.

Let us try stacking our RBM class. To be able to make the DBN we will need to define one more function in the RBM class, the output of the hidden of one RBM needs to be fed to the next RBM:

```
#Create expected output for our DBN
def rbm_output(self, X):
    out = tf.nn.sigmoid(tf.matmul(X, self.w) + self.hb)
    return out
```

Now we can just use the RBM class to create a stacked RBM structure. In the following code we create an RBM stack: the first RBM will have 500 hidden units, the second will have 200 hidden units, and the third will have 50 hidden units:

```
RBM_hidden_sizes = [500, 200 , 50 ] #create 2 layers of RBM with size
400 and 100

#Since we are training, set input as training data
inpX = train_data

#Create list to hold our RBMs
rbm_list = []

#Size of inputs is the number of inputs in the training set
input_size = train_data.shape[1]

#For each RBM we want to generate
for i, size in enumerate(RBM_hidden_sizes):
    print ('RBM: ',i,' ',input_size,'->', size)
    rbm_list.append(RBM(input_size, size))
    input_size = size

--------------------------------------------------------------------
```

RBM: 0   784 -> 500

RBM: 1   500 -> 200

RBM: 2   200 -> 50

For the first RBM, the MNIST data is the input. The output of the first RBM is then fed as input to the second RBM, and so on through the consecutive RBM layers:

```
#For each RBM in our list
for rbm in rbm_list:
    print ('New RBM:')
    #Train a new one
    rbm.train(tf.cast(inpX,tf.float32))
    #Return the output layer
```

```
inpX = rbm.rbm_output(inpX)
```

Our DBN is ready. The three stacked RBMs are now trained using unsupervised learning. DBNs can also be trained using supervised training. To do so we will need to fine-tune the weights of the trained RBMs and add a fully connected layer at the end.

Variational Autoencoders

Like DBNs and GANs, variational autoencoders are also generative models. **Variational Autoencoders (VAEs)** are a mix of the best of neural networks and Bayesian inference. They are one of the most interesting neural networks and have emerged as one of the most popular approaches to unsupervised learning. They are Autoencoders with a twist. Along with the conventional encoder and decoder network of Autoencoders (see *Chapter 8, Autoencoders*), they have additional stochastic layers. The stochastic layer, after the encoder network, samples the data using a Gaussian distribution, and the one after the decoder network samples the data using Bernoulli's distribution. Like GANs, VAEs can be used to generate images and figures based on the distribution they have been trained on. VAEs allow one to set complex priors in the latent and thus learn powerful latent representations. The following diagram describes a VAE:

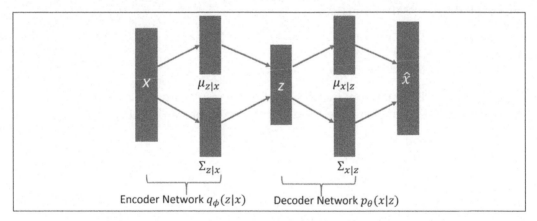

The Encoder network $q_\phi(z \mid x)$ approximates the true but intractable posterior distribution $p(z \mid x)$, where x is the input to the VAE and z is the latent representation. The decoder network $p\Theta(x \mid z)$ takes the d-dimensional latent variables (also called latent space) as its input and generates new images following the same distribution as $P(x)$. As you can see from the preceding diagram, the latent representation z is sampled from $z \mid x \sim N(\mu_{z \mid x}, \Sigma_{z \mid x})$, and the output of the decoder network samples $x \mid z$ from $x \mid z \sim N(\mu_{x \mid z}, \Sigma_{x \mid z})$.

Now that we have the basic architecture of VAEs, the question arises of how they can be trained, since the maximum likelihood of the training data and posterior density are intractable? The network is trained by maximizing the lower bound of the log data likelihood. Thus, the loss term consists of two components: generation loss, which is obtained from the decoder network through sampling, and the Kullback–Leibler (KL) divergence term, also called the latent loss.

Generation loss ensures that the image generated by the decoder and the image used to train the network are similar, and latent loss ensures that the posterior distribution $q(z\,|\,x)$ is close to the prior $p\theta(z)$. Since the encoder uses Gaussian distribution for sampling, the latent loss measures how closely the latent variables match this distribution.

Once the VAE is trained, we can use only the decoder network to generate new images. Let us try coding a VAE. This time we are using the Fashion-MNIST dataset; you learned about this dataset in *Chapter 5, Advanced Convolutional Neural Networks*. The dataset contains Zalando's (`https://github.com/zalandoresearch/fashion-mnist`) article images. The test-train split is exactly the same as for MNIST, that is, 60,000 train images and 10,000 test images. The size of each image is also 28×28, so you can easily replace the codes running on the MNIST dataset with the Fashion-MNIST dataset. The code in this section has been adapted from `https://github.com/dragen1860/TensorFlow-2.x-Tutorials`. As the first step we, as usual, import all the necessary libraries:

```
import  tensorflow as tf
import  numpy as np
from matplotlib import pyplot as plt
```

Let us fix the seeds for random number, so that the results are reproducible. We can also add an `assert` statement to ensure that our code runs on TensorFlow 2.0 or above:

```
np.random.seed(333)
tf.random.set_seed(333)
assert tf.__version__.startswith('2.'), "TensorFlow Version Below 2.0"
```

Before going ahead with making the VAE, let us also explore the Fashion-MNIST dataset a little. The dataset is available in the TensorFlow Keras API:

```
(x_train, y_train), (x_test, y_test) = tf.keras.datasets.fashion_
mnist.load_data()
x_train, x_test = x_train.astype(np.float32)/255., x_test.astype(np.
float32)/255.

print(x_train.shape, y_train.shape)
print(x_test.shape, y_test.shape)
-------------------------------------------------
```

```
(60000, 28, 28) (60000,)
(10000, 28, 28) (10000,)
```

We see some sample images:

```
number = 10  # how many digits we will display
plt.figure(figsize=(20, 4))
for index in range(number):
    # display original
    ax = plt.subplot(2, number, index + 1)
    plt.imshow(x_train[index], cmap='gray')
    ax.get_xaxis().set_visible(False)
    ax.get_yaxis().set_visible(False)
plt.show()
```

Figure 10: Sample images from the Fashion-MNIST dataset

Before we start, let us declare some hyperparameters like learning rate, dimensions of the hidden layer and the latent space, batch size, epochs, and so on:

```
image_size = x_train.shape[1]*x_train.shape[2]
hidden_dim = 512
latent_dim = 10
num_epochs = 80
batch_size = 100
learning_rate = 0.001
```

We use the TensorFlow Keras Model API to build a VAE model. The __init__() function defines all the layers that we will be using:

```
class VAE(tf.keras.Model):

    def __init__(self,dim,**kwargs):
        h_dim = dim[0]
        z_dim = dim[1]
        super(VAE, self).__init__(**kwargs)

        self.fc1 = tf.keras.layers.Dense(h_dim)
        self.fc2 = tf.keras.layers.Dense(z_dim)
        self.fc3 = tf.keras.layers.Dense(z_dim)

        self.fc4 = tf.keras.layers.Dense(h_dim)
        self.fc5 = tf.keras.layers.Dense(image_size)
```

We define the functions to give us the encoder output and decoder output and reparametrize. The implementation of the encoder and decoder functions are straightforward; however, we need to delve a little deeper for the `reparametrize` function. As you know, VAEs sample from a random node *z*, which is approximated by $q(z \mid \theta)$ of the true posterior. Now, to get parameters we need to use backpropagation. However, back propagation cannot work on random nodes. Using reparameterization, we can use a new parameter `eps` that allows us to reparametrize *z* in a way that will allow the back propagation through the deterministic random node (https://arxiv.org/pdf/1312.6114v10.pdf):

```python
def encode(self, x):
    h = tf.keras.nn.relu(self.fc1(x))
    return self.fc2(h), self.fc3(h)

def reparameterize(self, mu, log_var):
    std = tf.exp(log_var * 0.5)
    eps = tf.random.normal(std.shape)

    return mu + eps * std

def decode_logits(self, z):
    h = tf.nn.relu(self.fc4(z))
    return self.fc5(h)

def decode(self, z):
    return tf.nn.sigmoid(self.decode_logits(z))
```

Lastly, we define the `call()` function, which will control how signals move through different layers of the VAE:

```python
def call(self, inputs, training=None, mask=None):
    mu, log_var = self.encode(inputs)
    z = self.reparameterize(mu, log_var)
    x_reconstructed_logits = self.decode_logits(z)

    return x_reconstructed_logits, mu, log_var
```

Now we create the VAE model and declare the optimizer for it. You can see the summary of the model:

```python
model = VAE([hidden_dim, latent_dim])
model.build(input_shape=(4, image_size))
model.summary()
optimizer = tf.keras.optimizers.Adam(learning_rate)
```

```
Model: "vae"

Layer (type)                Output Shape              Param #
=================================================================
dense (Dense)               multiple                  401920

dense_1 (Dense)             multiple                  5130

dense_2 (Dense)             multiple                  5130

dense_3 (Dense)             multiple                  5632

dense_4 (Dense)             multiple                  402192
=================================================================
Total params: 820,004
Trainable params: 820,004
Non-trainable params: 0
```

Figure 11: Summary of the VAE model

Now we train the model. We define our loss function, which is the sum of the reconstruction loss and KL divergence loss:

```
dataset = tf.data.Dataset.from_tensor_slices(x_train)
dataset = dataset.shuffle(batch_size * 5).batch(batch_size)

num_batches = x_train.shape[0] // batch_size

for epoch in range(num_epochs):

    for step, x in enumerate(dataset):

        x = tf.reshape(x, [-1, image_size])

        with tf.GradientTape() as tape:

            # Forward pass
            x_reconstruction_logits, mu, log_var = model(x)

            # Compute reconstruction loss and kl divergence
            # Scaled by 'image_size' for each individual pixel.
            reconstruction_loss = tf.nn.sigmoid_cross_entropy_with_
logits(labels=x, logits=x_reconstruction_logits)
            reconstruction_loss = tf.reduce_sum(reconstruction_loss) /
batch_size

            kl_div = - 0.5 * tf.reduce_sum(1. + log_var -
tf.square(mu) - tf.exp(log_var), axis=-1)
            kl_div = tf.reduce_mean(kl_div)
```

```
# Backprop and optimize
loss = tf.reduce_mean(reconstruction_loss) + kl_div

gradients = tape.gradient(loss, model.trainable_variables)
for g in gradients:
    tf.clip_by_norm(g, 15)
optimizer.apply_gradients(zip(gradients, model.trainable_
variables))

if (step + 1) % 50 == 0:
    print("Epoch[{}/{}], Step [{}/{}], Reconst Loss: {:.4f},
KL Div: {:.4f}"
        .format(epoch + 1, num_epochs, step + 1, num_batches,
float(reconstruction_loss), float(kl_div)))
```

Once the model is trained it should be able to generate images similar to the original Fashion-MNIST images. To do so we need to use only the decoder network and we will pass to it a randomly generated *z* input:

```
z = tf.random.normal((batch_size, latent_dim))
out = model.decode(z)   # decode with sigmoid
out = tf.reshape(out, [-1, 28, 28]).numpy() * 255
out = out.astype(np.uint8)
```

In the following figure, you can see the result after 80 epochs; the generated images resemble the input space:

Figure 12: Results after 80 epochs

Summary

The chapter covered the major unsupervised learning algorithms. We went through algorithms best suited for dimension reduction, clustering, and image reconstruction. We started with the dimension reduction algorithm PCA, then we performed clustering using k-means and self-organized maps. After this we studied the restricted Boltzmann machine and saw how we can use it for both dimension reduction and image reconstruction. Next the chapter delved into stacked RBMs, that is, deep belief networks, and we trained a DBN consisting of three RBM layers on the MNIST dataset. Lastly, we learned about variational autoencoders, which, like GANs, can generate images after learning the distribution of the input sample space.

This chapter, along with chapters 6 and 9, covered models that were trained using unsupervised learning. In the next chapter, we move on to another learning paradigm: reinforcement learning.

References

1. `https://arxiv.org/abs/1404.1100`

2. `http://www.cs.otago.ac.nz/cosc453/student_tutorials/principal_components.pdf`

3. `http://mplab.ucsd.edu/tutorials/pca.pdf`

4. `http://projector.tensorflow.org/`

5. `http://web.mit.edu/be.400/www/SVD/Singular_Value_Decomposition.htm`

6. `https://www.deeplearningbook.org`

7. Kanungo, Tapas, et al. *An Efficient k-Means Clustering Algorithm: Analysis and Implementation.* IEEE transactions on pattern analysis and machine intelligence 24.7 (2002): 881-892.

8. Ortega, Joaquín Pérez, et al. *Research issues on K-means Algorithm: An Experimental Trial Using Matlab.* CEUR Workshop Proceedings: Semantic Web and New Technologies.

9. *A Tutorial on Clustering Algorithms,* `http://home.deib.polimi.it/matteucc/Clustering/tutorial_html/kmeans.html`.

10. Chen, Ke. *On Coresets for k-Median and k-Means Clustering in Metric and Euclidean Spaces and Their Applications.* SIAM Journal on Computing 39.3 (2009): 923-947.

11. `https://en.wikipedia.org/wiki/Determining_the_number_of_clusters_in_a_ data_set`.

12. *Least Squares Quantization in PCM,* Stuart P. Lloyd (1882), `http://www-evasion.imag.fr/people/Franck.Hetroy/Teaching/ProjetsImage/2007/Bib/lloyd-1982.pdf`

13. Dunn, J. C. (1973-01-01). *A Fuzzy Relative of the ISODATA Process and Its Use in Detecting Compact Well-Separated Clusters.* Journal of Cybernetics. 3(3): 32–57.

14. Bezdek, James C. (1981). *Pattern Recognition with Fuzzy Objective Function Algorithms.*

15. Peters, Georg, Fernando Crespo, Pawan Lingras, and Richard Weber. *Soft clustering–Fuzzy and rough approaches and their extensions and derivatives.* International Journal of Approximate Reasoning 54, no. 2 (2013): 307-322.

16. Sculley, David. *Web-scale k-means clustering.* In Proceedings of the 19th international conference on World wide web, pp. 1177-1178. ACM, 2010.

17. Smolensky, Paul. *Information Processing in Dynamical Systems: Foundations of Harmony Theory.* No. CU-CS-321-86. COLORADO UNIV AT BOULDER DEPT OF COMPUTER SCIENCE, 1986.

18. Salakhutdinov, Ruslan, Andriy Mnih, and Geoffrey Hinton. *Restricted Boltzmann Machines for Collaborative Filtering.* Proceedings of the 24th international conference on Machine learning. ACM, 2007.

19. Hinton, Geoffrey. *A Practical Guide to Training Restricted Boltzmann Machines.* Momentum 9.1 (2010): 926.

20. `http://deeplearning.net/tutorial/rbm.html`

Reinforcement Learning

This chapter introduces **reinforcement learning (RL)**—the least explored and yet most promising learning paradigm. Reinforcement learning is very different from both supervised and unsupervised learning models we have done in earlier chapters. Starting from a clean slate (that is, having no prior information), the RL agent can go through multiple stages of hit and trials, and learn to achieve a goal, all the while the only input being the feedback from the environment. The latest research in RL by OpenAI seems to suggest that continuous competition can be a cause for the evolution of intelligence. Many deep learning practitioners believe that RL will play an important role in the big AI dream: **Artificial General Intelligence (AGI)**. This chapter will delve into different RL algorithms, the following topics will be covered:

- What is RL and its lingo
- Learn how to use OpenAI Gym interface
- Deep Q-Networks
- Policy gradients

Introduction

What is common between a baby learning to walk, birds learning to fly, or an RL agent learning to play an Atari game? Well, all three involve:

- **Trial and error**: The child (or the bird) tries various ways, fails many times, and succeeds in some ways before it can really stand (or fly). The RL Agent plays many games, winning some and losing many, before it can become reliably successful.
- **Goal**: The child has the goal to stand, the bird to fly, and the RL agent has the goal to win the game.
- **Interaction with the environment**: The only feedback they have is from their environment.

So, the first question that arises is what is RL and how is it different from supervised and unsupervised learning? Anyone who owns a pet knows that the best strategy to train a pet is rewarding it for desirable behavior and punishing it for bad behavior. RL, also called **learning with a critic**, is a learning paradigm where the agent learns in the same manner. The agent here corresponds to our network (program); it can perform a set of **Actions (a)**, which brings about a change in the **State (s)** of the environment and, in turn, the agent receives a reward or punishment from the environment.

For example, consider the case of training a dog to fetch the ball: here, the dog is our agent, the voluntary muscle movements that the dog makes are the actions, and the ground (including person and ball) is the environment; the dog perceives our reaction to its action in terms of giving it a bone as a reward. RL can be defined as a computational approach to goal-directed learning and decision making, from interaction with the environment, under some idealized conditions. The **Agent** can sense the state of the **Environment**, and the **Agent** can perform specific well-defined actions on the **Environment**. This causes two things: first, a change in the state of the environment, and second, a reward is generated (under ideal conditions). This cycle continues, and in theory the agent learns how to more frequently generate a reward over time:

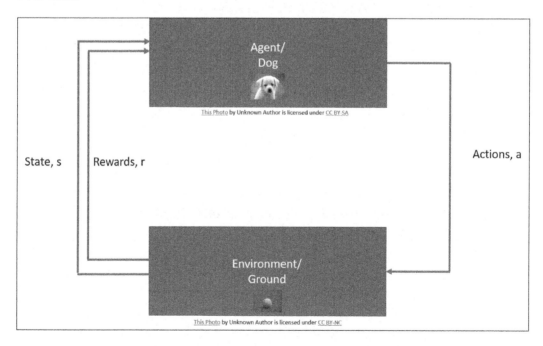

Unlike supervised learning, the **Agent** is not presented with any training examples; it does not know what the correct action is.

And unlike unsupervised learning, the agent's goal is not to find some inherent structure in the input (the learning may find some structure, but that isn't the goal); instead, its only goal is to maximize the rewards (in the long run) and reduce the punishments.

RL lingo

Before learning various RL algorithms, it is important we understand a few important terms. We will illustrate the terms with the help of two examples, first a robot in a maze, and second an agent controlling the wheels of a self-driving car. The two RL agents are shown as follows:

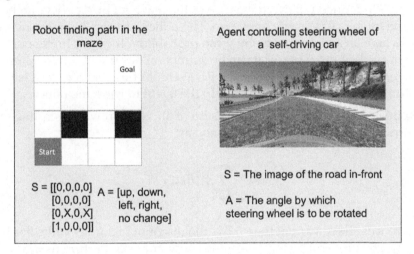

- **State**, S: State is the set of tokens (or representations) that can define all of the possible states the environment can be in. It can be continuous or discrete. In the case of the robot finding its path through a maze, the state can be represented by a 4 × 4 array, with elements telling whether that block is empty or occupied or blocked. A block with a value of 1 means it is occupied by the robot, 0 means it is empty, and X represents that the block is impassable. Each element in this array S, can have one of the three discrete values, so the state is discrete in nature. Next, consider the agent controlling the steering wheel of a self-driving car. The agent takes as an input the front view image. The image contains continuous valued pixels, so here the state is continuous.

- **Action**, $A(S)$: Actions are the set of all possible things that the agent can do in a particular state. The set of possible actions, A, depends on the present state, S. Actions may or may not result in a change of state. Like states, they can be discrete or continuous. The robot finding a path in the maze can perform five discrete actions [**up, down, left, right, no change**]. The SDC agent, on the other hand, can rotate the steering wheel in a continuous range of angles.

- **Reward** *R(S,A,S')*: Rewards are a scalar value returned by the environment based on the agent's action(s), here *S* is the present state and *S'* the state of the environment after action *A* is taken. It is determined by the goal; the agent gets a higher reward if the action brings it near the goal, and a low (or even negative) reward otherwise. How we define a reward is totally up to us—in the case of the maze, we can define the reward as the Euclidean distance between the agent's current position and goal. The SDC agent reward can be that the car is on the road (positive reward) or off the road (negative reward).

- **Policy** *π(S)*: Policy defines a mapping between each state and the action to take in that state. The policy can be *deterministic*—that is, for each state there is a well-defined policy. In the case of the maze robot, a policy can be that if the top block is empty, move up. The policy can also be *stochastic*—that is, where an action is taken by some probability. It can be implemented as a simple look-up table, or it can be a function dependent on the present state. The policy is the core of the RL agent. In this chapter, we'll learn about different algorithms that help the agent to learn the policy.

- **Return** *G*~t~: This is the discounted sum of all future rewards starting from current time, mathematically defined as:

$$G_t = \sum_{k=0}^{\infty} \gamma^k R_{t+k+1}$$

Here R_t is the reward at time *t*, *γ* is the discount factor; its value lies between (0,1). The discount factor determines how important future rewards are in deciding the policy. If it is near zero, the agent gives importance to the immediate rewards. A high value of discount factor, however, means the agent is looking far into the future. It may lose immediate reward in favor of the high future rewards, just as in the game chess you may sacrifice a pawn for checkmate of the opponent.

- **Value function** *V(S)*: This defines the "goodness" of a state in the long run. It can be thought of as the total amount of reward the agent can expect to accumulate over time, starting from the state, *S*. You can think of it as a long-term good, as opposed to an immediate, but short-lived good. What do you think is more important, maximizing immediate reward or value function? You probably guessed right: just as in chess, we sometimes lose a pawn to win the game a few steps later, and so the agent should try to maximize value function.

Normally, the value is defined either as the **State-Value function** $V^\pi(S)$ or **Action-Value function** $Q^\pi(S,A)$, where π is the policy followed. The state-value function is the expected return from the state S after following policy π:

$$V^\pi(S) = E_\pi[G_t|S_t = s]$$

Here E is the expectation, and $S_t=s$ is the state at time t. The action-value function is the expected return from the state S, taking an action $A=a$ and following the policy π:

$$Q^\pi(S,A) = E_\pi[G_t|S_t = s, A_t = a]$$

- **Model of the environment**: It's an optional element. It mimics the behavior of the environment, and it contains the physics of the environment; in other words, it tells how the environment will behave. The model of the environment is defined by the transition probability to the next state. This is an optional component; we can have a **model free** reinforcement learning as well where the transition probability is not needed to define the RL process.

In RL we assume that the state of the environment follows the **Markov property**, that is, each state is dependent solely on the preceding state, the action taken from the action space, and the corresponding reward. That is, if S^{t+1} is the state of the environment at time $t+1$, then it is a function of S^t state at time t, A^t is action taken at time t, and R^t is the corresponding reward received at time t, no prior history is needed. If $P(S^{t+1}|S^t)$ is the transition probability, mathematically the Markov property can be written as:

$$P(S^{t+1}|S^t) = P(S^{t+1}|S^1,S^2,...,S^t)$$

And thus, RL can be assumed to be a **Markov Decision Process** (MDP).

Deep reinforcement learning algorithms

The basic idea in **Deep Reinforcement Learning** (DRL) is that we can use a deep neural network to approximate either policy function or value function. In this chapter we will be studying some popular DRL algorithms. These algorithms can be classified in two classes, depending upon what they approximate:

- **Value-based methods**: In these methods, the algorithms take the action that maximizes the value function. The agent here learns to predict how good a given state or action would be. An example of the value-based method is the Deep Q-Network.

- Consider, for example, our robot in a maze: assuming that the value of each state is the negative of the number of steps needed to reach from that box to goal, then, at each time step, the agent will choose the action that takes it to a state with optimal value, as in the following diagram. So, starting from a value of **-6**, it'll move to **-5, -4, -3, -2, -1**, and eventually reach the goal with the value **0**:

-3	-2	-1	0
-4	-3	-2	-1
-5	■	-3	■
-6	-5	-4	-5

Each box has the value function:
Number of steps needed to reach goal (green box)

- **Policy-based methods**: In these methods, the algorithms predict the optimal policy (the one that maximizes the expected return), without maintaining the value function estimates. The aim is to find the optimal policy, instead of optimal action. An example of the policy-based method is policy-gradients. Here, we approximate the policy function, which allows us to map each state to the best corresponding action. One advantage of policy-based methods over value-based is that we can use them even for continuous action spaces.

Besides the algorithms approximating either policy or value, there are a few questions we need to answer to make reinforcement learning work:

- **How does the agent choose its actions, especially when untrained?**

  When the agent starts learning, it has no idea what is the best way in which to determine an action, or which action will provide the best Q-value. So how do we go about it? We take a leaf out of nature's book. Like bees and ants, the agent makes a balance between exploring the new actions and exploiting the learned ones. Initially when the agent starts it has no idea which action among the possible actions is better, so it makes random choices, but as it learns it starts making use of the learned policy. This is called the **Exploration vs Exploitation** [2] tradeoff. Using exploration, the agent gathers more information, and later exploits the gathered information to make the best decision.

- The next question that arises is, **how does the agent maintain a balance between exploration and exploitation?** There are various strategies; one of the most employed is the **Epsilon-Greedy** ($\epsilon - greedy$) policy. Here, the agent explores unceasingly, and depending upon the value of $\epsilon \in [0,1]$, at each step the agent selects a random action with probability ϵ, and with probability $1 - \epsilon$ selects an action that maximizes the value function. Normally, the value of ϵ decreases asymptotically. In Python the $\epsilon - greedy$ policy can be implemented as:

```
if np.random.rand() <= epsilon:
    a = random.randrange(action_size)
else:
    a = np.argmax(model.predict(s))
```

where `model` is the deep neural network approximating the value/policy function, `a` is the action chosen from the action space of size `action_size`, and `s` is the state. Another way to perform exploration is to use noise; researchers have experimented with both Gaussian and Ornstein-Uhlenbeck noise with success.

- **How to deal with the highly correlated input state space?**

The input to our RL model is the present state of the environment. Each action results in some change in the environment; however, the correlation between two consecutive states is very high. Now if we make our network learn based on the sequential states, the high correlation between consecutive inputs results in what is known in literature as Catastrophic Forgetting. To mitigate the effect of Catastrophic Forgetting, in 2018, David Isele and Akansel Cosgun proposed the **Experience Replay** [3] method.

In simplest terms, the learning algorithm first stores the MDP tuple: state, action, reward, and next state <S, A, R, S'> in a buffer/memory. Once a significant amount of memory is built, a batch is selected randomly to train the agent. The memory is continuously refreshed with new additions, and old deletions. The use of experience replay provides three-fold benefits:

  - First, it allows the same experience to be potentially used in many weight updates, hence increases data efficiency.
  - Second, the random selection of batches of experience removes the correlations between consecutive states presented to the network for training.
  - Third, it stops any unwanted feedback loops that may arise and cause the network to get stuck in local minima or diverge.

A modified version of experience replay is the **Prioritized Experience Replay (PER)**. Introduced in 2015 by Tom Schaul et al. [4], it derives from the idea that not all experiences (or, you might say, attempts) are equally important. Some attempts are better lessons than others. Thus, instead of selecting the experiences randomly, it will be much more efficient to assign higher priority to more educational experiences in selection for training. In the Schaul paper it was proposed that experiences in which the difference between the prediction and target is high should be given priority, as the agent could learn a lot in these cases.

- **How to deal with the problem of moving targets?**

  Unlike supervised learning, the target is not previously known in RL. With a moving target, the agent tries to maximize the expected return, but the maximum value goes on changing as the agent learns. In essence, this like trying to catch a butterfly yet each time you approach it, it moves to a new location. The major reason to have a moving target is that the same networks are used to estimate the action and the target values, and this can cause oscillations in learning.

  A solution to this was proposed by the DeepMind team in their 2015 paper, titled *Human-level Control through Deep Reinforcement Learning*, published in Nature. The solution is that now instead of a moving target, the agent has short-term fixed targets. The agent now maintains two networks, both are exactly the same in architecture, one called the local network, which is used at each step to estimate the present action, and one the target network, which is used to get the target value. However, both networks have their own set of weights. At each time step the local network learns in the direction such that its estimate and target are near to each other. After some number of time steps, the target network weights are updated. The update can be a **hard update**, where the weights of the local network are copied completely to the target network after N time steps, or it can be a **soft update**, in which the target network slowly (by a factor of Tau $\tau \epsilon [0,1]$) moves its weight toward the local network.

Reinforcement success in recent years

In the last few years, DRL has been successfully used in a variety of tasks, especially in game playing and robotics. Let us acquaint ourselves with some success stories of RL before learning its algorithms:

- **AlphaGo Zero**: Developed by Google's DeepMind team, the AlphaGo Zero paper *Mastering the game of Go without any human knowledge,* starts from an absolutely blank slate (**tabula rasa**). The AlphaGo Zero uses one neural network to approximate both the move probabilities and value.

This neural network takes as an input the raw board representation. It uses a Monte Carlo tree search guided by the neural network to select the moves. The reinforcement learning algorithm incorporates look-ahead search inside the training loop. It was trained for 40 days using a 40-block residual CNN and, over the course of training, it played about 29 million games (a big number!). The neural network was optimized on Google Cloud using TensorFlow, with 64 GPU workers and 19 CPU parameter servers. You can access the paper here: `https://www.nature.com/articles/nature24270`.

- **AI controlled sailplanes**: Microsoft developed a controller system that can run on many different autopilot hardware platforms such as Pixhawk and Raspberry Pi 3. It can keep the sailplane in the air without using a motor, by autonomously finding and catching rides on naturally occurring thermals. The controller helps the sailplane to operate on its own by detecting and using these thermals to travel without the aid of a motor or a person. They implemented it as a partially observable Markov decision process. They employed the Bayesian reinforcement learning and used the Monte Carlo tree search to search for the best action. They've divided the whole system into level planners—a high-level planner that makes a decision based on experience and a low-level planner that uses Bayesian reinforcement learning to detect and latch onto thermals in real time. You can see the sailplane in action at Microsoft News: `https://news.microsoft.com/features/science- mimics-nature-microsoft-researchers-test-ai-controlled-soaring- machine/`.

- **Locomotion behavior**: In the paper *Emergence of Locomotion Behaviours in Rich Environments* (`https://arxiv.org/pdf/1707.02286.pdf`), DeepMind researchers provided the agents with rich and diverse environments. The environments presented a spectrum of challenges at different levels of difficulty. The agent was provided with difficulties in increasing order; this led the agent to learn sophisticated locomotion skills without performing any reward engineering (that is, designing special reward functions).

It is really amazing to see how the DRL agent, without any implicit knowledge of the game, learns to play, and even beat, humans – in many specialized tasks. In the coming sections we will explore these fabulous DRL algorithms and see them play games with almost human efficiency within a few thousand epochs.

Introduction to OpenAI Gym

As mentioned earlier, **trial and error** is an important component of any RL algorithm. Therefore, it makes sense to train our RL agent firstly in a simulated environment.

Today there exists a large number of platforms that can be used for the creation of an environment. Some popular ones are:

- **OpenAI Gym**: It contains a collection of environments that we can use to train our RL agents. In this chapter, we'll be using the OpenAI Gym interface.

- **Unity ML-Agents SDK**: It allows developers to transform games and simulations created using the Unity editor into environments where intelligent agents can be trained using DRL, evolutionary strategies, or other machine learning methods through a simple-to-use Python API. It works with TensorFlow and provides the ability to train intelligent agents for 2D/3D and VR/AR games. You can learn more about it here: `https://github.com/Unity-Technologies/ml-agents`.

- **Gazebo**: In Gazebo, we can build three-dimensional worlds with physics-based simulation. Gazebo along with **Robot Operating System (ROS)** and the OpenAI Gym interface is gym-gazebo and can be used to train RL agents. To know more about this, you can refer to the white paper: `https://arxiv.org/abs/1608.05742`.

- **Blender learning environment**: It's a Python interface for the Blender game engine, and it also works over OpenAI Gym. It has at its base Blender: a free 3D modeling software with an integrated game engine. This provides an easy to use, powerful set of tools for creating games. It provides an interface to the Blender game engine, and the games themselves are designed in Blender. We can then create the custom virtual environment to train an RL agent on a specific problem (`https://github.com/LouisFoucard/gym-blender`).

- **Malmö**: Built by the Microsoft Team, Malmö is a platform for AI experimentation and research built on top of Minecraft. It provides a simple API for creating tasks and missions. You can learn more about Project Malmo here: `https://www.microsoft.com/en-us/research/project/project-malmo/`.

We will be using OpenAI Gym to provide an environment for our agent. OpenAI Gym is an open source toolkit to develop and compare RL algorithms. It contains a variety of simulated environments that can be used to train agents and develop new RL algorithms.

The first thing to do is install OpenAI Gym, the following command will install the minimal `gym` package:

```
pip install gym
```

If you want to install all (free) gym modules prefix it by `[all]`:

```
pip install gym[all]
```

The MuJoCo environment requires a purchasing license.

OpenAI Gym provides a variety of environments, from simple text-based to three-dimensional games. The environments supported can be grouped as follows:

- **Algorithms**: Contains environments that involve performing computations such as addition. While we can easily perform the computations on a computer, what makes these problems interesting as an RL problem is that the agent learns these tasks purely by example.

- **Atari**: This environment provides a wide variety of classic Atari/arcade games.

- **Box2D**: Contains robotics tasks in two-dimensions such as a car racing agent or bipedal robot walk.

- **Classic control**: This contains the classical control theory problems, such as balancing a cart pole.

- **MuJoCo**: This is proprietary (you can get a one-month free trial). It supports various robot simulation tasks. The environment includes a physics engine, hence, it's used for training robotic tasks.

- **Robotics**: This environment also uses the physics engine of MuJoCo. It simulates goal-based tasks for fetch and shadow-hand robots.

- **Toy text**: A simple text-based environment—very good for beginners.

You can get a complete list of environments from the gym website: https://gym.openai.com. To know the list of all available environments in your installation, you can use the following code:

```
from gym import envs
print(envs.registry.all())
```

This will output a list of all the installed environments along with their environment ID. The core interface provided by OpenAI Gym is the Unified Environment Interface. The agent can interact with the environment using three basic methods, that is, reset, step, and render. The reset method resets the environment and returns the observation. The step method steps the environment by one timestep and returns observation, reward, done, and info. The render method renders one frame of the environment, like popping a window. After importing the gym module, we can create any environment from the list of environments installed using the make command. Next, we create the "Breakout-v0" environment:

```
import gym
```

```
env_name = 'Breakout-v0'
env = gym.make(env_name)
```

Let's get an observation of the environment once it is reset:

```
obs = env.reset()
env.render()
```

You can see the Breakout environment in the following screenshot; the render function pops up the environment window:

The Breakout environment

Alternatively, you can use Matplotlib inline and change the render command to `plt.imshow(env.render(mode='rgb_array'))`. This will show the environment inline in the Jupyter Notebook.

You can learn more about the environment state space and its action space using `env.observation_space` and `env.action_space`. For our Breakout game we find that the state consists of a three-channel image of size 210 × 160, and the action space is discrete with four possible actions. Once you are done, do not forget to close the OpenAI using:

```
env.close()
```

Random agent playing Breakout

Let's have some fun and play the Breakout game. When I first played the game, I had no idea of the rules, or how to play, so I randomly chose the control buttons. Our novice agent will do the same; it will choose the actions randomly from the action space. Gym provides a function `sample()` which chooses a random action from the action space – we will be using this function. Also, we can save a replay of the game, to view it later. There are two ways to save the play, one using Matplotlib and another using OpenAI Gym Monitor wrapper. Let us first see the Matplotlib method.

We will first import the necessary modules; we will only need `gym` and `matplotlib` for now, as the agent will be playing random moves:

```
import gym
import matplotlib.pyplot as plt
import matplotlib.animation as animation
```

We create the Gym environment:

```
env_name = 'Breakout-v0'
env = gym.make(env_name)
```

Next we will run the game, one step at a time, choosing a random action, either for 300 steps or until the game is finished (whichever is earlier). The environment state (observation) space is saved at each step in the list `frames`:

```
frames = [] # array to store state space at each step

env.reset()
done = False
for _ in range(300):
    #print(done)
    frames.append(env.render(mode='rgb_array'))
    obs,reward,done, _ = env.step(env.action_space.sample())
    if done:
        break
```

Now comes the part of combining all the frames as a gif image using Matplotlib Animation. We create an image object, patch, and then define a function that sets image data to a particular frame index. The function is used by the Matplotlib `Animation` class to create an animation, which we finally save in the file `random_agent.gif`:

```
patch = plt.imshow(frames[0])
plt.axis('off')
def animate(i):
    patch.set_data(frames[i])
    anim = animation.FuncAnimation(plt.gcf(), animate, \
        frames=len(frames), interval=10)
    anim.save('random_agent.gif', writer='imagemagick')
```

Normally, a RL agent requires lots of steps for proper training, and as a result it is not feasible to store the state space at each step. Instead, we can choose to store after every 500th step (or any other number you wish) in the preceding algorithm. OpenAI Gym provides the Wrapper class to save the game as a video. To do so, we need to first import wrappers, then create the environment, and finally use Monitor.

By default, it will store the video of 1, 8, 27, 64, (episode numbers with perfect cubes), and so on and then every 1,000th episode; each training, by default, is saved in one folder. The code to do this is:

```
import gym
env = gym.make("Breakout-v0")
env = gym.wrappers.Monitor(env, 'recording', force=True)
observation = env.reset()
for _ in range(1000):
    #env.render()
    action = env.action_space.sample()
    # your agent here (this takes random actions)
    observation, reward, done, info = env.step(action)

    if done:
        observation = env.reset()
env.close()
```

 For Monitor to work one requires FFmpeg support, you may need to install it depending upon your OS, in case it is missing.

This will save the videos in mp4 format in the folder `recording`. An important thing to note here is that you have to set `force=True` option if you want to use the same folder for the next training session.

Deep Q-Networks

Deep Q-networks, **DQNs** for short, are deep learning neural networks designed to approximate the Q-function (value-state function), it is one of the most popular value-based reinforcement learning algorithms. The model was proposed by Google's DeepMind in NIPS 2013, in the paper entitled *Playing Atari with Deep Reinforcement Learning*. The most important contribution of this paper was that they used the raw state space directly as input to the network; the input features were not hand-crafted as done in earlier RL implementations. Also, they could train the agent with exactly the same architecture to play different Atari games and obtain state of the art results.

This model is an extension of the simple Q-learning algorithm. In Q-learning algorithms a Q-table is maintained as a cheat sheet. After each action the Q-table is updated using the Bellman equation [5]:

$$Q(S_t, A_t) = (1 - \alpha)Q(S_t, A_t) + \alpha(R_{t+1} + \gamma \, max_A Q(S_{t+1}, A_t))$$

The α is the learning rate, and its value lies in the range [0,1]. The first term represents the component of the old Q value and the second term the target Q value. Q-learning is good if the number of states and the number of possible actions are small, but for large state spaces and action spaces, Q-learning is simply not scalable. A better alternative would be to use a deep neural network as a function approximator, approximating the target Q-function for each possible action. The weights of the deep neural network in this case store the Q-table information. There is a separate output unit for each possible action. The network takes the state as its input and returns the predicted target Q value for all possible actions. The question arises: how do we train this network, and what should be the loss function? Well, since our network has to predict the target Q value:

$$Q_{target} = R_{t+1} + \gamma \, max_A Q(S_{t+1}, A_t)$$

the loss function should try and reduce the difference between the Q value predicted, $Q_{predicted}$ and the target Q, Q_{target}. We can do this by defining the loss function as:

$$loss = E_\pi \big[Q_{target}(S, A) - Q_{predicted}(S, W, A) \big]$$

Where W is the training parameters of our deep Q network, learned using gradient descent, such that the loss function is minimized. Following is the general architecture of a DQN. The network takes n-dimensional state as input, and outputs the Q value of each possible action in the m-dimensional action space. Each layer (including the input) can be a convolutional layer (if we are taking the raw pixels as input convolutional layers makes more sense) or can be dense layers:

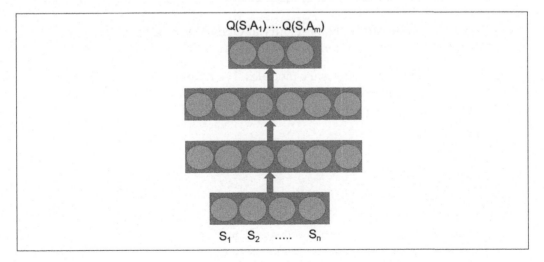

In the next section, we will try training a DQN, our agent task will be to stabilize a pole on a cart, the agent can move the cart left or right to maintain the balance.

DQN for CartPole

CartPole is a classic OpenAI problem with continuous state space and discrete action space. In it, a pole is attached by an un-actuated joint to a cart; the cart moves along a frictionless track. The goal is to keep the pole standing on the cart by moving the cart left or right. A reward of +1 is given for each time step the pole is standing. Once the pole is more than 15 degrees from the vertical, or the cart moves beyond 2.4 units from the center, the game is over:

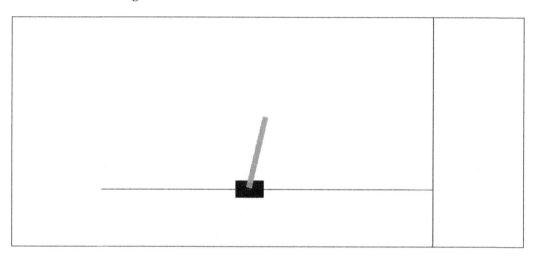

The code here is adapted from the best entry at OpenAI for the CartPole environment: https://gym.openai.com/envs/CartPole-v0/.

We start with importing the necessary modules. We require gym obviously to provide us with the CartPole environment, and tensorflow to build our DQN network. Besides these we need random and numpy modules:

```
import random
import gym
import math
import numpy as np
from collections import deque
import tensorflow as tf
from tensorflow.keras.models import Sequential
from tensorflow.keras.layers import Dense
from tensorflow.keras.optimizers import Adam
```

We set up the global values for the maximum episodes for which we will be training the agent (EPOCHS), the threshold value when we consider the environment solved (THRESHOLD) and a bool to indicate if we want to record the training or not (MONITOR). Please note that as per the official OpenAI documentation the CartPole environment is considered solved when the agent is able to maintain the pole in the vertical position for 195 time steps (ticks). In the following code for the sake of time we have reduced the THRESHOLD to 45:

```
EPOCHS = 1000
THRESHOLD = 195
MONITOR = True
```

Now let us build our DQN. We declare a class DQN and in its __init__() function declare all the hyperparameters and our model. We are creating the environment also inside the DQN class. As you can see, the class is quite general, and you can use it to train for any Gym environment whose state space information can be encompassed in a 1D array:

```
def __init__(self, env_string, batch_size=64):
        self.memory = deque(maxlen=100000)
        self.env = gym.make(env_string)
        self.input_size = self.env.observation_space.shape[0]
        self.action_size = self.env.action_space.n

        self.batch_size = batch_size
        self.gamma = 1.0
        self.epsilon = 1.0
        self.epsilon_min = 0.01
        self.epsilon_decay = 0.995

        alpha=0.01
        alpha_decay=0.01
        if MONITOR: self.env = gym.wrappers.Monitor(self.env, '../
data/'+env_string, force=True)

        # Init model
        self.model = Sequential()
        self.model.add(Dense(24, input_dim=self.input_size,
activation='tanh'))
        self.model.add(Dense(48, activation='tanh'))
        self.model.add(Dense(self.action_size, activation='linear'))
        self.model.compile(loss='mse', optimizer=Adam(lr=alpha,
decay=alpha_decay))
```

The DQN that we have built is a three-layered perceptron; in the following output you can see the model summary. We use Adam optimizer with learning rate decay:

```
Model: "sequential"

Layer (type)                 Output Shape              Param #
=================================================================
dense (Dense)                (None, 24)                120

dense_1 (Dense)              (None, 48)                1200

dense_2 (Dense)              (None, 2)                 98
=================================================================
Total params: 1,418
Trainable params: 1,418
Non-trainable params: 0
```

Figure 1: Summary of the DQN model

The variable list `self.memory` will contain our experience replay buffer. We need to add a method for saving the <S,A,R,S'> tuple into the memory and a method to get random samples from it in batches to train the agent. We perform these two functions by defining the class methods remember and replay:

```
def remember(self, state, action, reward, next_state, done):
        self.memory.append((state, action, reward, next_state, done))

def replay(self, batch_size):
        x_batch, y_batch = [], []
        minibatch = random.sample(self.memory, min(len(self.memory),
batch_size))
        for state, action, reward, next_state, done in minibatch:
            y_target = self.model.predict(state)
   y_target[0][action] = reward if done else reward + self.gamma *
np.max(self.model.predict(next_state)[0])
            x_batch.append(state[0])
            y_batch.append(y_target[0])

        self.model.fit(np.array(x_batch), np.array(y_batch), batch_
size=len(x_batch), verbose=0)
```

Our agent will use the **Epsilon Greedy policy** when choosing the action. This is implemented in the following method:

```
def choose_action(self, state, epsilon):
        if np.random.random() <= epsilon:
            return self.env.action_space.sample()
```

```
    else:
        return np.argmax(self.model.predict(state))
```

Next, we write a method to train the agent. We define two lists to keep track of the scores. First, we fill the experience replay buffer and then we choose some samples from it to train the agent and hope that the agent will slowly learn to do better:

```
def train(self):
    scores = deque(maxlen=100)
    avg_scores = []
    for e in range(EPOCHS):
        state = self.env.reset()
        state = self.preprocess_state(state)
        done = False
        i = 0
        while not done:
            action = self.choose_action(state,self.epsilon)
            next_state, reward, done, _ = self.env.step(action)
            next_state = self.preprocess_state(next_state)
            self.remember(state, action, reward, next_state, done)
            state = next_state
            self.epsilon = max(self.epsilon_min, self.epsilon_
decay*self.epsilon) # decrease epsilon
            i += 1
        scores.append(i)
        mean_score = np.mean(scores)
        avg_scores.append(mean_score)
        if mean_score >= THRESHOLD and e >= 100:
            print('Ran {} episodes. Solved after {} trials
√'.format(e, e - 100))
            return avg_scores
        if e % 100 == 0:
            print('[Episode {}] - Mean survival time over last 100
episodes was {} ticks.'.format(e, mean_score))

        self.replay(self.batch_size)
    print('Did not solve after {} episodes :('.format(e))
    return avg_scores
```

Now all necessary functions are done, we just need one more helper function to reshape the state of the CartPole environment so that the input to the model is in the correct shape. The state of the environment is described by four continuous variables: cart position ([-2.4-2.4]), cart velocity ([([$-\infty, \infty$])]), pole angle ([-41.8o-41.8o]) and pole velocity ([([$-\infty, \infty$])]):

```
def preprocess_state(self, state):
    return np.reshape(state, [1, self.input_size])
```

Let us now instantiate our agent for the CartPole environment and train it:

```
env_string = 'CartPole-v0'
agent = DQN(env_string)
scores = agent.train()
```

In the following screenshot you can see the agent being trained on my system. The agent was able to achieve our set threshold of 45 in 254 steps:

```
[Episode 0] – Mean survival time over last 100 episodes was 16.0 ticks.
[Episode 100] – Mean survival time over last 100 episodes was 17.47 ticks.
[Episode 200] – Mean survival time over last 100 episodes was 28.1 ticks.
Ran 254 episodes. Solved after 154 trials ✔
```

Figure 2: Agent training for the CartPole environment, achieving the target treshold within 254 steps

And the average reward plot as the agent learns is:

```
import matplotlib.pyplot as plt
plt.plot(scores)
plt.show()
```

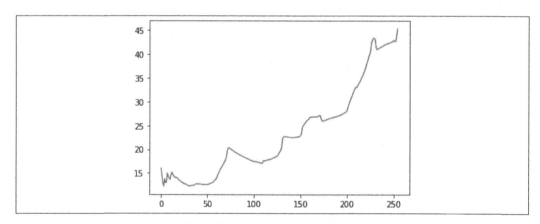

Figure 3: Average agent reward plot

Once the training is done you can close the environment:

```
agent.env.close()
```

You can see starting from no information about how to balance the pole, the agent using DQN is able to balance the pole for more and more time (on average) as it learns. Starting from the blank state, the agent is able to build information/ knowledge to fulfill the required goal. Remarkable!

DQN to play a game of Atari

In the preceding section we used DQN to train for balancing the CartPole. It was a simple problem, and thus we could solve it using a perceptron model. But imagine if the environment state was just the CartPole visual as we humans see it. With raw pixel values as the input state space, our previous DQN will not work. What we need is a convolutional neural network. Next, we build one based on the seminal paper on DQN, *Playing Atari with Deep Reinforcement Learning*.

Most of the code will be similar to the DQN for CartPole, but there will be significant changes in the DQN network itself, and how we preprocess the state that we obtain from the environment.

First, let us see the change in the way state space is processed. In the following screenshot you can see one of the Atari games, Breakout:

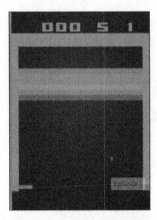

Figure 4: A screenshot of the Atari game, Breakout

Now, if you see the image, not all of it contains relevant information: the top part has redundant info about score, and bottom part has an unnecessary blank space, and the image is colored. To reduce the burden on our model, it is best to remove the unnecessary information, so we crop the image, convert it to grayscale, and make it a square of size 84 × 84 (as in the paper). Here is the code to preprocess the input raw pixels:

```
def preprocess_state(self, img):
    img_temp = img[31:195]  # Choose the important area of the image
    img_temp = tf.image.rgb_to_grayscale(img_temp)
    img_temp = tf.image.resize(img_temp, [self.IM_SIZE, self.IM_SIZE],
                               method=tf.image.ResizeMethod.NEAREST_
NEIGHBOR)
    img_temp = tf.cast(img_temp, tf.float32)
    return img_temp[:,:,0]
```

Another important issue is that just from the image at one time step, how can the agent know that the ball is going up or down? One way could be to use LSTM along with a CNN to keep a record of the past and hence ball movement. The paper, however, used a simple technique. Instead of single state frame, it concatenated the state space for the past four time steps together as one input to the CNN network, that is. the network sees four past frames of the environment as its input. The following is the code for combining the present and previous states:

```python
def combine_images(self, img1, img2):
    if len(img1.shape) == 3 and img1.shape[0] == self.m:
        im = np.append(img1[1:,:, :],np.expand_dims(img2,0), axis=2)
        return tf.expand_dims(im, 0)
    else:
        im = np.stack([img1]*self.m, axis = 2)
        return tf.expand_dims(im, 0)
```

The model was defined in the __init__ function. We modify the function to now have a CNN network with input of (84 × 84 × 4) representing four state frames each of size 84 × 84:

```python
def __init__(self, env_string,batch_size=64, IM_SIZE = 84, m = 4):
    self.memory = deque(maxlen=100000)
    self.env = gym.make(env_string)
    input_size = self.env.observation_space.shape[0]
    action_size = self.env.action_space.n
    self.batch_size = batch_size
    self.gamma = 1.0
    self.epsilon = 1.0
    self.epsilon_min = 0.01
    self.epsilon_decay = 0.995
    self.IM_SIZE = IM_SIZE
    self.m = m


    alpha=0.01
    alpha_decay=0.01
    if MONITOR: self.env = gym.wrappers.Monitor(self.env, '../
data/'+env_string, force=True)

    # Init model
    self.model = Sequential()
    self.model.add( Conv2D(32, 8, (4,4), activation='relu',padding='sa
me', input_shape=(IM_SIZE, IM_SIZE, m)))
    self.model.add( Conv2D(64, 4, (2,2), activation='relu',padding='v
alid'))
```

```
    self.model.add( Conv2D(64, 3, (1,1), activation='relu',padding='v
alid'))
    self.model.add(Flatten())
    self.model.add(Dense(512, activation='elu'))
    self.model.add(Dense(action_size, activation='linear'))
    self.model.compile(loss='mse', optimizer=Adam(lr=alpha,
decay=alpha_decay))
```

Lastly, we will need to make a minor change in the `train` function, we will need
to call the new `preprocess` function, along with the `combine_images` function to
ensure that four frames are concatenated:

```
def train(self):
    scores = deque(maxlen=100)
    avg_scores = []


    for e in range(EPOCHS):
        state = self.env.reset()
        state = self.preprocess_state(state)
        state = self.combine_images(state, state)
        done = False
        i = 0
        while not done:
            action = self.choose_action(state,self.epsilon)
            next_state, reward, done, _ = self.env.step(action)
            next_state = self.preprocess_state(next_state)
            next_state = self.combine_images(next_state, state)
            #print(next_state.shape)
            self.remember(state, action, reward, next_state, done)
            state = next_state
            self.epsilon = max(self.epsilon_min, self.epsilon_
decay*self.epsilon) # decrease epsilon
            i += reward

        scores.append(i)
        mean_score = np.mean(scores)
        avg_scores.append(mean_score)
        if mean_score >= THRESHOLD and e >= 100:
            print('Ran {} episodes. Solved after {} trials
✓'.format(e, e - 100))
            return avg_scores
        if e % 100 == 0:
            print('[Episode {}] - Score over last 100 episodes was
{}.'.format(e, mean_score))
```

```
        self.replay(self.batch_size)

    print('Did not solve after {} episodes :('.format(e))
    return avg_scores
```

That's all – you can now train the agent for playing Breakout. The complete code is available on GitHub of this chapter in the file DQN_Atari.ipynb.

DQN variants

After the unprecedented success of DQN, the interest in RL increased and many new RL algorithms came into being. Next, we see some of the algorithms that are based on DQN. They all use a DQN as the base and modify upon it.

Double DQN

In DQN, the agent uses the same Q value to both select an action and evaluate an action. This can cause a maximization bias in learning. For example, let us consider that for a state, S, all possible actions have true Q values of zero. Now our DQN estimates will have some values above and some values below zero, and since we are choosing the action with the maximum Q value and later evaluating the Q value of each action using the same (maximized) estimated value function, we are overestimating Q – or in other words, our agent is over-optimistic. This can lead to unstable training and a low-quality policy. To deal with this issue Hasselt et al. from DeepMind proposed the Double DQN algorithm in their paper *Deep Reinforcement Learning with Double Q-Learning*. In Double DQN we have two Q-networks with the same architecture but different weights. One of the Q-networks is used to determine the action using the epsilon greedy policy and the other is used to determine its value (Q-target).

If you recall in DQN the Q-target was given by:

$$Q_{target} = R_{t+1} + \gamma max_A Q(S_{t+1}, A_t)$$

Here the action A was selected using the same DQN network $Q(S,A;W)$ where W is the training parameters of the network; that is, we are writing the Q value function along with its training parameter to emphasize the difference between vanilla DQN and Double DQN:

$$Q_{target} = R_{t+1} + \gamma max_A Q(S_{t+1}, argmax_t Q(S, A; W); W)$$

In Double DQN, the equation for the target will now change. Now the DQN $Q(S,A;W)$ is used for determining the action and DQN $Q(S,A;W')$ is used for calculating the target (notice the different weights), then the preceding equation will change to:

$$Q_{target} = R_{t+1} + \gamma max_A Q(S_{t+1}, argmax_t Q(S, A; W); W')$$

This simple change reduces the overestimation and helps us to train the agent fast and more reliably.

Dueling DQN

This architecture was proposed by Wang et al. in their paper *Dueling Network Architectures for Deep Reinforcement Learning* in 2015. Like DQN and Double DQN it is also a model-free algorithm.

Dueling DQN decouples the Q-function into the value function and advantage function. The value function, which we have discussed earlier, represents the value of the state independent of any action. The advantage function, on the other hand, provides a relative measure of the utility (advantage/goodness) of action A in the state S. The Dueling DQN uses convolutional networks in the initial layers to extract the features from raw pixels. However, in the later stages it is separated into two different networks, one approximating the value and another approximating the advantage. This ensures that the network produces separate estimates for the value function and the advantage function:

$$Q(S, A) = A(S, A; \theta, \alpha) + V^{\pi}(S; \theta, \beta)$$

Here θ is an array of the training parameters of the shared convolutional network (it is shared by both V and A), α and β are the training parameters for the *Advantage* and *Value* estimator networks. Later the two networks are recombined using an aggregating layer to estimate the Q-value.

In the following diagram, you can see the architecture of Dueling DQN:

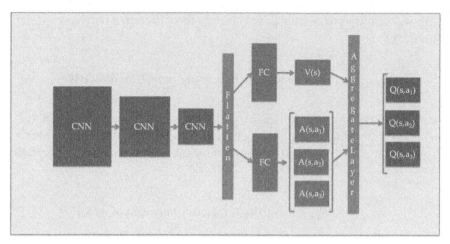

Figure 5: Visualizing the architecture of a Dueling DQN

You may be wondering, what is the advantage of doing all of this? Why decompose *Q* if we will be just putting it back together? Well, decoupling the value and advantage functions allow us to know which states are valuable, without having to take into account the effect of each action for each state. There are many states that, irrespective of the action taken, are good or bad states: for example, having breakfast with your loved ones in a good resort is always a good state, and being admitted to a hospital emergency ward is always a bad state. Thus, separating value and advantage allows one to get a more robust approximation of the value function. Next, you can see a figure from the paper highlighting how in the Atari game Enduro, the value network learns to pay attention to the road, and the advantage network learns to pay attention only when there are cars immediately in front, so as to avoid collision:

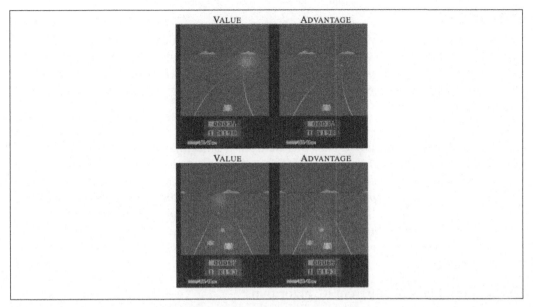

Image source: https://arxiv.org/pdf/1511.06581.pdf

The aggregate layer is implemented in a manner that allows one to recover both V and A from the given Q. This is achieved by enforcing that the advantage function estimator has zero advantage at the chosen action:

$$Q(S, A; \theta, \alpha, \beta) = A(S, A; \theta, \alpha) + V^{\pi}(S; \theta, \beta) - max_{a' \epsilon |A|} A(S, A'; \theta, \alpha)$$

In the paper, Wang et al. reported that the network is more stable if the max operation is replaced by the average operation. This is so because the speed of change in advantage is now the same as the change in average, instead of the optimal (max) value.

Rainbow

Rainbow is the current state of the art DQN variant. Technically, to call it a DQN variant would be wrong. In essence it is an ensemble of many DQN variants combined together into a single algorithm. It modifies the distributional RL [6] loss to multi-step loss and combines it with Double DQN using greedy action. Quoting from the paper:

> "*The network architecture is a dueling network architecture adapted for use with return distributions. The network has a shared representation $f\xi(s)$, which is then fed into a value stream v_η with N_{atoms} outputs, and into an advantage stream $a\xi$ with $N_{atoms} \times N_{actions}$ outputs, where $a_\xi^i(f_\xi(s), a)$ will denote the output corresponding to atom i and action a. For each atom z_i, the value and advantage streams are aggregated, as in Dueling DQN, and then passed through a softmax layer to obtain the normalised parametric distributions used to estimate the returns' distributions.*"

Rainbow combines six different RL algorithms:

- N-step returns
- Distributional state-action value learning
- Dueling networks
- Noisy networks
- Double DQN
- Prioritized Experience Replay

Deep deterministic policy gradient

DQN and its variants have been very successful in solving problems where the state space is continuous and action space is discrete. For example, in Atari games, the input space consists of raw pixels, but actions are discrete - [**up**, **down**, **left**, **right**, **no-op**]. How do we solve a problem with continuous action space? For instance, say an RL agent driving a car needs to turn its wheels: this action has a continuous action space One way to handle this situation is by discretizing the action space and continuing with DQN or its variants. However, a better solution would be to use a policy gradient algorithm. In policy gradient methods the policy $\pi(A|S)$ is approximated directly.

A neural network is used to approximate the policy; in the simplest form, the neural network learns a policy for selecting actions that maximize the rewards by adjusting its weights using steepest gradient ascent, hence, the name: policy gradients.

In this section we will focus on the **Deep Deterministic Policy Gradient (DDPG)** algorithm, another successful RL algorithm by Google's DeepMind in 2015. DDPG is implemented using two networks; one called the actor network and the other called the critic network.

The actor network approximates the optimal policy deterministically, that is it outputs the most preferred action for any given input state. In essence the actor is learning. The critic on the other hand evaluates the optimal action value function using the actor's most preferred action. Before going further, let us contrast this with the DQN algorithm that we discussed in the preceding section. In the following diagram, you can see the general architecture of DDPG:

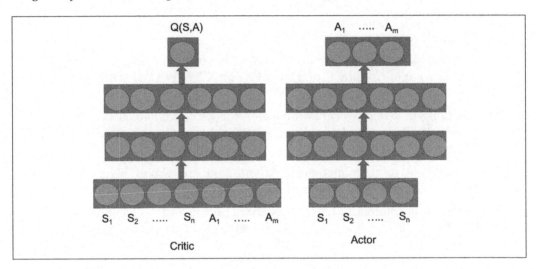

The actor network outputs the most preferred action; the critic takes as input both the input state and action taken and evaluates its Q-value. To train the critic network we follow the same procedure as DQN, that is we try to minimize the difference between the estimated Q-value and the target Q-value. The gradient of the Q-value over actions is then propagated back to train the actor network. So, if the critic is good enough, it will force the actor to choose actions with optimal value functions.

Summary

Reinforcement learning has in recent years seen a lot of progress, to summarize all of that in a single chapter is not possible. However, in this chapter we focused on the recent successful RL algorithms. The chapter started by introducing the important concepts in the RL field, its challenges, and the solutions to move forward. Next, we delved into two important RL algorithms: the DQN and DDPG algorithms. Toward the end of this chapter the book covered the important topics in the field of deep learning. In the next chapter, we will move into applying what we have learned to production.

References

1. https://www.technologyreview.com/s/614325/open-ai-algorithms-learned-tool-use-and-cooperation-after-hide-and-seek-games/?fbclid=IwAR1JvW-JTWnzP54bk9eCEvuJOq1y7vU4qz4OFfilWr7xHGHsILakKSD9UjY

2. Coggan, Melanie. *Exploration and Exploitation in Reinforcement Learning.* Research supervised by Prof. Doina Precup, CRA-W DMP Project at McGill University (2004).

3. Lin, Long-Ji. *Reinforcement learning for robots using neural networks.* No. CMU-CS-93-103. Carnegie-Mellon University Pittsburgh PA School of Computer Science, 1993.

4. Schaul, Tom, John Quan, Ioannis Antonoglou, and David Silver. *Prioritized Experience Replay.* arXiv preprint arXiv:1511.05952 (2015).

5. *Chapter 4, Reinforcement Learning*, Richard Sutton and Andrew Barto, MIT Press. https://web.stanford.edu/class/psych209/Readings/SuttonBartoIPRLBook2ndEd.pdf.

6. Dabney, Will, Mark Rowland, Marc G. Bellemare, and Rémi Munos. *Distributional Reinforcement Learning with Quantile Regression.* In Thirty-Second AAAI Conference on Artificial Intelligence. 2018.

7. Hessel, Matteo, Joseph Modayil, Hado Van Hasselt, Tom Schaul, Georg Ostrovski, Will Dabney, Dan Horgan, Bilal Piot, Mohammad Azar, and David Silver. *Rainbow: Combining improvements in Deep Reinforcement Learning.* In Thirty-Second AAAI Conference on Artificial Intelligence. 2018.

8. Pittsburgh PA School of Computer Science, 1993.

9. The details about different environments can be obtained from https://gym.openai.com/envs.

10. Wiki pages are maintained for some environments at https://github.com/openai/gym/wiki.

11. Details regarding installation instructions and dependencies can be obtained from `https://github.com/openai/gym`.

12. `https://arxiv.org/pdf/1602.01783.pdf`
`http://ufal.mff.cuni.cz/~straka/courses/npfl114/2016/sutton-bookdraft2016sep.pdf`
`http://karpathy.github.io/2016/05/31/rl/`

13. Xavier Glorot and Yoshua Bengio, *Understanding the difficulty of training deep feedforward neural networks*. Proceedings of the Thirteenth International Conference on Artificial Intelligence and Statistics, 2010, `http://proceedings.mlr.press/v9/glorot10a/glorot10a.pdf`.

14. A good read on why RL is still hard to crack: `https://www.alexirpan.com/2018/02/14/rl-hard.html`.

12
TensorFlow and Cloud

AI algorithms require extensive computing resources. With the availability of a large number of cloud platforms offering their services at competitive prices, cloud computing offers a cost-effective solution. In this chapter, we will talk about three main cloud platform providers that occupy the majority of the market share: **Amazon Web Services (AWS)**, Microsoft Azure, and Google Cloud Platform. Moreover, once you have trained your model on cloud, you can use **TensorFlow Extended (TFX)** to move your model to production. The chapter will cover:

- Creating and using virtual machines on cloud
- Creating and training directly on Jupyter Notebook on cloud
- Deploying the model on cloud
- Using TFX for production
- TensorFlow Enterprise

Deep learning on cloud

There was a time when, if you wanted to work in the field of deep learning, then you needed to shell out thousands of dollars to obtain the infrastructure required to train your deep learning model. Not anymore! Today, a large number of public cloud service providers offer affordable cloud computing services. Training your **Deep Learning (DL)** model on cloud offers various advantages:

- **Affordability**: Most cloud service providers offer a range of subscription options; you can choose from monthly subscriptions to pay-as-you-use options. Most also offer free credit for new users.
- **Flexibility**: You are no longer bound to a physical location; you can log in to the cloud from any physical location and continue your work.

- **Scalability**: As your need grows, you can scale your cloud resources as simply as requesting a quota increase or a change in subscription model.

- **Hassle-free**: Unlike your personal system, where everything from choice of hardware to the installation of software dependencies is your responsibility, the cloud services offer ready-made solutions in the form of premade system images. The images come installed with all the packages you might need for training your deep learning model.

- **Language support**: All services support a variety of computer languages. You can write your code in your favorite language.

- **API for deployment**: Most cloud services also allow you to embed your deep learning model directly into the applications and on the web.

Depending on the services offered, the cloud platform can be classified as:

- **Infrastructure as a Service (IaaS)**: In this case, the service provider only provides the physical infrastructure; things like virtual machines, data storage centers come in this.

- **Platform as a Service (PaaS)**: Here, the service provider provides a runtime environment, both hardware and software, for the development and deployment of applications. For example, web servers and data centers.

- **Software as a Service (SaaS)**: Here, the service provider provides a software application as a service, for example Microsoft Office 365 or the interactive Jupyter notebooks available on cloud.

Before delving into details about how to use different cloud services, let us go through some popular cloud service providers and their offerings. We will be considering Microsoft Azure, AWS, and Google Cloud platforms. All three of them provide facilities to build, deploy, and manage applications, additionally they can also provide services through the worldwide web.

Microsoft Azure

Microsoft Azure provides both PaaS and SaaS services. The Azure platform provides a myriad of services: virtual machines, networking, storage, and even IoT solutions. To access these services, you need to open an account with Azure. You will require an email address to do this. Go to the site: `https://azure.microsoft.com/en-in/` to open your account. The Azure platform also provides integration with GitHub, so if you already have a GitHub account you can use it to log in. Once you have successfully created the account and have logged in, you will see the following dashboard:

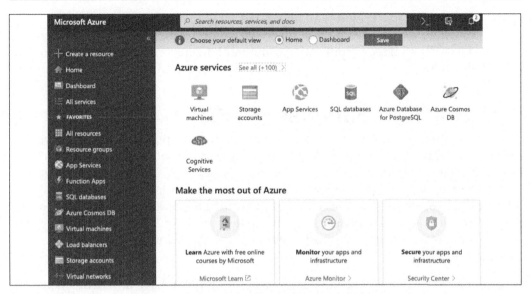

Figure 1: The Microsoft Azure dashboard

For new users, Azure offers a $200 credit, and a range of free services. For paid services, you can choose from a range (called "subscriptions" on the Azure platform) of monthly payment plans or "pay-as-you-go" options. You will need to provide your credit card information to access paid services. Some of the popular services offered by Azure are:

- **Virtual Machines**: You can create your own machines on the net, with up to 128 virtual CPUs (vCPUs) and up to 6 TB of memory. There is a wide range of virtual machine series offered by Azure. Since the topic of this book is deep learning, we will limit ourselves to N-series virtual machines offered by Azure, which are sufficient for our needs. In a later section, *Virtual machines on cloud*, you will learn the features of N-series and how to deploy one. To see the complete range of virtual machines offered please refer to: https://azure.microsoft.com/en-in/pricing/details/virtual-machines/series/.

- **Function**: Provides serverless architecture; one need not worry about hardware or networking, you just need to deploy your code, and Function takes care of the rest.

- **Storage Services**: Azure provides Blob storage to store any type of data in the cloud. The data stored on Blob can be used for content distribution, backup, and big data analytics.

- **IoT Hub**: Provides a central communication service to communicate between your IoT devices and code. Using IoT Hub, you can connect virtually any device to the cloud.

- **Azure DevOps**: Provides an integrated set of features that allow you to collaborate with a team. You can create a work plan, work together on code, develop and deploy applications, and implement continuous integration and deployment.

Amazon Web Services (AWS)

Since 2006, Amazon started offering its infrastructure on cloud to businesses, under the name Amazon Web Services. AWS offers a wide range of global cloud-based products. They include compute instances, storage services, databases, analytics, networking, mobile and developer tools, IoT, management tools, security, and enterprise applications. These services are available on-demand with pay-as-you-go pricing options or monthly subscriptions. There are over 140 AWS services offering data warehousing, directories, deployment tools, and content delivery to name a few.

Before using the AWS, you need to open an account. If you have an existing account you can log in using it, otherwise visit http://aws.amazon.com and click on **Create an AWS account** to create a new account, as seen in the following screenshot:

Figure 2: The "Create an AWS Account" tab.

The account can be created for free, and many of the services are available under the "free basic plan". To learn details about the free offerings you can visit: http://aws.amazon.com/free. Even though you may choose a free account and free services, the portal requires you to give credit/debit card details for verification purposes. Once you log in, you are led to a management console. Following is a screenshot of the management console:

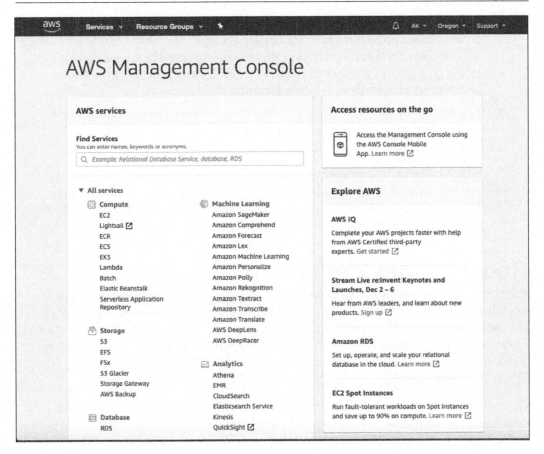

You can learn about all the services offered by AWS using this link: `https://docs.aws.amazon.com/index.html?nc2=h_ql_doc_do`. Let us now go through some of the important AWS services that we as deep learning engineers/researchers can use:

- **Elastic Compute Cloud** (**EC2**): Provides virtual computers. You can configure the hardware and software according to your infrastructural needs. You have an option to choose from CPU, GPU, storage, networking, and disk image configurations. We will talk about how to create an EC2 instance for deep learning in the next section.

- **Lambda**: The serverless computer service offered by Amazon. It lets you run code without provisioning or managing servers. You only need to pay for the compute time you consume – there is no charge when your code is not running. It allows one to run code for virtually any type of application or backend service, with zero administration requirements.

- **Elastic Beanstalk**: Provides quick and efficient services for deployment, monitoring, and scaling of your application.

- **AWS IoT**: Allows you to connect and manage devices in the cloud.

- **SageMaker**: A platform for developing and deploying machine learning models. With its prebuilt ML models, it allows you to train and deploy ML algorithms with ease. Later in this chapter we will learn how to use the integrated Jupyter Notebook of SageMaker to train our model on cloud.

Google Cloud Platform (GCP)

From computing infrastructure to software management, GCP provides a suite of cloud computing services. A complete list of all the services offered by GCP is available here: `https://cloud.google.com/docs/`. Google cloud offers the same infrastructure that it uses for its end-user products like Gmail, Google Search, and YouTube. Beside CPUs and GPUs, GCP also offers a choice of TPUs (*Chapter 16, Tensor Processing Unit*).

GCP allows you to open an account for free – you just need to register using an email address (or phone) and card (debit/credit) details. It offers a $300 credit to new users, which is valid for 12 months and can be used across its products. Once you log in to the Google console you can access all its services. Following is a screenshot of my Google console:

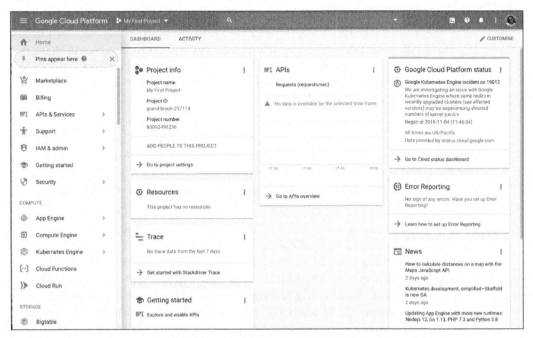

Figure 3: The console of the Google Cloud Platform

Like Azure and AWS, GCP also offers a plethora of services. Some of the services of interest to a deep learning scientist and engineer are (as defined in the latest Google GCP documentation):

- **Compute Engine** (https://cloud.google.com/compute/docs/): Compute Engine lets you create and run virtual machines on Google infrastructure. Compute Engine offers scale, performance, and value that allows you to easily launch large compute clusters on Google's infrastructure. There are no upfront investments and you can run thousands of virtual CPUs on a system that has been designed to be fast, and to offer strong consistency of performance.

- **Deep Learning Containers** (`https://cloud.google.com/ai-platform/deep-learning-containers/docs/`): AI Platform Deep Learning Containers provides you with performance optimized, consistent environments to help you prototype and implement workflows quickly. Deep Learning Containers images come with the latest machine learning data science frameworks, libraries, and tools preinstalled.

- **App Engine** (`https://cloud.google.com/appengine/docs/`): App Engine is a fully managed, serverless platform for developing and hosting web applications at scale. You can choose from several popular languages, libraries, and frameworks to develop your apps, then let App Engine take care of provisioning servers and scaling your app instances based on demand.

- **Cloud Functions** (`https://cloud.google.com/functions/docs/concepts/overview`): Google Cloud Functions is a serverless execution environment for building and connecting cloud services. With Cloud Functions you write simple, single-purpose functions that are attached to events emitted from your cloud infrastructure and services. Your function is triggered when an event being watched is fired. Your code executes in a fully managed environment. There is no need to provision any infrastructure or worry about managing any servers.

  Cloud Functions can be written using JavaScript, Python 3, or Go runtimes on Google Cloud Platform. You can take your function and run it in any standard Node.js (Node.js 6, 8 or 10), Python 3 (Python 3.7), or Go (Go 1.11) environment, which makes both portability and local testing a breeze.

- **Cloud IoT Core** (`https://cloud.google.com/iot/docs/`): Google Cloud Internet of Things (IoT) Core is a fully managed service for securely connecting and managing IoT devices, from a few to millions. Ingest data from connected devices and build rich applications that integrate with the other big data services of Google Cloud Platform.

- **Cloud AutoML** (`https://cloud.google.com/automl/docs/`): Cloud AutoML makes the power of machine learning available to you even if you have limited knowledge of machine learning. You can use AutoML to build on Google's machine learning capabilities to create your own custom machine learning models that are tailored to your business needs, and then integrate those models into your applications and web sites.

Having covered GCP, let's move on to another cloud service: IBM Cloud.

IBM Cloud

With about 190 cloud services, IBM allows one to create an account for free with a $200 credit (no cards required). You can open an account by giving your email and some additional details: `https://cloud.ibm.com/registration`. The best part of IBM cloud is that it provides access to Watson Studio, where one can leverage the Watson API and use its pretrained models to build and deploy applications. It also offers Watson Machine Learning, which allows you to build deep learning models from scratch.

Now that we've covered some cloud service providers, let's take a look at the virtual machines that we are able to utilize on these clouds.

Virtual machines on cloud

As the name suggests, **virtual machines** (**VMs**) are not real systems. Instead, they are a computer file, called an image, which emulates the behavior of an actual computer. Thus, we can create a virtual computer within a computer. It runs on your existing OS, almost like any other program, providing you the same experience as you would have on a physical system with the same configuration (albeit with some latency).

Each virtual machine has its own virtual hardware, including CPUs, GPUs, memory, hard drives, network interfaces, and other devices. The cloud service providers allow you to create a virtual machine on their physical hardware using VM services. This section will cover how to create a virtual machine on the three cloud service providers, and features offered by them.

EC2 on Amazon

To create a virtual machine on Amazon EC2 you will need to launch an Amazon EC2 instance by clicking on the **Launch Instance** button available in the EC2 dashboard, as shown in the following screenshot:

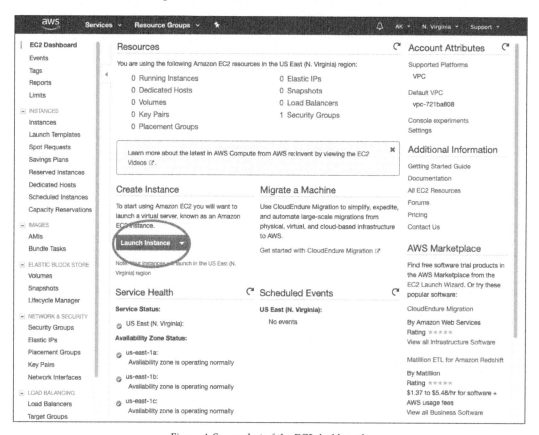

Figure 4: Screenshot of the EC2 dashboard

After clicking **Launch Instance**, you can create your virtual machine in two simple steps:

1. **Choose an Amazon Machine Image (AMI)**: Amazon offers a variety of prebuilt AMIs for Deep Learning (`https://aws.amazon.com/machine-learning/amis/`). The Conda AMIs (on AWS Linux, Ubuntu, and Windows OS) provide prebuilt Conda virtual environments for various Deep Learning frameworks including TensorFlow. The Base AMIs (on AWS Linux and Ubuntu) have various versions of CUDA preinstalled, and the user needs to enable the appropriate CUDA version and install the framework of choice.

 As of November 2019, the existing AMIs in Amazon Marketplace do not support TensorFlow 2.x.

2. **Choose the Instance type**: Amazon offers a wide range of instance selection, from general purpose computing to accelerated computing. For the purpose of deep learning we require instances with GPUs. P3, P2, G4, G3, and G2 instances have GPU support (`https://docs.aws.amazon.com/AWSEC2/latest/UserGuide/accelerated-computing-instances.html`). So, for DL projects you should select one of these. Please note that AWS has instance limits set on these, by default for all accelerated compute instances it is set to 0. You will need to first request for an increase in the instance limit (again remember each instance is not available in every region, so go through the documentation to know what regions to choose for your required instance).

Now unless you want to do advanced network and security settings, your machine is ready to launch. Just review your selections and launch it. Amazon EC2 allows you to communicate with your virtual machine through the command line via SSH or using a web browser.

An alternative to Amazon EC2 is Compute Instance, available on GCP.

Compute Instance on GCP

To access Compute instance, go to the Google Cloud Console and select Compute Engine, and you will reach the dashboard where you can select the configuration you want for your virtual machine. Following is a screenshot of the Compute Engine dashboard. Select **Create** or **Import** (if you already have a saved VM configuration) to create a new virtual machine instance:

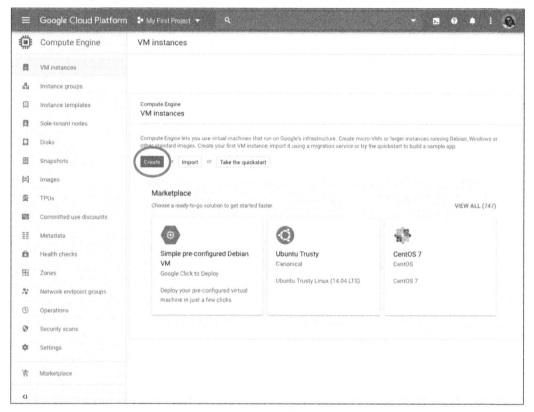

Figure 5: The Compute Engine dashboard

Alternatively, you can also choose the complete configuration from the **marketplace**, which will launch the environment with the corresponding (minimum) infrastructure. You then just need to deploy the instance. Each instance will have different price rating per month depending upon the compute resources it requires.

GCP Compute Engine offers two options for CPUs families, either Intel Skylake platform (also called N1; this series allows GPUs) or the Intel Cascade Lake platform. With your machine you have an option to add GPUs. At the time of writing this book, GCP offered four different GPUs (and TPUs; for more on TPUs refer to *Chapter 16, Tensor Processing Unit*):

- Nvidia Tesla K80
- Nvidia Tesla P4
- Nvidia Tesla T4
- Nvidia Tesla V100

Virtual machine on Microsoft Azure

For deep learning and prediction applications Azure provides machines with GPU capabilities. These are called N-series machines.

According to the Microsoft Azure site (`https://azure.microsoft.com/en-in/pricing/details/virtual-machines/series/`) there are three different N-series offerings, each aimed at specific workloads:

- **NC series**: It focuses on high-performance computing and machine learning applications. The latest version – NCsv3 – features Nvidia's Tesla V100 GPU.
- **ND series**: It focuses on training and inference scenarios for deep learning. It uses the Nvidia Tesla P40 GPUs. The latest version – NDv2 – features the Nvidia Tesla V100 GPUs.
- **NV series**: This supports powerful remote visualization applications and other graphics-intensive workloads backed by the Nvidia Tesla M60 GPU.

All of them also offer optional InfiniBand interconnect to enable scale-up performance. To create a virtual machine on Azure you need to follow three basic steps:

1. Log in to Azure portal
2. Select **Virtual machines** as a resource and then select **Create Virtual Machine**
3. Choose the configuration you require and launch it

In Azure also you need to request an increase in quota for certain compute instances.

Jupyter Notebooks on cloud

During development and testing of the model, many in the machine learning community find using Jupyter Notebooks handy; they provide an integrated environment to run and view the result. They are very useful when you are collaborating or want to discuss code with a client. With LaTeX support, many researchers are even shifting to present their research papers on Jupyter, and hence it makes sense to have Jupyter Notebook environment on cloud.

You just share the link and the other person can view it and run it, without any of the hassle of OS environment and software dependencies. In this section we will cover the Jupyter Notebook environments made available by three of the technological giants: Google, Microsoft, and Amazon.

SageMaker

Amazon SageMaker is a fully managed machine learning service. You can use it easily and quickly build and train machine learning models. The trained models can then be directly deployed into a production-ready hosted environment. SageMaker provides an integrated Jupyter notebook instance; this allows for easy access to data sources and provides a convenient coding platform for exploration and analysis, thus removing any need to manage servers.

An additional feature provided by SageMaker is the availability of optimized common machine learning algorithms. This allows users to run code efficiently, even when the dataset being used is extremely large. It offers flexible distributed training options that you can tailor according to your specific workflow. The trained model can later be deployed into a scalable and secure environment, with only a single click from the Amazon SageMaker console. Both training and hosting are billed according to the number of minutes used. There are no minimum fees and no upfront commitments. You can follow the Amazon documentation on how to setup SageMaker using this link: `https://docs.aws.amazon.com/sagemaker/latest/dg/gs.html`.

In order to load data and deploy your model, you will need to use SageMaker modules and functions. A good place to start will be this tutorial: `https://www.bmc.com/blogs/amazon-sagemaker/`. As you may gather from the tutorial, Amazon SageMaker is not free. Even experimenting on it to write code for this book required us to spend precious dollars. However, it offers ease of deployment.

Google Colaboratory

Google, along with the Jupyter development team, launched Google Colaboratory in 2014. Since then, the Colaboratory has grown in function and utility. Today, it supports GPU and TPU hardware acceleration. It supports Python (2.7 and 3.6 version). The Colab is integrated with Google Drive, so your notebooks are saved on your drive and you can also read data from your own drive (you will need to authorize the notebook first).

The best part of Google Colaboratory is that it is completely free. You can run your code continuously for 12 hours on it. To be able to work with Colaboratory, you need an account with Google. Your normal Gmail account will also work.

When you log in to Colaboratory at `https://colab.research.google.com/` `notebooks/intro.ipynb#recent=true`, you have the option to open an existing Jupyter Notebook from your drive or from GitHub. You can also upload an existing notebook from your computer or create a new notebook. For beginners, it also contains some example notebooks, as seen in the following screenshot:

Figure 6: A screenshot of the Colaboratory

You can create a new notebook as well, by clicking on the blue link in the bottom-right corner (in the preceding screenshot). This will create a Python 3 notebook.

 Jupyter plans to phase out Python 2 support by January 2020. Google too shall phase out the Python 2 support from Colaboratory after that.

To choose the hardware accelerator, you need to go to **Edit | Notebook Settings** and select the required hardware accelerator (None/GPU/TPU. For more information on TPUs refer to *Chapter 16, Tensor Processing Unit*). The Notebook environment comes installed with most useful Python packages (TensorFlow, NumPy, Matplotlib, Pandas, and so on).

In case you require to install a specific version or a module not part of the default Colaboratory environment you can use `pip install` or `apt-get install`. For example, the following command on being executed in the Colab notebook cell will install TensorFlow GPU 2.0 version:

```
! pip install tensorflow-gpu
```

 At the time of writing this book the default version of TensorFlow was 1.15, with a message that it will be shifting soon to TensorFlow 2.0, the NumPy version was 1.17.3, Matplotlib 3.1.1, and Pandas 0.25.3.

If you are interested to know the hardware details of the environment where Colaboratory notebooks run, you can get the info using the `cat` command:

For processor:

```
!cat /proc/cpuinfo
```

For memory:

```
!cat /proc/meminfo
```

To run these starting commands and get the version information for your region, you can use the following Colaboratory Notebook:

```
https://colab.research.google.com/drive/1i60H5hcJShrMKhytBUlItJ7Win0o
FjM6
```

Just like the standard Jupyter notebook, you can run the Unix command line commands directly in the Notebook prefixed by an exclamation mark "!".

You can also mount your Google Drive and access the files you have saved in your drive. To do this you will use:

```
from google.colab import drive
drive.mount('/content/drive/')
```

This will generate a link. After clicking the link you will get an authorization code, and entering the authorization code will give the notebook access to your drive. You can check the content of your drive using `!ls "/content/drive/My Drive"` and access any of the folders in it by specifying the path.

The Colab interface is very similar to Jupyter, so now you are all set to run your machine learning experiments on Colaboratory. One disadvantage of Colaboratory is that it does not work well in presentation mode. Fortunately, for that we have Azure Notebooks.

Microsoft Azure Notebooks

Microsoft offers Azure Notebooks, a free service for anyone to develop and run code in their web-browser using Jupyter. It supports Python 2, Python 3, R and F# and their popular packages. It is a general code authoring, executing, and sharing platform. According to Microsoft documentation, one can use Notebooks in diverse scenarios: like giving an online webinar, giving a PowerPoint-like presentation with executable codes in slides, or learning a new model. The service is free. However, to stop abuse, they have put network limitations; at present there is a 4 GB memory limit per user, and a 1 GB data limit.

Azure Notebooks is a thriving place, with many existing and exciting notebooks shared by the DL community. You can access them here: `https://github.com/jupyter/jupyter/wiki/A-gallery-of-interesting-Jupyter-Notebooks`.

Like Colaboratory, Azure Notebooks have most packages preinstalled, and if you require, you can install new packages via `!pip install`. You can run any Unix command line command with a prefixing exclamation mark. To be able to use Azure Notebooks, you will need to open an account. You can use your existing Microsoft account, or create a new one. It even offers an option to create a Child Account to encourage young people to learn programming, and these accounts have parental control.

 Some packages may not yet be available in Azure Notebooks.

You can access data directly through the notebook interface using upload/download commands. You can even download data from a URL using `!wget url_address`.

Now that we've looked at the cloud services and the VMs that can help us to perform our training, let's look at how we can move into the production stage, using TensorFlow Extended.

TensorFlow Extended for production

TFX is an end-to-end platform for deploying machine learning pipelines. A part of the TensorFlow ecosystem, it provides a configuration framework and shared libraries so as to integrate the common components needed to define, launch, and monitor software based on ML models. TFX includes many of the requirements for production software deployments and best practices, viz: scalability, consistency, testability, safety and security, and so on.

It starts with ingesting your data, followed by data validation, feature engineering, training, and serving. Google has created libraries for each major phase of the pipeline, and there are frameworks for a wide range of deployment targets. TFX implements a series of ML pipeline components. All of this is made possible by creating horizontal layers for things like pipeline storage, configuration, and orchestration. These layers are very important for managing and optimizing the pipelines and the applications that you run on them.

You will need to install it first. TensorFlow Extended can be installed using the `pip` command:

```
pip install tfx
```

In the following section we will cover the fundamentals of TFX, its architecture, and the various libraries available within it.

TFX Pipelines

The TFX pipeline consists of a sequence of components that implement an ML pipeline, specifically, ensuring the scalability and high performance of the underlined ML task. It includes modeling, training, inference, and deployment to web or mobile targets. A TFX pipeline includes several components, with each component consisting of three main elements: Driver, Executor, and and the Publisher. The driver queries the metadata store and supplies the resultant metadata to the executor, publisher accepts the results of the executor and saves then in metadata. The executor is the one performing all the processing. As an ML software developer, you will need to write code that runs in the executor depending upon the component class you are working with:

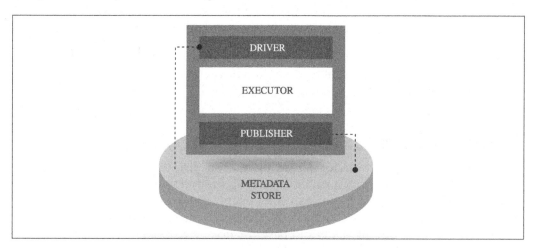

In a TFX pipeline, a unit of data, called an artifact, is passed between components. Normally a component has one input artifact and one output artifact. Every artifact has an associated metadata that defines its type and properties. The artifact type defines the ontology of artifacts in the entire TFX system, while the artifact property specifies the ontology specific to an artifact type. Users have the option to extend the ontology globally or locally.

TFX pipeline components

The following diagram shows the flow of data between different TFX components:

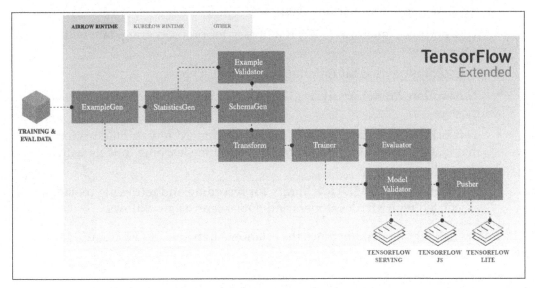

Flow of data between TFX components

 All the images in the TFX section have been adapted from the TensorFlow Extended official guide: https://www.tensorflow. org/tfx/guide.

To begin with we have ExampleGen, which ingests the input data, and can also split the input dataset. The data then flows to StatisticsGen, which calculates the statistics of the dataset. Then comes SchemaGen, which examines the statistics and creates a data schema; then an ExampleValidator, which looks for anomalies and missing values in the data; and Transform, which performs feature engineering in the dataset. The transformed dataset is then fed to the Trainer, which trains the model. The performance of the model is evaluated using Evaluator and ModelValidator. Finally, if all is well, the Pusher deploys the model on the serving infrastructure.

TFX libraries

TFX provides several Python packages that are used to create pipeline components. Quoting from the TensorFlow Extended User Guide (`https://www.tensorflow.org/tfx/guide`).

These packages are the libraries which you will use to create the components of your pipelines so that your code can focus on the unique aspects of your pipeline.

Different libraries included in TFX are:

- **TensorFlow Data Validation (TFDV)** is a library for analyzing and validating machine learning data

- **TensorFlow Transform (TFT)** is a library for preprocessing data with TensorFlow

- **TensorFlow** is used for training models with TFX

- **TensorFlow Model Analysis (TFMA)** is a library for evaluating TensorFlow models

- **TensorFlow Metadata (TFMD)** provides standard representations for metadata that are useful when training machine learning models with TensorFlow

- **ML Metadata (MLMD)** is a library for recording and retrieving metadata associated with ML developers and data scientists' workflows

The following diagram demonstrates the relationship between TFX libraries and pipeline components:

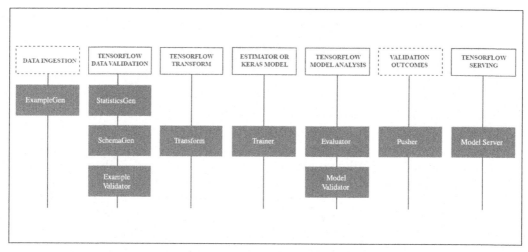

Figure 7: Relationships between TFX libraries and pipeline components, visualized

TFX uses the open source Apache Beam to implement data-parallel pipelines. Optionally TFX allows Apache Airflow and Kubeflow for easy configuration, operation, monitoring, and maintenance of the ML pipeline. Once the model is developed and trained, using TFX you can deploy it to one or more deployment target(s) where it will receive inference requests. TFX supports deployment to three classes of deployment targets: TensorFlow Serving (works with REST or gRPC interface), TensorFlow.js (for browser applications), and TensorFlow Lite (for native mobile and IoT applications). Trained models that have been exported as SavedModels can be deployed to any or all of these deployment targets.

TensorFlow Enterprise

TensorFlow Enterprise is the latest offering from Google that provides enterprise-grade support, cloud-scale performance, and managed services. TensorFlow Enterprise has been launched as a beta version. Its aim is to accelerate software development and ensure the reliability of launched AI applications. It is fully integrated with Google Cloud and its services, and introduces some improvements in the way TensorFlow Datasets reads data from Cloud Storage. TensorFlow Enterprise also introduces the BigQuery reader, which, as the name implies, allows the user to read data directly from BigQuery.

In ML tasks, speed is critical, and one of the major bottlenecks is the speed at which data is accessed for the training process. TensorFlow Enterprise provides optimized performance and easy access to data sources, making it extremely efficient on GCP.

Summary

In this chapter we explored different cloud service providers who could provide the computing power necessary to train, evaluate, and deploy your deep learning models. We started by first understanding the types of cloud computing services available today. The chapter explored the Amazon, Google, and Microsoft IaaS services for creating a virtual machine. The different infrastructure options available in each were discussed. Next, we moved to SaaS services, specifically Jupyter Notebook on cloud. The chapter covered the Amazon SageMaker, Google Colaboratory, and Azure Notebooks. Just training a model is not sufficient; eventually we want to deploy it in a scalable manner. Thus, we delved into TensorFlow Extended, which allows users to develop and deploy ML models in a scalable, safe, and secure manner. Lastly, we introduced TensorFlow Enterprise, the latest offering in the TensorFlow ecosystem, and briefly discussed its features.

References

1. To get a complete list of virtual machine types offered by Microsoft Azure: `https://azure.microsoft.com/en-in/pricing/details/virtual-machines/series/`

2. A good tutorial on Amazon SageMaker: `https://www.bmc.com/blogs/amazon-sagemaker/`

3. `https://colab.research.google.com/notebooks/intro.ipynb#recent=true`

4. A collection of interesting Azure Notebooks: `https://github.com/ipython/ipython/wiki/A-gallery-of-interesting-IPython-Notebooks`

5. Sculley, David, Gary Holt, Daniel Golovin, Eugene Davydov, Todd Phillips, Dietmar Ebner, Vinay Chaudhary, Michael Young, Jean-Francois Crespo, and Dan Dennison. *Hidden Technical Debt in Machine Learning Systems*. In *Advances in neural information processing systems*, pp. 2503-2511. 2015

6. TensorFlow Extended tutorials: `https://www.tensorflow.org/tfx/tutorials`

7. Baylor, Denis, Eric Breck, Heng-Tze Cheng, Noah Fiedel, Chuan Yu Foo, Zakaria Haque, Salem Haykal et al. *Tfx: A TensorFlow-Based Production-Scale Machine Learning Platform*. In *Proceedings of the 23rd ACM SIGKDD International Conference on Knowledge Discovery and Data Mining*, pp. 1387-1395. ACM, 2017.

8. A nice comparison between Google Colab and Azure Notebooks: `https://dev.to/arpitgogia/azure-notebooks-vs-google-colab-from-a-novices-perspective-3ijo`

9. TensorFlow Enterprise: `https://cloud.google.com/blog/products/ai-machine-learning/introducing-tensorflow-enterprise-supported-scalable-and-seamless-tensorflow-in-the-cloud`

13

TensorFlow for Mobile and IoT and TensorFlow.js

In this chapter we will learn the basics of TensorFlow for Mobile and **IoT** (**Internet of Things**). We will briefly present TensorFlow Mobile and we will introduce TensorFlow Lite in more detail. TensorFlow Mobile and TensorFlow Lite are open source deep learning frameworks for on-device inference. Some examples of Android, iOS, and Raspberry PI applications will be discussed, together with examples of deploying pretrained models such as MobileNet v1, v2, v3 (image classification models designed for mobile and embedded vision applications), PoseNet for pose estimation (a vision model that estimates the poses of people in image or video), DeepLab segmentation (an image segmentation model that assigns semantic labels (for example, dog, cat, car) to every pixel in the input image), and MobileNet SSD object detection (an image classification model that detects multiple objects with bounding boxes). This chapter will conclude with an example of federated learning, a new machine learning framework distributed over millions of mobile devices that is thought to respect user privacy.

TensorFlow Mobile

TensorFlow Mobile is a framework for producing code on iOS and Android. The key idea is to have a platform that allows you to have light models that don't consume too much device resources such as battery or memory. Typical examples of applications are image recognition on the device, speech recognition, or gesture recognition. TensorFlow Mobile was quite popular until 2018 but then became progressively less and less adopted in favor of TensorFlow Lite.

TensorFlow Lite

TensorFlow Lite is a lightweight platform designed by TensorFlow. This platform is focused on mobile and embedded devices such as Android, iOS, and Raspberry PI. The main goal is to enable machine learning inference directly on the device by putting a lot of effort in three main characteristics: (1) small binary and model size to save on memory, (2) low energy consumption to save on the battery, and (3) low latency for efficiency. It goes without saying that battery and memory are two important resources for mobile and embedded devices. In order to achieve these goals, Lite uses a number of techniques such as Quantization, FlatBuffers, Mobile interpreter, and Mobile converter, which we are going to review briefly in the following sections.

Quantization

Quantization refers to a set of techniques that constrains an input made of continuous values (such as real numbers) into a discrete set (such as integers). The key idea is to reduce the space occupancy of **Deep Learning** (**DL**) models by representing the internal weight with integers instead of real numbers. Of course, this implies trading space gains for some amount of performance of the model. However, it has been empirically shown in many situations that a quantized model does not suffer from a significant decay in performance. TensorFlow Lite is internally built around a set of core operators supporting both quantized and floating-point operations.

Model quantization is a toolkit for applying quantization. This operation is applied to the representations of weights and, optionally, to the activations for both storage and computation. There are two types of quantization available:

- Post-training quantization quantizes weights and the result of activations post training.
- Quantization-aware training allows for the training of networks that can be quantized with minimal accuracy drop (only available for specific CNNs). Since this is a relatively experimental technique, we are not going to discuss it in this chapter but the interested reader can find more information in [1].

TensorFlow Lite supports reducing the precision of values from full floats to half-precision floats (`float16`) or 8-bit integers. TensorFlow reports multiple trade-offs in terms of accuracy, latency, and space for selected CNN models (see *Figure 1*, source: `https://www.tensorflow.org/lite/performance/model_optimization`):

Model	Top-1 Accuracy (Original)	Top-1 Accuracy (Post Training Quantized)	Top-1 Accuracy (Quantization Aware Training)	Latency (Original) (ms)	Latency (Post Training Quantized) (ms)	Latency (Quantization Aware Training) (ms)	Size (Original) (MB)	Size (Optimized) (MB)
Mobilenet-v1-1-224	0.709	0.657	0.70	124	112	64	16.9	4.3
Mobilenet-v2-1-224	0.719	0.637	0.709	89	98	54	14	3.6
Inception_v3	0.78	0.772	0.775	1130	845	543	95.7	23.9
Resnet_v2_101	0.770	0.768	N/A	3973	2868	N/A	178.3	44.9

Figure 1: Trade-offs for various quantized CNN models

FlatBuffers

FlatBuffers (`https://google.github.io/flatbuffers/`) is an open source format optimized to serialize data on mobile and embedded devices. The format was originally created at Google for game development and other performance-critical applications. FlatBuffers supports access to serialized data without parsing/unpacking for fast processing. The format is designed for memory efficiency and speed by avoiding unnecessary multiple copies in memory. FlatBuffers works across multiple platforms and languages such as C++, C#, C, Go, Java, JavaScript, Lobster, Lua, TypeScript, PHP, Python, and Rust.

Mobile converter

A model generated with TensorFlow needs to be converted into a TensorFlow Lite model. The converter can introduce optimizations for improving the binary size and performance. For instance, the converter can trim away all the nodes in a computational graph that are not directly related to inference, but instead were needed for training.

Mobile optimized interpreter

TensorFlow Lite runs on a highly optimized interpreter that is used to optimize the underlying computational graphs (see *Chapter 2, TensorFlow 1.x and 2.x*), which in turn are used to describe the machine learning models. Internally, the interpreter uses multiple techniques to optimize the computational graph by inducing a static graph order and by ensuring better memory allocation. The Interpreter Core takes ~100 kb alone or ~300 kb with all supported kernels.

Supported platforms

On Android, TensorFlow Lite inference can be performed using either Java or C++. On iOS, TensorFlow Lite inference can run in Swift and Objective-C. On Linux platforms (such as Raspberry Pi), inferences run in C++ and Python. TensorFlow Lite for microcontrollers is an experimental port of TensorFlow Lite designed to run machine learning models on microcontrollers based on Arm Cortex-M (`https://developer.arm.com/ip-products/processors/cortex-m`) Series processors including Arduino Nano 33 BLE Sense (`https://store.arduino.cc/usa/nano-33-ble-sense-with-headers`), SparkFun Edge (`https://www.sparkfun.com/products/15170`), and the STM32F746 Discovery kit (`https://www.st.com/en/evaluation-tools/32f746gdiscovery.html`). These microcontrollers are frequently used for IoT applications.

Architecture

The architecture of TensorFlow Lite is described in *Figure 2* (from `https://www.tensorflow.org/lite/convert/index`). As you can see, both **tf.keras** (for example, TensorFlow 2.x) and **Low-level APIs** are supported. A standard TensorFlow 2.x model can be converted by using **TFLite Converter** and then saved in a **TFLite FlatBuffer** format (named `.tflite`), which is then executed by the **TFLite interpreter** on available devices (GPUs, CPUs) and on native device APIs. The concrete function in *Figure 2* defines a graph that can be converted to a TensorFlow Lite model or be exported to a **SavedModel**.

Using TensorFlow Lite

Using TensorFlow Lite involves the following steps:

1. **Model selection**: A standard TensorFlow 2.x model is selected for solving a specific task. This can be either a custom-built model or a pretrained model.

2. **Model conversion**: The selected model is converted with the TensorFlow Lite converter, generally invoked with a few lines of Python code.

3. **Model deployment**: The converted model is deployed on the chosen device, either a phone or an IoT device and then run by using the TensorFlow Lite interpreter. As discussed, APIs are available for multiple languages.

4. **Model optimization**: The model can be optionally optimized by using the TensorFlow Lite optimization framework:

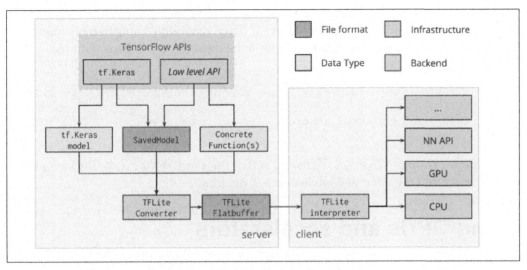

Figure 2: TensorFlow Lite internal architecture

A generic example of application

In this section we are going to see how to convert a model to TensorFlow Lite and then run it. Note that training can still be performed by TensorFlow in the environment that best fits your needs. However, inference runs on the mobile device. Let's see how with the following code fragment in Python:

```
import tensorflow as tf
converter = tf.lite.TFLiteConverter.from_saved_model(saved_model_dir)
tflite_model = converter.convert()
open("converted_model.tflite", "wb").write(tflite_model)
```

The code is self-explanatory. A standard TensorFlow 2.x model is opened and converted by using `tf.lite.TFLiteConverter.from_saved_model(saved_model_dir)`. Pretty simple! Note that no specific installation is required. We simply use the `tf.lite` API (https://www.tensorflow.org/api_docs/python/tf/lite). It is also possible to apply a number of optimizations. For instance, post-training quantization can be applied by default:

```
import tensorflow as tf

converter = tf.lite.TFLiteConverter.from_saved_model(saved_model_dir)
converter.optimizations = [tf.lite.Optimize.DEFAULT]
tflite_quant_model = converter.convert()
open("converted_model.tflite", "wb").write(tflite_quantized_model)
```

Once the model is converted it can be copied onto the specific device. Of course, this step is different for each different device. Then the model can run by using the language you prefer. For instance, in Java the invocation happens with the following code snippet:

```
try (Interpreter interpreter = new Interpreter(tensorflow_lite_model_
file)) {
   interpreter.run(input, output);
}
```

Again, pretty simple! What is very useful is that the same steps can be followed for a heterogeneous collection of Mobile and IoT devices.

Using GPUs and accelerators

Modern phones frequently have accelerators on board that allow floating-point matrix operations to be performed faster. In this case, the interpreter can use the concept of Delegate, and specifically `GpuDelegate()`, to use GPUs. Let's look at an example in Java:

```
GpuDelegate delegate = new GpuDelegate();
Interpreter.Options options = (new Interpreter.Options()).
addDelegate(delegate);
Interpreter interpreter = new Interpreter(tensorflow_lite_model_file,
options);
try {
   interpreter.run(input, output);
}
```

Again, the code is self-commenting. A new `GpuDelegate()` is created and then it is used by the Interpreter to run the model on a GPU.

An example of application

In this section, we are going to use TensorFlow Lite for building an example application that is later deployed on Android. We will use Android Studio (`https://developer.android.com/studio/`) to compile the code. The first step is to clone the repo with:

`git clone https://github.com/tensorflow/examples`

Then we open an existing project (see *Figure 3*) with the path `examples/lite/examples/image_classification/android`.

Then you need to install Android Studio from `https://developer.android.com/studio/install` and an appropriate distribution of Java. In my case, I selected the Android Studio MacOS distribution, and installed Java via `brew` with the following command:

```
brew tap adoptopenjdk/openjdk
```

```
brew cask install  homebrew/cask-versions/adoptopenjdk8
```

After that you can launch the `sdkmanager` and install the required packages. In my case, I decided to use the internal emulator and deploy the application on a virtual device emulating a Google Pixel 3 XL. The required packages are reported in *Figure 3*:

Figure 3: Required packages to use a Google Pixel 3 XL emulator

Then start Android Studio and select **Open an existing Android Studio project** as shown in *Figure 4*:

Figure 4: Opening a new Android project

Open the **Adv Manager** (under the **Tool** menu) and follow the instructions for how to create a virtual device, as the one shown in *Figure 5*:

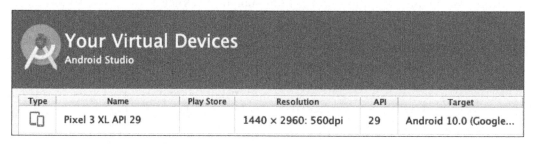

Type	Name	Play Store	Resolution	API	Target
⬚	Pixel 3 XL API 29		1440 × 2960: 560dpi	29	Android 10.0 (Google...

Figure 5: Creating a virtual device

Pretrained models in TensorFlow Lite

In many interesting use cases, it is possible to use a pretrained model that is already suitable for mobile computation. This is a field of active research with new proposals coming pretty much every month. TensorFlow Lite comes with a set of prebuilt models that are ready to use (`https://www.tensorflow.org/lite/models/`). As of October 2019, these include:

- **Image classification**: Used to identify multiple classes of objects such as places, plants, animals, activities, and people.
- **Object detection**: Used to detect multiple objects with bounding boxes.
- **Pose estimation**: Used to estimate poses with single or multiple people.
- **Smart reply**: Used to create reply suggestions for conversational chat messages.
- **Segmentations**: Identifies the shape of objects together with semantic labels for people, places, animals, and many additional classes.
- **Style transfers**: Used to apply artistic styles to any given image.
- **Text classification**: Used to assign different categories to textual content.
- **Question and answer**: Used to provide answers to questions provided by users.

In this section, we will discuss all the optimized pretrained models available in TensorFlow Lite out-of-the-box as of November 2019. These models can be used for a large number of mobile and edge computing use cases. Compiling the example code is pretty simple.

You just import a new project from each example directory and Android Studio will use Gradle (`https://gradle.org/`) for synching the code with the latest version in the repo and for compiling. If you compile all the examples, you should be able to see them in the emulator (see *Figure 6*). Remember to select **Build | Make Project**, and Android Studio will do the rest.

Edge computing is a distributed computing model that brings computation and data closer to the location where it is needed.

Figure 6: Emulated Google Pixel 3 XL with TensorFlow Lite example applications

Image classification

As of November 2019, the list of available models for pretrained classification is rather large, and it offers the opportunity to trade space, accuracy, and performance as shown in *Figure 7* (source: `https://www.tensorflow.org/lite/guide/hosted_models`):

Model name	Model size	Top-1 accuracy	Top-5 accuracy	TF Lite performance
Mobilenet_V1_0.25_128_quant	0.5 Mb	39.5%	64.4%	3.7 ms
Mobilenet_V1_0.25_160_quant	0.5 Mb	42.8%	68.1%	5.5 ms
Mobilenet_V1_0.25_192_quant	0.5 Mb	45.7%	70.8%	7.9 ms
Mobilenet_V1_0.25_224_quant	0.5 Mb	48.2%	72.8%	10.4 ms
Mobilenet_V1_0.50_128_quant	1.4 Mb	54.9%	78.1%	8.8 ms
Mobilenet_V1_0.50_160_quant	1.4 Mb	57.2%	80.5%	13.0 ms
Mobilenet_V1_0.50_192_quant	1.4 Mb	59.9%	82.1%	18.3 ms
Mobilenet_V1_0.50_224_quant	1.4 Mb	61.2%	83.2%	24.7 ms
Mobilenet_V1_0.75_128_quant	2.6 Mb	55.9%	79.1%	16.2 ms
Mobilenet_V1_0.75_160_quant	2.6 Mb	62.4%	83.7%	24.3 ms
Mobilenet_V1_0.75_192_quant	2.6 Mb	66.1%	86.2%	33.8 ms
Mobilenet_V1_0.75_224_quant	2.6 Mb	66.9%	86.9%	45.4 ms
Mobilenet_V1_1.0_128_quant	4.3 Mb	63.3%	84.1%	24.9 ms
Mobilenet_V1_1.0_160_quant	4.3 Mb	66.9%	86.7%	37.4 ms
Mobilenet_V1_1.0_192_quant	4.3 Mb	69.1%	88.1%	51.9 ms
Mobilenet_V1_1.0_224_quant	4.3 Mb	70.0%	89.0%	70.2 ms
Mobilenet_V2_1.0_224_quant	3.4 Mb	70.8%	89.9%	53.4 ms
Inception_V1_quant	6.4 Mb	70.1%	89.8%	154.5 ms
Inception_V2_quant	11 Mb	73.5%	91.4%	235.0 ms
Inception_V3_quant	23 Mb	77.5%	93.7%	637 ms
Inception_V4_quant	41 Mb	79.5%	93.9%	1250.8 ms

Figure 7: Space, accuracy, and performance trade-offs for various mobile models

MobileNet v1 is a quantized CNN model described in Benoit Jacob [2]. MobileNet V2 is an advanced model proposed by Google [3]. Online, you can also find floating-point models, which offer the best balance between model size and performance. Note that GPU acceleration requires the use of floating-point models. Note that recently AutoML models for mobile have been proposed based an automated **mobile neural architecture search (MNAS)** approach [4], beating the models handcrafted by humans.

We will discuss AutoML in *Chapter 14*, *An Introduction to AutoML*, and the interested reader can refer to MNAS documentation in the references [4] for applications to mobile.

Object detection

TensorFlow Lite comes with a pretrained model that can detect multiple objects within an image, with bounding boxes. 80 different classes of objects are recognized. The network is based on a pretrained quantized COCO SSD MobileNet v1 model. For each object, the model provides the class, the confidence of detection, and the vertices of the bounding boxes (https://www.tensorflow.org/lite/models/object_detection/overview).

Pose estimation

TensorFlow Lite includes a pretrained model for detecting parts of human bodies in an image or a video. For instance, it is possible to detect noses, left/right eyes, hips, ankles, and many other parts. Each detection comes with an associated confidence score (https://www.tensorflow.org/lite/models/pose_estimation/overview).

Smart reply

TensorFlow Lite has also a pretrained model for generating replies to chat messages. These replies are contextualized and similar to what is available on Gmail (https://www.tensorflow.org/lite/models/smart_reply/overview).

Segmentation

TensorFlow Lite has also a pretrained model (https://www.tensorflow.org/lite/models/segmentation/overview) for image segmentation, where the goal is to decide what the semantic labels (for example, person, dog, cat) assigned to every pixel in the input image are. Segmentation is based on the DeepLab algorithm [5].

Style transfer

TensorFlow Lite supports artistic style transfer (see *Chapter 5*, *Advanced Convolutional Neural Networks*) via a combination of a MobileNetV2-based neural network, which reduces the input style image to a 100-dimension style vector, and a style transform model, which applies the style vector to a content image to create the stylized image (https://www.tensorflow.org/lite/models/style_transfer/overview).

Text classification

TensorFlow Lite comes with a model for text classification and sentiment analysis (`https://www.tensorflow.org/lite/models/text_classification/overview`) trained on the Large Movie Review Dataset v1.0 (`http://ai.stanford.edu/~amaas/data/sentiment/`) with IMDb movie reviews that are positive or negative. An example of text classification is given in *Figure 8*:

Figure 8: An example of Text classification on Android with TensorFlow Lite

Question and answering

TensorFlow Lite also includes (`https://www.tensorflow.org/lite/models/bert_qa/overview`) a pretrained model for answering questions based on text fragments. The model is based on a compressed variant of BERT [6] (see *Chapter 7, Word Embeddings*) called MobileBERT [7], which runs 4x faster and has 4x smaller size. An example of Q&A is given in *Figure 9*:

Figure 9: An example of Q&A on Android with TensorFlow Lite and Bert

A note about using mobile GPUs

This section concludes the overview on pretrained models for mobile devices and IoT. Note that modern phones are equipped with internal GPUs. For instance, on Pixel 3, TensorFlow Lite GPU inference accelerates inference to 2–7x faster than CPUs for many models (see *Figure 10*, source: `https://medium.com/tensorflow/tensorflow-lite-now-faster-with-mobile-gpus-developer-preview-e15797e6dee7`):

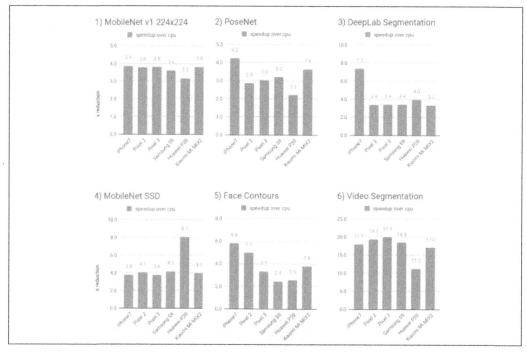

Figure 10: GPU speed-up over CPU for various learning models running on various phones

An overview of federated learning at the edge

As discussed, edge computing is a distributed computing model that brings computation and data closer to the location where it is needed.

Now, let's introduce **Federated Learning** (FL) [8] at the edge, starting with two use cases.

Suppose you built an app for playing music on mobile devices and then you want to add recommendation features aimed at helping users to discover new songs they might like. Is there a way to build a distributed model that leverages each user's experience without disclosing any private data?

Suppose you are a car manufacturer producing millions of cars connected via 5G networks, and then you want to build a distributed model for optimizing each car's fuel consumption. Is there a way to build such a model without disclosing the driving behavior of each user?

Traditional machine learning requires you to have a centralized repository for training data either on your desktop, or in your datacenter, or in the cloud. Federated learning pushes the training phase at the edge by distributing the computation among millions of mobile devices. These devices are ephemeral in that they are not always available for the learning process and they can disappear silently (for instance, a mobile phone can be switched off all of a sudden). The key idea is to leverage the CPUs and the GPU of each mobile phone that is made available for an FL computation. Each mobile device forming a part of a distributed FL training downloads a (pretrained) model from a central server and it performs local optimization based on the local training data collected on each specific mobile device. This process is similar to the transfer learning process (see *Chapter 5*, *Advanced Convolutional Neural Networks*), but it is distributed at the edge. Each locally updated model is then sent back by millions of edge devices to a central server to build an averaged shared model.

Of course, there are many issues to be considered. Let's review them:

1. **Battery usage**: Each mobile device that is part of an FL computation should save as much as possible on local battery usage.

2. **Encrypted communication**: Each mobile device belonging to an FL computation has to use encrypted communication with the central server to update the locally built model.

3. **Efficient communication**: Typically, deep learning models are optimized with optimization algorithms such as SGD (see *Chapter 1*, *Neural Network Foundations with TensorFlow 2.0*, and *Chapter 15*, *The Math Behind Deep Learning*). However, FL works with millions of devices and there is therefore a strong need to minimize the communication patterns. Google introduced a Federated Averaging algorithm [8], which is reported to reduce the amount of communication 10x-100x when compared with vanilla SGD. Plus, compression techniques [9] reduce the communication costs by an additional 100x with random rotations and quantization.

4. **Ensure user privacy**: This is probably the most important point. All local training data acquired at the edge must stay at the edge. This means that the training data acquired on a mobile device cannot be sent to a central server. Equally important, any user behavior learned in locally trained models must be anonymized so that it is not possible to understand any specific action performed by specific individuals.

Figure 11 shows a typical FL architecture (source [10]). An FL Server sends a model and a training plan to millions of devices. The training plan includes information on how frequently updates are expected and other metadata.

Each device runs the local training and sends a model update back to the global services. Note that each device has an FL runtime providing federated learning services to an app process that stores data in a local example store. The FL runtime fetches the training examples from the example store:

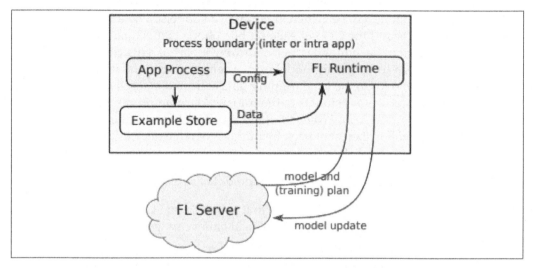

Figure 11: An example of federated learning architecture

TensorFlow FL APIs

The TensorFlow Federated (TTF) platform has two layers:

- **Federated learning (FL)**, a high-level interface that works well with `tf.keras` and non `tf.keras` models. In the majority of situations you will use this API for distributed training that is privacy preserving.

- **Federated core (FC)**, a low-level interface that is highly customizable and allows you to interact with low level communications and with federated algorithms. You will need this API only if you intend to implement new and sophisticated distributed learning algorithms. This topic is rather advanced, and we are not going to cover it in this book. If you wish to learn more, you can find more information online (`https://www.tensorflow.org/federated/federated_core`).

The FL API has three key parts:

1. **Models**: Used to wrap existing models for enabling federating learning. This can be achieved via the `tff.learning.from_keras_model()`, or via subclassing of `tff.learning.Model()`. For instance, you can have the following code fragment:

```
keras_model = …
keras_model.compile(...)
keras_federated_model = tff.learning.from_compiled_keras_
model(keras_model, ..)
```

2. **Builders**: This is the layer where the federated computation happens. There are two phases: compilation, where the learning algorithm is serialized into an abstract representation of the computation, and execution, where the represented computation is run.

3. **Datasets**: This is a large collection of data that can be used to simulate federated learning locally – a step useful for the initial fine tuning.

We conclude this overview by mentioning that you can find a detailed description (`https://www.tensorflow.org/federated/federated_learning`) of APIs online, and also a number of coding examples. The suggestion is to start by using the Colab notebook made available by Google (`https://colab.research.google.com/github/tensorflow/federated/blob/v0.10.1/docs/tutorials/federated_learning_for_image_classification.ipynb`). The framework allows us to simulate the distributed training before running it on a real environment. The library in charge of FL learning is `tensorflow_federated`. *Figure 12* discussed all the steps used in federated learning with multiple nodes, and it might be useful to better understand what has been discussed in this section. The next section will introduce TensorFlow.js, a variant of TensorFlow that can be used natively in JavaScript:

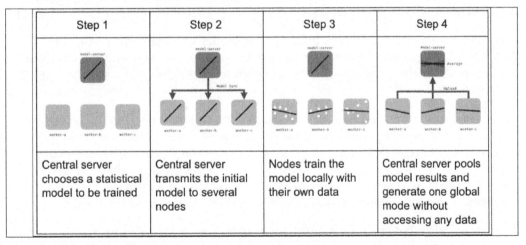

Step 1	Step 2	Step 3	Step 4
Central server chooses a statistical model to be trained	Central server transmits the initial model to several nodes	Nodes train the model locally with their own data	Central server pools model results and generate one global mode without accessing any data

Figure 12: An example of federated learning with multiple nodes (source: https://upload.wikimedia.org/wikipedia/commons/e/e2/Federated_learning_process_central_case.png)

TensorFlow.js

TensorFlow.js is a JavaScript library for machine learning models that can work either in vanilla mode or via Node.js. In this section we are going to review both of them.

Vanilla TensorFlow.js

TensorFlow.js is a JavaScript library for training and using **Machine Learning (ML)** models in a browser. It is derived from deeplearn.js, an open source, hardware-accelerated library for doing **Deep Learning (DL)** in JavaScript, and is now a companion library to TensorFlow.

The most common use of TensorFlow.js is to make pretrained ML/DL models available on the browser. This can help in situations where it may not be feasible to send client data back to the server due to network bandwidth or security concerns. However, TensorFlow.js is a full stack ML platform, and it is possible to build and train an ML/DL model from scratch, as well as fine-tune an existing pretrained model with new client data.

An example of a TensorFlow.js application is the TensorFlow Projector (`https://projector.tensorflow.org`), which allows a client to visualize their own data (as word vectors) in 3-dimensional space, using one of several dimensionality reduction algorithms provided. There are a few other examples of TensorFlow.js applications listed on the TensorFlow.js demo page (`https://www.tensorflow.org/js/demos`).

Similarly to TensorFlow, TensorFlow.js also provides two main APIs – the Ops API, which exposes low-level tensor operations such as matrix multiplication, and the Layers API, which exposes Keras-style high-level building blocks for neural networks.

At the time of writing, TensorFlow.js runs on three different backends. The fastest (and also the most complex) is the WebGL backend, which provides access to WebGL's low-level 3D graphics APIs and can take advantage of GPU hardware acceleration. The other popular backend is the Node.js backend, which allows the use of TensorFlow.js in server-side applications. Finally, as a fallback, there is the CPU-based implementation in plain JavaScript that will run in any browser.

In order to gain a better understanding of how to write a TensorFlow.js application, we will walk through an example of classifying MNIST digits using a **Convolutional Neural Network (CNN)** provided by the TensorFlow.js team (`https://storage.googleapis.com/tfjs-examples/mnist/dist/index.html`).

The steps here are similar to a normal supervised model development pipeline – load the data, define, train, and evaluate the model.

JavaScript works inside a browser environment, within an HTML page. The HTML file (named index.html) below represents this HTML page. Notice the two imports for TensorFlow.js (tf.min.js) and the TensorFlow.js visualization library (tfjs-vis.umd.min.js) – these provide library functions that we will use in our application. JavaScript code for our application comes from data.js and script.js files, located in the same directory as our index.html file:

```
<!DOCTYPE html>
<html>
<head>
  <meta charset="utf-8">
  <meta http-equiv="X-UA-Compatible" content="IE=edge">
  <meta name="viewport" content="width=device-width, initial-scale=1.0">

  <!-- Import TensorFlow.js -->
  <script src="https://cdn.jsdelivr.net/npm/@tensorflow/tfjs@1.0.0/
dist/tf.min.js"></script>
  <!-- Import tfjs-vis -->
  <script src="https://cdn.jsdelivr.net/npm/@tensorflow/tfjs-
vis@1.0.2/dist/tfjs-vis.umd.min.js"></script>

  <!-- Import the data file -->
  <script src="data.js" type="module"></script>
  <!-- Import the main script file -->
  <script src="script.js" type="module"></script>
</head>
<body>
</body>
</html>
```

For deployment, we will deploy these three files (index.html, data.js, and script.js) on a web server, but for development we can start a web server up by calling a simple one bundled with the Python distribution. This will start up a web server on port 8000 on localhost, and the index.html file can be rendered on the browser at http://localhost:8000:

python -m http.server

The next step is to load the data. Fortunately, Google provides a JavaScript script that we have called directly from our `index.html` file. It downloads the images and labels from GCP storage and returns shuffled and normalized batches of image and label pairs for training and testing. We can download this to the same folder as the `index.html` file using the following command:

```
wget https://raw.githubusercontent.com/tensorflow/tfjs-examples/master/
mnist-core/data.js
```

Model definition, training, and evaluation code is all specified inside the `script.js` file. The function to define and build the network is shown in the following code block. As you can see, it is very similar to the way you would build a sequential model with `tf.keras`. The only difference is the way you specify the arguments, as a dictionary of name-value pairs instead of a list of parameters. The model is a sequential model, that is, a list of layers. Finally, the model is compiled with the Adam optimizer:

```javascript
function getModel() {
  const IMAGE_WIDTH = 28;
  const IMAGE_HEIGHT = 28;
  const IMAGE_CHANNELS = 1;
  const NUM_OUTPUT_CLASSES = 10;

  const model = tf.sequential();
  model.add(tf.layers.conv2d({
    inputShape: [IMAGE_WIDTH, IMAGE_HEIGHT, IMAGE_CHANNELS],
    kernelSize: 5,
    filters: 8,
    strides: 1,
    activation: 'relu',
    kernelInitializer: 'varianceScaling'
  }));
  model.add(tf.layers.maxPooling2d({
    poolSize: [2, 2], strides: [2, 2]
  }));
  model.add(tf.layers.conv2d({
    kernelSize: 5,
    filters: 16,
    strides: 1,
    activation: 'relu',
    kernelInitializer: 'varianceScaling'
  }));
  model.add(tf.layers.maxPooling2d({
    poolSize: [2, 2], strides: [2, 2]
  }));
  model.add(tf.layers.flatten());
```

```
model.add(tf.layers.dense({
  units: NUM_OUTPUT_CLASSES,
  kernelInitializer: 'varianceScaling',
  activation: 'softmax'
}));

const optimizer = tf.train.adam();
model.compile({
  optimizer: optimizer,
  loss: 'categoricalCrossentropy',
  metrics: ['accuracy'],
});
return model;
}
```

The model is then trained for 10 epochs with batches from the training dataset and validated inline using batches from the test dataset. Best practice is to create a separate validation dataset from the training set. However, in order to keep our focus on the more important aspect of showing how to use TensorFlow.js to design an end-to-end DL pipeline, we are using the external `data.js` file provided by Google, which provides functions to return only a training and a test batch. In our example, we will use the test dataset for validation as well as evaluation later. This is likely to give us better accuracies compared to what we would have achieved with an unseen (during training) test set, but that is unimportant for an illustrative example such as this one:

```
async function train(model, data) {
  const metrics = ['loss', 'val_loss', 'acc', 'val_acc'];
  const container = {
    name: 'Model Training', styles: { height: '1000px' }
  };
  const fitCallbacks = tfvis.show.fitCallbacks(container, metrics);

  const BATCH_SIZE = 512;
  const TRAIN_DATA_SIZE = 5500;
  const TEST_DATA_SIZE = 1000;

  const [trainXs, trainYs] = tf.tidy(() => {
    const d = data.nextTrainBatch(TRAIN_DATA_SIZE);
    return [
      d.xs.reshape([TRAIN_DATA_SIZE, 28, 28, 1]),
      d.labels
    ];
  });
```

```
      const [testXs, testYs] = tf.tidy(() => {
        const d = data.nextTestBatch(TEST_DATA_SIZE);
        return [
          d.xs.reshape([TEST_DATA_SIZE, 28, 28, 1]),
          d.labels
        ];
      });

      return model.fit(trainXs, trainYs, {
        batchSize: BATCH_SIZE,
        validationData: [testXs, testYs],
        epochs: 10,
        shuffle: true,
        callbacks: fitCallbacks
      });
    }
```

Once the model finishes training, we want to make predictions and evaluate the model on its predictions. The following functions will do the predictions and compute the overall accuracy for each of the classes over all the test set examples, as well as produce a confusion matrix across all the test set samples:

```
    const classNames = [
      'Zero', 'One', 'Two', 'Three', 'Four',
      'Five', 'Six', 'Seven', 'Eight', 'Nine'];

    function doPrediction(model, data, testDataSize = 500) {
      const IMAGE_WIDTH = 28;
      const IMAGE_HEIGHT = 28;
      const testData = data.nextTestBatch(testDataSize);
      const testxs = testData.xs.reshape(
          [testDataSize, IMAGE_WIDTH, IMAGE_HEIGHT, 1]);
      const labels = testData.labels.argMax([-1]);
      const preds = model.predict(testxs).argMax([-1]);

      testxs.dispose();
      return [preds, labels];
    }

    async function showAccuracy(model, data) {
      const [preds, labels] = doPrediction(model, data);
      const classAccuracy = await tfvis.metrics.perClassAccuracy(
        labels, preds);
```

```
    const container = {name: 'Accuracy', tab: 'Evaluation'};
    tfvis.show.perClassAccuracy(container, classAccuracy, classNames);
    labels.dispose();
}

async function showConfusion(model, data) {
    const [preds, labels] = doPrediction(model, data);
    const confusionMatrix = await tfvis.metrics.confusionMatrix(
        labels, preds);
    const container = {name: 'Confusion Matrix', tab: 'Evaluation'};
    tfvis.render.confusionMatrix(
        container, {values: confusionMatrix}, classNames);
    labels.dispose();
}
```

Finally, the run() function will call all these functions in sequence to build an end-to-end ML pipeline:

```
import {MnistData} from './data.js';

async function run() {
    const data = new MnistData();
    await data.load();
    await showExamples(data);
    const model = getModel();
    tfvis.show.modelSummary({name: 'Model Architecture'}, model);
    await train(model, data);
    await showAccuracy(model, data);
    await showConfusion(model, data);
}

document.addEventListener('DOMContentLoaded', run);
```

Refreshing the browser location http://localhost:8000/index.html will invoke the run() method above. The table below shows the model architecture, and the plots below that show the progress of the training.

On the left are the loss and accuracy values on the validation dataset observed at the end of each batch, and on the right are the same loss and accuracy values observed on the training dataset (blue) and validation dataset (red) at the end of each epoch:

Model Architecture			
Layer Name	**Output Shape**	**# Of Params**	**Trainable**
conv2d_Conv2D1	[batch,24,24,8]	208	true
max_pooling2d_MaxPooling2D1	[batch,12,12,8]	0	true
conv2d_Conv2D2	[batch,8,8,16]	3,216	true
max_pooling2d_MaxPooling2D2	[batch,4,4,16]	0	true
flatten_Flatten1	[batch,256]	0	true
dense_Dense1	[batch,10]	2,570	true

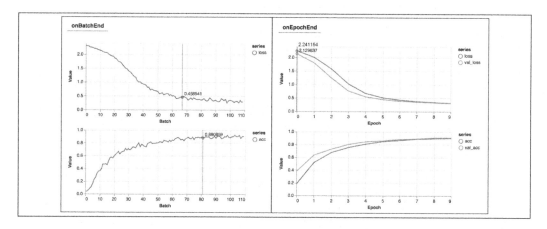

In addition, the following figure shows the accuracies across different classes for predictions from our trained model on the test dataset, as well as the confusion matrix of predicted versus actual classes for test dataset samples:

Accuracy

Class	Accuracy	# Samples
Zero	0.9636	55
One	0.9649	57
Two	0.9434	53
Three	0.9524	42
Four	0.9574	47
Five	0.7949	39
Six	0.902	51
Seven	0.9286	56
Eight	0.9038	52
Nine	0.8125	48

Confusion Matrix

label \ prediction	Class 0	Class 1	Class 2	Class 3	Class 4	Class 5	Class 6	Class 7	Class 8	Class 9
Class 0	51	0	0	0	0	0	1	0	0	0
Class 1	0	51	1	0	0	0	0	0	2	0
Class 2	0	0	42	0	0	0	0	0	3	0
Class 3	0	0	1	44	0	0	0	1	1	0
Class 4	0	0	0	0	44	0	0	0	0	2
Class 5	0	1	0	0	0	32	2	0	1	1
Class 6	0	0	0	0	1	0	47	0	0	0
Class 7	0	0	3	0	0	0	0	49	1	1
Class 8	1	0	0	1	2	0	0	1	42	0
Class 9	1	0	0	0	4	0	0	4	1	50

We have seen how to use TensorFlow.js within the browser. The next section will explain how to convert a model from Keras into TensorFlow.js.

Converting models

Sometimes it is convenient to convert a model that has already been created with `tf.keras`. This is very easy and can be done offline with the following command, which takes a Keras model from `/tmp/model.h5` and outputs a JavaScript model into `/tmp/tfjs_model`:

```
tensorflowjs_converter --input_format=keras /tmp/model.h5 /tmp/tfjs_model
```

The next section will explain how to use pretrained models in TensorFlow.js.

Pretrained models

TensorFlow.js comes with a significant number of pretrained models for deep learning with image, video, and text. The models are hosted on NPM, so it's very simple to use them if you are familiar with Node development.

The following table summarizes what is available as of November 2019 (source: `https://github.com/tensorflow/tfjs-models`):

Type	Model	Details	Install
Images	MobileNet (`https://github.com/tensorflow/tfjs-models/tree/master/mobilenet`)	Classify images with labels from the `ImageNet` database.	`npm i @tensorflow-models/mobilenet`
	PoseNet (`https://github.com/tensorflow/tfjs-models/tree/master/posenet`)	A machine learning model that allows for real-time human pose estimation in the browser; see a detailed description here: `https://medium.com/tensorflow/real-time-human-pose-estimation-in-the-browser-with-tensorflow-js-7dd0bc881cd5`.	`npm i @tensorflow-models/posenet`
	Coco SSD (`https://github.com/tensorflow/tfjs-models/tree/master/coco-ssd`)	Object detection model that aims to localize and identify multiple objects in a single image; based on the TensorFlow object detection API (`https://github.com/tensorflow/models/blob/master/research/object_detection/README.md`).	`npm i @tensorflow-models/coco-ssd`
	BodyPix (`https://github.com/tensorflow/tfjs-models/tree/master/body-pix`)	Real-time person and body-part segmentation in the browser using TensorFlow.js.	`npm i @tensorflow-models/body-pix`
	DeepLab v3 (`https://github.com/tensorflow/tfjs-models/tree/master/deeplab`)	Semantic segmentation	`npm i @tensorflow-models/deeplab`

Audio	Speech Commands (`https://github.com/tensorflow/tfjs-models/tree/master/speech-commands`)	Classify 1 second audio snippets from the speech commands dataset (`https://github.com/tensorflow/docs/blob/master/site/en/r1/tutorials/sequences/audio_recognition.md`).	`npm i @tensorflow-models/speech-commands`
Text	Universal Sentence Encoder (`https://github.com/tensorflow/tfjs-models/tree/master/universal-sentence-encoder`)	Encode text into a 512-dimensional embedding to be used as inputs to natural language processing tasks such as sentiment classification and textual similarity.	`npm i @tensorflow-models/universal-sentence-encoder`
	`Text Toxicity`	Score the perceived impact a comment might have on a conversation, from "Very toxic" to "Very healthy".	`npm i @tensorflow-models/toxicity`
General Utilities	KNN Classifier (`https://github.com/tensorflow/tfjs-models/tree/master/knn-classifier`)	This package provides a utility for creating a classifier using the K-nearest neighbors algorithm; it can be used for transfer learning.	`npm i @tensorflow-models/knn-classifier`

Each pretrained model can be directly used from HTML. For instance, this is an example with the KNN Classifier:

```html
<html>
  <head>
    <!-- Load TensorFlow.js -->
    <script src="https://cdn.jsdelivr.net/npm/@tensorflow/tfjs">
</script>
    <!-- Load MobileNet -->
    <script src="https://cdn.jsdelivr.net/npm/@tensorflow-models/
mobilenet"></script>
    <!-- Load KNN Classifier -->
    <script src="https://cdn.jsdelivr.net/npm/@tensorflow-models/knn-
```

```
classifier"></script>
  </head>
```

The next section will explain how to use pretrained models in Node.js.

Node.js

In this section we will give an overview of how to use TensorFlow with Node.js. Let's start:

The CPU package is imported with the following line of code, which will work for all Mac, Linux, and Windows platforms:

```
import * as tf from '@tensorflow/tfjs-node'
```

The GPU package is imported with the following line of code (as of November 2019 this will work only on a GPU in a CUDA environment):

```
import * as tf from '@tensorflow/tfjs-node-gpu'
```

An example of Node.js code for defining and compiling a simple dense model is reported below. The code is self-explanatory:

```
const model = tf.sequential();
model.add(tf.layers.dense({ units: 1, inputShape: [400] }));
model.compile({
  loss: 'meanSquaredError',
  optimizer: 'sgd',
  metrics: ['MAE']
});
```

Training can then start with the typical Node.js asynchronous invocation:

```
const xs = tf.randomUniform([10000, 400]);
const ys = tf.randomUniform([10000, 1]);
const valXs = tf.randomUniform([1000, 400]);
const valYs = tf.randomUniform([1000, 1]);

async function train() {
  await model.fit(xs, ys, {
    epochs: 100,
    validationData: [valXs, valYs],
  });
}
train();
```

In this section, we have discussed how to use TensorFlow.js with both vanilla JavaScript and with Node.js with sample applications for both the browser and for backend computation.

Summary

In this chapter we have discussed how to use TensorFlow Lite for mobile devices and IoT and deployed real applications on Android devices. Then, we also talked about Federated Learning for distributed learning across thousands (millions) of mobile devices, taking into account privacy concerns. The last section of the chapter was devoted to TensorFlow.js for using TensorFlow with vanilla JavaScript or with Node.js.

The next chapter is about AutoML, a set of techniques used to enable domain experts who are unfamiliar with machine learning technologies to use ML techniques easily.

References

1. *Quantization-aware training* https://github.com/tensorflow/tensorflow/tree/r1.13/tensorflow/contrib/quantize

2. *Quantization and Training of Neural Networks for Efficient Integer-Arithmetic-Only Inference*, Benoit Jacob, Skirmantas Kligys, Bo Chen, Menglong Zhu, Matthew Tang, Andrew Howard, Hartwig Adam, Dmitry Kalenichenko (Submitted on 15 Dec 2017); https://arxiv.org/abs/1712.05877

3. *MobileNetV2: Inverted Residuals and Linear Bottlenecks*, Mark Sandler, Andrew Howard, Menglong Zhu, Andrey Zhmoginov, Liang-Chieh Chen (Submitted on 13 Jan 2018 (v1), last revised 21 Mar 2019 (v4)) https://arxiv.org/abs/1806.08342

4. *MnasNet: Platform-Aware Neural Architecture Search for Mobile*, Mingxing Tan, Bo Chen, Ruoming Pang, Vijay Vasudevan, Mark Sandler, Andrew Howard, Quoc V. Le https://arxiv.org/abs/1807.11626

5. *DeepLab: Semantic Image Segmentation with Deep Convolutional Nets, Atrous Convolution, and Fully Connected CRFs*, Liang-Chieh Chen, George Papandreou, Iasonas Kokkinos, Kevin Murphy, and Alan L. Yuille, May 2017, https://arxiv.org/pdf/1606.00915.pdf

6. *BERT: Pre-training of Deep Bidirectional Transformers for Language Understanding*, Jacob Devlin, Ming-Wei Chang, Kenton Lee, Kristina Toutanova (Submitted on 11 Oct 2018 (v1), last revised 24 May 2019 v2)) https://arxiv.org/abs/1810.04805

7. *MOBILEBERT: TASK-AGNOSTIC COMPRESSION OF BERT BY PROGRESSIVE KNOWLEDGE TRANSFER,* Anonymous authors, Paper under double-blind review, `https://openreview.net/pdf?id=SJxjVaNKwB`, 25 Sep 2019 (modified: 25 Sep 2019)ICLR 2020 Conference Blind Submission Readers: Everyone

8. *Communication-Efficient Learning of Deep Networks from Decentralized Data,* H. Brendan McMahan, Eider Moore, Daniel Ramage, Seth Hampson, Blaise Agüera y Arcas (Submitted on 17 Feb 2016 (v1), last revised 28 Feb 2017 (this version, v3)) `https://arxiv.org/abs/1602.05629`

9. *Federated Learning: Strategies for Improving Communication Efficiency,* Jakub Konečný, H. Brendan McMahan, Felix X. Yu, Peter Richtárik, Ananda Theertha Suresh, Dave Bacon (Submitted on 18 Oct 2016 (v1), last revised 30 Oct 2017 (this version, v2)) `https://arxiv.org/abs/1610.05492`

10. *TOWARDS FEDERATED LEARNING AT SCALE: SYSTEM DESIGN,* Keith Bonawitz et al. 22 March 2019 `https://arxiv.org/pdf/1902.01046.pdf`

14

An introduction to AutoML

The goal of AutoML is to enable domain experts who are unfamiliar with machine learning technologies to use ML techniques easily.

In this chapter, we will go through a practical exercise using Google Cloud, and do quite a bit of hands-on work after briefly discussing the fundamentals. We will talk about automatic data preparation, automatic feature engineering, and automatic model generation. Then, we introduce AutoKeras and Cloud AutoML with its multiple solutions for Table, Vision, Text, Translation, and for Video processing.

What is AutoML?

During the previous chapters we have introduced several models used in modern machine learning and deep learning. For instance, we have seen architectures such as Dense networks, CNNs, RNNs, Autoencoders, and GANs.

Two observations are in order. First, these architectures are manually designed by deep learning experts, and are not necessarily easy to explain to non-experts. Second, the composition of these architectures themselves was a manual process, which involved a lot of human intuition and trial and error.

Today, one primary goal of artificial intelligence research is to achieve **Artificial General Intelligence (AGI)** – the intelligence of a machine that can understand and automatically learn any type of work or activity that a human being can do. However, the reality was very different before AutoML research and industrial applications started. Indeed, before AutoML, designing deep learning architectures was very similar to crafting – the activity or hobby of making decorative articles by hand.

Take for instance the task of recognizing breast cancer from X-rays. After reading the previous chapters, you will probably think that a deep learning pipeline created by composing several CNNs may be an appropriate tool for this purpose.

That is probably a good intuition to start with. The problem is that it is not easy to explain to the users of your model why a *particular* composition of CNNs works well within the breast cancer detection domain. Ideally, you want to provide easily accessible deep learning tools to the domain experts (in this case, medical professionals) without such a tool requiring a strong machine learning background.

The other problem is that it is not easy to understand whether or not there are variants (for example, different compositions) of the original manually crafted model that can achieve better results. Ideally, you want to provide deep learning tools for exploring the space of variants (for example, different compositions) in a more principled and automatic way.

So, the central idea of AutoML is to reduce the steep learning curve and the huge costs of handcrafting machine learning solutions by making the whole end-to-end machine learning pipeline more automated. To this end, we assume that the AutoML pipeline consists of three macro-steps: data preparation, feature engineering, and automatic model generation (see *Figure 1*). Throughout the initial part of this chapter, we are going to discuss these three steps in detail. Then, we will focus on Cloud AutoML:

Figure 1: Three steps of an AutoML pipeline

Achieving AutoML

How can AutoML achieve the goal of end-to-end automatization? Well, you are probably already guessing that a natural choice is to use machine learning – that's very cool – AutoML uses ML for automating ML pipelines.

What are the benefits? Automating the creation and tuning of the machine learning end-to-end offers produces simpler solutions, reduces the time to produce them, and ultimately might produce architectures that could potentially outperform the models that were crafted by hand.

Is this a closed research area? Quite the opposite. At the beginning of 2020, AutoML is a very open research field, which is not surprising, as the initial paper drawing attention to AutoML was published at the end of 2016.

Automatic data preparation

The first stage of a typical machine learning pipeline deals with data preparation (recall the pipeline of *Figure 1*). There are two main aspects that should be taken into account: data cleansing, and data synthesis.

Data cleansing is about improving the quality of data by checking for wrong data types, missing values, errors, and by applying data normalization, bucketization, scaling, and encoding. A robust AutoML pipeline should automate all of these mundane but extremely important steps as much as possible.

Data synthesis is about generating synthetic data via augmentation for training, evaluation, and validation. Normally, this step is domain-specific. For instance, we have seen how to generate synthetic CIFAR10-like images (*Chapter 4, Convolutional Neural Networks*) by using cropping, rotation, resizing, and flipping operations. One can also think about generate additional images or video via GANs (see *Chapter 6, Generative Adversarial Networks*) and using the augmented synthetic dataset for training. A different approach should be taken for text, where it is possible to train RNNs (*Chapter 9, Autoencoders*) to generate synthetic text or to adopt more NLP techniques such as BERT, seq2seq, or Transformers to annotate or translate text across languages and then translate back to the original one – another domain-specific form of augmentation.

A different approach is to generate synthetic environments where machine learning can occur. This became very popular in reinforcement learning and gaming, especially with toolkits such as OpenAI Gym, which aims to provide an easy-to-set-up simulation environment with a variety of different (gaming) scenarios.

Put simply, we can say that synthetic data generation is another option that should be provided by AutoML engines. Frequently, the tools used are very domain-specific and what works for image or video would not necessary work in other domains such as text. Therefore, we need a (quite) large set of tools for performing synthetic data generation across domains.

Automatic feature engineering

Featuring engineering is the second step of a typical machine learning pipeline (see *Figure 1*). It consists of three major steps: feature selection, feature construction, and feature mapping. Let's look at each of them in turn:

Feature selection aims at selecting a subset of *meaningful* features by discarding those that are providing little contribution to the learning task. In this context, meaningful is truly dependent on the application and the domain of your specific problem.

Feature construction has the goal of building new derived features, starting from the basic ones. Frequently, this technique is used to allow better generalization and to have a richer representation of the data.

Feature extraction aims at altering the original feature space by means of a mapping function. This can be implemented in multiple ways; for instance, it can use autoencoders (see *Chapter 9, Autoencoders*), PCA, or clustering (see *Chapter 10, Unsupervised Learning*).

In short, feature engineering is an art based on intuition, trial and error, and a lot of human experience. Modern AutoML engines aim to make the entire process more automated, requiring less human intervention.

Automatic model generation

Model generation and hyperparameter tuning is the typical third macro-step of a machine learning pipeline (see *Figure 1*).

Model generation consists of creating a suitable model for solving specific tasks. For instance, you will probably use CNNs for visual recognition, and you will use RNNs for either time series analysis or for sequences. Of course, many variants are possible, each of which is manually crafted through a process of trial and error, and works for very specific domains.

Hyperparameter tuning happens once the model is manually crafted. This process is generally very computationally expensive and can significantly change the quality of the results in a positive way. That's because tuning the hyperparameters can help to optimize our model further.

Automatic model generation is the ultimate goal of any AutoML pipeline. How can this be achieved? One approach consists in generating the model by combining a set of primitive operations including convolution, pooling, concatenation, skip connections, recurrent neural networks, autoencoders, and pretty much all the deep learning models we have encountered throughout this book. These operations constitute a (typically very large) search space to be explored, and the goal is to make this exploration as efficient as possible. In AutoML jargon, the exploration is called **NAS**, or **Neural Architecture Search**.

The seminal paper on AutoML [1] was produced in November 2016. The key idea (see *Figure 2*) is to use reinforcement learning (RL, see *Chapter 11, Reinforcement Learning*). An RNN acts as the controller and it generates the model descriptions of candidate neural networks. RL is used to maximize the expected accuracy of the generated architectures on a validation set.

On the CIFAR-10 dataset, this method, starting from scratch, designed a novel network architecture that rivals the best human-invented architecture in terms of test set accuracy. The CIFAR-10 model achieves a test error rate of 3.65, which is 0.09 percent better and 1.05x faster than the previous state-of-the-art model that used a similar architectural scheme. On the Penn Treebank dataset, the model can compose a novel recurrent cell that outperforms the widely used an LSTM cell (see *Chapter 9, Autoencoders*), and other state-of-the-art baselines. The cell achieves a test set perplexity of 62.4 on the Penn Treebank, which is 3.6 better than the previous state-of-the-art model.

The key outcome of the paper is shown in *Figure 2*. A controller network based on RNNs produces a sample architecture **A** with probability **p**. This candidate architecture **A** is trained by a child network to get a candidate accuracy **R**. Then a gradient of **p** is computed and scaled by **R** to update the controller. This reinforcement learning operation is computed in a cycle a number of times. The process of generating an architecture stops if the number of layers exceeds a certain value. The details of how a RL-based policy gradient method is used by the controller RNN to generate better architectures are in [1]. Here we emphasize the fact that NAS uses a meta-modeling algorithm based on Q-learning with $\epsilon - greedy$ exploration strategy and with experience replay (see *Chapter 11, Reinforcement Learning*) to explore the model search space:

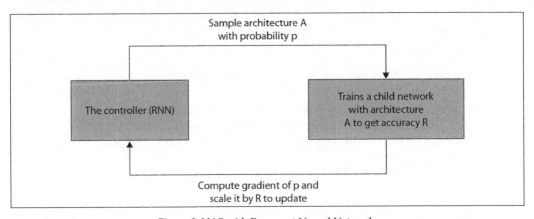

Figure 2: NAS with Recurrent Neural Networks

Since the original paper in late 2016, a Cambrian explosion of model generation techniques has been observed. Initially, the goal was to generate the entire model in one single step. Later, a *cell-based* approach has been proposed where the generation is divided into two macro-steps: first a cell structure is automatically built and then a predefined number of discovered cells are stacked together to generate an entire end-to-end architecture [2].

This **Efficient Neural Architecture Search (ENAS)** delivers strong empirical performance using significantly fewer GPU-hours compared with all existing automatic model design approaches, and notably, is 1000x less computationally expensive than standard Neural Architecture Search (in 2018). Here, the primary ENAS goal is to reduce the search space via hierarchical composition. Variants of the cell-based approach have been proposed, including pure hierarchical methods where higher-level cells are generated by incorporating lower-level cells iteratively.

Still considering NAS, a completely different idea is to use transfer learning (see *Chapter 5*, *Advanced Convolutional Neural Networks*) to transfer the learning of an existing neural network into a new neural network in order to speed up the design [3]. In other words, we want to use transfer learning in AutoML.

Another approach is based on **Genetic Programming (GP)** and **Evolutionary algorithms (EAs)** where the basic operations constituting the model search space are encoded into a suitable representation and then this encoding is gradually mutated to progressively better models in a way that resembles the genetic evolution of living beings [4].

Hyperparameter tuning consists of finding the optimal combination of hyperparameters both related to learning optimization (batch size, learning rate, and so on) and model-specific ones (kernel size; number of feature maps and so on for CNNs; number of neurons for dense or autoencoder networks, and so on). Again, the search space can be extremely large. There are two approaches generally used: grid search and random search.

Grid search divides the search space into a discrete grid of values and tests all the possible combinations in the grid. For instance, if there are three hyperparameters and a grid with only two candidate values for each of them, then a total of $2 \times 3 = 6$ combinations must be checked. There are also hierarchical variants of grid search, which progressively refine the grid for regions of the search space and provide better results. The key idea is to use a coarse grid first, and after finding a better grid region, implement a finer grid search on that region.

Random search performs a random sampling of the parameter search space, and this simple approach has been proven to work very well in many situations [5].

Now that we have briefly discussed the fundamentals we will do quite a bit of hands-on work on Google Cloud. Let's start.

AutoKeras

AutoKeras [6] provides functions to automatically search for the architecture and hyperparameters of deep learning models. The framework uses Bayesian optimization for efficient neural architecture search. You can install the alpha version by using `pip`:

```
pip3 install autokeras # for 0.4 version
pip3 install git+git://github.com/keras-team/autokeras@
master#egg=autokeras # for 1.0 version
```

The architecture is explained in *Figure 3* (taken from [6]):

1. The user calls the API

2. The searcher generates neural architectures on CPU

3. Real neural networks with parameters on RAM from the neural architectures

4. The neural network is copied to GPU for training

5. Trained neural networks are saved on storage devices

6. The searcher is updated based on the training results

Steps 2 to 6 will repeat until a time limit is reached:

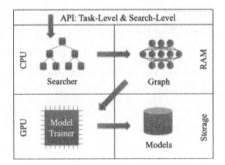

Figure 3: AutoKeras system overview

Google Cloud AutoML

Cloud AutoML (`https://cloud.google.com/automl/`) is a full suite of products for image, video, and text processing. As of the end of 2019, the suite consists of the following components, which do not require you to know how the deep learning networks are shaped internally:

AutoML Tables

- Enables you to automatically build and deploy state-of-the-art machine learning models on structured data used for general supervised classification and regression (see chapters 1, 2, and 3).

AutoML Vision

- **AutoML Vision**: Enables you to train machine learning models to classify your images according to your own defined labels.

- **AutoML Object Detection**: Used to automatically build a custom model to detect objects in an image with bounding boxes and labels, then deploy it to the cloud or on the edge.

AutoML Natural Language

- **AutoML Text Classification**: Used to automatically build a machine learning model to classify content into a custom set of categories.

- **AutoML Sentiment Analysis**: Used to automatically build a machine learning model to analyze the sentiment expressed within text.

- **AutoML Entity Extraction**: Used to automatically build a machine learning model to recognize a custom set of entities within text.

- **Cloud Natural Language API**: Use Google's proven pretrained model for general content classification, sentiment analysis, and entity recognition.

AutoML Video Intelligence

- **AutoML Video Intelligence Classification**: Used to automatically build a custom model to classify images, then deploy it to the cloud or on the edge.

AutoML Translation

- **AutoML Translation**: Build on top of Google's powerful Translation API with the words, phrases, and idioms that you need.

In the remainder of this chapter we will review five AutoML solutions: AutoML Tables, AutoML Vision, AutoML Text Classification, AutoML Translation, and AutoML Video Classification.

Using Cloud AutoML – Tables solution

Let's see an example of using Cloud AutoML Tables (see *Figure 4*). We'll aim to import some tabular data and train a classifier on that data; we'll use some marketing data from a bank. Note that this and the following examples might be charged by Google according to different usage criteria (please check online for latest cost estimations, at `https://cloud.google.com/products/calculator/`):

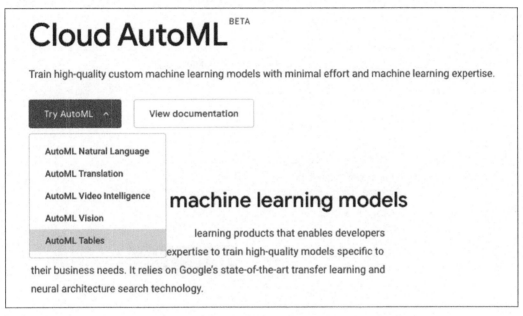

Figure 4: Google Cloud AutoML

As of the end of 2019, AutoML Tables is still in beta. Thus, we need to enable the beta API (see *Figure 5*):

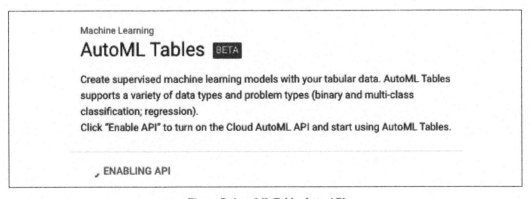

Figure 5: AutoML Tables beta API

Then, we can create a new dataset (see *Figure 6* and *7*) and import the data (see *Figure 8*):

Figure 6: AutoML Tables: the initial interface

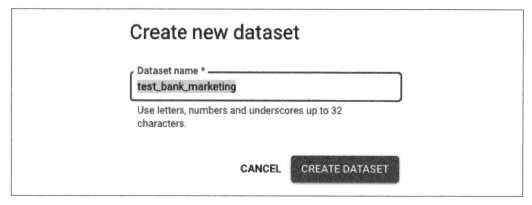

Figure 7: AutoML Tables: create a new dataset

For our example we use a demo dataset stored in Google Cloud storage inside the bucket `gs::://cloud-ml-tables-data/bank-marketing.csv`:

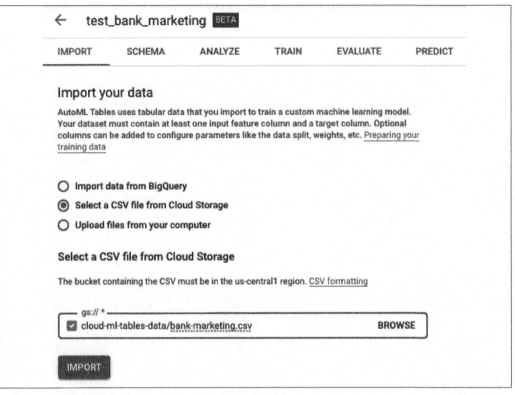

Figure 8: AutoML Tables: importing a csv dataset from cloud storage

Importing may require quite some time (see *Figure 9*):

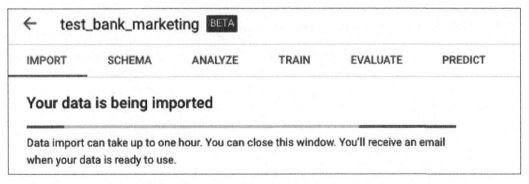

Figure 9: AutoML Tables – importing a CSV dataset

Once the data is imported, AutoML recognizes the type of each column (see *Figure 10*):

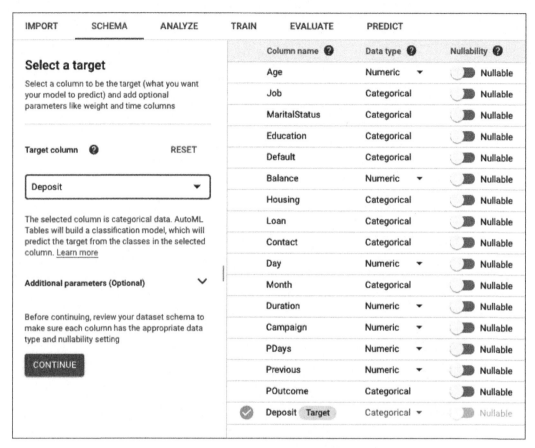

Figure 10: AutoML Tables: importing a CSV dataset

Let's select the target as the **Deposit** column. Since the selected column is categorical data, AutoML Tables will build a classification model. This will predict the target from the classes in the selected column. The classification is binary: 1 represents a negative outcome, meaning that a deposit is not made at the bank; 2 represents a positive outcome, meaning that a deposit is made at the bank.

The **ANALYZE** tab (see *Figure 11*) gives the opportunity to inspect the dataset with several metrics such as feature names, type, missing values, distinct values, invalid values, correlation with the target, mean, and standard deviation:

		Feature name ↑	Type	Missing ❓	Distinct values ❓	Invalid values ❓	Correlation with Target ❓	Mean ❓
All features	17	Age	Numeric	0% (0)	77	0	—	40.936
		Balance	Numeric	0% (0)	7,168	0	—	1,362.272
Numeric	7	Campaign	Numeric	0% (0)	48	0	—	2.764
		Contact	Categorical	0% (0)	3	0	—	—
Categorical	10	Day	Numeric	0% (0)	31	0	—	15.806
		Default	Categorical	0% (0)	2	0	—	—
		Deposit Target	Categorical	0% (0)	2	0	—	—
		Duration	Numeric	0% (0)	1,573	0	—	258.163
		Education	Categorical	0% (0)	4	0	—	—
		Housing	Categorical	0% (0)	2	0	—	—
		Job	Categorical	0% (0)	12	0	—	—
		Loan	Categorical	0% (0)	2	0	—	—
		MaritalStatus	Categorical	0% (0)	3	0	—	—
		Month	Categorical	0% (0)	12	0	—	—
		PDays	Numeric	0% (0)	559	0	—	40.198
		POutcome	Categorical	0% (0)	4	0	—	—
		Previous	Numeric	0% (0)	41	0	—	0.58

Rows per page: 50 ▼   1 – 17 of 17   ‹   ›

Figure 11: AutoML Tables: inspecting the dataset

It is now time to train the model by using the **TRAIN** tab (see *Figure 12*). In this example, we accept 1 hour as our training budget. During this time, you can go and take a coffee while AutoML works on your behalf (see *Figure 13*). The training budget is a number between 1 and 72 for the maximum number of node hours to spend training your model.

If your model stops improving before then, AutoML Tables will stop training and you'll only be charged the money corresponding to the actual node budget used:

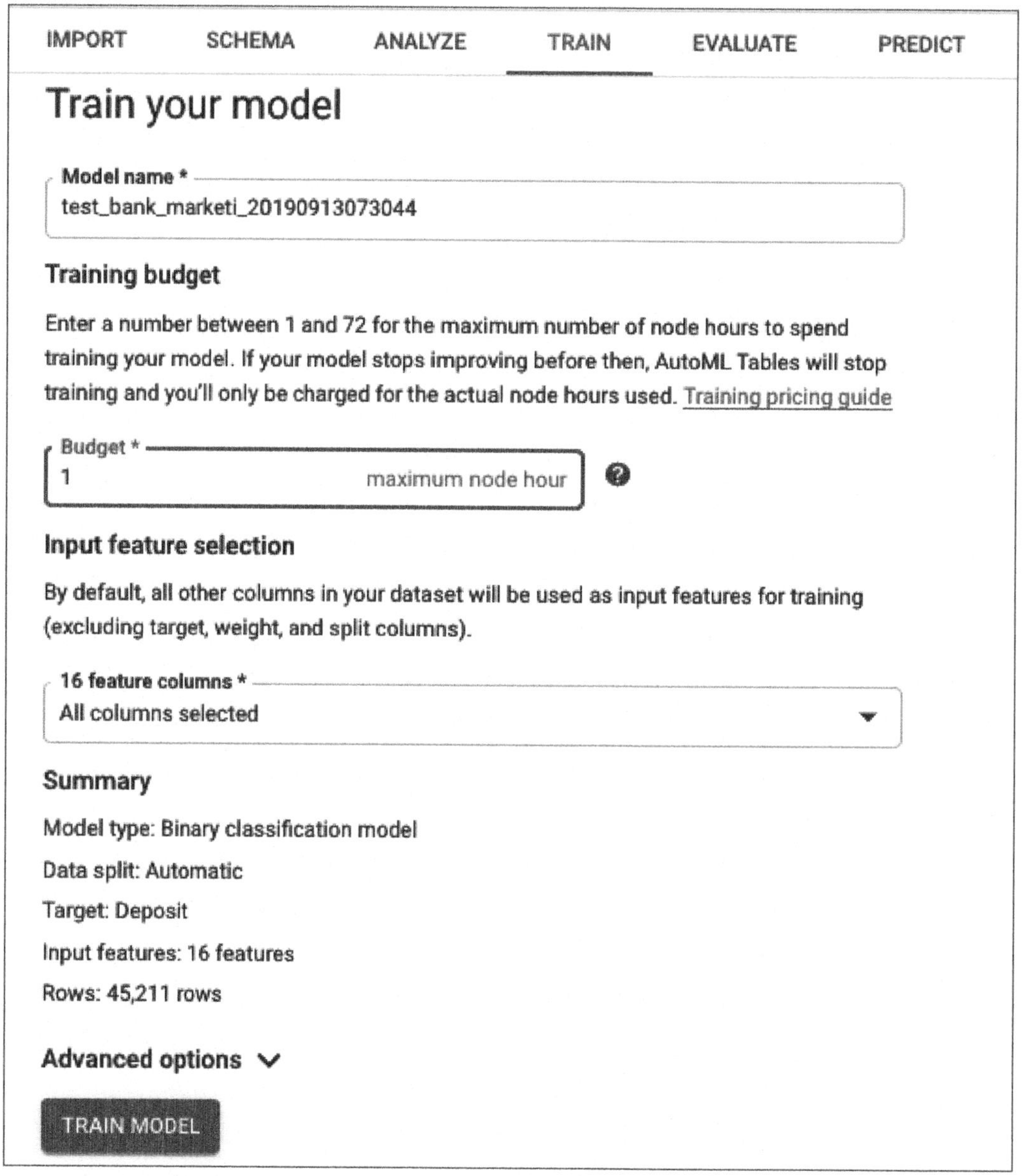

IMPORT   SCHEMA   ANALYZE   **TRAIN**   EVALUATE   PREDICT

Train your model

Model name *
test_bank_marketi_20190913073044

Training budget

Enter a number between 1 and 72 for the maximum number of node hours to spend training your model. If your model stops improving before then, AutoML Tables will stop training and you'll only be charged for the actual node hours used. Training pricing guide

Budget *
1   maximum node hour   ❓

Input feature selection

By default, all other columns in your dataset will be used as input features for training (excluding target, weight, and split columns).

16 feature columns *
All columns selected   ▼

Summary

Model type: Binary classification model

Data split: Automatic

Target: Deposit

Input features: 16 features

Rows: 45,211 rows

Advanced options ∨

TRAIN MODEL

Figure 12: AutoML Tables: preparing to train

Training a model costs around $20 per hour of compute resources, billed at the granularity of seconds.

This price includes the use of 92 n1-standard-4 equivalent machines in parallel. An initial six hours of free training are included:

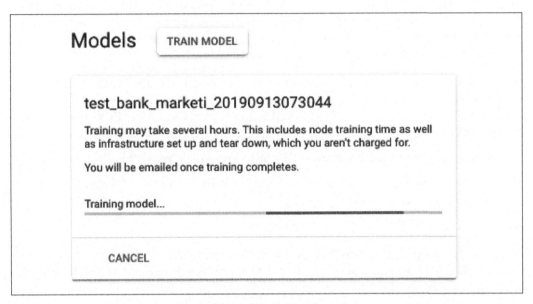

Figure 13: AutoML: training the model

After less than one hour, Google AutoML sent an email to my inbox (see *Figure 14*):

AutoML Tables finished training model "test_bank_marketi_20190913073044"

AutoML Tables <noreply-automl-tables@google.com>
to me ▾

Hello AutoML Tables Customer,

AutoML Tables finished training model "test_bank_marketi_20190913073044".
Additional Details:
Resource Name:
projects/655848112025/locations/us-central1/models/TBL5897749585064886272
Operation State: Succeeded

To continue your progress, go back to your model using
https://console.cloud.google.com/automl-tables/datasets/TBL8775197903233744896/train?project=655848112025

Sincerely,
The Google Cloud AI Team

Figure 14: AutoML Tables: training is concluded, and an email is sent to my account

Clicking on the suggested URL, it is possible to see the results of our training. The AutoML generated model reached an accuracy of 90% (see *Figure 15*). Remember that accuracy is the fraction of classification predictions produced by the model that were correct on a test set, which is held automatically. The log-loss (for example, the cross-entropy between the model predictions and the label values) is also provided. A lower value indicates a higher-quality model.

In addition, the **Area Under the Cover Receiver Operating Characteristic (AUC ROC)** curve is represented. This ranges from zero to one, and a higher value indicates a higher-quality model. This statistic summarizes a AUC ROC curve, which is a graph showing the performance of a classification model at all classification thresholds. The **True Positive Rate (TPR)** (also known as "recall") is: $TPR = \dfrac{TP}{TP + FN}$ where TP is the number of true positives and FN is the number of false negatives. The **False Positive Rate (FPR)** is: $FPR = \dfrac{FP}{FP + TN}$, where FP is the number of false positives and TN is the number of true negatives.

A ROC curve plots TPR versus FPR at different classification thresholds. In *Figure 15* you will see the **Area Under the Curve (AUC)** for one threshold of a ROC curve, whereas you can see the ROC curve itself in *Figure 17*.

It is possible to deep dive into the evaluation by accessing the evaluation tab and see additional information (see *Figure 16*) and access the confusion matrix (see *Figure 17*):

Figure 15: AutoML Tables: analyzing the results of our training

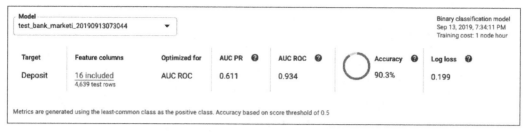

Figure 16: AutoML Tables: deep dive on the results of our training

Note that manually crafted models available in `https://www.kaggle.com/uciml/ adult-census-income/kernels` get to an accuracy of ~86-90%. Therefore, our model generated with AutoML is definitively a very good result!

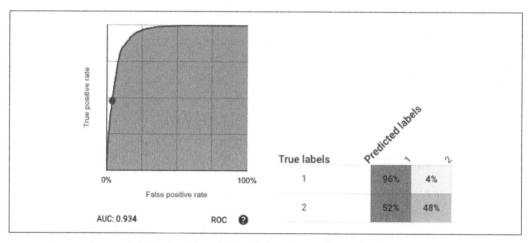

Figure 17: AutoML Tables: additional deep dive on the results of our training

If we are happy with our results, we can then deploy the model in production via the **PREDICT** tab (see *Figure 18*). Then it is possible to make online predictions of income by using a REST (`https://en.wikipedia.org/wiki/Representational_ state_transfer`) API, using this command for the example we're looking at in this chapter:

```
curl -X POST -H "Content-Type: application/json" \
  -H "Authorization: Bearer $(gcloud auth application-default print-
access-token)" \
https://automl.googleapis.com/v1beta1/projects/655848112025/locations/us-
central1/models/TBL5897749585064886272:predict \
  -d @request.json
```

You can use your command as generated by the console (see *Figure 19*) via JSON (see *Figure 20*):

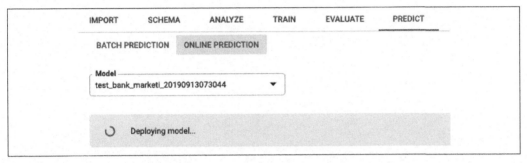

Figure 18: AutoML Tables: deploying in production

Execute the request

```
$ curl -X POST -H "Content-Type: application/json" \
    -H "Authorization: Bearer $(gcloud auth application-default prir
    https://automl.googleapis.com/v1beta1/projects/655848112025/loca
    -d @request.json
```

Figure 19: AutoML Tables: querying the deployed model in production

You can also predict via the web console (see *Figure 21*):

Access your model through a REST API

request.json

```
{
  "payload": {
    "row": {
      "values": [
        "39",
        "admin.",
        "married",
        "secondary",
        "no",
        "70",
        "yes",
        "no",
        "cellular",
        "31",
        "jul",
        "13",
        "11",
        "-1",
        "0",
        "unknown"
      ],
      "columnSpecIds": [
        "3086500662981165056",
        "8274647433711976448",
        "4815882919891435520",
        "204196901464047616",
        "5968804424498282496",
        "3230615851057020928",
        "7842301869484408832",
        "2077694346450173952",
        "4383537355663867904",
        "6689380364877561856",
        "8995223374091255808",
        "7121725929105129472",
        "2510039910677741568",
        "5392343672194859008",
        "7806576537674711104",
        "3662961415284588544"
      ]
    }
  }
}
```

Figure 20: AutoML Table: accessing the deployed model via REST API and JSON

IMPORT	SCHEMA	ANALYZE	TRAIN	EVALUATE	PREDICT

Predict label

Deposit

Prediction result

1
———————— Confidence score: 0.999

2
————————— Confidence score: 0.001

Feature column name	Data type	Status ↓	Value
Age	Numeric	Required	39
Balance	Numeric	Required	70
Campaign	Numeric	Required	11
Contact	Categorical	Required	cellular
Day	Numeric	Required	31
Default	Categorical	Required	no
Duration	Numeric	Required	13
Education	Categorical	Required	secondary
Housing	Categorical	Required	yes
Job	Categorical	Required	admin.

Rows per page: 10 ▼   1 – 10 of 16   ⟨ ⟩

PREDICT   RESET

Figure 21: AutoML Table: predicting deposit via the web console

Put simply, we can say that Google Cloud ML is very focused on simplicity of use and efficiency for AutoML. Let's summarize the main steps required (see *Figure 22*):

1. The dataset is imported
2. Your dataset schema and labels are defined
3. The input features are automatically recognized
4. AutoML performs the magic by automatically doing feature engineering, creating a model, and tuning the hyperparameters
5. The automatically built model can then be evaluated
6. The model is then deployed in production

Of course, it is possible to repeat in cycle 2-6 by changing the schema and the definition of the labels:

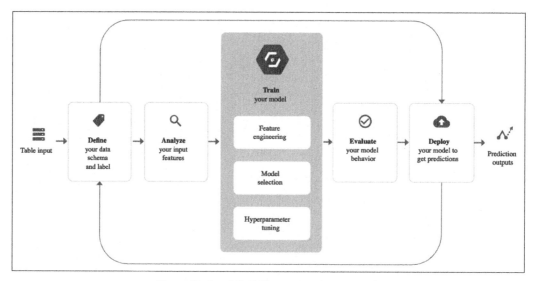

Figure 22: AutoML Table – main steps required

In this section we have seen an example of AutoML focused on easy of use and efficiency. The progress made is shown in Faes et al. [7], quoting the paper:

> *"We show, to our knowledge, a first of its kind automated design and implementation of deep learning models for health-care application by non-AI experts, namely physicians. Although comparable performance to expert-tuned medical image classification algorithms was obtained in internal validations of binary and multiple classification tasks, more complex challenges, such as multilabel classification, and external validation of these models was insufficient.*

We believe that AI might advance medical care by improving efficiency of triage to subspecialists and the personalisation of medicine through tailored prediction models. The automated approach to prediction model design improves access to this technology, thus facilitating engagement by the medical community and providing a medium through which clinicians can enhance their understanding of the advantages and potential pitfalls of AI integration."

In this case Cloud AutoML Vision has been used. So, let's look at an example.

Using Cloud AutoML – Vision solution

For this example, we are going to use the code made by Ekaba Bisong and available as open source under the MIT License (`https://github.com/dvdbisong/automl-medical-image-classification/blob/master/LICENSE`). Here the task is to classify images:

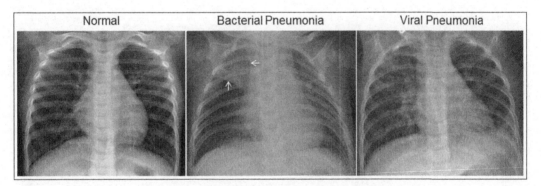

Figure 23: Lung chest X-rays

This type of classification requires expert knowledge when performed by humans. Using language typical of clinicians who are specialized in analyzing chest X-rays: "The normal chest X-ray (left panel) shows clear lungs with no areas of abnormal opacification. Bacterial pneumonia (middle) typically exhibits a focal lobar consolidation, in this case in the right upper lobe (see arrows), whereas viral pneumonia (right) manifests with a more diffuse "interstitial" pattern in both lungs". (Source: Kermany, D. S., Goldbaum M., et al. 2018. Identifying Medical Diagnoses and Treatable Diseases by Image-Based Deep Learning. Cell. `https://www.cell.com/cell/fulltext/S0092-8674(18)30154-5`)

Let's start. The first step is to activate the Image Classification option under AutoML Vision (see *Figure 24*):

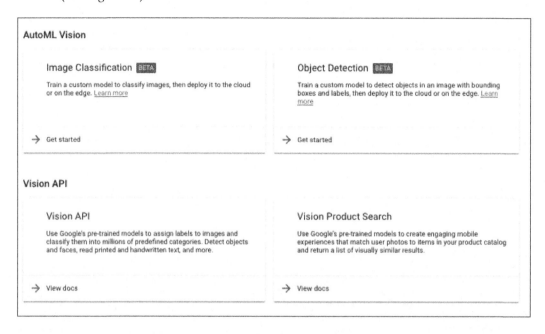

Figure 24: AutoML Vision – Image Classification

We can now create a new dataset (see *Figure 25*):

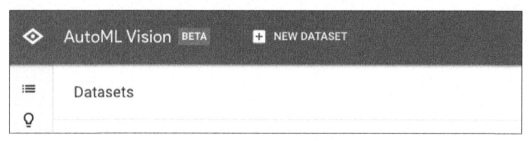

Figure 25: AutoML Vision – creating a new dataset

The dataset contains:

- 5,232 chest X-ray images from children
- 3,883 are samples of bacterial (2,538) and viral (1,345) pneumonia
- 1,349 samples are healthy lung X-ray images

The dataset is hosted on Kaggle, a web site dedicated to machine learning where people can compete in creating ML models shared with the community. The dataset can be accessed at `https://www.kaggle.com/paultimothymooney/chest-xray-pneumonia`. So, we need to get the dataset from Kaggle. Let's activate Cloud Shell from the upper-right corner of Google Cloud Console (see *Figure 26*):

Figure 26: AutoML Vision – activating Cloud Shell

Then, we can install Kaggle with pip (see *Figure 27*):

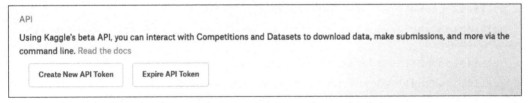

Figure 27: AutoML Vision - getting Kaggle data

```
sudo pip install kaggle
```

Now, we need to generate a token from Kaggle, which can be done by accessing `https://www.kaggle.com/<YourLogin>/account` (see *Figure 28*):

API

Using Kaggle's beta API, you can interact with Competitions and Datasets to download data, make submissions, and more via the command line. Read the docs

Create New API Token   **Expire API Token**

Figure 28: Kaggle – creating a new Kaggle API token

The token can be now uploaded on the cloud ephemeral VM via the console (see *Figure 29*):

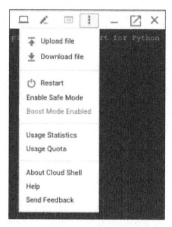

Figure 29: Kaggle – uploading the Kaggle token

Move the uploaded `kaggle.json` key to the directory. Download the dataset from Kaggle to Google Cloud Storage, unzip the archives, and move to a **Google Cloud Platform (GCP)** bucket, with the following commands:

 Instructions for creating cloud storage can be found at `https://cloud.google.com/storage/docs/quickstart-console`.

```
a_gulli@cloudshell:~$ mv kaggle.json .kaggle/

a_gulli@cloudshell:~$ kaggle datasets download paultimothymooney/chest-xray-pneumonia

a_gulli@cloudshell:~$ unzip chest-xray-pneumonia.zip

a_gulli@cloudshell:~$ unzip chest_xray.zip

a_gulli@cloudshell:~$ gsutil -m cp -r chest_xray gs://authentica-de791-vcm/chestXrays
```

Now we can create a new dataset for the visual training. We need a list of images on Google storage where each image is annotated with a label, as in the following example:

```
['gs://authentica-de791-vcm/chestXrays/train/NORMAL/IM-0115-0001.
jpeg', 'NORMAL']
['gs://authentica-de791-vcm/chestXrays/train/NORMAL/IM-0117-0001.
jpeg', 'NORMAL']
```

The first thing is to create a new notebook (see *Figure 30*):

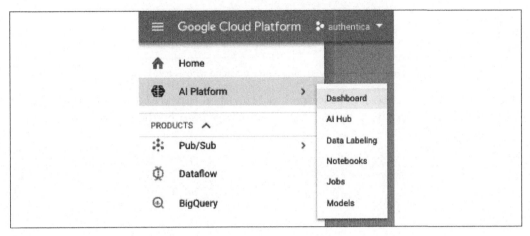

Figure 30: GCP – creating a new notebook

Then a new instance with TensorFlow 2.0 (see *Figure 31*):

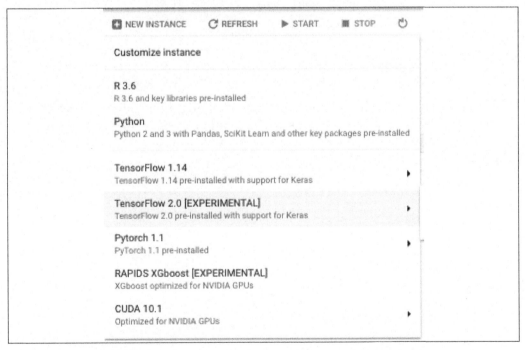

Figure 31: GCP – creating a new notebook instance with TensorFlow 2.0

This will create a new machine (see *Figure 32*):

Figure 32: GCP – provisioning a new machine with TensorFlow 2.0

Once the machine has been provisioned, we can open Jupyter Notebook (see *Figure 33*) and clone the repository by clicking the link provided by the environment in the UI (see *Figure 34*):

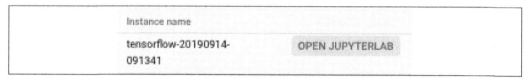

Figure 33: GCP – opening JupyterLab

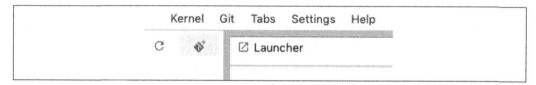

Figure 34: JupyterLab – cloning a Git repo by using the icon in grey

We can now preprocess all the images in our bucket by running all the cells in the notebook (see *Figure 35*). The notebook will help preprocessing them. Make sure that you customize the notebook to take into account your data paths, and GCP buckets:

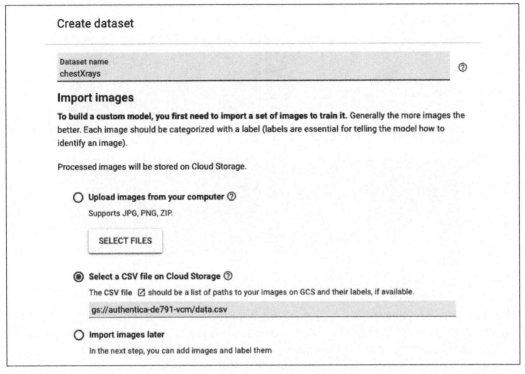

Figure 35: AutoML Vision – importing the dataset

It will take a while to import the data (see *Figure 36*). When concluded, an email is sent, and it is possible to browse the images (see *Figure 37*):

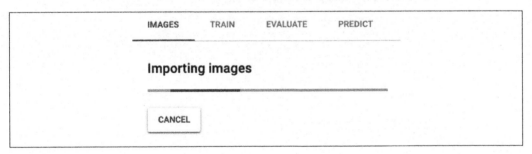

Figure 36: AutoML Vision – importing images

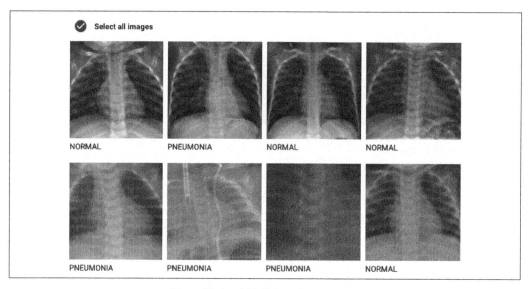

Figure 37: AutoML Vision – lung images

The next step is to start training (see *Figure 38*). Since at least 100 images are currently assigned to each label, there are enough images to start training. Images will be automatically split into training and test sets, so that it's possible to evaluate the model's performance. Unlabeled images will not be used:

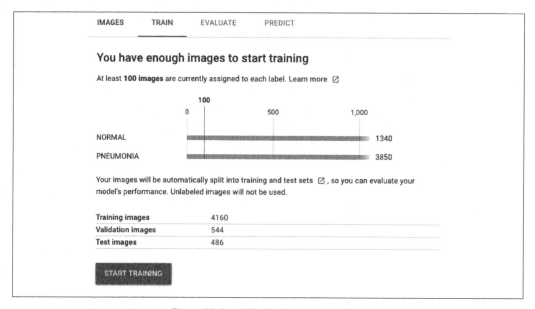

Figure 38: AutoML Vision – start training

There are two options: either the model is hosted in the cloud or it is optimized to run on the **Edge** (see *Figure 39*):

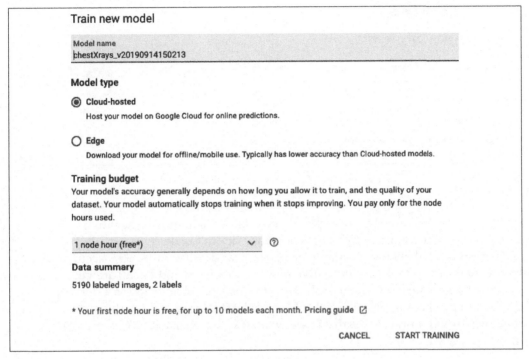

Figure 39: AutoML Vision – preparing to train the model

Training can take up from 15 minutes to several hours (see *Figure 40*):

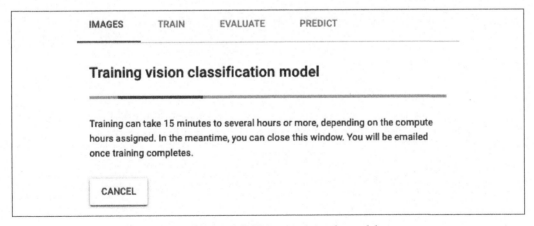

Figure 40: AutoML Vision – training the model

At the end we will receive an email and we can access the results (see *Figure 41*):

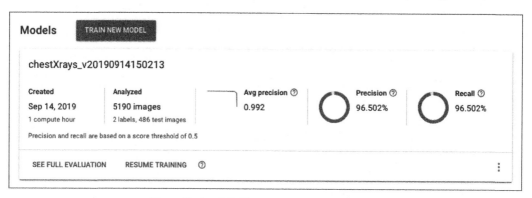

Figure 41: AutoML Vision – evaluating the results

When a particular problem includes an imbalanced dataset, accuracy isn't a good metric to look for. For example, if your dataset contains 95 negatives and 5 positives, having a model with 95% accuracy doesn't make sense at all. The classifier might label every example as negative and still achieve 95% accuracy. Hence, we need to look for alternative metrics. Precision and Recall are very good metrics to deal with such problems. It is also possible to access a detailed evaluation by clicking the **SEE FULL EVALUATION** link and see the precision, the **Precision@1**, and the **Recall@1** (see *Figure 42*) together with the confusion matrix (see *Figure 43*):

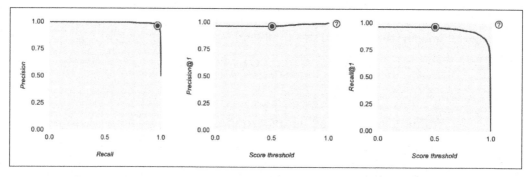

Figure 42: AutoML Vision – evaluating the results: Precision, Precision@1, Recall@1

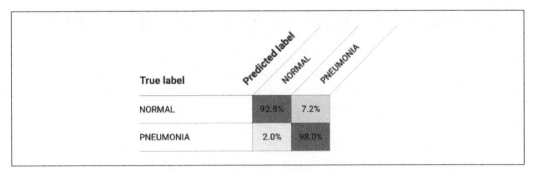

Figure 43: AutoML Vision – evaluating the results: confusion matrix

Note that again, the AutoML generated model is comparable or even better than the models manually crafted at the end of 2019. Indeed, the best model (`https://www.kaggle.com/aakashnain/beating-everything-with-depthwise-convolution`) available at the end of 2019 reached a recall of 0.98 and a precision of 0.79 (see *Figure 44*):

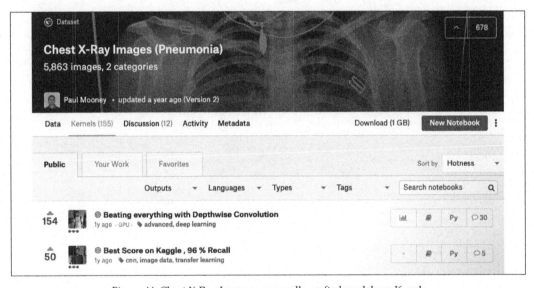

Figure 44: Chest X-Ray Images – manually crafted models on Kaggle

Using Cloud AutoML – Text Classification solution

In this section we are going to build a classifier using AutoML. Let's activate the text classification solution via `https://console.cloud.google.com/natural-language/` (see *Figure 45* and *46*):

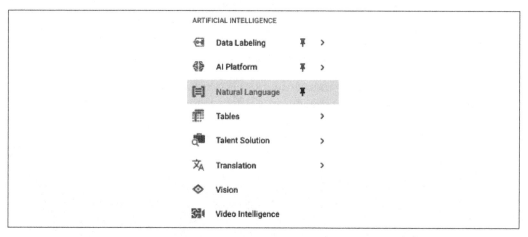

Figure 45: AutoML Text Classification – accessing the natural language interface

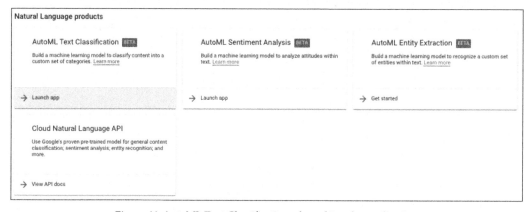

Figure 46: AutoML Text Classification – launching the application

We are going to use a dataset already available online (`https://cloud.google.com/natural-language/automl/docs/sample/happiness.csv`), load it into a dataset named "happiness," and perform a single-label classification (see *Figure 47*). The file is uploaded from my computer (see *Figure 48*):

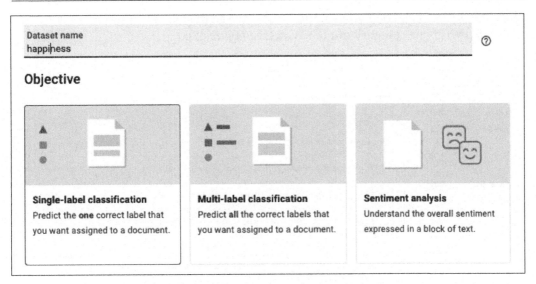

Figure 47: AutoML Text Classification – creating the dataset

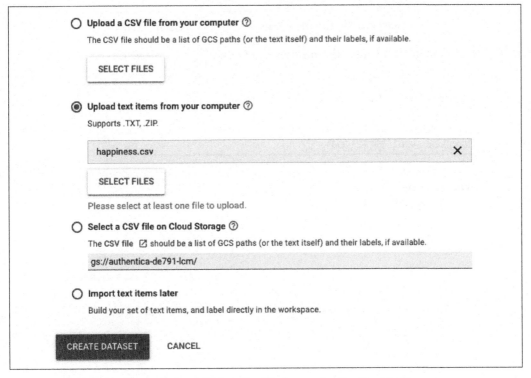

Figure 48: AutoML Text Classification – uploading the dataset

Once the dataset is loaded you should be able to see that each text fragment is annotated with one category out of seven (see *Figure 49*):

TEXT ITEMS	TRAIN	EVALUATE	PREDICT	

All texts	12663		Type to filter text items...	
Labeled	12663		**Text**	**Label**
Unlabeled	0			
		☐	I finished all of my work by the end of the day.	achievement
☐ Type to filter... ⋮		☐	An event that made me happy in the past 24 hours is getting free breakfast.	enjoy_the_moment
achievement	3931	☐	When I managed to get my custom PC up and running for the first time.	achievement
affection	4337			
bonding	1584	☐	My mother flew out of town to visit our family in KS. I was so happy to see her off on the plane and I could feel the joy she must have felt upon her way out there.	affection
enjoy_the_moment	1380			
exercise	196	☐ ›	Nowadays, happiness is a fuzzy concept and can mean many different things to many people. Part of the challenge of a science of happiness is to identify different concepts o...	enjoy_the_moment
leisure	986			
nature	249	☐	I was given a free dessert at a restaurant.	enjoy_the_moment
Add label		☐	I was nominated for an award.	achievement

Figure 49: AutoML Text Classification - sample of text and categories

It is now time to start training the model (see *Figure 50, 51,* and *52*):

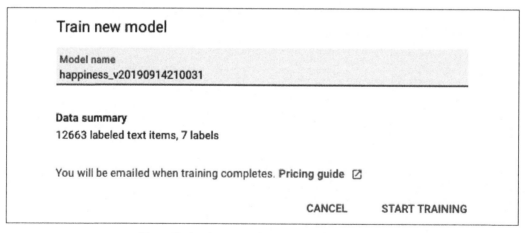

Figure 50: AutoML Text Classification – start training

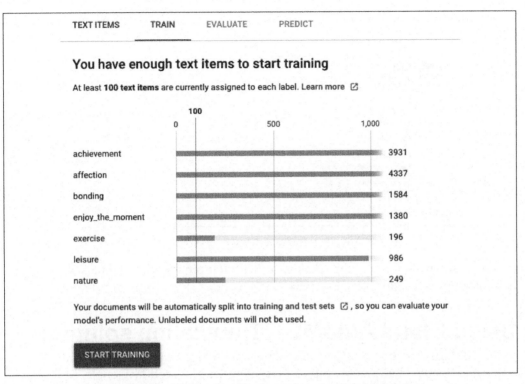

Figure 51: AutoML Text Classification – summary of label distribution

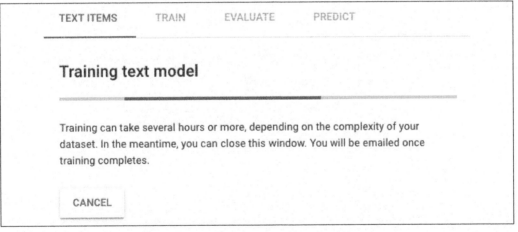

Figure 52: AutoML Text Classification – training a new model

At the end, the model is built and it achieves a good precision of 87.6% and recall of 84.1% (see *Figure 53*):

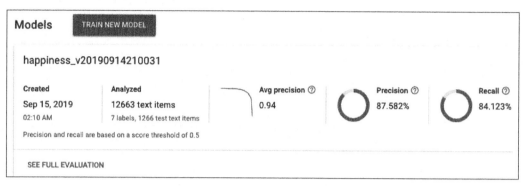

Figure 53: AutoML Text Classification – precision and recall

If you are interested in playing some more with happiness-related datasets, I suggest having a look at Kaggle: `https://www.kaggle.com/ritresearch/happydb`.

Using Cloud AutoML – Translation solution

In this solution, we are going to auto-create a model for translating text from English to Spanish built on the top of a large model provided by Google as the base.

As usual, the first step is to activate the solution (see *Figure 54*) and then create a dataset (see *Figure 55*):

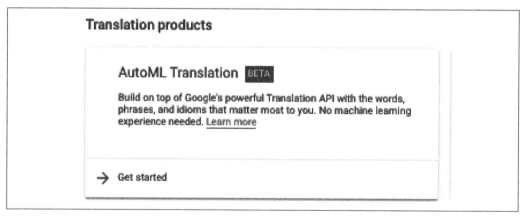

Figure 54: AutoML Text Translation – accessing the solution

Figure 55: AutoML Text Translation – creating a new dataset

For this simple example, we use a sample already available in `https://cloud.google.com/translate/automl/docs/sample/automl-translation-data.zip` and extract the file `en-es.tsv` from the archive. You should be able to see a few examples like the following:

```
Make sure all words are spelled correctly.    Comprueba que todas las
palabras están escritas correctamente.
Click for video information    Haz clic para ver la información en
vídeo
Click for product information    Haz clic para ver la información
sobre el producto
Check website for latest pricing and availability.    Accede al sitio
web para consultar la disponibilidad y el precio más reciente.
Tap and hold to copy link    Mantén pulsado el enlace para copiarlo
Tap to copy link    Toca para copiar el enlace
```

Then, you can create the dataset and select the source and the target language (see *Figure 56*):

Figure 56: AutoML Text Translation – choosing the language

As the next step, you can upload the training file (see *Figure 57*) and wait until the data is in (*Figure 58*):

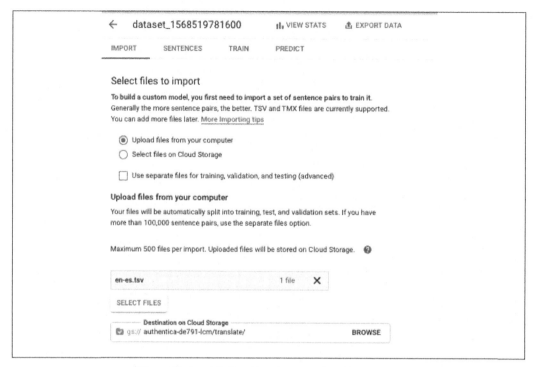

Figure 57: AutoML Text Translation – select files to train

Figure 58: AutoML Text Translation – examples of sentences

Next, choose a base model from which to start (see *Figure 59*). As of late 2019, there is only one base model available, named **Google Neural Machine Translation (Google NMT)**. This is the model used in production by Google for online translation. Now, you can start training (see *Figure 60*):

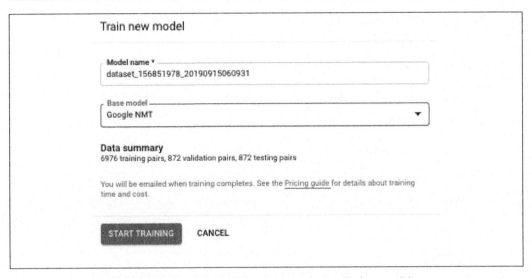

Figure 59: AutoML Text Translation – selecting the base model

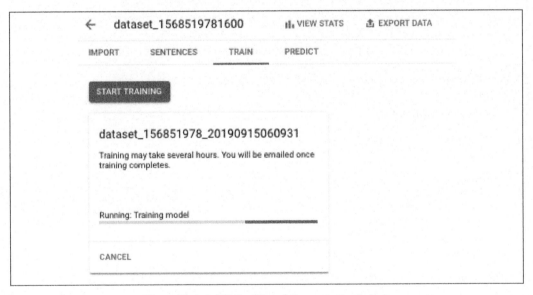

Figure 60: AutoML Text Translation – starting to train

Once the model is trained, we can use it and compare the results against the Google base model (see *Figure 61*):

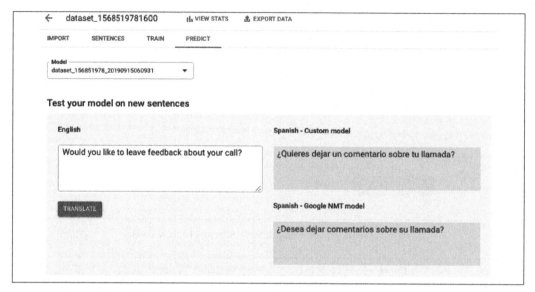

Figure 61: AutoML Text Translation – compare the Custom model and Google NMT model

The results are also accessible via a REST API (see *Figure 62*):

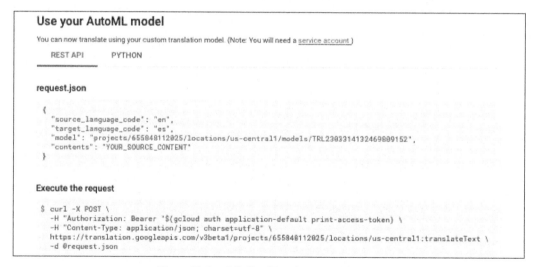

Figure 62: AutoML Text Translation – REST API

Using Cloud AutoML – Video Intelligence Classification solution

In this solution, we are going to automatically build a new model for video classification. The intent is to be able to sort different video segments into various categories (or classes) based on their content. The first step is to activate the solution (see *Figure 63*) and load a dataset (*Figure 64, 65,* and *66*). We are going to use a collection of about 5,000 videos available in a demo already stored in a GCP bucket on `gs://automl-video-demo-data/hmdb_split1_40_mp4.csv`:

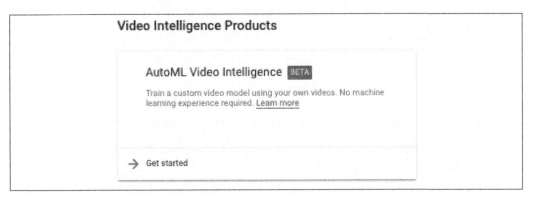

Figure 63: AutoML Video Intelligence – activating the solution

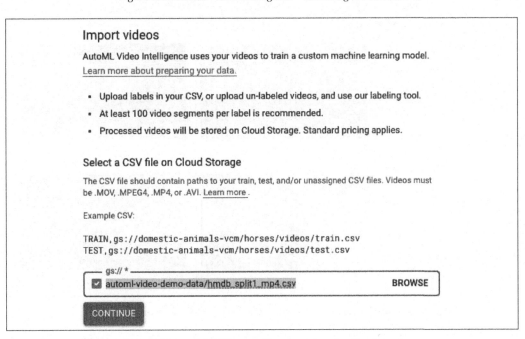

Figure 64: AutoML Video Intelligence – choosing the dataset

Figure 65: AutoML Video intelligence – starting to load the dataset

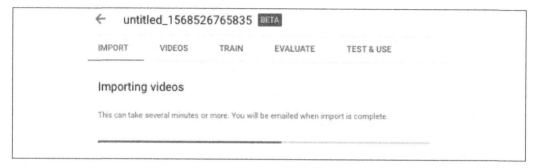

Figure 66: AutoML Video Intelligence – importing the videos

Once the videos are imported you should be able to preview them with their associated categories (see *Figure 67*):

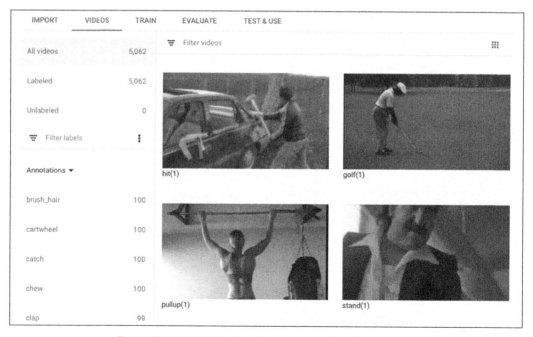

Figure 67: AutoML Video Intelligence – imported video preview

We can now start to build a model. In this case, the solution is warning that we don't have enough videos in some categories, and it is asking whether or not we want to add more videos. Let's ignore the warning for now (see *Figure 68*):

IMPORT	VIDEOS	TRAIN	EVALUATE	TEST & USE

Add more video segments before training

It is recommended that each label have at least 100 video segments assigned to it. Fewer video segments can result in an inaccurate model. Learn more To add more video segments, return to the Videos page.

Labels	Video segments		Train	Test
brush_hair		100	70	30
cartwheel		100	70	30
catch		100	70	30
chew		100	70	30
clap		99	70	29
climb		97	70	27
climb_stairs		100	70	30
dive		100	70	30
draw_sword		100	70	30

Figure 68: AutoML Video Intelligence – warning to get more videos

Now we can start training (see *Figure 69* and *70*):

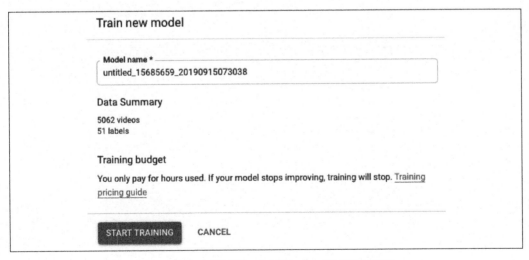

Train new model

Model name *
untitled_15685659_20190915073038

Data Summary

5062 videos
51 labels

Training budget

You only pay for hours used. If your model stops improving, training will stop. Training pricing guide

START TRAINING   CANCEL

Figure 69: AutoML Video Intelligence – starting to train

Once the model is trained you can access the results from the console (*Figure 68*). In this case we achieved a precision of 81.18% and a recall of 76.65%. You can play with the model, for instance increasing the number of labeled videos available, to see how the performance will change:

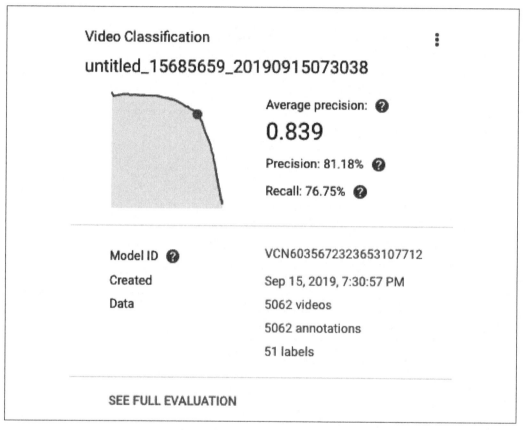

Figure 70: AutoML Video Intelligence – evaluating the results

Let's have a detailed look at the results via the **EVALUATE** tab. For instance, we can analyze the precision/recall graph for different levels of threshold (see *Figure 71*) and the confusion matrix showing examples of wrong classification of shots (see *Figure 72*):

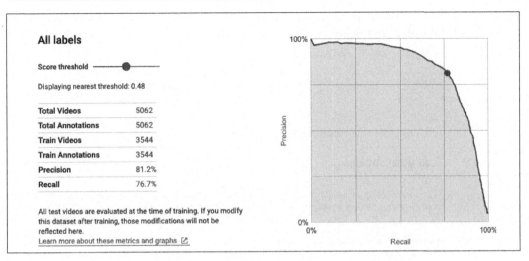

Figure 71: AutoML Video Intelligence – precision and recall

Confusion matrix

This table helps you understand where misclassifications occur (which labels get "confused" with each other). The top three misclassifications per label are shown here.

True Label ↑	Correct Prediction	Confused with...		
brush_hair	90%	wave : 6.67%	sit : 3.33%	
cartwheel	86.67%	flic_flac : 10%	handstand : 3.33%	
catch	96.67%	jump : 3.33%		
chew	90%	drink : 6.67%	eat : 3.33%	
clap	89.66%	throw : 6.9%	pick : 3.45%	
climb	100%			
climb_stairs	73.33%	run : 13.33%	walk : 6.67%	climb : 3.33%
dive	76.67%	climb : 10%	fall_floor : 6.67%	somersault : 3.33%

Figure 72: AutoML Video Intelligence – confusion matrix

We can also test the predictions of the model that was just created. In this case, we use a demo dataset available at `gs://automl-video-demo-data/hmdb_split1_test_gs_predict.csv` (see *Figure 73*):

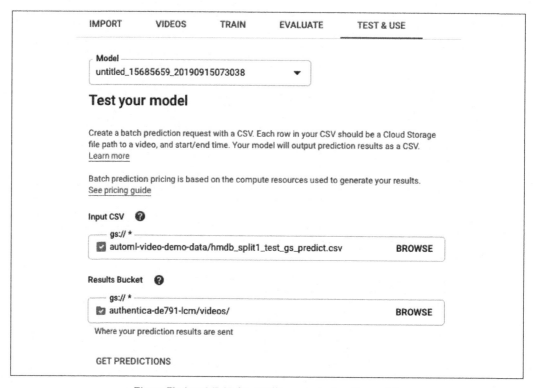

Figure 73: AutoML Video Intelligence – testing the model

This will start a batch process where all the videos in the test dataset are analyzed by our automatically generated model. Once done, you can inspect each video and get the prediction of what different video segments are all about (see *Figure 74*, where the prediction is "riding a horse"):

Figure 74: AutoML Video Intelligence – analyzing a video segment

Cost

Training on GCP has different costs depending upon the AutoML solution adopted; for example, training all the solutions presented in this chapter and serving models for testing had a cost of less than 10 dollars at the end of 2019. This is, however, not including the initial 6 hours of free discount that were available for the account (a grand total of less than $150). Depending on your organizational needs, this is likely to work out significantly less than the cost needed to buy expensive on-premises hardware.

The most expensive solutions for my datasets are reported in *Figure 75*. Of course, your costs may be different according to your specific needs and the models generated:

SKU	Product	SKU ID	Usage	Cost	One time credits	Discounts	↓ Subtotal
AutoML Content Classification Model Training Operations	Cloud Natural Language API	41FE-745B-850A	3.32 hour	$9.95	$0.00	–	$9.95
AutoML Tables Deployment	Cloud AutoML	3FEA-6ED1-509F	1,562,005,950 mebibyte second	$2.12	$0.00	–	$2.12
N1 Predefined Instance Core running in Americas	Compute Engine	2E27-4F75-95CD	35.17 hour	$1.11	$0.00	–	$1.11
N1 Predefined Instance Ram running in Americas	Compute Engine	6C71-E844-3BBC	131.88 gibibyte hour	$0.56	$0.00	–	$0.56
Class A Request Regional Storage	Cloud Storage	4DBF-185F-A41S	11,336 count	$0.03	$0.00	–	$0.03
AutoML Tables Online Prediction	Cloud AutoML	F664-BB0D-F8BE	0 hour	$0.00	$0.00	–	$0.00
Network Internet Egress from Americas to China	Compute Engine	9DE9-9092-B3BC	0 gibibyte	$0.00	$0.00	–	$0.00
AutoML Image Classification Model Training First Compute Hours	Cloud Vision API	8018-CE2C-1DF5	1 count	$0.00	$0.00	–	$0.00
AutoML Tables Training	Cloud AutoML	3B5C-4F27-B029	1 hour	$19.32	-$19.32	–	$0.00
Class B Request Regional Storage	Cloud Storage	7B70-010B-2763	641 count	$0.00	$0.00	–	$0.00

Figure 75: AutoML – example of costs

Bringing Google AutoML to Kaggle

On November 4th 2019, Google decided to integrate AutoML directly in Kaggle. To get started, you need to link your GCP account from Kaggle and authorize the access. This is easily done from a Kaggle Notebook as explained in *Figure 76*:

Figure 76: AutoML and Kaggle

The final step consists simply of activating AutoML (see *Figure 77*):

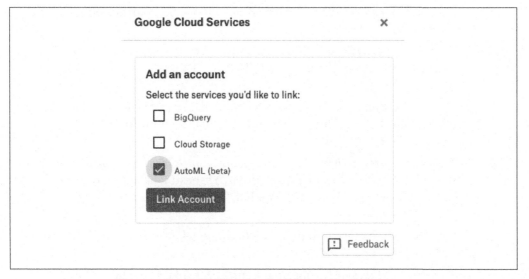

Figure 77: Activating AutoML from Kaggle

Summary

The goal of AutoML is to enable domain experts who are not familiar with machine learning technologies to use ML techniques easily. The primary goal is to reduce the steep learning curve and the huge costs of handcrafting machine learning solutions by making the whole end-to-end machine learning pipeline (data preparation, feature engineering, and automatic model generation) more automated.

After reviewing the state-of-the-art solution available at the end of 2019, we discussed how to use Cloud AutoML for text, videos, and images, achieving results comparable to the ones achieved with handcrafted models. AutoML is probably the fastest growing research topic and the interested reader can understand the latest results at `https://www.automl.org/`.

The next chapter discusses the math behind deep learning, a rather advanced topic that is recommended if you are interested in understanding what is going on "under the hood" when you play with neural networks.

References

1. *Neural Architecture Search with Reinforcement Learning*, Barret Zoph, Quoc V. Le; 2016, `http://arxiv.org/abs/1611.01578`.

2. *Efficient Neural Architecture Search via Parameter Sharing*, Hieu Pham, Melody Y. Guan, Barret Zoph, Quoc V. Le, Jeff Dean, 2018, `https://arxiv.org/abs/1802.03268`.

3. *Transfer NAS: Knowledge Transfer between Search Spaces with Transformer Agents*, Zalán Borsos, Andrey Khorlin, Andrea Gesmundo, 2019, `https://arxiv.org/abs/1906.08102`.

4. *NSGA-Net: Neural Architecture Search using Multi-Objective Genetic Algorithm*, Zhichao Lu, Ian Whalen, Vishnu Boddeti, Yashesh Dhebar, Kalyanmoy Deb, Erik Goodman, Wolfgang Banzhaf, 2018 `https://arxiv.org/abs/1810.03522`.

5. *Random Search for Hyper-Parameter Optimization*, James Bergstra, Yoshua Bengio, 2012, `http://www.jmlr.org/papers/v13/bergstra12a.html`.

6. *Auto-Keras: An Efficient Neural Architecture Search System*, Haifeng Jin, Qingquan Song and Xia Hu, 2019, `https://www.kdd.org/kdd2019/accepted-papers/view/auto-keras-an-efficient-neural-architecture-search-system`.

7. *Automated deep learning design for medical image classification by health-care professionals with no coding experience: a feasibility study*, Livia Faes et al, The Lancet Digital Health Volume 1, Issue 5, September 2019, Pages e232-e242 `https://www.sciencedirect.com/science/article/pii/S2589750019301086`.

15

The Math Behind
Deep Learning

In this chapter we discuss the math behind deep learning. This topic is quite advanced and not necessarily required for practitioners. However, it is recommended reading if you are interested in understanding what is going on *under the hood* when you play with neural networks. We start with an historical introduction, and then we will review the high school concept of derivatives and gradients. We will also introduce the gradient descent and backpropagation algorithms commonly used to optimize deep learning networks.

History

The basics of continuous backpropagation were proposed by Henry J. Kelley [1] in 1960 using dynamic programming. Stuart Dreyfus proposed using the chain rule in 1962 [2]. Paul Werbos was the first proposing to use backpropagation for neural nets in his 1974 PhD Thesis [3]. However, it was only in 1986 that backpropagation gained success with the work of David E. Rumelhart, Geoffrey E. Hinton, and Ronald J. Williams published in Nature [4]. Only in 1987, Yan LeCun described the modern version of backpropagation currently used for training neural networks [5].

The basic intuition of SGD was introduced by Robbins and Monro in 1951 in a context different from neural networks [6]. Only in 2012 – or 52 years after the first time backpropagation was first introduced – AlexNet [7] achieved a top-5 error of 15.3% in the ImageNet 2012 Challenge using GPUs. According to The Economist [8], "Suddenly people started to pay attention, not just within the AI community but across the technology industry as a whole." Innovation in this field was not something that happened overnight. Instead it was a long walk lasting more than 50 years!

Some mathematical tools

Before introducing backpropagation, we need to review some mathematical tools from calculus. Don't worry too much; we'll briefly review a few areas, all of which are commonly covered in high school-level mathematics.

Derivatives and gradients everywhere

Derivatives are a powerful mathematical tool. We are going to use derivatives and gradients for optimizing our network. Let's look at the definition. The derivative of a function $y = f(x)$ of a variable x is a measure of the rate at which the value y of the function changes with respect to the change of the variable x. If x and y are real numbers, and if the graph of f is plotted against x, the derivative is the "slope" of this graph at each point.

If the function is linear, $y = f(x) = ax + b$, the slope is $a = \dfrac{\Delta y}{\Delta x}$. This is a simple result of calculus that can be derived by considering that:

$$y + \Delta(y) = f(x + \Delta x) = a(x + \Delta x) + b = ax + a\Delta x + b = y + a\Delta x$$

$$\Delta(y) = a\Delta(x)$$

$$a = \frac{\Delta y}{\Delta x}$$

In *Figure 1* we show the geometrical meaning of Δ_x, Δ_y and the angle Θ between the linear function and the x-cartesian axis:

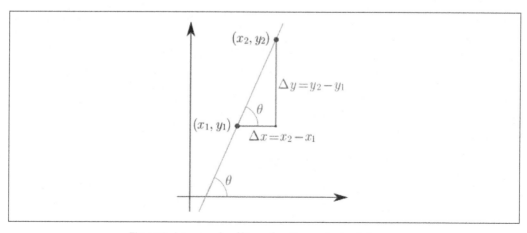

Figure 1: An example of linear function and rate of change

If the function is not linear then the intuition is to compute the rate of change as the mathematical limit value of the ratio of the differences $\frac{\Delta y}{\Delta x}$ as $\Delta(x)$ becomes infinitely small. Geometrically, this is the tangent line at $(x, y = f(x))$ as shown in *Figure 2*:

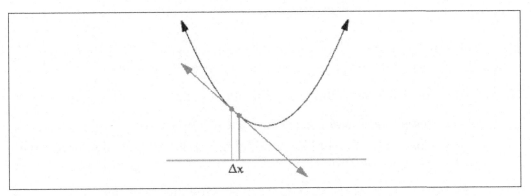

Figure 2: Rate of change for $f(x) = x^2$ and tangential line as $\Delta x \rightarrow 0$

For instance, considering $f(x) = x^2$ and the derivative $f'(x) = 2x$ in a given point, say $x = 2$, we have that the derivative is positive $f'(2) = 4$ (see *Figure 3*):

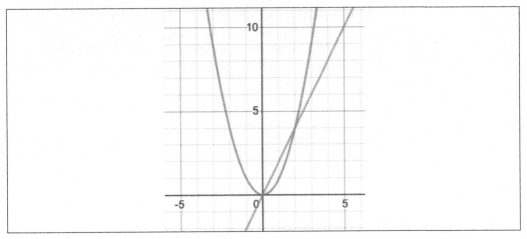

Figure 3: $f(x) = x^2$ and $f'(x) = 2x$

Gradient is a generalization of the derivative for multiple variables. Note that the derivative of a function of a single variable is a scalar-valued function, whereas the gradient of a function of several variables is a vector-valued function. The gradient is denoted with an upside-down delta ∇, and called *del.* or *nabla* from the Greek alphabet. This makes sense as delta indicates change in one variable, and the gradient is the change in all variables.

Suppose $x \in \mathbb{R}^m$ (for example, the space of real numbers with m dimensions) and f maps from $\mathbb{R}^n$ to $\mathbb{R}$; the gradient is defined as follows:

$$\nabla(f) = \left(\frac{\partial f}{\partial x_1}, \dots, \frac{\partial f}{\partial x_m} \right)$$

In math, a partial derivative $\frac{\partial f}{\partial x_i}$ of a function of several variables is its derivative with respect to one of those variables, with the others held constant.

Note that it is possible to show that the gradient is a vector (a direction to move) that:

- Points in the direction of greatest increase of a function.
- Is 0 at a local maximum or local minimum. This is because if it is 0, it cannot increase or decrease further.

The proof is left as an exercise to the interested reader. (Hint: consider *Figure 2* and *3*.)

Gradient descent

If the gradient points in the direction of greatest increase for a function, then it is possible to move towards a local minimum for the function by simply moving in a direction opposite to the gradient. That's the key observation used for gradient descent algorithms, which will be used shortly. An example is provided in *Figure 4*:

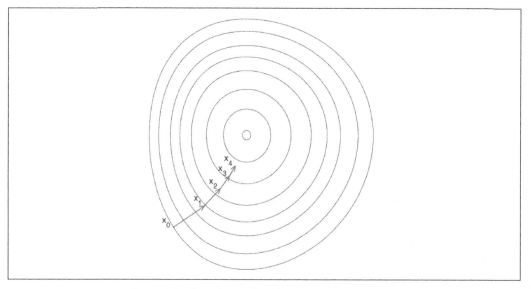

Figure 4: Gradient descent for a function in three variables

Chain rule

The chain rule says that if we have a function $y = g(x)$ and $z = f(g(x)) = f(y)$ then the derivative is defined as follows:

$$\frac{dz}{dx} = \frac{dz}{dy}\frac{dy}{dx}$$

This can be generalized beyond the scalar case. Suppose $x \in \mathbb{R}^m$ and $y \in \mathbb{R}^n$ with g which maps from $\mathbb{R}^m$ to $\mathbb{R}^n$, and f, which maps from $\mathbb{R}^n$ to $\mathbb{R}$, and with $y = g(x)$ and $z = f(y)$; then we have:

$$\frac{\partial z}{\partial x_i} = \sum_j \frac{\partial z}{\partial y_j}\frac{\partial y_j}{\partial x_i}$$

The generalized chain rule using partial derivatives will be used as a basic tool for the backpropagation algorithm when dealing with functions in multiple variables. Stop for a second and make sure that you fully understand it.

A few differentiation rules

It might be useful to remind ourselves of a few additional differentiation rules that will be used later:

- Constant differentiation: $c' = 0$, with c constant
- Differentiation variable: $\frac{\partial y}{\partial z}z = 1$, when deriving the differentiation variable
- Linear differentiation: $[af(x) + bg(x)] = af'(x) + bg'(x)$
- Reciprocal differentiation: $\left[\frac{1}{f(x)}\right]' = \frac{f'(x)}{f(x)^2}$
- Exponential differentiation: $[f(x)^n]' = n * f(x)^{n-1}$

Matrix operations

There are many books about matrix calculus. Here we focus only on only a few basic operations used for neural networks. Let us recall that a matrix $m \times n$ can be used to represent the weights w_{ij} with $0 \le i \le m, 0 \le j \le n$ associated with the arcs between two adjacent layers.

Note that by adjusting the weights we can control the "behavior" of the network and that a small change in a specific w_{ij} will be propagated through the network following its topology (see *Figure 5*, where the edges in bold are the ones impacted by the small change in a specific w_{ij}):

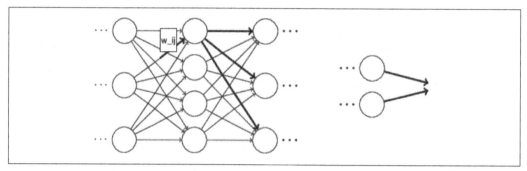

Figure 5: Propagating w_{ij} changes through the network via the edges in bold

Now that we have reviewed some basic concepts of calculus let's start applying them to deep learning. The first question is how to optimize activation functions. Well, I am pretty sure that you are thinking about computing the derivative, so let's do it!

Activation functions

In *Chapter 1, Neural Network Foundations with TensorFlow 2.0*, we have seen a few activation functions including sigmoid, tanh, and ReLU. In the following section we compute the derivative of these activation functions.

Derivative of the sigmoid

Remember that the sigmoid is defined as $\sigma(z) = \dfrac{1}{1 + e^{-z}}$ (see *Figure 6*):

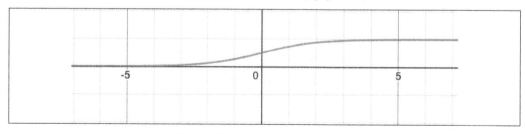

Figure 6: Sigmoid activation function

The derivative can be computed as follows:

$$\sigma'(z) = \frac{d}{dz}\left(\frac{1}{1+e^{-z}}\right) = \frac{1}{(1+e^{-z})^{-2}}\frac{d}{dz}(e^{-z}) = \frac{e^{-z}}{(1+e^{-z})}\frac{1}{(1+e^{-z})} =$$

$$\frac{e^{-z}+1-1}{(1+e^{-z})}\frac{1}{(1+e^{-z})} = \left(\frac{(1+e^{-z})}{(1+e^{-z})} - \frac{1}{(1+e^{-z})}\right)\frac{1}{(1+e^{-z})} =$$

$$\left(1 - \frac{1}{(1+e^{-z})}\right)\left(\frac{1}{(1+e^{-z})}\right)$$

$$\left(1 - \sigma(z)\right)\sigma(z)$$

Therefore the derivative of $\sigma(z)$ can be computed as a very simple form $\sigma'(z) = \left(1 - \sigma(z)\right)\sigma(z)$.

Derivative of tanh

Remember that the arctan function is defined as, $\tanh(z) = \dfrac{e^z - e^{-z}}{e^z + e^{-z}}$ as seen in *Figure 7*:

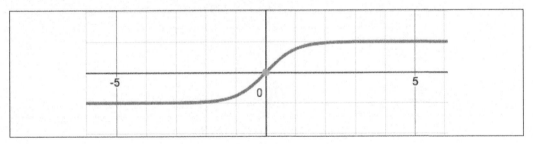

Figure 7: Tanh activation function

If you remember that $\dfrac{d}{dz}e^z = e^z$ and $\dfrac{d}{dz}e^{-z} = -e^{-z}$, then the derivative is computed as:

$$\frac{d}{dz}\tanh(x) = \frac{(e^z + e^{-z})(e^z + e^{-z}) - (e^z - e^{-z})(e^z - e^{-z})}{(e^z + e^{-z})^2} =$$

$$1 - \frac{(e^z - e^{-z})^2}{(e^z + e^{-z})^2} = 1 - \tanh^2(z)$$

Therefore the derivative of *tanh(z)* can be computed as a very simple form: $tanh'(z) = 1 - tanh^2(z)$.

Derivative of ReLU

The ReLU function is defined as $f(x) = max(0, x)$ (see *Figure 8*). The derivative of ReLU is:

$$f'(x) = \begin{cases} 1, & if\, x > 0 \\ 0, & otherwise \end{cases}$$

Note that ReLU is non-differentiable at zero. However, it is differentiable anywhere else, and the value of the derivative at zero can be arbitrarily chosen to be a 0 or 1, as demonstrated in *Figure 8*:

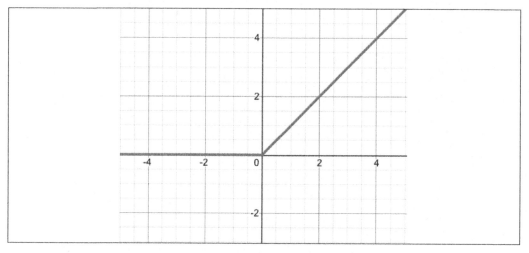

Figure 8: ReLU activation function

Backpropagation

Now that we have computed the derivative of the activation functions, we can describe the backpropagation algorithm – the mathematical core of deep learning. Sometimes, backpropagation is called *backprop* for short.

Remember that a neural network can have multiple hidden layers, as well as one input layer and one output layer.

In addition to that, recall from *Chapter 1*, *Neural Network Foundations with TensorFlow 2.0*, that backpropagation can be described as a way of progressively correcting mistakes as soon as they are detected. In order to reduce the errors made by a neural network, we must train the network. The training needs a dataset including input values and the corresponding true output value. We want to use the network for predicting the output as close as possible to the true output value. The key intuition of the backpropagation algorithm is to update the weights of the connections based on the measured error at the output neuron(s). In the remainder of this section, we will explain how to formalize this intuition.

When backpropagation starts, all the weights have some random assignment. Then the net is activated for each input in the training set: values are propagated forward from the input stage through the hidden stages to the output stage where a prediction is made (note that we keep the following figure simple by only representing a few values with green dotted lines, but in reality all the values are propagated forward through the network):

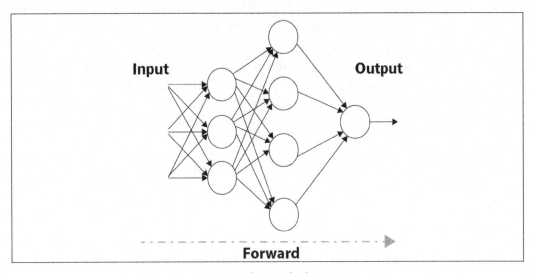

Figure 9: Forward step in backpropagation

Since we know the true observed value in the training set, it is possible to calculate the error made in prediction.

The easiest way to think about backtracking is to propagate the error back (see *Figure 10*), using an appropriate optimizer algorithm such as a gradient descent to adjust the neural network weights with the goal of reducing the error (again for the sake of simplicity only a few error values are represented here):

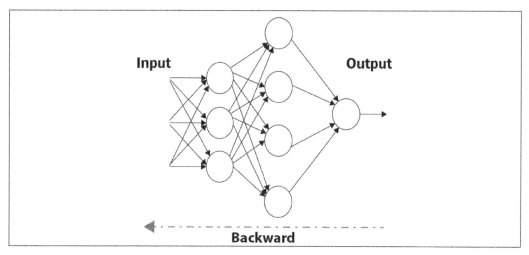

Figure 10: Backward step in backpropagation

The process of forward propagation from input to output and backward propagation of errors is repeated several times until the error goes below a predefined threshold. The whole process is represented in *Figure 11*. A set of features is selected as input to a machine learning model, which produces predictions. The predictions are compared with the (true) label and the resulting loss function is minimized by the optimizer, which updates the weights of the model:

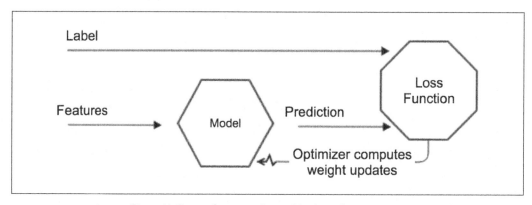

Figure 11: Forward propagation and backward propagation

Let's see in detail how the forward and backward steps are realized. It might be useful to have a look back at *Figure 5* and recall that a small change in a specific w_{ij} will be propagated through the network following its topology (see *Figure 5*, where the edges in bold are the ones impacted by the small change in a specific weight).

Forward step

During the forward steps the inputs are multiplied with the weights and then they all are summed together. Then the activation function is applied (see *Figure 12*). This step is repeated for each layer, one after another. The first layer takes the input features as input and it produces its output. Then, each subsequent layer takes as input the output of the previous layer:

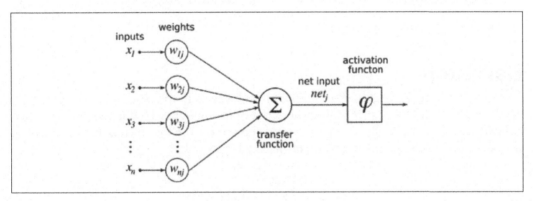

Figure 12: Forward propagation

If we look at one single layer, mathematically we have two equations:

1. The transfer equation: $z = \sum_i w_i x_i + b$, where x_i are the input values, w_i are the weights, and b is the bias. In vector notation $z = W_T X$. Note that b can be *absorbed* in the summatory by setting $w_0 = b$ and $x_0 = 1$.

2. The activation function: $y = \sigma(z)$, where σ is the chosen activation function.

An artificial neural network consists of an input layer I, an output layer O and any number of hidden layers H_i situated between the input and the output layers. For the sake of simplicity let's assume that there is only one hidden layer, since the results can be easily generalized.

As shown in *Figure 12*, The features x_i from the input layer are multiplied by a set of fully-connected weights w_{ij} connecting the input layer to the hidden layer (see the left side of *Figure 12*). The weighted signals are summed together with the bias to calculate the result $z_j = \sum_i w_i x_i + b_j$ (see the center of *Figure 12*).

The result is passed through the activation function $y_j = \sigma_j(z_j)$ which leaves the hidden layer to the output layer (see the right side of *Figure 12*).

Summarizing, during the forward step we need to run the following operations:

- For each neuron in a layer, multiply each input by its corresponding weight.
- Then for each neuron in the layer, sum all input x weights together.
- Finally, for each neuron, apply the activation function on the result to compute the new output.

At the end of the forward step, we get a predicted vector y_o from the output layer o given the input vector x presented at the input layer. Now the question is: how close is the predicted vector y_o to the true value vector t?

That's where the backstep comes in.

Backstep

For understanding how close the predicted vector yo is to the true value vector t we need a function that measures the error at the output layer o. That is the *loss function* defined earlier in the book. There are many choices for the loss function. For instance, we can define the **Mean Squared Error (MSE)** as follows:

$$E = \frac{1}{2}\sum_o (y_o - t_o)^2$$

Note that E is a quadratic function and, therefore, the difference is quadratically larger when t is far away from y_o, and the sign is not important. Note that this quadratic error (loss) function is not the only one that we can use. Later in this chapter we will see how to deal with cross-entropy.

Now, remember that the key point is that during the training we want to adjust the weights of the network in order to minimize the final error. As discussed, we can move towards a local minimum by moving in the opposite direction to the gradient $-\nabla w$. Moving in the opposite direction to the gradient is the reason why this algorithm is called *gradient descent*. Therefore, it is reasonable to define the equation for updating the weight w_{ij} as follows:

$$w_{ij} \leftarrow w_{ij} - \nabla w_{ij}$$

For a function in multiple variables, the gradient is computed using partial derivatives. We introduce the hyperparameter η – or, in ML lingo, the learning rate – to account for how large a step should be taken in the direction opposite to the gradient.

Considering the error, E, we have the equation:

$$\nabla w = -\eta \frac{\partial E}{\partial w_{ij}}$$

The preceding equation is simply capturing the fact that a slight change will impact the final error, as seen in *Figure 13*:

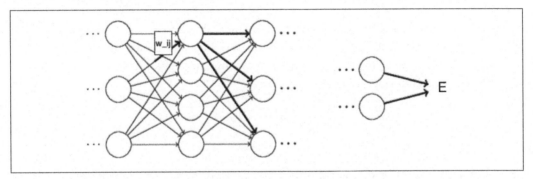

Figure 13: A small change in w_{ij} will impact the final error, E

Let's define the notation used throughout our equations in the remaining section:

- z_j is the input to node j for layer l
- δ_j is the activation function for node j in layer l (applied to z_j)
- $y_j = \delta_j(z_j)$ is the output of the activation of node j in layer l
- w_{ij} is the matrix of weights connecting the neuron i in layer l – 1 to the neuron j in layer l
- b_j is the bias for unit j in layer l
- t_o is the target value for node o in the output layer

Now we need to compute the partial derivative for the error at the output layer ∂E when the weights change by ∂w_{ij}. There are two different cases:

Case 1: Weight update equation for a neuron from hidden (or input) layer to output layer.

Case 2: weight update equation for a neuron from hidden (or input) layer to hidden layer.

We'll begin with case 1.

Case 1 – From hidden layer to output layer

In this case, we need to consider the equation for a neuron from hidden layer j to output layer o. Applying the definition of E and differentiating we have:

$$\frac{\partial E}{\partial w_{jo}} = \frac{\partial \frac{1}{2}\Sigma_o(y_o - t_o)^2}{\partial w_{jo}} = (y_o - t_o)\frac{\partial(y_o - t_o)}{\partial w_{jo}}$$

Here the summation disappears because when we take the partial derivative with respect to the j-th dimension, the only term not zero in the error is the j-th. Considering that differentiation is a linear operation and that $\frac{\partial t_o}{\partial w_{jo}} = 0$ – because the true t_o value does not depend on w_{jo} – we have:

$$\frac{\partial(y_o - t_o)}{\partial w_{jo}} = \frac{\partial y_o}{\partial w_{jo}} - 0$$

Applying the chain rule again and remembering that $y_o = \delta_o(z_o)$, we have:

$$\frac{\partial E}{\partial w_{jo}} = (y_o - t_o)\frac{\partial y_o}{\partial w_{jo}} = (y_o - t_o)\frac{\partial \delta_o(z_o)}{\partial w_{jo}} = (y_o - t_o)\delta'_o(z_o)\frac{\partial z_o}{\partial w_{jo}}$$

Remembering that $z_o = \sum_j w_{jo}\delta_j(z_j) + b_o$ we have: that

$$\frac{\partial z_o}{\partial w_{jo}} = \delta_j(z_j)$$

Again because when we take the partial derivative with respect to the j-th dimension, the only term not zero in the error is the j-th. By definition $\delta_j(z_j) = y_j$, so putting everything together we have:

$$\frac{\partial E}{\partial w_{jo}} = (y_o - t_o)\delta'_o(z_o)y_j$$

The gradient of the error E with respect to the weights w_j from the hidden layer j to the output layer o is therefore simply the product of three terms: the difference between the prediction y_o and the true value to, the derivative $\delta'_o(z_o)$ of the output layer activation function, and the activation output y_j of node j in the hidden layer. For simplicity we can also define $v_o = (y_o - t_o)\delta'_o(z_o)$ and get:

$$\frac{\partial E}{\partial w_{jo}} = v_o y_j$$

In short, for case 1 the weight update equation for each of the hidden-output connections is:

$$w_{jo} \leftarrow w_{jo} - \eta \frac{\partial E}{\partial w_{jo}}$$

 If we want to explicitly compute the gradient with respect to the output layer biases, the steps to follow are similar to the one above with only one difference.

$$\frac{\partial z_o}{\partial b_o} = \frac{\partial \sum_j w_{jo}\delta_j(z_j) + b_o}{\partial b_o} = 1$$

So in this case $\dfrac{\partial E}{\partial b_o} = v_o$.

Next, we'll look at case 2.

Case 2 – From hidden layer to hidden layer

In this case, we need to consider the equation for a neuron from a hidden layer (or the input layer) to a hidden layer. *Figure 13* showed that there is an indirect relationship between the hidden layer weight change and the output error. This makes the computation of the gradient a bit more challenging. In this case, we need to consider the equation for a neuron from hidden layer i to hidden layer j. Applying the definition of E and differentiating we have:

$$\frac{\partial E}{\partial w_{ij}} = \frac{\partial \frac{1}{2}\sum_o(y_o - t_o)^2}{\partial w_{ij}} = \sum_o (y_o - t_o)\frac{\partial(y_o - t_o)}{\partial w_{ij}} = \sum_o (y_o - t_o)\frac{\partial y_o}{\partial w_{ij}}$$

In this case the sum will not disappear because the change of weights in the hidden layer is directly affecting the output. Substituting $y_o = \delta_o(z_o)$ and applying the chain rule, we have:

$$\frac{\partial E}{\partial w_{ij}} = \sum_o (y_o - t_o) \frac{\partial \delta_o(z_o)}{\partial w_{ij}} = \sum_o (y_o - t_o) \delta'_o(z_o) \frac{\partial z_o}{\partial w_{ij}}$$

The indirect relation between z_o and the internal weights w_{ij} (*Figure 13*) is mathematically expressed by the expansion:

$$z_o = \sum_j w_{jo} \delta_j(z_j) + b_o =$$

$$\sum_j w_{jo} \delta_j \left(\sum_i w_{ij} z_i + b_i \right) + b_o$$

$$\text{since } z_j = \sum_i w_{ij} z_i + b_i$$

This suggests applying the chain rule again:

$$\frac{\partial z_o}{\partial w_{ij}} = \text{(chain rule)}$$

$$= \frac{\partial z_o}{\partial y_j} \frac{\partial y_j}{\partial w_{ij}} = \text{(substituting } z_o)$$

$$= \frac{\partial y_j w_{jo}}{\partial y_j} \frac{\partial y_j}{\partial w_{ij}} = \text{(deriving)}$$

$$= w_{jo} \frac{\partial y_j}{\partial w_{ij}} = \text{(substituting } y_j = \delta_j(z_j))$$

$$= w_{jo} \frac{\partial \delta_j(z_j)}{\partial w_{ij}} = \text{(chain rule)}$$

$$= w_{jo} \delta'_j(z_j) \frac{\partial z_j}{\partial w_{ij}} = \text{(substituting } z_j = \sum_i y_i w_{ij} + b_i)$$

$$= w_{jo}\delta'_j(z_j) \frac{\partial(\sum_i y_i w_{ij} + b_i)}{\partial w_{ij}} = \text{(derivation)}$$

$$= w_{jo}\delta'_j(z_j)y_i$$

Now we can combine the preceding two results:

$$\frac{\partial E}{\partial w_{ij}} = \sum_o (y_o - t_o)\delta'_o(z_o) \frac{\partial z_o}{\partial w_{ij}}$$

$$\frac{\partial z_o}{\partial w_{ij}} = w_{jo}\delta'_j(z_j)y_i$$

and get:

$$\frac{\partial E}{\partial w_{ij}} = \sum_o (y_o - t_o)\delta'_o(z_o)w_{jo}\delta'_j(z_j)y_i = y_i\delta'_j(z_j)\sum_o (y_o - t_o)\delta'_o(z_o)w_{jo}$$

Remembering the definition $v_o = (y_o - t_o)\delta'_o(z_o)$ we get:

$$\frac{\partial E}{\partial w_{ij}} = \sum_o (y_o - t_o)\delta'_o(z_o)w_{jo}\delta'_j(z_j)y_i = y_i\delta'_j(z_j)\sum_o v_o w_{jo}$$

This last substitution with v_o is particularly interesting because it back-propagates the signal v_o computed in the subsequent layer. The rate of change ∂E with respect to the rate of change of the weights w_{ij} is therefore the multiplication of four factors: the output activations y_i from the layer below, the derivative of hidden layer activation function δ'_j and the sum of the back-propagated signal v_o previously computed in the subsequent layer weighted by w_{jo}. We can use this idea of backpropagating the error signal by defining $v_j = \delta'_j(z_j)\sum_o v_o w_{jo}$ and therefore $\frac{\partial E}{\partial w_{ij}} = y_i v_j$. This suggests that in order to calculate the gradients at any layer l in a deep neural network, we can simply multiply the back propagated error signal v_j and multiply it by the feed-forward signal y_{l-1} arriving at the layer l. Note that the math is a bit complex but the result is very simple indeed! The intuition is given in *Figure 14*. Given a function $z = f(x, y)$ computed locally to a neuron with the inputs x and y, the gradients $\frac{\partial L}{\partial z}$ are backpropagated. Then, they combine via chain rule with the local gradients $\frac{\partial z}{\partial x}$ and $\frac{\partial z}{\partial y}$ for further backpropagation.

Here, L denotes the error from the generic previous layer:

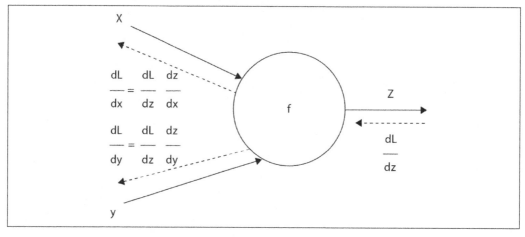

Figure 14: An example of the math behind backpropagation

 If we want to explicitly compute the gradient with respect to the output layer biases, it can be proven that $\frac{\partial E}{\partial b_i} = v_j$. We leave this as an exercise for the reader.

In short, for case 2 (hidden-to-hidden connection) the weight delta is $\Delta w = \eta v_j y_i$ and the weight update equation for each of the hidden-hidden connections is simply:

$$w_{ij} \leftarrow w_{ij} - \eta \frac{\partial E}{\partial w_{ij}}$$

We have arrived at the end of this section and all the mathematical tools are defined to make our final statement. The essence of backstep is nothing other than applying the weight update rules one layer after another, starting from the last output layer and moving back toward the first input layer. Difficult to derive, to be sure, but extremely easy to apply once defined. The whole forward-backward algorithm at the core of deep learning is then the following:

1. Compute the feed-forward signals from the input to the output.

2. Compute the output error E based on the predictions y_o and the true value t_o.

3. Backpropagate the error signals; multiply them with the weights in previous layers and with the gradients of the associated activation functions.

4. Compute the gradients $\frac{\partial E}{\partial \theta}$ for all of the parameters θ based on the back-propagated error signal and the feed-forward signals from the inputs.

5. Update the parameters using the computed gradients $\theta \leftarrow \theta - \eta \frac{\partial E}{\partial \theta}$.

Note that the above algorithm will work for any choice of differentiable error function E and for any choice of differentiable activation δ_l function. The only requirement is that both must be differentiable.

Limit of backpropagation

Gradient descent with backpropagation is not guaranteed to find the global minimum of the loss function, but only a local minimum. However, this is not necessarily a problem observed in practical application.

Cross entropy and its derivative

Gradient descent can be used when cross entropy is adopted as the loss function. As discussed in *Chapter 1, Neural Network Foundations with TensorFlow 2.0*, the logistic loss function is defined as:

$$E = L(c,p) = -\sum_i [c_i \ln(p_i) + (1 - c_i) \ln(1 - p_i)]$$

Where c refers to one-hot encoded classes (or labels) whereas p refers to softmax-applied probabilities. Since cross entropy is applied to softmax-applied probabilities and to one-hot-encoded classes, we need to take into account the chain rule for computing the gradient with respect to the final weights, $score_i$. Mathematically, we have:

$$\frac{\partial E}{\partial score_i} = \frac{\partial E}{\partial p_i} \frac{\partial p_i}{\partial score_i}$$

Computing each part separately, let's start from $\frac{\partial E}{\partial p_i}$:

$$\frac{\partial E}{\partial p_i} = \frac{\partial(-\Sigma[c_i \ln(p_i) + (1 - c_i) \ln(i - p_i)])}{\partial p_i} = \frac{\partial(-c_i \ln(p_i) + (1 - c_i) \ln(i - p_i)])}{\partial p_i}$$

(Note that for a fixed ∂p_i all the terms in the sum are constant except the chosen one.)

Therefore, we have:

$$-\frac{\partial c_i \ln p_i}{\partial p_i} - \frac{\partial(1-c_i)\ln(1-p_i)}{\partial p_i} = -\frac{c_i}{p_i} - \frac{(1-c_i)}{(1-p_i)}\frac{\partial(1-p_i)}{\partial p_i}$$

(Applying the partial derivative to the sum and considering that $\ln'(x) = \frac{1}{x}$.)

Therefore, we have:

$$\frac{\partial E}{\partial p_i} = -\frac{c_i}{p_i} + \frac{(1-c_i)}{(1-p_i)}$$

Now let's compute the other part $\frac{\partial p_i}{\partial score_i}$ where p_i is the softmax function defined as $\sigma(x_j) = \frac{e^{x_i}}{\sum_i e^{x_i}}$.

The derivative is:

$$\frac{\partial \sigma(x_j)}{\partial x_k} = \sigma(x_j)(1 - \sigma(x_j)) \quad \text{if } j = k$$

$$\text{and } \frac{\partial \sigma(x_j)}{\partial x_k} = -\sigma(e^{x_i})\sigma(e^{x_k}) \text{ if } j \neq k.$$

Using the Kronecker delta $\delta_{ij} = \begin{cases} 1 & \text{for } j = k \\ 0 & \text{ow} \end{cases}$ we have:

$$\frac{\partial \sigma(x_j)}{\partial x_k} = \sigma(x_j)(\delta_{ij} - \sigma(x_j))$$

Therefore, considering that we are computing the partial derivative, all the components are zeroed with the exception of only one, and we have:

$$\frac{\partial p_i}{\partial score_i} = p_i(1 - p_i)$$

Combining the results, we have:

$$\frac{\partial E}{\partial score_i} = \frac{\partial E}{\partial p_i}\frac{\partial p_i}{\partial score_i} = \left[-\frac{c_i}{p_i} + \frac{(1-c_i)}{(1-p_i)}\right][p_i(1-p_i)] =$$

$$-\frac{c_i[p_i(1-p_i)]}{p_i} + \frac{(1-c_i)p_i(1-p_i)}{1-p_i} =$$

$$-c_i(1-p_i) + (1-c_i)p_i =$$

$$-c_i + c_ip_i + p_i - c_ip_i =$$

$$= p_i - c_i$$

Where c_i denotes the one-hot-encoded classes and p_i refers to the softmax probabilities. In short, the derivative is both elegant and easy to compute:

$$\frac{\partial E}{\partial score_i} = p_i - c_i$$

Batch gradient descent, stochastic gradient descent, and mini-batch

If we generalize the preceding discussion, then we can state that the problem of optimizing a neural network consists of adjusting the weights w of the network in such a way that the loss function is minimized. Conveniently, we can think about the loss function in the form of a sum, as in this form it's indeed representing all the loss functions commonly used:

$$Q(w) = \frac{1}{n}\sum_{i=1}^{n} Q_i(w)$$

In this case, we can perform a derivation using steps very similar to those discussed in the previous paragraph, where η is the learning rate and ∇ is the gradient:

$$w = w - \eta\nabla Q(w) = w - \eta\sum_{i=1}^{n} \nabla Q_i(w)$$

In many cases, evaluating the above gradient might require expensive evaluation of the gradients from all summand functions. When the training set is very large, this can be extremely expensive. If we have three million samples, we have to loop through three million times or use the dot product. That's a lot! How can we simplify this? There are three types of gradient descent, each different in the way they handle the training dataset:

Batch Gradient Descent (BGD)

Batch gradient descent computes the change of error, but updates the whole model only once the entire dataset has been evaluated. Computationally it is very efficient, but it requires that the results for the whole dataset be held in the memory.

Stochastic Gradient Descent (SGD)

Instead of updating the model once the dataset has been evaluated, it does so after every single training example. The key idea is very simple: SGD samples a subset of summand functions at every step.

Mini-Batch Gradient Descent (MBGD)

This is the method that is very frequently used in deep learning. MBGD (or mini-batch) combines BGD and the SGD in one single heuristic. The dataset is divided into small batches of about size bs, which is generally from 64 to 256. Then each of the batches are evaluated separately.

Note that *bs* is another hyperparameter to fine tune during training. MBGD lies between the extremes of BGD and SGD – by adjusting the batch size and the learning rate parameters, we sometimes find a solution that descends closer to the global minimum than can be achieved by either of the extremes.

In contrast with gradient descent, where the cost function minimized more smoothly, the mini-batch gradient has a bit more of a noisy and bumpy descent, but the cost function still trends downhill. The reason for the noise is that mini-batches are a sample of all the examples and this sampling can cause the loss function to oscillate.

Thinking about backpropagation and convnets

In this section we want to give an intuition behind backpropagation and convnets. For the sake of simplicity we will focus on an example of convolution with input X of size 3×3, one single filter W of size 2×2 with no padding, stride 1, and no dilation (see *Chapter 5, Advanced Convolutional Neural Networks*). The generalization is left as an exercise.

The standard convolution operation is represented in *Figure 15*. Simply put, the convolutional operation is the forward pass:

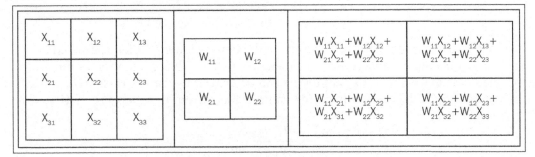

Figure 15: Forward pass for our convnet toy example

Following the intuition of *Figure 15*, we can now focus our attention to the backward pass for the current layer. The key assumption is that we receive a backpropagated signal $\frac{\partial L}{\partial h_{ij}}$ as input, and we need to compute $\frac{\partial L}{\partial w_{ij}}$ and $\frac{\partial L}{\partial x_{ij}}$. This computation is left as an exercise but please note that each weight in the filter contributes to each pixel in the output map or, in other words, any change in a weight of a filter affects all the output pixels.

Thinking about backpropagation and RNNs

As you remember from *Chapter 8, Recurrent Neural Networks*, the basic equation for an RNN is $s_t = \tanh(U_{xt} + W_{st-1})$, the final prediction is $\hat{y}_t = softmax(Vs_t)$ at step t, the correct value is y_t, and the error E is the cross-entropy. Here U, V, W are learning parameters used for the RNNs' equations. These equations can be visualized as in *Figure 16* where we unroll the recurrency. The core idea is that total error is just the sum of the errors at each time step.

If we used SGD, we need to sum the errors and the gradients at each timestep for one given training example:

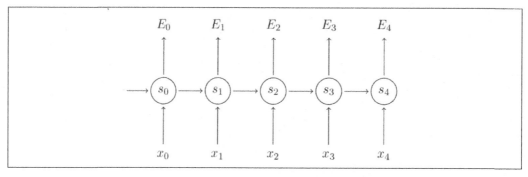

Figure 16: Recurrent neural network unrolled with equations

We are not going to write all the tedious math behind all the gradients, but rather focus only on a few peculiar cases. For instance, with math computations similar to the one made in the previous chapters, it can be proven by using the chain rule that the gradient for V depends only on the value at the current timestep s_3, y_3 and $\widehat{y}_3$:

$$\frac{\partial E_3}{\partial V} = \frac{\partial E_3}{\partial \widehat{y}_3}\frac{\partial \widehat{y}_3}{\partial V} = \frac{\partial E_3}{\partial \widehat{y}_3}\frac{\partial \widehat{y}_3}{\partial z_3}\frac{\partial z_3}{\partial V} = (\widehat{y}_3 - y_3)s_3$$

However, $\frac{\partial E_3}{\partial W}$ has dependencies carried across timesteps because for instance $s_3 = \tanh\left(U_{x_t} + W_{s_2}\right)$ depends on s_2 which depends on W_2 and s_1. As a consequence, the gradient is a bit more complicated because we need to sum up the contributions of each time step:

$$\frac{\partial E_3}{\partial W} = \sum_{k=0}^{3} \frac{\partial E_3}{\partial \widehat{y}_3}\frac{\partial \widehat{y}_3}{\partial s_3}\frac{\partial s_3}{\partial s_k}\frac{\partial s_k}{\partial W}$$

In order to understand the preceding equation, you can think that we are using the standard backpropagation algorithm used for traditional feed-forward neural networks, but for RNNs we need to additionally add the gradients of W across timesteps. That's because we can effectively make the dependencies across time explicit by unrolling the RNN. This is the reason why backpropagation for RNNs is frequently called **Backpropagation Through Time (BTT)**. The intuition is shown in *Figure 17* where the backpropagated signals are represented:

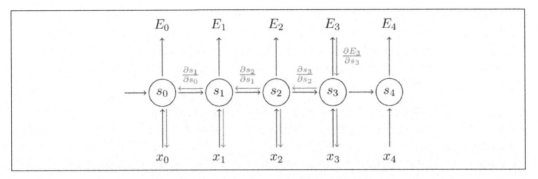

Figure 17: RNN equations and back propagated signals

I hope that you are following up to this point because now the discussion will be slightly more difficult. If we consider:

$$\frac{\partial E_3}{\partial W} = \sum_{k=0}^{3} \frac{\partial E_3}{\partial \widehat{y_3}} \frac{\partial \widehat{y_3}}{\partial s_3} \frac{\partial s_3}{\partial s_k} \frac{\partial s_k}{\partial W}$$

Then we notice that $\frac{\partial s_3}{\partial s_k}$ should be again computed with the chain rule producing a number of multiplications. In this case, we take the derivative of a vector function with respect to a vector, so we need a matrix whose elements are all the pointwise derivatives (in math, this matrix is called a Jacobian). Mathematically, it can be proven that:

$$\frac{\partial s_3}{\partial s_k} = \prod_{j=k+1}^{3} \frac{\partial s_j}{\partial s_{j-1}}$$

Therefore, we have:

$$\frac{\partial E_3}{\partial W} = \sum_{k=0}^{3} \frac{\partial E_3}{\partial \widehat{y_3}} \frac{\partial \widehat{y_3}}{\partial s_3} (\prod_{j=k+1}^{3} \frac{\partial s_j}{\partial s_{j-1}}) \frac{\partial s_k}{\partial W}$$

The multiplication in the preceding equation is particularly problematic since both the sigmoid and *tanh* get saturated at both ends and their derivative goes to 0. When this happens, they drive other gradients in previous layers towards 0. This makes the gradient vanish completely after a few time steps and the network stops learning from "far away."

Chapter 8, Recurrent Neural Networks, discussed how to use LSTMs and GRUs to deal with the problem of vanishing gradients and efficiently learn long-range dependencies. In a similar way, the gradient can explode when one single term in the multiplication of the Jacobian matrix becomes large. *Chapter 8, Recurrent Neural Networks*, discussed how to use gradient clipping to deal with this problem.

We now come to the conclusion of this journey, and you should now better understand how backpropagation works and how it is applied in neural networks for dense networks, CNNs, and RNNs. In the next section, we will discuss how TensorFlow computes gradients, and why this is useful for backpropagation.

A note on TensorFlow and automatic differentiation

TensorFlow can automatically calculate derivatives, a feature called Automatic Differentiation. This is achieved by using the chain rule. Every node in the computational graph (see *Chapter 2, TensorFlow 1.x and 2.x*) has an attached gradient operation for calculating the derivatives of input with respect to output. After that, the gradients with respect to parameters are automatically computed during backpropagation.

Automatic differentiation is a very important feature because you do not need to handcode new variations of backpropagation for each new model of a neural network. This allows quick iteration and running many experiments faster.

Summary

In this chapter we discussed the math behind deep learning. Put simply, a deep learning model computes a function given an input vector to produce the output. The interesting part is that we can literally have billions of parameters (weights) to be tuned. Backpropagation is a core mathematical algorithm used by deep learning for efficiently training artificial neural networks following a gradient descent approach that exploits the chain rule. The algorithm is based on two steps repeated alternatively: the forward step and the backstep.

During the forward step inputs are propagated through the network in order to predict outputs. These predictions might be different from the true values given to assess the quality of the network. In other words, there is an error and our goal is to minimize it. This is where the backstep plays a role, by adjusting the weights of the network to minimize the error.

The error is computed via loss functions such as MSE, or cross-entropy for noncontinuous values such as Booleans (*Chapter 1, Neural Network Foundations with TensorFlow 2.0*). A gradient-descent-optimization algorithm is used to adjust the weight of neurons by calculating the gradient of the loss function. Backpropagation computes the gradient, and gradient descent uses the gradients for training the model. Reduction in the error rate of predictions increases accuracy, allowing machine learning models to improve. Stochastic gradient descent is the simplest thing you could possibly do by taking one step in the direction of the gradient. This chapter does not cover the math behind other optimizers such as Adam and RMSProp (chapter 1). However, they involve using the first and the second moments of the gradients. The first moment involves the exponentially decaying average of the previous gradients and the second moment involves the exponentially decaying average of the previous squared gradients.

There are three big properties of your data that justify using deep learning, otherwise you might just use regular machine learning: (1) very-high-dimensional input (text, images, audio signals, videos, and temporal series are frequently a good example), (2) dealing with complex decision surfaces that cannot be approximated with a low-order polynomial function, and (3) having a large amount of training data available.

Deep learning models can be thought of as a computational graph made up by stacking together several basic components such as Dense (chapter 1), CNNs (chapters 4 and 5), Embeddings (chapter 6), RNNs(chapter 7), GANs (chapter 8), Autoencoders (chapter 9) and, sometimes, adopting shortcut connections such as "peephole", "skip", and "residual" because they help data flow a bit more smoothly (chapter 5 and 7). Each node in the graph takes tensors as input and produces tensors as output. As discussed, training happens by adjusting the weights in each node with backpropagation, where the key intuition is to reduce the error in the final output node(s) via gradient descent. GPUs and TPUs (chapter 16) can significantly accelerate the optimization process since it is essentially based on (hundreds of) millions of matrix computations.

There are a few other mathematical tools that might be helpful to improve your learning process. Regularization (L1, L2, Lasso, from chapter 1) can significantly improve the learning by keeping weights normalized. Batch normalization (chapter 1) helps to basically keep track of the mean and the standard deviation of your dataset across multiple deep layers. The key intuition is to have data resembling a normal distribution while it flows through the computational graph. Dropout (chapters 1, 4, and 5) helps by introducing some elements of redundancy in your computation; this prevents overfitting and allows better generalization.

This chapter has presented the mathematical foundation behind the intuition. As discussed, this topic is quite advanced and not necessarily required for practitioners. However, it is recommended reading if you are interested in understanding what is going on "under the hood" when you play with neural networks.

The next chapter will introduce the **Tensor Processing Unit (TPU)**, a special chip developed at Google for ultra-fast execution of many mathematical operations described in this chapter.

References

1. Kelley, Henry J. (1960). *Gradient theory of optimal flight paths*. ARS Journal. 30 (10): 947–954. Bibcode:1960ARSJ...30.1127B. doi:10.2514/8.5282.

2. Dreyfus, Stuart (1962). *The numerical solution of variational problems*. Journal of Mathematical Analysis and Applications. 5 (1): 30–45. doi:10.1016/0022-247x(62)90004-5.

3. Werbos, P. (1974). *Beyond Regression: New Tools for Prediction and Analysis in the Behavioral Sciences*. PhD thesis, Harvard University.

4. Rumelhart, David E.; Hinton, Geoffrey E.; Williams, Ronald J. (1986-10-09). *Learning representations by back-propagating errors*. Nature. 323 (6088): 533–536. Bibcode:1986Natur.323..533R. doi:10.1038/323533a0.

5. LeCun, Y. (1987). *Modèles Connexionnistes de l'apprentissage (Connectionist Learning Models)*, Ph.D. thesis, Universite' P. et M. Curie, 1987

6. Herbert Robbins and Sutton Monro *A Stochastic Approximation Method The Annals of Mathematical Statistics*, Vol. 22, No. 3. (Sep., 1951), pp. 400-407.

7. Krizhevsky, Alex; Sutskever, Ilya; Hinton, Geoffrey E. (June 2017). *ImageNet classification with deep convolutional neural networks* (PDF). Communications of the ACM. 60 (6): 84–90. doi:10.1145/3065386. ISSN 0001-0782.

8. *From not working to neural networking*. The Economist. 25 June 2016

16
Tensor Processing Unit

This chapter introduces the **Tensor Processing Unit (TPU)**, a special chip developed at Google for ultra-fast execution of neural network mathematical operations. Similarly to **Graphic Processing Units (GPUs)**, the idea here is to have a special processor focusing only on very fast matrix operations with no support for all the other operations normally supported by **Central Processing Units (CPUs)**. However, the additional improvement with TPUs is to remove from the chip any hardware support for graphics operation normally present in GPUs (rasterization, texture mapping, frame buffer operations, and so on). Think of a TPU as a special purpose co-processor specialized for deep learning, being focused on matrix or tensor operations. In this chapter we are going to compare CPUs and GPUs with the three generations of TPUs and Edge TPUs. All these accelerators are available as November 2019. The chapter will include code examples of using TPUs. So with that, let's begin.

C/G/T processing units

In this section we discuss CPUs, GPUs, and TPUs. Before discussing TPUs, it will be useful for us to review CPUs and GPUs.

CPUs and GPUs

You are probably somewhat familiar with the concept of a CPU, a general-purpose chip sitting in each computer, tablet, and smartphone. CPUs are in charge of all of the computations: from logical controls, to arithmetic, to register operations, to operations with memory, and much more. CPUs are subject to the well-known Moore's law [1], which states that the number of transistors in a dense integrated circuit doubles about every two years.

Many people believe that we are currently in an era where this trend cannot be sustained for long, and indeed it has already declined during the past few years. Therefore, we need some additional technology if we want to support the demand for faster and faster computation to process the ever-growing amount of data that is available out there.

One improvement came from so-called GPUs: special purpose chips that are perfect for fast graphics operations such as matrix multiplication, rasterization, frame buffer manipulation, texture mapping, and many others. In addition to computer graphics where matrix multiplications are applied to pixels of images, GPUs also turned out to be a great match for deep learning. This is a funny story of serendipity: a great example of a technology created for one goal and then meeting staggering success in a domain completely unrelated to the one they were originally envisioned for.

 Serendipity is the occurrence and development of events by chance in a happy or beneficial way.

TPUs

One problem encountered in using GPUs for deep learning is that these chips are made for graphics and gaming, not only for fast matrix computations. This would of course be the case, given that the G in GPU stands for Graphics! GPUs led to unbelievable improvements for deep learning but, in the case of tensor operations for neural networks, large parts of the chip are not used at all. For deep learning, there is no need for rasterization, no need for frame buffer manipulation, and no need for texture mapping. The only thing that is necessary is a very efficient way to compute matrix and tensor operations. It should be no surprise that GPUs are not **necessarily** the ideal solution for deep learning, since CPUs and GPUs were designed long before deep learning became successful.

Before going into the technical details, let's first discuss the fascinating genesis of Tensor Processing Unit version 1, or TPU v1. In 2013, Jeff Dean, the Chief of Brain Division at Google, estimated (see *Figure 1*) that if all the people owning a mobile phone were talking only three minutes more per day, then Google would have needed two times or three times more servers to process this data. This would have been an unaffordable case of success-disaster, that is, where great success has led to problems that cannot be properly managed.

It was clear that neither CPUs nor GPUs were a suitable solution. So, Google decided that they needed something completely new; something that would allow a 10x growth in performance with no significant cost increase. That's how TPU v1 was born! What is impressive is that it took only 15 months from initial design to production. You can find more details about this story in Jouppi et al., 2014 [3] where a detailed report about different inference workloads seen at Google in 2013 is also reported:

Name	LOC	Layers					Nonlinear function	Weights	TPUv1 Ops / Weight Byte	TPUv1 Batch Size	% Deployed
		FC	Conv	Vector	Pool	Total					
MLP0	0.1k	5				5	ReLU	20M	200	200	61%
MLP1	1k	4				4	ReLU	5M	168	168	
LSTM0	1k	24		34		58	sigmoid, tanh	52M	64	64	29%
LSTM1	1.5k	37		19		56	sigmoid, tanh	34M	96	96	
CNN0	1k		16			16	ReLU	8M	2888	8	5%
CNN1	1k	4	72		13	89	ReLU	100M	1750	32	

Figure 1: Different inference workloads seen at Google in 2013 (source [3])

Let's talk a bit about the technical details. TPU v1 is a special device (or an **Application-Specific Integrated Circuit**, also known as **ASIC**) designed for super-efficient tensor operations. TPUs follow the philosophy *less is more*. This philosophy has an important consequence: TPUs do not have all the graphic components that are needed for GPUs. Because of this, they are both very efficient from an energy consumption perspective, and frequently much faster than GPUs. So far, there have been three generations of TPUs. Let's review them.

Three generations of TPUs and Edge TPU

As discussed, TPUs are domain-specific processors expressly optimized for matrix operations. Now, you might remember that the basic operation of a matrix multiplication is a dot product between a line from one matrix and a column from the other matrix. For instance, given a matrix multiplication $Y=X*W$, computing $Y[i,0]$ is:

$$Y[i, 0] = X[i, 0] * W[0,0] + X[i, 1] * W[1,0] + X[i, 2] * W[2,0] + \cdots + X[i, n] * W[n, 0]$$

The sequential implementation of this operation is time consuming for large matrices. A brute-force computation has time complexity of $O(n^3)$ for $n \times n$ matrices, so it's not feasible for running large computations.

First-generation TPU

The first-generation TPU (TPU v1) was announced in May 2016 at Google I/O. TPU v1 [1] supports matrix multiplication using 8-bit arithmetic. TPU v1 is specialized for deep learning inference but it does not work for training. For training there is a need to perform floating-point operations, as discussed in the following paragraphs.

A key function of TPU is the "systolic" matrix multiplication. Let's see what this means. Remember that the core of deep learning is a core product $Y=X*W$, where, for instance, the basic operation to compute $Y[i,0]$ is:

$$Y[i, 0] = X[i, 0] * W[0,0] + X[i, 1] * W[1,0] + \cdots + X[i, n] * W[n, 0]$$

"Systolic" matrix multiplication allows multiple $Y[i, j]$ values to be computed in parallel. Data flows in a coordinated manner and, indeed, in medicine the term "systolic" refers to heart contractions and how blood flows rhythmically in our veins. Here systolic refers to the data flow that pulses inside the TPU. It can be proven that a systolic multiplication algorithm is less expensive than the brute force one [2]. TPU v1 has a **Matrix Multiply Unit** (**MMU**) running systolic multiplications on 256×256 cores so that 641,000 multiplications can be computed in parallel in one single shot. In addition, TPU v1 sits in a rack and it is not directly accessible. Instead, a CPU acts as the host controlling data transfer and sending commands to the TPU for performing tensor multiplications, for computing convolutions, and for applying activation functions.

The communication CPU ↔ TPU v1 happens via a standard PCIe 3.0 bus. From this perspective, TPU v1 is closer in spirit to an **FPU** (**floating-point unit**) coprocessor than it is to a GPU. However, TPU v1 has the ability to run whole inference models to reduce dependence on the host CPU. *Figure 2* represents TPU v1, as shown in [3]. As you see in the figure, the processing unit is connected via a PCI port, and it fetches weights via a standard DDR4 DRAM Chip. Multiplication happens within the MMU with systolic processing. Activation functions are then applied to the results. MMU and the unified buffer for activations take up a large amount of space. There is an area where the activation functions are computed:

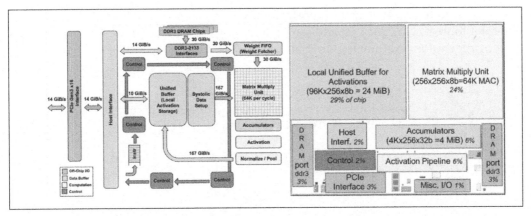

Figure 2: TPU v1 design schema (source [3])

TPU v1 is manufactured on a 28 nm process with a die size ≤ 331 mm2, clock
speed of 700 MHz, 28 MB of on-chip memory, 4 MB of 32-bit accumulators,
and a 256×256 systolic array of 8-bit multipliers. For this reason, we can get
700Mhz*65536 (multipliers) → 92 Tera operations/sec. This is an amazing
performance for matrix multiplications: *Figure 3* shows the TPU circuit board
and flow of data for the systolic matrix multiplication performed by the MMU.
In addition, TPU v1 has an 8 GB dual-channel 2133 MHz DDR3 SDRAM offering
34 GB/s of bandwidth. The external memory is standard, and it is used to store and
fetch the weights used during the inference. Notice also that TPU v1 has a thermal
design power of 28-40 Watts, which is certainly low consumption compared to
GPUs and CPUs. Moreover, TPU v1 are normally mounted in a PCI slot used for
SATA disks so they do not require any modification in the host server [3]. Up to 4
cards can be mounted in each server. *Figure 3* shows TPU v1 card and the process of
systolic computation:

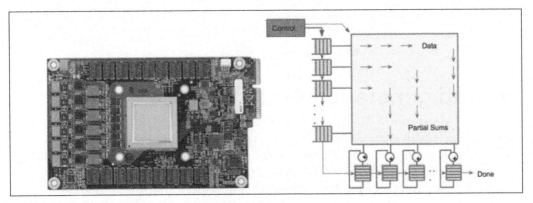

Figure 3: On the left you can see a TPU v1 board, and on the right an example of how the data is processed
during the systolic computation

If you want to have a look at TPU performance compared to GPUs and CPUs, we can refer Jouppi et al., 2014 [3] and see (in a log-log scale graph) that the performance is two orders of magnitude higher than a Tesla K80 GPU.

 The graph shows a "rooftop" performance that is growing until the point where it reaches the peak and then it is constant. The higher the roof the merrier for performance.

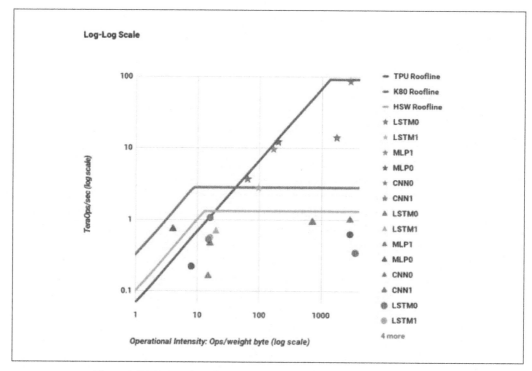

Figure 4: TPU v1 peak performance can be up to 3x higher than a Tesla K80

Second-generation TPU

The second-generation TPUs (TPU2) were announced in 2017. In this case, the memory bandwidth is increased to 600 GB/s and performance reaches 45 TFLOPS. 4 TPU2s are arranged in a module with 180 TFLOPS performance. Then 64 modules are grouped into a pod with 11.5 PFLOPS of performance. TPU2s adopt floating-point arithmetic and therefore they are suitable for both training and inference.

TPU2 has MMU for matrix multiplications of 128x128 cores and a **Vector Processing Unit (VPU)** for all other tasks such as applying activations. The VPU handles `float32` and `int32` computations. The MXU on the other hand operates in a mixed precision 16-32 bit floating point format.

Each TPU v2 chip has two cores, and up to 4 chips are mounted in each board. In TPU v2, Google adopted a new floating-point model called bfloat 16. The idea is to sacrifice some resolution but still be very good for deep learning. This reduction in resolution allows you to improve the performance of the v2 TPUs, which are more power efficient than v1. Indeed, it can be proven that a smaller mantissa helps reducing the physical silicon area and multiplier power. Therefore, the bfloat16 uses the same standard IEEE 754 single-precision floating-point format, but it truncates the mantissa field from 23 bits to just 7 bits. Preserving the exponent bits allows the format to keep the same range as the 32-bit single precision. This allows for relatively simpler conversion between the two data types:

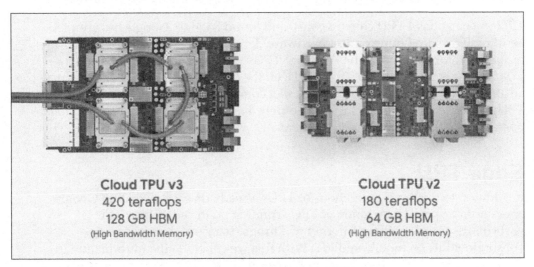

Figure 5: Cloud TPU v3 and Cloud TPU v2

Google offers access to these TPU v2 and TPU v3 via **Google Compute Engine (GCE)** and on **Google Kubernetes Engine (GKE)**. Plus, it is possible to use them for free via Colab.

Third-generation TPU

The third-generation TPUs (TPU3) were announced in 2018 [4]. TPU3s are 2x faster than TPU2 and they are grouped in 4x larger pods. In total, this is a performance increase of 8x. Cloud TPU v3 pods can deliver more than 100 PetaFLOPS of computing power.

On the other hand, Cloud TPU v2 pods released in alpha in 2018 can achieve 11.5 PetaFLOPS; another impressive improvement. As of 2019 both TPU2 and TPU3 are in production with different prices:

Figure 6: Google announced TPU v2 and v3 Pods in beta at the Google I/O 2019

TPU v3 board has 4 TPU chips, 8 cores, and liquid cooling. Google has adopted an ultra-high-speed interconnect hardware derived from supercomputer technology, for connecting thousands of TPUs with very low latency. Each time a parameter is updated on a single TPU, all the others are informed via a reduce-all algorithm typically adopted for parallel computation. So, you can think about TPU v3 as one of the fastest supercomputers available today for matrix and tensor operations with thousands of TPUs inside it.

Edge TPU

In addition to the three generations of TPUs already discussed, in 2018 Google announced a special generation of TPUs running on the edge. This TPU is particularly appropriate for **Internet of Things (IoT)** and for supporting TensorFlow Lite on mobile and IoT. With this we conclude the introduction to TPU v1, v2, and v3. In the next section we will briefly discuss performance.

TPU performance

Discussing performance is always difficult because it is important to first define the metrics that we are going to measure, and the set of workloads that we are going to use as benchmarks. For instance, Google reported an impressive linear scaling for TPU v2 used with ResNet-50 [4] (see *Figure 7*).

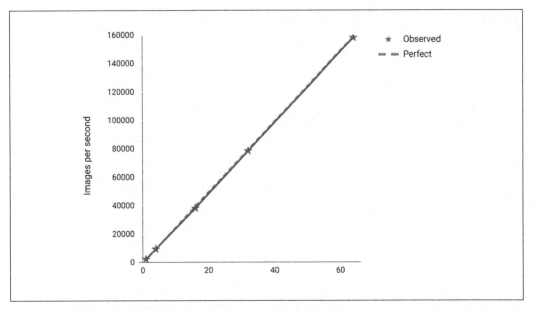

Figure 7: Linear scalability in the number of TPUs v2 when increasing the number of images

In addition, you can find online a comparison of ResNet-50 [4] where a Full Cloud TPU v2 Pod is >200x faster than a V100 Nvidia Tesla GPU for ResNet-50 training:

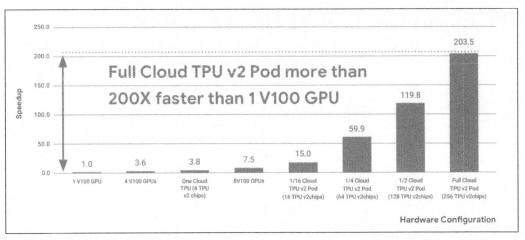

Figure 8: A Full Cloud TPU v2 Pod is >200x faster than a V100 Nvidia Tesla GPU for training a ResNet-50 model

In December 2018, the MLPerf initiative was announced. MLPerf [5] is a broad ML benchmark suite created by a large set of companies. The goal is to measure the performance of ML frameworks, ML accelerators, and ML cloud platforms.

How to use TPUs with Colab

In this section, we show how to use TPUs with Colabs. Just point your browser to `https://colab.research.google.com/` and change the runtime from the runtime menu as shown in *Figure 9*:

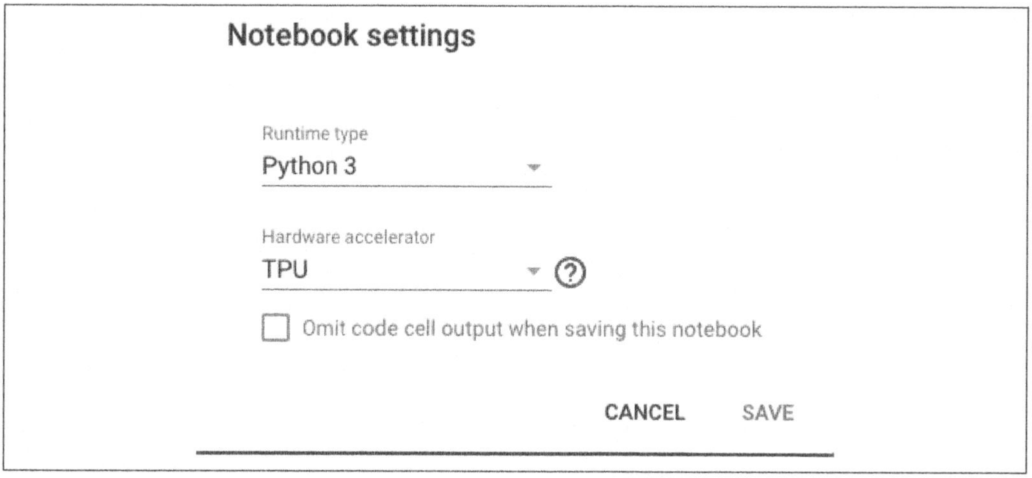

Figure 9: Setting TPU as runtime in Colab

Checking whether TPUs are available

First of all, let's check if there is a TPU available by using this simple code fragment that returns the IP address assigned to the TPU. Communication between CPU and TPU happens via `grpc`:

```
import os
try:
    device_name = os.environ['COLAB_TPU_ADDR']
    TPU_ADDRESS = 'grpc://' + device_name
    print('Found TPU at: {}'.format(TPU_ADDRESS))

except KeyError:
    print('TPU not found')
```

```
Found TPU at: grpc://10.91.166.82:8470
```

We've confirmed that a TPU is available! Now, we'll continue to explore how we can make use of it.

Loading data with tf.data

Our goal is to implement a simple CNN on MNIST data (see *Chapter 4, Convolutional Neural Networks*). Then we want to run the model on a TPU. To do this, we must load the data with tf.data libraries. Hence, we need to define a training and test function (see *Chapter 2, TensorFlow 1.x and 2.x*) as shown in the following code:

```
# training input function
def train_input_fn(batch_size=1024):
    # Convert the inputs to a Dataset.
    dataset = tf.data.Dataset.from_tensor_slices((x_train,y_train))
    # Shuffle, repeat, and batch the examples.
    dataset = dataset.cache() # Loads the data into memory
    dataset = dataset.shuffle(1000, reshuffle_each_iteration=True)
    dataset = dataset.repeat()
    dataset = dataset.batch(batch_size, drop_remainder=True)
    return dataset

# testing input function
def test_input_fn(batch_size=1024):
    dataset = tf.data.Dataset.from_tensor_slices((x_test,y_test))
    # Shuffle, repeat, and batch the examples.
    dataset = dataset.cache()
    dataset = dataset.shuffle(1000, reshuffle_each_iteration=True)
    dataset = dataset.repeat()
    dataset = dataset.batch(batch_size, drop_remainder=True)
    return dataset
```

Where `(x_train, y_train), (x_test, y_test) = mnist.load_data()`. Note that `drop_remainder=True` is an important parameter that forces the batch method to pass **fixed shapes** expected by the TPUs. Note that TPU v2 has an MMU with 128 × 128 multipliers. Usually you get the best performance by setting the batch size to 128 per TPU core. With 10 TPU cores, for instance, the batch size would be 1,280.

Building a model and loading it into the TPU

As of November 2019, TensorFlow 2.0 does not fully support TPUs. They are available in TensorFlow 1.5.0, and with the nightly build. Let's first see an example with TensorFlow 1.5, and the example with the nightly build will be shown later.

Note that full support for `TPUDistributionStrategy` is planned for TensorFlow 2.1. 2.0 has limited support, and the issue is tracked in `https://github.com/tensorflow/tensorflow/issues/24412`.

So, let's define a standard CNN model made up of three convolutional layers, alternated with max-pooling layers and followed by two dense layers with a dropout in the middle. For the sake of brevity, the definition of `input_shape`, `batch_size` is omitted. In this case, we use the functional `tf.keras` API (see *Chapter 2, TensorFlow 1.x and 2.x*):

```
Inp = tf.keras.Input(name='input', shape=input_shape, batch_
size=batch_size, dtype=tf.float32)
x = Conv2D(32, kernel_size=(3, 3), activation='relu',name = 'Conv_01')
(Inp)
x = MaxPooling2D(pool_size=(2, 2),name = 'MaxPool_01')(x)
x = Conv2D(64, (3, 3), activation='relu',name = 'Conv_02')(x)
x = MaxPooling2D(pool_size=(2, 2),name = 'MaxPool_02')(x)
x = Conv2D(64, (3, 3), activation='relu',name = 'Conv_03')(x)
x = Flatten(name = 'Flatten_01')(x)
x = Dense(64, activation='relu',name = 'Dense_01')(x)
x = Dropout(0.5,name = 'Dropout_02')(x)
output = Dense(num_classes, activation='softmax',name = 'Dense_02')(x)
model = tf.keras.Model(inputs=[Inp], outputs=[output])
```

Let's now use Adam optimizer and compile the model:

```
#Use a tf optimizer rather than a Keras one for now
opt = tf.train.AdamOptimizer(learning_rate)

model.compile(
    optimizer=opt,
    loss='categorical_crossentropy',
    metrics=['acc'])
```

Then, we call `tpu.keras_to_tpu_model` to convert to a TPU model and then we use the `tpu.TPUDistributionStrategy` for running on a TPU. It's as simple as that; we just need to take the appropriate strategy with `TPUDistributionStrategy()` and all the rest is done transparently on our behalf:

```
tpu_model = tf.contrib.tpu.keras_to_tpu_model(
    model,
    strategy=tf.contrib.tpu.TPUDistributionStrategy(
        tf.contrib.cluster_resolver.TPUClusterResolver(TPU_ADDRESS)))
```

The execution is super-fast on a TPU as every single iteration takes about 2 seconds:

```
Epoch 1/10
INFO:tensorflow:New input shapes; (re-)compiling: mode=train (# of
cores 8), [TensorSpec(shape=(1024,), dtype=tf.int32, name=None),
TensorSpec(shape=(1024, 28, 28, 1), dtype=tf.float32, name=None),
TensorSpec(shape=(1024, 10), dtype=tf.float32, name=None)]
INFO:tensorflow:Overriding default placeholder.
INFO:tensorflow:Remapping placeholder for input
Instructions for updating:
Use tf.cast instead.
INFO:tensorflow:Started compiling
INFO:tensorflow:Finished compiling. Time elapsed: 2.567350149154663 secs
INFO:tensorflow:Setting weights on TPU model.
60/60 [==============================] - 8s 126ms/step - loss: 0.9622 -
acc: 0.6921
Epoch 2/10
60/60 [==============================] - 2s 41ms/step - loss: 0.2406 -
acc: 0.9292
Epoch 3/10
60/60 [==============================] - 3s 42ms/step - loss: 0.1412 -
acc: 0.9594
Epoch 4/10
60/60 [==============================] - 3s 42ms/step - loss: 0.1048 -
acc: 0.9701
Epoch 5/10
60/60 [==============================] - 3s 42ms/step - loss: 0.0852 -
acc: 0.9756
Epoch 6/10
60/60 [==============================] - 3s 42ms/step - loss: 0.0706 -
acc: 0.9798
Epoch 7/10
60/60 [==============================] - 3s 42ms/step - loss: 0.0608 -
acc: 0.9825
Epoch 8/10
60/60 [==============================] - 3s 42ms/step - loss: 0.0530 -
acc: 0.9846
Epoch 9/10
60/60 [==============================] - 3s 42ms/step - loss: 0.0474 -
acc: 0.9863
```

```
Epoch 10/10
60/60 [==============================] - 3s 42ms/step - loss: 0.0418 -
acc: 0.9876

<tensorflow.python.keras.callbacks.History at 0x7fbb3819bc50>
```

As you can see, running a simple MNIST model on TPUs is extremely fast. Each iteration is around 3 seconds even if we have a CNN with 3 convolutions followed by two dense stages.

Using pretrained TPU models

Google offers a collection of models pretrained with TPUs available on GitHub TensorFlow/tpu repo (`https://github.com/tensorflow/tpu`). Models include image recognition, object detection, low-resource models, machine translation and language models, speech recognition, and image generation. Whenever it is possible, my suggestion is to start with a pretrained model [6], and then fine tune it or apply some form of transfer learning. As of September 2019, the following models are available:

Image Recognition, Segmentation, and more	Machine Translation and Language Models	Speech Recognition	Image Generation
Image Recognition • AmoebaNet-D • ResNet-50/101/152/2000 • Inception v2/v3/v4 Object Detection • RetinaNet • Mask R-CNN Image Segmentation • Mask R-CNN • DeepLab • RetinaNet Low-Resource Models • MnasNet • MobileNet • SqueezeNet	Machine Translation (transformer based) Sentiment Analysis (transformer based) Question Answer Bert	ASR Transformer	Image Transformer DCGAN GAN

Table 1: State-of-the-art collection of models pretrained with TPUs available on GitHub

The best way to play with the repository is to clone it on Google Cloud Console and use the environment available at `https://github.com/tensorflow/tpu/blob/master/README.md`.

You should be able to browse what is shown in *Figure 10*. If you click the button **OPEN IN GOOGLE CLOUD SHELL**, then the system will clone the Git repo into your Cloud Shell and then open the shell (see *Figure 11*). From there, you can play with a nice Google Cloud TPU demo for training a ResNet-50 on MNIST with a TPU Flock – a Compute Engine VM and Cloud TPU pair (see *Figure 12*). I will leave this training demo to you, if you are interested in looking it up:

Cloud TPUs

This repository is a collection of reference models and tools used with Cloud TPUs.

The fastest way to get started training a model on a Cloud TPU is by following the tutorial. Click the button below to launch the tutorial using Google Cloud Shell.

Note: This repository is a public mirror, pull requests will not be accepted. Please file an issue if you have a feature or bug request.

Running Models

To run models in the `models` subdirectory, you may need to add the top-level `/models` folder to the Python path with the command:

```
export PYTHONPATH="$PYTHONPATH:/path/to/models"
```

Figure 10: State-of-the-art collection of models pretrained with TPUs available on GitHub

ssh.cloud.google.com/cloudshell/editor?shellonly=true
Cloud Shell
cloudshell
cloudshell
To set your Cloud Platform project in this session use "gcloud config set project [PROJECT_ID]"
a_gulli@cloudshell:~$ cloudshell_open --repo_url "https://github.com/tensorflow/tpu" --page "shell" --tutorial "tools/ctpu/tutorial.md"
You have already cloned this repo into directory tpu. Would you like to:
[1] cd into that directory
[2] cd into that directory and `git pull`
[3] git clone a new copy
Enter your choice [default 1]: 1
cd-ing into tpu
a_gulli@cloudshell:~/tpu$

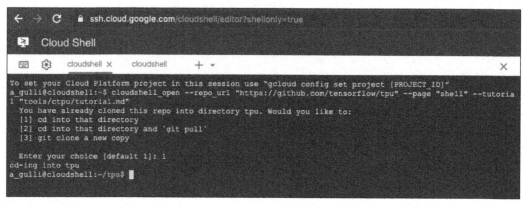

Figure 11: Google Cloud Shell with tpu git repo cloned on your behalf

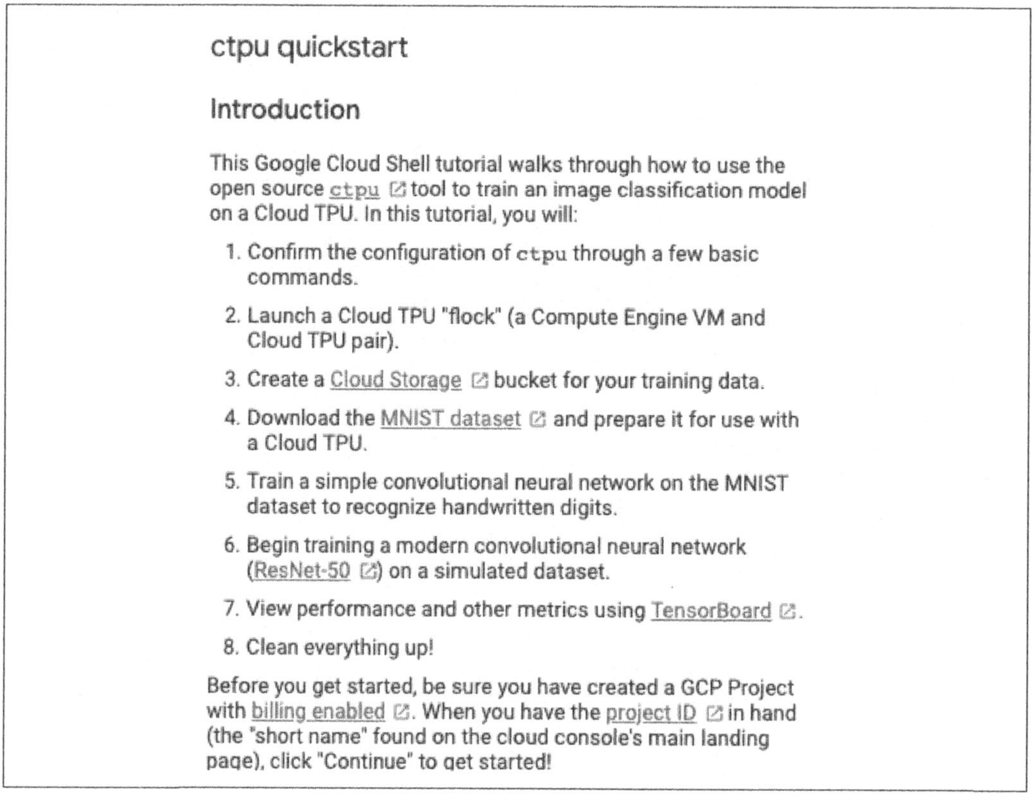

ctpu quickstart
Introduction
This Google Cloud Shell tutorial walks through how to use the open source ctpu tool to train an image classification model on a Cloud TPU. In this tutorial, you will:
1. Confirm the configuration of ctpu through a few basic commands.
2. Launch a Cloud TPU "flock" (a Compute Engine VM and Cloud TPU pair).
3. Create a Cloud Storage bucket for your training data.
4. Download the MNIST dataset and prepare it for use with a Cloud TPU.
5. Train a simple convolutional neural network on the MNIST dataset to recognize handwritten digits.
6. Begin training a modern convolutional neural network (ResNet-50) on a simulated dataset.
7. View performance and other metrics using TensorBoard.
8. Clean everything up!
Before you get started, be sure you have created a GCP Project with billing enabled. When you have the project ID in hand (the "short name" found on the cloud console's main landing page), click "Continue" to get started!

Figure 12: Google Cloud TPU demo for training a ResNet-50 on MNIST with a TPU Flock

Using TensorFlow 2.1 and nightly build

As of November 2019, you can get full TPU support only with the latest TensorFlow 2.x nightly build. If you use the Google Cloud Console (https://console.cloud.google.com/) you can get the latest nightly build. Just, go to **Compute Engine | TPUs | CREATE TPU NODE**. The version selector has a "nightly-2.x" option. Martin Görner has a nice demo at http://bit.ly/keras-tpu-tf21 (see *Figure 13*). This is used for classifying images of flowers:

Figure 13: Martin Görner on Twitter on Full Keras/TPU support

Note that both Regular Keras using model.fit() and custom training loop, distributed are supported. You can refer to http://bit.ly/keras-tpu-tf21. Let's look at the most important parts of the code related to TPUs. First at all, the imports:

```
import re
import tensorflow as tf
import numpy as np
from matplotlib import pyplot as plt
print("Tensorflow version " + tf.__version__)
```

Then the detection of the TPUs, and the selection of TPU strategy:

```
try:
    tpu = tf.distribute.cluster_resolver.TPUClusterResolver()
# TPU detection
    print('Running on TPU ', tpu.cluster_spec().as_dict()['worker'])
except ValueError:
    tpu = None

if tpu:
    tf.config.experimental_connect_to_cluster(tpu)
    tf.tpu.experimental.initialize_tpu_system(tpu)
    strategy = tf.distribute.experimental.TPUStrategy(tpu)
else:
    strategy = tf.distribute.get_strategy()

print("REPLICAS: ", strategy.num_replicas_in_sync)
```

Then the usage of TPUs, where the appropriate TPU strategy is used:

```
with strategy.scope():
    model = create_model()
    model.compile(optimizer=tf.keras.optimizers.SGD(nesterov=True,
momentum=0.9),
                loss='categorical_crossentropy',
                metrics=['accuracy'])
    model.summary()
```

In short, it is extremely simple to use TPUs with the upcoming TensorFlow 2.1, and if you want to experiment immediately you can use TensorFlow 2.0 nightly build. Martin reports typical run times for his specific model:

- GPU (V100): 15s per epoch

- TPU v3-8 (8 cores): 5s per epoch

- TPU pod v2-32 (32 cores): 2s per epoch

Summary

TPUs are very special ASIC chips developed at Google for executing neural network mathematical operations in an ultra-fast manner. The core of the computation is a systolic multiplier that computes multiple dot products (row * column) in parallel, thus accelerating the computation of basic deep learning operations. Think of a TPU as a special-purpose coprocessor for deep learning, which is focused on matrix or tensor operations. Google has announced three generations of TPUs so far, plus an additional Edge TPU for IoT. Cloud TPU v1 is a PCI-based specialized co-processor, with 92 TeraFLOPS and inference only. Cloud TPU v2 achieves 180 TeraFLOPS and it supports training and inference. Cloud TPU v2 pods released in alpha in 2018 can achieve 11.5 PetaFLOPS. Cloud TPU v3 achieves 420 TeraFLOPS with both training and inference support. Cloud TPU v3 pods can deliver more than 100 PetaFLOPS of computing power. That's a world-class supercomputer for tensor operations!

References

1. Moore's law `https://en.wikipedia.org/wiki/Moore%27s_law`.

2. *Forty-three ways of systolic matrix multiplication*, I.Ž. Milovanović, et al., Article in International Journal of Computer Mathematics 87(6):1264-1276 May 2010.

3. *In-Datacenter Performance Analysis of a Tensor Processing Unit*, Norman P. Jouppi, and others, 44th International Symposium on Computer Architecture (ISCA), June 2014.

4. Google TPU v2 performance `https://storage.googleapis.com/nexttpu/index.html`.

5. MLPerf site `https://mlperf.org/`.

6. Collection of models pretrained with TPU `g.co/cloudtpu`.

Other Books You May Enjoy

If you enjoyed this book, you may be interested in these other books by Packt:

Python Machine Learning - Third Edition

Sebastian Raschka, Vahid Mirjalili

ISBN: 978-1-78995-575-0

- Master the frameworks, models, and techniques that enable machines to 'learn' from data
- Use scikit-learn for machine learning and TensorFlow for deep learning
- Apply machine learning to image classification, sentiment analysis, intelligent web applications, and more

- Build and train neural networks, GANs, and other models
- Add machine intelligence to web applications
- Clean and prepare data for machine learning
- Classify images using deep convolutional neural networks
- Best practices for evaluating and tuning models
- Predict continuous target outcomes using regression analysis
- Uncover hidden patterns and structures in data with clustering
- Dig deeper into textual and social media data using sentiment analysis

AI Crash Course

Hadelin de Ponteves

ISBN: 978-1-83864-535-9

- Master the key skills of deep learning, reinforcement learning, and deep reinforcement learning
- Understand Q-learning and deep Q-learning
- Learn from friendly, plain English explanations and practical activities
- Build fun projects, including a virtual-self-driving car
- Use AI to solve real-world business problems and win classic video games
- Build an intelligent, virtual robot warehouse worker

Dancing with Qubits

Robert S. Sutor

ISBN: 978-1-83882-736-6

- See how Quantum Computing works, what makes it different, and why it could be so powerful

- Discover the complex, mind-bending mechanics that underpin quantum systems

- Understand the necessary concepts behind classical and quantum computing

- Refresh and extend your grasp of computing, quantum theory, and quantum computing

- Explore the main applications of quantum computing to scientific computing, AI, and elsewhere

- Comprehend the detailed overview of qubits, quantum circuits, and quantum algorithm

Leave a review - let other readers know what you think

Please share your thoughts on this book with others by leaving a review on the site that you bought it from. If you purchased the book from Amazon, please leave us an honest review on this book's Amazon page. This is vital so that other potential readers can see and use your unbiased opinion to make purchasing decisions, we can understand what our customers think about our products, and our authors can see your feedback on the title that they have worked with Packt to create. It will only take a few minutes of your time, but is valuable to other potential customers, our authors, and Packt. Thank you!

Index

X

Y